EYEWITNESS TRAVEL

SOUTH AFRICA

GAUTENG AND SUN CITY
Pages 252–271

BLYDE RIVER CANYON AND KRUGER
Pages 272–289

Polokwane
Nelspruit
PRETORIA
Johannesburg
MBABANE
SWAZILAND

Kimberley
Bloemfontein

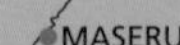

LESOTHO
Durban

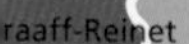

Port
izabeth

DURBAN AND ZULULAND
Pages 224–243

THE SOUTHERN CAPE
Pages 164–177

THE GARDEN ROUTE TO GRAHAMSTOWN
Pages 178–199

WILD COAST, DRAKENSBERG AND MIDLANDS
Pages 208–223

EYEWITNESS TRAVEL

SOUTH AFRICA

MAIN CONTRIBUTORS:
MICHAEL BRETT, BRIAN JOHNSON-BARKER
AND MARIËLLE RENSSEN

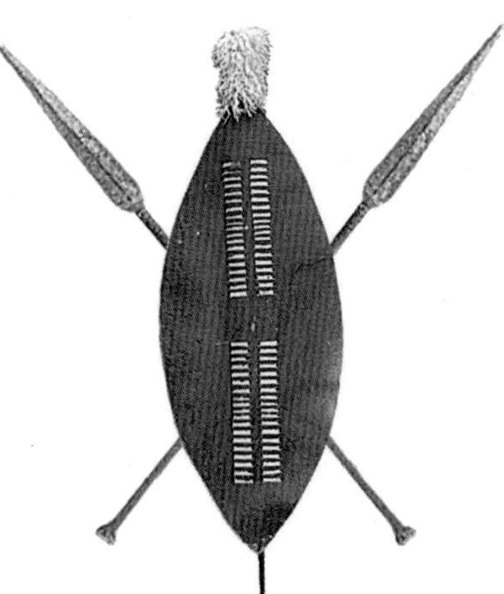

LONDON, NEW YORK,
MELBOURNE, MUNICH AND DELHI
www.dk.com

Produced by Struik New Holland Publishing (Pty) Ltd,
Cape Town, South Africa

MANAGING EDITOR Claudia Dos Santos
MANAGING ART EDITORS Peter Bosman, Trinity Loubser-Fry
EDITORS Gill Gordon, Gail Jennings
DESIGNERS Simon Lewis, Mark Seabrook
MAP CO-ORDINATOR John Loubser
PRODUCTION Myrna Collins
PICTURE RESEARCHER Carmen Watts
RESEARCHER Jocelyn Convery

Dorling Kindersley Limited
EDITORIAL DIRECTOR Vivien Crump
ART DIRECTOR Gillian Allan
MAP CO-ORDINATOR David Pugh

MAIN CONTRIBUTORS
Michael Brett, Brian Johnson-Barker, Mariëlle Renssen

PHOTOGRAPHERS
Shaen Adey, Roger de la Harpe, Walter Knirr

ILLUSTRATORS
Bruce Beyer, Annette Busse, Bruno de Robillard,
Steven Felmore, Noel McCully, Dave Snook

Reproduced in Singapore by Colourscan
Printed and bound by South China Printing Co. Ltd., China

First published in Great Britain in 1999
by Dorling Kindersley Limited
80 Strand, London WC2R 0RL

Reprinted with revisions 2001, 2002, 2003, 2005, 2007

A CIP CATALOGUE RECORD IS AVAILABLE FROM THE BRITISH LIBRARY.

ISBN 978 1 40532 109 9

FLOORS ARE REFERRED TO THROUGHOUT IN ACCORDANCE WITH EUROPEAN USAGE; IE THE "FIRST FLOOR" IS THE FLOOR ABOVE GROUND LEVEL.

Front cover main image: Silhouette of two quivertrees

The information in this DK Eyewitness Travel Guide is checked regularly.

Every effort has been made to ensure that this book is as up-to-date as possible at the time of going to press. Some details, however, such as telephone numbers, opening hours, prices, gallery hanging arrangements and travel information are liable to change. The publishers cannot accept responsibility for any consequences arising from the use of this book, nor for any material on third party websites, and cannot guarantee that any website address in this book will be a suitable source of travel information. We value the views and suggestions of our readers very highly. Please write to: Publisher, DK Eyewitness Travel Guides, Dorling Kindersley, 80 Strand, London WC2R 0RL, Great Britain.

◁ **Stampeding eland in the Pilanesberg National Park near Sun City**

CONTENTS

Vasco Da Gama

INTRODUCING SOUTH AFRICA

CAPE TOWN

Camps Bay Beach, Cape Town

Red Disas on Table Mountain

A male leopard patrols his territory at Londolozi Game Reserve

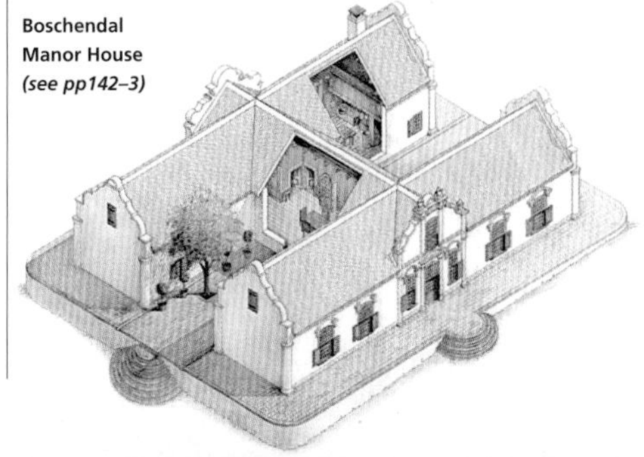

Boschendal Manor House *(see pp142–3)*

HOW TO USE THIS GUIDE

This guide helps you to get the most from a visit to South Africa, providing expert rec ommendations and detailed practical information. *Introducing South Africa* maps the country and sets it in its historical and cultural context. The four regional sections, plus *Cape Town*, describe important sights, using photographs, maps and illustrations. Throughout, features cover topics from food and wine to wildlife and culture. Restaurant and hotel recommendations can be found in *Travellers' Needs*. The *Survival Guide* contains practical tips on everything from transport to personal safety.

CAPE TOWN

The "mother city" has been divided into three sightseeing areas. Each has its own chapter opening with a list of the sights described. The *Further Afield* section covers many peripheral places of interest. All sights are numbered and plotted on an *Area Map*. Information on the sights is easy to locate as it follows the numerical order used on the map.

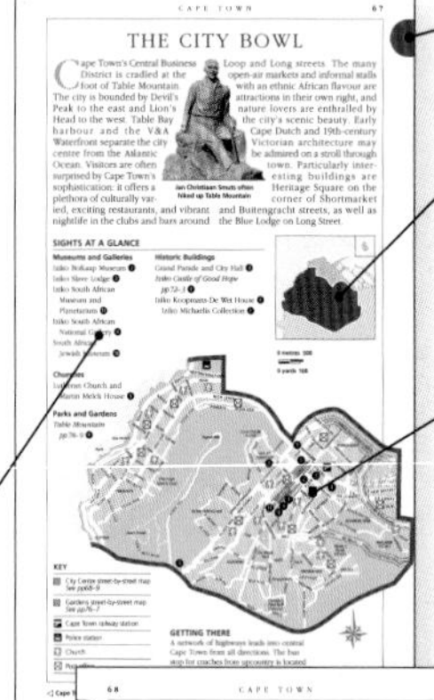

THE CITY BOWL

All pages relating to Cape Town have red thumb tabs.

A locator map shows clearly where the area is in relation to other areas of the city.

1 Area Map
For easy reference, sights are numbered and located on a map. City centre sights are also marked on the Cape Town Street Finder *maps* (see pp115–23).

Sights at a Glance lists the chapter's sights by category: Museums and Galleries, Churches, Parks and Gardens, Historic Buildings etc.

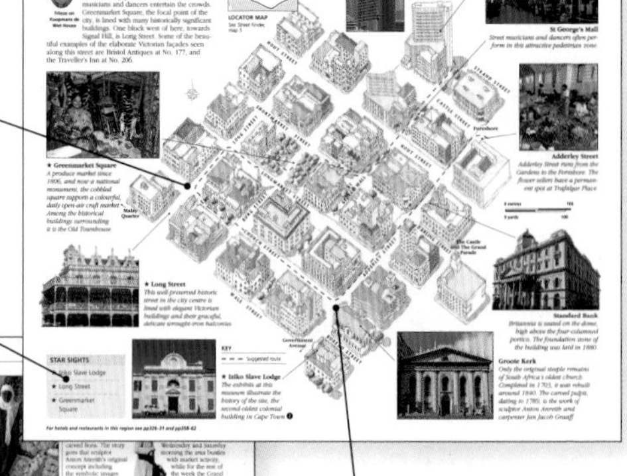

Street-by-street: City Centre

2 Street-by-Street Map
This gives a bird's-eye view of the key areas in each sightseeing area.

Stars indicate the sights that no visitor should miss.

A suggested route for a walk covers the more interesting streets in the area.

3 Detailed Information
All the sights in Cape Town are described individually. Addresses, telephone numbers and other practical information are also provided for each entry. The key to the symbols used in the information block is shown on the back flap.

1 Introduction
A general account of the landscape, history and character of each region is given here, explaining both how the area has developed over the centuries and what attractions it has to offer visitors today.

SOUTH AFRICA AREA BY AREA

Apart from Cape Town, the rest of the country has been divided into ten regions, each of which has a separate chapter. The most interesting towns and sights to visit are numbered on a *Regional Map* at the beginning of each chapter.

Each area of South Africa can be easily identified by its colour coding, shown on the inside front cover.

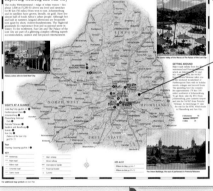

2 Regional Map
This shows the main road network and gives an illustrated overview of the whole region. All interesting places to visit are numbered and there are also useful tips on getting to, and around, the region.

Story boxes explore specific subjects further.

3 Detailed Information
All the important towns and other places to visit are described individually. They are listed in order, following the numbering on the Regional Map. *Within each entry, there is further detailed information on important buildings and other sights.*

For all the top sights, a Visitors' Checklist provides the practical information you will need to plan your visit.

4 South Africa's Top Sights
The historic buildings are dissected to reveal their interiors; national parks have maps showing facilities and trails. The most interesting towns or city centres have maps, with sights picked out and described.

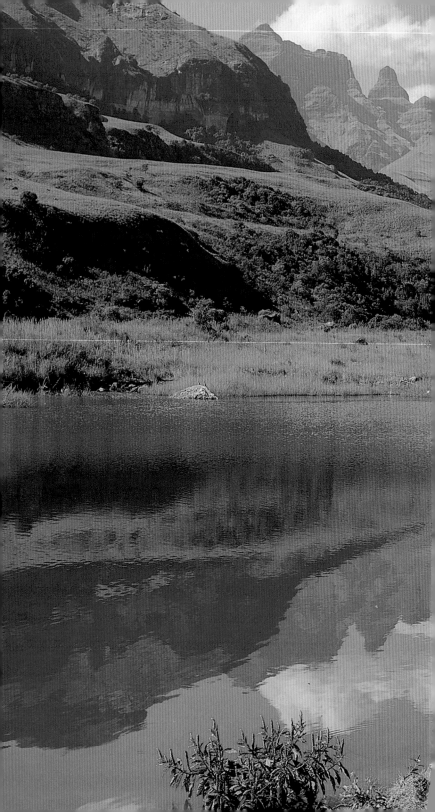

INTRODUCING SOUTH AFRICA

DISCOVERING SOUTH AFRICA

South Africa – the "Rainbow Nation" – has been described as offering the whole world in one country. The variety of scenery is outstanding: from beautiful forests to dramatic coastlines and vibrant cities. This is also a country with 11 official languages and a multifaceted culture as a result. Whether you want to experience exciting extreme sports, outstanding wine tours or fantastic shopping opportunities, South Africa will deliver. However, no trip would be complete without visiting one of the national parks for a chance to see the majestic lions, elephants and other animals that these reserves protect. The following pages will help you to plan and make the most out of this incredible country.

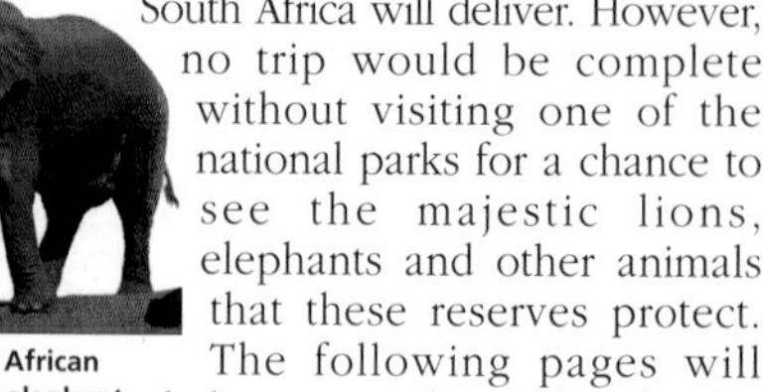

An African bush elephant

Aerial view of Cape Town from Green Point

CAPE TOWN

- **Shopping at the V&A Waterfront**
- **The legislative capital**
- **Dramatic Table Mountain**
- **Outstanding beaches**

Set against the ocean and overlooked by the imposing Table Mountain, Cape Town is arguably the most scenic city in South Africa. It has always been a cosmopolitan place, and this is reflected in the shops at the **V&A Waterfront** *(see pp82–4)*, which will impress even the most discerning of visitors.

The grand public buildings and excellent museums, such as the **Castle of Good Hope** *(see pp72–3)*, are indicative of Cape Town's importance as South Africa's legislative capital, as are the imposing statues and monuments that punctuate the many parks and gardens. Cape Town also offers some of the best national parks in the country. **Table Mountain** *(see pp78–9)* is easily reached by cable car, and it provides breathtaking panoramic views. Make sure to check the weather forecast first, however, since the summit can be shrouded in mist. Further along the coast lies the **Cape Riviera** *(see p93)*, which boasts excellent beaches that are very popular with both tourists and locals. Be aware that traffic can get congested along the coast, although the beaches are well worth the effort.

CAPE WINELANDS

- **Fascinating wine tours**
- **Cape Dutch architecture**
- **Historic Stellenbosch**

With a history in wine-making stretching back more than 350 years, it is not surprising that South Africa offers such excellent **wine tours** *(see p140 and p147)*. The visits provide a fascinating insight into the industry, not to mention the opportunity to sample the end product.

The Cape Winelands are blessed with a landscape of green rolling hills overlooked by jagged mountain peaks. The architectural heritage left by the Dutch and French adds to the region's charm. A particularly good example of the style is **Boschendal Manor House** *(see pp142–3)*. The larger towns are just as picturesque as the white-washed farmhouses that dot the area. **Stellenbosch** *(see pp136–9)*, in particular, is worth visiting for the different styles of Cape Dutch architecture that line the peaceful streets. Other attractions include the **Kleinplasie Open-Air Museum** *(see pp150–51)*, the enticing wayside inns and some of the best restaurants in the country.

Terraced vineyards in the Cape Winelands region

The vast underground complex of the Cango Caves

WESTERN COASTAL TERRACE

- **Floral Namaqualand**
- **Towering Cedarberg Mountains**
- **Seafood fresh from the sea**

The best time to visit the Western Coastal Terrace is in the spring (August–October), when most of the sparse annual rainfall occurs. This is when **Namaqualand** *(see pp162–3)* bursts into colourful bloom. The **Cedarberg Mountains** *(see pp160–61)* are a spectacular, if surreal, sight. Formed from tectonic activity, the twisted landscape is perfect for hiking explorations.

Colourful Namaqualand

The **West Coast National Park** *(see pp158–9)* is one of South Africa's most important wetlands. But this is not the only delight the ocean has to offer. The open-air *skerm* (restaurants) serve a range of delicious fresh seafood, and are the perfect place to stop for an informal meal.

SOUTHERN CAPE

- **The spectacular Four Passes**
- **Wild coastline**
- **Exploring Cango Caves**
- **Whale watching at Hermanus**

A rural wonderland, the Southern Cape is shadowed by the great ridge of the Overberg Mountains. The **Four Passes** *(see pp174–5)*, which traverse the peaks, are some of the world's most scenic mountain drives.

The coastline is equally dramatic, culminating in the wild **Cape Agulhas** *(see p171)*. Here the cold Atlantic Ocean crashes into the warmer waters of the Indian Ocean, producing treacherous conditions for even the most experienced of sailors and swimmers.

For the more intrepid visitor, the **Cango Caves** *(see p175)* are an excellent day out. The cathedral-like vastness of the Great Hall ends with a claustrophobic hole in the rock known as The Letterbox, through which visitors can "post" themselves.

Hermanus *(see pp168–9)* is world-renowned as one of the finest on-shore sites for whale watching. The best time to visit is during October, when there is a peak in whale numbers. The town is well set up for viewing these stately creatures.

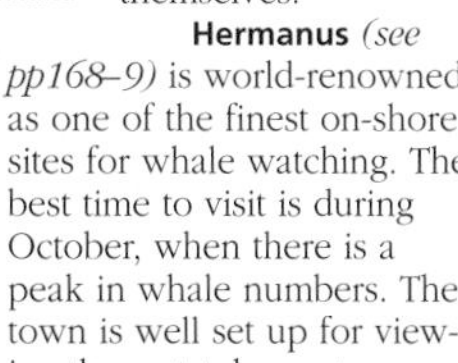

GARDEN ROUTE TO GRAHAMSTOWN

- **Exotic flowers and forests**
- **Tsitsikamma National Park**
- **Excellent hiking trails**
- **Port Elizabeth's golden beaches**

Never was an area more aptly named than the exotic and beautiful Garden Route. There are many cultivated blooms to see here, but the real draw are the forests of indigenous African hardwoods found in **Tsitsikamma National Park** *(see pp190–91)*. Two of the most popular hiking trails in the country can be found here, but visitors should be aware that they must carry all their provisions with them.

The year-round balmy weather and well-planned trails through unspoilt woodlands have also contributed to making this one of the best regions for hiking. The seven-day, 165-km (65-mile) **Outeniqua Hiking Trail** *(see p187)* leads walkers through the forests that surround **Knysna** *(see pp186–7)*.

The ocean is never far away in the Garden Route, and there are many places to stop and enjoy the coastline. **Port Elizabeth** *(see pp192–5)* is one of the friendliest cities in South Africa. The golden beaches are understandably popular, but don't miss out on the city's beautiful architecture, or the exciting dolphin and seal shows at **Bayworld** *(see p195)*.

A scenic stretch of coastline in the Garden Route region

WILD COAST, DRAKENSBERG AND MIDLANDS

- **Mighty Ukhahlamba Peaks**
- **Historic battlefield tours**
- **Mountainous Lesotho**
- **Gandhi statue in Pietermaritzburg**

Known to the Zulu as *Ukhahlamba* – "a barrier of spears" – the mighty Drakensberg Mountains look down on the lush valleys that have long provided rich grazing. The hunter-gatherer San Bushmen made this region their home, and traces of their lives can be seen in the beautiful rock art in the **Natal Drakensberg Park** *(see pp216–17)*. The area was later colonized by Xhosa, Zulu, Afrikaner and British people, leading to a succession of fierce conflicts. A **battlefields tour** *(see p220)* takes in such immortal sites as Blood River, Rorke's Drift and Ladysmith.

Though entirely surrounded by South Africa, **Lesotho** *(see 214–15)* is an independent country, and the mountain refuge of the self-governing Basotho tribe. Abundant flora, fauna, rock art and fossil deposits make this the perfect destination for anyone who loves outdoor pursuits. **Pietermaritzburg** *(see pp222–3)* has many interesting monuments, including one of Gandhi, who began his fight against racial inequality here.

The rugged landscape of the Drakenberg Mountains

High-rise buildings dominating the Johannesburg skyline

A group of Zulu warriors performing a tribal dance

DURBAN AND ZULULAND

- **Bustling Durban**
- **Thrilling game parks**
- **Zulu heritage**

The country's biggest port, and third-largest city, **Durban** *(see pp228–33)* is a popular destination in KwaZulu-Natal. The city's large Indian population adds another dimension to the nation's rich cultural mix, and the beautiful **Juma Musjid Mosque** *(see p230)* and **Temple of Understanding** *(see p231)* are well worth visiting. Durban has a fairly high crime rate, so it is best for visitors to stay within the main tourist areas.

The region is also home to some of South Africa's best game parks. Situated in the north are rich reserves of bush and grassland that are the perfect habitat for the "Big Five": lion, leopard, rhino, buffalo and elephant. **Hluhluwe-Umfolozi Park** *(see p240)* and **Itala Game Reserve** *(see p240–41)* offer excellent opportunities to view these wild creatures.

The legacy of the Zulu warriors is never far away, and **Shakaland** *(see p239)* is a fantastic reconstruction of a typical village.

GAUTENG AND SUN CITY

- **Big business in Jo'burg**
- **Vibrant Soweto**
- **Pretoria/Tshwane – the administrative capital**
- **The Palace of the Lost City**

Dynamic **Johannesburg** *(see pp256–9)* is a city of contrasts, with affluence and poverty found within a short distance of each other. **Sandton** *(see p263)* has become a wealthy suburb with great shopping and entertainment, but **Soweto** *(see p263)* has yet to feel the effects of the improved economy. The township can be visited as part of a guided tour, and it's worth joining one for the vibrant music and art. It is not advisable, however, to go on your own.

The administrative capital, **Pretoria/Tshwane** *(see pp266–7)*, has many elegant monuments and buildings. Less expected are the purple jacaranda trees, which burst into bloom each spring.

An alternative to cultural pursuits is the **Palace of the Lost City** casino *(see pp270–71)*, which is devoted to all forms of entertainment.

BLYDE RIVER CANYON AND KRUGER

- **Scenic Panorama Route**
- **Incredible national parks and reserves**
- **The waterfalls tour**
- **Beautiful Swaziland**

Some of the most incredible landscapes in South Africa are found where the land drops from the northern peaks of the imposing Drakensberg Mountains to the seemingly endless bushlands of the veld far below. A spectacular scenic drive known as the **Panorama Route** *(see p279)* provides a good overview, with plenty of pull-in points to take in the view. **Kruger National Park** *(see pp284–7)*, the oldest and largest game reserve in the world, offers the same beautiful scenery, but with the added attraction of the "Big Five". It can be easy to concentrate on just these wonderful animals, but be aware that the park is also home to many other species, including cheetah, crocodile and baboon.

Scoured by a fast-flowing river, the **Blyde River Canyon** *(see p279)* is vast in extent, and there are more waterfalls here than in any other area of South Africa. **Lisbon Falls** *(see p277)* is the highest, with an impressive 90-m (295-ft) drop. The beautiful kingdom of **Swaziland** *(see pp288–9)* provides excellent hiking opportunities through highlands and nature reserves.

A flock of Karoo lamb at a farm in the town of Graaff-Reinet

SOUTH OF THE ORANGE

- **Unique Karoo landscape**
- **Vast sheep ranches**
- **Graaff-Reinet's architecture**
- **Hardy mountain zebras**

The Orange River is the largest and longest river in South Africa, but to the immediate south is a scrubland area where water is always scarce. Named by the Khoina Tribe, the Karoo ("land of great thirst") may seem inhospitable, but it supports many plant and animal species. The **Karoo National Park** and **Karoo Nature Reserve** *(see p302)* were set up to conserve the region's unique heritage.

The area is also home to large sheep ranches that produce huge quantities of mutton and wool. **Cradock** *(see p306)* is the hub of the sheep-farming business and has a lovely church modelled on London's St-Martin-in-the-Fields. **Graaff-Reinet** *(see pp304–5)* grew up around the magistrate's court that was established here in 1786. The town is known for its beautiful Cape Dutch architecture. The **Mountain Zebra National Park** *(see p306)* was created to save the Cape mountain zebra from extinction. The park has been successful in its efforts, and there is now a population of over 250 animals.

Lions relaxing in the sands of the Kalahari Desert

NORTH OF THE ORANGE

- **Kimberley's diamond rush**
- **Bloemfontein – the judicial capital**
- **Wild Kalahari Desert**

Formerly a quiet farming district, **Kimberley** *(see pp316–17)* was the scene of the world's greatest diamond rush. The famed Big Hole is a vast man-made crater that yielded an incredibly rich haul, including the Cullinan Diamond, the largest gem of this type ever found.

Bloemfontein *(see pp318–19)* is the judicial capital of South Africa and has an entirely different atmosphere. There are many grand buildings here, including the Old Presidency and the Appeal Court. The cool and leafy King's Park provides a respite from the formal architecture and is a pleasant place to stop for lunch.

The Kalahari Desert has been protected by the formation of the **Kgalagadi Transfrontier Park** *(see p315)*, Africa's largest national park. The desert is home to 19 species of carnivore, including lion, cheetah, brown hyena and tawny eagle.

Putting South Africa on the Map

The southernmost country on the African continent, South Africa is roughly five times the size of Britain. It covers an area of 1,223,201 sq km (472,156 sq miles), and has a population of around 46 million. The sovereign kingdoms of Swaziland and Lesotho lie within its borders. The Atlantic, which washes its western shores, and the Indian Ocean, which laps the East Coast, meet at Cape Agulhas, Africa's most southerly tip. To the north of South Africa lie the independent neighbouring states of Namibia, Botswana, Zimbabwe and Mozambique.

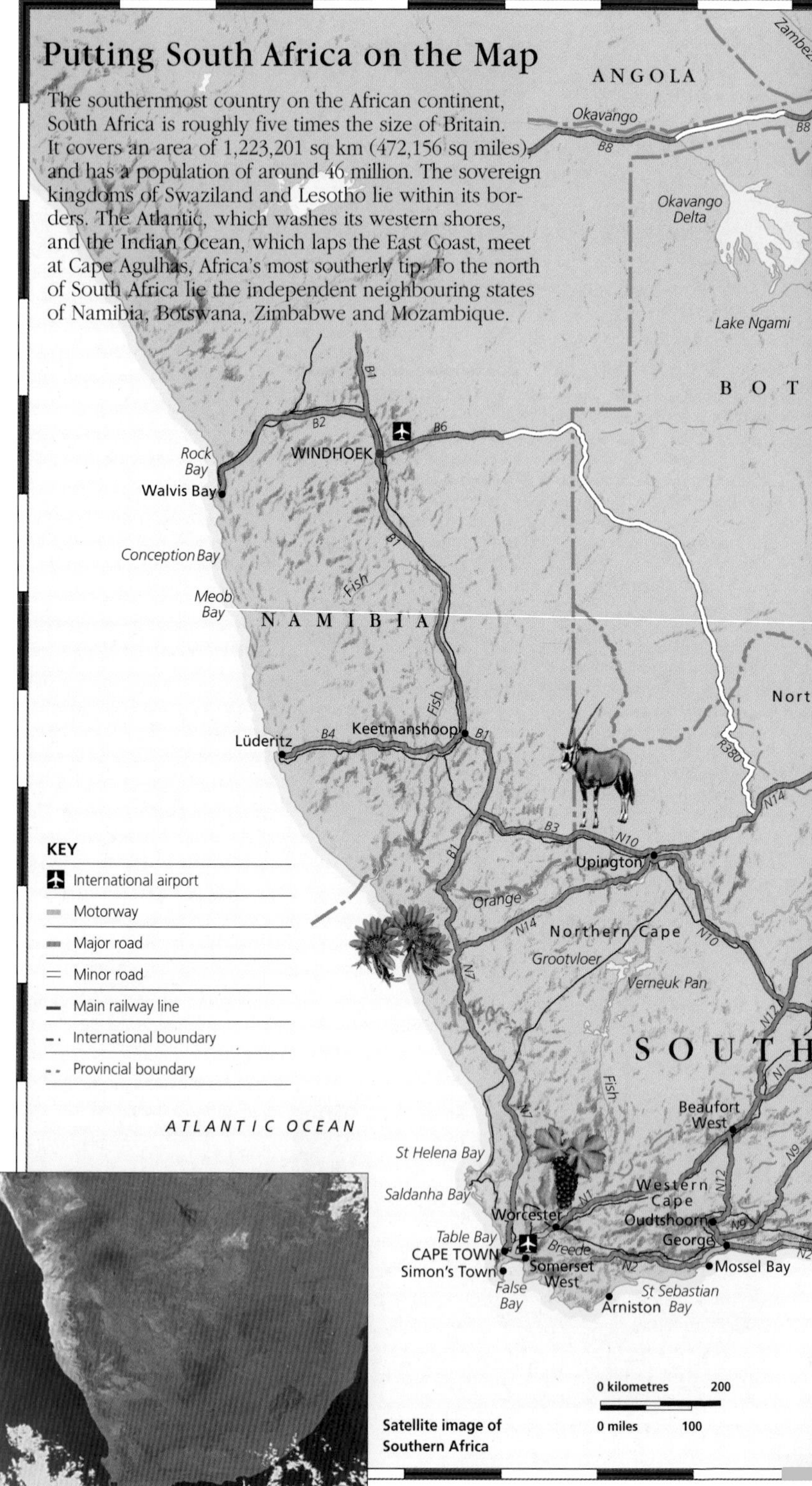

Satellite image of Southern Africa

◁ Formations of the Drakensberg mountain range

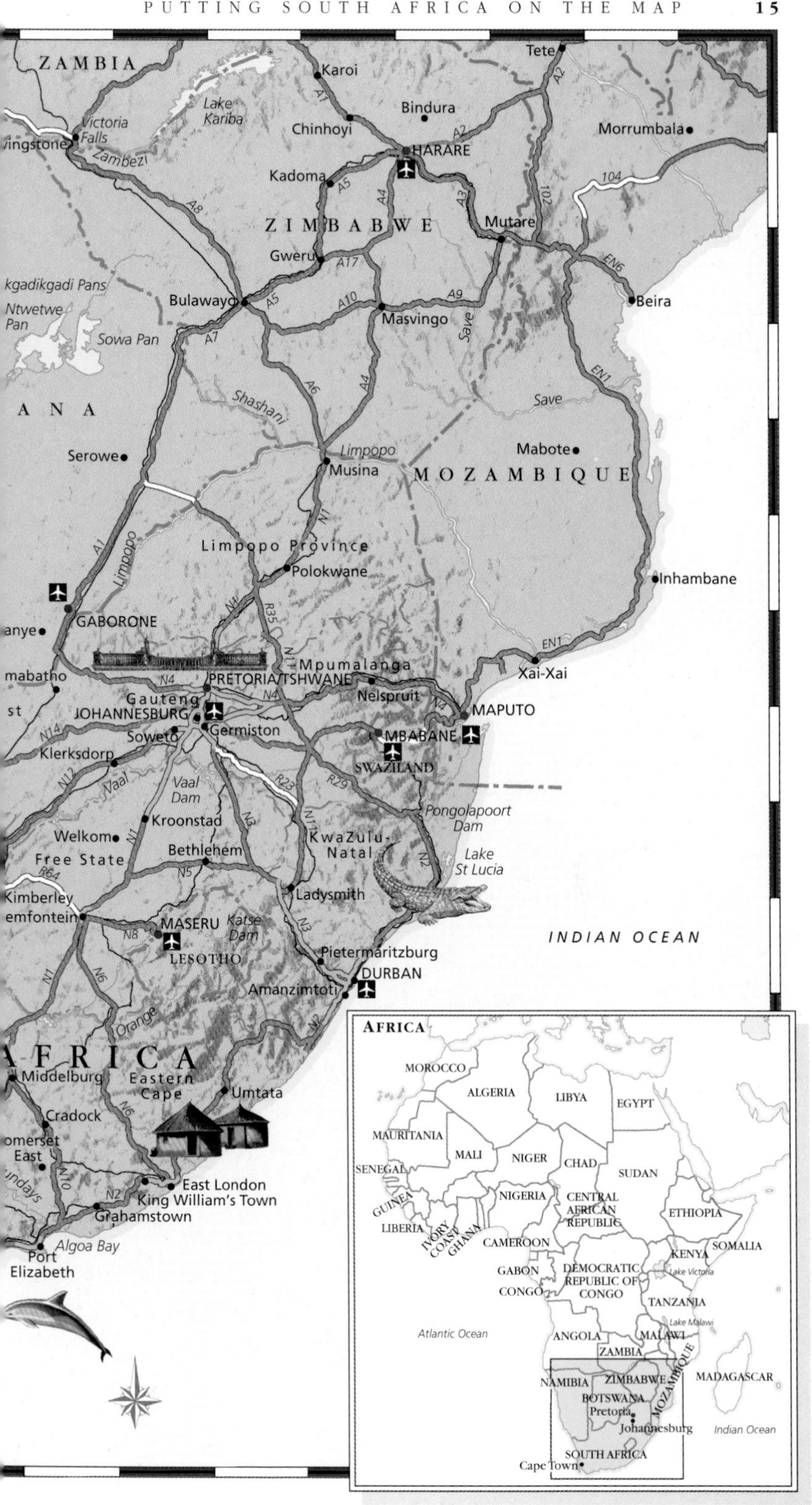
ZAMBIA
Lake Kariba
Victoria Falls
Zambezi
Karoi
Bindura
Chinhoyi
Tete
Morrumbala
HARARE
Kadoma
ZIMBABWE
Mutare
Gweru
Beira
Bulawayo
Masvingo
Sowa Pan
Ntwetwe Pan
Shashani
Save
Limpopo
Mabote
Serowe
Musina
MOZAMBIQUE
Limpopo Province
Polokwane
Inhambane
GABORONE
Mpumalanga
Xai-Xai
PRETORIA/TSHWANE
Nelspruit
Gauteng
JOHANNESBURG
MAPUTO
Germiston
Soweto
MBABANE
SWAZILAND
Klerksdorp
Vaal Dam
Kroonstad
Pongolapoort Dam
Welkom
KwaZulu-Natal
Lake St Lucia
Free State
Bethlehem
Kimberley
Ladysmith
MASERU
Katse Dam
LESOTHO
INDIAN OCEAN
Pietermaritzburg
DURBAN
Amanzimtoti
Orange
AFRICA
Middelburg
Eastern Cape
Umtata
Cradock
East London
King William's Town
Grahamstown
Algoa Bay
Port Elizabeth
AFRICA
MOROCCO
ALGERIA
LIBYA
EGYPT
MAURITANIA
MALI
NIGER
CHAD
SUDAN
SENEGAL
NIGERIA
CENTRAL AFRICAN REPUBLIC
ETHIOPIA
GUINEA
LIBERIA
IVORY COAST
GHANA
CAMEROON
SOMALIA
KENYA
GABON
DEMOCRATIC REPUBLIC OF CONGO
Lake Victoria
CONGO
TANZANIA
Atlantic Ocean
Lake Malawi
ANGOLA
MALAWI
ZAMBIA
NAMIBIA
ZIMBABWE
MADAGASCAR
BOTSWANA
Pretoria
MOZAMBIQUE
Johannesburg
Indian Ocean
SOUTH AFRICA
Cape Town

Road Map of South Africa

International airports at Johannesburg, Cape Town and Durban link South Africa with the rest of the world, while domestic airports serve many of the smaller centres. International ocean liners dock at the ports of Cape Town, Durban and Port Elizabeth. An efficient road network spans the vast interior, linking cities and towns. This book divides the country into ten regions, with a separate chapter for Cape Town. Officially South Africa has nine provinces.

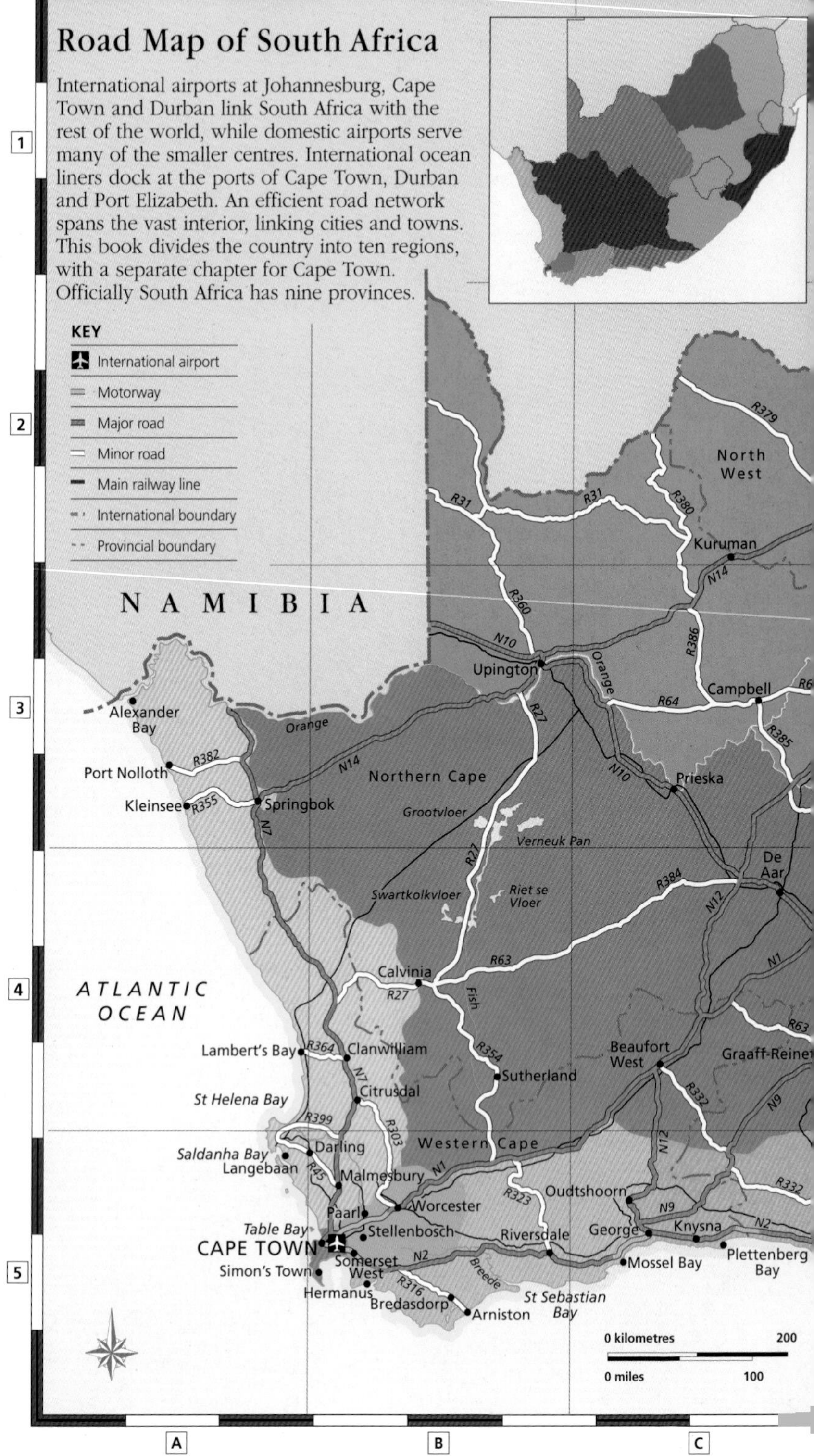

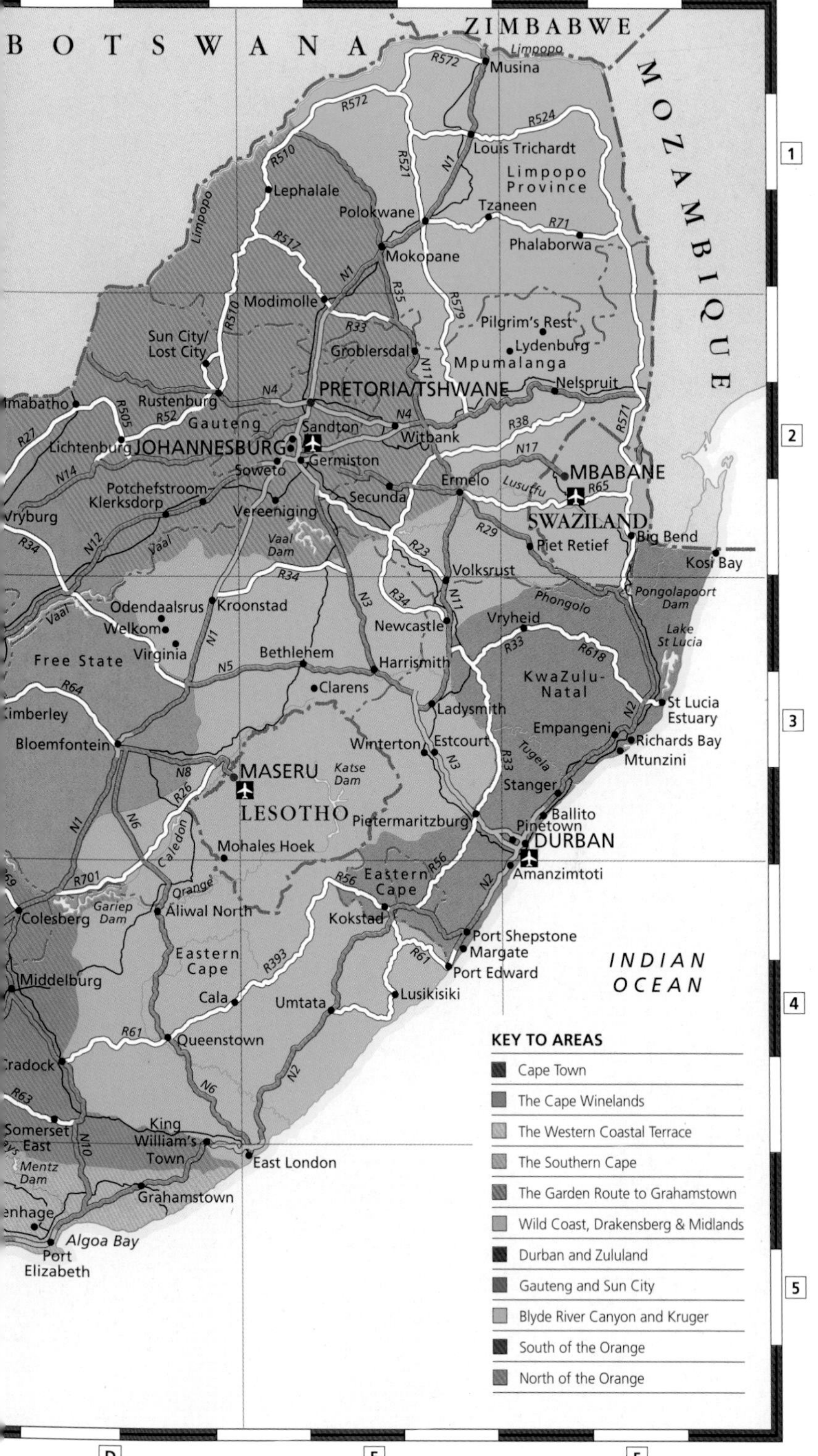
BOTSWANA
ZIMBABWE
MOZAMBIQUE
SWAZILAND
LESOTHO
INDIAN OCEAN
Limpopo Province
Mpumalanga
Gauteng
Free State
KwaZulu-Natal
Eastern Cape
PRETORIA/TSHWANE
JOHANNESBURG
MBABANE
MASERU
DURBAN
Musina
Louis Trichardt
Tzaneen
Phalaborwa
Lephalale
Polokwane
Mokopane
Modimolle
Sun City/ Lost City
Groblersdal
Pilgrim's Rest
Lydenburg
Nelspruit
Rustenburg
Sandton
Witbank
Germiston
Soweto
Lichtenburg
Potchefstroom
Klerksdorp
Vereeniging
Secunda
Ermelo
Vryburg
Piet Retief
Big Bend
Kosi Bay
Volksrust
Kroonstad
Odendaalsrus
Welkom
Virginia
Newcastle
Vryheid
Bethlehem
Harrismith
Clarens
Ladysmith
Winterton
Estcourt
Bloemfontein
Pietermaritzburg
Mohales Hoek
Empangeni
Richards Bay
Mtunzini
St Lucia Estuary
Stanger
Ballito
Pinetown
Amanzimtoti
Kokstad
Aliwal North
Colesberg
Port Shepstone
Margate
Port Edward
Lusikisiki
Umtata
Cala
Middelburg
Queenstown
Cradock
Somerset East
King William's Town
East London
Grahamstown
Port Elizabeth
Algoa Bay
Vaal Dam
Katse Dam
Gariep Dam
Mentz Dam
Pongolapoort Dam
Lake St Lucia
Limpopo
Vaal
Orange
Caledon
Tugela
Phongolo
Lusutfu
KEY TO AREAS
Cape Town
The Cape Winelands
The Western Coastal Terrace
The Southern Cape
The Garden Route to Grahamstown
Wild Coast, Drakensberg & Midlands
Durban and Zululand
Gauteng and Sun City
Blyde River Canyon and Kruger
South of the Orange
North of the Orange

A PORTRAIT OF SOUTH AFRICA

Blue skies, game parks, wilderness areas, and the promise of a sun-drenched holiday are what draws most visitors to South Africa. While the country continues to be troubled by deep-rooted racial divisions, the determination of her people to begin anew makes it an inspiring and beautiful place to explore.

South Africa, roughly the size of Spain and France combined, encompasses an astonishing diversity of environments: from the dramatic arid moonscapes of the northwest to the forest-fringed coastline of the Garden Route; from the flat, dry Karoo interior to the craggy Drakensberg in the east; the manicured vineyards of the Cape to the spring flower fields of Namaqualand. South Africa is the only country in the world that can lay claim to an entire floral kingdom within its borders. Centred on a small area in the Western Cape, *fynbos* (literally "fine-leaved bush") comprises a unique variety of proteas, ericas and grasses.

King protea

The many wildlife parks further north are home to the Big Five: buffalo, elephant, leopard, lion and rhino, while the wetlands and marine reserves along the east coast teem with sea creatures and colourful birds, great and small, that are often overlooked.

And then there are the beaches, favourite holiday destination of the locals, for boardsailing, swimming, surfing, angling, and suntanning.

The "rainbow people of God" is how former Anglican Archbishop Desmond Tutu described the newly liberated South African nation – this conglomeration of beliefs, traditions, and heritages living within a country of breathtaking natural wonders.

Acacia trees survive along the parched fringes of the Kalahari desert

◁ A young Zulu dancer in traditional costume

Groote Schuur Hospital, where the world's first successful heart transplant was carried out in 1967

Yet, these stark contrasts do not exist in scenery alone. Many observers speak of two worlds within one country: a first and a third. Although 60 per cent of the continent's electricity is generated in South Africa, more than half of the nation's households still have to rely on paraffin, wood and gas for light, cooking, and heating their homes.

The modern South African state began as a halfway station. Dutch traders of the 17th century, on long sea voyages to their colonies in the East, replenished their stores at the Cape. A fertile land, South Africa is still largely self-reliant today, compelled to become so as a result of the long period of international political isolation that resulted from its former policy of racial discrimination known as *apartheid* (apartness).

Pouring gold bars

South Africa became a world producer of gold and petroleum. Impressive advances were made in communication, weapons technology and mining, but apartheid stood in the way of harmony and economic growth. In the late 1960s, while the world's first human heart transplant was performed at Groote Schuur Hospital in Cape Town, the majority of South Africans struggled to fulfill their most basic needs of food, shelter and education.

Farm labourers relaxing on a hay wagon, West Coast

PEOPLE AND SOCIETY

Living in a land of such differences, it is hardly surprising that South Africans lack a collective identity. In 1994, English, Afrikaans, and nine Bantu tongues were recognized as official languages. Afrikaans, derived from Dutch and altered through contact with other tongues, is spoken by 18 per cent of the population.

South Africa's cultural mix has its roots in a colonial past. The original hunter-gatherer inhabitants of the Cape were joined, about 1,000 years ago, by migrating Bantu-speakers from the north. In the 17th century, European settlers appeared – first the Dutch, then the British and French – with their slaves from Indonesia, Madagascar, and India. Later followed indentured labourers from India. Settlers and slaves alike brought with them their culinary traditions, and if there is a national cuisine it is Cape Malay: mild lamb and fish curries sweetened with spiced fruit. Although seafood is relished, South Africans are really a meat-loving nation. The outdoor *braai* (barbecue) is popular all around the globe, but no one does it quite like South Africans, with fiercely guarded secret recipes, and competitions for the best *boerewors* (spicy sausage) and *potjiekos* (a tasty stew prepared in a three-legged cast iron pot).

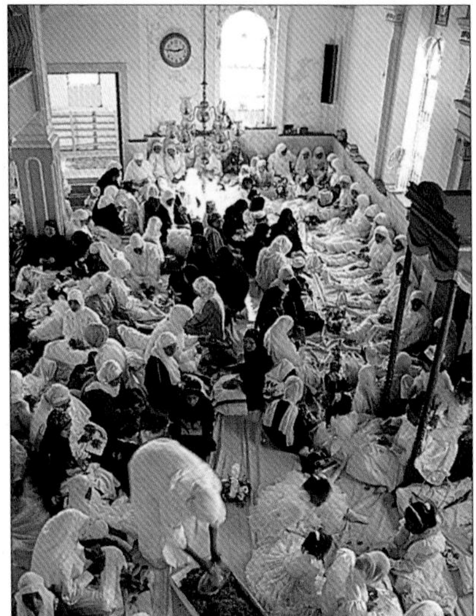

Feast day preparations in a Cape Town mosque

Religion crosses many of the cultural and social divides. The African independent churches have a large following, as their approach includes aspects of tribal mysticism, and a firm belief in the influence of ancestral spirits. The Dutch Reformed, Roman Catholic, Presbyterian, and Anglican churches draw worshippers from all population groups. Islam is strongly represented in the Western Cape, while Buddhists and Hindus are mainly found in Durban.

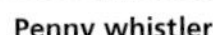

Penny whistler

CULTURE AND SPORT

A new awareness of African identity is increasingly apparent. Music, which has always played a central part in traditional ceremony and celebration, clearly leads the way. Regular church choir-festivals attest to the popularity of, especially, gospel and choral harmony. The distinctive sound of Zulu *mbube* (unaccompanied choral singing) has become one of South Africa's best known exports.

African choir performing gospel and harmonies

Sindiwe Magona is the author of several books about her life as a black South African woman

The natural African gift for rhythm and harmony easily made the transition from rural area to city. Although the tunes are much influenced by popular North American music, jazz, soul, *kwela* (the inimitable piercing sound of the penny whistle), *kwaito* (transient pop), rock and reggae all have a determined local flavour.

The white Afrikaner's cultural heritage, accumulated over centuries of isolation from the European motherland, today embraces a powerful body of prose and poetry, and a very distinctive musical tradition. Afrikaans songs tend to be rather nostalgic, often evoking gentler times. By contrast, the music of the coloured people is lively, distinguished by bouncy melodies and cheerful, racy lyrics that belie the sadness and indignities of the past.

Cape minstrel

During the long, dark years of apartheid, oppression and suffering offered much ready-made source material for the arts. Although older South African literature undoubtedly has its luminaries *(see pp30–31)*, modern writers are moving away from racial introspection towards more universal themes.

Most South Africans are passionate about sport – whether they are participating or watching. This ardour has increased since the end of the sports boycott. The Rugby World Cup, which was held in Cape Town and other cities in 1995 and won by a jubilant South Africa, probably did more to unite the nation than anything else. South Africans countrywide celebrated their national team's victory. Soccer, cricket, boxing, horse racing and athletics also draw the expectant crowds.

Faces blazing with pride, a jubilant nation celebrates its Rugby World Cup victory in 1995

South Africans enjoy the outdoors, as here, on popular Clifton beach in Cape Town

SOUTH AFRICA TODAY

Perhaps the best starting point from which to chart the end of apartheid is the announcement of then President FW de Klerk regarding the unbanning of the African National Congress (ANC), and the Communist Party and Pan-Africanist Congress (PAC). On 11 February 1990, Nelson Mandela was released from the Victor Verster Prison near Paarl. He had been imprisoned since 1963.

South Africa's children have a special place in *"Madiba's"* heart

Amid escalating violence, negotiations began for a peaceful transition to democracy. Finally, on 27 April 1994, all South Africans voted. Five days later the results were announced: the ANC had secured 63 per cent of the votes, and Nelson Mandela became the first Black president of the "New South Africa".

The new constitution was approved in May 1996 and has, arguably, the most enlightened Bill of Rights in the world. It outlaws discrimination on the grounds of ethnic or social origin, religion, gender, sexual orientation, and language. Yet, many citizens still live very close to poverty. Despite the country's many natural resources, advanced technology and sophisticated infrastructure, the gap between South Africa's privileged and its poor is widening. Jobs are in very short supply and tough times lie ahead, but the nation looks to the future applying its president's maxim: "It is not easy to remain bitter if one is busy with constructive things."

A bold mural in Johannesburg portrays the multicultural nation

The Contrasting Coasts

Two ocean currents influence the coastal climate of South Africa: the tropical Agulhas Current, which flows south down the East Coast, and the cold, north-flowing Benguela Current along the western shores. The two merge somewhere off lonely Cape Agulhas, Africa's most southerly cape. Together with the winds and mountains, these ocean movements determine the region's coastal variance: the aridity of the west versus the luxuriant forest in the east. The coastal fauna and flora, both terrestrial and aquatic, display interesting variations. Here, too, the west differs substantially from the east, as plants and animals have adapted to their specific environments.

Blue whales, *at 33 m (108 ft) the largest mammals on earth, are one of the whale species that frequent South African coastal waters during the Arctic winter.*

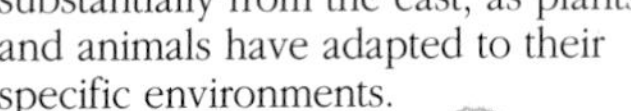

Drosanthemums *are low-growing plants, well adapted to arid West Coast conditions. They store precious water in their small, thick leaves and flower between August and October.*

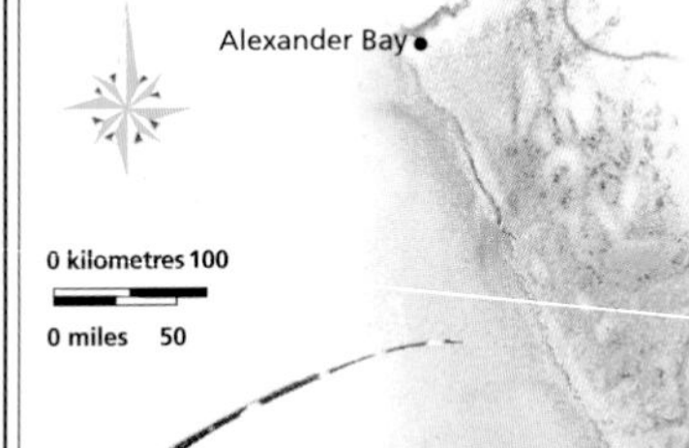

The black korhaan *inhabits dry coastal scrubland. The males are strikingly coloured and protect their territory with raucous calls. Females are an inconspicuous mottled brown and avoid detection by standing perfectly still.*

West Coast rock lobster, *important to the region's economy, are harvested under special licence. They are not reared on a commercial basis.*

The Benguela Current flows north, carrying cold water from the Antarctic.

At Cape Agulhas, the waters of the two currents converge.

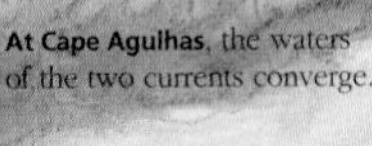

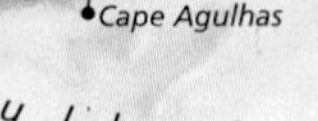

THE WEST COAST

Even in summer, water temperatures average only 14°C (57°F). This precludes the formation of rain-bearing clouds, and annual precipitation is below 250 mm (10 in). The lack of fresh water means that only tough succulents survive on dew from sea mists. The sea water, full of nutrients, sustains a rich and varied marine life.

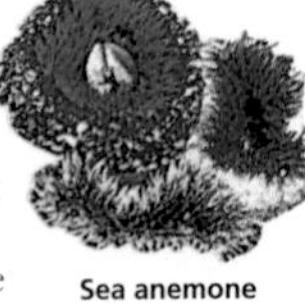

Sea anemone

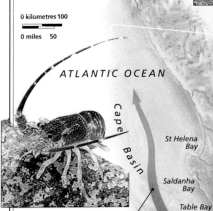

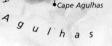

Memorial plaque at Cape Agulhas

CAPE AGULHAS

The southernmost point of the African continent is not Cape Point, but unassuming Cape Agulhas on the rocky east side of the windswept, shallow Danger Point headland. The Portuguese word *agulhas*, from which it gets its name, means "needles". It was here, early navigators discovered, that the compass needle was not affected by magnetic deviation, but pointed true north. A plaque is set into the rock and markers give the distances to international cities.

Various dolphin species *can be seen frolicking in the warm currents off towns like Durban and Margate. They usually occur in groups of 10 to 15 individuals.*

The genus *Crinum* *(amaryllis family) is commonly seen in swampy grassland along the East Coast. It flowers in summer.*

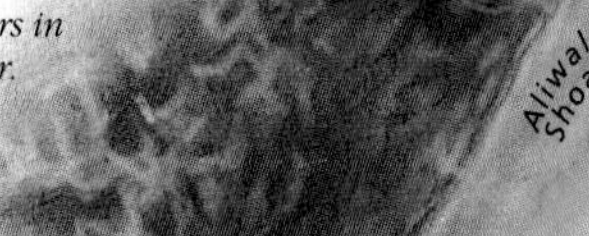

The Grass owl *(Tyto capensis) occurs in swampy grassland along the east coast of South Africa.*

The warm Agulhas Current causes humid conditions along the East Coast.

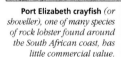

Port Elizabeth crayfish *(or shoveller), one of many species of rock lobster found around the South African coast, has little commercial value.*

THE EAST COAST

The warm Agulhas Current that flows south through the Mozambique Channel creates hot, humid conditions along the East Coast. Vegetation is subtropical and mangrove forests flourish in the Umgeni River Estuary near Durban. The annual migration of big pilchard shoals is eagerly awaited by fish, bird and man. Coral reefs, rare in South African waters, are found in the St Lucia Marine Reserve.

Nudibranch

The Landscapes and Flora of South Africa

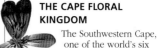

South Africa's flora has charmed visitors and intrigued botanists for years. Many species are widely distributed within the country, but each region has produced distinct characteristics, the result of varying geographic, climatic and soil conditions. In the more arid western reaches of the country, plants tend to be small and low-growing, flowering briefly after the winter rains, while further east open grassland and bushveld dominate. Along the East Coast grow lush subtropical coastal forests.

Aloe flower

THE CAPE FLORAL KINGDOM

Pelargonium

The Southwestern Cape, one of the world's six floral kingdoms, boasts around 8,500 different plants in an area less than four per cent of the Southern African land surface. This so-called *fynbos* (fine-leaved bush) includes some 350 species of protea, as well as pelargoniums, ericas, reeds and irises. Most are endemic to the area, and is well represented in the Kirstenbosch National Botanical Garden *(see pp104–5)*.

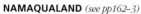

SEMI-DESERT

Succulent

In Southern Africa, true desert is confined to the Namib. The semi-desert Great Karoo region covers about one-third of South Africa. Its flora has evolved to withstand aridity and extreme temperatures. Many succulents, including the aloes, mesembryanthemums, euphorbias and stapelias, store water in their thick leaves or roots. The seeds of daisy-like ephemeral plants may lie dormant for years, only to germinate and flower briefly when the conditions are favourable *(see pp162–3)*. Trees tend to grow along seasonal river courses.

NAMAQUALAND *(see pp162–3)*

Many succulent plants in this region survive only through the condensation of nightly mists that roll in from the Atlantic Ocean. Adaptation has led to many bizarre species, such as the *kokerboom* (quiver tree), *half-mens* (half-human), and the insectivorous plants of the Stapelia family. Dwarf shrubs and scraggy bushes are widely spaced over dusty land that is bare for most of the year, until even modest winter rains raise dense, multi-hued crops of daisy-like *vygie* blossoms.

Vygies

TEMPERATE FOREST

Dense evergreen forests thrive in the high-rainfall area around Knysna *(see pp186–7)*. They produce lovely rare hardwoods such as stinkwood and yellowwood, two types that also occur along the subtropical coastal belt of KwaZulu-Natal. Knysna's temperate forests have a characteristic undergrowth of shrubs, ferns, fungi, and creepers, such as the wispy "old man's beard". Mature trees may reach a height of 60 m (195 ft), with a girth of seven metres (23 ft).

Forest fungus

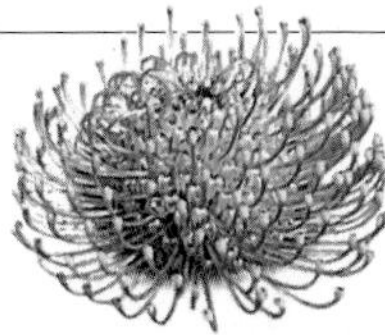

***Pincushion proteas** bloom from June to December in colours ranging from yellow to deep red. Flower heads last for up to three weeks and attract sunbirds and insects.*

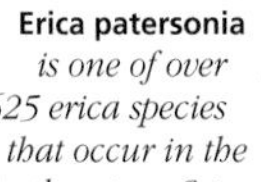

***Erica patersonia** is one of over 625 erica species that occur in the Southwestern Cape. It is mainly found along streams.*

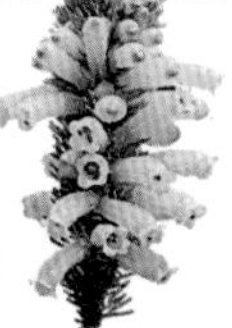

***Protea grandiceps** is one of the most widely distributed of its species. It grows at the higher altitudes of coastal mountains.*

***Ericas** are found on Table Mountain, where* Erica dichrus *provides dense red splashes of colour.*

***Yellow pincushion proteas** grow on a tall, shrub that is found near the coast.*

BUSHVELD

Large tracts of the interior are covered with tall grasses and low trees, most of them deciduous, fine-leaved and thorny. The Kruger National Park *(see pp284–7)* is an excellent example of several transitional types occurring between sparse shrub and savanna; here shrubs grow densely and larger tree types include marula, mopane and baobab. The large acacia family is characterized by pod-bearing trees and shrubs with clusters of small, golden-yellow flowers.

"Weeping boerbean" pod

HIGH MOUNTAIN

Mountain flora, zoned according to altitude and increasing severity of the environment, rises from dense heath to mixed scrub and grasses. A relatively small subalpine belt, 2,800 m (9,000 ft) above sea level, is confined to the Drakensberg region *(see pp216–17)*. Characteristic floral species are Helichrysum ("everlastings"), sedges and ericas. In many areas, annuals make brief, colourful spring appearances. Among the proteas growing in this region is the rare snow protea on the high peaks of the Cedarberg *(see pp160–61)*.

Watsonia

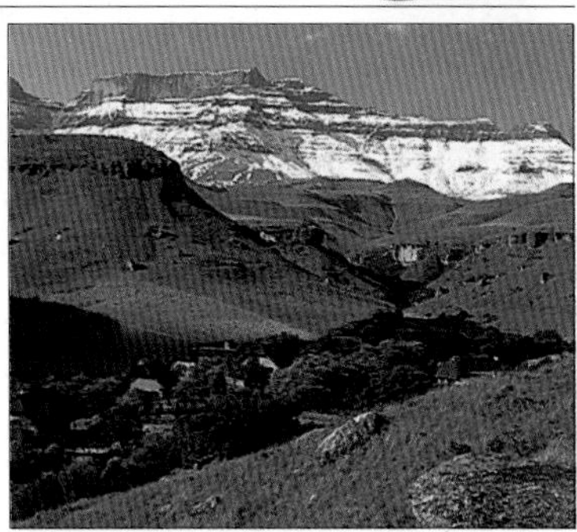

SUBTROPICAL COASTAL BELT

Brackish swamps, saline estuaries and lush plant growth are characteristic of the KwaZulu-Natal coast. Mangroves anchor themselves to their unstable habitat with stilt-like roots, while higher up on the banks grow palms and the broad-leaved wild banana of the Strelitzia family. A good example of typical East Coast vegetation can be seen at Kosi Bay *(see p243)*, where swamps surround lakes that are overgrown with water lilies and reeds. Dune forests and grasslands are dotted with wild palms.

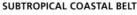

Water lily

South Africa's Wildlife Heritage

Before the arrival of the white colonists, nomadic Khoina hunted wild animals for food, while to the east Zulu and Venda traded in ivory and organized ceremonial hunts – but their spears and pitfall traps had little impact. In comparison to 17th-century Europe, South Africa's wildlife seemed inexhaustible, and by the mid-19th century, the settlers' weapons had seen to it that the vast herds had disappeared – many species were in danger of extinction. Conservation measures over the past century have brought about a spectacular recovery, and South Africa's wildlife reserves are now among the finest in the world.

Giraffe

The klipspringer, *agile and sure-footed, o ccurs in mountainous areas throughout the country.*

Bee-eaters, *one of around 840 bird species recorded in the country, gather in flocks along rivers in the Kruger National Park. They catch flying insects and return to their perch to consume their prey.*

Blue wildebeest

Zebra

Nyala bulls can be distinguished from the similar-looking kudu by the orange colour of their lower legs.

Warthog

Princeps demodocus demodocus*, the attractive Christmas butterfly, is also known as the citrus swallowtail, and can be seen throughout South Africa from September to April. As its name suggests, the species often occurs in citrus groves.*

AT THE WATERHOLE

In the dry winter months (May to September), an ever-changing wildlife pageant unfolds as animals gather at waterholes to drink. Wooden hides have been erected at waterholes in KwaZulu-Natal's Hluhluwe-Umfolozi *(see p240)* and Mkuzi game reserves, while the rivers in the Kruger National Park offer the best vantage points.

AFRICA'S BIG FIVE

This term originated from hunting jargon for the most dangerous and sought-after trophy animals. Today, they are still an attraction, with Kruger National Park *(see pp284–7)* the prime Big-Five viewing destination. Hluhluwe-Umfolozi, and the Pilanesberg and Madikwe reserves, too, are well-known sanctuaries.

Lions, *the largest of the African cats, live in prides of varying size controlled by one or more dominant males.*

The black rhinoceros *is in serious danger of extinction. It is distinguished from the white rhino by its longer upper lip.*

THE FIRST WILDLIFE RESERVES

By the mid-19th century, hunters had decimated the big game. Subspecies like the quagga (relative of the zebra) and Cape lion had become extinct. As towns expanded people began to view wildlife as an asset and, in 1889, the Natal *Volksraad* (people's council) agreed to establish a wildlife reserve. In 1894, a strip of land between KwaZulu-Natal and Swaziland became the Pongola Game Reserve, Africa's first conservation area. Four years later, President Paul Kruger signed a proclamation that established the forerunner of a sanctuary that was later named Kruger National Park in his honour.

Quagga

Early 19th-century hunting party

Female impala

Nyala cows, usually accompanied by dominant bulls, are often spotted in the woodlands of northern KwaZulu-Natal.

Waterholes dry out rapidly in the summer heat and the animals suffer much hardship.

Vervet monkeys usually avoid the arid habitats.

The hunt *is a brutal, yet timeless African sequence. Cheetah mainly prey on smaller gazelles, like springbok and impala.*

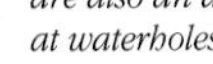

Oxpeckers and kudu *are an example of the symbiosis that has evolved between different animals under the harsh African conditions. The birds free the antelope of parasites and are also an alarm system at waterholes.*

Spotted hyena *are one of the most interesting of African predators. Loose family groups are led by females who, due to high levels of male hormones, also have male genitalia. Powerful pack hunters, they can bring down animals as large as buffalo.*

Buffalo *are the most abundant of the Big Five and occur in large herds. Old bulls become loners and may be extremely dangerous.*

Leopards *are shy cats that are largely nocturnal and often rest on tree branches.*

Elephants *live in tight-knit family groups led by a matriarch. The bulls remain solitary or may band together to form bachelor herds.*

Literary South Africa

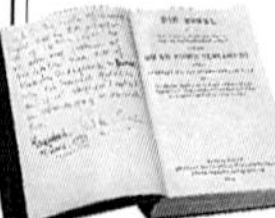
Afrikaans Bible

A rich literary tradition exists in all 11 national languages, which include nine Bantu tongues, mostly from the Nguni and Sotho branches. Most books were published in Afrikaans or English, while much of the African heritage was handed down orally. Books in African tongues are now beginning to enjoy a wider circulation, both locally and abroad, and are also appearing in foreign translation. Over the years, South Africa has inspired a number of outstanding authors and poets, among them Sir Percy FitzPatrick, Olive Schreiner, Sir Laurens van der Post, Nadine Gordimer and Mzwakhe Mbuli.

CJ Langenhoven wrote *Die Stem*, one of the two national anthems

Painting by Credo Mutwa, taken from the book *African Proverbs*

TRADITIONAL AFRICAN STORIES

Many African communities have an oral tradition of entertaining, informative stories, genealogies, proverbs and riddles that have been passed on from generation to generation.

Izibongo, simplistically translated as praise songs, are very complex oral presentations delivered by a skilled performer known as *mbongi*. This rhythmic form of poetry uses exalted language, rich in metaphor and parallelisms. At the inauguration of Nelson Mandela, two *izibongo* were performed in Xhosa.

Among the best written works are SEK Mqhayi's historic *Ityala Lamawele* (Lawsuit of the Twins) and A Jordan's *Ingqumbo Yeminyanya* (The Wrath of the Ancestors), both in Xhosa, and Thomas Mofolo's *Chaka* in Sotho, BW Vilakazi's *Noma nini* in Zulu, and Sol Plaatjie's *Mhudi* in Tswana.

English publications of traditional African tales, novels and poetry include *Indaba my Children* and *African Proverbs* by Credo Mutwa.

Actor Patrick Mynhardt dramatizes Herman Charles Bosman's *A Sip of Jerepigo*

AFRIKAANS LITERATURE

The Dutch spoken by the colonial authorities formed the basis of a local tongue that became known as Afrikaans, or simply *die taal* (the language). Efforts to translate the Bible into Afrikaans led to a vigorous campaign to have the language formally recognized. A direct result of these tireless efforts was the publication of almost 100 books before 1900.

The descriptive prose and lyrical poetry of literary greats like Gustav Preller, CJ Langenhoven, DF Malherbe and Totius (Jacob Daniël du Toit), who delighted in the use of their new language, helped to establish Afrikaans as the lingua franca.

Later writers, like PG du Plessis and Etienne Le Roux, placed Afrikaans literature in a wider context, while Adam Small and Breyten Breytenbach used it as a form of political and social protest against the white Afrikaner establishment.

"Afrikanerisms", deliberate use of Afrikaans words and sentence construction when writing in English, is a literary device used in Pauline Smith's *The Beadle*, and in Herman Charles Bosman's humorous short story *A Cask of Jerepigo*. Both works describe the life, joys and hardships of a rural Afrikaner community.

Afrikaans became a hated symbol of oppression during the apartheid years yet, today, it is more widely spoken than any other local tongue.

The 1924 publication of *The Flaming Terrapin* established Roy Campbell as a leading poet. Although the hardships of black South Africans had been highlighted in Herbert Dhlomo's short stories and Peter Abrahams's *Mine Boy*, it was the subject matter of race relations in *Cry the Beloved Country* (1948) by Alan Paton that attracted the world's attention.

Among several superb female writers, Nadine Gordimer (*A Sport of Nature* and *July's People*, among others) became the recipient of a Nobel Prize for Literature in 1991. The author contributed greatly to the standard of writing in South Africa, and her struggle against another of the apartheid era's crippling laws – censorship – paved the way for many others. Rose Zwi's *Another Year in Africa* is an insight into the life of South Africa's Jewish immigrants, while the autobiographical *To my Children's Children* is Sindiwe Magona's account of a youth spent in the former homeland of Transkei, and of the daily struggle in Cape Town's townships.

Jock of the Bushveld statue in the Kruger National Park

ENGLISH POETRY AND PROSE

Olive Schreiner's *Story of an African Farm* (1883), first published under a male pseudonym, presented the rural Afrikaner to an international audience for the first time. The book was startling, also, for its advanced views on feminism – sentiments that the author expanded on in *Woman and Labour* (1911).

Percy FitzPatrick's *Jock of the Bushveld* (1907) became one of the best-known of all South African titles. A blend of romantic adventure and realism, it tells the story of a transport rider and his dog on the early gold fields.

Later popular authors who achieved international sales include Geoffrey Jenkins, and Wilbur Smith whose novels, such as *Where the Lion Feeds*, have made him one of the world's best-selling writers. A more thought-provoking genre is that of Stuart Cloete's *The Abductors*, once banned in South Africa, and Sir Laurens van der Post's touching description of a dying culture in *Testament to the Bushmen*.

The works of André P Brink and JM Coetzee dealt mainly with social and political matters that were often viewed by the apartheid regime as attacks on the establishment. Brink's critical *Looking on Darkness* (1963) became the first Afrikaans novel to be banned in South Africa.

Local edition of *A Sport of Nature*

CONTEMPORARY LITERATURE

Autobiographies and travelogues, popular genres for modern local writers, offer insights into the lives of South Africans. Nelson Mandela's *Long Walk to Freedom* was a national bestseller. *Country of my Skull* is Antjie Krog's narrative of her two years spent reporting on the Truth and Reconciliation Commission, while *Beckett's Trek* and *Madibaland* by Denis Beckett, and Sarah Penny's *The Whiteness of Bones* are entertaining jaunts through South Africa and its neighbours. Zakes Mda's award-winning *Ways of Dying* gives the reader a glimpse of the professional mourner, while Ashraf Jamal's *Love Themes for the Wilderness* takes a life-affirming trip into contemporary urbanity.

STRUGGLE POETRY

During the apartheid years, conflict and the repression of Africans provided recurring themes. Produced orally in various Bantu tongues and in written form in English, the new means of expression was termed "Struggle Poetry". Oswald Mtshali's Sounds of a Cowhide Drum (1971) signalled the shift in black poetry from lyrical themes to indirect political messages in free verse. Other creators of this form of protest were Mzwakhe Mbuli, known as "the people's poet", Mafika Gwala, James Matthews, Sipho Sepamla, Njabulo Ndebele and Mongane Wally Serote. Their verse expressed disapproval of the socio-political conditions in the country and was, at the same time, a conscious attempt to raise the level of awareness among their people.

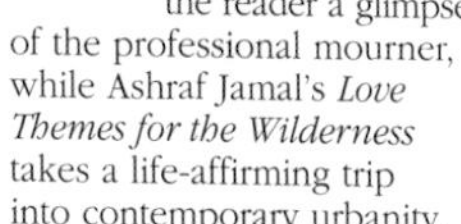

Mongane Wally Serote, poet and politician

South African Architecture

Diverse factors have influenced building styles in South Africa: climate, social structure, and the state of the economy have all shaped the country's homes. In earlier days, when suitable raw materials were often unavailable, ingenious adaptations resulted. Variations include the *hartbeeshuisie* (hard-reed house), a pitched-roof shelter built directly on the ground, and the beehive-shaped "corbelled" huts, built of stone in areas where structural timber was unobtainable, as in the Northern Cape. Modern South African building and engineering skills have kept abreast with international trends, and many different styles can be seen throughout the country.

Weaving the reed fence surrounding a traditional Swazi village

INDIGENOUS ARCHITECTURAL STYLES

Most traditional rural dwellings, often called "rondavels", are circular in shape. The conical roofs are traditionally constructed of a tightly woven reed or grass thatch, while the walls may be made of mud blocks mixed with cow dung, or consist of a framework of woven branches and covered with animal hide. Most of these homes, except the *matjieshuise* of the arid Namaqualand nomads for whom rain was no threat, are well insulated and waterproof. In recent times, materials like corrugated iron, plastic sheeting and cardboard have become popular, especially in informal settlements on the outskirts of cities.

Zulu "beehives" *are a community effort. The stick framework is erected by the men, and the women thatch it.*

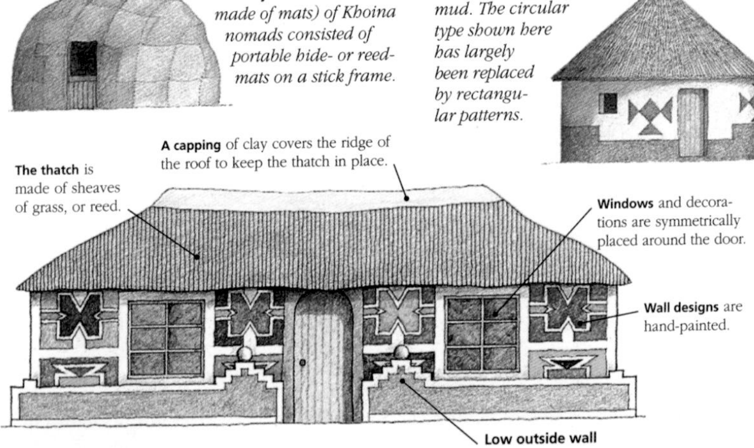

A capping of clay covers the ridge of the roof to keep the thatch in place.
The thatch is made of sheaves of grass, or reed.
Windows and decorations are symmetrically placed around the door.
Wall designs are hand-painted.
Low outside wall

The *matjieshuise* *(houses made of mats) of Khoina nomads consisted of portable hide- or reed-mats on a stick frame.*

Xhosa huts *are built of mud. The circular type shown here has largely been replaced by rectangular patterns.*

Ndebele homes *are, perhaps, the most eye-catching local style. The walls of the rectangular structures are traditionally painted by women, using bright primary colours. No stencils are used for the bold geometric motifs.*

Ndebele wall detail

Basotho huts, *originally circular, are built of blocks of turf, mud, or stone, and plastered with mud. In rural areas, walls are still decorated with pebbles, but the use of paint is spreading.*

CAPE DUTCH ARCHITECTURE

The vernacular of the Western Cape, recognized by its symmetrical design and prominent gables, evolved around the mid-18th century from a simple row of thatched rooms whose sizes depended on the length of the available beams. The forms of the gables were derived from the Baroque architecture of Holland. End gables prevented the roof from being torn off by high winds, while the centre gable let light into the attic.

Gable of Franschhoek Town Hall

Thatching reed was widely available in the *vleis* (swamps).

Sash windows had many small panes, and only the lower half could be opened.

Rhone, *near Franschhoek, is a good example of an 18th-century homestead. The front gable dates back to 1795.*

The front gable

Stable-type door

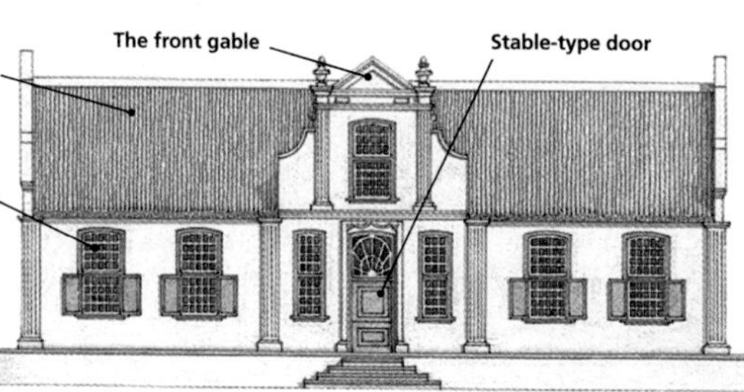

GEORGIAN ARCHITECTURE

Modest examples of 18th-century Georgian-style architecture, with plain front pediments and flat roofs, survive along the narrow, cobbled streets of Cape Town's Bo-Kaap, or "Malay Quarter".

The neighbourhood of Artificers' Square in Grahamstown also has fine examples. Here, the houses display typical many-paned, sliding sash windows, plain parapets and a fanlight above the entrance.

Geometric brick detail

The chimney was designed to complement the house.

The roof is protected by slate tiles.

Bertram House, *completed in 1839, is Cape Town's only surviving brick Georgian house.*

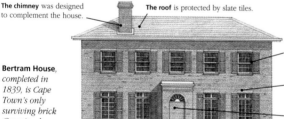

Louvre shutters reduce the harsh glare of the sun.

Precise brick-laying adds attractive detail.

The wind lobby excludes draughts.

VICTORIAN ARCHITECTURE

The romantic Victorian style with its decorative cast-iron detail, brass fittings, and stained-glass windows became extremely popular, especially in Cape Town, around the turn of the century. Here, too, terrace housing, pioneered in 18th-century England by the Adam Brothers, provided affordable housing for a burgeoning middle-class. Fine examples may be seen in suburbs like Woodstock, Observatory, Mowbray and Wynberg.

***Broekie* lace detail, Prince Albert**

Cast-iron decorations were called *broekie* lace, because they resembled the lacy edging of ladies' drawers.

Oom Samie se Winkel (see p136)*, in Stellenbosch, displays a marked Cape Dutch influence. The porch encouraged patrons to linger.*

Ornamental gable

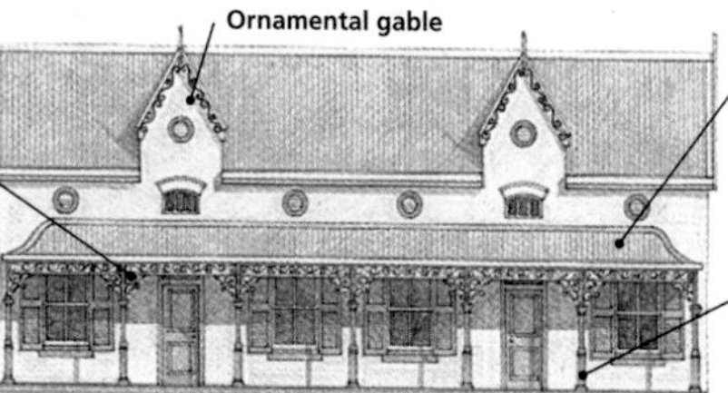

A corrugated iron awning covers the verandah.

Cast-iron supports hold up the awning.

Multicultural South Africa

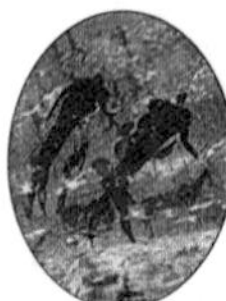

San Bushman rock painting

The South African nation is composed of a medley of different beliefs and cultures. Early influences, such as the languages and religions of slaves from India, Madagascar, Indonesia, West and East Africa and Malaysia, are preserved by their descendants. South Africa's mineral wealth drew settlers from other parts of Africa, as well as Asia, America and Europe – heritages still reflected in today's faces. Most coloured people live in the former slave-owning Western Cape area, while many Indians live around Durban, where their ancestors worked on sugar plantations.

Very few San Bushmen still hunt and live in the traditional way

THE KHOINA

Khoina rock paintings, often found in caves overlooking the plains below, offer tantalizing evidence of the practical skills and the spiritual nature of the people who were almost certainly South Africa's original human inhabitants. *(See Drakensberg pp216–17 and Kagga Kamma p160.)* Many were hunter-gatherers, living lightly on the natural bounty of the land.

Under pressure from more material cultures, some Khoina withdrew inland, where their descendants (the San Bushmen) are still today found in parts of Namaqualand and in the Northern Cape.

Other Khoina eventually threw in their lot with the Dutch settlers. Many of today's Cape Coloured people are descended from them.

THE BANTU-SPEAKERS

The Bantu languages are indigenous to Africa, although not related to those of the Khoina. Each group has its own complex system of cultures and relationships, although Westernized culture is replacing many of the older, traditional ways. Cattle and cattle pens *(kraals)* have an important place in Zulu, Xhosa and Ndebele cultures, and Zulu handicrafts include works in earthenware, iron and wood. Basket-making and weaving are other skills. The Xhosa, most of whom live in the Eastern Cape, are known for their beautifully designed and executed beadwork. The Ndebele of the Limpopo Province and Gauteng are renowned for their remarkably colourful and intricate beadwork, and their decorative painting applied to buildings is particularly eye-catching.

Many Xhosa women smoke long-stemmed pipes

Weaving is an important skill, and many Sotho, Xhosa and Tswana wear patterned or sombre ochre blankets as over-garments. In the northerly parts of Northern Province live the Venda, with a tradition, unusual in South Africa, of building in stone. The Venda are one of the few groups that traditionally used a drum as a musical instrument. Wood sculptures by leading Venda artists are treasured pieces.

The Wartburger Hof in KwaZulu-Natal looks like an alpine lodge

THE EUROPEAN COLONISTS

The first European settlers, in 1652, were Dutch and German. European politics further affected the composition of the Cape population, when French Huguenots were settled here from 1688, and French and German regiments were periodically brought in to boost the local defences against Britain. The British, however, took permanent possession of the Cape in 1806 and, during the depression that followed the Napoleonic Wars, dispatched several thousand settlers to farm in the Eastern Cape. More (pro-British) German settlers arrived after the Crimean War, and many British ex-soldiers elected to stay in South Africa, or returned to it, after the South African War of 1899–1902 and the World Wars. The British custom of hot Christmas dinner, for example, prevails in many quarters, despite its unsuitability in the stifling local climate.

Franschhoek, near Cape Town, retains some of the atmosphere of a French wine-growing region, while Eastern Cape villages settled by Germans still carry the names of German cities, such as Berlin and Hamburg.

ASIAN ORIGINS

East Indian islanders who opposed Dutch colonization of their territory in the 17th and 18th centuries were banished to the Cape of Good Hope. Slaves imported from Indonesia and the Indian subcontinent swelled the size of the oppressed minority. Nearly all of them belonged to the Islamic faith, while many others converted.

During the 19th century, thousands of indentured Indians worked in the sugar cane fields of KwaZulu-Natal, and elected to stay on at the end of their contract. In KwaZulu-Natal, Cape Town and Gauteng, the striking Eastern mosques and temples are a noteworthy architectural feature. Religious festivals are regularly observed, and the bustling oriental markets yield a treasure trove of spices, jewellery and handicrafts.

AFRIKANERS

The term "Afrikaner" was first recorded in 1706, as referring to a South African-born, Afrikaans- (or Dutch-) speaking white person. In more recent times, however, just the first-language use of Afrikaans has become the identifying factor. Afrikaner men are often associated with a love for outdoor sport (especially rugby) and a passion for the *braai* (barbecue).

During Afrikaner festivals, traditional costumes are worn

The tunes delivered by a *Boere-orkes* (literally "farmers' band") consist of concertina, banjo, piano accordion, and fiddles, and bear great similarity to North American "country" music.

THE COLOURED PEOPLE

The term "Cape Coloured" has now been in use for almost two centuries to define members of what is sometimes called "the only truly indigenous population".

Many of these people are descended from relationships between settlers, slaves and local tribes, and many slave names survive in the form of surnames such as Januarie, November, Titus, Appollis, Cupido and Adonis.

Temple dancing is still being taught in Durban

The most skilled fishermen, livery men as well as artisans were traditionally found in the Asian and Coloured communities, and many of the Cape's beautiful historic buildings were their creations.

A young Muslim girl prepares flower decorations for a festival

FROM ALL QUARTERS

Compared with other countries such as the United States and Australia, South Africa offered little scope for unskilled or semi-skilled white labour from Europe. However, small but steady numbers of immigrants did arrive, especially from Eastern European countries like Yugoslavia, Poland and Bulgaria.

South Africa has many citizens from Italy, Greece, Portugal and the Netherlands, as well as Jewish communities. These and other groups have formed common-interest societies seen at their most picturesque during colourful community carnivals.

Sport in South Africa

Given the country's favourable climate, sport plays a major role in the lives of many South Africans. In recent years, generous government funding and corporate sponsorship have resulted in the development of sporting facilities in the previously disadvantaged communities, encouraging much as yet unexplored talent. Sports events that are held in the major centres take place in world-class stadiums with superb facilities. Seats for the important matches are best bought through Computicket *(see p377)*, while those for lesser events are obtainable directly at the respective venues.

Soccer attracts spectators from all sectors of South African society

SOCCER

Without question the country's most popular sport, soccer is played all over South Africa, in dusty township streets and in the elite professional clubs. The most popular clubs attract huge spectator and fan followings, and can easily fill 80,000-seat stadiums for top matches. The soccer leagues are contested by clubs, and, unlike other major sports such as rugby and cricket, there is little emphasis on representation at provincial level.

The national soccer team, known as Bafana Bafana, has had success in the biennial African Cup of Nations, winning the contest in 1995 (when South Africa hosted the tournament) and reaching the finals in 1998. The team, ranked among the world's top 40, qualified for the World Cup Finals for the first time in 1998. Except for the hottest summer months (Dec–Feb), soccer is played year round.

RUGBY UNION

Rugby is played at all levels – from school to regional club, and from provincial to national stage.

Teams from the 14 provincial unions contest the Currie Cup every season. These 14 unions supply players to the five regional teams that fight for victory in the Super 14, an international and regional tournament involving South Africa, as well as Australia and New Zealand.

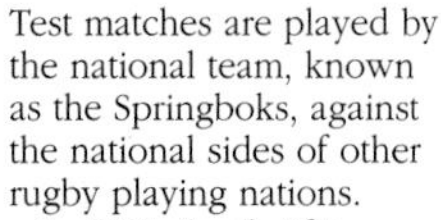

Test matches are played by the national team, known as the Springboks, against the national sides of other rugby playing nations.

In 1995, South Africa was winner of the Rugby World Cup (contested every four years). The local rugby season begins in early February, continuing through the winter months and ending, in late October, with the Currie Cup Finals *(see p38)*.

CRICKET

South Africa has long been a major force in the world of cricket. Played during the summer months, cricket is a sport enjoyed by thousands of players and spectators at various levels, from club and provincial competitions to international test matches.

Development programmes have discovered great talent among the youth of once-disadvantaged communities.

Four-day provincial games and the more popular one-day matches are held, while five-day tests are contested between South Africa and visiting national teams. One-day and day/night limited-overs international and provincial matches are particularly popular, usually played to packed stands.

The demand for tickets to these games is high, and advance booking is available through Computicket outlets countrywide or the cricket union hosting the match.

Rugby games draw crowds of up to 50,000 to the provincial stadiums

Two Oceans Marathon runners pass the crowds at Constantia Nek

MARATHONS AND ULTRA-MARATHONS

Long-distance running is both a popular pastime and a serious national sport. South Africa boasts a number of the world's fastest marathon runners, such as Josiah Thugwane who won a gold medal in the 1996 Olympics.

The strenuous 56-km (35-mile) Two Oceans Marathon, which takes place around the Cape Peninsula on Easter Saturday, and the energy-sapping 85-km (53-mile) long Comrades Marathon, run between the KwaZulu-Natal cities of Durban and Pietermaritzburg in June, are two of the most difficult, yet popular, ultra-marathons in the country. Both events attract thousands of international and local entrants.

With its excellent training facilities and fine summer weather, South Africa is a popular place for European athletes to train during the winter months in Europe. During this season, the international Engen Grand Prix Athletics Series is held in various South African cities.

GOLF

South Africa boasts some of the finest golf courses in the world, and has also produced some of the world's finest golfers. The golfing prowess of Gary Player is legendary, while youthful Ernie Els ranks among the top three golfers in the world. Every December, Sun City hosts the Nedbank Golf Challenge *(see p39)*, where 12 contestants compete for the largest prize in the world – 2 million dollars. The South African Golf Tour also attracts professional golfers from around the globe.

Two local events, the South African Open and the Alfred Dunhill PGA, are both held in mid- to late January.

CYCLING

Apart from various local professional events, the Cape Peninsula hosts the largest timed cycle race in the world, the annual Cape Argus Pick 'n Pay Cycle Tour. Over 35,000 sweaty cycling enthusiasts, some dressed in flamboyant costumes, race or trundle 105 km (65 miles) around the Peninsula on the second Sunday in March. About one third of the contestants is from overseas.

EQUESTRIAN SPORTS

Horse racing, until recently the only legal form of gambling in the country, has been an enormous industry for many years. The "Met" (Metropolitan Stakes) held in Cape Town in January, and the Durban July are major social events, with fashion and high stakes the order of the day. Show jumping and horse trials attract crowds every spring to venues such as Inanda near Johannesburg.

The Cape to Rio race leaves Table Bay with huge fanfare

WATERSPORTS

South Africa's coastline offers superb opportunities for sports enthusiasts. The Gunston 500 surfing event, held in Durban each July, is a major attraction. Cape Town is a popular port of call for round-the-world yacht races, and is also the starting point for the Cape to Rio event that takes place early in January every three years.

Sun City's Golf Course hosts the Nedbank Golf Challenge

SOUTH AFRICA THROUGH THE YEAR

Though organized festivals are a relatively new feature in South Africa, long, sunny days have given rise to a number of festivities, many of them outdoors. Cities, towns and villages host festivals to celebrate a variety of occasions: the start of the oyster and wildflower seasons; the citrus, apple or grape harvest; even the arrival of the southern right whale from its arctic breeding grounds – all are reason for celebration. The arts, music, religion, language and sport also take their places on the calendar of events. The diversity of festivals emphasizes the disparate origins of South Africa's many peoples and their gradual coming together as a single nation.

Dancers, FNB Vita Dance Umbrella

SPRING

All across the country, but especially noticeable in the semi-arid Western and Northern Cape regions, the onset of warmer weather raises colourful fields of wildflowers. In wildlife reserves throughout South Africa, the newborn of various species will soon be seen.

SEPTEMBER

Arts Alive *(Sep)*, Johannesburg *(see pp256–7)*. An exciting urban arts festival, with performers ranging from world-class musicians to children eager to show off the skills they have acquired at the workshops.

Guinness Jazz Festival *(Sep–Oct)*, Johannesburg *(see pp256–7)*. Local and international musicians provide a jazz extravaganza.

Wildflower Festival *(second week in Sep)*. The town of Caledon *(see p166)* celebrates its varied indigenous flora.

Wildflower Show *(late Sep)*, Darling *(see p157)*. The show displays the unique West Coast flora and cultivated orchids.

Whale Festival *(last week in Sep)*, Hermanus *(see p168)*. From early spring onwards, the southern right whales and their calves can be seen close to shore in and around Walker Bay.

Prince Albert Agricultural Show *(Sep)*, Prince Albert *(see p173)*. The people of Prince Albert proudly celebrate their agricultural heritage with this show featuring arts and crafts, horse displays, food stalls and entertainment.

Magoebaskloof Spring Festival *(Sep–Oct)*, Magoebaskloof. A bustling arts, crafts and entertainment fair, held in a forest setting.

Orchids from Darling

OCTOBER

Currie Cup Finals *(late Oct)*, The location varies from year to year. Rugby match between the two best provincial teams.

The Johannesburg Biennale *(Oct of alternating years)*, Johannesburg *(see pp256–7)*. Various activities are held throughout the city.

Raisin Festival *(second Sat in Oct)*, Upington *(see p314)*. Music, choir contests and fun on the Orange River.

Bosman Weekend *(Oct)*, Groot Marico. A celebration of writer Herman Charles Bosman in the town where many of his stories are set.

The Oude Libertas open-air amphitheatre

NOVEMBER

Cherry Festival *(third week in Nov)*, Ficksburg. Celebrate South Africa's commercially grown cherries and asparagus.

National Choir Festival *(Nov–Dec)*, Standard Bank Arena, Johannesburg *(see pp256–7)*. The culmination of a national competition.

Nedbank Summer Concert Season *(Nov–Feb)*, Josephine Mill, Cape Town *(see p102)*. Delightful outdoor concerts.

SUMMER

Most tourists visit South Africa during the long summer months. The local long school holidays extend from December well into January. With many South African families traditionally heading for the seaside and wildlife reserves, this is when the roads are at their busiest. Summer is a season spent outdoors. Christmas lunch is more likely to be celebrated around an informal *braai* (barbecue) than at a dining table. Over much of the country, summer rain arrives in the form of short, noisy thunder showers.

Carols by Candlelight

DECEMBER

Carols by Candlelight *(pre-Christmas)*. These colourful Advent celebrations take place in all of the major towns and cities.

Helderberg Festival of Lights *(Dec–Jan)*, Somerset West *(see p134)*. Main Street display of festive lights in rural Somerset West.

The Spier Summer Festival *(Dec–Mar)*, Spier, Stellenbosch *(see p140)*. A celebration featuring local and international opera, music, dance, comedy and drama.

Miss South Africa, Sun City *(see p268)*. A glittering, old-fashioned beauty pageant for the nine provincial beauty queens, one of whom will be crowned Miss South Africa.

Shooting the Camps Drift rapids on the Duzi River

Nedbank Golf Challenge, Sun City *(see p268)*. An internationally renowned golfing event with 12 of the world's best golfers.

JANUARY

Summer Sunset Concerts *(every Sun evening, Jan–Mar)*, Kirstenbosch National Botanical Gardens, Cape Town *(see pp104–5)*. Musical performances are held on the Gardens' verdant lawns.

Duzi Canoe Marathon *(second week in Jan)*, Pietermaritzburg *(see pp222–3)*. A three-day canoe marathon to the mouth of the Umgeni River.

Maynardville Open-Air Theatre *(Jan–Feb)*, Wynberg, Cape Town *(see p110)*. Shakespearean plays are performed in a city park.

Oude Libertas Arts Programme *(Jan–Mar)*, Stellenbosch *(see pp138–9)*. Performances in an amphitheatre among the vines.

Minstrel Carnival *(2 Jan)*, Cape Town *(see p22)*. A colourful musical procession culminates in concerts at Green Point Stadium.

Cherries

FEBRUARY

FNB Vita Dance Umbrella *(Feb–Mar)*, Braamfontein, Johannesburg *(see pp256–7)*. One of the most important dance events in South Africa.

Prickly Pear Festival *(early Feb)*, Willem Prinsloo Agricultural Museum, Pretoria/Tshwane *(see pp266–7)*. A showcase of 19th-century lifestyles and farming practices.

Kavady Festival *(Jan–Feb)*, Durban *(see pp228–31)*. A Hindu festival during which many penitents pierce their flesh with hooks and draw beautifully decorated carts through the streets.

Cape Town's minstrels are a colourful sight in early January

AUTUMN

When deciduous trees and grapevines begin to shed their leaves, a new round of country fairs is ushered in. The harvest festivals of many small towns celebrate crops like potatoes and olives; even sheep and gems are cause for cheerful get-togethers. A number of wine festivals are held from Paarl in the fertile Western Cape to Kuruman in the arid Northern Cape.

Over a million followers of the Zionist Church gather at Easter

MARCH

Rand Show *(Mar–Apr)*, Johannesburg *(see pp256–7)*. What began as an agricultural show has become a blend of entertainment and consumerism.

Cape Town Jazz Festival *(last weekend in Mar)*, Cape Town *(see pp78–81)*. This annual jazz festival is a two-day affair featuring nearly 40 international and African acts performing on five stages to an audience of 15,000. The musical extravaganza is accompanied by a series of photographic and art exhibitions.

APRIL

Zionist Church gathering *(Easter)*, near Polokwane (formerly Pietersburg, *see p274)* in the Northern Province. More than a million followers of this African Christian church gather at Moria (also known as Zion City) over the Easter weekend.

Festival of Light *(Good Friday)*, Pietermaritzburg *(see pp222–3)*. At the Sri Siva, Soobramoniar and Marriamen temples, visitors witness the grand and costly fireworks display.

Fire-walking *(Easter)*, Umbilo Hindu Temple, Durban *(see pp228–31)*. Devout Hindus, after careful spiritual preparation, walk uninjured across a bed of red-hot coals.

Devotee, Festival of Light

Two Oceans Marathon *(Easter)*, Cape Town. This 56-km (35-mile) marathon *(see p37)* around the Cape Peninsula is a qualifying race for the Comrades' Marathon.

Klein Karoo Arts Festival *(Apr)*, Oudtshoorn *(see p176)*. A mainly Afrikaans cultural festival.

Ladysmith Show *(Apr)*, Ladysmith, KwaZulu-Natal. An agricultural show with many craft stalls and entertainment.

Tulbagh Goes Dutch *(Apr)*, Tulbagh. A two-day festival featuring cultural activities, food stalls, a Dutch beer garden and a tulip exhibition.

Splashy Fen Music Festival *(last weekend in Apr)*, Splashy Fen Farm, Underberg, KwaZulu-Natal. Mainstream, alternative, folk and traditional music styles.

Amusement park at the Rand Show in Johannesburg

MAY

Pink Loerie Mardi Gras *(May)*, Knysna *(see p186)*. A four-day gay festival.

Prince Albert Olive, Food & Wine Festival *(May)*, Prince Albert. *(see p173)*. Live music, a cycle race, and an olive-stone spitting competition plus food and wine tastings.

Sabie Forest Fair *(May)* Sabie. This fair offers arts-and-crafts stalls and local entertainment around a unique Forestry Museum.

WINTER

Dry season for most of the country, only the winter-rainfall area along the South-western and Southern Cape coast is lush and green at this time. Inland, days are typically warm, although nightly frosts are common in high-lying areas. Snowfalls occur on the mountains of the Western and Eastern Cape and in the KwaZulu-Natal and Lesotho highlands. Late winter is particularly good for game-watching, as the thirsty wildlife gathers around waterholes.

JUNE

Comrades' Marathon *(mid-Jun)*, between Durban and Pietermaritzburg. This ultra long-distance running event attracts top-class runners from all over the world *(see p37)*.

JULY

National Arts Festival *(early to mid-Jul)*, Grahamstown *(see pp198–9)*. An extremely popular two weeks of local and international drama, film, dance, visual arts and music.

Hibiscus Festival *(Jul)*, South Coast of KwaZulu-Natal *(see pp234–5)*. Colourful craft stalls and plenty of entertainment.

Safari wildlife-viewing drive at Sabi Sabi, Mpumalanga

High fashion, July Handicap

July Handicap *(first Sat in Jul)*, Greyville Race Course, Durban *(see pp228–9)*. This is the glamour event of the South African horse-racing fraternity.

Knysna Oyster Festival *(early Jul)*, Knysna *(see p186)*. The festival, centred on the commercial oyster beds in Knysna Lagoon, coincides with a forest marathon.

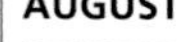

Knysna oyster

Berg River Canoe Marathon *(Jul)*, Paarl *(see pp146–7)*. A strenuous four-day canoe race that provides some high excitement and is staged annually when the river is in full flood.

Calitzdorp Port Festival *(late Jul)*, Karoo *(see p174)*. A celebration of the region's famous port-style wine.

Mr Price Pro *(see pp206–7) (mid-Jul)*, Durban *(see pp228–31)*. This popular week-long surfing championship attracts the world's best surfers and hordes of spectators.

AUGUST

Agricultural and Wildflower Show *(late Aug)*, Piketberg. The quality of this flower show, as well as the vividness of the colours and the range of species on display, depends entirely on the rainfall during the preceding winter.

Hantam Vleisfees, *(last weekend in Aug)*, Calvinia. Located in the Northern Cape, Calvinia is sheep country. The festival is a celebration of meat in all its forms: stewed, curried or grilled. First held in 1989, the three-day event also offers music concerts, a vintage-car rally, and the glittering Miss Vleisfees competition.

Cars-in-the-Park *(early Aug)*, Pretoria/Tshwane *(see pp266–7)*. Gleaming vintage vehicles are displayed by proud owners.

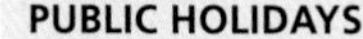

PUBLIC HOLIDAYS

New Year's Day (1 Jan)
Human Rights Day (21 Mar)
Good Friday (Apr)
Family Day (Apr)
Freedom Day (27 Apr)
Workers' Day (1 May)
Youth Day (16 Jun)
National Women's Day (9 Aug)
Heritage Day (24 Sep)
Day of Reconciliation (16 Dec)
Christmas Day (25 Dec)
Day of Goodwill (26 Dec)

National Arts Festival, Grahamstown

The Climate of South Africa

Situated halfway between the Equator and the Antarctic, South Africa has a temperate climate with short-term exceptions in certain locations. Day temperatures can soar to 50°C (122°F) over low-lying coastal plains in summer and drop to -16°C (3°F) during a winter's night over the higher plateau areas. Rainfall increases from west to east. The most popular time of year to visit South Africa is during the summer months, from December to February, but winter days are sunny and cool and best for game viewing.

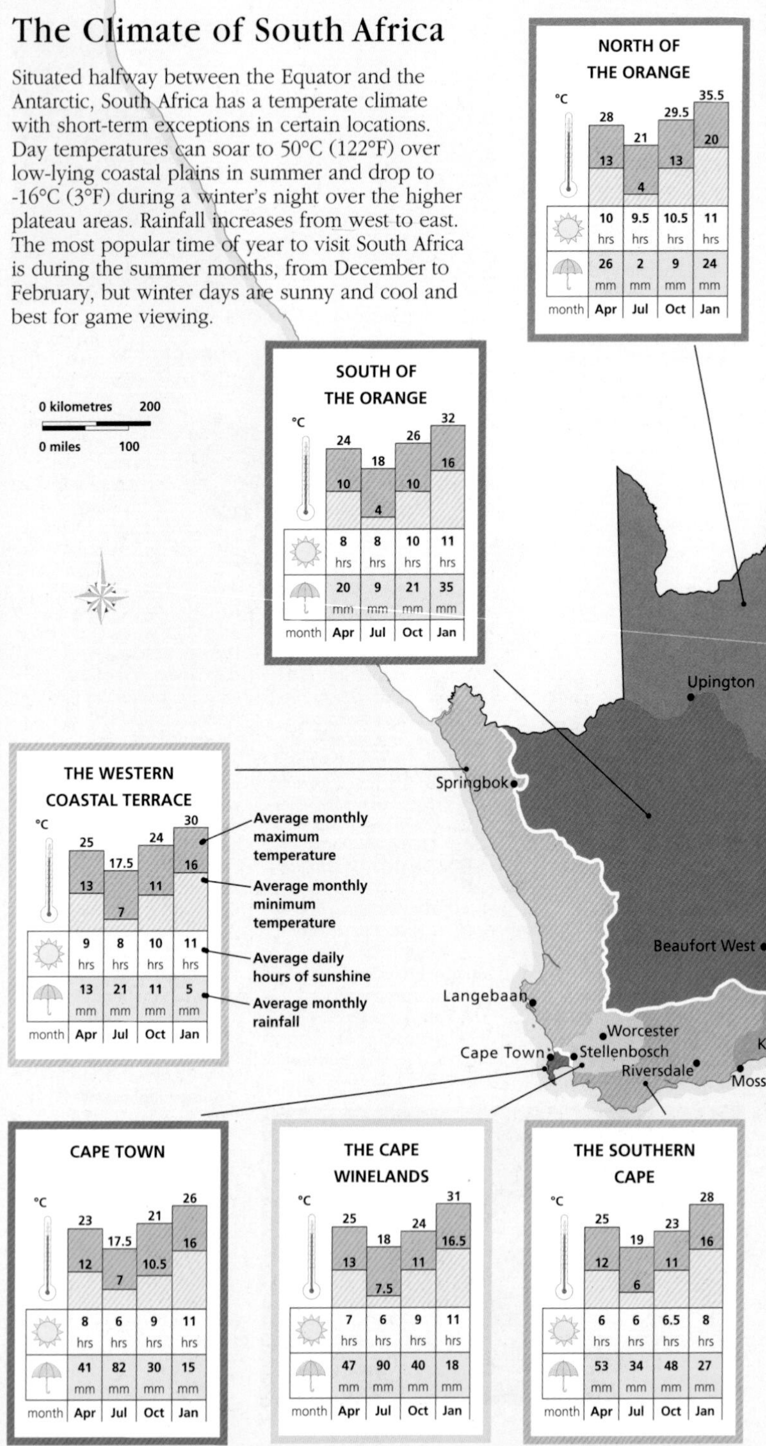

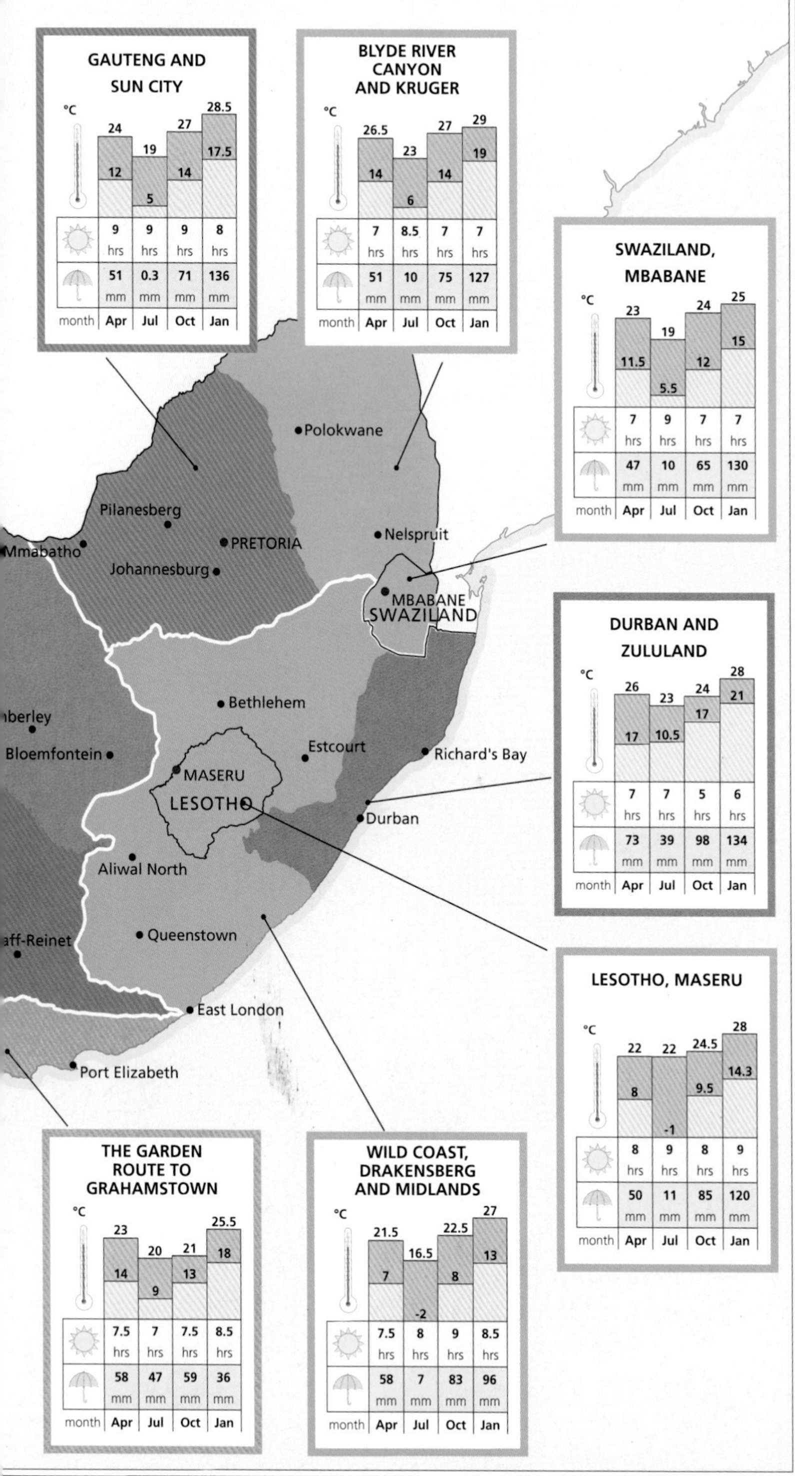
GAUTENG AND SUN CITY
°C
24 19 27 28.5
12 5 14 17.5
9 hrs 9 hrs 9 hrs 8 hrs
51 mm 0.3 mm 71 mm 136 mm
month Apr Jul Oct Jan
BLYDE RIVER CANYON AND KRUGER
°C
26.5 23 27 29
14 6 14 19
7 hrs 8.5 hrs 7 hrs 7 hrs
51 mm 10 mm 75 mm 127 mm
month Apr Jul Oct Jan
SWAZILAND, MBABANE
°C
23 19 24 25
11.5 5.5 12 15
7 hrs 9 hrs 7 hrs 7 hrs
47 mm 10 mm 65 mm 130 mm
month Apr Jul Oct Jan
DURBAN AND ZULULAND
°C
26 23 24 28
17 10.5 17 21
7 hrs 7 hrs 5 hrs 6 hrs
73 mm 39 mm 98 mm 134 mm
month Apr Jul Oct Jan
LESOTHO, MASERU
°C
22 22 24.5 28
8 -1 9.5 14.3
8 hrs 9 hrs 8 hrs 9 hrs
50 mm 11 mm 85 mm 120 mm
month Apr Jul Oct Jan
THE GARDEN ROUTE TO GRAHAMSTOWN
°C
23 20 21 25.5
14 9 13 18
7.5 hrs 7 hrs 7.5 hrs 8.5 hrs
58 mm 47 mm 59 mm 36 mm
month Apr Jul Oct Jan
WILD COAST, DRAKENSBERG AND MIDLANDS
°C
21.5 16.5 22.5 27
7 -2 8 13
7.5 hrs 8 hrs 9 hrs 8.5 hrs
58 mm 7 mm 83 mm 96 mm
month Apr Jul Oct Jan
Polokwane
Pilanesberg
PRETORIA
Nelspruit
Mmabatho
Johannesburg
MBABANE
SWAZILAND
Bethlehem
berley
Bloemfontein
Estcourt
Richard's Bay
MASERU
LESOTHO
Durban
Aliwal North
Queenstown
aff-Reinet
East London
Port Elizabeth

THE HISTORY OF SOUTH AFRICA

The ancient footprints discovered at Langebaan, a cast of which is now in the South African Museum in Cape Town, were made 117,000 years ago. They are the world's oldest traces of anatomically modern man, *Homo sapiens sapiens*. Other early hominid remains found at the Sterkfontein caves in Gauteng and at Taung near Bloemfontein belong to the group known as *Australopithecus africanus*.

Jan van Riebeeck, the founder of Cape Town

The African and European civilization drifted towards a cultural collision when the Dutch East India Company set up a refreshment station in Table Bay. The year was 1652, and the colonizers had come not just to visit, but to stay. On the whole, the Dutch sought to establish amicable relationships with the local Khoina, but a natural wariness and the inability to understand one another doomed many attempts and the pattern of relations over the subsequent centuries was set. Rivalry over water and grazing soon turned into open hostility, first around the bay and then further afield as Dutch "burghers" sought new land. Their trails initiated a wave of migration inland. Isolated clashes with indigenous groups escalated into the bitter frontier wars of the 18th and 19th centuries, a situation further aggravated by the arrival of the 1820 British settlers. Although outnumbered, the settlers' muskets, cannons and horses were an advantage that led to a prevailing sense of white supremacy, with both colonial and republican governments denying people of colour their rights.

Ironically, it was the exploitation of black labour in the mines of Kimberley and Johannesburg that ignited the spark of African nationalism, while the apartheid laws of the mid-1900s focused world attention and pressure on South Africa. The release of Nelson Mandela in 1990 was the beginning of a transformation that set the country on a new course: the road to democracy.

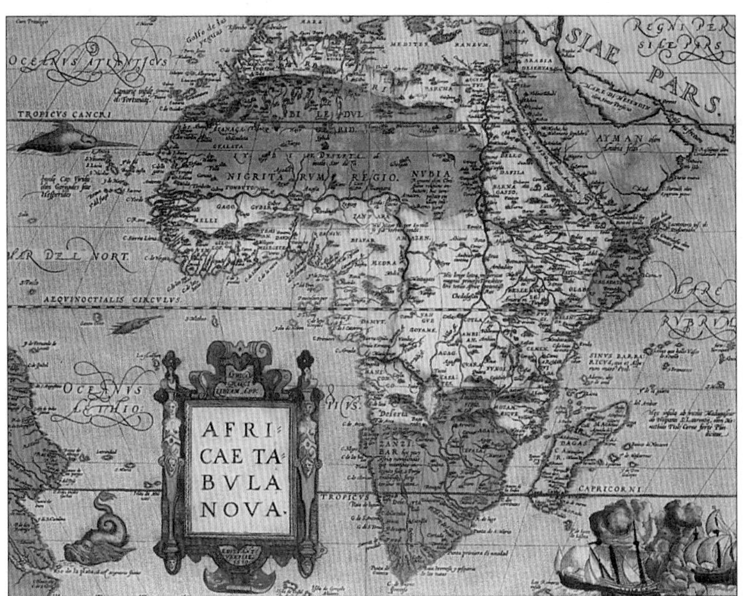

This surprisingly accurate map was produced in 1570 by Abraham Ortelius from Antwerp

◁ Ancient San Bushman paintings adorn many rock walls like this one in the Cedarberg, Western Cape

Prehistoric South Africa

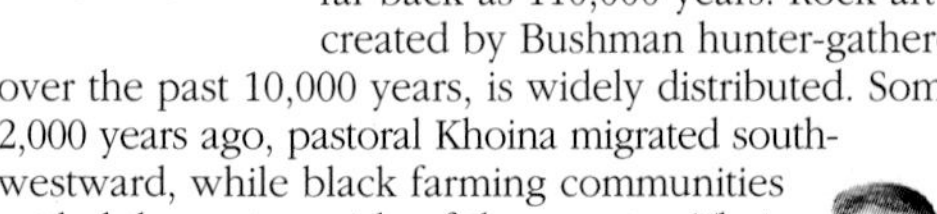

Stone Age grinding tool

Some 2–3 million years ago, long after the dinosaurs, *Australopithecus africanus* inhabited South Africa's plains. *Australopithecines* were the ancestors of anatomically modern people whose remains in South Africa date at least as far back as 110,000 years. Rock art created by Bushman hunter-gatherers over the past 10,000 years, is widely distributed. Some 2,000 years ago, pastoral Khoina migrated southwestward, while black farming communities settled the eastern side of the country. Their descendants were encountered by the 15th-century Portuguese explorers.

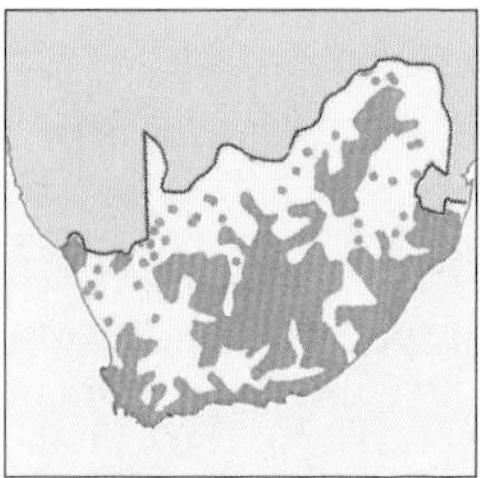

EARLY MAN

▪ *Distribution in South Africa*

Australopithecus africanus
In 1925, Professor Raymond Dart, then dean of the University of the Witwatersrand's medical faculty, first identified man's ancestor based on the evidence of a skull found near Taung, North West Province.

Langebaan Footprints
Homo sapiens *tracks at Langebaan Lagoon are around 117,000 years old. They are the world's oldest fossilized trail of anatomically modern human beings.*

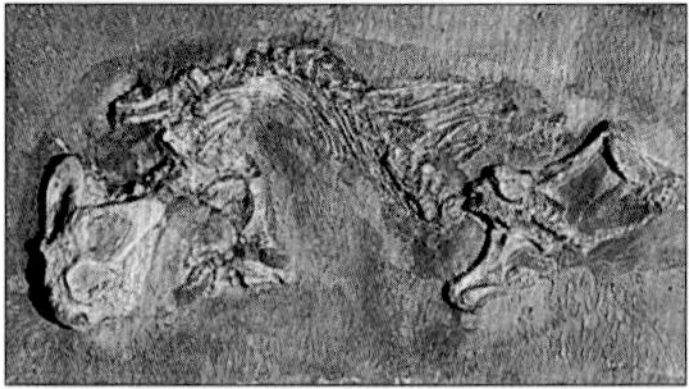

Karoo Fossils
Diictodon *skeletons found in the Karoo* (see p302) *belonged to mammal-like reptiles that tunnelled into the mud along river banks some 255 million years ago.*

CRADLE OF MANKIND

Based on the evidence of fossilized remains from the Sterkfontein caves *(see p264)* and other sites in South and East Africa, palaeontologists believe that people evolved in Africa. Stone tools and bone fragments indicate that modern humans lived and hunted in South Africa some 110,000 years ago.

TIMELINE

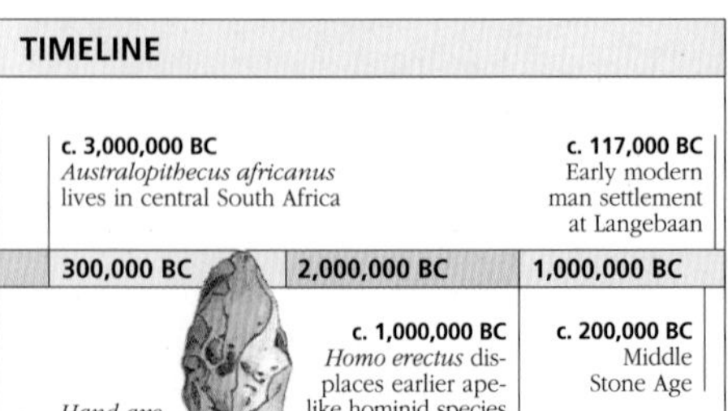

c. 3,000,000 BC *Australopithecus africanus* lives in central South Africa

c. 117,000 BC Early modern man settlement at Langebaan

300,000 BC | 2,000,000 BC | 1,000,000 BC

Hand axe

c. 1,000,000 BC *Homo erectus* displaces earlier ape-like hominid species

c. 200,000 BC Middle Stone Age

c. 35,000 BC Start of Late Stone Age, man uses refined tools and weapons

Spear head

40,000 BC | 30,000 BC | 20,000

c. 38,000 BC Iron ore is mined for its pigment at Ngwenya in Swaziland

c. 26,000 BC Earliest known example of rock art (Namibia)

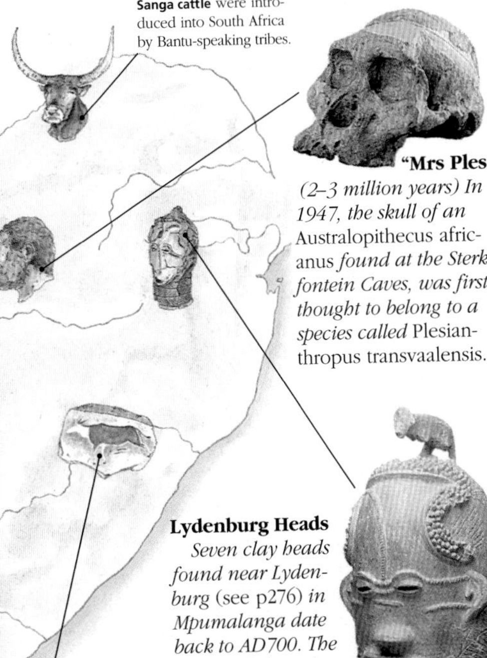

Early Goldsmiths
Gold ornaments, discovered in Mapungubwe grave sites in 1932, belonged to an Iron Age civilization that flourished until the end of the 12th century.

Sanga cattle were introduced into South Africa by Bantu-speaking tribes.

"Mrs Ples"
(2–3 million years) In 1947, the skull of an Australopithecus africanus *found at the Sterkfontein Caves, was first thought to belong to a species called* Plesianthropus transvaalensis.

Lydenburg Heads
Seven clay heads found near Lydenburg (see p276) *in Mpumalanga date back to AD700. The experts believe they were used in rituals.*

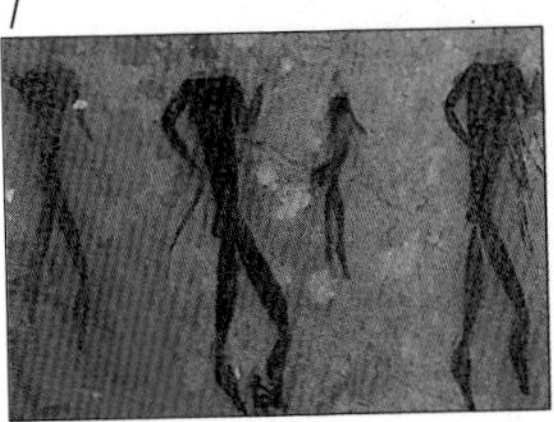

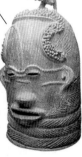

Rock Paintings
South Africa is a rich storehouse of prehistoric art. Some paintings are thought to date back 10,000 years, while others were painted as little as 200 years ago.

WHERE TO SEE PREHISTORIC SOUTH AFRICA

The Natal Museum in Pietermaritzburg *(p223)*, McGregor Museum in Kimberley *(p316)* and Transvaal Museum in Pretoria/Tshwane *(p267)* hold important collections of rock art, archaeological and palaeontological artifacts. Rock paintings can be seen in the Cedarberg of the Western Cape *(p161)* and in the Drakensberg in Lesotho *(pp214–15)* and KwaZulu-Natal *(pp216–17)*. The South African Museum in Cape Town *(p76)* has dioramas of early people. Bloemfontein's National Museum *(p318)* and the museum in Lydenburg *(p276)* exhibit fossil finds. The Sterkfontein Caves *(p264)*, where Mrs Ples was found, are near Krugersdorp. Many of these museums can assist visitors with information on outings to individual sites.

Bushman Cave Museum *is an open-air site in the Giant's Castle Reserve* (see pp216–17).

The Sudwala Caves (see p276) *feature an interesting timeline display on the evolution of man.*

c. 8,000 BC Microlithic ...ne toolkit of the Bushman culture

10,000 BC

AD 1 | **AD 350** | **AD 700** | **AD 1050** | **AD 1400**

c. AD 200 Black farmers and iron-workers settle south of the Limpopo River and plant sorghum crops

Sorghum

San Bushman bow and arrows

c. AD 1 Nomadic Khoina herders, originally from Botswana, move southwest into Cape coastal territory

c. 1400 Stone settlements of Sotho people expand from the Highveld into present-day Free State

Explorers and Colonizers

Bartolomeu Dias (1450–1500)

Portuguese navigators pioneered the sea route to India, but it was the Dutch who set up a fortified settlement at the Cape in 1652. The indigenous Khoina who initially welcomed the trade opportunities were quickly marginalized. Some took service with the settlers, while others fled from the Dutch *trekboers* (migrant graziers). In 1688, the arrival of French Huguenot families swelled the numbers of the white settlers, driving even more Khoina away from their ancestral land.

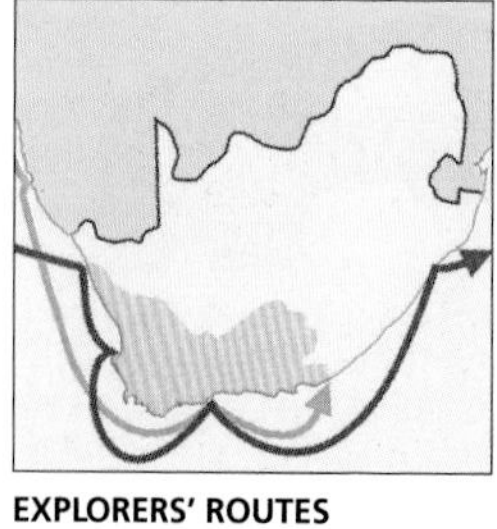

EXPLORERS' ROUTES

Dias 1488 *Da Gama 1498*

Cape colony 1795

The Caravels of Dias

In 1988, a replica of the ship commanded by Bartolomeu Dias 500 years before retraced his voyage from Lisbon to Mossel Bay. The ship is now housed in Mossel Bay's Bartolomeu Dias Museum complex (see pp182–3).

Unique Early Postal Systems

In the 15th and 16th centuries, Portuguese captains anchored in Mossel Bay and left messages for each other engraved on flat rocks. The stones soon became a type of post box, with letters stored beneath them.

JAN VAN RIEBEECK'S ARRIVAL

On 6 April 1652, Jan van Riebeeck landed at the Cape to establish a permanent settlement for the Dutch East India Company. The first commander of the new outpost and his wife, Maria de la Quellerie, are commemorated by statues erected near the site of their historic landing.

TIMELINE

1400 | 1450 | 1500 | 1550

1486 Portuguese sail as far as today's Namibia.

1498 Vasco da Gama discovers the route to India around the Cape of Good Hope

Vasco da Gama

c. 1500 Shipwrecked Portuguese sailors encounter Iron Age farmers along South Africa's south coast.

1510 Dom Francisco d'Almeida, viceroy of Portuguese India, and 57 of his men are killed by Khoina in Table Bay

The Vereenigde Oost-Indische Compagnie (VOC)
Several small trading companies joined in 1602 to form the Dutch East India Company (VOC). It was granted a charter to trade, draw up treaties and maintain an army and a fleet. The VOC was dissolved in 1798.

ds and trinkets e offered as gifts he Khoina.

Autshumao, leader of the local *Strandlopers* (a people living near the sea who ate mainly fish and mussels) had been taken to Java by the British in 1631. He had a basic knowledge of English and was able to negotiate with the Dutch.

Animal skins were worn by the native peoples of the Cape.

Superior Weaponry
Matchlocks secured the settlers' advantage over the clubs and throwing-spears of the Hottentots, and the bows and poisoned arrows used by the San Bushmen.

Almond Hedge
A remnant of the hedge that was planted to discourage unauthorized trading with the Khoina can be seen at Kirstenbosch National Botanical Gardens (see pp104–5).

WHERE TO SEE EXPLORERS AND COLONIZERS

Mossel Bay's museum complex houses a replica of Dias's caravel *(pp182–3)*, as well as the old milkwood tree in which passing sailors left messages for their fellow mariners. The Castle of Good Hope in Cape Town *(pp72–3)* is South Africa's oldest surviving structure. The Huguenot Memorial Museum in Franschhoek *(p144)* honours the French heritage of the town and contains antique furniture and paintings. Early colonial artifacts are on display at the Iziko Slave Lodge in Cape Town *(p70)*.

The De Kat Balcony, at the Castle of Good Hope in Cape Town, was designed by sculptor Anton Anreith.

The French Huguenots
Fleeing from religious persecution in France, about 200 Huguenots arrived at the Cape of Good Hope in 1688. They were assigned farms around Franschhoek (see pp144–5), *where they planted vineyards.*

1594 Portuguese barter with Khoina in Table Bay

Maria de la Quellerie

1652 Jan van Riebeeck and his wife, Maria de la Quellerie, arrive in Table Bay.

1693 Sheik Yusuf is exiled to the Cape after instigating a rebellion in Java. His *kramat* (shrine) near Faure (Western Cape) is revered by Muslims

1600 | **1650** | **1700** | **1750**

1608 The Dutch barter with Khoina clans for food

1658 War against Khoina follows cattle raids and killing of settlers

1688 Huguenot refugees settle at the Cape

1713 Smallpox epidemic kills unknown hundreds of Khoina, as well as many white settlers

British Colonization

Hitching post, Graaff-Reinet

By 1778, settler expansion had reached the Eastern Cape and the Great Fish River was proclaimed the eastern boundary of the Cape Colony. As this was Xhosa territory, local herdsmen were deprived of their pastures and a century of bitter "frontier wars" ensued. In 1795, following the French Revolution, British forces were able to occupy the Cape. Having returned it to the Netherlands in 1802, they reclaimed it in 1806 and instituted a government-sponsored programme that assigned farms in the Zuurveld area to British settlers. To the east, Shaka Zulu was just beginning to build a powerful empire.

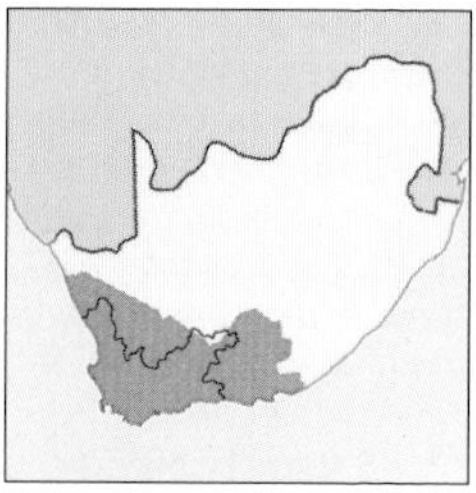

SETTLER EXPANSION

▪ *1814* — *Cape today*

Battle of Muizenberg (1795)
In this battle for possession of the Cape, British warships bombarded Dutch outposts at Muizenberg (see p99). *Britain was victorious and thus acquired a halfway station en route to India.*

Blockhouse ruins

FORT FREDERICK

In the 19th century, many private homes were fortified, and a succession of outposts and frontier forts were built in the Eastern Cape. Few were attacked; almost all are now in ruin. Fort Frederick in Port Elizabeth *(see pp192–3)* has been restored and is a superb example of what these frontier fortifications looked like.

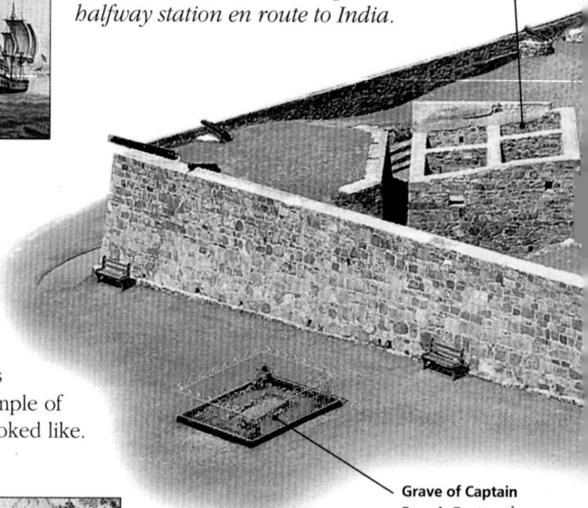

Grave of Captain Francis Evatt, who oversaw the landing of the 1820 settlers.

Rustenburg House
After the battle of Muizenberg, the Dutch surrendered the Cape to Britain. The treaty was signed in this house in Rondebosch, Cape Town. Its present Neo-Classical façade probably dates from around 1803.

TIMELINE

1750 Worldwide, Dutch influence begins to wane

1751 Rijk Tulbagh appointed Dutch Governor of the Cape (1751–71)

1760

1770 Gamtoos River made boundary of Cape Colony

1778 Fish River made boundary of Cape Colony

1779 A year after it is made boundary of the Cape Colony, settlers and Xhosa clash at the Fish River – the first of nine frontier wars

1780

1789 Merino sheep are imported from Holland and thrive in South Africa

Merino sheep

Battle of Blaauwberg (1806)
This battle between the Dutch and the British was fought at the foot of the Blouberg, out of range of British warships. Outnumbered and poorly disciplined, the Dutch defenders soon broke rank and fled.

The 1820 Settlers
About 4,000 Britons, mostly artisans with little or no farming experience, settled around Grahamstown (see pp198–9).

The Powder Magazine could hold some 900 kg (2,000 lb) of gunpowder.

Entrance

The Xhosa
The Xhosa had farmed in the Zuurveld (present Eastern Cape) for centuries. The arrival of the 1820 Settlers caused friction and dispute.

Shaka Zulu
This gifted military strategist became Zulu chief after the death of Senzangakona in 1815. Shaka introduced the assegaai *(short spear) and united lesser clans into a Zulu empire.*

WHERE TO SEE BRITISH COLONIZATION

The museums in Umtata (the capital of the former Transkei) and the University of Fort Hare in Alice (in the former Ciskei) have interesting collections of colonial artefacts. Old weapons and ammunition, uniforms, maps, and even letters and medical supplies are displayed in the Military Museum at the Castle of Good Hope in Cape Town *(pp72–3)*. The museums in King William's Town, Queenstown and Grahamstown all *(pp198–9)* exhibit collections of frontier-war memorabilia. The excellent MuseuMAfricA in Johannesburg *(p256)* has a superb collection of old prints and paintings.

MuseuMAfricA has three permanent exhibitions and various temporary displays.

Typical settler house

1795 Battle of Muizenberg and first British occupation

1800 The *Cape Town Gazette* and *African Advertiser* are first published

1806 Battle of Blaauwberg. Second British occupation of the Cape

1818 Shaka's military conquests in Zululand begin

1820 4,000 British settlers arrive in Grahamstown

1829 The Khoina are released from having to carry passes. The University of Cape Town is founded

1800 | **1810** | **1820** | **1830**

3 Lombard k, the first k in the ntry, opens ape Town

1802 Lady Anne Barnard, whose letters and diaries give an insight into colonial life, leaves the Cape

1814 British occupation of the Cape is ratified by the Congress of Vienna

1815 The Slagter's Nek rebellion, led by anti-British frontiersmen, ends with judicial executions near Cookhouse (Eastern Cape)

1828 Shaka is murdered by his half-brother, Dingane

Colonial Expansion

A Voortrekker woman's bonnet

The British colonial administration met with hostility from the Cape's Dutch-speaking community. Dissatisfied Voortrekkers (Boer pioneers) headed east and north in an exodus that became known as the Great Trek. In 1838, Zulu chief Dingane had one group of Voortrekkers killed, but in the subsequent Battle of Blood River his own warriors were beaten. A short-lived Boer republic, Natalia, was annexed by Britain in 1843. By 1857, two new Boer states, Transvaal and Orange Free State, landlocked and impoverished but independent, had been consolidated north of the Orange and Vaal rivers.

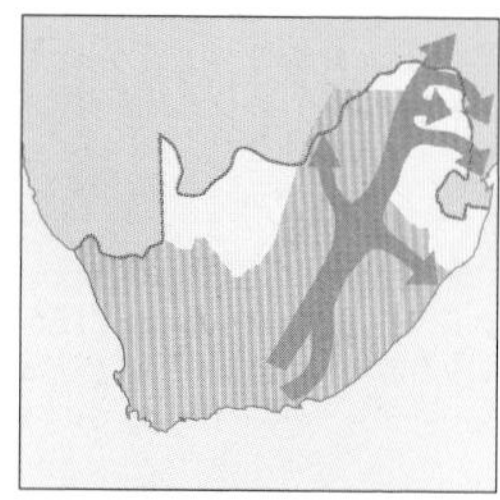
VOORTREKKER MOVEMENT

1836 Great Trek

British territory by 1848

Emancipated Slaves
The freeing of 39,000 Cape Colony slaves in 1834 angered Boer farmers who relied on slave labour. The British decision was not due entirely to philanthropism, it was simply cheaper to employ free labour.

The Battle of Vegkop
In 1836 the Ndebele found themselves in the path of trekker expansion northwards. Traditional weapons were no match for blazing rifles: the 40 Voortrekkers beat off an attack by 6,000 Ndebele warriors at Vegkop, killing 430, but losing most of their own sheep, cattle and trek oxen.

THE GREAT TREK

Dissatisfied with the British administration, convoys of Boer ox wagons trekked inland to seek new territory. The pioneers, armed with cannons and muskets, were accompanied by their families, black and coloured retainers and livestock. Each wagon was "home" for the duration of the journey and contained all that the family owned. At night, or under attack, the convoy would form a laager – a circle of wagons lashed together with chains.

Barrels were used to store food, water and gunpowder.

Wagon chest

The drive shaft was attached to the yoke which was placed around the neck of the oxen.

TIMELINE

1830

1834 Slaves freed subject to a four-year "apprenticeship". Sixth Frontier War erupts; Voortrekkers travel to present-day Free State, KwaZulu-Natal, Northern Province and Namibia

1835

1836 The Great Trek begins

1838 Battle of Blood River follows the murder of Voortrekker leader, Piet Retief, and his men

Dingane

1839 Boer Republic of Natalia is proclaimed

1840

The Battle of Blood River
On 16 December 1838, the river ran red with blood as a 468-strong burgher commando defeated 12,500 Zulu warriors in retribution for the killing of Piet Retief.

Tallow candles provided light.
A protective cover made of tanned hide sheltered the occupants inside.
Quilts were very often highly prized, complex pieces of craftsmanship.
Large wheels enabled the drivers to negotiate rough terrain without damaging the wagon.
Water barrel

Nongqawuse
In 1857, a Xhosa seer predicted that her people would regain their former power if they destroyed all their herds and crops, but the resulting famine further weakened their position.

WHERE TO SEE THE COLONIAL EXPANSION

British colonial history is well covered in cultural history and battle site museums nationwide. Museums at Grahamstown *(pp198–9)*, Port Elizabeth *(pp192–3)*, King William's Town and East London have displays of old weapons, maps and pioneer artifacts. MuseuMAfricA *(p256)* in Johannesburg exhibits historic documents, war memorabilia and maps. Kleinplasie Open-air Museum *(pp150–51)* is a living showcase of the lifestyles and farming processes of the Voortrekkers.

The Battle of Blood River Memorial, Dundee, shows a recreated, life-size laager.

The Kat River Rebellion
Khoina settlers on the Kat River in the Cape had fought for the government without compensation, but rebelled in the war of 1850. With their defeat, their land passed to white ownership.

846 Seventh 'rontier War Var of the Axe)

1850 Eighth Frontier War, in which the Kat River Khoina join the Xhosa

1854 Britain withdraws from the Orange River Sovereignty

1856 British and German settlers placed on Eastern Cape border; the Colony of Natal is granted a representative government

845 | **1850** | **1855** | **1860**

1852 The Cape is granted representative government by Britain. Zuid-Afrikaansche Republiek (Transvaal) is formed

1853 Stamps available in the Cape Colony for the first time

First postage stamp

1857 Thousands of Xhosa living between the Keiskamma and Great Kei rivers (Eastern Cape) perish in a famine resulting from an ill-advised prophecy

Clash for Gold and Diamonds

The crown of England

The discovery of diamonds in the Northern Cape laid the foundation for South Africa's economy and created a massive migrant labour system. Subsequent strikes of gold in the east of the country promised an untold source of wealth best exploited under a single British authority. African kingdoms and two Boer republics were coerced to join a British confederation. Resistance to the British masterplan led to a series of skirmishes that culminated in the South African (Boer) War of 1899–1902.

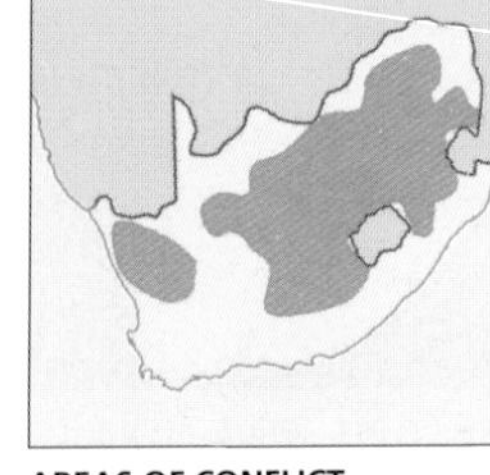

AREAS OF CONFLICT

Boer strongholds, war zones

Gold Fever
Finds of alluvial gold at Pilgrim's Rest (see p277) *and Barberton preceded the 1886 discovery of Johannesburg's Main Reef.*

Leander Jameson (1853–1917)
After the discovery of the Transvaal gold reefs, Jameson masterminded a revolt intended to topple President Paul Kruger of the Transvaal Republic.

Cecil John Rhodes (1853–1902)
This ruthless financier became involved in organizing the Jameson Raid in 1896, while he was prime minister of the Cape. The interference in the affairs of another state effectively ended his political career.

TIMELINE

1860 | 1865 | 1870 | 1875

1867 A 21-carat diamond is found near Hopetown in the Northern Cape

1871 Diamonds found at Colesberg Kopje (Kimberley). Gold found in Pilgrim's Rest

1877 Britain annexes South African Republic

1878 Walvis Bay (in today's Namibia) is proclaimed British territory

1879 Britain invades the Zulu kingdom of Cetshwayo, adjoining their colony of Natal

Cut diamond

Jan Christiaan Smuts
General Smuts (1870–1950) played prominent roles in the South African War and in both World Wars. He also helped to draft the United Nations Charter, and was twice elected as prime minister of South Africa (1919–24 and 1939–48).

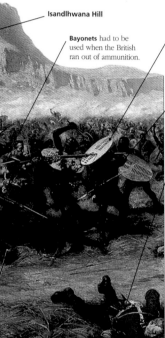

WHERE TO SEE THE CLASH FOR GOLD AND DIAMONDS

Coach tours include the major sites on the Battlefields Route *(p220)* in KwaZulu-Natal. Audiotapes for self-guided tours are available at the Talana Museum *(p220)*. Gold Reef City *(pp260–61)* is an evocative re-creation of Johannesburg in the 1890s. The Kimberley Mine Museum *(p317)* is one of several excellent historic sites in Kimberley.

Kimberley Mine Big Hole in Kimberley, Northern Cape.

Isandlhwana Hill

Bayonets had to be used when the British ran out of ammunition.

Shields covered with cow hide were used to ward off the bayonets.

The *assegaai* (short stabbing spear) was useful in close combat.

British casualties were high; only a handful of men escaped alive.

BATTLE OF ISANDHLWANA

In an effort to subjugate the fiercely independent Zulu, British officials provoked several incidents. In 1879, a 1,200-strong British and colonial force was annihilated by 20,000 Zulu warriors at Isandhlwana Hill.

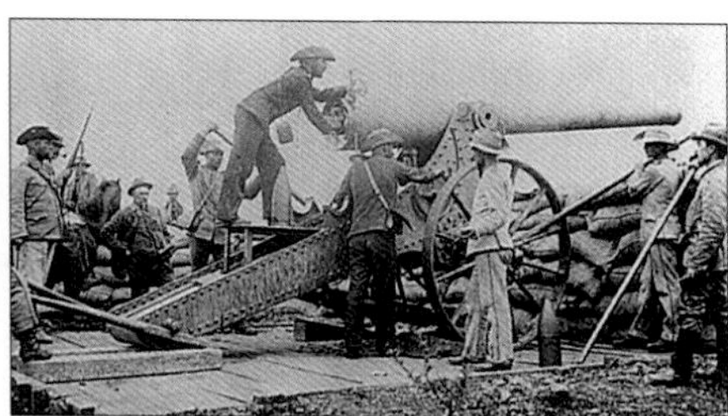

Modern Warfare
The South African War (1899–1902) was the first fought with high-velocity rifles and mechanical transport. Although the Boers were good shots and horsemen and could live off the land, limited man-power as well as the loose and informal structure of their armies counted against them.

884 Lesotho ecomes British rotectorate

1886 Discovery of the Main Reef on Witwatersrand (Gauteng)

1894 Kingdom of Swaziland becomes British protectorate

1896 Jameson Raid into Transvaal fails. Rinderpest kills countless head of cattle as well as wild animals

1902 South African War ends

880 | 1885 | 1890 | 1895 | 1900

81 ›ers ›feat itish my at ıjuba

1883 Olive Schreiner publishes *Story of an African Farm*

1885 Britain annexes part of Bechuanaland (Botswana)

Mahatma Gandhi

1893 Mohandas Karamchand Gandhi arrives in Durban to practise law

Winston Churchill as war correspondent in South Africa

1899 Start of South African War. Sabie Game Reserve declared (forerunner of today's Kruger National Park)

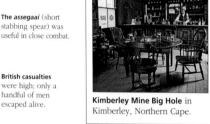

The Apartheid Years

"Free Mandela"

In 1910, the Union of South Africa became a self-governing colony within the British Commonwealth. The future of black South Africans was largely left undecided, leading to the founding of the South African Native National Congress (later known as the ANC) in 1912. The Great Trek centenary of 1938 renewed the white Afrikaner's hope for self-determination. In 1948, the Afrikaner-based National Party (NP) came to power and, by manipulating the composition of parliament, managed to enforce a series of harsh laws that stripped black South Africans of most of their basic human rights. In 1961 Prime Minister Verwoerd led the country out of the Commonwealth and into increasing political isolation.

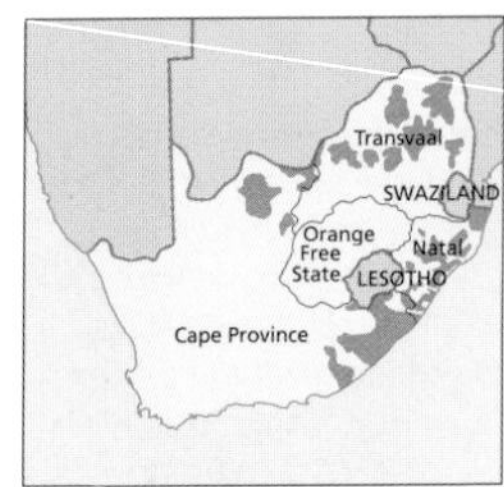

APARTHEID SOUTH AFRICA

— *Provincial boundaries (1994)*

■ *Homelands up to 1984*

Delville Wood
One of the most vicious battles of World War I was fought at Delville Wood, in France. For five days, 3,000 South African soldiers held out against the German line.

BURNING PASS BOOKS
The 1952 Natives Act required all black people over 16 to carry a pass book (permit to work in a "white" area) at all times, and present it to the police on demand. In 1960, thousands assembled at township police stations countrywide to burn their pass books. The law was repealed in 1986.

The Great Trek Centenary
The ox wagons rolled again in 1938, headed for a solemn celebration in Pretoria, where the first stone of the Voortrekker Monument (see p267) *was laid. This re-enactment of the Great Trek was an impressive display of Afrikaner solidarity, patriotism and political strength.*

TIMELINE

1905 Cullinan Diamond found at Premier Diamond Mine

1907 Sir James Percy FitzPatrick writes *Jock of the Bushveld*

1912 south African Native National Congress founded (later becomes ANC)

1928 Kirstenbosch Botanical Gardens and University of South Africa founded

1936 F printing the Bible Afrika

1900 | **1910** | **1920** | **1930**

1904 President Paul Kruger dies.

President Paul Kruger

1910 Formation of the Union of South Africa

1914 South Africa declares war on Germany. Boer rebellion put down by Union government. The first National Party formed in Bloemfontein

1922 Miners' rebellion breaks out at coal mines in Witbank

1927 Compulsory racial segregation declared in many urban areas

APARTHEID

Afrikaans for "segregation", this word describes the government policy in force after 1948. In keeping with racial classification laws, skin colour dictated where people were allowed to live, work and even be buried. It determined where children were taught and influenced the quality of their education. Sex "across the colour bar" was punishable by imprisonment. Loss of land was among the system's most terrible inflictions.

Security police "house calls" enforced apartheid laws

WHERE TO SEE THE APARTHEID YEARS

District Six Museum, located on the edge of this former Cape Town precinct, shows what life was like in this largely Muslim community before it was cleared under the Group Areas Act, starting in 1966. Exhibits at the Mayibuye Centre, University of the Western Cape, depict the oppression and struggle for democracy. The Iziko Slave Lodge *(p70)* in Cape Town and MuseuMAfricA *(p256)* in Johannesburg also have interesting displays. In Pretoria/Tshwane, the Voortrekker Museum and Monument *(p267)* offer an insight into the driving force behind Afrikaner Nationalism.

MuseuMAfricA in Johannesburg shows the living conditions in a township like Sophiatown.

District Six, "the life and soul of Cape Town", was declared a white area in 1966.

African Nationalism
Drum, first published in the 1950s, was important for black journalists. Not afraid to criticize the white regime, they rekindled African Nationalism.

Apartheid's Architects
Dutch-born Hendrik Verwoerd (1901–66), prime minister from 1958 until his assassination, and Charles Robberts Swart (1894–1982), the minister of justice, implemented many apartheid measures.

First edition of Afrikaans Bible

1939 South Africa declares war on Germany

1940

1948 National Party elected as the country's government

1949 Prohibition of Mixed Marriages Act, the first of many apartheid laws, is passed by Parliament

1950

1950 Communism is outlawed

1955 Petrol is made from coal for the first time in South Africa

1958 Hendrik Verwoerd becomes prime minister of South Africa

1960

1960 Police shoot 69 demonstrators at Sharpeville. Whites-only referendum opts for a republic

Age of Democracy

The laws imposed by the white Nationalist government outraged black African societies, and the decree that Afrikaans be the language of instruction at black schools sparked off the revolt of 1976. States of emergency came and went, and violence increased. It became clear that the old system of administration was doomed. In 1990, State President Frederik Willem de Klerk undertook the first step towards reconciliation by unbanning the ANC, Communist Party and 34 other organizations, and announcing the release of Nelson Mandela.

Buttonhole, 1992 Referendum

THE NEW SOUTH AFRICA

— *Provincial boundaries*

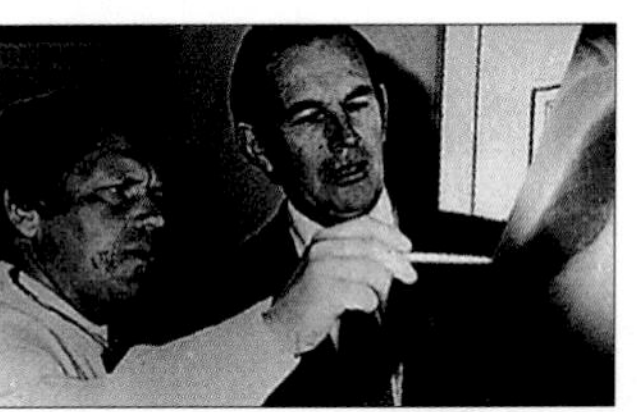

A World First
Christiaan Barnard (right) made medical history in 1967 when he transplanted a human heart.

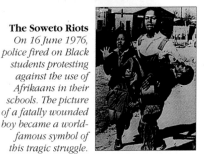

Desmond Tutu won a Nobel Peace Prize (1984) and Martin Luther King Peace Prize (1986) for his dedicated anti-apartheid campaign.

The Soweto Riots
On 16 June 1976, police fired on Black students protesting against the use of Afrikaans in their schools. The picture of a fatally wounded boy became a world-famous symbol of this tragic struggle.

Arts Against Apartheid
The Black Christ (by Ronald Harrison) was inspired by the Sharpeville Massacre and banning of the then ANC president Chief Albert Luthuli (depicted as Christ). Banned for years, it now hangs in the Iziko South African National Gallery *(see p77)*.

DEMOCRATIC ELECTION

On 27 April 1994, South Africans went to the polls – many for the first time. Five days later the result was announced: with 63 per cent of votes in its favour, the African National Congress (ANC) had achieved victory in all but two provinces and Nelson Mandela was the new State President.

TIMELINE

1961 South Africa becomes a republic outside the British Commonwealth

Old flag

1971 International Court and UN Security Council recognize Namibia and revoke South Africa's mandate on the country

1980 ANC bombs Sasolburg Oil Refinery in the Free State

1960 | 1965 | 1970 | 1975 | 1980

1962 Nelson Mandela jailed. Start of UN-imposed sanctions

1963 Guerrilla war begins in South West Africa (Namibia)

1966 Prime Minister Verwoerd assassinated. Lesotho gains its independence

1968 Swaziland gains independence

1976 Soweto riots erupt. Flight of foreign capital from South Africa

1984 New constitution for tricameral parliament

Kwaito – Sound of a New Generation
Boomshaka sings kwaito, *a uniquely South African sound that was born in the townships of Gauteng. The lyrics, influenced by* toyi-toyi *(protest) chants, have a similar repetitive quality.*

Free At Last
On 11 February 1990, after almost three decades in custody, Nelson Mandela emerged from the Victor Verster prison near Paarl. The high-profile event was watched by millions around the world.

Cricket World Cup 1992
Political change in South Africa saw the national cricket team included in a world event for the first time in over 20 years.

Independent Electoral Commission monitor

Ballot paper

Sealed ballot box

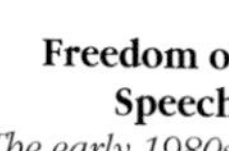

Sanctions Lifted
In 1993, trade sanctions (introduced in 1986) were lifted and brands became available again.

Freedom of Speech
The early 1980s saw flamboyant Evita Bezuidenhout (see p157) *on stage for the first time. Her outspoken, satirical views on internal politics made her famous in South Africa and abroad.*

The Truth and Reconciliation Commission (TRC)
Established in 1994 under the chairmanship of former Archbishop of Cape Town Desmond Tutu, the aim of this commission was to establish the motives behind political crimes committed during the apartheid years.

) Namibian ependence. unbanned. on Mandela released

1994 ANC wins SA's first democratic election. Nelson Mandela becomes president

1995 South Africa hosts and wins the Rugby World Cup

2003 Walter Sisulu, a key member of the ANC and Nelson Mandela's mentor, dies at the age of 91

2005 The Geographical Names Committee recommends that Pretoria change its name to Tshwane

1990 **1995** **2000** **2005** **2010**

92 Referendum held rding FW de Klerk's cy of change. South a participates in the pic Games, the first time since 1960

The new flag

1999 Second democratic election

1998 Truth and Reconciliation Commission hearings begin

2004 The ruling party, ANC, wins a landslide election, taking 70 per cent of the votes

CAPE TOWN

Cape Town at a Glance

Cape Town lies on a small peninsula at the southern tip of Africa which juts into the Atlantic Ocean. It is South Africa's premier tourist destination and its fourth largest urban centre. Enriched by Dutch, British and Cape Malay influences, the cosmopolitan atmosphere is a unique blend of cultures. Lying at the foot of its most famous landmark, Table Mountain, Cape Town has a host of well-preserved historical buildings. Many, such as the Old Townhouse on Greenmarket Square, now house museums. Outside the city, attractions include Chapman's Peak Drive along a winding coastline, where sheer cliffs drop to the swirling sea below, and a tour of the vineyards around Franschhoek and Stellenbosch.

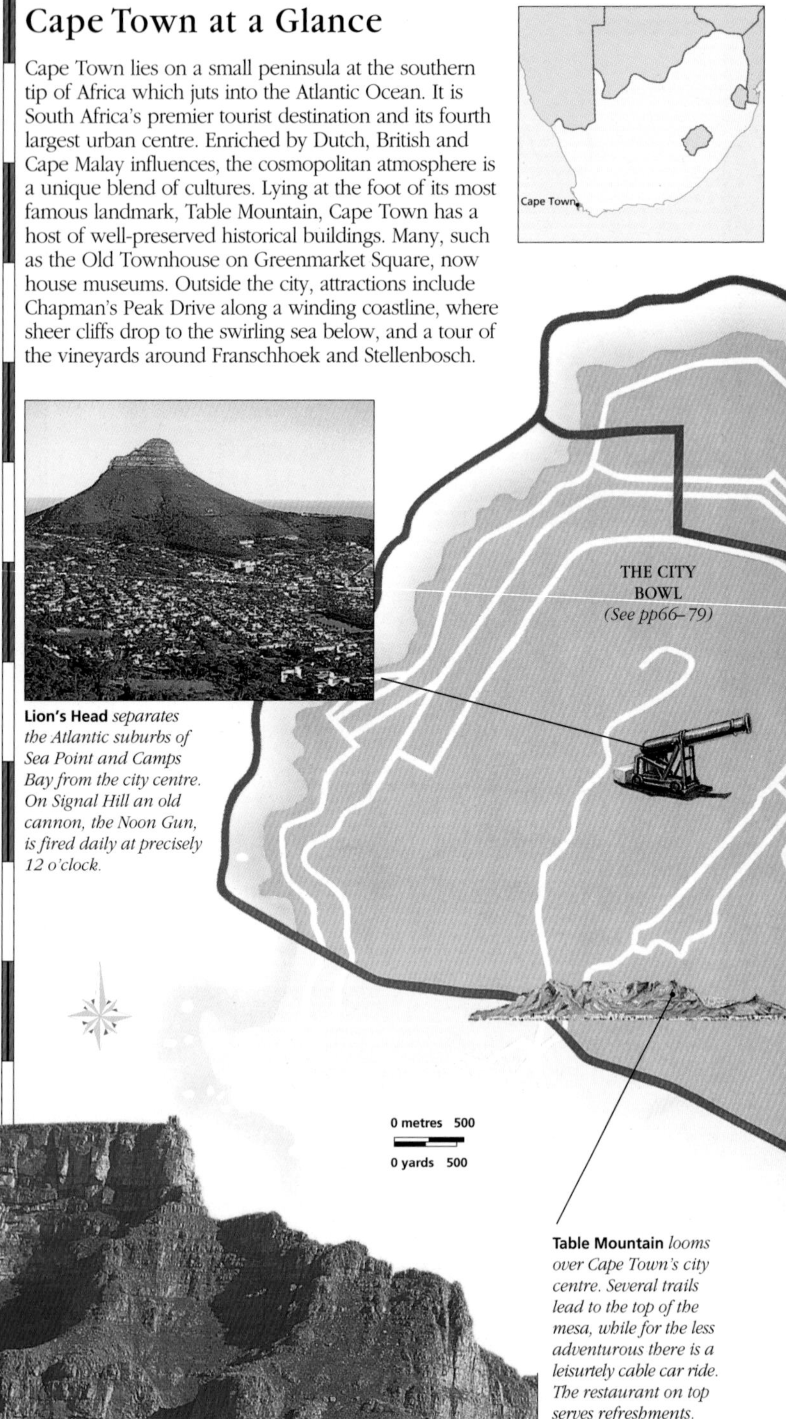

Lion's Head *separates the Atlantic suburbs of Sea Point and Camps Bay from the city centre. On Signal Hill an old cannon, the Noon Gun, is fired daily at precisely 12 o'clock.*

Table Mountain *looms over Cape Town's city centre. Several trails lead to the top of the mesa, while for the less adventurous there is a leisurtely cable car ride. The restaurant on top serves refreshments.*

◁ **Campus Bay beach, on the Atlantic seaboard, is a popular spot for sunbathing and people-watching**

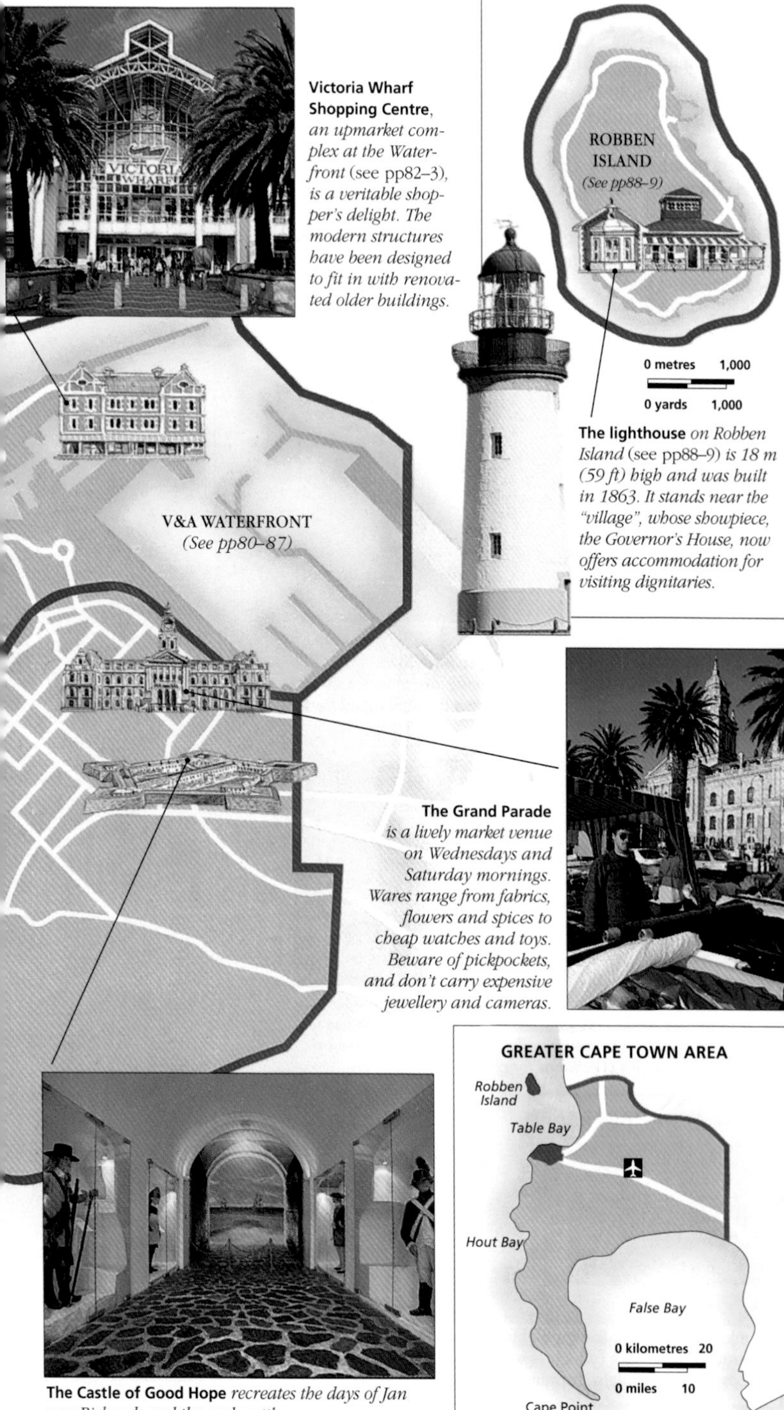

Victoria Wharf Shopping Centre, *an upmarket complex at the Waterfront* (see pp82–3), *is a veritable shopper's delight. The modern structures have been designed to fit in with renovated older buildings.*

The lighthouse *on Robben Island* (see pp88–9) *is 18 m (59 ft) high and was built in 1863. It stands near the "village", whose showpiece, the Governor's House, now offers accommodation for visiting dignitaries.*

The Grand Parade *is a lively market venue on Wednesdays and Saturday mornings. Wares range from fabrics, flowers and spices to cheap watches and toys. Beware of pickpockets, and don't carry expensive jewellery and cameras.*

The Castle of Good Hope *recreates the days of Jan van Riebeeck and the early settlers.*

Street-by-street: City Centre

Frieze on Koopmans de Wet House

The compact city centre lends itself to walking, because most of its major sights are easily accessible. Cape Town is dissected by a number of thoroughfares, one of which is Adderley Street. The parallel St George's Mall is a lively pedestrian zone where street musicians and dancers entertain the crowds. Greenmarket Square, the focal point of the city, is lined with many historically significant buildings. One block west of here, towards Signal Hill, is Long Street. Some of the beautiful examples of the elaborate Victorian façades seen along this street are Bristol Antiques at No. 177, and the Traveller's Inn at No. 206.

ROBBEN ISLAND
V&A WATERFRONT
CITY CENTRE

LOCATOR MAP
See Street Finder, map 5

HOUT STREET
SHORTMARKET STREET
LONG STREET
LONGMARKET STREET
BURG STREET
CHURCH STREET
WALE STREET

★ Greenmarket Square
A produce market since 1806, and now a national monument, the cobbled square supports a colourful, daily open-air craft market. Among the historical buildings surrounding it is the Old Townhouse.

Malay Quarter

★ Long Street
This well-preserved historic street in the city centre is lined with elegant Victorian buildings and their graceful, delicate wrought-iron balconies.

Government Avenue

STAR SIGHTS

- ★ Iziko Slave Lodge
- ★ Long Street
- ★ Greenmarket Square

KEY

– – – Suggested route

★ Iziko Slave Lodge
The exhibits at this museum illustrate the history of the site, the second-oldest colonial building in Cape Town ❷

For hotels and restaurants in this region see pp326–31 and pp358–62

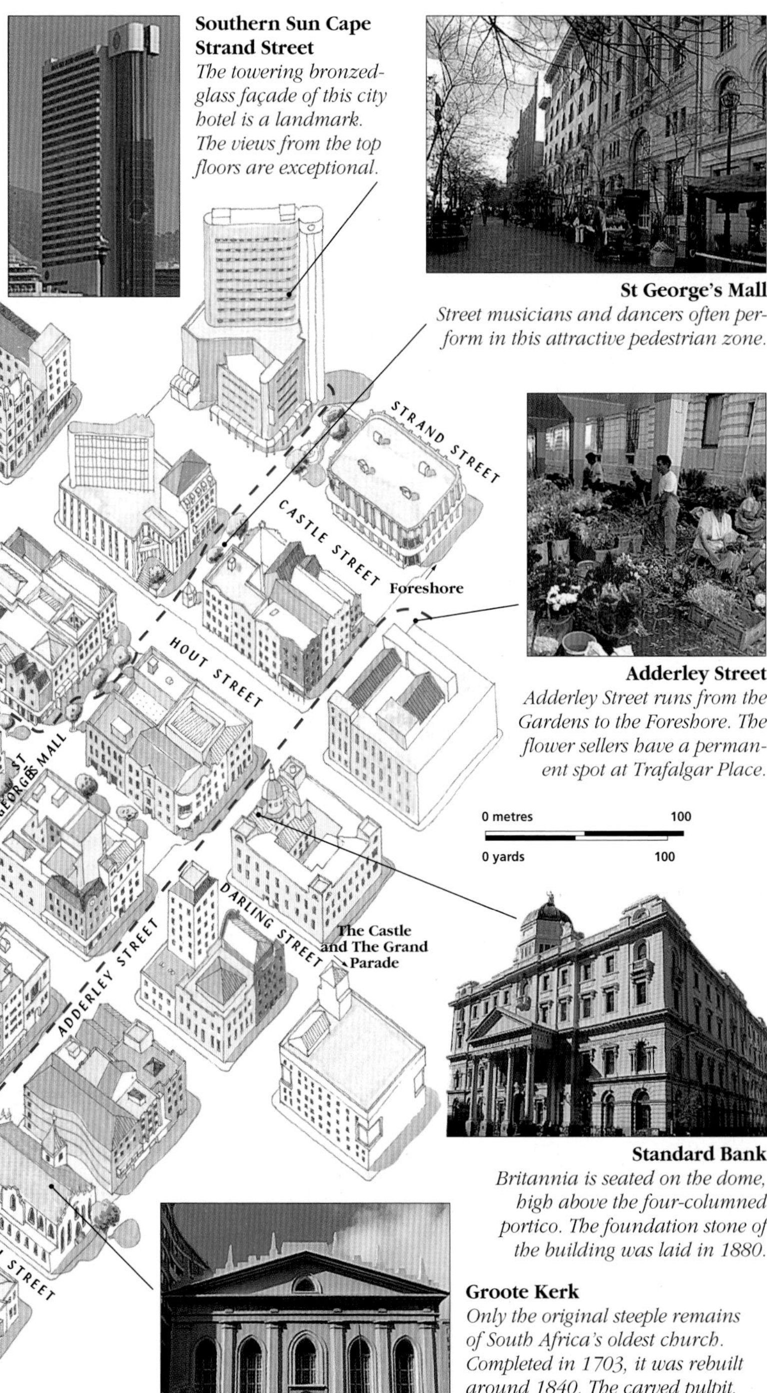

Southern Sun Cape Strand Street
The towering bronzed-glass façade of this city hotel is a landmark. The views from the top floors are exceptional.

St George's Mall
Street musicians and dancers often perform in this attractive pedestrian zone.

Adderley Street
Adderley Street runs from the Gardens to the Foreshore. The flower sellers have a permanent spot at Trafalgar Place.

Standard Bank
Britannia is seated on the dome, high above the four-columned portico. The foundation stone of the building was laid in 1880.

Groote Kerk
Only the original steeple remains of South Africa's oldest church. Completed in 1703, it was rebuilt around 1840. The carved pulpit, dating to 1789, is the work of sculptor Anton Anreith and carpenter Jan Jacob Graaff.

The Old Town House, where the Iziko Michaelis Collection is kept

Iziko Michaelis Collection ❶

Greenmarket Square. **Map** 5 B1. ***Tel*** *(021) 481-3933.* *10am–5pm Mon–Fri, 10am–4pm Sat.* *Good Friday, 25 Dec.*

This national monument on Greenmarket Square was built in 1755, in the Cape Rococo style, and initially served as the "*Burgherwacht Huys*" (house of the night patrol) and the magistrate's court until 1839, when it was claimed as a town hall by the newly formed municipality. After renovations in 1915, the building was handed over to the Union Government for use as an art gallery.

The original collection was donated to the city by the wealthy financier Sir Max Michaelis in 1914. It was added to by Lady Michaelis after the death of her husband in 1932.

The collection consists of a world-renowned selection of Dutch and Flemish art from the 17th-century Golden Age. The portraits are particularly interesting, offering an insight into Dutch society at the time.

In addition to the permanent collection, the gallery has a series of temporary exhibitions that have been designed to appeal to both locals and visitors alike.

After hours, the gallery becomes an active cultural centre, hosting chamber-music concerts, and interesting lectures.

Iziko Slave Lodge ❷

Cnr Wale & Adderley sts. **Map** 5 B2. ***Tel*** *(021) 460-8200.* *9:30am–4:30pm daily.*

The first building on this site was a lodge that housed the slaves who worked in the Company's Garden *(see pp76–7)*. It was built around 1679 on land that originally formed part of the garden.

By 1807, new premises from which to administer the Cape colony were needed, and the Slave Lodge suited most requirements. Many slave inhabitants of the lodge were sold, while others were moved to the west wing of the building. The vacated area was turned into offices. In 1811, the west wing was also converted.

The people responsible for the conversion were the builder Herman Schutte, the sculptor Anton Anreith and the architect Louis Michel Thibault. As well as government offices, the lodge also housed the Supreme Court, the post office and the public library. The present building once extended into Adderley Street, but this portion had to be demolished when the road was widened. However, the original façade, designed by Thibault, has been restored to its former splendour.

Plaque on the Iziko Slave Lodge

Iziko Museums of Cape Town is working on transforming the Slave Lodge into a major site that increases public awareness of slavery, cultural diversity and the struggle for human rights in South Africa. The history of slavery at the Cape is illustrated with three-dimensional and audiovisual displays along with text, images and maps. A section that focuses on life at the lodge is currently being developed, based on archaeological and archival sources, as well as the memories of people who trace their roots to the time of slavery in the Cape.

THE MICHAELIS COLLECTION

This important art collection was established in 1914, when Sir Max Michaelis donated 68 paintings collected by Lady Phillips and Sir Hugh Lane. The gallery formally opened three years later, and today comprises some 104 paintings and 312 etchings. It includes works by Frans Hals, Rembrandt, van Dijck, David Teniers the Younger, Jan Steen and Willem van Aelst. Although the collection is rather small in comparison to international galleries, it presents a valuable source of reference of the evolution of Dutch and Flemish art over two centuries. One of the most famous paintings in the collection is the *Portrait of a Lady* by Frans Hals.

***Portrait of a Lady*, Frans Hals (1640)**

Many Cape Muslims have greengrocer stalls on the Grand Parade

Across the road from the Old Slave Lodge is the **Groote Kerk** (big church). Soon after their arrival at the Cape, the Dutch held religious services on board of Jan van Riebeeck's ship, *Drommedaris*.

Later, they used a small side room at Castle Good Hope. However, when need arose for a decent burial place, a permanent site had to be chosen. The first, temporary structure at the northeast end of the Company's Gardens was replaced by a thatched church on the same site in 1700, at the order of Governor Willem Adriaan van der Stel.

The church was completely rebuilt in the 19th century, and the new building dedicated in 1841. All that remains of the original church today is the Baroque belfry, which, unfortunately, is now almost obscured by tall modern buildings.

Of interest in the church is the splendid original pulpit supported by carved lions. The story goes that sculptor Anton Anreith's original concept including the symbolic images of Hope, Faith and Charity was rejected as being too papist.

The façade of the church has high Gothic windows divided by bold pilasters. In front of the building is a statue of Andrew Murray, minister of the Dutch Reformed Church in Cape Town from 1864–71.

Andrew Murray (1828–1917)

Groote Kerk
Adderley St. **Map** *5 B2.* ***Tel*** *(021) 422-0569.* *10am–2pm Mon–Fri .*

Grand Parade and City Hall ❸

Darling St. **Map** 5 C2. ***Tel*** City Hall: *(021) 400-2230.* *7:30am–5:30pm Mon–Sat.*

The grand parade was the site van Riebeeck selected for his first fort in 1652. The structure was levelled in 1674 when the Castle of Good Hope *(see pp72–3)* was completed; until 1821 the area was used as parade and exercise ground for the troops. As buildings went up around the perimeter, greengrocers established fruit stalls, precursors of today's fleamarket. Every Wednesday and Saturday morning the area bustles with market activity, while for the rest of the week the Grand Parade serves as a pay-and-display car park.

Overlooking the Grand Parade is Cape Town's large City Hall. Built in 1905 in the elaborate Italian Renaissance style, it presents its elegant façades on four different streets. A 39-bell carillion tower was added in 1923. The walls of the City Hall regularly resound to the soaring orchestral strains of the Cape Town Philharmonic, formerly known as the Cape Town Symphony Orchestra. It is well worth getting tickets for the popular lunchtime and evening concerts, which can be booked through any branch of Computicket *(see p110)*.

Iziko Castle of Good Hope ❹

See pp72–3.

Cape Town's City Hall opposite the Grand Parade

Iziko Castle of Good Hope ❹

Dutch East India (VOC) monogram, 17th century

Cape Town's Iziko Castle of Good Hope is South Africa's oldest structure. Built between 1666–79, it replaced an earlier clay-and-timber fort erected by Commander Jan van Riebeeck *(see p48)* in 1652. The Castle overlooks the Grand Parade and is now a museum that also houses traditional Cape regiments and units of the National Defence Force.

Dolphin Pool
Descriptions and sketches made by Lady Anne Barnard (see p102) *in the 1790s enabled the reconstruction of the dolphin pool over two hundred years later.*

The Castle Moat
The restoration of the moat, which is a relatively recent addition to the Castle, was completed in 1999.

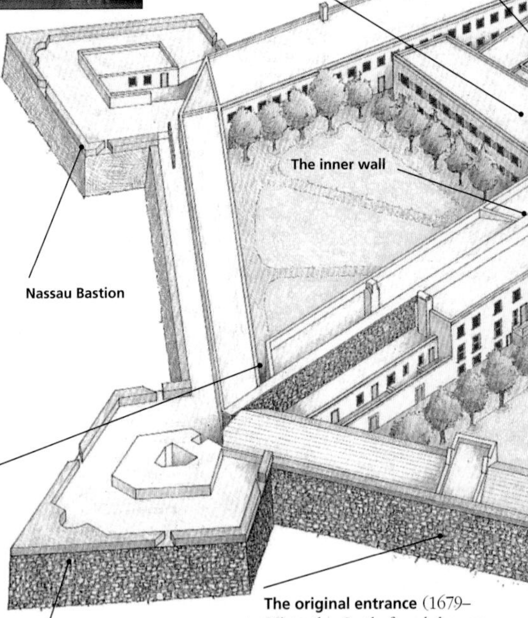

The original entrance (1679–82) to the Castle faced the sea, but has since been closed.

The Archway
Slate, taken from a quarry on Robben Island (see pp88–9) *in the 17th century, was used for the paving stones inside the Castle.*

STAR FEATURES

- ★ The Castle Military Museum
- ★ William Fehr Collection
- ★ De Kat Balcony

★ The Castle Military Museum
On display is an array of military artifacts, as well as weapons and uniforms from the VOC and British periods of occupation of the Cape.

★ William Fehr Collection
Exhibits include paintings by old masters such as Thomas Baines, as well as period furniture, glass, ceramics and metalware.

VISITORS' CHECKLIST

Cnr Darling & Buitenkant sts.
Map 5 C2. ***Tel*** *(021) 787-1249.*
Cape Town station.
9am–4pm daily;
Key Ceremony *10am, noon.*
1 Jan, 25 Dec. *11am, noon, 2pm Mon–Sat.*
www.iziko.org.za

Oranje Bastion

Entrance Gable
A teak copy of the original VOC gable reflects martial symbols: a banner, flags, drums and cannon balls.

Leerdam Bastion
Leerdam, Oranje, Nassau, Catzenellenbogen and Buuren were titles held by Prince William of Orange.

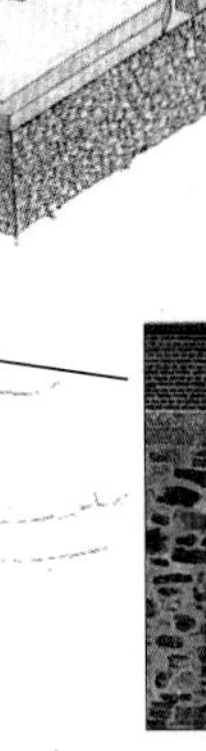

Colonnaded verandah

Moat

The Castle Entrance
The original bell, cast in Amsterdam in 1697, still hangs in the belfry. The coat of arms of the United Netherlands can be seen on the pediment above the gate.

Buuren Bastion

★ De Kat Balcony
The original staircase, built in 1695 as part of a defensive crosswall, divided the square into an inner and outer court, and was remodelled between 1786 and 1790.

Lutheran Church and Martin Melck House ❺

Strand St. **Map** 5 B1. ***Tel*** *(021) 421-5854.* ◯ *10am–2pm Mon–Fri.*

Since the ruling authority was intolerant of any religion other than that of the Dutch Reformed Church, the Lutheran Church began as a "storeroom". Wealthy Lutheran businessman, Martin Melck, built it with the intention of modifying it into a place of worship once the religious laws were relaxed, and the first service was held in 1776. A few years later, the sexton's house was added.

From 1787–92, the German-born sculptor Anton Anreith embellished the church and added a tower. Today, both the church and the sexton's house are national monuments. The Martin Melck House, next door, was built in 1781 and declared a national monument in 1936. The building is a rare example of an 18th-century Cape town-house that features an attic.

In April 2001, the Gold of Africa Museum opened next door (Tel: (021) 405-1540), featuring a collection of over 350 19th- and 20th-century gold objects from Mali, Senegal, Ghana and the Ivory Coast. Plans for expansion include the acquisition of further treasures from the entire African continent, a training studio and boutique.

The Lutheran Church in Strand Street

The dining room in Iziko Koopmans-De Wet House

Iziko Koopmans-De Wet House ❻

35 Strand St. **Map** 5 B1. ***Tel*** *(021) 481-3935.* ◯ *9:30am–4pm Tue–Thu.*

This neo-classical home was built in 1701 when Strand Street, then close to the shore, was the most fashionable part of Cape Town. The building was enlarged in subsequent centuries; a second storey was added, and renowned French architect Louis Michel Thibault remodelled the façade around 1795 in Louis XVI-style. The De Wet family was the last to own the house. After the death of her husband, Johan Koopmans, Maria de Wet lived here with her sister, from 1880 until her death in 1906. Over the years, the De Wet sisters assembled the many fine antiques that can still be seen in the museum today. Maria de Wet, apart from being a renowned society hostess who entertained guests like President Paul Kruger *(see p251)* and mining magnate Cecil John Rhodes *(see p54)*, was also responsible for taking the first steps to protect Cape Town's many historic buildings. It was thanks to her intervention that the destruction of part of the Castle was prevented when the new railway lines were being

Iziko Bo-Kaap Museum ❼

71 Wale St. **Map** 5 A1. ***Tel*** *(021) 481-3939.* ◯ *9am–4pm Mon–Sat.* ● *Eid-ul-Fitr, Eid-ul-Adha, Good Fri, 25 Dec.*

The Iziko Bo-Kaap Museum, which dates back to the 1760s, is the oldest house in the area still in its original form. The characteristic features are a *voorstoep* (front terrace) and a courtyard at the back, both emphasizing the social aspect of Cape Muslim culture. The museum focuses on the history of Islam in the Cape of Good Hope, highlighting its local cultural expressions.

The Bo-Kaap area has traditionally been associated with the Muslim community of South Africa, and the oldest mosque in the country is located on Dorp Street, just behind the museum.

Table Mountain ❽

See pp78–9.

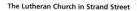

Malay Culture in Cape Town

The original Malays were brought to the Cape from 1658 onwards by the Dutch East India Company. Most of them were Muslims from Sri Lanka, Indonesian islands and India. A large proportion of them were slaves, while others were political exiles of considerable stature. After the abolition of slavery in the early 1830s, the Cape Malays (or Cape Muslims as they now prefer to be called) settled on the slope of Signal Hill in an area called Bo–Kaap ("above Cape Town") to be near the mosques that had been built there (Auwal Mosque dates from 1794). The Malays had a significant influence on the Afrikaans tongue, and many of their culinary traditions *(see pp354–5)* were absorbed by other cultures. Today, the Muslim community is very much a part of Cape Town: the muezzins' haunting calls, ringing out from minarets to summon the faithful, are an integral part of the city.

Mango atchar

STREETS OF THE BO-KAAP

Just above modern Cape Town, within easy walking distance of the city centre, lies the traditional home of the Cape Muslims. Here, narrow-fronted houses in pastel colours open onto cobbled streets.

Ornate parapets and plasterwork adorn the houses, most of which date from around 1810.

Cobbled streets still exist, but many of them have now been tarred.

Muslim tradition *dictates that formal attire be worn on festive occasions. This includes the traditional fez for men, while women don the characteristic* chador *(full-length veil or shawl).*

The fez, *of Turkish origin, is still worn occasionally, but knitted, or cloth, caps are more common nowadays.*

Signal Hill *is the traditional home of the Cape Muslim community. Many of the quaint, Bo-Kaap cottages have been replaced by modern apartment blocks higher up.*

The Mosque in Longmarket Street, *like many of the Bo-Kaap's mosques, stands wedged in-between the homes of residents. Religion is a fundamental part of every devout Muslim's life.*

Street-by-Street: Gardens

Jan van Riebeeck's famous vegetable garden, established in 1652 to provide ships rounding the Cape of Good Hope with fresh supplies, is still today known as the "Company's Garden". It is a leafy, tranquil area that contains an array of exotic shrubs and trees, an aviary (records show that a "menagerie" existed here during the time of governor Simon van der Stel), a conservatory and a sun dial dating back to 1787. There is also an open-air restaurant. Nearby stands a Saffren pear tree, planted soon after the arrival of Jan van Riebeeck, which makes it the oldest cultivated tree in South Africa. Look out for the disused old well, and the tap that protrudes from the gnarled tree nearby.

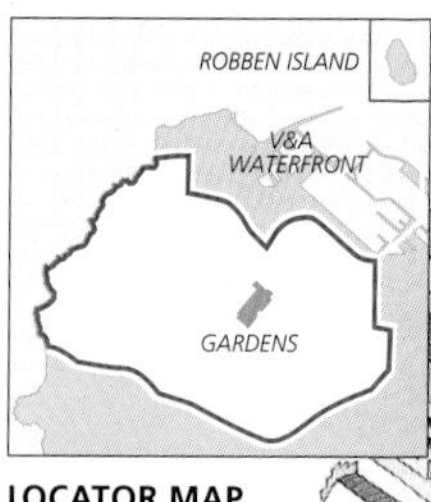

LOCATOR MAP
See Street Finder, map 5

KEY

— — — Suggested route

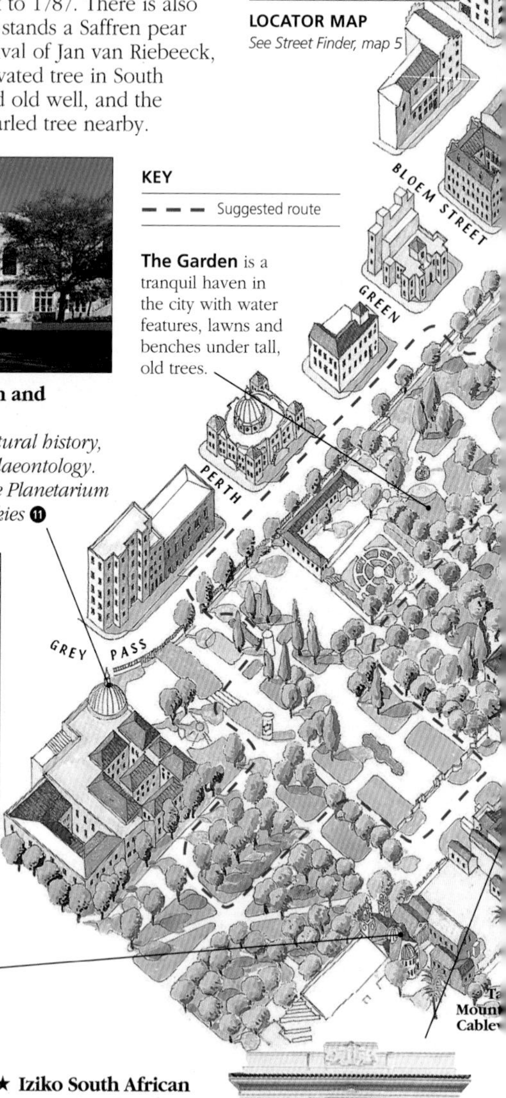

The Garden is a tranquil haven in the city with water features, lawns and benches under tall, old trees.

★ Iziko South African Museum and Planetarium
The museum concentrates on natural history, archaeology, entomology and palaeontology. The sophisticated equipment in the Planetarium reconstructs the southern night skies ⓫

South African Jewish Museum
The entrance to this museum is situated in the Old Synagogue, the first synagogue built in South Africa in 1863 ❿

STAR SIGHTS

- ★ Iziko South African National Gallery
- ★ Iziko South African Museum & Planetarium
- ★ Government Avenue

★ Iziko South African National Gallery
Temporary exhibitions of contemporary local artists augment the permanent collection of 6,500 paintings ❾

For hotels and restaurants in this region see pp326–31 and pp358–62

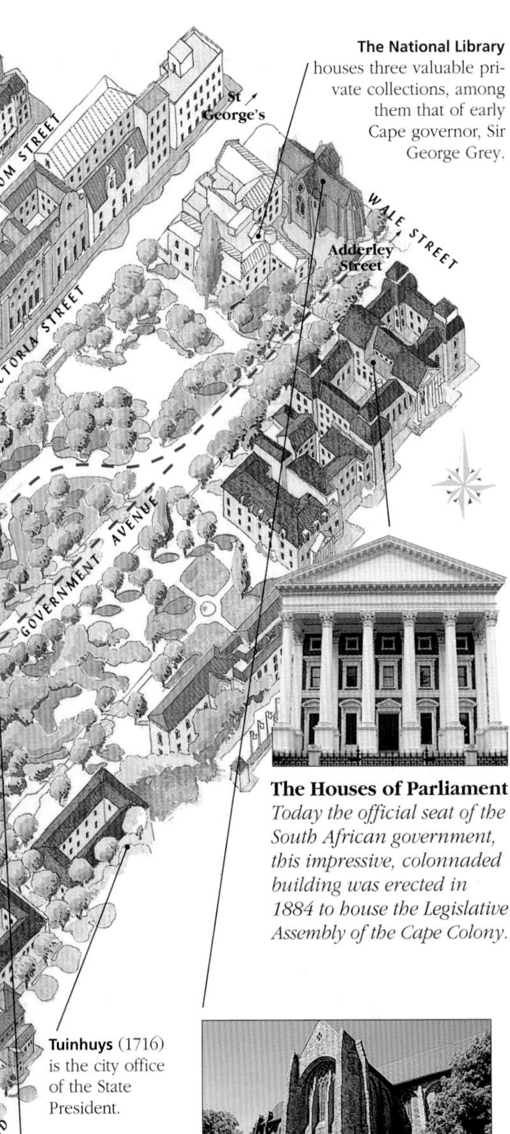

The National Library houses three valuable private collections, among them that of early Cape governor, Sir George Grey.

The Houses of Parliament
Today the official seat of the South African government, this impressive, colonnaded building was erected in 1884 to house the Legislative Assembly of the Cape Colony.

Tuinhuys (1716) is the city office of the State President.

St George's Cathedral
This Anglican cathedral (1901) features stained glass by Gabriel Loire of Chartres and a Rose Window by F Spear.

★ Government Avenue
The original lemon tree lane has been replaced by tall, shady oak trees.

0 metres 100
0 yards 100

Iziko South African National Gallery ❾

Off Government Ave. **Map** 5 B2. ***Tel*** *(021) 467-4660.* *10am–5pm Tue–Sun.* *public hols.* **www**.iziko.org.za

South Africa's premier art museum houses outstanding collections of British, French, Dutch, Flemish and South African paintings. Selections from the permanent collection change regularly to allow for a full programme of temporary exhibitions of contemporary photography, sculpture, beadwork, and textiles. They provide a great insight into the extraordinary range of artworks produced in this country, the African continent and further afield.

South African Jewish Museum ❿

84 Hatfield St. **Map** 5 A2. ***Tel*** *(021) 465-1546.* *10am–5pm Mon–Thu, Sun; 10am–2pm Fri.* *Jewish hols.* **www**.sajewishmuseum.co.za

This museum narrates the story of South African Jewry from its beginnings, setting it against the backdrop of the country's history. The exhibits celebrate the pioneering spirit of the early Jewish immigrants and their descendants.

The new building, opened in 2000 by Nelson Mandela, makes full use of interactive media to present the exhibits.

Iziko South African Museum and Planetarium ⓫

25 Queen Victoria St. **Map** 5 A2. ***Tel*** *(021) 481-3800.* *10am–5pm daily.* *Good Fri, 25 Dec.* *free on Sat.*

Of special interest here are the whale skeletons, the coelacanth, reptile fossils from the Karoo, and the Shark World exhibition. There are also exceptional examples of rock art, including whole sections from caves.

The Planetarium offers daily shows for various age groups.

Table Mountain ❽

Cable car

The Cape Peninsula mountain chain is a mass of sedimentary sandstone lying above ancient shales that were deposited some 700 million years ago, as well as large areas of granite. The sandstone sediment, which forms the main block of the mountain, was deposited about 450 million years ago when the Peninsula, then a part of Gondwana, lay below sea level. After the subsidence of the primeval ocean, the effects of wind, rain, ice and extreme temperatures caused erosion of the softer layers, leaving behind the characteristic mesa of Table Mountain.

Royal Visitors
In 1947, King George VI and the future Queen Mother accompanied Prime Minister Smuts on a bike.

Kirstenbosch National Botanical Garden
The garden (see pp104–5) *nestles at the foot of the Peninsula range. Three major trails and numerous paths lead up the mountain slopes.*

King's Blockhouse
This is the best preserved of the three 18th-century stone forts that were built during the first British occupation of the Cape (see pp50–51).

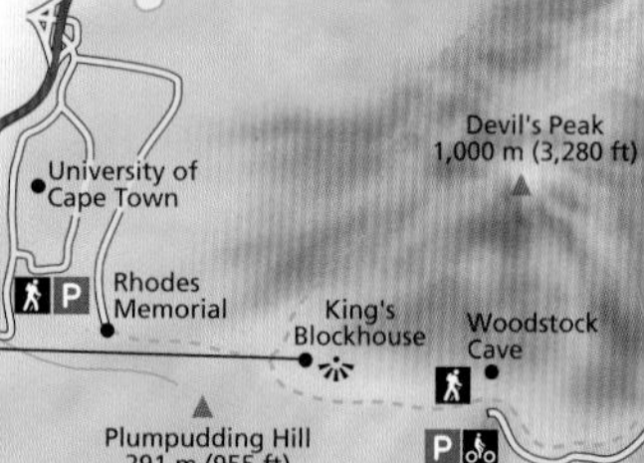

KEY

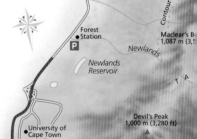

- Major road
- Road
- Hiking trail
- Viewpoint
- Hiking trail starting point
- Mountain bike access
- Wildflowers
- Parking

TABLE MOUNTAIN FAUNA AND FLORA

Disa orchid

Over 1,500 plant species of the 2,285 that make up the Cape Floral Kingdom of the Peninsula can be found in the protected natural habitat of Table Mountain. They include *Disa uniflora* (also called Pride of Table Mountain), which mostly grows near streams and waterfalls, and several members of the regal protea family. Wildlife, consisting mostly of small mammals, reptiles and birds, includes the rare and secretive ghost frog that is found in a few perennial streams on the plateau.

Ghost frog

The Plateau
The high plateau affords superb views of the Hely-Hutchinson reservoir and the Back Table, and southwards to False Bay and Cape Point.

VISITORS' CHECKLIST

Map 4 D5, E5, F5. The Table Mountain Aerial Cableway Company, *(021) 424-0015. Cable cars depart every 10–15 mins.* daily. winds over 80 km (50 miles) per hour. Adderley St or taxi from city centre. **www.**cpnp.co.za

De Villiers Dam
Original Disa
Alexandra Reservoir
Victoria Reservoir
Reserve Peak 844 m (2,769 ft)
Ravine
Disa Stream
Hely-Hutchinson Reservoir
Woodhead Reservoir
Junction Peak 919 m (3,015 ft)
Kasteelpoort
Orion's Cave
Pipe Track
Platteklip Gorge
Upper Cableway Station
Upper Contour Path
Platteklip
Lower Cableway Station
CAMPS BAY
Mocke Reservoir
SEA POINT AND CLIFTON
CITY CENTRE
Lion's Head 669 m (2,195 ft)
RUMP
LION'S
Signal Hill 350 m (1,148 ft)

0 kilometres 3
0 miles 1

Viewing Platform
In 1998, extensive upgrading of the Table Mountain Cableway as well as the lower and upper stations resulted in special reinforced viewing platforms at strategic vantage points.

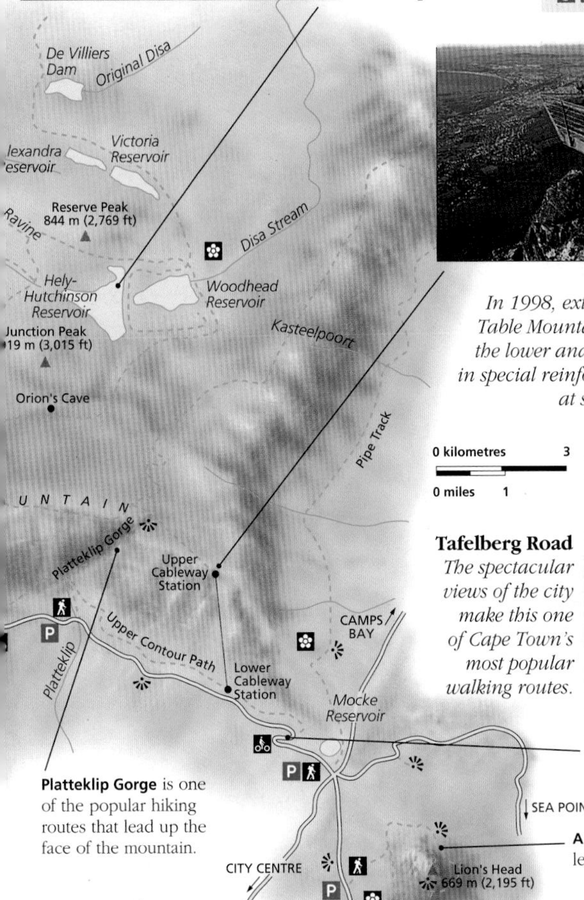

Tafelberg Road
The spectacular views of the city make this one of Cape Town's most popular walking routes.

Platteklip Gorge is one of the popular hiking routes that lead up the face of the mountain.

A circular route leads up Lion's Head

Kramat
This burial place of Goolam Muhamed Soofi is one of six Muslim shrines that form a holy circle around the Cape Peninsula.

TIPS FOR WALKERS

Several well-marked trails, graded according to their degree of difficulty, lead to the summit. All hikers must wear proper walking boots and are advised to check with the Lower Cableway Station before setting out, as weather conditions may deteriorate without warning. Hiking on windy or misty days is not recommended.

Hikers on the plateau

V&A WATERFRONT

Logo of the V&A Waterfront

Cape Town's successful Waterfront project was named after the son of Queen Victoria. In 1860, a young Prince Alfred initiated the construction of the first breakwater in stormy Table Bay, by toppling a load of rocks that had been excavated from the sea floor into the water. The Alfred Basin, which was subsequently created, successfully protected visiting ships from the powerful gales howling around the Cape in winter that had previously caused an alarming number of vessels to founder.

Increased shipping volumes led to the building of the Victoria Basin to ease the pressure on Alfred. From the 1960s, the basins and surrounding harbour buildings gradually fell into disrepair. Then, in November 1988, the Waterfront Company set out to modernize, upgrade and develop the site. Today, visitors can stroll through the shopping areas and enjoy a meal in one of the many eateries, while watching the daily workings of the harbour.

In Table Bay, some 11 km (7 miles) north of the Waterfront lies Robben Island, the political enclave that gained international fame for the high-profile exiles incarcerated there. For most of its recorded history, the island has served as a place of confinement – for early slaves, convicts, lepers and the mentally unstable. In 1961, however, it became a maximum-security prison for leading political activists, among them Nelson Mandela. Today, the island is a protected area, and the former prison a museum.

SIGHTS AT A GLANCE

V&A Waterfront pp82–3 ❶ *Robben Island pp88–9* ❷

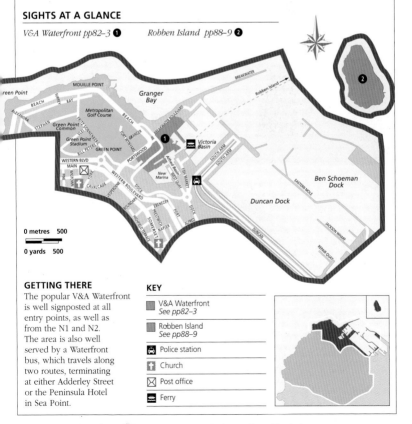

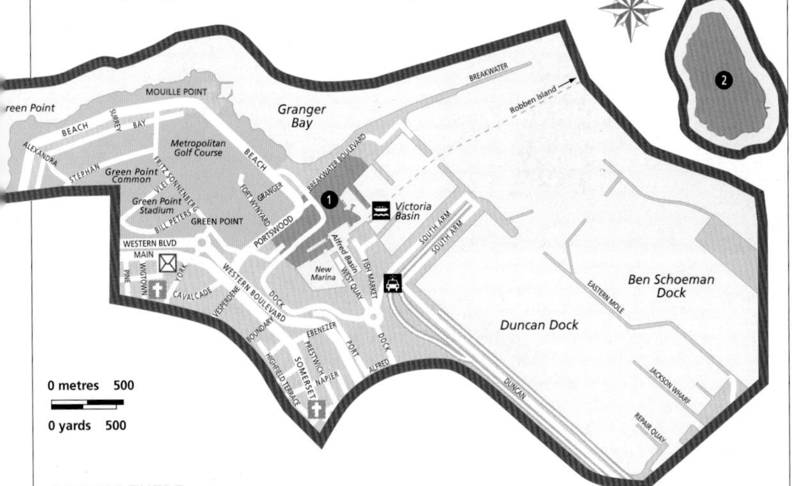

0 metres 500

0 yards 500

GETTING THERE

The popular V&A Waterfront is well signposted at all entry points, as well as from the N1 and N2. The area is also well served by a Waterfront bus, which travels along two routes, terminating at either Adderley Street or the Peninsula Hotel in Sea Point.

KEY

- V&A Waterfront *See pp82–3*
- Robben Island *See pp88–9*
- Police station
- Church
- Post office
- Ferry

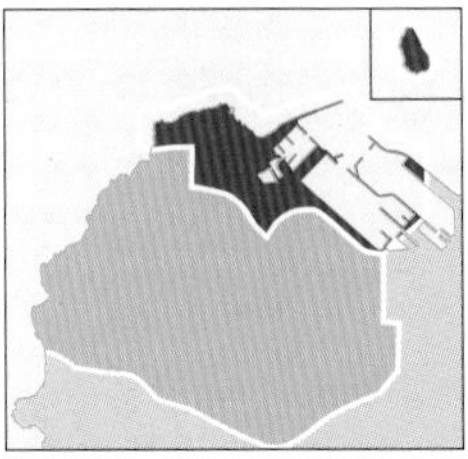

◁ **The V&A Waterfront shopping and entertainment complex is part of a working harbour**

The V&A Waterfront ❶

The V&A Waterfront is a shopper's haven, offering designer boutiques and others selling quirky hand-painted clothing, health and beauty shops, homeware and gift speciality stores, and over 40 ethnically diverse food outlets. Most eating places have harbour views, and alfresco dining on the wharfs and waterside platforms is extremely popular. Many bars and bistros offer live music, with excellent jazz at the Green Dolphin, while regular outdoor concerts are staged at the Waterfront Amphitheatre. Excursions of all kinds start at the Waterfront, from boat tours around the harbour and to Robben Island, helicopter flips over the peninsula to sunset champagne cruises off Clifton Beach. The Waterfront also boasts luxurious hotel accommodation.

LOCATOR MAP

Illustrated Area

Extent of V&A Waterfront

Granger Bay and Sea Point

BREAKW

★ BMW Pavilion
This modern BMW showroom displays the company's latest models and is open late into the evening.

Sea Point

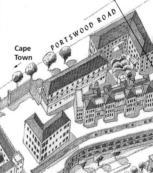

The Scratch Patch affords visitors the opportunity to their own selection of polished semi-precious stones, such as amethyst and tiger's-eye.

BEACH

PORTSWOOD ROAD

Cape Town

★ Two Oceans Aquarium
Shatterproof glass tanks and tunnels are filled with shoaling fish such as yellowtail, steenbras, *and musselcracker, as well as turtles, and even a short-tailed stingray.*

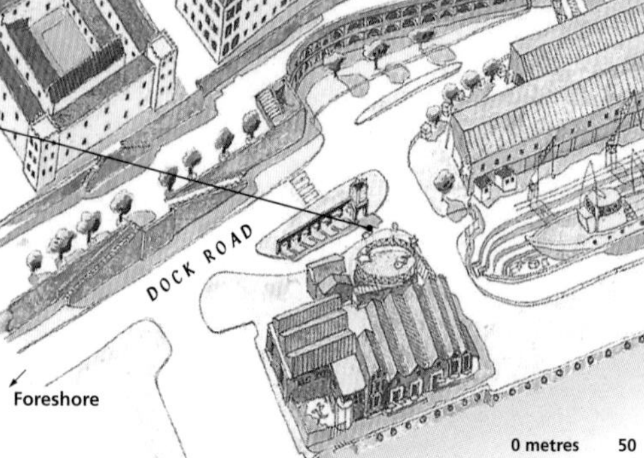

0 metres 50

0 yards 50

STAR FEATURES

- ★ Two Oceans Aquarium
- ★ BMW Pavilion
- ★ Victoria Wharf Shopping Centre

For hotels and restaurants in this region see pp326–31 and pp358–62

Table Bay Hotel
One of the best-appointed establishments at the V&A Waterfront, the glamorous Table Bay Hotel offers the ultimate in comfort and luxury. Each room has wonderful views of Table Mountain and the busy harbour.

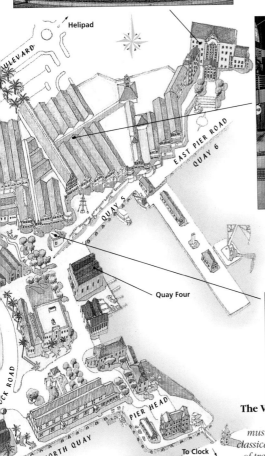

Helipad

ULEVARD

EAST PIER ROAD

QUAY 6

QUAY 5

Quay Four

★ Victoria Wharf Centre
Exclusive shops, boutiques, cosy eateries and informal "barrow" stalls give this shopping centre a festive, market-day feel.

The V&A Waterfront Amphitheatre
This venue offers a vast array of musical and other events. Jazz, rock, classical concerts and even the rhythms of traditional drumming appear here.

CK ROAD

PIER HEAD

NORTH QUAY

To Clock Tower Centre

The Cape Grace Hotel
Another of the V&A Waterfront's fine accommodation offerings, The Cape Grace on West Quay has wonderful views.

VISITORS' CHECKLIST

Cape Town harbour. **Map** 2 D3–4, E3–4. *Visitors' Centre (021) 408-7600. Minibus taxi service operates daily between city centre and Waterfront. to Robben Island; N Mandela Gateway (see p89). 9am–midnight. Cape To Rio (Jan, every three years); Wine Festival (May); Dragon Boat Races (Nov).* **www**.waterfront.co.za

Exploring the Waterfront

The V&A Waterfront is one of Cape Town's most visited attractions. The multibillion-rand redevelopment scheme incorporates ideas from other ventures, like San Francisco's harbour project. Easily accessible, it has its own bus service running to and from the city centre, and provides ample covered and open-air parking for vehicles. Major stores are open from 9am to 9pm, and most restaurants close well after midnight. Some of the city's newest hotels are here.

Whitbread Round-the-World racers moor at the Waterfront

Two Oceans Aquarium

Dock Rd. **Map** 2 D4. ***Tel*** *(021) 418-3823.* *9:30am–6pm daily.* **www**.aquarium.co.za

The aim of this complex is to introduce visitors to the incredible diversity of sealife which occurs in the ocean around the Cape coast. A world first is the interesting exhibit of a complete river ecosystem that traces the course of a stream from its mountain source down to the open sea. One of the most fascinating features is a ceiling-high glass tank that holds various shoals of line fish, like Red Roman, swimming among the waving tangles of a kelp forest. Apart from waterbirds like wagtails, there is a resident colony of jackass penguins, a tank full of mischievous seals and the touch pool, which has wide-eyed children exploring delicate underwater creatures like crabs, starfish and sea urchins.

Victorian clocktower

Alfred Basin (West Quay)

Off Dock Rd. **Map** 2 E4.

Alfred Basin forms a crucial part of the working harbour as fishing boats chug to the Robinson Graving Dock for repair and maintenance. Alongside the dry dock is the Waterfront Craft Market, one of South Africa's largest indoor markets. Available here are handcrafted gifts ranging from toys and furniture to candles and art. Adjoining the blue craft shed is the **Iziko South African Maritime Museum**, which contains South Africa's largest model ship collection. The SAS *Somerset*, a former naval defence vessel, is part of the museum. Visits to the ship are included in the entrance fee.

Iziko South African Maritime Museum
Shop 17, Dock Rd. ***Tel*** *(021) 464-1267.* *9:30am–5pm daily.* *Good Fri, 25 Dec.*

Victoria Basin

Map 2 E3.

The Waterfront's most popular venue, Quay Four Restaurant, is located at the edge of the basin, with superb views of the harbour and its constant boat traffic. The large Agfa Amphitheatre regularly stages free recitals and concerts, from the Cape Town Philharmonic Orchestra to African musicians and their energetic dance routines. In the **Red Shed Craft Workshop**, visitors can observe glass-blowers at work, buy handmade pottery and ceramics, leathercraft, hand-painted fabrics, jewellery and gifts. Nearby, in the **King's Warehouse**, the catch of the day is stacked side by side with crisp vegetables and fragrant herbs. Equally tempting is the aroma of exotic crushed spices and the many deli luxuries, such as freshly made Italian biscotti.

Red Shed Craft Workshop
Opposite Imax. ***Tel*** *(021) 408-7846.* *9am–9pm daily.*

King's Warehouse
Breakwater Blvd.
9am–9pm daily.

Inside the BMW Pavilion

BMW Pavilion

Cnr. Portswood & Dock rds. **Map** 2 D3. ***Tel*** *(021) 418-4200.* *until 11pm.*

The BMW Pavilion is a modern building that serves as a showroom for the company's latest cars. BMW's ritziest new models are immaculately presented here and, with the centre open late into the evening, visitors are free to roam and admire the collection at their leisure.

The pavilion provides a well-equipped conference centre and is also used to host temporary exhibitions from time to time.

Exhibits at the Two Oceans Aquarium

An innovative approach to education has assured the popularity and success of this venture. The complex is constantly upgraded to accommodate new exhibits, such as the recently installed jellyfish tank. Future displays will include an unusual quarantine section. All the exhibits introduce the public to unfamiliar aspects of the fragile marine environment and the need for its preservation. Young visitors, in particular, enjoy the hands-on experience. Alpha Activities Centre offers an interesting daily programme in the vicinity of the entertaining seal tank. Novel "sleep-overs" in front of the Predator Tank are a hit with children between the ages of six and 12. Adventurous visitors in possession of a valid scuba licence may book dives during the day, although not during feeding sessions in the Predator and Kelp tanks.

Starfish

THE DISPLAYS

The aquarium's displays are well planned and create an interesting, stimulating environment. Quite a few of them are interactive, offering visitors the opportunity to experience sealife at first hand. The latest technology is used to reveal the secrets of even the tiniest of sea creatures.

The interior *of the aquarium has been carefully designed to recreate various ocean and riverine habitats.*

The I & J Predator Tank *is a two-million-litre exhibit protected by shatterproof glass. Open to the sea, the tides constantly wash in fresh sea water for the turtles, yellowtails and ragged tooth sharks.*

The Touch Pool *invites children to handle and examine sea creatures like crabs and starfish.*

Jackass penguins, *rescued from oil spills, have a small colony in the aquarium complex.*

The Intertidal Pool *contains mussels, barnacles, starfish, sea anemones and various sponges.*

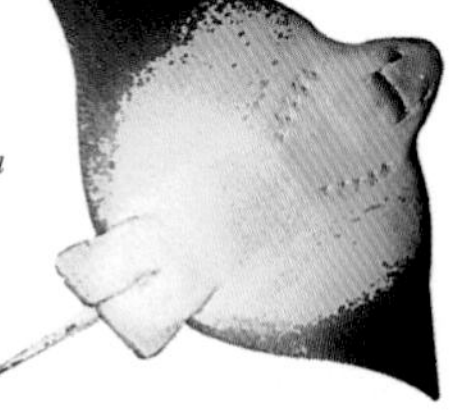

A short-tailed stingray, *like this one, can be seen in the Predator Tank.*

The V&A Waterfront is a hive of activity until late at night ▷

SEALINK
TOURS

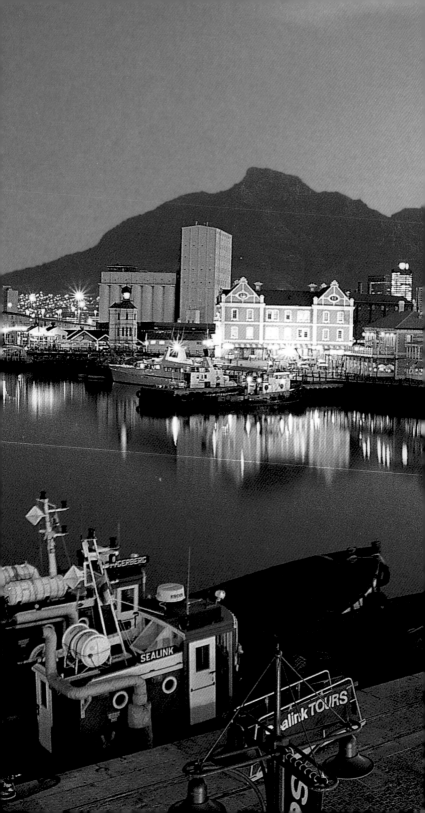

Robben Island ❷

World War II battery

Named "Robbe Eiland" (seal island) by the Dutch in the mid-17th century due to its large seal population, Robben Island has seen much human suffering. As early as 1636 it served as a penal settlement, and was taken over by the South African Prisons Service in 1960. When the last political prisoners were released in 1991, the South African Natural Heritage Programme nominated the island for its significance as a seabird breeding colony – it hosts more than 130 bird species, including the migrant Caspian tern and the jackass penguin. Today, the island is an important ecological and historical heritage site.

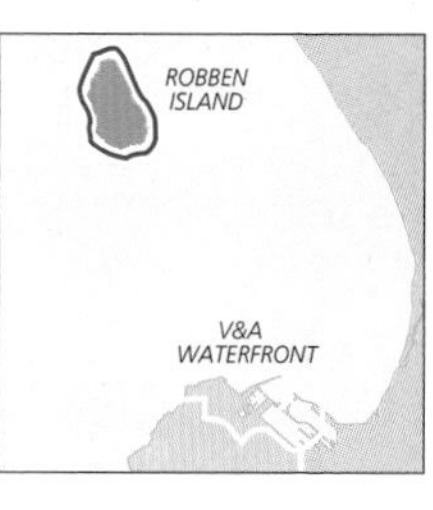

★ Governor's House
This splendid Victorian building dates from 1895 and was originally the home of the Island Commissioner. Today it serves as a conference centre and provides upmarket accommodation for visiting dignitaries and VIPs.

0 metres 500
0 yards 150

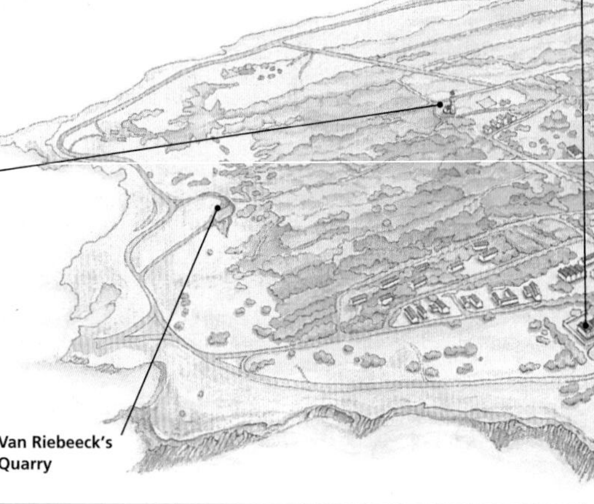

The Lighthouse
This lighthouse was built in 1863 to replace the fire beacons in use until then. It is 18 m (59 ft) high, and its beam can be seen from a distance of 25 km (15 miles).

STAR FEATURES

- ★ Governor's House
- ★ The Prison
- ★ Lime Quarry

POLITICAL PRISONERS

In the 18th century, high-ranking princes and sheikhs from India, Malaysia and Indonesia were sent to Robben Island by the Dutch East India Company for inciting resistance against their European overlords. The British banished rebellious Xhosa rulers to the island in the early 1800s. And in 1963, Nelson Mandela and seven other political activists were condemned to life imprisonment here by the South African government.

Exiled Xhosa chiefs, Robben Island, 1862

Offshore Island
This flat, rocky island lies 11 km (7 miles) north of Cape Town in the icy Atlantic Ocean. Composed mainly of blue slate, it is only 30 m (98 ft) above sea level at its highest point. None of the trees on the island are indigenous.

VISITORS' CHECKLIST

Road map B5. ***Tel*** *(021) 409-5100. N Mandela Gateway, V&A Waterfront 9, 10 & 11am, noon, 1, 2 & 3pm. rough seas. obligatory; book 2 days in advance. inform ticket office in advance.*
@ info@robben-island.co.za

Caspian Tern
This endangered migrant bird species breeds on the northern part of the island.

★ The Prison
Robben Island served as a place of banishment from 1658, when Jan van Riebeeck sent his interpreter here. The maximum security prison was completed in 1964.

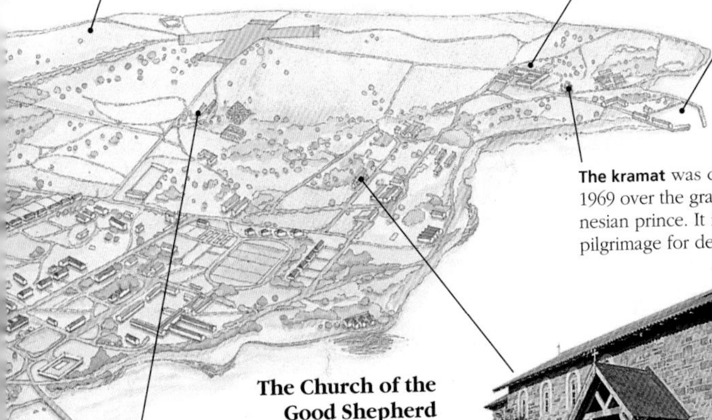

Murray's Bay Harbour

The kramat was constructed in 1969 over the grave of an Indonesian prince. It is a place of pilgrimage for devout Muslims.

The Church of the Good Shepherd
Designed by Sir Herbert Baker, this stone church was built by lepers in 1895, for use by men only. Worshippers had to stand or lie because there were no pews.

Faure Jetty

★ Lime Quarry
Political prisoners, required to work in this quarry for at least six hours a day, suffered damage to their eyesight due to the constant dust and the glare of the sunlight on the stark white lime cliffs.

FURTHER AFIELD

In summer, the compact City Bowl bakes at the foot of Table Mountain's northern slopes, initiating a migration to the superb beaches of the Cape Riviera: Clifton, Camps Bay and Llandudno. Parking space is at a premium as sunseekers move on to the coastal villages of Hout Bay, Kommetjie and Scarborough, as well as Cape Point, with its dramatic ocean views. The wooded southern slopes of Table Mountain are cooler – it is known to rain in Newlands while the beaches of the Cape Riviera bask under clear skies. Also on the cool southern incline is Kirstenbosch National Botanical Garden with its 7,000 plant species, and the world-famous wine estate Groot Constantia. On the popular False Bay coast, the water at Fish Hoek and Muizenberg is up to 5°C (10°F) warmer than along the western side of the Cape Peninsula.

Chacma baboons, Cape Point

SIGHTS AT A GLANCE

Historic Buildings
Iziko Groot Constantia pp100–1 ⑩
Mostert's Mill ⑬
Rhodes Memorial ⑭
South African Astronomical Observatory ⑮

Parks and Gardens
Kirstenbosch National Botanical Garden pp104–5 ⑪
Ratanga Junction ⑯

Suburbs
Green Point and Sea Point ①
Cape Riviera ②
Hout Bay ③
Noordhoek ⑤
Simon's Town ⑦
Fish Hoek ⑧
Muizenberg ⑨
Newlands ⑫

Nature Reserves
Cape of Good Hope Nature Reserve ⑥

Driving Tours
The Cape Peninsula ④

20 km = 12 miles

KEY
- Main sightseeing area
- Built-up area
- Reserve boundary
- International airport
- Motorway
- Major road
- Minor road

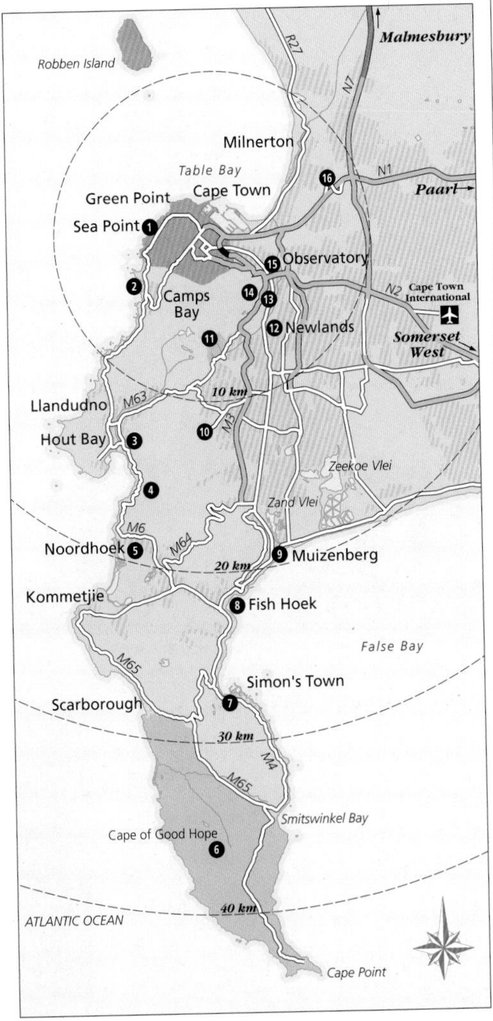

Robben Island
Malmesbury
Milnerton
Table Bay
Paarl
Green Point
Cape Town
Sea Point
Observatory
Camps Bay
Cape Town International
Newlands
Somerset West
Llandudno
Hout Bay
Zeekoe Vlei
Zand Vlei
Noordhoek
Muizenberg
Kommetjie
Fish Hoek
False Bay
Simon's Town
Scarborough
Smitswinkel Bay
Cape of Good Hope
ATLANTIC OCEAN
Cape Point
10 km
20 km
30 km
40 km

◁ **Around 28 different indigenous cycad species can be seen at Kirstenbosch National Botanical Garden**

An aerial view of Sea Point on Cape Town's Atlantic seaboard

Green Point and Sea Point ❶

Main or Beach rds. **Map** 1 B4, 3 C1.

Since the development of the V&A Waterfront began in 1995, the real estate value in neighbouring seaside suburbs like Green Point and Mouille Point has soared. Beach Road, only a stone's throw from the sea, is today lined with a row of expensive high-rise apartments, as well as trendy restaurants and modern, upmarket office blocks.

Green Point Common backs the residential strip. It started in 1657 as a farm granted to Jan van Riebeeck, but the soil proved unfit for cultivation. The sports complex that was built on the common comprises hockey, soccer, rugby and cricket fields, bowling greens, tennis and squash courts, a sports stadium and an 18-hole golf course. Green Point's red and white candy-striped lighthouse, built in 1824, is still functional. Its resonant foghorn is notorious for keeping Mouille Point's residents awake when mist rolls in from the sea.

Further on along Beach Road lies the suburb of Sea Point. It, too, has undergone intensive development over the years and sports towering apartment blocks, hotels and offices. Sea Point used to be Cape Town's most popular entertainment strip. However, the opening of the V&A Waterfront provided a new and more convenient attraction, with its upmarket eateries, pubs and amphitheatre, so Sea Point's glamour has faded somewhat, although the suburb still teems with restaurants, bars, and night spots.

All day long, the 3-km (2-mile) Sea Point promenade is abuzz with joggers, rollerbladers, children, tanned people-watchers and older residents strolling along with their lap dogs.

The promenade ends with a pavilion which adjoins a large parking area and the open-air **Sea Point Swimming Pool**, which is filled with filtered seawater.

Small sandy coves (packed with sunbathers in summer) dot the rocky shoreline. The tidal pools among the rocks are always a source of amazement, particularly for children, who enjoy scrambling around looking for sea anemones, tiny starfish, shells and the occasional octopus. Graaff's Pool is a secluded bathing spot. It is open to the sea and, by tradition, for men only.

Mouille Point lighthouse has a foghorn to warn ships at sea

Sea Point Swimming Pool
Beach Rd. ***Tel*** *(021) 434-3341.*
Dec–Jan: 7am–7pm daily; Feb–Nov: 7am–4:30pm daily.
only in bad weather.

LION'S HEAD AND SIGNAL HILL

A relatively easy climb to the top of Lion's Head, 670 m (2,198 ft) high, affords breathtaking views of the City Bowl and Atlantic coastline. Climbers can leave their cars at a parking area along Signal Hill Road (take the right-hand fork at the top of Kloof Nek Road), which opens to the contour path that encircles Lion's Head. At the end of Signal Hill Road is a viewpoint and another parking area. This spot is popular for its night vistas of the city. Signal Hill is the site of Cape Town's noon gun, a battery originally built by the British in 1890 to defend the harbour. Every day the cannon is loaded with 1.5 kg (3 lb) of gunpowder and fired off at precisely noon.

The view from Lion's Head is spectacular

For hotels and restaurants in this region see pp326–31 and pp358–62

Cape Riviera ❷

Victoria Rd. **Map** 3 B2–5.

Shortly after the Sea Point Swimming Pool, Beach Road runs via Queens into Victoria Road. Bantry Bay, Clifton and Llandudno are the desirable addresses along this steep stretch of coast, which is known as the "Riviera" of Cape Town because of the million-dollar homes that flank it. With incomparable views and beautiful beaches right on their doorsteps, this is the haunt of the wealthy.

The coastal route extends all the way to idyllic Hout Bay, which lies over the saddle that separates the Twelve Apostles mountain range from the peak of Little Lion's Head. The 12 impressive sandstone buttresses, named after the biblical apostles by Sir Rufane Donkin, one-time governor of the British Cape Colony, flank the Riviera's suburbs. First is **Bantry Bay**, whose luxury apartments, many supported on concrete stilts, are built into the steep mountain slope.

Trendy **Clifton** follows, with its four famous small beaches separated by granite boulders. Fourth Beach is popular especially among families, as it has a car park nearby, while the other three are only accessible from the road via steep flights of stairs. The Atlantic's waters are icy but the beaches are sheltered from the strong southeaster gales by Lion's Head, so during the summer months all of the four beaches are tremendously popular with sunseekers and the resulting traffic congestion is enormous.

A good meal and sweeping sea views at "Blues" in Camps Bay

Victoria Road continues along the shore past **Maiden's Cove**, which has a tidal pool and good public facilities, and **Glen Beach**, which has no amenities but is frequented nonetheless by surfers and sunbathers. At **Camps Bay**, the broad sweep of beach lined with tall, stately palms is another very popular spot, although the southeaster tends to bluster through here quite strongly, especially during the summer months. Backed by Lion's Head and the mountain chain known as the Twelve Apostles, Camps Bay's lovely setting has been the inspiration for the establishment of a superb hotel, The Bay *(see p327)*, and a string of good restaurants, most of which offer unrivalled sea views.

Strolling along Camps Bay Beach

Arguably the city's most beautiful little beach, **Llandudno**, lies about 10 km (6 miles) east of Camps Bay. The small elite residential area, settled on a rocky promontory at the foot of the mountain known as Little Lion's Head, is first spotted from the cliff top. Its curve of pristine white beach and distilled turquoise sea is a favourite spot to toast the sunset. A 20-minute walk to the west over the rocky shore leads to secluded and sheltered **Sandy Bay**, Cape Town's nudist beach.

Camps Bay beach with the Twelve Apostles in the background

Hout Bay ❸

The World of Birds logo

Since the 1940s, Hout Bay has been an important fishing centre. It is also a pretty residential area and a popular weekend resort. Its name derives from a diary entry made by Jan van Riebeeck in July 1653, in which he refers to "t'houtbaaijen", the wooded bays in the area. Hout Bay's fisheries centre on snoek and rock lobster, and include canning factories, a fishmeal plant and a fresh fish market. The 1-km-long (half-mile) beach is backed by low, scrub-covered dunes and flanked by tall mountains. To the west, the Karbonkelberg mountain range culminates in the towering 331-m (1,086-ft) Sentinel peak. To the east rises the Chapman's Peak range, along the slopes of which snakes a world-famous scenic drive.

A colourful fishing trawler at the Hout Bay harbour

Exploring Hout Bay

Road map B5. 20 km (12 miles) S of Cape Town on M6 or M63. *from Cape Town station, Adderley St.*

The green valleys of Hout Bay are threaded with oak-lined roads. Horse paddocks and stables are prolific, many local riding centres offer instruction and recreational horse riding. Residents walk their dogs on Hout Bay beach in the early mornings, or watch the sun set behind the Sentinel. Besides the swimmers who brave the cold waters, the beach is also frequented by paddlesurfers, and, at its westernmost end, windsurfers and Hobie Cat sailors. At the eastern edge of the bay, a 1.4-m (4.5-ft) high bronze statue of a leopard is perched on a rock pinnacle. It was executed in 1963 by the late Ivan Mitford-Barberton, a local artist. The village of Hout Bay itself offers a great variety of small coffee shops, restaurants, clothing and curio shops. Closer to the harbour there are a number of pubs, including the popular Dirty Dick's Tavern, which has an open verandah that overlooks the harbour.

At the start of the scenic coastal drive, Chapman's Peak Hotel is very well-positioned, with beautiful views across the bay, and its terrace is especially popular in summer for seafood lunches and relaxed sundowners.

A work sculpted in memory of the mountain leopards

A hiker's view of Hout Bay, seen from Chapman's Peak

Mariner's Wharf

Harbour Road. ***Tel*** *(021) 790-1100.* *daily.*

Mariner's Wharf was built by a local family, the Dormans, whose predecessors farmed in the Hout Bay valley during the 1900s. A little farm stall on Hout Bay Road that sells delicious home-baked biscuits and breads as well as fresh fruit and vegetables is named Oakhurst after the original family farm.

Mariner's Wharf, which lies sandwiched between Hout Bay's beach and the busy little fishing harbour. It offers an open-air bistro, an upstairs seafood restaurant, a shop that sells marine-related curios and an excellent fresh- and shellfish market. Visitors can also enjoy a stroll along the pier that juts out into the sea and is flanked by moored fishing boats.

From the harbour, a number of tour operators launch regular cruises that take visitors out to watch sea birds and to photograph the Cape fur seal colony on Duiker Island. The ever-popular sunset cruises are also on offer and various local game-fishing companies organize expeditions off Hout Bay's shores to catch a variety of gamefish such as yellowfin and longfin tuna, broadbill swordfish and marlin.

For hotels and restaurants in this region see pp326–31 and pp358–62

Mariner's Wharf has an excellent fresh fish market

Hout Bay Museum
4 Andrews Rd. ***Tel*** *(021) 790-3270.* *8am–4pm Mon–Thu, 8:30am–4pm Fri.* *public hols.*

This museum has interesting displays on the history of the Hout Bay valley and its people, focusing on forestry, mining and the fishing industry up to modern times. The museum also organizes weekly guided nature walks into the surrounding mountains.

Environs: Just north of Hout Bay, the remarkable **World of Birds Wildlife Sanctuary** is presently the largest bird sanctuary in Africa and the second largest in the world. The high, landscaped, walk-through aviaries feature 450 bird species. Around 3,000 individual birds are kept in the sanctuary for rehabilitation purposes, many of them brought in injured. Others are endangered species which are introduced for a captive breeding programme. Wherever possible, birds are released into their natural habitat again once they are fit to survive.

Visitors can watch them feed, build nests and incubate their eggs. The World of Birds also plays an important secondary role in educating the public on conservation and other environmental matters. Among the endangered bird species that have benefited from special breeding projects are the Egyptian vulture, which is extinct in South Africa, the blue crane and the citron-crested cockatoo.

Rare primates can also be seen at the sanctuary, among these the endangered pygmy marmoset and Geoffrey's tufted-ear marmoset.

World of Birds Wildlife Sanctuary
Valley Rd. ***Tel*** *(021) 790-2730.* *9am–5pm daily.*
www.worldofbirds.co.za

Black-shouldered kite

LINEFISH OF THE WESTERN CAPE

The cold, nutrient-bearing water along the West Coast results in a greater number of fish than off the East Coast, but not as great a variety. The biggest catches are of red roman, kabeljou and white stumpnose. The uniquely South African national fish, the galjoen, has now become very rare. The deep gulleys along the rocky shores of the Western Cape, with their characteristic kelp beds, are perfect fishing spots for anglers.

Red Roman *Particularly tasty when stuffed and baked, this fish is found in great numbers off the Cape reefs.*

Snoek *Winter and early spring see the "snoek run", when this predatory fish migrates south in search of its prey – pilchards. Its rich, rather oily flesh is either canned, smoked or dried.*

Kabeljou (kob) *One of the most common food fishes, this is invariably served as the "linefish catch of the day".*

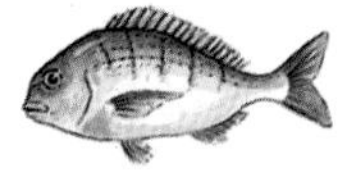

White stumpnose *A delicious sport fish, it is eagerly sought by ski-boat anglers.*

Yellowtail *This is one of the finest seasonal gamefish available in South African waters. The flesh is very firm and tasty, but can be coarse, especially in older and larger fish.*

Cape salmon *Its flesh is similar to that of its cousin, the kob, but more flavourful.*

Touring the Cape Peninsula ❹

Tours of the Cape Peninsula should start on the Atlantic coast and include Chapman's Peak Drive, a scenic route that took seven years to build. The drive, cut into the cliff face, has splendid lookout points with picnic sites. A highlight of the tour is the panorama at Cape Point, where the peninsula juts into the sea. The views encompass False Bay, the Hottentots Holland mountains and Cape Hangklip, 80 km (50 miles) away. The return journey passes the penguin colony at Boulders and goes through charming Simon's Town.

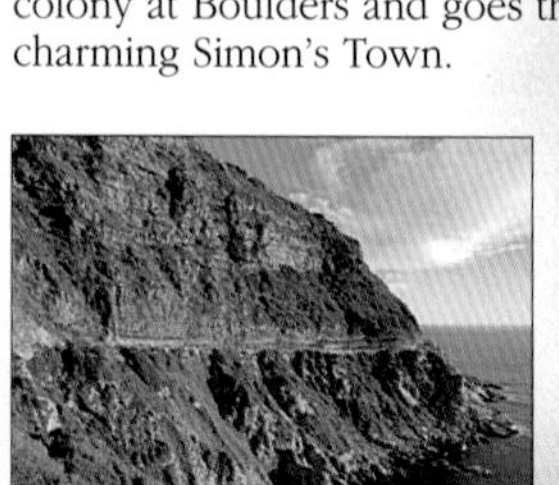

Chapman's Peak ①
The highest point rises to 592 m (1,942 ft). An observation platform is on sheer cliffs which drop 160 m (525 ft) to the swirling seas below.

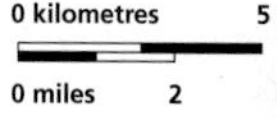

Kommetjie ②
Flashes from the powerful beams of Slangkop Lighthouse can be seen from Hout Bay at night.

KEY

- Tour route
- Other roads
- Park or reserve boundary
- Viewpoint
- Shore-based whale watching

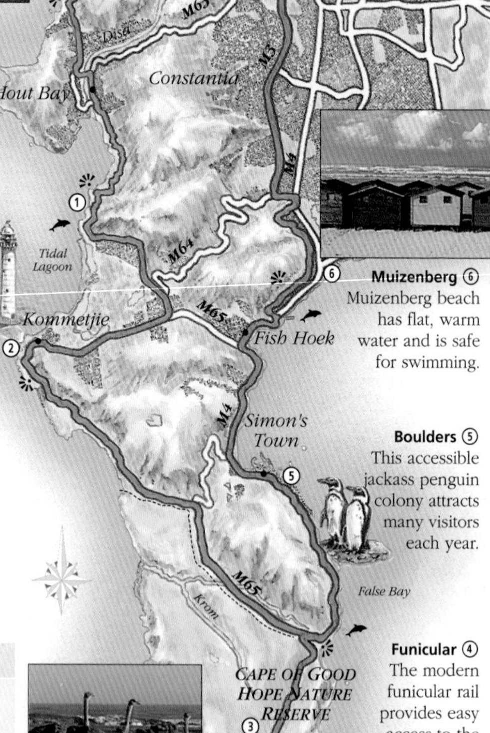

Muizenberg ⑥
Muizenberg beach has flat, warm water and is safe for swimming.

Boulders ⑤
This accessible jackass penguin colony attracts many visitors each year.

Funicular ④
The modern funicular rail provides easy access to the lookout atop Cape Point.

Cape of Good Hope Nature Reserve ③
The reserve is home to several animal species, among them ostriches.

TIPS FOR DRIVERS

Length: *160 km (99 miles). From De Waal Drive via Camps Bay and Chapman's Peak Drive to Cape Point, returning through Simon's Town and Muizenberg, then back to the city via the M3.*
Duration of journey: *To fully appreciate the beauty of both coastlines, Cape Point and the peninsula, it is advisable to do the route in two stages.*

Horse riding on Noordhoek Beach is a popular pastime

Noordhoek ❺

Road map B5. Via Chapman's Peak Drive or Ou Kaapse Weg.

The best feature of this little coastal settlement is its 6-km (4-mile) stretch of pristine white beach. Strong currents make the water unsafe for swimming but it is popular with surfers and paddleskiers. The shore is good for horse riding and long walks (tourists are advised to walk in groups) while along its length lies the wreck of the *Kakapo,* a steamer that was beached here during a storm in 1900. Part of the Hollywood movie *Ryan's Daughter* was filmed here.

Environs: Another coastal hamlet, **Kommetjie**, adjoins a tidal lagoon situated inland from Noordhoek Beach. Long Beach, which stretches north as far as Klein Slangkop Point, is a venue for surfing championships and is very popular among boardsailors.

Scarborough, at the mouth of the Schuster's River, is a sought-after residential area. In summer, the seasonal lagoon is very popular.

Cape of Good Hope Nature Reserve ❻

Road map B5. M4 via Simon's Town. ***Tel*** *(021) 780-9100 (from 9am–5pm).* Main gate: *Oct–Mar: 6am–6pm (spring/summer) daily; Apr–Sep: 7am–5pm (autumn/winter) daily. The gate closes at 6pm in winter & sunset in summer.*

Named *Cabo Tormentoso* (Cape of Storms) by Bartolomeu Dias in 1488, the peninsula was later renamed *Cabo de Boa Esperança* (Cape of Good Hope) by King John of Portugal, who saw it as a positive omen for a new route to India.

The reserve that now exists on the tip of the peninsula is exposed to gale-force winds. As a result, the vegetation is limited to hardy milkwood trees and *fynbos*. Small antelope such as eland, bontebok, grey rhebok and grysbok occur here, as do Cape mountain zebra. Visitors will also encounter troops of chacma baboons, which can be aggressive as a result of unlawful feeding by humans.

To view the point from the upper station, the visitor can either climb aboard the funicular or walk the steep, paved pathway to the top. From here, the views are marvellous and the sea pounds relentlessly against the rocks some 300 m (98 ft) below.

The original lighthouse, whose base still stands at the viewpoint, always used to be swathed in fog. The *Lusitania*, a Portuguese liner, was wrecked on Bellows Rock, directly below this lighthouse, in April 1911. As a result, the present lighthouse was constructed lower down on the Cape Point promontory in 1911.

Along the reserve's east coast, the tidal pools at Venus Pool, Bordjiesrif and Buffels Bay and the numerous picnic spots attract hordes of holidaymakers. Buffels Bay has public facilities and a boat-launching ramp. A number of easy and scenic walking trails along the west coast include the Thomas T Tucker shipwreck trail and the path to Sirkelsvlei; maps are available at the reserve's entrance gate.

Bontebok, Cape of Good Hope

The Flying Dutchman

THE FLYING DUTCHMAN

This legend originated in 1641, when the Dutch captain Hendrick van der Decken was battling wild seas off Cape Point while sailing home. No match against the storm, his battered ship started sinking, but Van der Decken swore that he would round the Cape, whether it took him until Judgement Day. Since then many sight ings of a phantom ship, its masts smashed and sails in shreds, have been reported in bad weather. The most significant was recorded in July 1881 in the diary of a certain midshipman sailing on HMS *Bacchante*. He was crowned King George V of England in 1910.

For hotels and restaurants in this region see pp326–31 and pp358–62

Classic architecture along the main road in Simon's Town

Simon's Town ❼

Road map B5. 14,000. from Cape Town station, Adderley St. *111 St George's St, Simon's Town, (021) 786-1011.* **www**.simonstown.com

Picturesque Simon's Town in False Bay has been the base of the South African navy since 1957. It was named after Simon van der Stel *(see p100)*, who visited this sheltered little spot around 1687.

Jackass penguin

Since the Cape's winter storms caused extensive damage to the ships that were anchored in Table Bay, the Dutch East India Company decided, in 1743, to make Simon's Bay their anchorage point in winter.

From 1814, until handover to South Africa, it served as the British Royal Navy's base in the South Atlantic. The town's characterful hotels and bars have been frequented by generations of seamen.

Simon's Town's naval history is best absorbed by joining one of the interesting **Historical Walks** that take place every Tuesday and Saturday morning. The walks begin near the railway station and end at the Martello Tower on the East Dockyard, taking in the **Simon's Town Museum**, the South African Naval Museum, and the Warrior Toy Museum. The Simon's Town Museum is housed in The Residency, believed to be the town's oldest building. It was built in 1777 as weekend retreat for Governor Joachim van Plettenberg. Later, it also served as a naval hospital. Among the exhibits is a replica of a World War II royal naval pub and the cramped quarters of the original slave lodge. Martello Tower, the walk's endpoint, was built in 1796 as a defence against the French.

Historical Walk
Tel *Simon's Town station, (021) 786-1805. 10am Tue and Sat.*

Simon's Town Museum
Court Rd. ***Tel*** *(021) 786-3046. 9am–4pm Mon–Fri, 10am–4pm Sat, 11am–4pm Sun and pub hols. 1 Jan, Good Fri, 25 Dec. Donations.*

Environs: Between Simon's Town and the Cape of Good Hope Nature Reserve, the M4 passes through charming settlements that offer safe swimming and snorkelling in a number of protected bays such as Froggy Pond, Boulders and Seaforth. The big granite rocks after which Boulders is named provide excellent shelter when the southeaster blows. A walk along the beach between Boulders and Seaforth leads to secluded little coves. A major attraction at Boulders is the protected, land-based colony of over 2,300 jackass penguins.

Further south, Miller's Point has grassed picnic areas, a slipway, and tidal rock pools. The Black Marlin Restaurant here is loved for its views and fresh seafood. At Smitswinkel Bay, a lovely cove lies at the foot of a very steep path.

ABLE SEAMAN JUST NUISANCE

In Jubilee Square, overlooking Simon's Bay's naval harbour, stands the statue of a Great Dane. During World War II this dog was the much-loved mascot of British sailors based in Simon's Town. Just Nuisance, formally enrolled in the Royal Navy, was given the title Able Seaman. When he died in a Simon's Town naval hospital, he was honoured with a full military funeral, which was attended by 200 members of the British Royal Navy. One room at the Simon's Town Museum is filled with memorabilia of the unusual cadet.

Just Nuisance and friend

Fish Hoek 8

Road map B5. M4, False Bay. *11,000.* from Cape Town station, Adderley St. *11 First Avenue.* ***Tel** (021) 782-4531.*

Only recently was liquor allowed to be sold in Fish Hoek; until then it was a "dry" municipality. This condition had been written into a property grant made by Governor Lord Charles Somerset in 1818, and was only repealed in the 1990s.

The broad stretch of Fish Hoek beach is lined with changing rooms, cafés and a yacht club, and is popular with families and the sailing fraternity. Regattas are held regularly, and catamarans and Hobie Cats often line the beach. Jager's Walk, a pleasant pathway overlooking sea and beach, runs along the edge of the bay.

Environs: The M4 continues northwards, staying close to the shore. It passes through the seaside suburb of St James which has a small, safe family beach and is characterized by a row of wooden bathing huts that have all been painted in bright primary colours.

At the picturesque little fishing harbour of Kalk Bay, the daily catches of fresh fish, particularly snoek, are sold directly from the boats. The height of the snoek season varies, but usually extends from June to July. The Brass Bell restaurant, sandwiched between the railway station and the rocky shore, has a popular pub, good seafood, and at high tide, waves crash against the breakwater between the restaurant and the sea. Kalk Bay is also popular for its many antique and art shops that line Main Road.

Muizenberg's beachfront seen from Boyes Drive

Muizenberg 9

Road map B5. M4, False Bay. *5,800.* from Cape Town station, Adderley St. *Beach Rd.* ***Tel** (021) 422-4611.* *9am–5:30pm Mon–Fri, 9am–1pm Sat.*

The name Muizenberg comes from the Dutch phrase *Muijs zijn berg*, meaning "Muijs's mountain". Wynand Willem Muijs was a sergeant who, from 1743, commanded a military post on the mountain overlooking the beach.

Muizenberg's white sands, which curve for 40 km (25 miles) around False Bay as far as the town of Strand, rightly earned the town its status as the country's premier holiday retreat in the 19th century. Traces of this early popularity are still visible in the now-shabby façades of once-grand beach mansions. Today a fast-food pavilion, seawater pool and wide lawns attract young and old alike.

The railway station perches on a rocky section of shoreline, where the curve of the bay is known as Surfer's Corner, due to its popularity among novice surfers.

Rhodes Cottage

Environs: Cecil John Rhodes, prime minister of the Cape Colony from 1890–5, started a fashion trend when he bought Barkly Cottage in Muizenberg in 1899. Soon, holiday mansions began to mushroom at the seaside resort, although most were in stark contrast to his simple, stone-walled, thatch cottage. The cottage is today a museum in Main Road and has been renamed **Rhodes Cottage**.

It contains photographs and personal memorabilia of the powerful empire builder and statesman, including his diamond-weighing scale and the chest in which he carried his personal belongings.

Rhodes Cottage
Main Rd. ***Tel** (021) 788-1816.* *9:30 am–4:30pm daily.* *25 Dec.*

Fish Hoek beach offers safe bathing

Iziko Groot Constantia ⑩

Newly appointed Commander of the Cape Simon van der Stel named this farm Constantia; it was the first piece of land granted to him in 1685. The most likely of several theories regarding the origin of the name is that it honours the daughter of Rijckloff van Goens, who supported the governor's land application. After Van der Stel's death in 1712, the farm was subdivided into three. The portion with the manor house, built around 1685, was renamed Groot Constantia. Hendrik Cloete bought the estate in 1778. His family owned it for three generations thereafter, and was responsible for the present appearance of the buildings.

Carriage Museum
A collection of simple carts and other implements tells the story of transport in the Cape's early colonial days.

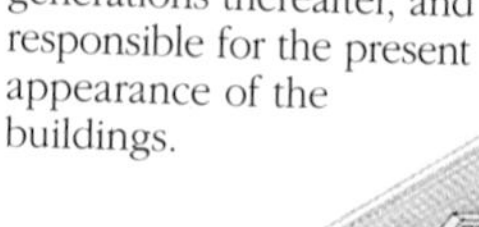

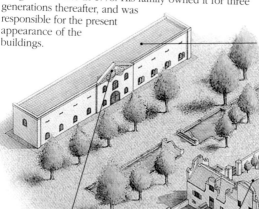

★ Cloete Wine Cellar
This façade, commissioned by Hendrik Cloete and built in 1791, is attributed to Louis Thibault. The Rococo pediment was sculpted by Anton Anreith.

Cape Gable
The very tall gable of the manor house was added between 1799 and 1803. The sculpted figure of Abundance that decorates its lofty niche is the work of respected sculptor, Anton Anreith.

★ Manor House
This museum contains an authentic representation of a wealthy, 19th-century farming household. Most of the antiques were donated by Alfred A de Pass, member of a Dutch family.

STAR FEATURES

- ★ Manor House
- ★ Cloete Wine Cellar
- ★ Jonkershuis

For hotels and restaurants in this region see pp326–31 and pp358–62

Groot Constantia
The Mediterranean climate of temperate summers and cool, rainy winters has ensured the success of the vines planted on this estate.

VISITOR'S CHECKLIST

Road map B5. Groot Constantia off-ramp from M3 (Van der Stel Freeway) onto Ladies Mile. ***Tel*** *(021) 794-5128.* 9am–6pm *daily (to 5pm May–Nov).* 1 Jan, *Good Fri, 25 Dec.* *cellar: (021) 794-5128. 10am–4pm daily.*

Vin de Constance
This naturally sweet Muscat de Frontignan by Klein Constantia (until 1712 part of the Groot Constantia estate) is made in the style of the early 18th-century wines.

★ Jonkershuis
Once the abode of the estate owner's bachelor sons, the quaint Jonkershuis is now a restaurant that serves traditional Cape dishes.

Trees in the front garden included oak, chestnut, olive and banana. By 1695, some 8,401 had been planted.

THE DEVELOPMENT OF GABLE DESIGN

Government House (1756) is an example of the concave, or lobed, gable style.

Libertas (1771) has a convex-concave gable style, also called the Cape Baroque.

Klein Constantia (1799) has a classical gable, inspired by the Italian Renaissance.

Nederburg (1800) has a convex-concave outline, broken pediment and low pilasters.

Newlands Forest, a popular destination for weekend excursions

Kirstenbosch National Botanical Garden ⓫

See pp104–5.

Newlands ⓬

Road map B5. *fm Cape Town station, Adderley St.* *Terminus in Strand St to Mowbray station.*

An exclusive suburb nestled at the foot of Table Mountain's southern slopes, Newlands is the headquarters for the Western Province rugby and cricket unions. The big Newlands sports grounds, which were renamed Newlands-Norwich in 1996, have served as the venue for many international matches. The rugby stadium can hold up to 50,000 spectators, and hosted the opening game of the 1995 Rugby World Cup *(see p36)*.

Newlands Forest runs along the edge of the M3, a major route that links Muizenberg with the southern suburbs and the city centre. Local residents love to take long walks and exercise their dogs through the forest's tall blue gums, pines and silver trees, which are watered by the Newlands stream.

Exhibits at the small **Rugby Museum**, situated close to the Newlands-Norwich sports grounds, include boots, jerseys, blazers, ties and caps worn by South Africa's rugby greats, past and present.

Some 1,500 photos depict various national teams, as well as individual players of note. A vast collection of related mementos includes items that date back to 1891, when South Africa played their first international match against Britain.

A little further on stands a beautifully restored national monument, **Josephine Mill**. This mill with its cast-iron wheel was built in 1840 by the Swede, Jacob Letterstedt, on the bank of the Liesbeeck River, to grind wheat. It was named after the Swedish Crown Princess, Josephine.

Josephine Mill

Today, the mill is managed by Cape Town's Historical Society, and is Cape Town's only surviving operational mill. Demonstrations take place on request and fresh biscuits and flour are for sale.

The society also arranges guided walks along the Liesbeeck River, and during the summer months (Nov–Feb) Sunday evening concerts are held on the river banks.

Rugby Museum
Boundary Rd. ***Tel*** *(021) 686-2151.*
8:30am–5pm Mon–Fri.

Josephine Mill
Boundary Rd. ***Tel*** *(021) 686-4939.*
9am–4pm Mon–Fri. *weekends and public hols.*

Mostert's Mill ⓭

Road map B5. Rhodes Drive. *Golden Acre terminus in Strand St to Mowbray station.* ***Tel*** *(021) 762-5127.* *phone to book.*

This old-fashioned windmill dates to 1796 and stands on part of the Groote Schuur estate bequeathed to the country's people by financier Cecil John Rhodes *(see p54)*. Rhodes bought the estate in 1891, donating a portion to the University of Cape Town, which today sprawls across the lower slopes of the mountain, its red-tiled roofs and ivy-covered walls an unmistakable landmark above Rhodes Drive (M3). The mill was restored in 1936 with aid from the Netherlands. There is no guide on the site.

Environs: Directly east of Mostert's Mill, in the suburb of Rosebank, is the **Irma Stern Museum**, dedicated to one of South Africa's most talented and prolific modern

LADY ANNE BARNARD (1750–1825)

A gracious Cape Georgian homestead in Newlands, now the Vineyard Hotel, was once the country home of 19th-century hostess, Lady Anne Barnard, who lived at the Cape from 1797 to 1802 with her husband Andrew, the colonial secretary. A gifted writer, she is remembered for her witty and astute accounts of life in the new colony. She was also a talented artist: dainty sketches often accompanied her letters and the entries in her personal journal.

Lady Anne Barnard

Mostert's Mill dates back to 1796

painters, who died in 1966. Her magnificent home, The Firs, is filled with 200 paintings and her valuable personal collection of antiques.

Travelling northwest from Mostert's Mill along the busy M3 that leads into town, the road curves around Devil's Peak to become De Waal Drive, which heads into the city centre. On the right-hand side is the famous **Groote Schuur Hospital** where, in 1967, the world's first heart transplant was performed by Professor Christiaan Barnard.

Irma Stern Museum
Cecil Rd, Rosebank. ***Tel*** *(021) 685-5686.* *10am–5pm Tue–Sat.* *public hols.*

Rhodes Memorial ⓮

Road map B5. Groote Schuur Estate. Exit off M3. *(021) 689-9151.*

Directly opposite Groote Schuur homestead – the state president's official Cape Town residence – the Rhodes Memorial overlooks the busy M3, and affords sweeping views of the southern suburbs.

The white granite, Doric-style temple on the slopes of Devil's Peak was designed by Sir Herbert Baker as a tribute to Cecil John Rhodes, and unveiled in 1912. It contains a bust of Rhodes by JM Swan, who also sculpted the eight bronze lions which guard the stairs. Beneath the bust is an inscription from "The Burial" written by one of Rhodes' good friends, Rudyard Kipling. The focus of the memorial, however, is the bronze equestrian statue, titled "Physical Energy", which was executed by George Frederic Watts.

The sweeping views from the monument across the southern suburbs and out to the distant Hottentots Holland mountains are superb. Mixed oak and pine woodlands cover the mountain slopes around the memorial. They still harbour a small, free-living population of fallow deer, as well as a few Himalayan tahrs, first introduced on Groote Schuur estate in the 1890s by Cecil John Rhodes.

South African Astronomical Observatory ⓯

Road map B5. Off Liesbeeck Pkway, Observatory Rd. ***Tel*** *(021) 447-0025.* *8pm on 2nd Sat of every month.* *groups of 10 or more must book.*

The site for the Royal Observatory was selected in 1821 by the first Astronomer Royal stationed at the Cape, Reverend Fearon Fellows. Today, as the national headquarters for astronomy in South Africa, it controls the Sutherland laboratory in the Great Karoo and is responsible for transmitting the electronic impulse that triggers off the daily Noon Day Gun on Signal Hill *(see p79)*, thus setting standard time for the entire country.

Ratanga Junction ⓰

Road map B5. Off N1, 10 km (6 miles) N of Cape Town. ***Tel*** *086 120 0300.* *10am–5pm Wed–Sun.* *25 Dec.* **www**.ratanga.co.za

Ratanga Junction theme park logo

Ratanga Junction is the country's first full-scale theme park. The highly imaginative venue is situated some 12 km (7 miles) from the city centre on the N1, at the Century City shopping, hotel and office complex.

Ratanga Junction provides entertainment for the entire family. Chief among its many attractions are the thrilling tube ride through Crocodile Gorge, the spine-chilling Cobra rollercoaster, and a breath-taking 18.5-m (60-ft) log-flume drop on Monkey Falls.

Also on offer are various shows, "jungle cruises", fun rides specifically designed for younger children, and the usual host of fast-food outlets. There is also plenty for adult visitors, with over 20 themed restaurants, a cinema complex, laser shows, cabaret and comedy performances, a 3-D theatre, and an array of bars, pubs and games venues.

The Rhodes Memorial, designed by Sir Herbert Baker

Kirstenbosch National Botanical Garden ⓫

Daisy

In July 1913, the South African government handed over the running of Kirstenbosch estate (which had been bequeathed to the state by Cecil John Rhodes in 1902) to a board of trustees. The board established a botanical garden that preserves and propagates rare indigenous plant species. Today, the world-renowned garden covers an area of 5.3 sq km (2 sq miles), of which 7 per cent is cultivated and 90 per cent is covered by natural *fynbos* and forest. Kirstenbosch is spectacular from August to October when the garden is ablaze with spring daisies and gazanias.

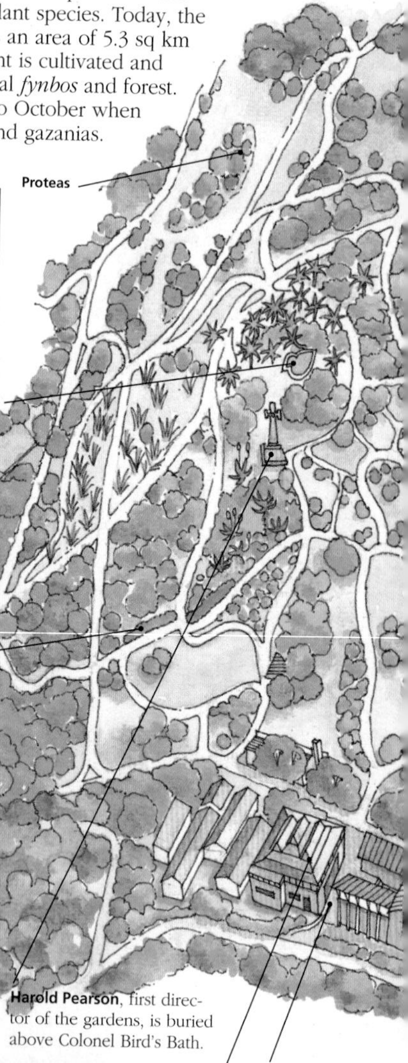

Proteas

★ Colonel Bird's Bath
Tree ferns and Cape Holly trees surround this pool, named after Colonel Bird, deputy colonial secretary in the early 1800s.

Van Riebeeck's Almond hedge
In the 1650s a hedge was planted to keep the Khoina out of the settlement and discourage illegal trading.

Birds
Proteas attract the indigenous sugarbirds.

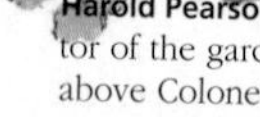
Harold Pearson, first director of the gardens, is buried above Colonel Bird's Bath.

Main entrance

★ Conservatory
This glasshouse, with a baobab at its centre, displays all the floral regions of the country, from lush coastal forest to arid and alpine.

STAR FEATURES

- ★ Conservatory
- ★ Colonel Bird's Bath
- ★ Camphor Avenue

For hotels and restaurants in this region see pp326–31 and pp358–62

Braille Trail
A guide rope leads visually impaired visitors along this interesting 470-m (1,542-ft) long walk through a wooded area. Signs in large print and braille describe the plant species that grow along the trail.

VISITORS' CHECKLIST

Road map B5. Rhodes Ave turnoff on M3. *Mowbray Station.* *Fm Golden Acre in Adderley St and Mowbray Station.* **Tel** *Mon–Fri: (021) 799-8899, Sat–Sun: (021) 761-4916.* *Apr–Aug: 8am–6pm daily; Sep–Mar: 8am–7pm daily.* *10am Tue & Sat.* **www**.nbi.ac.za

Floral Splendour
After the winter rains, carpets of indigenous Namaqualand daisies and gazanias echo the flower display found along the West Coast (see p162).

Two Gift Shops
The shop located at the upper entrance to the Gardens sells indigenous plants and seeds, while the lower shop offers a variety of natural history books, gifts and novelty items.

★ Camphor Avenue
This avenue of camphor trees was planted by Cecil John Rhodes around the end of the 19th century to link his cottage in Muizenberg with his Groote Schuur estate.

SHOPPING IN CAPE TOWN

Cape Town is known as the international gateway to Africa, and the vast array of appealing shopping options supports its reputation. The bustling V&A Waterfront *(see pp82–4)*, in convenient proximity to the city centre, is just one of several large, sophisticated shopping complexes that offer everything under one roof – from fresh produce to high fashion and gourmet dining. Old and new contend for centre stage in the city centre; antique jewellery and modern art are both worth searching for. The lively Long and Kloof streets, pedestrianized St George's Mall and the informal Greenmarket Square houses shops with a strong local flavour. The streetside art displays, buskers and stalls offering African masks, beadwork and carvings add to the vibrant atmosphere. Surrounding suburbs like Hout Bay regularly host outdoor craft stalls and noisy fish markets.

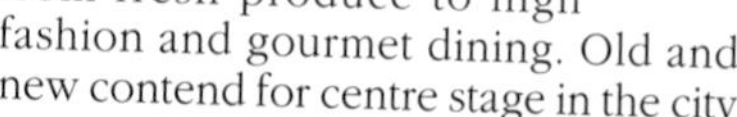

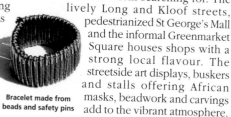

Bracelet made from beads and safety pins

OPENING HOURS

Most shops in the city centre and in the suburbs are open from 9am–5pm on weekdays, and from 9am–1pm on Saturdays. Major malls open at 9am and close between 7pm–9pm throughout the week and on most public holidays. Fridays are usually the busiest time of the week and many shops stay open until 9pm, although Muslim-owned businesses are closed between noon and 2pm. Supermarkets and many delis are open on Sundays.

A relaxing corner of the busy Cape Quarter shopping mall

SHOPPING MALLS

Cape Town's malls offer one-stop dining, entertainment, banking and shopping, with convenient parking facilities.

Canal Walk, the largest, has more than 400 upmarket shops open till 9pm every day, and is a ten minute drive from the city centre. With its children's entertainment options and massive food court, it's an excellent choice for families.

One of Cape Town's many malls

The 185 shops in elegant **Cavendish Square** stock a range of high fashion, homewares and gourmet fare. The **V&A Waterfront**, a unique centre in the heart of the old harbour, is an attractive modern shopping venue offering outstanding jewellery, curios, make-up stores, restaurants and supermarkets.

Fashionable Capetonians prefer to browse at **Lifestyles on Kloof** and **Cape Quarter** in Green Point, which house home decor, art, fashion, beauty, health and lifestyle-related shops in a unique Cape Malay style building.

MARKETS

The cobblestoned **Greenmarket Square**, in the centre of Cape Town, is a vibrant craft market held Monday to Saturday, weather permitting. Here one can buy African carvings, masks, drums, beadwork, jewellery, leatherwork, ceramics and handmade clothing.

The **Red Shed Craft Workshop** and the **Waterfront Craft Market**, both at the V&A Waterfront, are indoor venues open all week. Clothing, jewellery, mosaics and an array of textiles and artwork are available here.

On Sundays the best place to head to is the **Greenpoint Market**, in the parking area of the Greenpoint stadium, which has everything from arts and crafts to plants and car parts are up for sale. **Milnerton Flea Market**, also held on weekends, is great for true bargain hunters, who can rummage through the junk to look for precious finds.

For African baskets, ceramics and shell art, visit the **Lion's Club of Hout Bay Arts and Craft Market** (open Sundays). The **Constantia Country**

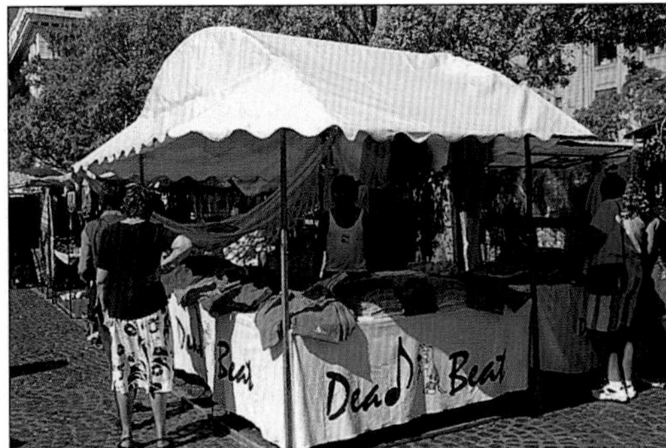

Cobbled Greenmarket Square is one of the city's most popular markets

Living Market, held the third Saturday of the month, sells quality handwork.

Open-air markets also take place in Rondebosch and Kirstenbosch. The latter is a favourite with families, as children can play on the grass within sight of their parents. Remember to take cash with you: many markets don't accept credit cards.

The entrance to African Image

AFRICAN CRAFTS

African Image and the **Pan African Market** stock choice fabrics, ethnic furniture, beads, utensils and sculptures. **Africa Nova** specializes in locally produced handmade art, beautiful textiles from all over Africa and a range of unusual ceramic designs. **Heartworks** offers colourful beads, bags and glass, as well as innovative wood, wire and ceramic items.

In Newlands, the **Montebello Design Centre** is home to several artisan studios producing jewellery, textiles and pottery. The items made on-site are sold in the shop.

There is also a pleasant restaurant situated in the shade of several oak trees.

Another working artists' studio is **Streetwires**, which boasts more than 80 wire and bead artists under one roof, all creating enchanting items. The studio is open to visitors, and the artists chat to their clients while they work. **Monkeybiz**, with its distinctive yellow building painted with red monkeys, sells one-off beaded products made by township women in their homes rather than in factories. Profits from the beadwork support the Monkeybiz Wellness Clinic for HIV/AIDS-affected women.

Township tour itineraries often include a visit to the Khayelitsha Craft Market and the Sivuyile Craft Centre in Gugulethu *(see pp382)*.

BOOKS AND MUSIC

The most comprehensive bookstore chain in South Africa, **Exclusive Books** stocks newspapers, maps, guides, novels, CDs and a wide range of magazines. Some branches also have an in-store coffee shop.

Long Street is renowned for its bookstores. **Select Books** and **Clarke's Bookshop** both sell a variety of new, second-hand and collector's editions of Southern African books; Clarke's also specializes in books on Southern African art.

The **Traveller's Bookshop** offers an inspiring selection of travel guides and maps for all destinations. The book store at the **Kirstenbosch Botanical Gardens** sells travel, plant and wildlife guides specific to South Africa, as well as a range of titles for children. Fans of comic books, graphic novels and action figures will adore **Reader's Den** in Claremont.

There are a number of music megastores offering a range of commercial and more alternative CDs. **Look & Listen**, open till late, is the largest in Cape Town. At the small, centrally located **African Music Store**, visitors are introduced to the exciting sounds of Africa. Specialist stores such as **Syndicate Records** are worth a visit for their second-hand CDs at low prices.

FOOD AND WINE

New York Bagel in Sea Point has delicious bagels and a superb deli area. Head to **Mariner's Wharf Fish Market** for supplies of tasty fresh fish, and to **Melissa's The Food Shop** for an extensive range of attractively packaged handmade products.

Many supermarkets stock wine, but specialist shops can offer advice and freight facilities, and they are able to suggest Wine Route itineraries. **Vaughn Johnson's Wine & Cigar Shop** stocks a number of unusual Cape wines, such as Meerlust, Cordoba and Welgemeend. **Caroline's Fine Wine Cellar** stocks more than a thousand bottles, including classic imported wines from France, Italy, Spain and Australia. The shop also holds regular wine-tasting evenings.

Vaughn Johnson's Wine & Cigar Shop

Entrance to Naartjie, a popular children's clothes shop

HOMEWARE AND GIFTS

Imaginative homeware is readily available in Cape Town and shoppers will be spoiled for choice. In recent years, the city has witnessed a steady rise in lifestyle stores selling everything from kitsch china to stylish teapots.

The **Carrol Boyes Shop**, a perfect stop for gift shopping, sells designer cutlery, tableware and household items in silver, pewter, aluminium and steel.

Cape to Cairo, in Kalk Bay, offers a range of decorative objects from around the world, from Cuban antiques to Russian art. **Clemintina Ceramics** stocks a selection of contemporary South African ceramics, which are sure to cheer up any kitchen.

Two household names in South Africa are the chains **@ Home**, ideal for trendy homeware and creative pieces for the bathroom, bedroom and kitchen; and **Mr Price Home**, which is equally popular. Its wide range of fashionable household goods are sold at very reasonable prices.

ANTIQUES AND JEWELLERY

Quality antiques do not come cheap in Cape Town, but there is no shortage of wonderful items to buy. Those in search of genuine South African pieces – such as early Cape Dutch furniture – can find superb quality antiques at **Deon Viljoen**.

In the city centre, both casual shoppers and serious collectors will enjoy browsing **Church Street Antique Market**, as well as the **Long Street Antique Arcade**, with its 12 antique shops. **Kay's Antiques** specializes in period jewellery from the Victorian to the Art Deco era.

Private Collections, in Green Point, has a fascinating stock of colonial Indian artifacts. Nearby, **Trade Roots** has a fine collection of antique Chinese country furniture and artifacts. Both are worth visiting just to browse through their interesting pieces.

Ye Olde Artifact Cove and Shipwreck in Hout Bay is a very unusual shop, specializing in maritime memorabilia, nautical antiques and fascinating shipwreck finds.

An unusual teapot from Carrol Boyes

Cape Town is renowned for its gold and jewellery, and the V&A Waterfront is a particularly good place to browse; **Olga Jewellery Design Studio** and **Uwe Koetter** are popular choices.

Both the **Diamond Works** and **Prins & Prins**, among others, offer tourists the chance to learn the art of diamond cutting, from the design stage to the finished product. At the end of the tour visitors can view a special collection of diamonds, with no obligation to buy.

CLOTHES AND ACCESSORIES

Cape Town has an eclectic collection of clothing shops. **India Jane** is the place to go for beautiful feminine clothes by celebrated South African designers Amanda Laird Cherry and Maya Prass.

The **Young Designers Emporium (YDE)** showcases South Africa's younger design talent and offers the latest fashions at reasonable prices. **Hip Hop** has everything from custom-made suits to unique evening dresses described as, "classic with a twist". **Klûk** is known for its exquisite couture and bridal wear; designer Malcolm Klûk apprenticed under John Galliano. Classic, well-cut garments can be found at **Hilton Weiner** and **Jenny Button**, and a selection of quality menswear stores can also be found in the major shopping malls.

Families may want to take some time to explore the children's clothes shops, which are excellent in Cape Town. **Naartjie** is one of the most popular, the 100 per cent cotton items come in bright colours and cute designs.

Shoppers who want to pick up bags, hats and scarves, but are on a limited budget, should copy the locals and buy their accessories at factory shops. These outlets sell end of season stock often at huge discounts. Contact Cape Town Tourism for a list of stores.

The streamlined interior of Carrol Boyes Shop at the V&A Waterfront

DIRECTORY

SHOPPING MALLS

Canal Walk
Century City.
Tel (021) 555-4444.

Cape Quarter
Waterkant St. **Map** 2 D5.
Tel (021) 421-0737.

Cavendish Square
Dreyer St, Claremont.
Tel (021) 657-5620.

Lifestyles on Kloof
50 Kloof St. **Map** 5 A2.

V&A Waterfront
Map 2 D3.
Tel (021) 408-7600.

MARKETS

Constantia Country Living Market
Cape Academy, Firgrove Way. *Tel (021) 712-2124.*

Greenmarket Square
Cnr Shortmarket & Burg sts. **Map** 5 B1.

Greenpoint Market
Green Point Stadium. **Map** 1 C3. *Tel (021) 439-4805.*

Lion's Club of Hout Bay Arts and Craft Market
Village Green, Main Rd.
Tel (021) 790-3474.

Milnerton Flea Market
Racecourse Rd, Milnerton.
Tel (021) 550-1383.

Red Shed Craft Workshop
V&A Waterfront. **Map** 2 D3. *Tel (021) 408-7846.*

Waterfront Craft Market
V&A Waterfront. **Map** 2 D3. *Tel (021) 408-7600.*

AFRICAN CRAFTS

African Image
Cnr Church & Burg sts.
Map 5 B1.
Tel (021) 423-8385.

Africa Nova
Cape Quarter, Green Point.
Map 2 D5.
Tel (021) 425-5123.

Heartworks
V&A Waterfront. **Map** 2 E3. *Tel (021) 421-5939.*

Monkeybiz
Rose St, Bo-Kaap.
Tel (021) 426-0636.

Montebello Design Centre
Newlands Ave, Newlands.
Tel (021) 685-6445.

Pan African Market
Long St. **Map** 5 A2.
Tel (021) 426-4478.

Streetwires
Shortmarket St, Bo-Kaap.
Map 5 B1.
Tel (021) 426-2475.

BOOKS AND MUSIC

African Music Store
Long St. **Map** 5 B1.
Tel (021) 426-0857.

Clarke's Bookshop
Long St. **Map** 5 B1.
Tel (021) 423-5739.

Exclusive Books
Cavendish Sq, Claremont.
Tel (021) 674-3030.

Kirstenbosch Botanical Gardens
Rhodes Drive, Newlands.
Tel (021) 799-8899.

Look & Listen
Cavendish Sq, Claremont.
Tel (021) 683-1810.

Reader's Den
Main Rd, Claremont.
Tel (021) 671-9551.

Select Books
Long St. **Map** 5 B1.
Tel (021) 424-6955.

Syndicate Records
Shortmarket St. **Map** 5 B1.
Tel (021) 424-9165.

Traveller's Bookshop
King's Warehouse, V&A Waterfront. **Map** 2 E3.
Tel (021) 425-6880.

FOOD AND WINE

Caroline's Fine Wine Cellar
King's Warehouse, V&A Waterfront. **Map** 1 B1.
Tel (021) 425-5701.

Mariner's Wharf Fish Market
Harbour Rd, Hout Bay.
Tel (021) 790-1100.

Melissa's The Food Shop
Kloof St, Gardens. **Map** 5 A2. *Tel (021) 424-5540.*

New York Bagel
Regent Rd, Sea Point. **Map** 3 C1. *Tel (021) 439-7523.*

Vaughn Johnson's Wine & Cigar Shop
Pierhead, Dock Rd, V&A Waterfront. **Map** 2 E3.
Tel (021) 419-2121.

HOMEWARE AND GIFTS

@ Home
Canal Walk, Century City.
Tel (021) 529-3156.

Cape to Cairo
Main Rd, Kalk Bay.
Tel (021) 788-4571.

Carrol Boyes Shop
Victoria Wharf, V&A Waterfront. **Map** 2 E3.
Tel (021) 418-0595.

Clemintina Ceramics
Main Rd, Kalk Bay.
Tel (021) 788-5849.

Mr Price Home
Dreyer St, Claremont.
Tel (021) 671-3968.

ANTIQUES AND JEWELLERY

Church Street Antique Market
Church St Mall. **Map** 5 B1. *Tel (021) 438-8566.*

Deon Viljoen
Palmboom Rd, Newlands.
Tel (021) 762-9870.

Diamond Works
Coen Steytler Ave.
Map 2 E5.
Tel (021) 425-1970.

Kay's Antiques
Cavendish Sq, Claremont.
Tel (021) 671-8998.

Long Street Antique Arcade
Long St. **Map** 5 A2.
Tel (021) 423-2504.

Olga Jewellery Design Studio
Victoria Wharf, V&A Waterfront. **Map** 2 E3.
Tel (021) 419-8016.

Prins & Prins
Cnr Hout & Loop sts.
Map 5 B1.
Tel (021) 422-1090.

Private Collections
Cnr Hudson & Waterkant sts, Green Point.
Tel (021) 421-0298.

Trade Roots
Hudson St, Green Point.
Tel (021) 421-0401.

Ye Olde Artifact Cove & Shipwreck in Hout Bay
Mariner's Wharf, Hout Bay Harbour.
Tel (021) 790-1100.

Uwe Koetter
Alfred Mall, V&A Waterfront.
Map 2 E4.
Tel (021) 421-1039.

CLOTHES AND ACCESSORIES

Hilton Weiner
Burg St. **Map** 5 B1.
Tel (021) 424-1023.

Hip Hop
Cavendish St, Claremont.
Tel (021) 674-4605.

India Jane
Cape Quarter, Green Point. **Map** 2 D5.
Tel (021) 421-3517.

Jenny Button
Cavendish St, Claremont.
Tel (021) 683-9504.

Klûk
Jarvis St, De Waterkant.
Map 2 D5.
Tel (021) 425-8926.

Naartjie
Canal Walk, Century City.
Tel (021) 551-6317.

Young Designers Emporium (YDE)
Cavendish Sq, Claremont.
Tel (021) 683-6177.

ENTERTAINMENT IN CAPE TOWN

Much of Cape Town's leisure activity centres on the beaches and mountains, but the city is developing a fine reputation for its nightlife and vibrant cultural events. Some of the best entertainment is found alfresco, with buskers and local beat poets fighting it out on the streets of the city. The grand flagship venue is the Artscape Theatre Centre, which draws audiences to local and international music performances, dance, cabaret, theatre and comedy. Cape Town has its own original form of jazz, which can be found in many of the restaurants, bars and clubs in and around Long Street. Capetonians are known to be laid-back and enjoy dinner followed by a visit to the cinema, but the city also caters for serious clubbers. Much of the action is concentrated on the trendy clubs and bars in the city centre and at the V&A Waterfront.

Ster Kinekor company logo

INFORMATION

For details of entertainment in the city, check the daily and weekend newspapers. They review and list events in the cinema, arts and theatre. Good choices include the *Cape Times*, *Cape Argus* on Tuesdays, *Mail & Guardian* on Fridays and *Weekend Argus*. Reviews and listings also appear in the magazine – *Cape Etc*. The Cape radio station Good Hope FM mentions events from time to time, and the websites: www.tonight.co.za and www.mg.co.za may be helpful. For details of nightlife events, flyers are the best bet and are found all over the city. Try www.thunda.com and www.clubbersguide.co.za for more information. Many venues have leaflets about forthcoming attractions, and the major venues have information telephone lines and websites.

Computicket booking office, V&A Waterfront

For information on comedy performances, contact the **Cape Comedy Collective** and for any other specific questions, **Cape Town Tourism** is also very helpful.

BOOKING TICKETS

Theatre seats can be reserved by calling **Computicket** or logging onto Computicket online. They have branches in all the major centres country wide, which are open all day and some into the night. To book a theatre and dance performance at the Artscape theatre, contact **Dial-A-Seat**.

Telephone bookings for Ster-Kinekor cinemas can be made by calling **Ticketline**. There is also a dedicated phoneline, **Tele-Ticket** for bookings and information on Nu Metro films. Most theatres and cinemas don't accept telephone bookings without a payment by credit card.

The Baxter Theatre in Rondebosch

DISABLED VISITORS

In general, most public buildings, museums and top visitor attractions cater for wheelchairs. **Kirstenbosch National Botanical Gardens** provides good access for the disabled, and even has a special "touch and smell" area for visually impaired visitors. The **V&A Waterfront** also has specially designed parking bays, ramps and broad walkways. Most theatres are suitable for those in wheelchairs. The Baxter Theatre has wheelchair positions located in certain areas; however, it's important to tell Computicket at the time of booking if a space is required. There are also adapted toilets and a lift to the restaurant.

At the back of specific Ster-Kinekor cinemas there is an area where people can comfortably sit in their wheelchairs – check out the film section in newspapers to see which theatres are wheelchair-friendly. **Flamingo Tours** and Titch Travel organize holidays and tours for people with disabilities, and will be able to outline suitable venues.

BUDGET ENTERTAINMENT

Film-lovers on a budget will be happy to know that going to the cinema is a far cheaper activity in South Africa than in most other countries, and a bonus is that Tuesday is cut-price day at most cinemas.

On the music front, St George's Cathedral Choir gives performances free of charge – watch the press for details or telephone Computicket. From time to time, there are also free lunchtime concerts at the Baxter Theatre, showcasing the work of students from Cape Town University's **South African College of Music**.

The AGFA Amphitheatre at the V&A Waterfront often hosts free performances. On Heritage Day (24 September) look out for many free music festivals that are advertised by local press and radio.

Several word-class galleries offer free entrance, including **Joao Ferreira Gallery** (viewing of the gallery collection is by appointment only), **Bell-Roberts Gallery** and **Everard Read**.

It is also well worth considering buying the reasonably priced **Cape Town Pass** that allows free entry to over 50 of Cape Town's best attractions, as well as some 20 special offers and discounts.

Summer concert, Kirstenbosch Gardens

OPEN-AIR ENTERTAINMENT

From December to March Kirstenbosch Gardens host the Summer Sunset Concert series where a wide variety of music is presented, from opera to rock and the local Philharmonic Orchestra. This is a great event for families, and spectators will enjoy the fresh air and attractive surroundings. Warm clothing is an essential as the weather can change suddenly.

Performances hosted by the University of Cape Town's **Little Theatre** and **Maynardville Open-air Theatre** take place in January and February, when Shakespearean plays are performed under the stars. These open-air events are very special and many theatre-goers take along a pre-performance picnic to enjoy in the park.

Other outdoor entertainments on offer include breathtaking acrobatic performances by the **South African National Circus School** in Observatory, and relaxing Sunday evening concerts at the **Josephine Mill** on the river bank.

Open-air concert at the AGFA Amphitheatre, the V&A Waterfront

CINEMA

Mainstream Hollywood productions are extremely popular and the main fare in Cape Town's **Ster-Kinekor** and **Nu Metro** cinema complexes, as well as at **Cinema Prive**, which is more expensive but has big, comfortable seats and oak side-tables for drinks.

Art-house cinemas in Cape Town specialize in thought-provoking, independent films along with international art releases. **Cinema Nouveau** at the V&A Waterfront and **Cavendish Square** (the biggest non-mainstream cinema in the city) offer refreshing alternatives to the usual Hollywood fare. **Cinema Starz** at the Grandwest Casino is another independent cinema, but tends to screen Hollywood films. The charming **Labia Theatre**, originally an Italian embassy ballroom, has operated as an art-house cinema since the 1970s and caters for the more discerning viewer.

For an exclusive experience, consider a private viewing at **Cine 12**, ideal for small groups.

Cape Town Philharmonic Orchestra and choir, Centenary performance

CLASSICAL MUSIC AND OPERA

Cape Town City Hall offers classical music and opera performances in majestic surroundings. The Artscape is the home of the **Cape Town Philharmonic Orchestra**, which usually gives performances on Thursday evenings. Occasionally, rather different concert venues are chosen, such as the Two Oceans Aquarium or the South African Museum. The Artscape stages opera and musicals, as well as popular lunchtime and Sunday afternoon concerts. There are 1,200 seats in the Opera House and the view is exceptional from every angle.

The Baxter Theatre Complex is where the South African College of Music performs its repertoire of chamber music, string ensembles, organ recital and orchestral productions. It is also the venue for recitals by visiting soloists and chamber ensembles and it hosts occasional lunchtime concerts. **Cape Town Opera**, with its black soloists and chorus members, creates an inspiring listening experience. They perform at the Artscape and Baxter and give additional performances at the V&A Waterfront in February.

THEATRE AND DANCE

The **Artscape** also hosts world-class performances of drama, ballet and satire, as well as experimental theatre, community and children's productions. It is one of the few venues in Southern Africa with the facilities to stage internationally known musicals such as *Les Miserables*, *Cats* and *Phantom of the Opera*, as well as big touring shows including *Spirit of Dance*, *Tap Dogs* and the St Petersburg State Academic Ballet. A calendar of events is available from the box office.

Another theatre and dance venue is the **Baxter Theatre Complex** in Rondebosch. The Main Theatre and Concert Hall show mainstream productions, whereas the intimate Studio Theatre hosts more challenging works.

In addition to the impressive **Cape Town City Ballet**'s contemporary and classical performances, Cape Town has a great variety of jazz, contemporary dance and hip hop companies performing styles such as African dancing, gumboots and Pantsula.

COMEDY

At the **Theatre on the Bay** in Camps Bay, farce is the standard fare, while at **Evita Se Perron** in the town of Darling *(see p157)*, a short drive from Cape Town, the cutting wit of Pieter-Dirk Uys launches amusing attacks on current political issues. Both venues, along with the popular **On Broadway** in Shortmarket Street, also have excellent cabaret and drag troupes.

Black comedians with one-man shows include Marc Lottering and Kurt Schoonraad. They are part of a new comedy trend that is replacing white and often racist comedians.

For fun interactive comedy, **Theatresports** takes place every Tuesday at **Kalk Bay Theatre** and every Thursday evening at the SABC Auditorium in Sea Point. It is all improvised by a team of professional actors.

Theatre on the Bay, Camps Bay

JAZZ, AFRICAN AND ROCK MUSIC

Cape Town's unique, indigenous style of jazz is heavily influenced by traditional African sounds. The legendary Jazz musician Abdullah Ibrahim and other greats can be found playing at many of the venues around town. A fashionable spot is the **Winchester Mansions**

Cape Town City Ballet production of Giselle

Live sax playing at a Cape Town jazz festival

Hotel, especially good for lazy Saturday afternoons. **Heritage Square** offers alfresco dining to live jazz over the weekends, and during the summer St George's Mall buzzes with street music.

The V&A Waterfront is where you will find the popular **Green Dolphin**, an excellent restaurant and cocktail bar that provides live jazz performances every night. In the vicinity is the **West End**, a great dancing venue that is best on Fridays and Saturdays.

There are unbelievably good jazz bars in the surrounding townships, such as **Keith's Jazz Pub and Grill** in Khayelitsha, but it's advisable to experience them on an organized township tour.

Two of the main Jazz festivals are the Jazzathon at the V&A Waterfront in January and the Cape Town International Jazz Festival (previously known as the North Sea Jazz festival) at the International Convention Centre at the end of March, which is the greatest Jazz event on the continent.

The **Marimba Restaurant & Cigar Bar** is not to be missed on a Tuesday night with its sounds of the African marimba fusing with jazz. It is a good idea to book early as it can be sold out weeks in advance. The famous **Drum Café** specializes in interactive drum circles. Each guest is given a drum and the group is taught to play together. It is a powerful experience and the Saturday afternoon session at 3pm is ideal for families.

International live acts often perform at the **Belville Velodrome**, while local rock bands favour the **Mercury Live and Lounge**, which is the leading live rock venue.

CHILDREN'S ENTERTAINMENT

There is no need to worry that children will be bored in Cape Town. In addition to the endless outdoor activities that the city has to offer, there are plenty of family-friendly attractions too. For many kids, the thrilling amusement park, Ratanga Junction *(see p103)* is top of the list, but **Laserquest** and the indoor adventure playground in Claremont are also big hits with children. The **ice-skating rink** at the Grandwest Casino keeps kids occupied as the adults gamble.

Canal Walk offers **Boogaloos Skate Park** for skaters and **MTN Sciencentre,** which is a great complex with about 300 interactive displays. Another educational option is the **Planetarium**, where shows are held daily and at weekends.

The V&A Waterfront stages concerts and events during the holidays and the Zip Zap Circus at Easter is very popular.

Scratch 'n' Dive at the Waterfront and in Simon's Town is a fantastic activity. It involves digging for semi-precious gems at the scratch patch – and kids get to keep what they have found.

CLUBS, BARS AND CAFÉS

It is not always easy to distinguish between the clubs and bars of Cape Town, as drinking and dancing usually take place in the same venue.

Trendy bars along the Camps Bay strip offer cocktails and sundowners – try **Caprice** if you're up for a showy summer scene or **Sand Bar**, a casual pavement café. **La Med Beach Bar** in Clifton, a long-time favourite with the locals, is perfect for a just off-the-beach drink. Long Street in the City Centre provides an eclectic mix of places. Try the **Po Na Na Bar** with its view over Heritage Square, or the **Fireman's Arms** – a fun 1906 vintage-style bar.

For sophisticated cocktails, champagne, caviar and oysters in an upmarket ambience, head straight to **Planet Champagne & Cocktail Bar** at Mount Nelson Hotel, or **Asoka Son of Dharma** in arty Kloof street.

There are hundreds of clubs in Cape Town, varying from your standard disco-playing dance fare to profoundly alternative clubs, and the scene continues to grow. With a cigar bar, whisky lounge and regular events and DJs, one of the most fashionable is **Opium**. The gay and lesbian scene in Cape Town is big and there's a wealth of clubs to choose from on the outskirts of the city centre, on the "Green Mile" strip in Green Point.

Long Street has some of the best bars and clubs in Cape Town

DIRECTORY

INFORMATION

Cape Comedy Collective
Tel (021) 789-1665

Cape Town Tourism
www.cape-town.org

BOOKING TICKETS

Computicket
Tel (083) 915-8000

Dial-A-Seat
Tel (021) 421-7695

Tele-Ticket (Nu Metro)
Tel (0861) 100-220

Ticketline (Ster-Kinekor)
Tel (0861) 300-444

DISABLED VISITORS

Flamingo Tours
Tel (021) 557-4496
www.flamingotours.co.za

Kirstenbosch National Botanical Garden
Rhodes Dr, Newlands.
Tel (021) 799-8899

V&A Waterfront
Map 2 D3
Tel (021) 408-7600

BUDGET ENTERTAINMENT

Bell-Roberts Gallery
Tel (021) 422-1100

Cape Town Pass
www.thecapetownpass.co.za

Everard Read
Tel (021) 418-4527

Joao Ferreira Gallery
Tel (021) 423-5403

South African College of Music
Tel (021) 650-2640

OPEN-AIR ENTERTAINMENT

Josephine Mill
Boundary Rd, Newlands.
Tel (021) 686-4939

Little Theatre
Orange St. **Map** 5 A3
Tel (021) 480-7129

Maynardville Open-air Theatre
Church St, Wynberg.
Tel (021) 421-7695

South African National Circus School
Willow Rd, Observatory.
Tel (021) 692-4287

CINEMA

Cavendish Square
Dreyer St, Claremont.
Tel (0861) 300-444

Cine 12
12 Apostles Hotel, Victoria Rd, Camps Bay. **Map** 3B5
Tel (021) 437-9000

Cinema Nouveau
V&A Waterfront.
Map 2 E3
Tel (0861) 300-444

Cinema Prive
Canal Walk, Century City.
Tel (021) 555-2510

Cinema Starz
Grandwest Casino.
Tel (021) 534-0250

Labia Theatre
Orange St and Kloof St.
Map 5 A2
Tel (021) 424-5927

Nu Metro
www.numetro.co.za

Ster-Kinekor
www.sterkinekor.com

CLASSICAL MUSIC & OPERA

Cape Town Opera
Tel (021) 410-9807
www.capetownopera.co.za

Cape Town Philharmonic
Tel (021) 410-9809
http://www.cpo.org.za/

THEATRE & DANCE

Artscape Theatre Centre
DF Malan St, Foreshore.
Map 5 C1
Tel (021) 410-9800

Baxter Theatre Complex
Main Rd, Rondebosch.
Tel (021) 685-7880

Cape Town City Ballet
Tel (021) 650-2400
www.capetowncityballet.org.za

COMEDY

Evita Se Perron
Darling Station, Darling.
Tel (022) 492-2831

Kalk Bay Theatre
Main Rd, Kalk Bay.
Tel (073) 220-5430

On Broadway
Shortmarket St. **Map** 5B1
Tel (021) 424-1194

Theatre on the Bay
Link St, Camps Bay.
Tel (021) 438-3301

Theatresports
Tel (021) 447-5510
www.theatresports.co.za

JAZZ, AFRICAN & ROCK MUSIC

Belville Velodrome
Willie Van Der Schoor Rd, Belville.
Tel (021) 949-7450

Drum Café
Tel (021) 462-1064
www.drumcafe.co.za

Green Dolphin
V&A Waterfront. **Map** 2 E4 *Tel (021) 421-7471*

Heritage Square
Cnr Shortmarket and Bree sts. **Map** 5 B1
Tel (021) 422-0221

Keith's Jazz Pub and Grill
Mncedisi St, Khayelitsha.
Tel (021) 361-0525

Marimba Restaurant and Cigar Bar
Cape Town International Convention Centre, Lower Long St.
Map 5 A2
Tel (021) 418-3366

Mercury Live & Lounge
De Villiers St, Zonnebloem.
Map 5 C3
Tel (021) 465-2106

West End
College Rd, Rynlands.
Tel (021) 637-9133

Winchester Mansions Hotel
Beach Rd. **Map** 1 B3
Tel (021) 434-2351

CHILDREN'S ENTERTAINMENT

Boogaloos Skate Park
Canal Walk, Century City.
Tel (021) 555-2895

Ice-skating
Grandwest Casino.
Tel (021) 535-2260

Laserquest
Main Rd, Claremont.
Tel (021) 683-7296

MTN Sciencentre
Canal Walk, Century City.
Tel (021) 529-8100

Planetarium
Queen Victoria St.
Map 5 B2
Tel (021) 481-3900

Scratch 'n' Dive
V&A Waterfront.
Tel (021) 419-9429

CLUBS, BARS & CAFES

Asoka Son of Dharma
Kloof St. **Map** 4 F3
Tel (021) 422-0909

Caprice
Victoria Rd. **Map** 3 B5
(021) 438-8315

Fireman's Arms
Lower Buitengracht St.
Map 5 A1
Tel (021) 419-1513

La Med
Victoria Rd. **Map** 3 B4
Tel (021) 438-5600

Planet Champagne & Cocktail Bar
Orange St. **Map** 5 A2
Tel (021) 483-1000

Po Na Na
Shortmarket St. **Map** 5 B1
Tel (021) 423-4889

Opium
Dixon St. **Map** 2 D5
Tel (021) 425-4010

Sand Bar
Victoria Rd. **Map** 3 B5
Tel (021) 438-8836

CAPE TOWN STREET FINDER

The map references appearing with the sights, shops and entertainment venues that are mentioned in the Cape Town chapter refer to the maps in this section. The key map below shows the areas covered including: the City Bowl, the Central Business District, the historical Gardens area and the V&A Waterfront. All the principal sights mentioned in the text are marked, as well as useful information like tourist information offices, police stations, post offices and public parking areas, always at a premium in the inner city. A full list of symbols appears in the key. Map references for Cape Town's hotels *(see pp-326–31)* and restaurants *(see pp358–62)* have been included in the Travellers' Needs section.

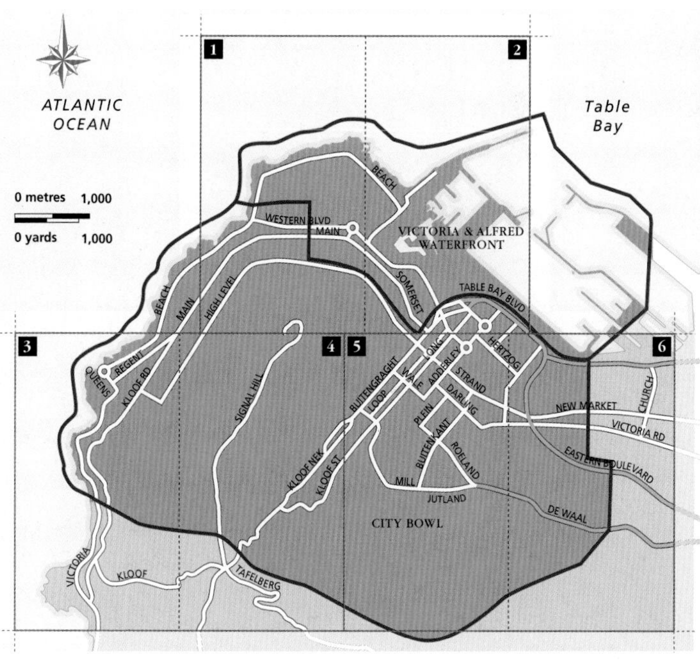

KEY

- Major sight
- Place of interest
- Other building
- Transnet station
- Bus terminus
- Minibus terminus
- Ferry boarding point
- Taxi rank
- Parking
- Tourist information
- Hospital with casualty unit
- Police station
- Mountain biking access
- Bathing beach
- Church
- Mosque
- Synagogue
- Post office
- Viewpoint
- Railway line
- Pedestrianized street
- Road (no public access)

SCALE FOR STREET FINDER PAGES

0 metres 400

0 yards 400

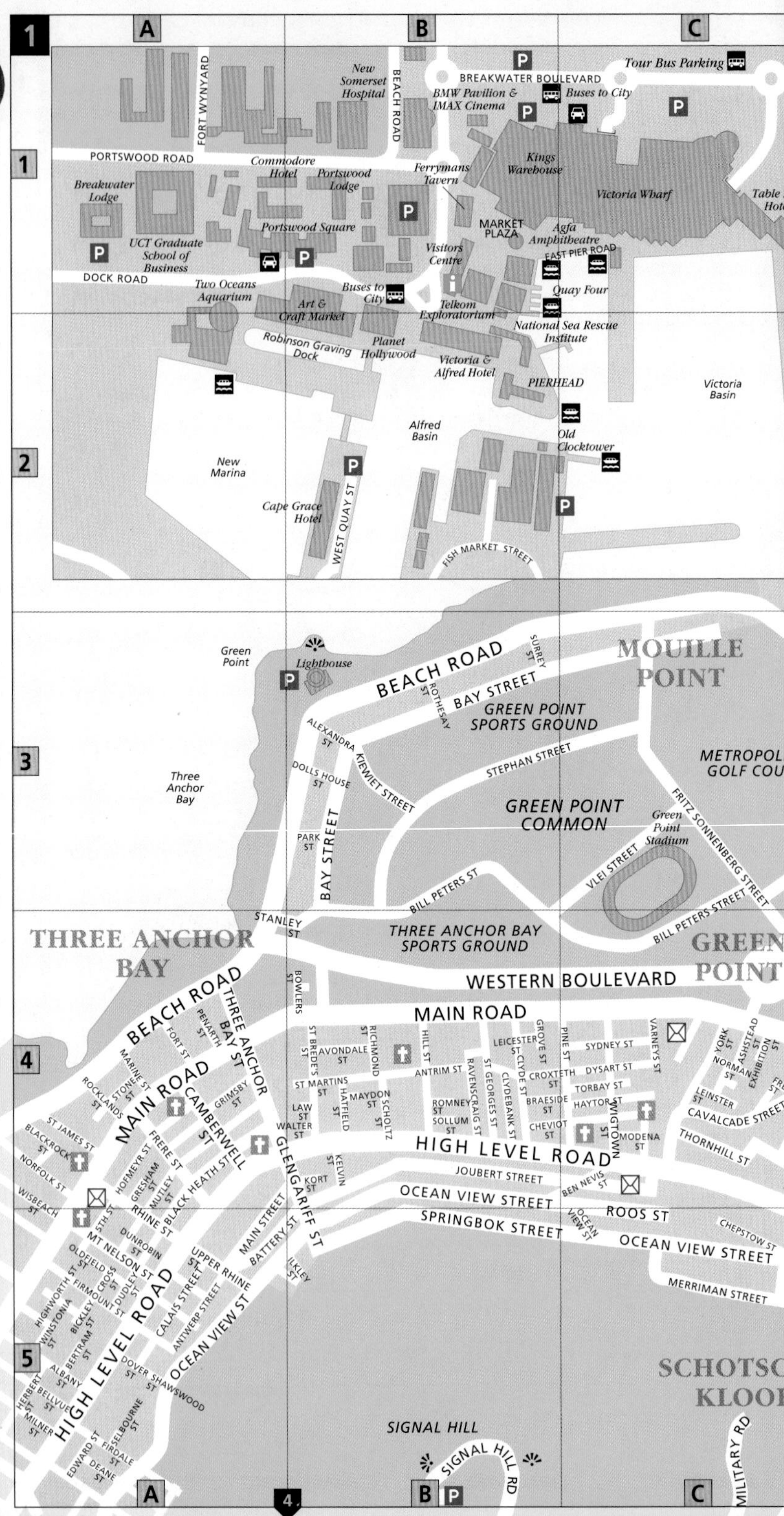

1
A
B
C
Tour Bus Parking
BREAKWATER BOULEVARD
New Somerset Hospital
BEACH ROAD
FORT WYNYARD
BMW Pavilion & IMAX Cinema
Buses to City
PORTSWOOD ROAD
Commodore Hotel
Portswood Lodge
Ferrymans Tavern
Kings Warehouse
Victoria Wharf
Table Bay Hotel
Breakwater Lodge
UCT Graduate School of Business
Portswood Square
MARKET PLAZA
Agfa Amphitheatre
EAST PIER ROAD
Visitors Centre
DOCK ROAD
Two Oceans Aquarium
Buses to City
Quay Four
Art & Craft Market
Telkom Exploratorium
National Sea Rescue Institute
Robinson Graving Dock
Planet Hollywood
Victoria & Alfred Hotel
PIERHEAD
Victoria Basin
Alfred Basin
Old Clocktower
New Marina
Cape Grace Hotel
WEST QUAY ST
FISH MARKET STREET
2
Green Point
Lighthouse
BEACH ROAD
SURREY ST
MOUILLE POINT
BAY STREET
ROTHESAY ST
GREEN POINT SPORTS GROUND
ALEXANDRA ST
3
Three Anchor Bay
DOLLS HOUSE ST
KIEWIET STREET
STEPHAN STREET
METROPOLITAN GOLF COURSE
GREEN POINT COMMON
FRITZ SONNENBERG STREET
Green Point Stadium
PARK ST
BAY STREET
VLEI STREET
BILL PETERS ST
BILL PETERS STREET
STANLEY ST
THREE ANCHOR BAY
THREE ANCHOR BAY SPORTS GROUND
GREEN POINT
BOWLERS ST
WESTERN BOULEVARD
BEACH ROAD
THREE ANCHOR BAY ST
PENARTH ST
FORT ST
MAIN ROAD
4
MARINE ST
ROCKLANDS ST
STONE ST
MAIN ROAD
CAMBERWELL ST
GRIMSBY ST
ST BREDE'S ST
AVONDALE ST
RICHMOND ST
HILL ST
ANTRIM ST
LEICESTER ST
GROVE ST
PINE ST
SYDNEY ST
VARNEYS ST
YORK ST
ASHSTEAD ST
EXHIBITION ST
NORMAN ST
ST MARTINS ST
HATFIELD ST
MAYDON ST
SCHOLTZ ST
RAVENSCRAIG ST
ST GEORGES ST
CLYDE ST
CLYDEBANK ST
CROXTETH ST
DYSART ST
TORBAY ST
LEINSTER ST
LAW ST
WALTER ST
ROMNEY ST
SOLLUM ST
BRAESIDE ST
HAYTOR ST
CHEVIOT ST
WIGTOWN ST
MODENA ST
CAVALCADE STREET
THORNHILL ST
ST JAMES ST
BLACKROCK ST
NORFOLK ST
FRERE ST
HOFMEYR ST
GRESHAM ST
MUTLEY ST
BLACK HEATH ST
GLENGARIFF ST
HIGH LEVEL ROAD
KELVIN ST
KORT ST
JOUBERT STREET
BEN NEVIS ST
WISBEACH ST
5TH ST
RHINE ST
OCEAN VIEW STREET
ROOS ST
OCEAN VIEW ST
SPRINGBOK STREET
CHEPSTOW ST
OCEAN VIEW STREET
MT NELSON ST
DUNROBIN ST
MAIN STREET
BATTERY ST
UPPER RHINE ST
ILKLEY ST
MERRIMAN STREET
OLDFIELD ST
HIGHWORTH ST
CROSS ST
FIRMOUNT ST
DUDLEY ST
CALAIS STREET
ANTWERP STREET
OCEAN VIEW ST
HIGH LEVEL ROAD
WINSTONIA ST
BICKLEY ST
BERTRAM ST
5
SCHOTSCHE KLOOF
ALBANY ST
DOVER ST
SHAWSWOOD
HERBERT ST
BELLVUE ST
MILNER ST
SELBOURNE ST
EDWARD ST
FIRDALE ST
DEANE ST
SIGNAL HILL
SIGNAL HILL RD
MILITARY RD
A
4
B
C

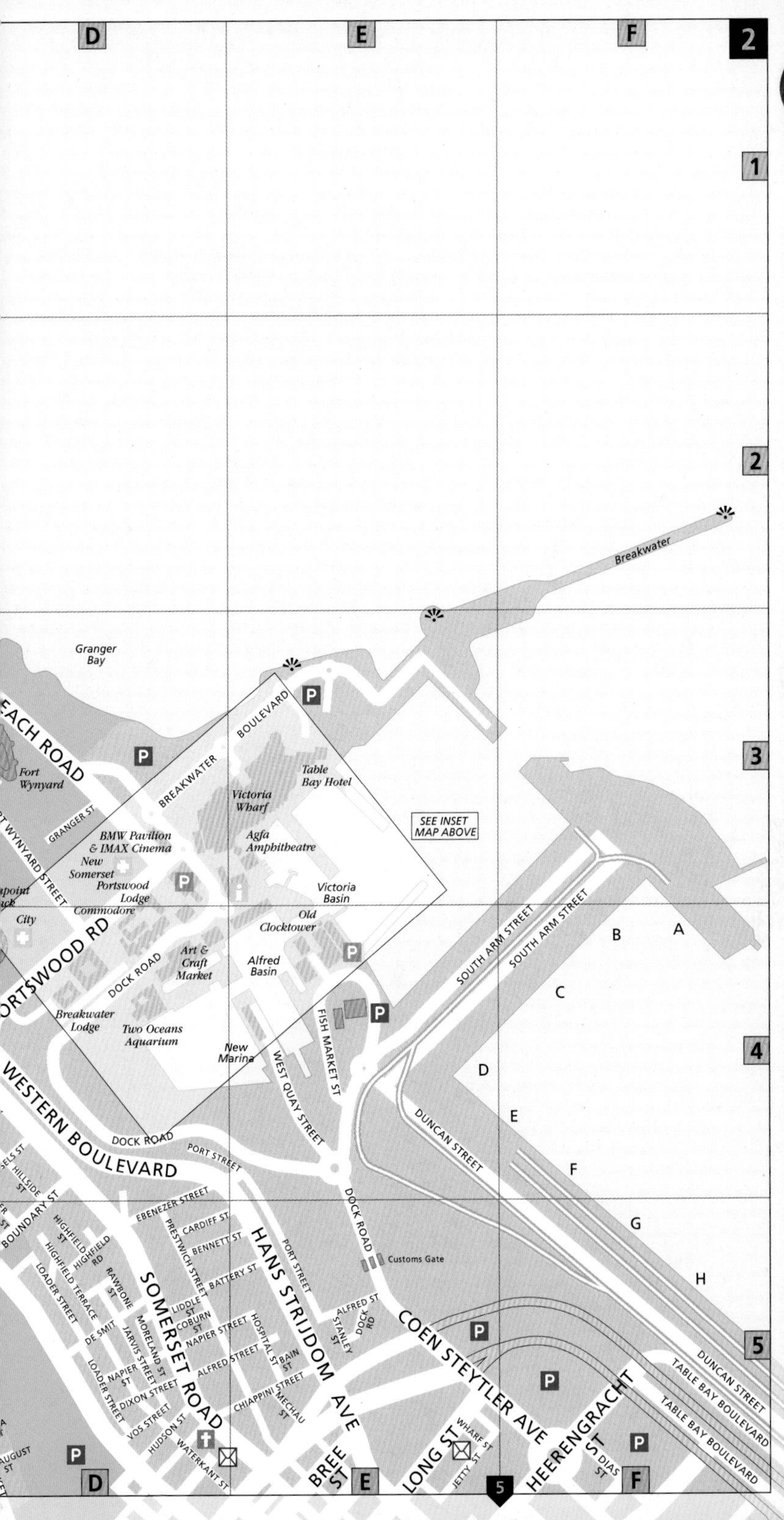

D
E
F
2
1
2
3
4
5
Breakwater
Granger Bay
BEACH ROAD
Fort Wynyard
GRANGER ST
FORT WYNYARD STREET
BREAKWATER BOULEVARD
Table Bay Hotel
Victoria Wharf
SEE INSET MAP ABOVE
BMW Pavilion & IMAX Cinema
Agfa Amphitheatre
New Somerset
Portswood Lodge
Victoria Basin
Commodore
City
Old Clocktower
PORTSWOOD RD
Art & Craft Market
Alfred Basin
DOCK ROAD
Breakwater Lodge
Two Oceans Aquarium
New Marina
FISH MARKET ST
WEST QUAY STREET
SOUTH ARM STREET
SOUTH ARM STREET
A
B
C
D
E
F
G
H
DUNCAN STREET
WESTERN BOULEVARD
DOCK ROAD
PORT STREET
HILLSIDE ST
BOUNDARY ST
EBENEZER STREET
CARDIFF ST
BENNETT ST
BATTERY ST
PRESTWICH STREET
HANS STRIJDOM AVE
PORT STREET
DOCK ROAD
Customs Gate
HIGHFIELD ST
HIGHFIELD RD
HIGHFIELD TERRACE
LOADER STREET
RAWBONE ST
SOMERSET ROAD
LIDDLE ST
COBURN ST
NAPIER STREET
HOSPITAL ST
BAIN ST
ALFRED ST
STANLEY ST
DOCK RD
COEN STEYTLER AVE
DE SMIT
MORELAND ST
JARVIS STREET
NAPIER ST
LOADER STREET
DIXON STREET
ALFRED STREET
CHIAPPINI STREET
MECHAU ST
VOS STREET
HUDSON ST
WATERKANT ST
AUGUST ST
BREE ST
LONG ST
WHARF ST
JETTY ST
HEERENGRACHT ST
DIAS ST
DUNCAN STREET
TABLE BAY BOULEVARD
TABLE BAY BOULEVARD
5

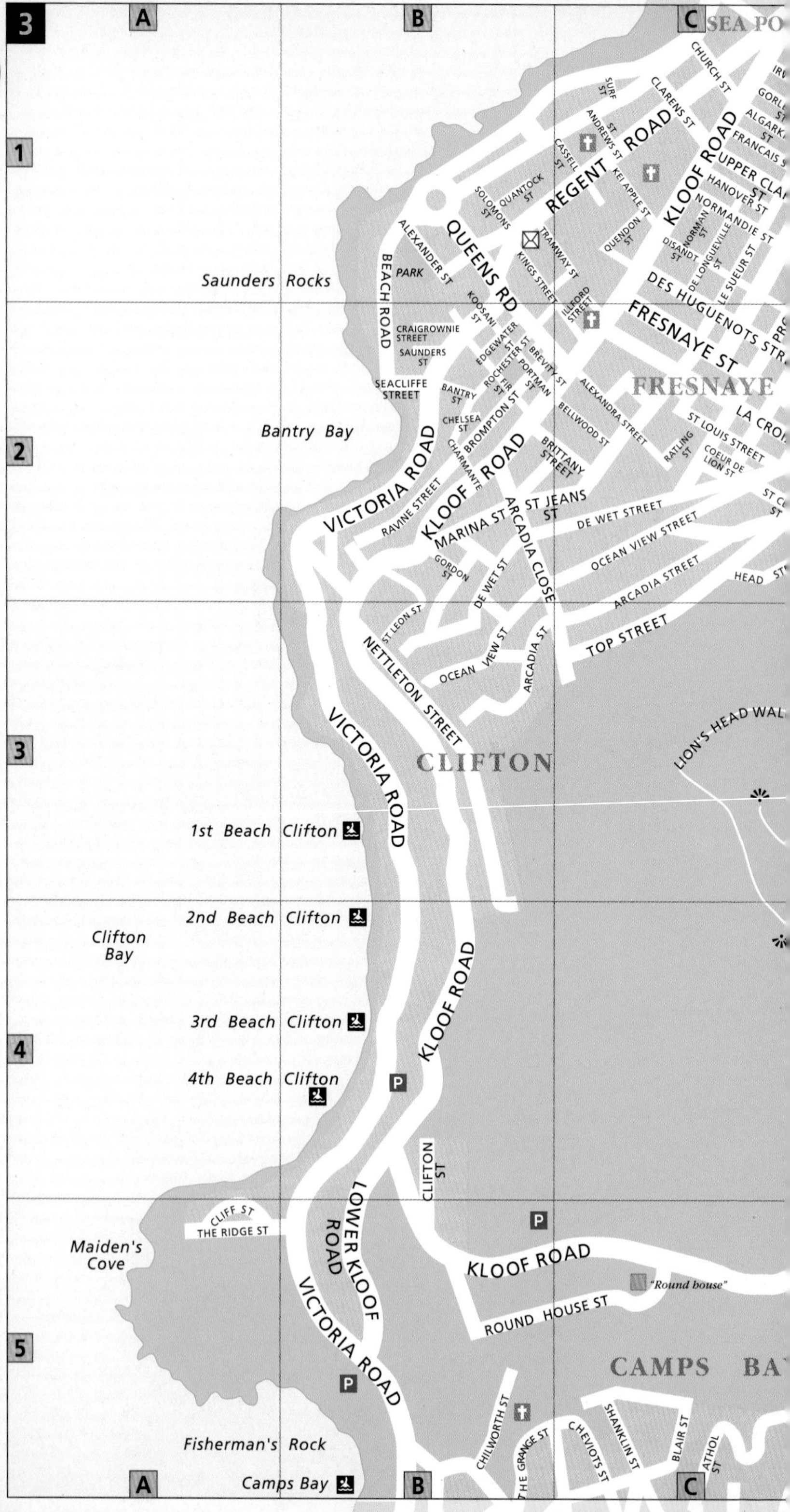
3
A
B
C
1
2
3
4
5
SEA PO
FRESNAYE
CLIFTON
CAMPS BA
Saunders Rocks
Bantry Bay
1st Beach Clifton
2nd Beach Clifton
Clifton Bay
3rd Beach Clifton
4th Beach Clifton
Maiden's Cove
Fisherman's Rock
Camps Bay
CHURCH ST
CLARENS ST
SURF ST
ST ANDREWS ST
REGENT ROAD
KLOOF ROAD
UPPER CLA
HANOVER ST
NORMANDIE ST
CASSELL ST
QUANTOCK ST
SOLOMONS ST
KEI APPLE ST
QUENDON ST
DISANDT ST
NORMAN ST
DE LONGUEVILLE ST
LE SUEUR ST
ALEXANDER ST
QUEENS RD
TRAMWAY ST
KINGS STREET
BEACH ROAD
PARK
KOOSANI ST
ILLFORD STREET
DES HUGUENOTS STR
FRESNAYE ST
CRAIGROWNIE STREET
SAUNDERS ST
EDGEWATER ST
ROCHESTER ST
BREVITY ST
FIR ST
PORTMAN ST
SEACLIFFE STREET
BANTRY ST
BROMPTON ST
ALEXANDRA STREET
BELLWOOD ST
CHELSEA ST
ST LOUIS STREET
RATLING ST
COEUR DE LION ST
LA CROI
CHARMANTE
BRITTANY STREET
VICTORIA ROAD
RAVINE STREET
ST JEANS ST
DE WET STREET
MARINA ST
ARCADIA CLOSE
OCEAN VIEW STREET
GORDON ST
DE WET ST
ARCADIA STREET
HEAD ST
ST LEON ST
TOP STREET
NETTLETON STREET
OCEAN VIEW ST
ARCADIA ST
LION'S HEAD WAL
P
CLIFTON ST
LOWER KLOOF ROAD
CLIFF ST
THE RIDGE ST
"Round house"
ROUND HOUSE ST
CHILWORTH ST
THE GRANGE ST
CHEVIOTS ST
SHANKLIN ST
BLAIR ST
ATHOL ST

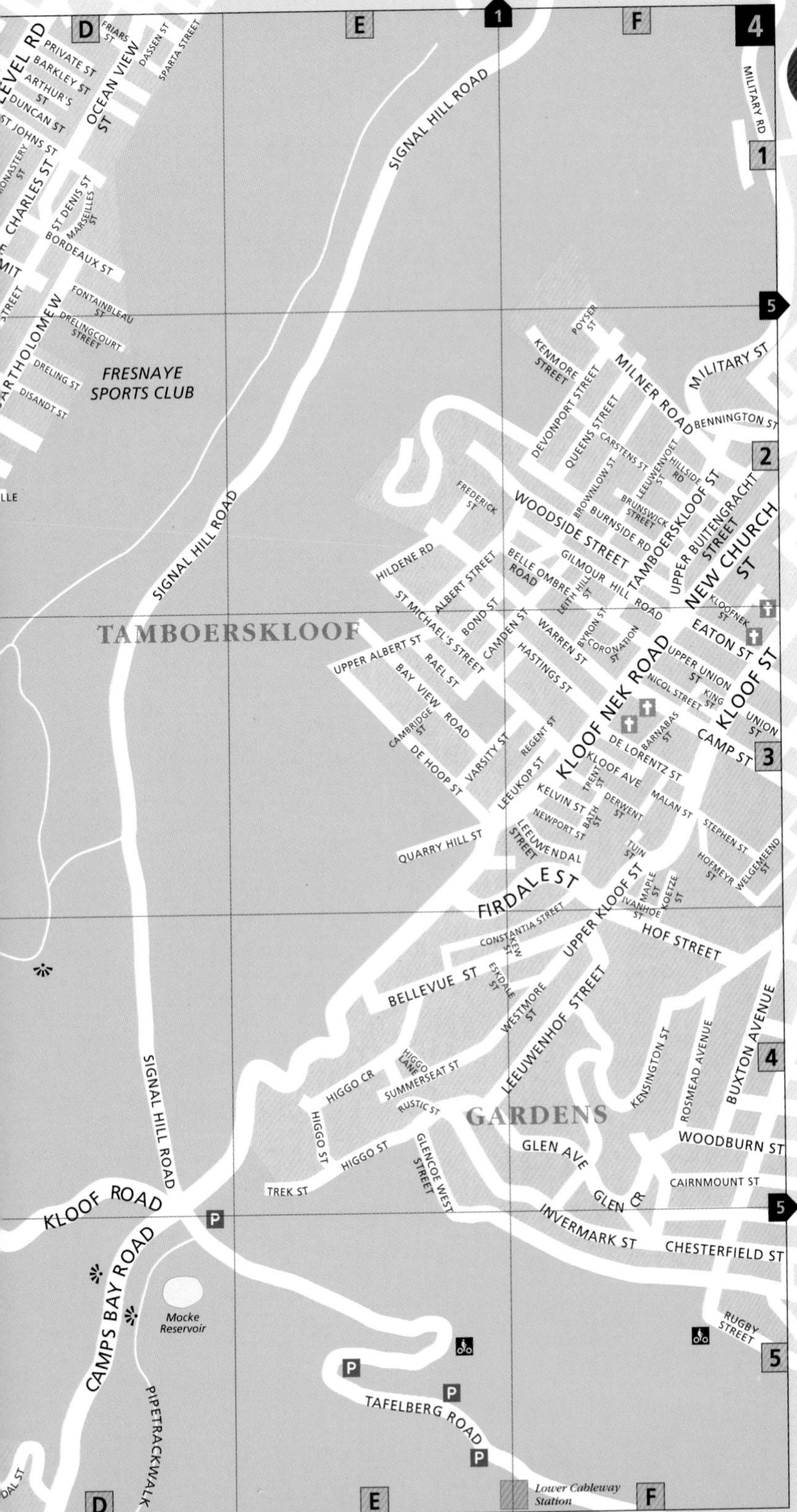

D
E
1
F
4
1
2
3
4
5
5
TAMBOERSKLOOF
GARDENS
FRESNAYE SPORTS CLUB
SIGNAL HILL ROAD
KLOOF ROAD
CAMPS BAY ROAD
PIPETRACKWALK
Mocke Reservoir
TAFELBERG ROAD
Lower Cableway Station
KLOOF NEK ROAD
KLOOF ST
NEW CHURCH ST
UPPER BUITENGRACHT STREET
TAMBOERSKLOOF ST
WOODSIDE STREET
MILNER ROAD
MILITARY RD
MILITARY ST
BENNINGTON ST
KENMORE STREET
POYSER ST
DEVONPORT STREET
QUEENS STREET
CARSTENS ST
BROWNLOW ST
LEEUWENVOET ST
HILLSIDE RD
BURNSIDE RD
BRUNSWICK STREET
FREDERICK ST
HILDENE RD
ALBERT STREET
BELLE OMBRE ROAD
GILMOUR HILL ROAD
LEITH HILL ST
ST MICHAEL'S STREET
BOND ST
CAMDEN ST
WARREN ST
BYRON ST
CORONATION ST
KLOOFNEK ST
EATON ST
UPPER UNION ST
NICOL STREET
KING ST
UNION ST
CAMP ST
UPPER ALBERT ST
RAEL ST
BAY VIEW ROAD
HASTINGS ST
CAMBRIDGE ST
DE HOOP ST
VARSITY ST
REGENT ST
BARNABAS ST
DE LORENTZ ST
KLOOF AVE
TRENT ST
LEEUKOP ST
KELVIN ST
NEWPORT ST
BATH ST
DERWENT ST
MALAN ST
STEPHEN ST
QUARRY HILL ST
LEEUWENDAL STREET
TUIN ST
HOFMEYR ST
WELGEMEEND ST
FIRDALE ST
UPPER KLOOF ST
MAPLE ST
IVANHOE ST
KOETZE ST
CONSTANTIA STREET
KEW ST
HOF STREET
BELLEVUE ST
ESKDALE ST
WESTMORE ST
LEEUWENHOF STREET
KENSINGTON ST
ROSMEAD AVENUE
BUXTON AVENUE
HIGGO CR
HIGGO LANE
SUMMERSEAT ST
RUSTIC ST
HIGGO ST
TREK ST
GLENCOE WEST STREET
GLEN AVE
GLEN CR
WOODBURN ST
CAIRNMOUNT ST
INVERMARK ST
CHESTERFIELD ST
RUGBY STREET
LEVEL RD
PRIVATE ST
BARKLEY ST
ARTHUR'S ST
DUNCAN ST
ST JOHNS ST
OCEAN VIEW ST
FRIARS ST
DASSEN ST
SPARTA STREET
CHARLES ST
ST DENIS ST
MARSEILLES ST
BORDEAUX ST
FONTAINBLEAU ST
DRELINGCOURT STREET
DRELING ST
DISANDT ST
P

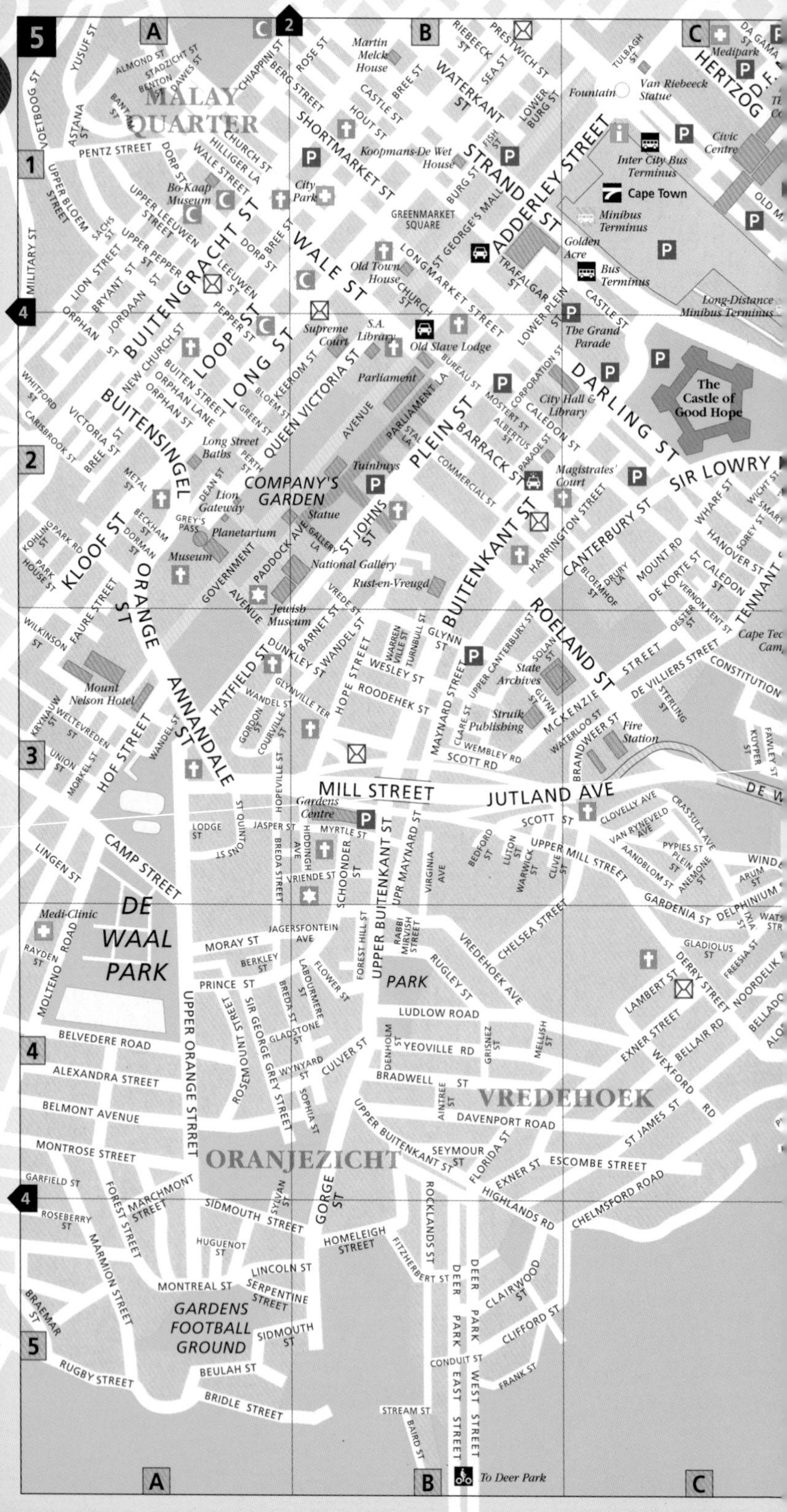
5
MALAY QUARTER
COMPANY'S GARDEN
The Castle of Good Hope
The Grand Parade
City Hall & Library
Cape Town
Inter City Bus Terminus
Minibus Terminus
Bus Terminus
Long-Distance Minibus Terminus
Golden Acre
Civic Centre
Medipark
Van Riebeeck Statue
Fountain
Martin Melck House
Koopmans-De Wet House
Bo-Kaap Museum
City Park
Greenmarket Square
Old Town House
Supreme Court
S.A. Library
Old Slave Lodge
Parliament
Tuinhuys
Magistrates' Court
Long Street Baths
Lion Gateway
Planetarium
Museum
Statue
National Gallery
Rust-en-Vreugd
Jewish Museum
State Archives
Struik Publishing
Fire Station
Mount Nelson Hotel
Gardens Centre
Medi-Clinic
DE WAAL PARK
PARK
VREDEHOEK
ORANJEZICHT
GARDENS FOOTBALL GROUND
Cape Technikon Campus
To Deer Park
ADDERLEY STREET
STRAND ST
WALE ST
LONG ST
LOOP ST
BUITENGRACHT ST
BUITENSINGEL
QUEEN VICTORIA ST
PLEIN ST
DARLING ST
SIR LOWRY RD
BUITENKANT ST
ROELAND ST
KLOOF ST
ORANGE ST
ANNANDALE ST
HOF STREET
MILL STREET
JUTLAND AVE
CAMP STREET
UPPER ORANGE STREET
UPPER BUITENKANT ST
HERTZOG BLVD
SHORTMARKET ST
LONGMARKET STREET
HOPE STREET
CANTERBURY ST
DE VILLIERS STREET
CONSTITUTION
TENNANT
BELVEDERE ROAD
ALEXANDRA STREET
BELMONT AVENUE
MONTROSE STREET
DAVENPORT ROAD
ESCOMBE STREET
HIGHLANDS RD
CHELMSFORD ROAD
DEER PARK EAST STREET
DEER PARK WEST STREET
RUGBY STREET
BRIDLE STREET
A
B
C
1
2
3
4
5

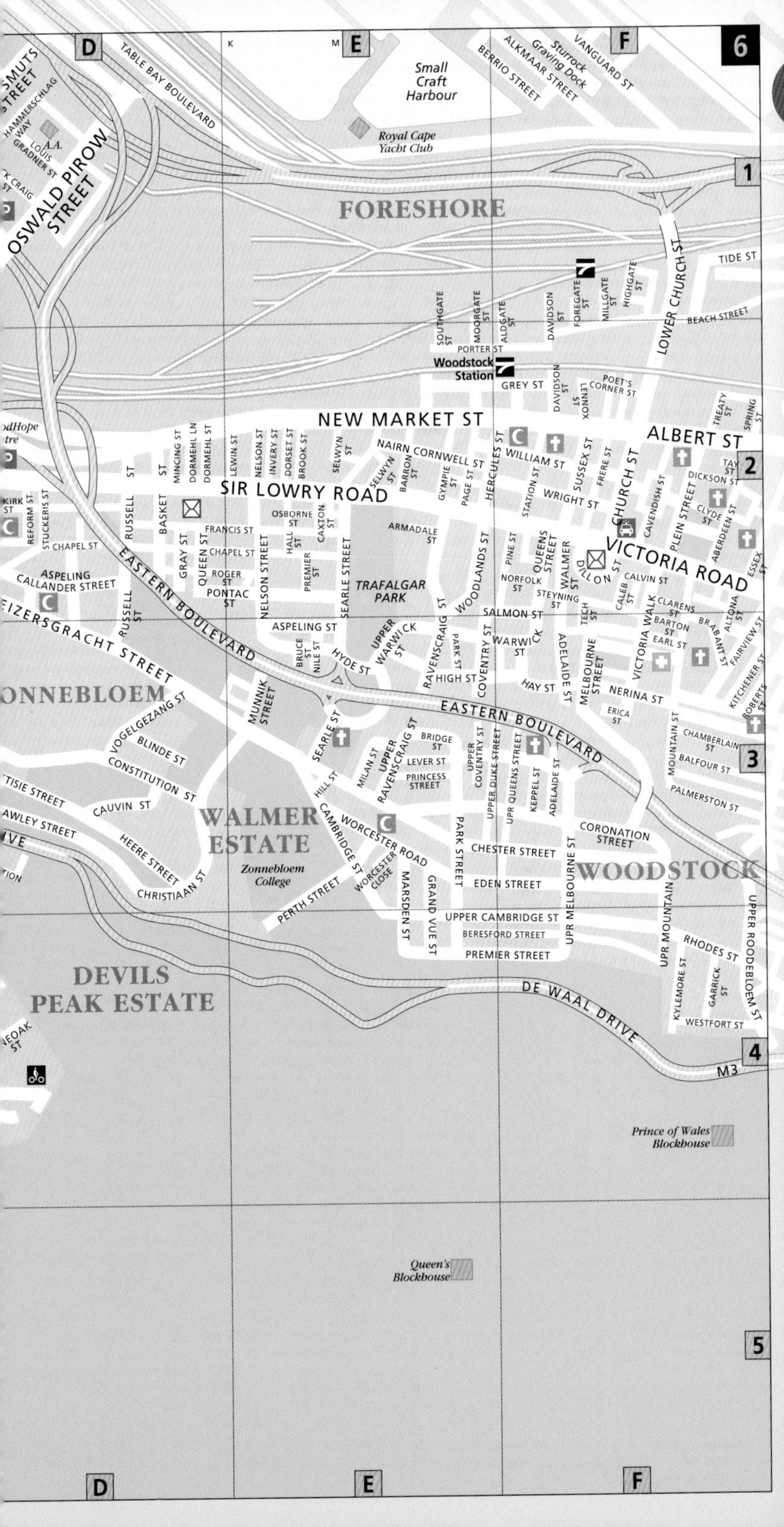
6
D
E
F
Small Craft Harbour
Royal Cape Yacht Club
FORESHORE
OSWALD PIROW STREET
TABLE BAY BOULEVARD
NEW MARKET ST
SIR LOWRY ROAD
ALBERT ST
VICTORIA ROAD
EASTERN BOULEVARD
TRAFALGAR PARK
Woodstock Station
LOWER CHURCH ST
WALMER ESTATE
Zonnebloem College
WOODSTOCK
DEVILS PEAK ESTATE
DE WAAL DRIVE
M3
Prince of Wales Blockhouse
Queen's Blockhouse
1
2
3
4
5

Cape Town Street Finder Index

THE WESTERN & SOUTHERN CAPE

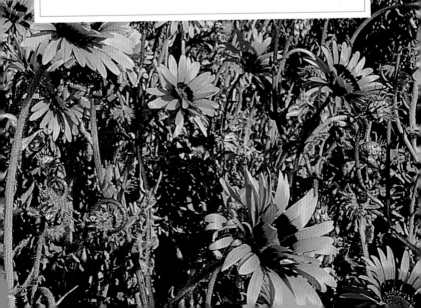

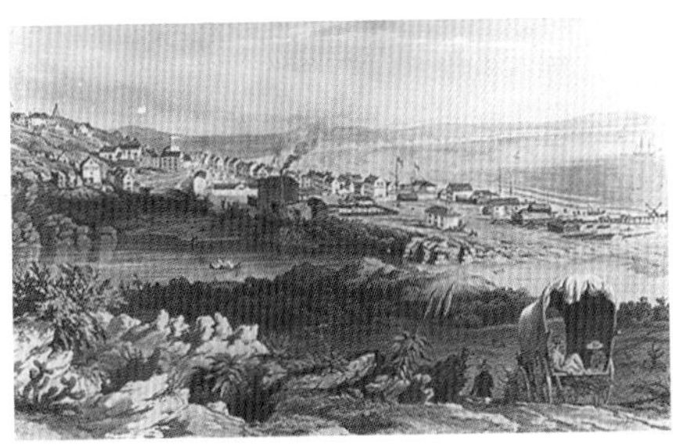

Introducing the Western and Southern Cape

This region is dominated by a rugged mountain chain, comprising what is geologically known as the Cape folded mountains. The landscapes found in this territory are diverse. The arid and rather barren West Coast gives way to fertile winelands, cradled by jagged mountains. Beyond the terraced valleys, dramatic passes that traverse the massive mountain ranges of the Southern Cape are a testament to the efforts of early road builders. The spectacular Cango Caves lie here and, on the other side of the mountains, the spectacular Garden Route. All along the rocky coastline, which is one of the most dangerous in the world and where swells can reach up to 30 m (98 ft) in height, fishermen reap the harvest of the sea.

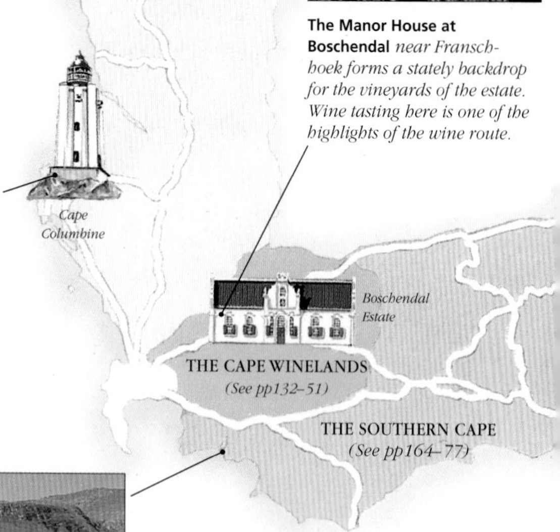

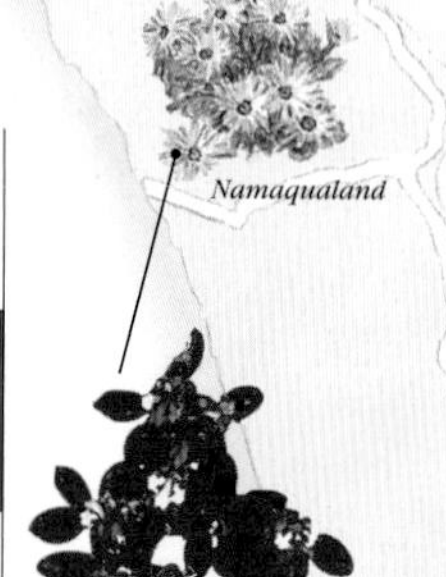

Namaqualand

0 kilometres 50

0 miles 25

A myriad wildflowers *occurs in this region after good spring rains, when the dry West Coast comes alive with colour.*

THE WESTERN COASTAL TERRACE

(See pp152–63)

The Manor House at Boschendal *near Franschhoek forms a stately backdrop for the vineyards of the estate. Wine tasting here is one of the highlights of the wine route.*

Cape Columbine

Cape Columbine lighthouse *on the West Coast warns ships of the dangerous rocks along the shore. It is the last manned lighthouse in South Africa.*

Boschendal Estate

THE CAPE WINELANDS

(See pp132–51)

THE SOUTHERN CAPE

(See pp164–77)

Hermanus *is best known for the southern right whales that come here to give birth to their calves. The best time of the year for whale watching is around September.*

◁ **In spring, double Namaqualand daisies provide carpets of colour**

Knysna Forest *is known for its tall stinkwood trees and ancient yellowwoods, some of which are 650 years old. The dense canopy is alive with birds, such as the elusive, emerald-green lourie.*

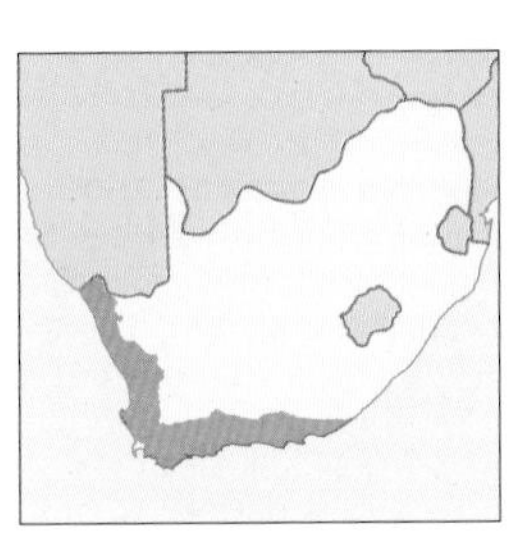

Addo Elephant National Park *in the Eastern Cape is a major tourist attraction. The park is home to around 300 elephants.*

Port Elizabeth's *attractions include an aquarium on the beachfront, where dolphin shows are the most popular event. In the city, a host of historic buildings and statues date back to British colonial times.*

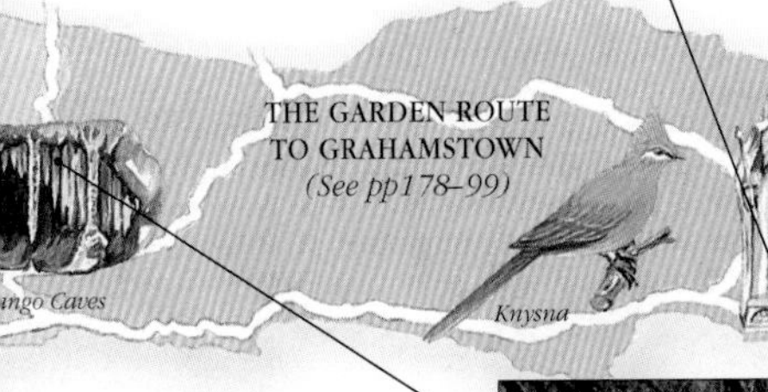

The Cango Caves *near Oudtshoorn contain many fascinating dripstone formations, caused by the constant percolation of water through limestone.*

Pinotage Wine-Making

Pinotage is a unique South African cultivar that was developed in 1925 by Stellenbosch University professor Abraham Perold, from a cross of pinot noir and cinsaut (then called hermitage). The world's first commercially bottled pinotage was released in 1961 under the Lanzerac label. The fruity, purple-red wine has, since then, achieved international acclaim. Pinotage comprises only a small percentage of South African total grape plantings, with most of the crop grown around Stellenbosch. In recent years, cuttings have been exported to California and New Zealand.

Old grape press in the Stellenryck Museum, Stellenbosch

Pinot noir

Cinsaut

Pinotage

THE PINOTAGE CULTIVARS

Pinot noir, the noble cultivar from France's famous Burgundy district, contributed complexity, flavour, and colour, while cinsaut improved the yield. Today, pinotage is an early ripening cultivar that results in a light- to medium-bodied wine with unique flavour characteristics.

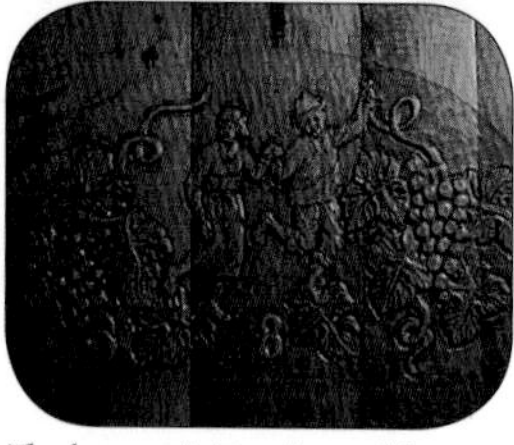

The large **oak barrels** *used for maturation and storage of red wines are often decorated with hand-carved designs, like this beautiful example from the Delheim cellar in Stellenbosch.*

Stellenbosch *(see pp136–40)* is surrounded by gentle hills that are ideal for growing pinotage.

PINOTAGE INTERNATIONAL AWARDS

1987: Kanonkop (1985) – Beyers Truter voted Diners' Club "Winemaker of the Year"
1991: Kanonkop (1989 Reserve) – Robert Mondavi Trophy (USA)
1996: Kanonkop (1992) – Perold Trophy (International Wine and Spirit Competition)
1997: L'Avenir (1994) – Perold Trophy
1997: Jacobsdal (1994) – gold medal at Vin Expo Competition (France)

Two of South Africa's well-known pinotage labels

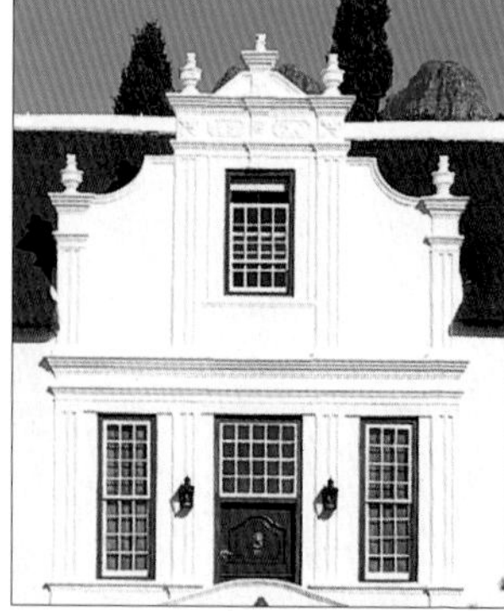

Lanzerac, in Stellenbosch, combines a luxury country hotel with a working winery. Pinotage is one of a range of wines made by the estate.

THE RED WINE-MAKING PROCESS

Wine is a natural product and winemakers take great care during harvesting, production and maturation to ensure that their wines are of a high quality and meet the requirements of the consumer. Modern trends call for minimal interference in the vineyard and cellar in order to allow the wines to "speak" for themselves.

Harvesting *is carefully timed to achieve the best flavours and characters from the grape. Red wines are traditionally harvested later than white wines, to allow the development of riper and more concentrated fruit.*

Grapes are cut off the vine with sharp shears to minimize damage to the mature berries

Destalking *removes the stems, whose high tannin content influences the wine's flavour. The grapes are then lightly crushed before being put into a vat for fermentation to begin.*

Destalker and crusher

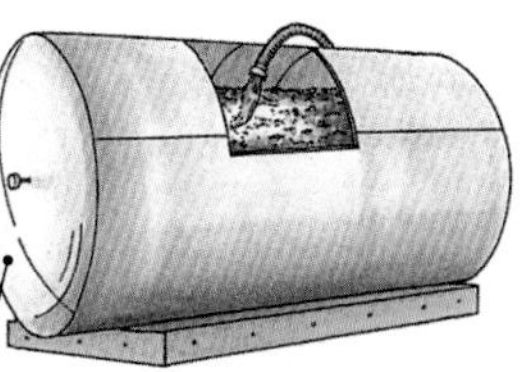

Fermentation tank

Fermentation *occurs over three to five days. The juice is periodically pumped over the "cap" formed by the skins to extract the desired amount of colour and tannin. After fermentation, the juice is separated from the skins, and matured before blending and bottling.*

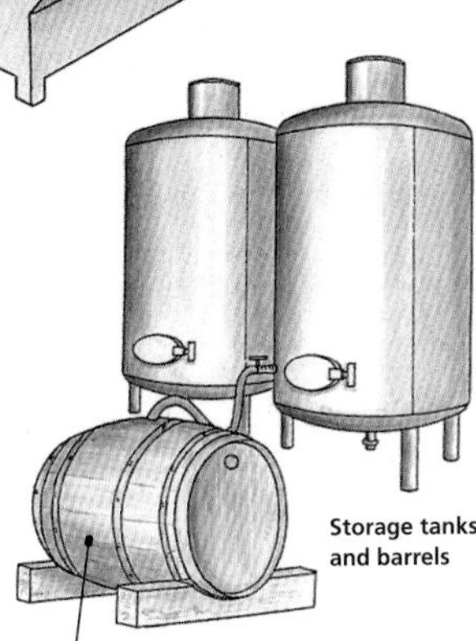

Storage tanks and barrels

Racking *is the transfer of fermented wine from one tank or cask to another to remove the "lees", sediments that would cause the end product to appear cloudy. Filtration and fining, often using egg whites, removes impurities.*

Maturation *of pinotage takes 12–15 months. Traditionally, big vats were used, but the modern trend is to use small barrels made of French or American oak. The size of the barrel, type of wood and maturation time combine to shape the character of the wine. Once matured, the red wines are ready for bottling.*

Wooden maturation barrels

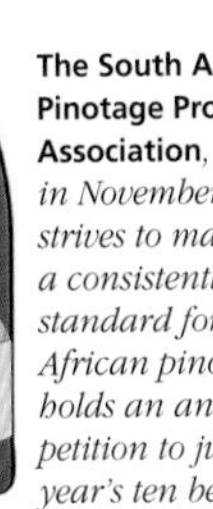

The South African Pinotage Producers, Association, *formed in November 1995, strives to maintain a consistently high standard for South African pinotage. It holds an annual competition to judge the year's ten best wines.*

Over 130 pinotages are made in South Africa

Whale-Watching

Shop sign in Hermanus

Some 37 whale and dolphin species and around 100 different types of shark occur in Southern African waters. Only a small number come in close to the coast however. Of the dolphins, bottlenose, common and Heaviside's are the most prolific, while common predatory sharks include the great white, tiger, ragged-tooth, oceanic white tip, bull (Zambezi), and mako. A large portion of the world's 4,000–6,000 southern right whales migrates north annually, with numbers increasing by seven per cent every year. They leave their subantarctic feeding grounds from June onwards to mate and calve in the warmer waters of the protected rocky bays and inlets that occur along the South African coastline.

WHALE-WATCHING

Best vantage points

Callosities *are tough, wart-like growths on the whale's skin, not barnacles as is often thought. Scientists use these unique markings to distinguish between individuals.*

An albino calf was born in Hermanus in 1997.

THE SOUTHERN RIGHT WHALE

Early whalers named this species "southern right" *(Eubalaena australis)* because it occurred south of the Equator and was the perfect quarry. Its blubber was rich in oil, the baleen plates supplied whalebone for corsets, shoe horns and brushes, and when dead it floated, unlike other whales which sank. A protected species, they can migrate by up to 2,600 km (1,615 miles) annually.

A characteristic V-shaped "blow" *can be seen when the southern right exhales. The vapour is produced by condensation, as warm breath comes into contact with cooler air.*

The "Whale Crier" *patrols the streets of Hermanus, blowing a kelp horn to inform passers-by of the best sightings of the day.*

WHALE ANTICS

The reasons for some types of whale behaviour are, as yet, unclear. Breaching, for example, may either indicate aggression, or joyfulness; it may also simply help the animal get rid of lice.

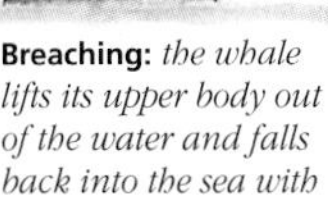

Breaching: *the whale lifts its upper body out of the water and falls back into the sea with a massive splash.*

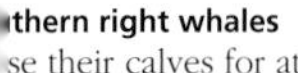

Lobtailing: *the flukes slap on the surface to produce a loud clap.*

Spyhopping: *the whale lifts its head vertically from the sea to observe what is happening on the surface.*

thern right whales se their calves for at st six months.

Shore-based whale watching is superb at Hermanus.

Humpback whales *are well known for their spectacular breaching behaviour, lifting their bodies well above the water. A striking feature of this species is its extremely long flippers.*

WHALE EXPLOITATION

In the years from 1785 to around 1805, some 12,000 southern right whales were killed off the Southern African coast, but the northern right whale was the most ruthlessly hunted and is virtually extinct today. After the introduction of cannon-fired harpoons, humpbacks were the first large whale to be exploited. Some 25,000 were killed between 1908 and 1925. By 1935, when the League of Nations' Convention for the Regulation of Whaling came into effect, fewer than 200 southern right whales remained in Southern African waters. Although numbers are increasing steadily, today's total population is only a fraction of what it once was.

Early whalers in False Bay

THE CAPE WINELANDS

The Cape's Winelands are a scenically enchanting region of lofty mountains and fertile valleys and slopes planted with orchards and vines. Nestled in the valleys are graceful Cape Dutch manor houses, of which stately Nederburg in Paarl (which hosts a famous wine auction), elegant Boschendal near Franschhoek and the charming Lanzerac Hotel in Stellenbosch are the best known.

Stellenbosch was the first of the wineland towns to be established by Simon van der Stel, who had succeeded Jan van Riebeeck as governor in 1679. After Van der Stel visited the area in November of that year and proclaimed it to be well watered and fertile, the first free burghers (early Dutch settlers who were granted tracts of land together with implements and oxen to help them establish farms) were sent to this valley to start a new life. Settlement in the Franschhoek valley followed with the arrival of the French Huguenots (Protestant refugees from Europe), and later Dutch as well as French pioneers established themselves in the Paarl area. The temperate Mediterranean climate of the Cape has ensured the survival of the early wine-making traditions.

The cool mountain and sea breezes create diverse conditions, and variable soil types – from the acidic and sandy alluvial soils of Stellenbosch to the lime-rich soils of Robertson – ensure a wide range of superb wines, both red and white, making South Africa the world's eighth-largest producer. Well over 100 estates, 66 co-operatives and more than 100 private cellars in the Western Cape support about 300,000 farm workers and their dependents.

Most of the estates and co-ops offer tastings, and the architectural legacy of the settlers is evident on a drive through any of the Wineland towns.

Klein Constantia in Cape Town is a particularly picturesque wine estate

◁ The Gazebo at Boschendal estate on the Franschhoek wine route

Exploring the Cape Winelands

After Table Mountain, the V&A Waterfront and Cape Point, the winelands are the Western Cape's most popular attraction. The towns of Stellenbosch and Paarl are special for their elegant, gabled architecture, while Franschhoek enjoys an exquisite valley setting. Viewed from majestic mountain passes, the vineyards of Worcester and Robertson fit together like puzzle pieces, and the drawcard of Tulbagh *(see p157)* is its row of quaint, historical houses, meticulously restored after a devastating earthquake in 1969.

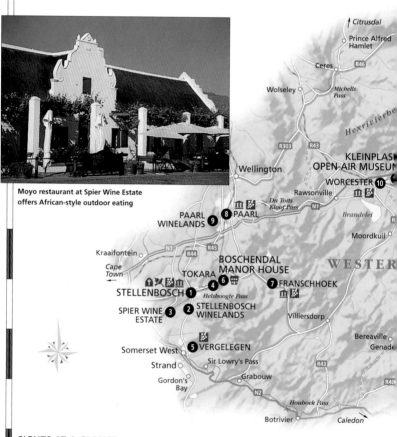

Moyo restaurant at Spier Wine Estate offers African-style outdoor eating

Citrusdal
Prince Alfred Hamlet
Ceres
R46
Wolseley
Michells Pass
Hexrivierbe
R303
R43
KLEINPLASIE OPEN-AIR MUSEUM
Wellington
WORCESTER 10
Rawsonville
Du Toits Kloof Pass
N1
Brandvlei
PAARL WINELANDS 9
8 PAARL
Moordkuil
N1
R45
R44
Kraaifontein
Cape Town
BOSCHENDAL MANOR HOUSE
TOKARA
WESTERN
6
4
7 FRANSCHHOEK
STELLENBOSCH 1
Helshoogte Pass
SPIER WINE ESTATE 3
2 STELLENBOSCH WINELANDS
Villiersdorp
Bereaville
Genade
5 VERGELEGEN
Somerset West
Strand
Sir Lowry's Pass
Gordon's Bay
Grabouw
R43
R40
N2
Houhoek Pass
Botrivier
Caledon

SIGHTS AT A GLANCE

Boschendal Manor House pp142–3 ❻
Franschhoek ❼
Kleinplasie Open-Air Museum pp150–51 ⓫
Montagu ⓭
Paarl ❽
Robertson ⓬
Spier ❸
Stellenbosch pp136–9 ❶
Tokara ❹
Vergelegen ❺
Worcester ❿

Tours and Trails

Boesmanskloof Traverse p149 ⓮
Paarl Winelands Tour p147 ❾
Stellenbosch Winelands p140 ❷

SEE ALSO

- ***Where to Stay*** pp332–4
- ***Where to Eat*** pp363–4

Delheim's vineyards, Stellenbosch

GETTING AROUND

The winelands are served by two major national routes, the N1 and N2. All of the connecting principal roads are clearly signposted. Franschhoek, Paarl and Worcester are accessed from the N1, Stellenbosch from either the N1 or N2 national route. Robertson is reached from Worcester via the R60.

The scenic mountain passes are well worth an excursion and own transport is essential if you wish to tour these areas. Alternatively, visitors can join one of the coach tours organized by major tour operators like Intercape (see p409) and Mainline Passenger Services (see p407). Cape Town International is the closest airport.

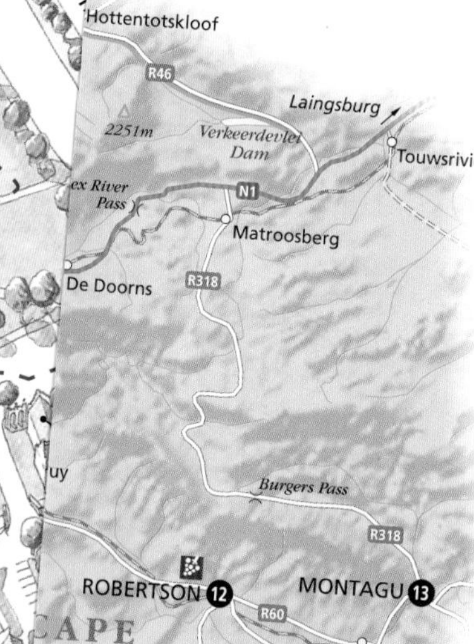

Montagu is renowned for its hot springs

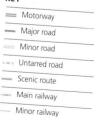

0 kilometres 50

0 miles 25

KEY

 Motorway

Major road

Minor road

Untarred road

Scenic route

Main railway

Minor railway

Pass

Rhebokskloof has converted a cellar into a cosy wine-tasting venue

Exploring Stellenbosch

The heart of the Winelands, this beautiful university town is also the historical cradle of Afrikaans culture. Founded in 1679, the town's proud educational heritage began in 1863 with the establishment of the Dutch Reformed Theological Seminary. The Stellenbosch College was completed in 1886, the forerunner of the university, which was established in 1918. Today, the university buildings are beautifully integrated with the surrounding historical monuments, reinforcing the town's dignified atmosphere of culture and learning.

Rhenish Complex

Herte St. *Opening times of buildings vary and are subject to change.* ***Tel*** *(021) 883-3584 for information.*

This lovely group of old buildings, which is flanked by two modern educational centres – the Rhenish Primary School and the Rhenish Institute – is representative of most of all the architectural styles that have appeared in Stellenbosch over the centuries.

Parts of the Cape Dutch-style Rhenish parsonage are much older than the date of 1815 noted on the building's gable. The parsonage houses a museum of miniature rooms fitted with period furniture and a 50-sq-m (538-sq-ft) model railway set in a diminutive reconstruction of the landscape around Stellenbosch.

Leipoldt House, which was built around 1832, is an interesting combination of Cape Dutch and English Georgian architectural styles, while the Rhenish Church, facing Bloem Street, was erected in 1823 by the Missionary Society of Stellenbosch as a training centre and school for slaves and "coloured" people.

Oom Samie se Winkel

Oom Samie se Winkel

84 Dorp St. ***Tel*** *(021) 887-0797.* *8:30am–5:30pm (6pm summer) Mon–Fri, 9am–5pm (5:30pm summer) Sat, Sun.* *1 Jan, Good Fri, 25 Dec.*

This charming, restored Victorian shop, whose name means "Uncle Samie's Store", has been operating as a general store since 1904. Its original proprietor, bachelor Samie Volsteedt, used to live in the house next door. The store, a Stellenbosch institution and a national monument, has bric-a-brac ranging from bottled preserves, basketry, candles and curios to 19th-century butter churns, plates and kitchen utensils. Visitors may also browse in Samie's Victorian Wine Shop for a special vintage or take tea under the leafy pergolas of the Koffiehuis restaurant.

Toy and Miniature Museum

Market St (next to tourist information office). ***Tel*** *(021) 887-9433.* *9:30am–5pm Mon–Sat, 2–5pm Sun.* *Sun (May–Aug).* **www**.museums.org.za/stellmus

The Toy and Miniature Museum offers a world of enchantment for both young and old and is well worth a visit. Housed in the old Rhenish Parsonage of 1815, the museum is the first of its kind in Africa. On display is an amazing collection of historical toys, including antique dolls and Dinky Toy motor cars, as well as a model railway-layout and miniature houses. The museum also boasts a number of finely detailed and exquisite 1:12 scale miniature rooms, each with delicate filigree work.

On sale in the small museum shop are furniture and accessories for dolls' houses, as well as momentos of the museum's unique treasures.

The Stellenbosch Village Museum

18 Ryneveld St. ***Tel*** *(021) 887-2902.* *9am–5pm Mon–Sat, 2–5pm Sun.* *Good Fri, 25 Dec.*

This complex features houses from Stellenbosch's early settlement years to the 1920s, although the Edwardian and other early 20th-century houses are not open to the public. The museum includes four buildings. Schreuder House was built in 1709 by Sebastian Schreuder. It is the oldest of the houses and shows the spartan, simple lifestyle of the early settlers. Bletterman House, erected in 1789, belonged to Hendrik Bletterman, a wealthy *landdrost* (magistrate). Parts of

The Rhenish Complex, a splendid example of Cape Dutch architecture

For hotels and restaurants in this region see pp332–4 and pp363–4

ARTS AND CRAFTS IN STELLENBOSCH

Nurtured by Stellenbosch's environment of culture and learning, a community of artists, graphic designers, ceramists and screen-printers has settled in the town. Multiple galleries and studios such as the Dorp Street Gallery at 176 Dorp Street and the Stellenbosch Art Gallery at 34 Ryneveld Street show the works of respected contemporary South African and local artists. Outside Stellenbosch, off Devon Valley Road, the Jean Craig Pottery Studio showcases all stages of its pottery production, and on Annandale Road, off the R310, visitors can watch spinners and weavers at work at Dombeya Farm. A detailed arts and crafts brochure is available from the Stellenbosch tourist information centre.

Work by Hannetjie de Clerq

The 18th-century middle-class Schreuder House at the Village Museum

Grosvenor House, the most elegant of the four, date back to 1782, but later additions to the house represent the Classicism of the 1800s. The house has period furnishings of the 1800s.

Constructed in 19th-century Victorian style, the interiors of Bergh House, occupied by Olof Marthinus Bergh from 1837 to 1866, accurately reflect the comfortable lifestyle of a wealthy burgher of the 1850s.

Sasol Art Museum

Eben Donges Centre, 52 Ryneveld St. ***Tel*** *(021) 808-3695.* *9am–4pm Tue–Fri, 9am–5pm Sat.* *Good Fri, 25 Dec.*

The interesting exhibition at the Sasol Art Museum focuses on anthropology, cultural history and art. Of particular interest to many visitors are the prehistoric artifacts, reproductions of San rock art and crafted utensils and ritual objects from South, West and Central Africa.

Van Ryn Brandy Cellar

R310 from Stellenbosch, exit 33. ***Tel*** *(021) 881-3875.* *9am–4:30pm Mon–Fri, 9am–2:30pm Sat.* *public hols.*

At this cellar just southwest of Stellenbosch, where the well-known local brands Van Ryn and Viceroy are made, guided tours introduce the visitor to the intricate art of brandy production. Brandy courses are offered and include a lecture, an audio-visual presentation, as well as a brandy tasting and dinner.

Environs: The **Jonkershoek Nature Reserve** lies in a valley 10 km (6 miles) southeast of Stellenbosch that is flanked by the scenic Jonkershoek and Stellenbosch mountain ranges. The scenery is characterized by wooded ravines, pine plantations and montane *fynbos*, which in spring and summer includes tiny pink and white ericas, blushing bride *(Serruria florida)* and the king protea. The waterfalls and streams of the Eerste River provide abundant water for hikers, mountain bikers and horse riders. For the less energetic, there is a 12-km (7.5-mile) scenic drive into the mountains. Baboons and dassies may be sighted, and sometimes the elusive klipspringer. Of the many bird species in the reserve, the Cape sugarbird and malachite and orange-breasted sunbirds are most likely to be seen.

Jonkershoek Nature Reserve

Jonkershoek Rd. ***Tel*** *(021) 866-1560.* *8am–6pm daily.* *heavy rains (Jun–Aug).* **www**.capenature.org.za

The sandstone mountains of the Jonkershoek Nature Reserve

Stellenbosch Winelands ❷

The Stellenbosch wine route was launched in April 1971 by the vintners of three prominent estates: Spier, Simonsig and Delheim. Today, the route comprises a great number of estates and co-operatives. Tasting, generally for a small fee, and cellar tours are offered throughout the week at most of the vineyards. A few of them can be visited by appointment only and many are closed on Sundays, so phoning ahead is advisable.

Delheim ⑦
Particularly atmospheric is Delheim's wine cellar with its brick arches, wooden benches and mellow light.
Tel *(021) 888-4600.*

Saxenburg ①
Established as a farm in 1693, Saxenburg was turned into a wine estate some 20 years ago. It has since become a beacon of quality, winning many accolades for its wines.
Tel *(021) 903-6113.*

Morgenhof ⑥
Established in 1692, this historic farm is owned by the Huchon-Cointreau family of Cognac, in France.
Tel *(021) 889-5510.*

Thelema ⑤
A family-run estate, Thelema is renowned for producing quality wines.
Tel *(021) 885-1924.*

Neethlingshof ②
The Lord Neethling restaurant in the old manor house serves Thai, Indonesian and Vietnamese cuisine.
Tel *(021) 883-8988.*

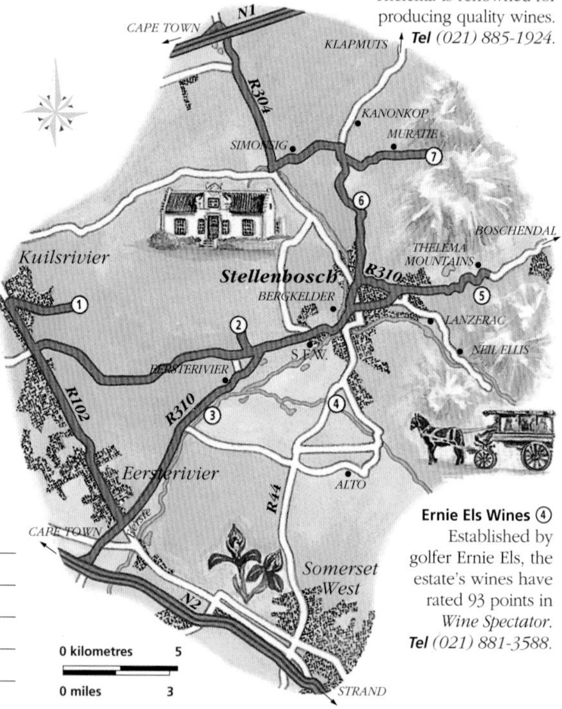

KEY

- Motorway
- Tour route
- Other roads
- Viewpoint

0 kilometres 5

0 miles 3

Ernie Els Wines ④
Established by golfer Ernie Els, the estate's wines have rated 93 points in *Wine Spectator.*
Tel *(021) 881-3588.*

Spier Estate ③
This complex consists of the manor house, a riverside pub, farm stall, three restaurants, wine centre, a dam and an open-air amphitheatre.

TIPS FOR DRIVERS

Tour length: *Due to the great number of wine estates, most visitors tour three or four cellars, stopping for lunch at one of the superb estate restaurants.*
Getting there: *Visitors need a car, unless they join one of the coach tours* (see p409).

Spier Wine Estate ❸

Road map B5. Stellenbosch. N2, then R310. ***Tel*** *(021) 809-1100.* *Spier. Vintage Train from Cape Town. Phone estate for schedules.* *tastings: 10am–4pm daily.* **www**.spier.co.za

Bounded by the Eerste River, this extensive complex is the result of major renovations undertaken since 1993 after businessman Dick Enthoven purchased the estate from the Joubert family.

The Spier development also includes an experimental farm that was previously owned by the University of Stellenbosch. Future plans are to extend the present vineyards with mainly red grape varietals – merlot, cabernet, shiraz and pinotage – to be planted by 2002. Spier has three excellent restaurants; the Jonkershuis offers a superb Indonesian and Cape Malay buffet.

Very popular with visitors are picnics on the rolling lawns surrounding the lake, after having stocked up on the mouthwatering delicacies available at Spier's farm stall.

In summer, the 1,075-seat open-air amphitheatre stages live entertainment ranging from opera, jazz and classical music to ballet and stand-up comedy.

Spier operates a luxury train, the Spier Vintage Train, which departs from its own private station close to the main Cape Town Station and delivers guests directly to the estate.

The vineyards surrounding the Tokara estate

Tokara ❹

Road map B5. Stellenbosch. Off R310, on Helshoogte Pass. ***Tel*** *(021) 808-5900.* *9am–5pm Mon–Fri, 10am–3pm Sat & Sun.*

Merchant banker GT Ferreira swapped his Sandton office for the fresh Simonsberg air in the early 1990s. Investment and development at this estate have been on a scale seldom seen in South Africa.

Located up on the Helshoogte Pass, Tokara offers great views, art exhibitions, fine food, olive oil and, above all, excellent wines. The first bottling, in 2000, was under the Zondernaam ("without name") label: it was an immediate success, winning a string of medals.

With industry stalwarts such as cellar master Gyles Webb (from neighbouring Thelema) and winemaker Miles Mossop at the helm, the estate is destined to continue going from strength to strength.

Vergelegen ❺

Road map B5. Somerset West. Lourensford Rd from R44. ***Tel*** *(021) 847-1334.* *9:30am–4:30pm daily.* *Good Fri, 1 May, 25 Dec.* *10:30am, 11:30am, 3pm.*

Choice white wine of the area

The vines and the five old camphor trees in front of the manor house were planted in 1700, when the farm belonged to Willem Adriaan van der Stel. Today, Vergelegen is the property of the Anglo American Group. The estate boasts a unique cellar, built into the slopes of Helderberg Mountain. The ripe grapes are fed into underground destalking, crushing and steel maturation tanks from above the ground, thus maximizing the effect of gravity and minimizing bruising. This results in a special brand of velvet-smooth wines.

The estate also has a wine museum and serves light lunches in the charming Lady Phillips Tea Garden (Lady Florence Phillips lived here from 1917 to 1940). The extensive renovations undertaken by the Phillips couple revealed the foundations of an octagonal garden, built by Willem van der Stel, which has now been restored.

Visitors enjoying an outdoor meal at the Spier estate

For hotels and restaurants in this region see pp332–4 and pp363–4

Boschendal Manor House ❻

Boschendal picnic basket

In 1685, Simon van der Stel granted the land on which the manor house stands to the French Huguenot Jean le Long. Originally named "Bossendaal" (which literally means "forest and valley"), the property was transferred in 1715, together with adjacent fertile farmland, to another Huguenot settler, Abraham de Villiers. It remained in the wine-farming De Villiers family for 100 years. Jan de Villiers built the wine cellar and coach house in 1796. His youngest son, Paul, was responsible for Boschendal Manor House in its present H-shaped form, which he built in 1812. Today, this historic estate belongs to DGB, a consortium of local business people who bought Boschendal from Anglo-American in 2003.

The Back Entrance
Visitors to Boschendal enter the elegant Manor House via the gabled back door.

Crafted Room Dividers
Screens divided the front and back rooms in elegant Cape Dutch homes. Boschendal's original teak-and-yellowwood screen is decorated with geometric designs in dark ebony.

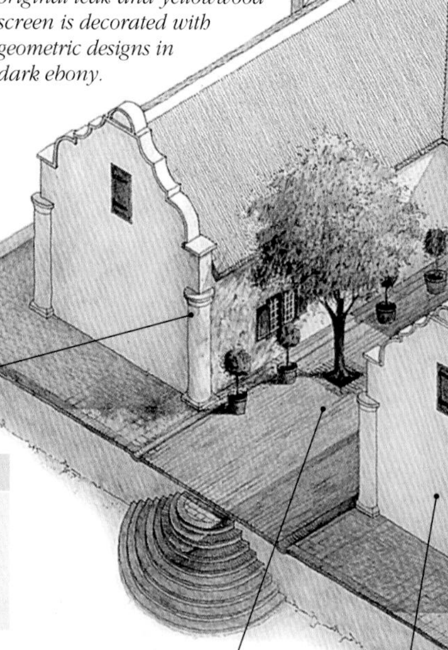

Rounded pilasters supported the end gables. The front and back pilasters have a more classic design.

Brick-paved courtyard

STAR FEATURES

- ★ Master Bedroom
- ★ Kitchen
- ★ Sitting Room

★ Master Bedroom
This antique stinkwood four-poster bed was crafted in 1810 by local artisans. It is decorated with a hand-crocheted lace hanging and a light, embroidered cotton bedspread, both of which date from around 1820.

For hotels and restaurants in this region see pp332–4 and pp363–4

VISITORS' CHECKLIST

Road map B5. On R45 from Stellenbosch. ***Tel*** *(021) 870–4272.* *9:30am–5pm daily.*
www.boschendal.com

★ Kitchen
The original clay floor was washed with a mixture of water and cow dung to keep it cool and vermin-free. Walls were painted dark brown or red to hide the dirt.

Long-Case Clock
This Dutch clock, made in 1748, shows the date, day of the week, month, zodiac sign, moon phases and the tide in Amsterdam.

The sash windows are all mounted by similarly curved mouldings that reflect the shape of the gables.

★ Sitting-Room
A gabled armoire, crafted in oak with a walnut veneer, contains a collection of Ming Dynasty porcelain (1573–1620) created for the Chinese export market.

The reception room has an original section of the 1812 wall frieze.

The drop-fanlight had to be raised to allow visitors to enter.

The Gift and Wine Shop
Boschendal wines, as well as preserves, souvenirs and gifts are sold at this shop.

FRIEZES

Painted wall decoration using oil-based pigments is a craft believed to derive from Europe. Pilasters and swags would feature in reception and dining rooms, entwined roses in drawing rooms and, in less important rooms, a dado of a single colour on a plain background would suffice. The original 1812 wall frieze (in the reception rooms) of black acorns and green leaves was discovered during restoration in 1975.

Franschhoek ❼

Farms in this beautiful valley encircled by the Franschhoek and Groot Drakenstein mountains were granted to several French Huguenot families *(see p49)* by the Dutch East India Company (VOC) in 1694. The new settlers brought with them considerable skill as farmers, crafters and viticulturalists, leaving a marked influence on the area, which the Dutch named *De Fransche Hoek* (French Corner).

Victory statue

A collection of period furniture in the Franschhoek Huguenot Museum

Exploring Franschhoek

Upon arrival, the town's French heritage is immediately evident in lilting names like Haute Cabrière, La Provence and L'Ormarins. The main attraction, besides an exquisite setting, is its gourmet cuisine, accompanied by the area's excellent wines. Around 30 restaurants *(see p363)* offer superb Malay, country and Provençale dishes.

Franschhoek's wine route was established in 1980 by Michael Trull, a former Johannesburg advertising executive. He formed the Vignerons de Franschhoek, with five founder cellars; today there are 20 estates.

A unique experience is a visit to **Cabrière Estate**. After an interesting cellar tour, host Achim von Arnim cleanly shears the neck off a bottle of his Pierre Jourdan sparkling wine with a sabre, an old technique known as *sabrage*, before serving the wine.

Visible at the top end of the main street is the **Huguenot Monument**, unveiled in 1948 to commemorate the arrival of the French settlers. Among the lawns and fragrant rose beds, a wide semi-circular colonnade forms an amphitheatre for three tall arches. They are representative of the Holy Trinity and rise behind the figure of a woman who stands on a globe with her feet on France. On a tall spire that surmounts the central arch is the "Sun of Righteousness".

VISITORS' CHECKLIST

Road map B5. N1, exit 47, R45. *8,000.* *Cape Town 79 km (49 miles) E.* *Huguenot St, (021) 876-3603.* *9am–5pm daily.* *Bastille Day (14 Jul).*

Cabrière Estate

Tel *(021) 876-2630.* *9am–5pm Mon–Fri, 11am–1pm Sat. Wine tasting: 11am, 3pm Mon–Fri & 11am Sat.* *for groups (by advance booking only).*

Huguenot Memorial Museum

Lambrecht St. ***Tel*** *(021) 876-2532.* *9am–5pm Mon–Sat, 2–5pm Sun.* *Good Fri, 25 Dec.*

This museum was inaugurated in 1967 and functions primarily as a research facility covering the history and genealogy of the Cape's Huguenot families and their descendants. Among the exhibits are 18th-century furniture, Huguenot graphics, title deeds, and other early documents and letters. Of special note is a copy of the Edict of Nantes (1598), which permitted freedom of worship to Protestants in France.

There is also a fine collection of old Bibles, one of which was printed in 1636.

The Huguenot Monument in Franschhoek was built in 1943

Franschhoek's French Heritage

Franschhoek is a charming little country town with a distinctly French character. Wine-making traditions introduced by the early French Huguenot settlers are still pursued by viticulturalists with surnames like Malherbe, Joubert and du Toit. Restaurants called Le Quartier Français and La Petite Ferme offer Provençale cuisine in light-filled, airy interiors, while Chez Michel flies the French flag and serves delicacies like escargots, and Camembert marinated in Calvados brandy. Architecturally, the influence of French Classicism is evident in the graceful lines of the historic buildings. A good example is the Huguenot Memorial Museum, which was based on a design by the 18th-century French architect Louis Michel Thibault.

The emblem of Cabrière Estate

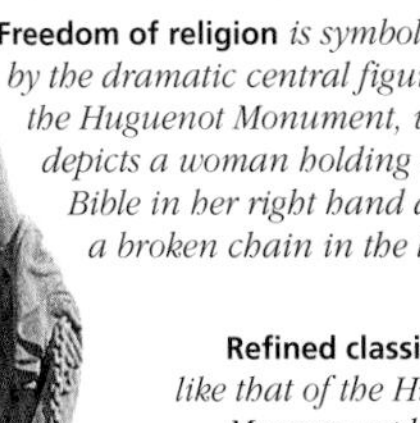

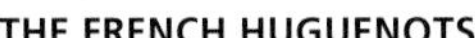

Freedom of religion *is symbolized by the dramatic central figure at the Huguenot Monument, which depicts a woman holding a Bible in her right hand and a broken chain in the left.*

Refined classic gables *like that of the Huguenot Museum replaced the Baroque exuberance of earlier gables.*

THE FRENCH HUGUENOTS

After King Louis XIV of France revoked the Edict of Nantes in 1685, countless French Huguenots were forced to flee to Protestant countries. The Dutch East India Company's offer of a new life at the Cape of Good Hope was eagerly accepted by some 270 individuals.

Powdered wig

The tricorn was worn by gentlemen.

Mother-of-pearl buttons on garments were very fashionable.

Many Khoina were employed as slaves.

Hoop skirts were reinforced by stiff petticoats made from whalebone.

Restaurants *in Franschhoek exude typical French joie* de vivre *and ambience.*

Rocco Catoggio *(1790–1858), depicted here with his grandson Rocco Cartozia de Villiers, married into a prominent Huguenot family.*

Grape presses *like this one, which stands outside the Huguenot Museum, were used by the French settlers to produce the first wines of the region.*

The road to Worcester leads through the scenic Du Toit's Kloof Pass

Worcester ⑩

Road map B5. N1 from Cape Town via Du Toit's Kloof Pass. *94,000.* *Worcester Station.* *Worcester Information Center, (023) 348-2795.*

Worcester, named after the Marquis of Worcester, the brother of one-time Cape governor Lord Charles Somerset lies some 110 km (68 miles) east of Cape Town. It is the biggest centre in the Breede River Valley and the largest producer of table grapes in South Africa. Its wineries produce about one quarter of the country's wine. Several of the estates, such as Nuy and Graham Beck, are open to the public for tastings and sales.

The attraction of a trip to Worcester is the drive through the Du Toit's Kloof Pass, which climbs to a height of 823 m (2,700 ft). Construction of the Huguenot Tunnel in 1988 shortened the pass by 11 km (7 miles), but the route still affords scenic views of Paarl and the Berg River Valley.

At Church Square in the town, there is a Garden of Remembrance designed by Hugo Naude. The World War I Memorial is also here, along with a stone cairn erected at the time of the symbolic *Ossewa* (ox wagon) Trek of 1938 *(see p56)* that was undertaken to commemorate the historic Great Trek *(see pp52–3)*.

Hugo Naude House, located two blocks further south of Church Square, was the artist's home until his death in 1941. Today, it is an art gallery that hosts various revolving exhibitions featuring works by various contemporary South African artists. The exhibitions are changed monthly.

Northeast of Church Square, in a building known as Beck House, is the **Worcester Museum**, furnished like a late-19th-century home.

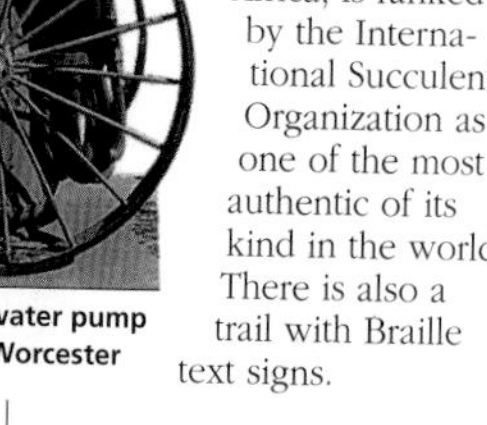
Old water pump in Worcester

Worcester Museum
Cnr Church and Baring sts.
Tel *(023) 342-2225.*
9am–4:30pm Mon–Sat.
public hols.

Hugo Naude House
Russell St. ***Tel*** *(023) 342-5802.*
8:30am–4:30pm Mon–Fri, 9:30am–noon Sat.
pub hols.

Environs: The **Karoo National Botanical Garden**, some 3 km (2 miles) north of Worcester, contains plants that thrive in a semi-desert environment.

Jewel-bright mesembryanthemums are lovely in spring, while the unusual year-round species include the prehistoric welwitschias, and the *halfmens* (half-human) and quiver trees. One section features plants grouped together according to regional and climatic zones. The succulent plant collection, the largest in Africa, is ranked by the International Succulent Organization as one of the most authentic of its kind in the world. There is also a trail with Braille text signs.

Karoo National Botanical Garden
Roux Rd, Worcester. ***Tel*** *(023) 347-0785.* *8am–7pm daily.*
(Aug–Oct only)

Kleinplasie Open-Air Museum ⑪

See pp150–51.

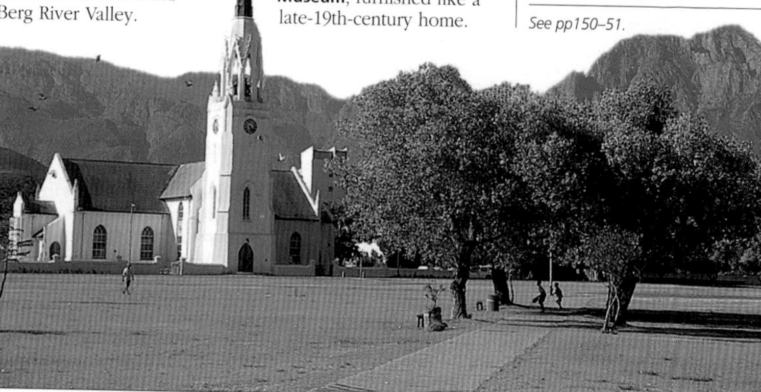
The Dutch Reformed Church in Worcester

Robertson's Dutch Reformed Church

Robertson ⓬

Road Map B5. R60 from Worcester or Swellendam. *21,000.* *Cnr Reitz and Voortrekker sts, (023) 626-4437.* **www**.robertsonr62.com

Robertson lies in the Breede River Valley where sunny slopes create perfect conditions for vineyards and orchards. In addition to wine and table grapes, dried fruit is a major industry. The Robertson Wine Route comprises 24 private and co-operative cellars, many of which, like van Loveren, are acclaimed for their choice Chardonnays.

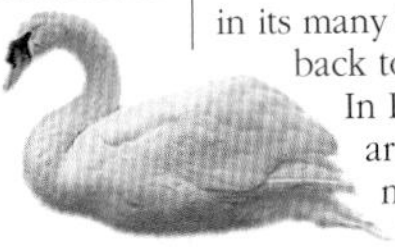

Swan, Montagu Inn

Montagu ⓭

Road Map B5. N15 fm Robertson. *11,000.* *Bath St, (023) 614-2471.*

The charm of Montagu lies in its many houses dating back to the early 1850s. In Long Street alone are 14 national monuments. The best known feature is the thermal springs (at a constant 43°C, 109°F), situated 2 km (1 mile) from town. The hotel and timeshare resort nearby offer a comfortable stay.

The scenery of the northern edge of the Langeberg range has led to the establishment of trails for hikers, mountain bikers and 4WD enthusiasts.

The route to Montagu from Robertson passes through a 16-m (52-ft) long tunnel, above which stands the ruined Sidney Fort built by the British during the South African War.

Avalon hot springs in Montagu

The start of the hiking trail from Greyton

BOESMANSKLOOF TRAVERSE ⓮

This popular five-hour walking trail follows a gap through the Riviersonderend mountains. It runs between the rustic hamlets of Greyton and McGregor and can be tackled from either village. Hikers will need to be reasonably fit as the trail ascends and descends the mountainside. The views here are impressive, and the stream running along the scenic McGregor section of the trail ensures an abundant water supply. The Oakes Falls, 9 km (6 miles) from Greyton, a series of waterfalls and pools, are ideal for swimming. There are no overnight huts.

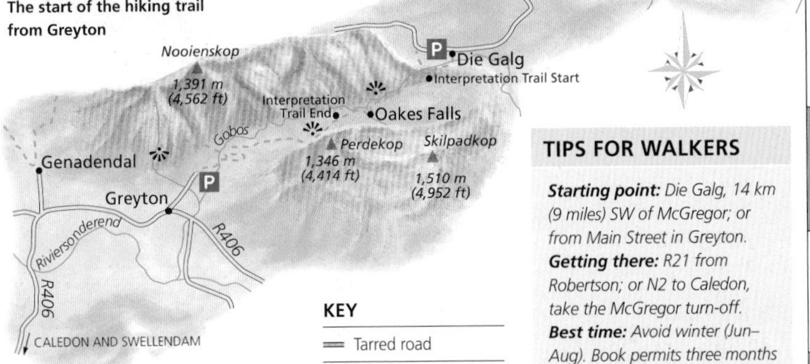

ROBERTSON
McGregor
Takkap
BONNIEVALE
Hoeks
Die Galg
Interpretation Trail Start
Nooienskop
1,391 m (4,562 ft)
Interpretation Trail End
Oakes Falls
Gobos
Perdekop
1,346 m (4,414 ft)
Skilpadkop
1,510 m (4,952 ft)
Genadendal
Greyton
Riviersonderend
R406
CALEDON AND SWELLENDAM

KEY
Tarred road
Trail
Viewpoint

0 kilometres 4
0 miles 2

TIPS FOR WALKERS

Starting point: *Die Galg, 14 km (9 miles) SW of McGregor; or from Main Street in Greyton.*
Getting there: *R21 from Robertson; or N2 to Caledon, take the McGregor turn-off.*
Best time: *Avoid winter (Jun–Aug). Book permits three months ahead from Vrolijkheid Nature Reserve.* ***Tel*** *(023) 625-1671.*

Kleinplasie Open-Air Museum ⓫

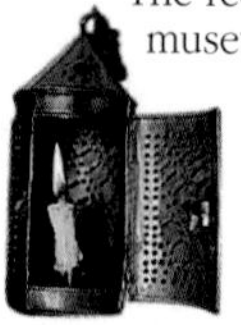

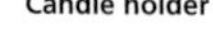

Candle holder

The recreated buildings of this living "little farm" museum, which opened in 1981, portray the lifestyle of the early Cape pioneer farmer. Each one houses a particular home industry activity that was practised between 1690 and 1900. Here, visitors can watch cows being milked, wholewheat bread and traditional *melktert* (milk tart) being baked in an outdoor oven and the making of tallow candles and soap. At times the museum hosts seasonal activities such as wheat threshing and winnowing, grape treading and the distilling of *witblits* (a potent homemade brandy).

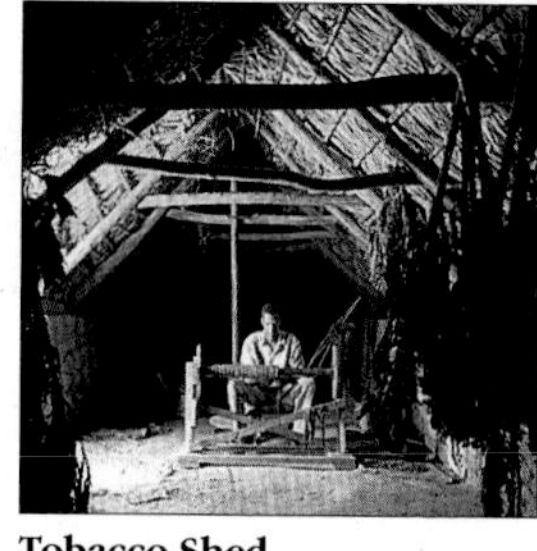

Tobacco Shed
Dried tobacco leaves are twisted together in this 19th-century, windowless farm shed.

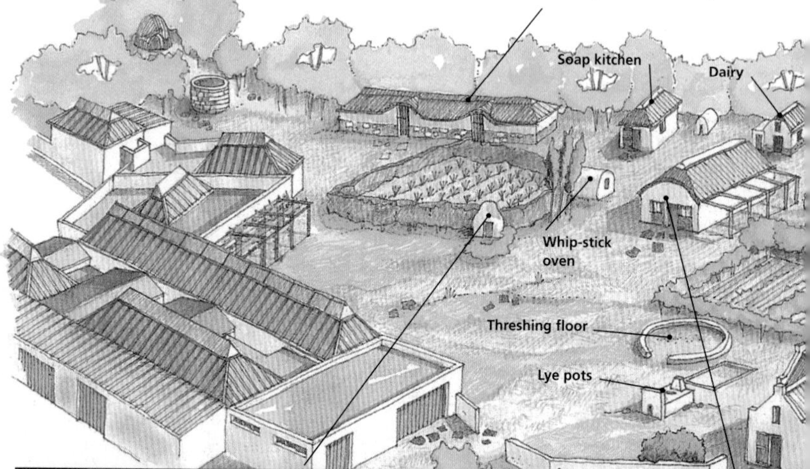

Soap kitchen
Dairy
Whip-stick oven
Threshing floor
Lye pots

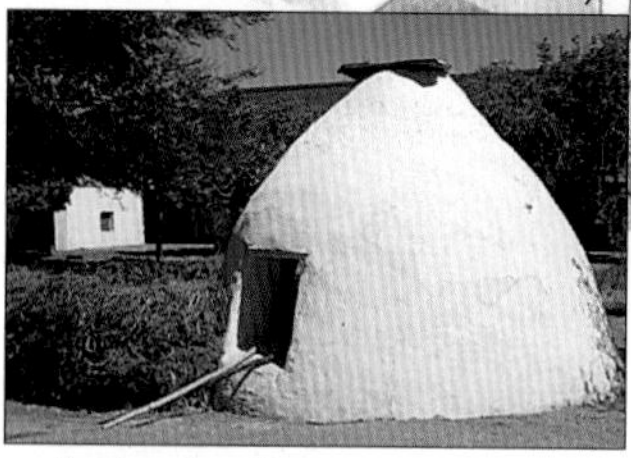

★ Shepherd's Hut
Shepherds who tended distant flocks lived in temporary shelters like this one. In the treeless Karoo, domed stone roofs were used instead of wooden beams and trusses.

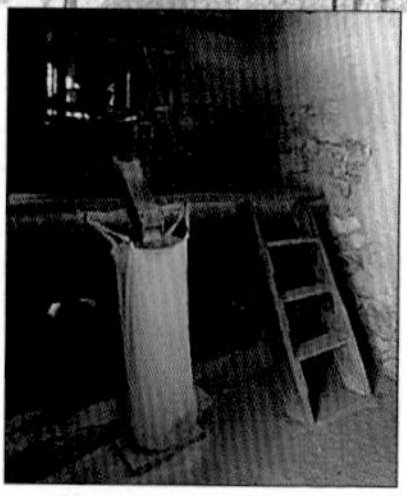

The Horse-Mill
Back in 1850, most farmers relied on horse-drawn mills to grind flour, a slow, laborious process.

STAR FEATURES

- ★ Shepherd's Hut
- ★ The Blacksmith
- ★ Labourer's Cottage

NECTAR
OXO cubes

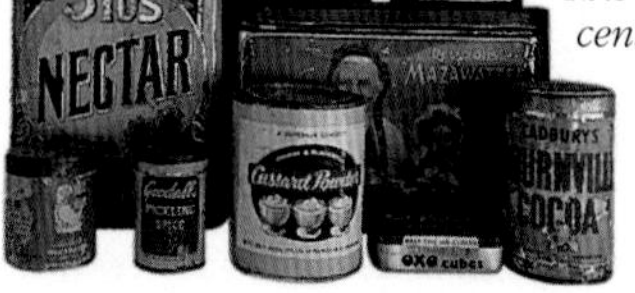

Canisters
This collection of 19th-century storage tins is displayed in the museum restaurant. Occasionally, these tins are found in "junk" stores today.

For hotels and restaurants in this region see pp332–4 and pp363–4

★ The Blacksmith
The smithy door, as well as the bellows used by the blacksmith, date from 1820. The rest of the building has walls cast in clay and gables built in raw brick. The blacksmith can be seen daily, forging nails, hinges, forks and tripods.

VISITORS' CHECKLIST

Road Map B5. N1, signposted fm Worcester. ***Tel*** *(023) 342-2225.* *9am–4:30pm Mon–Sat.* *Good Friday, 25 Dec.* www.worcester.org.za/kleinplasie

★ Labourer's Cottage
Simply furnished and thatched with rye straw, one-roomed dwellings like this one date from the mid-19th century. They housed farm labourers and their families.

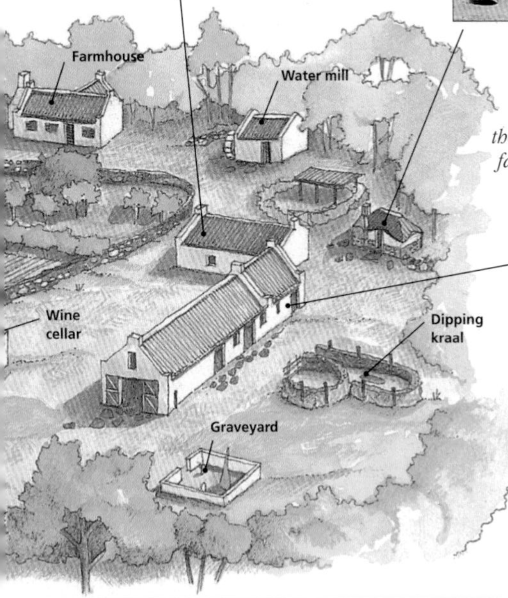

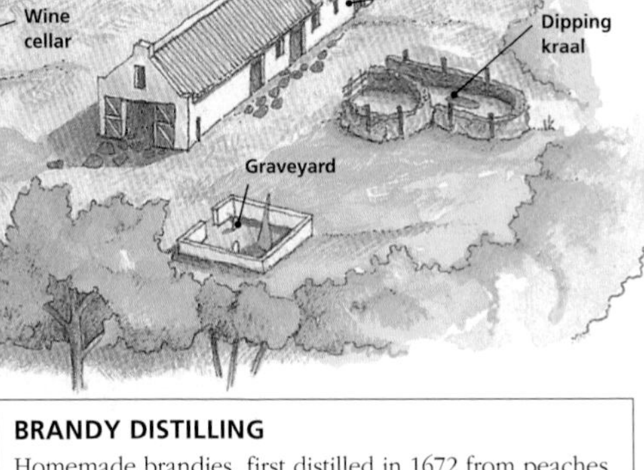

Harness Room
This is a replica of an 1816 coach house, stable and harness room. The tanning of skins took place here, too.

Donkey Power
To draw water, a donkey rotated the bucket pump. Small buckets on a looped chain scooped water from the well and emptied it into irrigation furrows.

BRANDY DISTILLING

Homemade brandies, first distilled in 1672 from peaches and apricots, became known as *witblits* (white lightning). To create this potent liquor, crushed fruit is fermented in large vats for ten days. The pulp is then poured into a brandy still and heated so that the alcohol evaporates. The resulting vapour is conducted from the dome of the still into a water-cooled condensation spiral, which causes the alcohol to become liquid again. The first extraction, called the "heads", is discarded. Only the second, "the heart", is bottled; the rest is used as liniment.

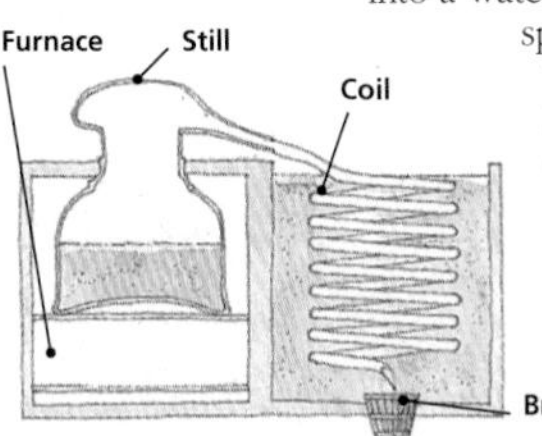

Exploring the Western Coastal Terrace

Although first appearances seem to indicate that the West Coast is a hot, barren wilderness, it is a magnet to visitors during the spring months when flowering daisies and gazanias paint the landscape with bold colour splashes. The region is also known for its spectacular walking and hiking trails in the Cedarberg mountains, which are famous for their contorted rock formations and breathtaking views. Along the coastline, the cold waters of the Atlantic yield a vast array of delicious seafood, from rock lobster and black mussels to fresh linefish, which can be sampled at a number of *skerms* (open-air restaurants) that have been established on the beaches.

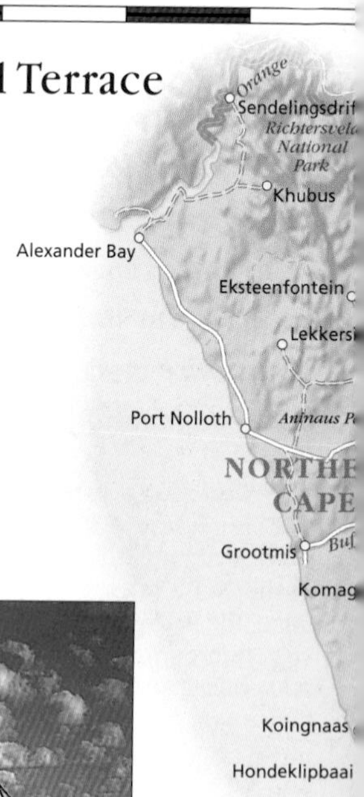

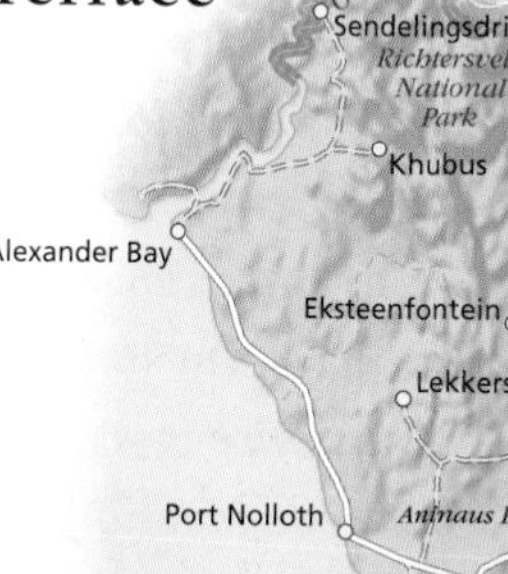

Fishing trawlers at anchor in Lambert's Bay harbour

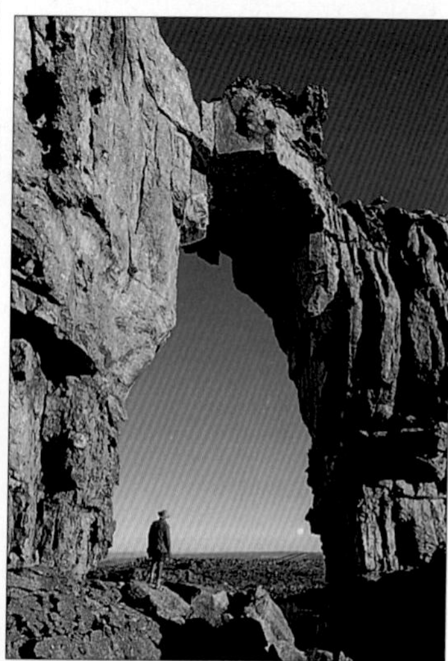

The Wolfberg Arch in the Cedarberg

SIGHTS AT A GLANCE

Cedarberg 9
Citrusdal 7
Clanwilliam 8
Darling 4
Lambert's Bay 3
Malmesbury 5
Tulbagh 6
West Coast 1
West Coast National Park pp158–9 2

Driving Tour

Namaqualand Tour 10

GETTING AROUND

A car is essential for touring this region as no regular public transport service exists. Private coach companies do operate along this section of coast however. During the flower season, a large number of organized coach tours are available from operators based in Cape Town. The N7, a major national route, runs straight up the West Coast from Cape Town to the Namibian border, with main roads leading off to the coast and interior. Between Cape Town and St Helena Bay, the R27 offers a more scenic route with intermittent views of the coastline. The closest international airport is in Cape Town.

For additional map symbols *see back flap*

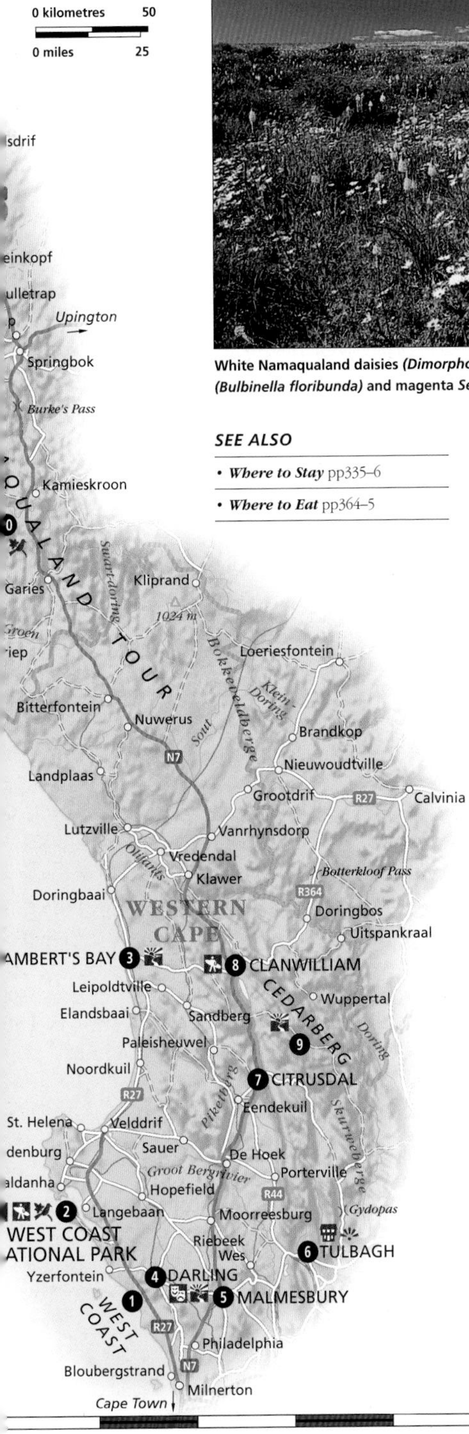

0 kilometres 50
0 miles 25

White Namaqualand daisies *(Dimorphotheia pluvialis)*, tall yellow bulbinellas *(Bulbinella floribunda)* and magenta *Senecio* open their petals to the sun

SEE ALSO

- ***Where to Stay*** pp335–6
- ***Where to Eat*** pp364–5

KEY

- Major road
- Minor road
- Untarred road
- Scenic route
- Main railway
- Minor railway
- International border
- Provincial border
- Summit
- Pass

Upington
Springbok
Burke's Pass
Kamieskroon
Kliprand
1024 m
Garies
Loeriesfontein
Bitterfontein
Nuwerus
Brandkop
Nieuwoudtville
Landplaas
Grootdrif
Calvinia
Lutzville
Vanrhynsdorp
Vredendal
Klawer
Botterkloof Pass
Doringbaai
WESTERN CAPE
Doringbos
Uitspankraal
AMBERT'S BAY 3
8 CLANWILLIAM
CEDARBERG
Leipoldtville
Wuppertal
Elandsbaai
Sandberg
Paleisheuwel
9
Noordkuil
7 CITRUSDAL
Eendekuil
St. Helena
Velddrif
Sauer
De Hoek
Porterville
Hopefield
Langebaan
Moorreesburg
Gydopas
2 WEST COAST
ATIONAL PARK
Riebeek Wes
6 TULBAGH
Yzerfontein
4 DARLING
1 WEST COAST
5 MALMESBURY
Philadelphia
Bloubergstrand
Milnerton
Cape Town

Lookout, West Coast National Park

Fishermen drag their boat to the water at Paternoster

The West Coast ❶

Road map A4, A5.

From Cape Town, the R27 leads up the West Coast to the Olifants River, linking the coastal towns. Between Milnerton, Bloubergstrand and Melkbosstrand, Marine Drive (M14), which becomes Otto Du Plessis Drive, is a scenic road with wonderful views of the dunes and sea. Travelling north, the village of Bloubergstrand, today a sought-after residential area, is famous for its unsurpassed views of Table Mountain seen across the 16-km (10-mile) wide expanse of Table Bay, and lies at the foot of the Blouberg (blue mountain). The broad beaches and bays of Bloubergstrand are popular with watersports enthusiasts and families, although south-easterly summer gales can create windy conditions.

Heading north along the R27, silver domes come into view. They belong to **Koeberg Nuclear Power Station**, the only nuclear facility in Africa, which offers guided tours.

A left turn from the R27 onto the R315 leads to Yzerfontein, whose claim to fame is its prolific crayfish (rock lobster) reserves. The sweet-tasting flesh of this shellfish is a sought-after local delicacy and during the crayfishing season (Dec–Apr), the local campsite attracts countless divers and their families. Permits, allowing daily catches of four crayfish per person, are obtainable at any post office.

Continuing north on the R27, past the industrial fishing hub and harbour of Saldanha, is Vredenburg. From here, a 16-km (10-mile) drive leads to Paternoster, a typical little wind-blown fishing village with whitewashed cottages. Legend recounts that the Portuguese sailors shipwrecked here recited the Paternoster (Our Father) to give thanks for their survival.

Around a rocky headland, the village of **St Helena** perches at the edge of a sheltered bay. Just before the village a signposted turnoff leads to the monument commemorating Portuguese navigator Vasco da Gama's landing on these shores on St Helena's Day, 7 November, in 1497.

The fishing industry here benefits from the cold, north-flowing Benguela Current. It ensures a ready supply of rich nutrients that sustain the vast populations of anchovies and other shoals of pelagic fish.

Koeberg Nuclear Power Station
Tel *(021) 550-4089.* ◯ *7:30am–4:30pm Mon–Fri.* ● *public hols.* *ring to book.*

OPEN-AIR SEAFOOD FEASTS

Along the West Coast, restaurateurs have established open-air eating places known as *skerms* (Afrikaans for "shelters") with names like Die Strandloper *(see p365)*, in Langebaan, and Die Muisbosskerm *(see p364)*, in Lambert's Bay. Reed roofs provide shade and mussel shells are used as utensils, but the major appeal is the fresh seafood on offer: smoked angelfish, *snoek* (a large gamefish that tastes best when barbecued), spicy mussel stews, thin slices of *perlemoen* (abalone), and calamari.

Lunch at Die Strandloper

West Coast National Park ❷

See pp158–9.

A seal pup relaxes on the rocks of Bird Island, Lambert's Bay

Lambert's Bay ❸

Road map A4. *7,000.* *Church St, Lambert's Bay (027) 432-1000. Lambert's Bay Charter Office (083) 726-2207.* ◯ *8am daily (groups only).*

This little fishing town, a two-hour drive north of St Helena on a gravel road, was named after Rear-Admiral Sir Robert Lambert. This senior Royal Navy officer who was stationed in Durban, monitored the marine survey of this section of coastline.

For visitors, the main attraction is **Bird Island**, which lies about 100 m (328 ft) offshore and is accessible via a breakwater-cum-harbour wall.

The island is a breeding ground for thousands of jackass penguins, Cape cormorants and the striking Cape gannet with its painted face. A viewing tower allows visitors to remain unobtrusive while observing the birds' behaviour.

The Lambert's Bay Charter Office offers one-hour trips on a boat called *Wolf-T*, which leaves at 8am every day. From August to October, groups of visitors are taken out to spot southern right whales, while penguins, Cape fur seals and Heaviside's dolphins, endemic to the West Coast, can be seen throughout the year. Guided excursions through the striated dunes in the southernmost reaches of the Namib desert are unfortunately no longer available.

Darling ❹

Road map B5. R307. 6,000. *Cnr Pastorie & Hill sts, (022) 492-3361.*

Darling is surrounded by a farming region of wheatfields, vineyards, sheep and dairy cattle, but the small town is best known for its annual springflower show *(see p38)*. The first show was held in 1917, and the tradition has been maintained ever since.

Darling also lays claim to satirist Pieter-Dirk Uys *(see p111)*, who gained fame for the portrayal of his female alter ego, Evita Bezuidenhout, fictitious ambassadress of the equally fictitious homeland called Baphetikosweti. **Evita se Perron** (Evita's platform) is situated on a defunct railway platform and draws crowds to hear the hilarious, razor-sharp analyses of local politics.

A National Monument on historical Church Street in Tulbagh

Evita se Perron
Tel *(022) 492-2831.*

Malmesbury ❺

Road map B5. *21,000.*
Bokomo Rd.
De Bron Centre, (022) 487-1133.

Malmesbury, the heart of South Africa's wheatland, lies in the *Swartland* (black country), a term that has, at times, been attributed to the region's soil, at others to its renosterbush, a local shrub that turns a dark hue in winter. This town is South Africa's major wheat distributor and site of one of its largest flour mills. The surrounding wheatfields undergo constant metamorphosis, and the velvety shoots rippling in the breeze or cropped furrows with bales piled high are a lovely sight.

Tulbagh ❻

Road map B5. R44. *18,000.*
Station Rd. *along Church St.*
4 Church St, (023) 230-1348.

In 1700, Governor Willem Adriaan van der Stel initiated a new settlement in the Breede River Valley, naming it Tulbagh after his predecessor.

Encircled by the Witzenberg and Winterhoek mountains, the town made headlines in 1969 when it was hit by an earthquake measuring 6.3 on the Richter scale. Eight people died and many historic buildings were badly damaged. The disaster resulted in a five-year restoration project undertaken along Church Street, lined with no less than 32 18th- and 19th-century Victorian and Cape Dutch homes. The oldest building, Oude Kerk (old church) Volksmuseum, dates back to 1743 and contains the original pulpit, pews and Bible. De Oude Herberg, Tulbagh's first boarding house (1885), is now a guest house and art gallery.

Cape gannets populate Bird Island in their thousands

West Coast National Park ❷

Watch out – tortoises on the road

The West Coast National Park encompasses Langebaan Lagoon, the islands Schaapen, Jutten, Marcus and Malgas, and the Postberg Nature Reserve, which is opened to the public each spring (Aug–Sep) when it is carpeted with colourful wildflowers like daisies and gazanias. The park is one of South Africa's most important wetlands, harbouring some 250 000 waterbirds including plovers, herons, ibis, and black oystercatchers. Antelope species such as eland, kudu and zebra can also be seen. Accommodation in the park consists of a guesthouse, cottages and a houseboat on the lagoon.

Cape Cormorants
Abundant on the coast, they feed on pelagic shoaling fish, but have been affected by overfishing.

SEABIRDS

Langebaan Lagoon, 15 km (9 miles) long, at an average depth of 1 m (3 ft), offers a sheltered haven for a great number of seabirds, including waders, gulls, flamingos, and pelicans. Resident and migrant species take advantage of the Atlantic's nutrient-rich water to rear their chicks.

The curlew sandpiper's curved bill enables it to probe for small crustaceans.

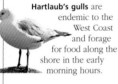

Hartlaub's gulls are endemic to the West Coast and forage for food along the shore in the early morning hours.

Lesser flamingos, distinguished from greater flamingos by their smaller size and red bill, often congregate in large flocks.

White Pelicans
Langebaan Lagoon is home to one of only a handful of white pelican breeding colonies in Southern Africa. The species feeds on fish, which it scoops up in the large pouch under its beak. Pelicans fly and feed in formation.

★ Geelbek Goldfields Environmental Centre
This educational centre in the park is a mine of fascinating information on the fauna, flora and ecology of the region. Birdwatchers can observe many different species from the nearby hide.

STAR FEATURE

★ Geelbek Goldfields Environmental Centre

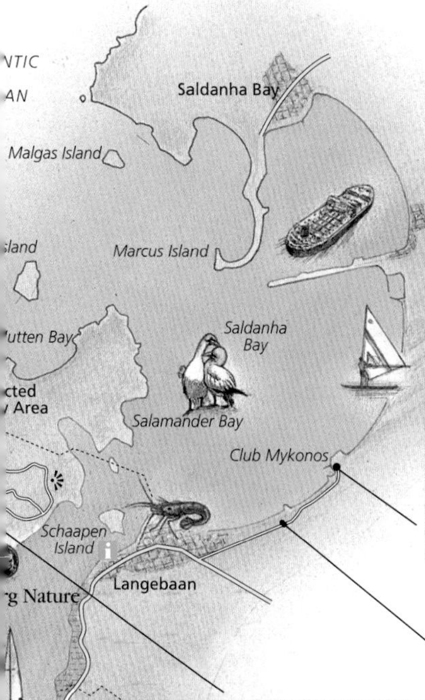

VISITORS' CHECKLIST

Road map A5. Yzerfontein and Langebaan. *Geelbek Goldfields Environmental Centre, (022) 772-2798/99. 7:30am–4pm daily. Accommodation: book through the Geelbek Goldfields Environmental Centre.*
Postberg Nature Reserve *7:30am–5pm Aug–Sep.*

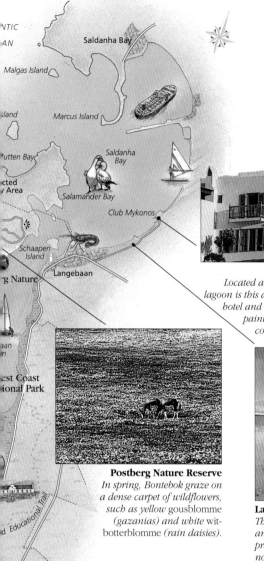

Club Mykonos
Located at the water's edge north of the lagoon is this attractive Mediterranean-style hotel and timeshare resort. The brightly painted cluster complex offers self-contained units with balconies.

Postberg Nature Reserve
In spring, Bontebok graze on a dense carpet of wildflowers, such as yellow gousblomme *(gazanias) and white* wit-botterblomme *(rain daisies).*

Langebaan Beach
This beach is very popular with anglers, who use mainly sand prawns to catch white stump-nose, kob, elf, and skates.

KEY

- Tarred road
- Untarred road
- Trail
- Information
- Viewpoint

Catamaran on the beach

WATERSPORTS AT LANGEBAAN

Ideal conditions have attracted the attention of international organizations: the 1995 Windsurfing World Cup was held at Langebaan Lagoon, and in 1998 it was nominated to host the prestigious Production-Board World Championships. In order to protect the natural environment without curtailing the activities of other interest groups, the lagoon has been zoned into three recreational areas, with the northern tip demarcated for all watersports enthusiasts and the central part of the lagoon out of bounds for motorboats.

Zinc-roofed houses along Church Street in Clanwilliam

Citrusdal ❼

Road map B4. *2,900.* *fm Cape Town station to Church St.* ***Tel*** *Voortrekker St, (022) 921-3210.*

Frost-free winters and the Olifants River Irrigation Scheme have made Citrusdal South Africa's third-largest citrus district. The first orchard was planted with seedlings from Van Riebeeck's garden at the foot of Table Mountain *(see pp78–9)*. One tree, after bearing fruit for some 250 years, is now a national monument.

The Goede Hoop Citrus Co-operative has initiated scenic mountain bike trails around Citrusdal, like the old Ceres and Piekenierskloof passes.

Clanwilliam ❽

Road map B4. *4,000.* *fm Cape Town station.* ***Tel*** *Main Rd, (027) 482-2024.*

Clanwilliam is the headquarters of the *rooibos* (red bush) tea industry. The shoots of the wild shrub are used to make a caffeine-free tea that is low in tannins and also considered to have medicinal properties *(see p354)*.

Clanwilliam Dam, encircled by the Cedarberg Mountains, stretches for 18 km (11 miles) and is popular with water-skiers. Wooden holiday cabins line the banks, and an attractive campsite has been established right at the water's edge.

Cedarberg ❾

Road map B4. *Ceres. Algeria Cape Nature Conservation turnoff fm N7.* *(027) 482-2812. Anyone wishing to hike or stay in the Cedarberg area will require a permit.*

From the north, the Cedarberg is reached via Pakhuis Pass and the Biedouw Valley, 50 km (31 miles) from Clanwilliam. Coming from the south, take the N7 from Citrusdal. The Cedarberg range is a surreal wilderness of sandstone peaks that have been eroded into jagged formations. It is part of the Cedarberg Wilderness Area which was proclaimed in 1973 and covers 710 sq km (274 sq miles). The attraction of the range is its recreational appeal – walks, hikes, camping and wonderful views. The southern part, in particular, is popular for its dramatic rock formations: the Maltese Cross, a 20-m (66-ft) high pillar, and the Wolfberg Arch with its sweeping views of the area. At the Wolfberg Cracks, the main fissure measures over 30 m (98 ft). The snow protea *(Protea cryophila)*, endemic to the upper reaches of the range, occurs on the Sneeuberg which, at 2,028 m (6,654 ft), is the highest peak.

Road marker at Kagga Kamma

The Clanwilliam cedar, after which the area was named, is a species that is protected in the Cedarberg Wilderness Area. At the southern end of the Cedarberg lies the **Kagga Kamma** reserve where some of the last Bushman families live. Tours allow you to interact with members of the clan and observe fire-making and beadcraft skills. Artifacts are for sale (a portion of the proceeds goes back to the community). Game drives are arranged and cottages and huts offer accommodation.

Kagga Kamma
Southern Cedarberg.
Tel *Tour reservations (021) 872-4343 (to be prebooked).* *daily.* *(meals included).*

Scenic view over Clanwilliam Dam to the Cedarberg mountains

For hotels and restaurants in this region see pp335–6 and pp364–5

Rock Formations of the Cedarberg

During the Palaeozoic pre-Karoo era several hundred million years ago, the formations that over time became the Cape Folded Mountains were under water. Of the sandstones, shales and quartzites of these Cape formations, Table Mountain sandstone was the most resilient. In the Karoo Period, tectonic forces produced the crumpled folds of the Cape mountains. Subsequent erosion wore away the soft rock, leaving the harder layer. The resulting formations can be seen today in the Cedarberg's twisted landscape. The original grey-coloured sandstone of the bizarre terrain has frequently been stained a rich red by iron oxides.

THE MALTESE CROSS

This unusual 20-m (66-ft) high rock formation, a day hike from Dwarsrivier Farm (Sanddrif), consists partly of Table Mountain sandstone. More resistant to erosion, it forms the upper portion of the cross.

Hiking
Paths made by woodcutters some 100 years ago now provide access for hikers.

Softer layers erode faster, causing a thinner base.

Cedarberg Cedar
Some 8,000 trees are planted annually to ensure the survival of this endemic species. The cedars were once popularly used as telephone poles.

The scree slope, composed of fallen debris from above.

Wolfberg Cracks
Lovely views greet hikers at the Wolfberg Cracks, a 75-minute walk from the Wolfberg Arch.

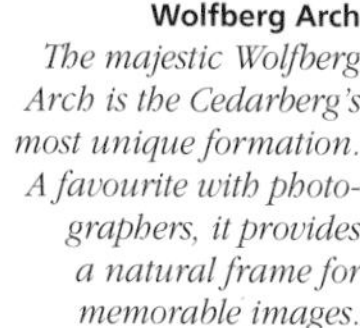

Wolfberg Arch
The majestic Wolfberg Arch is the Cedarberg's most unique formation. A favourite with photographers, it provides a natural frame for memorable images.

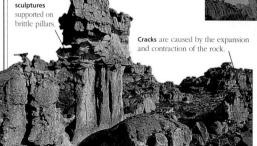

The Arch, 30 m (98 ft) high, overlooks a region known as the Tankwa Karoo.

Bizarre rock sculptures supported on brittle pillars.

Cracks are caused by the expansion and contraction of the rock.

Erosion
Over aeons, wind and water have carved the Cedarberg into a fairytale landscape. Pinnacles, arches and fissures resemble the strange castles of another world, while the rock outcrops seem alive with gargoyles and goblins.

Namaqualand Tour ⑩

Gazania krebsiana

Namaqualand, an area of about 48,000 sq km (18,500 sq miles), from the Orange River in the north to the mouth of the Olifants River in the south, is a region of sharp contrasts. In spring, this scrub-covered, arid land blazes with colour – from fuchsia pinks to neon yellows and oranges – as a myriad daisies and flowering succulents open their petals to the sun. The seeds of the drought-resistant plants lie dormant in the soil during the dry months, but if the first rains (usually around March and April) are good, they burst into bloom from August to October.

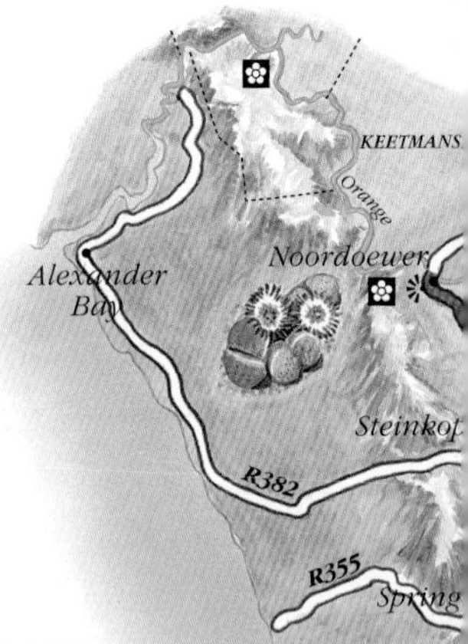

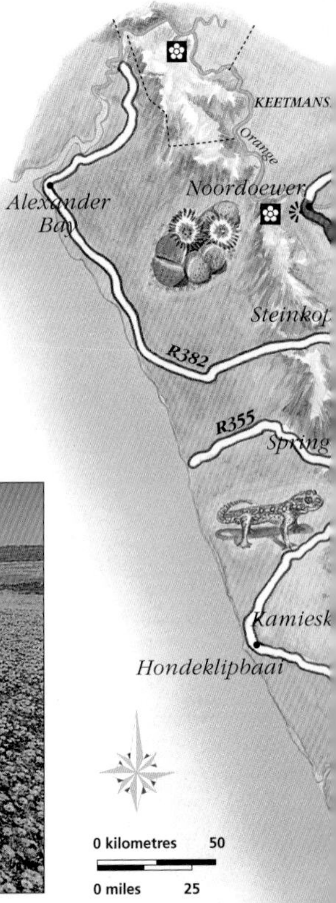

0 kilometres 50

0 miles 25

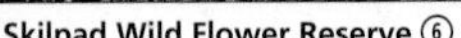

Skilpad Wild Flower Reserve ⑥
Lying 17 km (11 miles) west of Kamieskroon, the reserve was purchased by WWF-SA (World Wide Fund for Nature in South Africa) in 1993 to protect the area's plant life. The higher rainfall resulting from the reserve's proximity to the West Coast guarantees excellent displays. Bright orange daisies *(Ursinia sp)* and gazanias are at their most spectacular here.

Tienie Versveld Reserve ①
After attending the Darling wildflower and orchid shows, visitors can drive to this nearby reserve and view expanses of wildflowers in their natural habitat. Namaqualand's best displays vary from season to season, depending on the rainfall patterns.

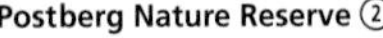

Postberg Nature Reserve ②
This is the most popular flower-viewing spot among locals, as it is an easy day-trip from Cape Town, and visitors are not often disappointed at its multicoloured bands of annuals stretching as far as the eye can see.

KEY

- Tour route
- Other roads
- Park boundary
- Viewpoint
- Wildflower viewing

Goegap Nature Reserve ⑦
Situated 15 km (9 miles) east of Springbok, the "capital" of Namaqualand, the Goegap Nature Reserve's flat plains and granite koppies support hundreds of succulents. Over the years, the reserve has recorded 580 plant species within its boundaries.

Nieuwoudtville Wildflower Reserve ⑤
This reserve contains the world's largest concentration of geophytes (plants with bulbs, corms or tubers). Of the 300 plant species, the more prominent ones are the irises and lily family.

Vanrhynsdorp ④
This town is situated in the stony *Knersvlakte* (a name that literally translates as "gnashing plains"). Spring ushers in dramatic displays of succulents such as *vygies*, and annuals like *botterblom* and *gousblom (Ursinia* sp).

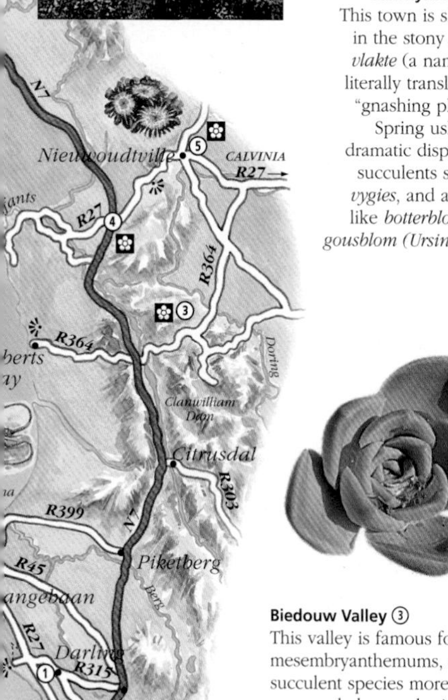

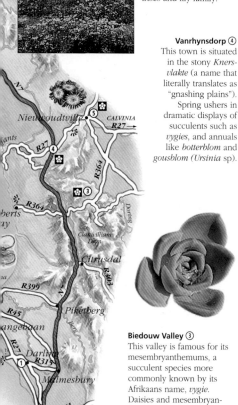

Biedouw Valley ③
This valley is famous for its mesembryanthemums, a succulent species more commonly known by its Afrikaans name, *vygie*. Daisies and mesembryanthemums form the major group of Namaqualand's 4,000 floral species.

TIPS FOR DRIVERS

Tour length: *Due to the extent of the area, trips can vary from one to three days. For details of coach tours, call Captour.* ***Tel*** *(021) 426-4260.*
When to go: *Flowers bloom Aug–Oct – call Namaqualand Information Bureau for the best viewing areas. Flowers only open on sunny days, and are best between 11am and 4pm; drive with the sun behind you and flowers facing you.*
Where to stay and eat: *Each town has its own hotel, as well as guesthouses and a campsite. Private homes may also offer accommodation.*
Namaqualand Information Bureau, (0277) 12-8000.

THE SOUTHERN CAPE

The Southern Cape's interior is characterized by its towering mountains, whose high-walled passes offer visitors a number of awe-inspiring scenic drives. The region's largest town, Oudtshoorn, upholds its reputation as ostrich farming capital, while on the coast, tourists are drawn to Hermanus every year to watch southern right whales from excellent vantage points along the coast.

The quaint seaside towns of the Southern Cape lie in a region known as the Overberg, which extends east of the Hottentots Holland mountains and is defined to the north by the Riviersonderend mountains and the Langeberg and Outeniqua ranges. Along the coast, the Overberg stretches to the mouth of the Breede River, just north of the De Hoop Nature Reserve. Sir Lowry's Pass, a circuitous road that winds high above Gordon's Bay and offers splendid views across the False Bay coastline, is the gateway to the Overberg.

Early European settlers were prevented from crossing this formidable mountain barrier until Sir Lowry's Pass was constructed by Major Charles Michell in 1828. Before this, the Overberg was populated by the nomadic Khoina *(see pp48–9)*, attracted by abundant mountain water and grazing for their herds. Elephant and other wildlife also roamed the area; in fact, the pass follows an ancient migratory trail, named *gantouw* (eland's path) by the indigenous peoples. As the settlers penetrated further into unexplored territory they faced another mountain barrier: north over the Langeberg and Outeniqua lay the Little Karoo, protected by the Swartberg mountains. It was in this territory that two of South Africa's greatest road builders, Andrew Geddes Bain and his son, Thomas Bain, made their fame. The spectacular Four Passes Tour *(see pp174–5)* is a worthwhile excursion; visitors can detour to the exquisite dripstone formations of the nearby Cango Caves or ride a giant bird at Oudtshoorn's ostrich farms.

At the coast, windswept Cape Agulhas marks the meeting point of the cold Atlantic and warm Indian oceans.

Thatched fishermen's cottages at Arniston (Waenhuiskrans)

◁ **An ancient stalagmite is bathed in eerie light at the Cango Caves, near Oudtshoorn**

Exploring the Southern Cape

An alternative route to the N2 over Sir Lowry's Pass, which drops down into wheatfields and farmland dotted with cattle and woolly merino sheep, is the R44, a scenic road that hugs the coastline from Gordon's Bay to Hermanus. Coastal hamlets like Cape Agulhas – official meeting point of two oceans – offer a calm contrast to the majestic passes that lead through the mountains. Oudtshoorn is where the mansions of former "ostrich barons" can be seen, and nearby lies the underground splendour of the Cango Caves.

Wind-blown sand dunes at De Hoop Nature Reserve

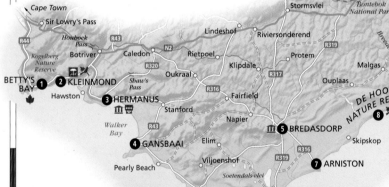

Matjiesfontein
N1
Worcester
Witteberg
1382 m
Touws
Boerboonfontein
Marloth Nature Reserve
R62
Barr
Trad
SWELLENDAM 9
Bontebok National Park
Stormsvlei
Cape Town
Sir Lowry's Pass
R44
Houhoek Pass
R43
Lindeshof
Riviersonderend
Breede
N2
R319
Kogelberg Nature Reserve
Botriver
Caledon
Rietpoel
Protem
R320
Klipdale
Malgas
BETTY'S BAY 1
2 KLEINMOND
Shaw's Pass
Oukraal
R317
Ouplaas
R316
Hawston
3 HERMANUS
Fairfield
DE HOOP NATURE RES
Stanford
8
Napier
Walker Bay
R43
5 BREDASDORP
4 GANSBAAI
Elim
Skipskop
R316
R319
7 ARNISTON
Viljoenshof
Pearly Beach
Soetendals-vlei
Struis Bay
Struisbaai
Quoin Point
6 CAPE AGULHAS

Rocky beach near Arniston's cave

GETTING AROUND

The N2 over Sir Lowry's Pass cuts right across the South Cape to Riversdale, where the R323 heads north to Oudtshoorn, the Cango Caves and the country's most dramat passes, which are linked by the R328. All of the coastal towns are accessed via main routes feeding off the N2. The De Hoop Nature Reserve can be reached via an untarred road from both Bredasdorp and the N2. Coach tours offer day trips, otherwise public transport services are severely limited, so a car is essential for touring this region. The closest international airport is in Cape Town

For additional map symbols *see back flap*

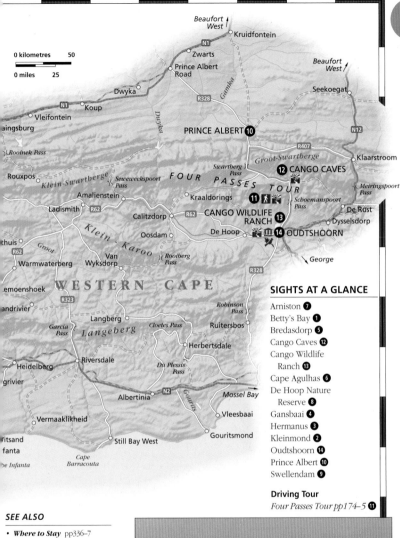

SIGHTS AT A GLANCE

Arniston 7
Betty's Bay 1
Bredasdorp 5
Cango Caves 12
Cango Wildlife Ranch 13
Cape Agulhas 6
De Hoop Nature Reserve 8
Gansbaai 4
Hermanus 3
Kleinmond 2
Oudtshoorn 14
Prince Albert 10
Swellendam 9

Driving Tour

Four Passes Tour pp174–5 11

SEE ALSO

- ***Where to Stay*** pp336–7
- ***Where to Eat*** p365

KEY

- Major road
- Minor road
- Untarred road
- Scenic route
- Main railway
- Minor railway
- Summit
- Pass

A group of residents at High Gate Ostrich Farm, near Oudtshoorn

Betty's Bay ❶

Road map B5. R44 SE of Gordon's Bay. *300.* *Cape Town International.* *Kleinmond, (028) 271-5657.*

This seaside village, named after Betty Youlden, the daughter of a property developer who lived here in the 1900s, is a popular weekend retreat. People cherish its remote solitude, a testament to which is the fact that electrification of some local homes occurred only in 1993.

Of significance is the **Harold Porter National Botanical Garden** on the slopes of the Kogelberg which rises behind Betty's Bay. Harold Porter, a partner in a property agents' business in the town, bought this tract of land in 1938 to preserve the rich mountain and coastal *fynbos* vegetation. Over 1,600 species of ericas, proteas and watsonias – one of the densest concentrations in the Western Cape – attract sugarbirds and sunbirds. A permit is required for the Leopard Kloof Trail that runs through dense riverine forest to a picturesque waterfall. The penguin reserve at Stoney Point protects a small breeding colony of African jackass penguins.

Erica, Harold Porter Gardens

Harold Porter National Botanical Garden
Tel *(028) 272-9311.* *8am–4:30pm (7pm summer) daily.*

Wide lagoon mouth and beach at Kleinmond

Kleinmond ❷

Road map B5. R44 E of Betty's Bay. *2,900.* *Spar Centre (028) 271-5657.*

Surrounding Kleinmond, the stony hills with their thin green veneer of *fynbos* scrub once harboured small bands of Khoina and runaway slaves.

In the 1920s Kleinmond, at the foot of the Palmietberg, was a fishing settlement; today it is a holiday spot where rock angling for *kabeljou* (kob), and fishing for yellowtail and tunny are popular pastimes. Kleinmond Lagoon, where the Palmiet River reaches the sea, offers safe swimming and canoeing.

Visitors can appreciate the beautiful sea and mountain vistas from a well-planned network of hiking trails in the **Kogelberg Nature Reserve** and maybe even glimpse some of the dainty, shy gazelle species like klipspringer, as well as grysbok and steenbok that occur in the coastal fynbos and on the lower slopes of the mountain.

Kogelberg Nature Reserve
Betty's Bay. ***Tel*** *(028) 271-5138.* *8am–5pm daily.*

Hermanus ❸

Road map B5. *55,000.* *Bot River 30 km (18 miles) N on N2.* *Hermanus Stn, Mitchell Street, (028) 312-2629.*

Originally established as a farming community by Hermanus Pieters, the town became a fashionable holiday and retirement destination due to the sunny climate and attractive location. Fisherman and sailors also found a relatively easy life, while visitors frequented the Windsor, Astoria and other august hotels. Today the town's grandeur is a little faded, but it still has plenty to offer most tourists.

The focal point of the town is the **Old Harbour Museum**, which traces the history of the town's whaling days, and contains a whale skull and old weapons. Fishermen's boats dating from 1850 to the mid-1900s lie restored and hull-up on the old ramp. On the higher rocks are *bokkom* stands, racks on which fish are hung to dry in the sun.

Today, Hermanus is famous for its superb whale-watching sites. Every year, southern right whales *(see p130–31)* migrate

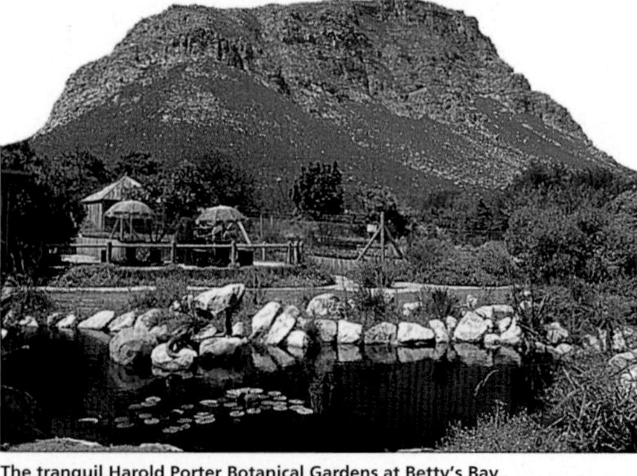

The tranquil Harold Porter Botanical Gardens at Betty's Bay

from the sub-Antarctic to calve in the shelter of Walker Bay. They arrive in June and leave again by December, but the peak whale-watching season is from September to October, when visitors are guaranteed daily sightings of the large mammals frolicking offshore. The town's official whale crier blows his kelp horn as he walks along Main Street, bearing a signboard that shows the best daily sighting places.

Despite having lost some of its charm to development and the influx of tourists, Hermanus has a beautiful coastline. Unspoilt beaches such as Die Plaat, a 12-km (7-mile) stretch from Klein River Lagoon to De Kelders, are perfect for walks and horseriding. A clifftop route extends from New Harbour to Grotto Beach; the regularly placed benches allow walkers to rest and enjoy the superb views. Swimming is generally safe, and there is a tidal pool below the Marine Hotel, to the east of the old harbour.

Activities near Hermanus include the Rotay Way, a 10-km (six-miles) scenic drive, and the Hermanus Wine Route, which features four vineyards tucked away in the pretty Hemel en Arde Valley.

The popular Marine Hotel in Hermanus

Approximately 20 km (12.5 miles) east of Hermanus lies **Stanford**, a rustic crafts centre. The heart of this little village contains many historical homes built in the late 1800s and early 1900s, and has been proclaimed a national conservation area. The early school building and Anglican Church both date back to 1880, while the reputedly haunted Spookhuis (ghost house) is dated about 1885.

Fernkloof Nature Reserve boasts 40 km (25 miles) of waymarked footpaths, a 4.5-km (three-mile) circular nature trail and more than a thousand species of *fynbos*.

Old Harbour Museum
Market Place.
Tel *(028) 312-1475.*
9am–4:30pm Mon–Sat, noon–4pm Sun. public hols.

WHALE WATCHING IN HERMANUS

The World Wide Fund for Nature (WWF) has recognized Hermanus as one of the best land-based whale-watching spots on earth. October sees a peak in whale numbers (from 40 to 70 have been recorded). The mammals can be seen as close as 10 m (11 yd) away. Particularly special is the Old Harbour Museum's sonar link-up. A hydrophone buried in the seabed transmits the whale calls to an audio room on shore.

Whale Route logo

The rocky coastline around Hermanus offers good vantage points for whale watchers

Coming face to face with a great white on a shark-diving expedition

Gansbaai ❹

Road map B5.
R43 SE of Hermanus. *22,000.*
Cnr Main Rd & Berg St, (028) 384-1439.

The name Gansbaai (Bay of Geese) originates from the flocks of Egyptian geese that used to breed here.

Gansbaai is renowned for the tragedy of HMS *Birkenhead*. In February 1852, this ship hit a rock off Danger Point, 9 km (6 miles) away, and sank with 445 men – all the women and children were saved. To this day, the phrase "Birkenhead Drill" describes the custom of favouring women and children in crisis situations.

From Gansbaai there are several boat trips to Dyer Island, where you can watch great white sharks feed on the seals that breed on nearby Geyser Island. This area is also home to large numbers of African penguins, another food source for the great whites that congregate here. Nicknamed "Shark Alley", the channel between the islands and the mainland is a popular destination for water safaris and shark-diving expeditions.

Bredasdorp ❺

Road map B5. *9,800.*
Lang St, (028) 424-2584.

Bredasdorp lies in a region of undulating barley fields and sheep pasture. The town is a centre for the wool industry, but serves mainly as an access route to Cape Agulhas (via the R319) and Arniston (via the R316).

The town's most interesting feature is the **Shipwreck Museum**, which pays tribute to the southern coast's tragic history. This treacherous length of coastline has been labelled the "graveyard of ships" as its rocky reefs, gale-force winds and powerful currents make it one of the most dangerous in the world. Since 1552, more than 130 ships have foundered here, an average of one wreck per kilometre of coast.

The best time to visit the Bredasdorp Mountain Reserve is from mid-September to mid-October, when the countryside becomes bathed in colour from hundreds of blooms bursting into flower. An attractive, small garden has been created especially to showcase the indigenous wildflowers that are found here.

Figurehead, Shipwreck Museum

Shipwreck Museum

Independent St. ***Tel** (028) 424-1240.* *9am–4:45pm Mon–Fri, 11am–3:45pm Sat & Sun.*

This museum was officially opened in April 1975 and is housed in an old rectory and church hall, both of which have been declared national monuments.

The rectory, built in 1845, is furnished like a 19th-century townhouse typical of South Africa's southern coast. The interiors and furnishings were influenced by the many shipwrecks that occurred along this capricious stretch of coastline. The salvaged wood, as well as ships' decor, frequently reappeared in door and window frames and in the ceiling rafters.

Many of the maritime artifacts that were donated have been incorporated into the refurbished home. The beautiful marble-topped washstand in the bedroom was salvaged from the *Queen of the Thames*, which sank in 1871, while the medicine chest came from the *Clan MacGregor*, which was shipwrecked in 1902.

The church hall, dating back to 1864, is now called the Shipwreck Hall. Its rather gloomy interior is a suitable environment for the interesting and diverse relics displayed in glass-cases, all of which were recovered from major shipwrecks in the area.

A 19th-century kitchen in the Shipwreck Museum at Bredasdorp

For hotels and restaurants in this region see pp336–7 and p365

Arniston's fishermen live in Kassiesbaai

Cape Agulhas ❻

Road map B5. R319, 45 km (28 miles) S of Bredasdorp. *Lang St, (028) 424-2584.*

Cape Agulhas was named by early Portuguese navigators, the first to round Africa in the 15th century. At the southernmost point of their journey, the sailors noticed that their compass needles were unaffected by magnetic deviation, pointing true north instead. They called this point the "Cape of Needles".

At this promontory, where the tip of the African continental shelf disappears undramatically into the sea to form what is known as the Agulhas Bank *(see p24)*, the Atlantic and Indian oceans merge. The only physical evidence of this convergence is a simple stone cairn.

This is one of the world's most treacherous stretches of coast. The often-turbulent waters are shallow, rock-strewn and subject to heavy swells and strong currents. This is the graveyard for more than 250 once-proud vessels, including the Japanese trawler *Meisho Maru 38*, whose rusting wreck can be seen 2 km (1 mile) west of the Agulhas lighthouse.

Lighthouse and Museum

***Tel** (028) 435-6078. 9am–4:30pm daily.*

Agulhas Lighthouse, whose design is based on the Pharos lighthouse of Alexandria in Egypt, was built in 1848. After the Green Point lighthouse, it is the oldest working lighthouse in Southern Africa. It fell into disuse, but was restored and reopened in 1988. Today, its 7.5 million-candlepower lamp is visible for 30 nautical miles.

The museum, attached to the lighthouse was opened in 1994. There are 71 steps to the top of the tower, which affords superb views of the coast and seascape.

A plaque at Cape Agulhas

Agulhas Lighthouse is at the southernmost point of Africa

Arniston ❼

Road map B5. *1,500. Lang St, Bredasdorp, (028) 424-2584.*

Arniston's name originates from the British vessel, *Arniston*, which was wrecked east of the settlement in May 1815. Tragically, of the 378 soldiers, homebound from Ceylon (Sri Lanka), only six survived.

The little fishing settlement is located some 24 km (15 miles) southeast of Bredasdorp off the R316 and is characterized by its turquoise waters. The locals call the village Waenhuiskrans (wagonhouse cliff), after a cave that is large enough to accommodate several fully spanned ox-wagons and is situated 2 km (1 mile) south of the modern Arniston Hotel. The cave is accessible only at low tide, however, and visitors should beware of freak waves washing over the slippery rocks.

Kassiesbaai is a cluster of rough-plastered and thatched fishermen's cottages with traditional tiny windows to keep out the midday heat. This little village lies to the north of Arniston, very close to undulating white sand dunes. Further to the south lies Roman Beach, which is especially good for youngsters, with its gently sloping seabed, rock pools and caves. Continuing further from here is a windy, wild rocky point that attracts many hopeful anglers.

Mountain-biking in the De Hoop Nature Reserve

De Hoop Nature Reserve 8

Road map B5. R319, 56 km (35 miles) W of Bredasdorp. ***Tel*** *(028) 425-5020. 7am–6pm daily. Permits required.*

This reserve, located some 15 km (9 miles) north of Arniston, encompasses a 50-km (30-mile) stretch of coastline, weathered limestone cliffs and spectacular sand dunes, some of which tower as high as 90 m (295 ft). De Hoop's main attraction is a 14-km (8-mile) wetland that is home to 12 of South Africa's 16 waterfowl species.

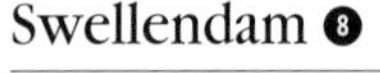

Eland at the De Hoop Nature Reserve

Thousands of red-knobbed coot, yellow-billed duck and Cape shoveller, as well as Egyptian geese, can be seen here, although populations do fluctuate with the water level of the marshland. The bird-watching is best between the months of September and April, when migrant flocks of Palaearctic waders arrive. Of the 13 species that have been recorded, visitors may expect to see ringed plover, wood and curlew sandpiper, greenshank, and little stint.

The rich variety of *fynbos* species includes the endemic Bredasdorp sugarbush *(Protea obtusfolia)*, stinkleaf sugarbush *(Protea susannae)* and pincushion protea *(Leucospermum oliefolium)*.

Wildlife can also be seen in the reserve, and there is a short circular drive from the rest camp to Tierhoek. Species to look out for are the rare Cape mountain zebra and small gazelle, like bontebok, grey rhebok and the rather shy and elusive mountain reedbuck.

For visitors who enjoy cycling, a mountain-bike trail traverses the Potberg section of the reserve, which contains a breeding colony of the rare Cape vultures. However, to avoid disturbing the birds the sites are not accessible.

Comfortable campsites and self-catering cottages are available for visitors who wish to stay overnight and experience the spectacular southern night sky almost free of light pollution.

Swellendam 8

Road map B5. *31,000.* *Oefeningshuis, Voortrek Street, (028) 514-2770.* **www.** swellendamtourism.co.za

Nestling in the shadow of the imposing Langeberg Mountains, Swellendam is one of South Africa's most picturesque small towns. The country's third-oldest town, after Cape Town and Stellenbosch, Swellendam was founded by the Dutch in 1742 and named after the governor and his wife.

The attractive thatched-roofed and whitewashed **Drostdy** was built by the Dutch East India Company in 1747 as the seat of the *landdrost*, or magistrate. It now serves as a museum of Dutch colonial life. Built shortly afterwards the Old Gaol is situated at the rear of the Drostdy. Originally it was a simple, single-storey building with lean-to cells, but it was subsequently enlarged to include an enclosed courtyard created by linking the two cell blocks with high walls.

Near the museum is the *Ambagswerf* (trade yard), which features a smithy and wagonmaker's shop, a mill and bakery, a tannery, a cooperage and a coppersmith. Crafts demonstrations are held here regularly. Also on site is the pretty Mayville Cottage. Built between 1853 and 1855, it represents a transition of architectural styles, using both Cape Dutch and Cape Georgian influences. Outside the cottage is a well-designed rose garden featuring several heritage species.

Swellendam is renowned for its many fine old buildings, including the imposing Dutch Reformed church, with a whitewashed façade and an elegant clock tower. The **Oefeningshuis**, built in 1838 as a school for freed slaves, now serves as a tourist information centre. An interesting feature of the building is the clock designed for the illiterate: when the time painted on the sculpted

The whitewashed Dutch Reformed church in Swellendam

For hotels and restaurants in this region see pp336–7 and p365

Scenic view of the Swartberg Pass from the village of Prince Albert

clock face matches that on the real clock below, then it is time for worship.

Also of note are the splendid wrought-iron balconies and fittings of the Buirski & Co shop, which opened for trade in 1880 opposite the Oefeningshuis, and the elegant Auld House on the same street.

Drostdy

18 Swellengrebel Street. *Tel 028) 514-1138.* *9am–4:45pm Mon–Fri, 10am–3:45pm Sat & Sun.* *Good Fri, 25 Dec, 1 Jan. &*

Environs: Bontebok National Park is 6 km (3.7 miles) outside of Swellendam. This scenic wilderness was set up to protect the endangered species of antelope after which it was named. The bontebok has since recovered enough to share the habitat with several other introduced animals. Most of the park is accessible by car, and there are also several excellent self-guided walking trails. The more challenging 74-km (46-mile) Swellendam Trail takes in the Marloth Nature Reserve, which is situated along the southern slopes of the Langenberg Mountains.

Prince Albert 8

Road map C5. *5,700.* *Fransie Pienaar Museum, Kerkstraat (023) 541-1366.* **www**.patourism.co.za

This pretty village, which is part of the Four Passes tour *(see pp174–5)*, has several attractions. The **Fransie Pienaar Museum**, which hosts one of the world's largest fossil collections, also houses the tourist information centre, where guided walking tours of Prince Albert can be booked.

The **Prince Albert Gallery**, opposite the museum, was set up by local artists who wanted to find a venue to show their work. There are regular exhibits of paintings, sculpture and photographs. On Saturday mornings, in the square opposite the museum, there is a food and crafts market, and each May Prince Albert holds a popular olive, food and wine festival *(see p40)*. Apart from the stalls of local produce, there are also workshops, children's activities and guided walks.

Environs: The spectacular Swartberg Pass, key to the Karoo Desert, starts just 2 km (1.2 miles) from Prince Albert. The slopes of the pass provide the irrigation that makes the village an oasis in this arid area. The pass was built by the road engineer Thomas Bain after heavy floods in 1875 swept away the previous road, depriving local farmers of their link with the nearest seaports.

Nearby Sutherland houses the **South African Astronomical Observatory**, which boasts the largest telescope in the southern hemisphere. There are two guided tours daily; booking is essential.

Fransie Pienaar Museum

42 Church St. *Tel (023) 541-1172.* *9am–12:30pm, 2–5pm Mon–Fri, 9am–noon Sat, 10am–noon Sun.* *public hols.*

Prince Albert Gallery

Seven Arches, Church St. *Tel (023) 541-1057.* *10am–12:30pm, 2–4pm Mon–Fri, 10am–noon Sat.* *Wed pm, public hols.*

South African Astronomical Observatory

Tel (023) 571–2436.

Beautiful proteas blooming on the Swartberg Pass

Visitors can get close to nature stroking tame cheetahs

Cango Wildlife Ranch ⓭

Road map C5. R328 to Cango Caves. ***Tel*** *(044) 272-5593.*
8am–5pm daily.
www.cango.co.za

The ranch lies 3 km (2 miles) north of Oudtshoorn. Since the establishment of the Cheetah Conservation Foundation in 1993, the ranch has ranked among the leading cheetah breeders in Africa and is one of the world's top five protection institutions. The breeding enclosure is not accessible, but visitors may enter a fenced area to interact with tame cheetahs. Other thrills include crocodile cage diving, the opportunity to play with tiger or lion cubs and for the younger visitor a pygmy hippo encounter. The centre has also recently started a Bengal tiger breeding programme: there are eight tigers at the ranch, including a rare white Bengal tiger.

Walkways elevated over a natural bushveld environment allow the visitor close-up views of some other powerful hunters: lion, jaguar and puma. Crocodiles and alligators, of which there are over 400, are also bred at the ranch, and exotic snakes on show include a South American albino python, a 4-m (13-ft) boa constrictor and a copperhead viper. There is a further breeding programme under way for the endangered Cape wild dog.

The ranch has a well regarded programme of tours and special events, and a fully licensed restaurant that serves, among other things, crocodile and ostrich meat.

Nile crocodile at the Cango Wildlife Ranch

Oudtshoorn ⓮

Road map C5. N12 from George.
123,500. *Baron van Reede St, (044) 279-2532.*
www.oudtshoorn.co.za

The town of Oudtshoorn was established in 1847 at the foot of the Swartberg Mountains, to cater to the needs of the Little Karoo's growing farming population. It gained prosperity when the demand for ostrich feathers – to support Victorian, and later Edwardian fashion trends – created a sharp rise in the industry in 1870–80.

The Karoo's hot, dry climate proved suitable for big-scale ostrich farming – the loamy soils yielded extensive crops of lucerne, which forms a major part of the birds' diet, and the ground was strewn with the small pebbles that are a vital aid to their somewhat unusual digestive processes.

Oudtshoorn's importance as an ostrich-farming centre continued for more than 40 years, and the town became renowned for its sandstone mansions, built by wealthy ostrich barons. But World War I and changes in fashion resulted in the industry's decline and unfortunately many farmers went bankrupt. Ostrich farming eventually recovered in the 1940s with the establishment of the tanning industry. Today, ostrich products include eggs and leather, meat and bonemeal. The town also produces crops of tobacco, wheat and grapes.

A sandstone "feather palace" on the outskirts of Oudtshoorn

TTING AROUND
: N2 traverses the entire leng
Garden Route, from Mossel
Port Elizabeth and beyond, c
y up the east coast. Althoug
ch tours to the area are ava
el by car is ideal as it allow
tor to explore the pretty co
ns along the way at leisure
en- and five-day hiking trai
Tsitsikamma, as well as sh
est walks, may also entice v
inger. There are domestic a
Port Elizabeth and George.

0 kilometres

0 miles 25

A view of Knysna L

The early 20th-century sandstone façade of the CP Nel Museum

CP Nel Museum

3 Baron van Reede St. ***Tel*** *(044) 272-7306.* *9am–5pm Mon–Sat.* *public hols.*

This building, formerly the Boys' High School of Oudtshoorn, was designed in 1906 by the local architect Charles Bullock. Its green-domed sandstone façade is considered to be one of the best examples of stone masonry found anywhere in South Africa. The school hall was designed in 1913 by JE Vixseboxse.

The museum was named in honour of its founder, Colonel CP Nel. A series of dioramas traces the history of ostriches and the impact of ostrich farming on the town and its community. Displays also depict the cultural history and lifestyle of the people of the Klein Karoo region, and the museum prides itself on its excellent replica of an early 20th-century pharmacy. There is a section devoted to the vital role played by the Jewish community in the development of Oudtshoorn's feather industry.

A carved ostrich egg lamp

Le Roux Townhouse

146 High St. ***Tel*** *(044) 272-3676.* *8am–1pm and 2–5pm, Mon–Fri, Sat & Sun by app.* *public hols.*

Built around 1895, this is an outstanding example of the feather palaces of the time. An annex of the CP Nel Museum, its exhibits include authentic European furniture from the period 1900–20 and a collection of porcelain, glassware and pieces made from Cape silver.

THE OSTRICH'S UNUSUAL EATING HABITS

Ostriches have neither teeth nor a crop, so have developed the habit of eating stones, which help to grind and digest their food. Perhaps by extension of this habit, or perhaps because they are naturally curious, there is little that an ostrich won't eat. A few years ago, an Oudtshoorn farmer was mystified by the theft of his washing – shirts, socks, trousers vanished every washday, until the death of one of his ostriches revealed the culprit! The birds have also been seen to eat babies' shoes, combs, sunglasses, buttons and earrings (ripped from the shirts and ears of tourists).

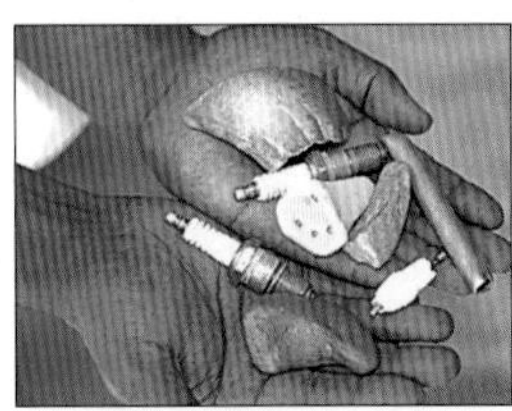
Spark plugs and bullet cases – ostriches eat almost anything

Highgate Ostrich Show Farm

Off R328 to Mossel Bay. ***Tel*** *(044) 272-7115.* *7:30am–5pm daily.* multilingual.

Located 10 km (6 miles) south of Oudtshoorn, this large farm offers a tour of its ostrich breeding facilities where visitors can learn more about the various stages of the bird's development, and have an opportunity to cuddle the chicks, handle the eggs and visit an ostrich pen. The adventurous may even ride an ostrich. Those who don't have the nerve, can watch jockeys take part in an ostrich derby. The tour length is 1.5 to 2 hours and the fee includes refreshments.

The curio shop offers ostrich feather products, handbags, wallets, belts and shoes.

Coloured ostrich plumes are available in stores in Oudtshoorn

Safari Show Farm

Off R328 to Mossel Bay. ***Tel*** *(044) 272-7311/2.* *8am–4:30pm daily.*

Situated 5 km (3 miles) from Oudtshoorn, this show farm has over 2,500 ostriches. The conducted tours leave every half-hour and include an ostrich race and visits to the breeding camp and museum.

Place your bet on the race winner at one of the ostrich farms

Bartolomeu Dias Museum Complex (Mossel Bay) ❶

The Bartolomeu Dias Museum Complex, established in 1988, celebrates the 500th anniversary of Dias's historic landfall. A full-sized replica of his ship was built in Portugal in 1987 and set sail for Mossel Bay, arriving on 3 February 1988. Here, the 25-ton vessel was lifted from the water and lowered into the specially altered museum with its high, angled roof, clerestory windows and sunken floor for the keel.

★ The Caravel

The intrepid Spanish and Portuguese seafarers of the 15th and 16th centuries sailed into the unknown in small two- or three-masted ships like this.

Portuguese flag

Lateen sails are characteristic of Mediterranean ships.

Letter Box

Mail posted in this unusual post box in the museum complex is marked with a special postmark.

Post Office Tree

The 16th-century seafarers left messages for each other in a shoe suspended from a milkwood tree like this one, next to the museum building.

Rudder

Barrels filled with fresh water were stored in the hold.

Crew Cabin

Cramped confines in the crew's quarters left little room for privacy on sea voyages that often lasted many months.

STAR FEATURES

★ The Caravel

★ Stained-Glass Windows

VISITORS' CHECKLIST

Road map C5. Mossel Bay. *(044) 691-2202.* **Museum *Tel*** *(044) 691-1067.* *9am–4:45pm daily (to 3:45pm Sat & Sun).* **www**.gardenroute.net/mby

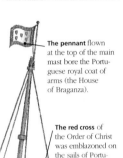

★ Stained-Glass Windows
Three beautiful windows by Ria Kriek commemorate the early voyages of discovery. Shown here are the sails of the Dias caravel.

The pennant flown at the top of the main mast bore the Portuguese royal coat of arms (the House of Braganza).

The red cross of the Order of Christ was emblazoned on the sails of Portuguese sailing vessels.

THE EPIC VOYAGE OF DIAS

A small fleet left Portugal around August 1487 under the command of Bartolomeu Dias *(see p48)*. The explorer made several landfalls on the West African coast, erecting *padrões* (stone crosses) along the way. In February 1488, he dropped anchor off the South African coast. The inlet he named after São Bras (St Blaize) is today called Mossel Bay.

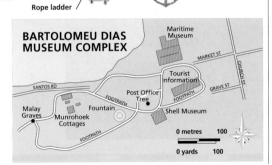

Pulleys and ropes enabled sailors to furl and unfurl the sails at great speed.

Anchor

Rope ladder

BARTOLOMEU DIAS MUSEUM COMPLEX

Maritime Museum
Market St
Church St
Tourist Information
Grave St
Santos Rd
Post Office Tree
Footpath
Fountain
Shell Museum
Malay Graves
Munrohoek Cottages
0 metres 100
0 yards 100

Exploring Mossel Bay and the Bartolomeu Dias Museum Complex

One of the main attractions in the seaside town of Mossel Bay, situated 397 km (246 miles) east of Cape Town, is the interesting museum complex and the historic centre, both overlooking the harbour.

Seafaring history is the subject at the Bartolomeu Dias Museum Complex. Apart from the outstanding reconstruction of Dias's caravel, there are old maps, photographs and documents detailing the first explorations around the tip of Africa. The complex also includes the **Old Post Office Tree Manor**, which commemorates the custom of early navigators who left messages for each other in a shoe.

The town is probably best known for its controversial and costly Mossgas development, initiated by the discovery of natural offshore gas fields.

But the real charm of the settlement lies in its natural beauty – fine beaches and walks. The 15-km (9-mile) St Blaize Hiking Trail winds along an unspoilt stretch of coastline from Bat's Cave to Dana Bay. Santos Beach, the only north-facing beach in South Africa, guarantees sunny afternoons and safe swimming.

Regular cruises take visitors out to **Seal Island**, while **Shark Africa** offers the excitement of a shark cage dive or snorkelling and certification diving courses.

Romonza–Seal Isle Trips
Tel *(044) 690-3101.*

Shark Africa
Cnr Upper Cross & Kloof sts. ***Tel*** *(044) 691-3796, (082) 455 2438.*

The Old Post Office Tree Manor

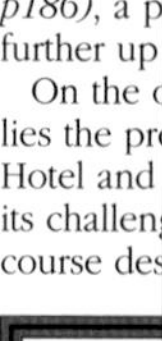

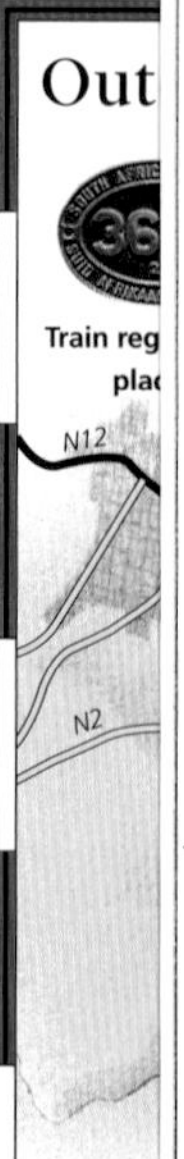

Tsitsikamma National Park ❼

Cape clawless otter

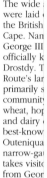

The Tsitsikamma National Park, designated in 1964, extends for 68 km (42 miles) from Nature's Valley to Oubosstrand and stretches seawards for some 5.5 km (3 miles), offering licensed snorkellers and divers a unique "underwater trail". Within the park's boundaries lie two of South Africa's most popular hikes, the Tsitsikamma and Otter trails. Primeval forest, rugged mountain scenery, an abundance of water from rivers and streams, and panoramic views contribute to their popularity with hikers.

★ Yellowwood trees
Once considered inferior and used for building, today yellowwood is highly valued.

Fynbos
The typical vegetation of this area is coastal fynbos which consists of low-growing species of ericas and proteas.

Bloukrans River gorge is the site of an overnight trail hut.

Common dolphins
Hikers on the Otter Trail are sure to see dolphins frolicking in the waves.

STAR FEATURES

★ Otter Trail

★ Yellowwood trees

★ Tsitsikamma Trail

★ Otter Trail
This five-day coastal hike was the country's first official trail and stretches from the mouth of the Storm's River to the superb beach at Nature's Valley. Hikers may spot whales, dolphins, seals and Cape clawless otters along the way.

★ Tsitsikamma Trail

The relatively easy inland walking route leads 60 km (37 miles) through fynbos and indigenous forest in the Tsitsikamma mountains and takes five days to complete.

VISITORS' CHECKLIST

Road map C5. Keurboomstrand 14 km (8 miles) E of Plettenberg Bay on N2. *Plettenberg Bay.* *Hopper and Baz buses to De Vasselot camp.* *National Parks Board Reservations national numbers: (011) 678-8870, (012) 428-9111.* *7:30am–5pm.* **Otter Trail:** *41 km (25 miles).* **Tsitsikamma Trail:** *60 km (37 miles).* *(permit required for trails).* **www**.saparks.co.za

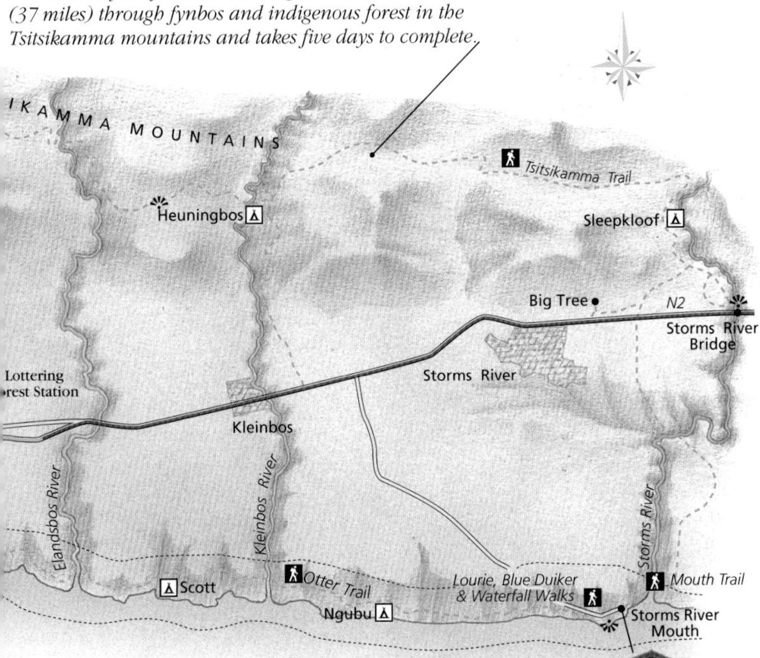

IKAMMA MOUNTAINS
Tsitsikamma Trail
Heuningbos
Sleepkloof
Big Tree
N2
Storms River Bridge
Storms River
Lottering Forest Station
Kleinbos
Elandsbos River
Kleinbos River
Storms River
Scott
Otter Trail
Ngubu
Lourie, Blue Duiker & Waterfall Walks
Mouth Trail
Storms River Mouth

Storms River Rest Camp

Rustic log cabins provide cozy accommodation at the start of the Otter Trail.

0 kilometres 5
0 miles 5

KEY

- Motorway
- Major road
- Tarred road
- Trail
- Viewpoint
- Hiking
- Overnight trail huts

TIPS FOR WALKERS

En route to Storms River Mouth

Visitors should be fit, and sturdy walking shoes are essential. For the longer hikes, all provisions as well as cooking gear and sleeping bags must be carried, as the overnight huts are only equipped with mattresses. The Bloukrans River along the Otter Trail can only be forded by swimming or wading, so waterproof backpacks are advised.

Street-by-Street: Port Elizabeth ❽

Statue of Queen Victoria

The third-largest port and fifth-largest city in the country, Port Elizabeth faces east across the 60-km (38-mile) wide sweep of Algoa Bay. Many of its attractions are concentrated along the seafront. Modern Port Elizabeth has spread inland and northward along the coast from the original settlement. It is often referred to as the "Friendly City" and its wide open beaches are popular with visitors. Among the many attractions in this major tourist centre are a host of well-preserved historic buildings, splendid architecture, Bayworld, Snake Park, Donkin Reserve and Happy Valley.

Donkin Lighthouse
Built in 1861, the lighthouse is in the Donkin Reserve.

CHAPEL STREET

DONKIN STREET

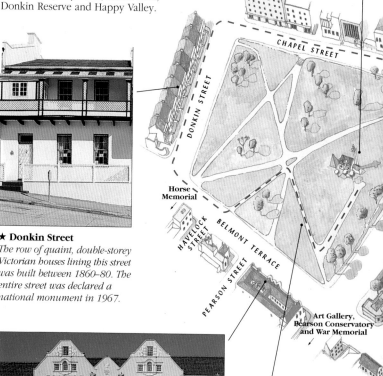

Horse Memorial

HAVELOCK STREET

BELMONT TERRACE

PEARSON STREET

Art Gallery, Pearson Conservatory and War Memorial

★ Donkin Street
The row of quaint, double-storey Victorian houses lining this street was built between 1860–80. The entire street was declared a national monument in 1967.

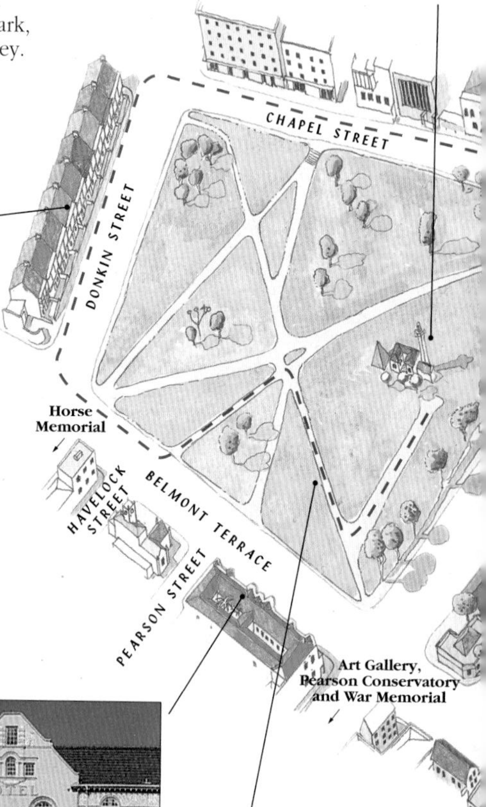

Donkin Reserve is situated on a hillside overlooking the city.

Protea Hotel Edward
This well-preserved Edwardian building is a city landmark, located in the heart of Port Elizabeth's historical district. The hotel is renowned for its sumptuous breakfasts and has a vintage lift that is still fully operational.

STAR SIGHTS

- ★ Donkin Street
- ★ City Hall
- ★ Fort Frederick

For hotels and restaurants in this region see pp337–40 and pp365–7

The Campanile
Built in 1923 to commemorate the arrival of the 1820 British Settlers, this 52-m (168-ft) high tower has a spiral staircase leading to a viewing platform.

VISITORS' CHECKLIST

Road map D5. 2 million. *Port Elizabeth International, 4 km (2.5 miles) NW.* *Strand St, (041) 507-2662.* *Greenacres Shopping Centre, Newton Park, and city centre.* *Port Elizabeth railway station.* *Donkin Reserve, (041) 585-8884.* *8am–4:30pm Mon–Fri, 9:30am–3:30pm Sat–Sun.* *25 Dec, 1 Jan.* *Shakespeare Festival (Feb), Vodacom Splash (Easter), Summer Holiday Programme (Dec).* **www**.nmbt.co.za

KEY

Suggested route

0 metres 100

0 yards 100

★ City Hall
The City Hall was built between 1858–62, and the clock tower was added in 1883. A replica of the 1488 Dias cross can be seen here (see pp182–3).

No. 7 Castle Hill, built in 1827, is one of the city's oldest surviving Settler cottages. It is now a museum.

★ Fort Frederick
The first stone structure in the district, this fort (see pp50–51) *was built in 1799 by British soldiers who feared an attack by French forces. No shot was ever fired from it.*

The Drill Hall (1882) was the headquarters of Prince Alfred's Guard, a volunteer regiment founded in 1856.

Exploring Port Elizabeth

Signpost

Modern Port Elizabeth sprawls inland and northward on the windy shores of Algoa Bay. Many of the city's most popular attractions, such as Bayworld with its dolphin and seal shows, can be found along Humewood Beach. Port Elizabeth is very proud of its settler heritage and a wealth of historic buildings and museums, as well as memorials and statues, await exploration further inland.

Donkin Reserve

Belmont Terrace. (041) 585-8884. *8am–4:30pm Mon–Fri; 9:30am–3:30pm Sat–Sun.* *25 Dec, 1 Jan.*

In this attractive park-like reserve is the pyramid-shaped memorial that then acting governor of the Cape, Sir Rufane Donkin, dedicated to his late wife in 1820. A few days earlier he had named the settlement Port Elizabeth in her honour.

The adjacent lighthouse was completed in 1861. The entire site was declared a national monument in 1938.

Donkin Memorial

The Horse Memorial

Horse Memorial

Cape Road.

During the South African War, Port Elizabeth was the port of entry for the horses of British soldiers. After the war, local resident Harriet Meyer raised money to honour the estimated 347,000 horses that had died. The statue by sculptor Joseph Whitehead, unveiled in 1905, was relocated to its present site in 1957. The inscription reads: "The greatness of a nation consists not so much in the number of its people or the extent of its territory as in the extent and justice of its compassion."

St George's Park

Park Drive.

The setting of the well-known play, *Master Harold and the Boys,* by Athol Fugard, this lovely park is home to the oldest cricket ground and bowling green in South Africa. It also contains tennis courts, a swimming pool, a botanic garden and several historic monuments, like the War Memorial in the north-east corner of the park.

The Pearson Conservatory, named after Henry Pearson who served as mayor of the city for 16 terms, was completed in 1882 and houses a collection of exotic plants.

Main Public Library

Market Square. ***Tel*** *(041) 585-8133.*

Work on the building, located on the corner of Whites Road and Main Street, began in 1935. The attractive terracotta façade was made in England, shipped out, and the numbered segments assembled on site. The lovely stained-glass dome on the second floor is a masterpiece. A statue of Queen Victoria, one of at least three in South Africa, stands right in front of the entrance to the building.

Fort Frederick

Belmont Terrace.

In 1799, a British garrison was sent to Algoa Bay to prevent an invasion by French troops supporting the rebel republic of Graaff-Reinet *(see pp304–5).* Small, square Fort Frederick *(see pp50–51)* was built on a low hill overlooking the mouth of the Baakens River, and named after the Duke of York, who was commander-in-chief of the British army at the time. Although it was defended by eight cannons, no salvoes were ever fired from them in an act of war. The arrival of the English settlers in 1820 was supervised by the commander of the garrison, Captain Francis Evatt, whose grave can be seen at the fort.

Humewood Beach

2 km (1 mile) S of the city centre.

The recreation hub of Port Elizabeth, Humewood Beach is bordered by Marine Drive, which provides quick access to all the attractions that line the shore. An attractive covered promenade provides welcome shelter from the wind and hosts a fleamarket over weekends. There is also an inviting freshwater and tidal pool complex nearby.

The Queen Victoria statue in front of the Main Public Library

The all-important "19th hole" at Humewood Golf Course

Lifeguards are stationed at all the main beaches. Sailing and scuba diving are popular here, and the windy expanse of Algoa Bay is often punctuated by the white sails of yachts.

Many hotels and holiday apartments line Marine Drive and there are numerous little restaurants and eateries, especially at Brookes Pavilion near the Museum Complex.

The jetty at Humewood Beach

The Museum Complex and Bayworld is the flagship of the beachfront, and also includes a snake park and Tropical House. The entrance to the museum itself is lined with several open enclosures containing water birds. The interesting exhibits inside include a marine gallery containing salvaged items, fully rigged models of early sailing ships, and a fascinating display of the Xhosa people.

Tropical House is well worth a visit. Numerous forest bird species scurry through the dense undergrowth or roost in tree tops in this spacious exhibit. A path circles the rocky 7-m (23-ft) high man-made hill at the centre of the building, offering a bird's-eye view of, among others, crocodiles and flamingos.

On view at the Snake House are snakes from around the world, including South African species like the puffadder.

Bayworld's dolphin and seal shows always attract the crowds. The "stars" were all born in captivity, and are not replaced when they die.

The Museum Complex and Bayworld
Marine Drive. ***Tel*** *(041) 584-0650.*
9am–4:30pm daily. Shows at 11am and 3pm.
www.bayworld.co.za

Happy Valley
3 km (2 miles) S of the city centre.
A sandy underpass connects Humewood Beach and Happy Valley, an attractive, tranquil park in a shallow valley. Several walking paths meander across the well-kept lawns, past a little stream, lily ponds and small waterfalls.

Environs: The championship **Humewood Golf Course**, some 3 km (2 miles) south along the coast from Humewood is considered to be one of the best in South Africa. At the clubhouse, golfers can enjoy a well-earned drink and marvel at the splendid views across the bay.

A lovingly restored little narrow-gauge steam train that has been named the Apple Express occasionally departs from Humewood Station on weekends. It puffs to the village of Thornhill, 48 km (30 miles) east of Port Elizabeth, and completes the return journey to the city after lunch.

About 3 km (2 miles) south of Humewood lies the cape that marks the entrance to Algoa Bay. **Cape Recife** and its surrounding nature reserve are an ideal destination for bird spotting and exploring the unspoilt rocky shore.

A 9-km-long (6-mile) hiking trail explores the reserve and traverses several different coastal habitats that include redbuds and dune vegetation. The route passes the Cape Recife lighthouse, a spot that is a favourite with divers. A rocky outcrop near the lighthouse shelters a small colony of Jackass penguins.

Of the number of ships that have been wrecked at Cape Recife, the Greek vessel *Kapodistrias* was the most recent casualty. The bulk carrier struck Thunderbolt Reef in July 1985.

Humewood Golf Course
Tel *(041) 583-2137.*

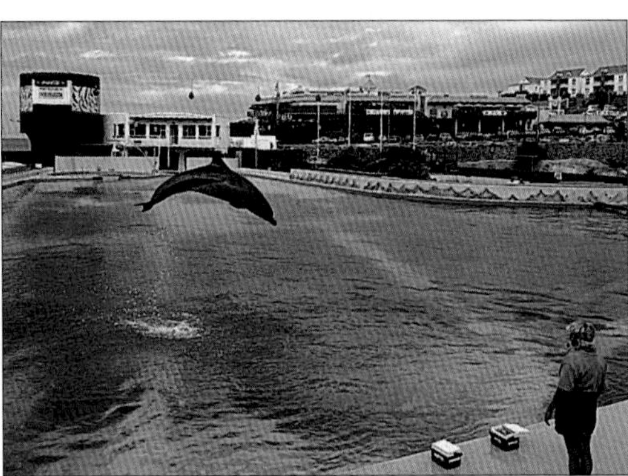
One of the performing bottlenose dolphins at Bayworld

Addo Elephant National Park ❾

Road map D5. 50 km (31 miles) NE of Port Elizabeth. ***Tel*** *(042) 233-0556. Reservations: (012) 428-9111.* *7am–7pm daily.* **www**.addoelephantpark.com

In the past, elephants lived throughout the Cape Colony, but as the land was settled they were hunted to extinction. In 1919 Major Philip Pretorius was appointed to exterminate the last survivors and succeeded in shooting 120 over 11 months. Only 15 terrified elephants survived in the densest thickets.

When public opinion turned in their favour, a 68 sq km (26 sq mile) tract of surplus land was declared national park territory in 1931. However, the animals raided nearby farms at night and a suitable fence was needed to prevent escapes.

After numerous experiments, warden Graham Armstrong constructed a guard from railway tracks and elevator cables. By 1954, some 23 sq km (9 sq miles) had been fenced in this way and the elephants were safely contained.

For many years, Addo resembled a large zoo. Oranges were placed below the rest camps at night to lure the shy beasts out of the bush, while the stout fences separated visitors and animals. The herd responded well to protection – increasing to 265 by 1998 – making it necessary to enlarge their territory. Today, the park includes the Zuurberg mountains to the north, and its size has increased to 600 sq km (232 sq miles). South African National Parks plans to quadruple it in size.

Addo's main focus is the rest camp that offers a restaurant, shop, swimming pool, caravan park and 24 comfortable Cape Dutch chalets. A network of game-viewing roads allows visitors to explore the southern region of the park. Kadouw Lookout is one of several from which to view the elephants.

Dung beetles are protected in the park

Among the other animals inhabiting the dense thicket are buffalo, black rhino, kudu, eland, hartebeest and bushbuck. But visitors tend to overlook one of the park's smallest and most fascinating creatures. The flightless dung beetle is virtually restricted to Addo. Signs warn motorists not to drive over them.

Addo's dense *spekboom (Portulacaria afra)* bushland sustains the highest concentration of large mammals in the country. To monitor the effects that the elephant, black rhino and buffalo populations have on the vegetation, a botanical reserve has been established. A 6-km (4-mile) trail explores this reserve, in which many of the indigenous trees have been labelled.

A herd of elephants at a waterhole in the Addo Elephant National Park

A rustic chalet in the Addo Elephant National Park

Shamwari Game Reserve ❿

Road map D5. 72 km (44 miles) N of Port Elizabeth. ***Tel*** *(042) 203-1111.* *11am–6pm daily (booking essential; lunch included).* **www**.shamwari.com

At 140 sq km (54 sq miles), Shamwari is the largest private reserve in the Eastern Cape and the only one in the province where the Big Five *(see pp28–9)* can be seen. It consists of undulating bushveld country in the catchment area of the Bushmans River. The recipient of four international awards, Shamwari is the brainchild of entrepreneur Adrian Gardiner, who originally bought the ranch in the hills near Paterson as a retreat for his family. Over the years, several neighbouring farms were incorporated and wildlife re-introduced. The reserve is now home to 33 elephant, 12 white rhino, buffalo, zebra, giraffe and 16 antelope species including eland, kudu, impala, gemsbok, hartebeest, springbok and black wildebeest.

Shamwari is the only private reserve in the Eastern Cape where the endangered black rhino is found. Five were translocated from

KwaZulu-Natal and, as the reserve's vegetation provides an ideal habitat, four calves have thus far been born. The lion pride, once kept in a separate camp, now roams the entire reserve.

The reserve offers luxury accommodation *(see p340)* and an African wildlife experience that has attracted many famous visitors, including the late Princess Diana. Rangers conduct game-viewing drives in open vehicles twice daily.

White Rhino, Shamwari Game Reserve

Alexandria ⓫

Road map D5. R72, E of Port Elizabeth.

Alexandria was founded in 1856 around a Dutch Reformed Church. A dirt road, just west of town, crosses chicory fields before entering the enchanting Alexandria forest. Superb specimens of yellowwood, one of the 170 tree species found here, tower above the road. The forest and the largest active dune system in South Africa are protected by the 240 sq km (93 sq miles) **Alexandria State Forest**. The two-day, 35-km (22-mile) Alexandria Hiking Trail, one of the finest coastal walks in South Africa, passes through gloomy, dense indigenous forest to reach sand dunes rising to 150 m (488 ft) above the sea, before returning via a circular route. Overnight huts are located at the start and at Woody Cape.

Alexandria State Forest
8 km (5 miles) off R72.
Tel *(046) 653-0601.*
7am–7pm daily.

Port Alfred ⓬

Road map D5. R72, 150 km (93 miles) E of Port Elizabeth.
18,000. *Halyards Hotel*
Causeway Rd, (046) 624-1235.

Port Alfred, a charming seaside resort in the Eastern Cape, is well known for its superb beaches. Those west of the river mouth are more developed, while those to the east are unspoilt and excellent for long walks. Kelly's Beach offers safe bathing. The entire stretch of coast is perfect for surfing and also popular with rock and surf fishermen.

Outside the **Kowie Museum**, which preserves the town's history is, a figurehead from an old sailing ship.

Environs: The Kowie River is navigable for 25 km (16 miles) upriver in small vessels. The two-day Kowie Canoe Trail allows canoeists to savour the beauty of the river and the forested hills that surround it. At the overnight stop, 21 km (13 miles) upstream in the Waters Meeting Nature Reserve, a footpath explores the dense bush and forest, and a variety of birds and small animals can be seen.

Kowie Museum
Pascoe Crescent. ***Tel*** *(046) 624-4713.* *10am–1pm Mon–Fri.*
public hols.

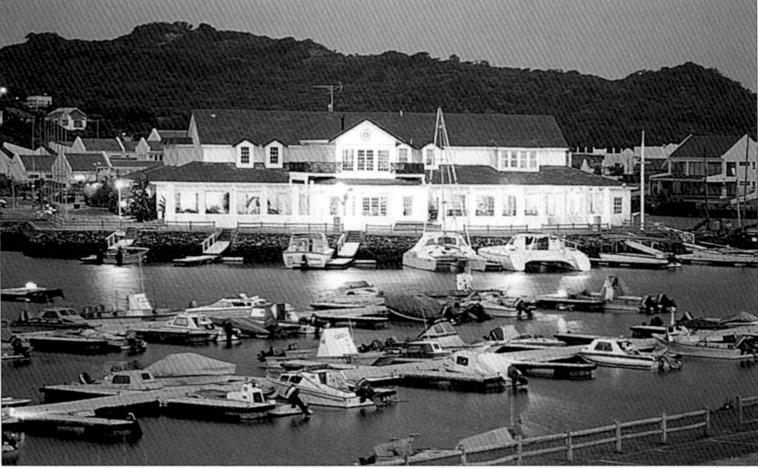

Many luxury yachts, catamarans and fishing vessels are moored at Port Alfred's marina

Grahamstown ⓭

Arts Festival logo

After the fourth Frontier War of 1812, Colonel John Graham established a military post on an abandoned farm near the southeast coast. In an attempt to stabilize the region, the Cape government enticed 4,500 British families to the farmlands. Many of these "1820 Settlers" prefered an urban life, and Grahamstown became a thriving trading centre, home to the largest concentration of artisans outside Cape Town.

Exploring Grahamstown

Grahamstown is known for its over 50 churches, university and superb schools. Its major attractions lie within a 500-m (1,625-ft) walk from the **City Hall** in High Street. Some 60 buildings have been declared national monuments, and a host of beautifully restored Georgian and Victorian residences line the streets.

Cathedral of St Michael and St George

High St. ***Tel*** *(046) 622-3976.*
8am–4:30pm daily.

The cathedral is the town's most prominent landmark – its spire towers 51 m (166 ft) above the town centre. The original St George's Church, built in 1824, is the oldest Anglican Church in South Africa, and the massive organ is one of the finest in the country.

Methodist Church

Bathurst St. ***Tel*** *(046) 622-7210.* *daily.*

The Commemoration Church is noted for its Gothic Revival façade and lovely stained-glass windows. It was completed in 1850.

Albany Museum Complex

Tel *(046) 622-2312.*

The complex incorporates five separate venues. Two of them, the **History and Natural Sciences museums** display fossils, settler artifacts and Xhosa dress. Another, the **Old Provost**, opposite Rhodes University, was built in 1838 as a military prison. **Drostdy Gateway**, which frames the university entrance, is all that remains of the 1842 magistrate's offices. **Fort Selwyn** *(see pp50–51)*, adjacent to the 1820 Settlers Monument, was built in 1836 and offers scenic views of the town.

History and Natural Sciences museums

Somerset Street.
Tel *(046) 622-2312.*
9am–1pm, 2–5pm Mon–Fri; 9am–1pm Sat. *Good Fri, 25 Dec.*

Old Provost

Lucas Avenue. ***Tel*** *(046) 622-2312.* *9am–1pm Fri.* *Sat–Thu, Good Fri, 25 Dec.*

Fort Selwyn

Fort Selwyn Drive.
Tel *(046) 622–2312.*
by appointment only.

The Cathedral of St Michael and St George in High Street

Drostdy Gateway, the entrance to Rhodes University

Observatory Museum

Bathurst Street. ***Tel*** *(046) 622-2312.*
9am–1pm, 2–5pm Mon–Fri; 9am–1pm Sat. *Good Fri, 25 Dec.*
(except turret).

The attraction at this historic home and workshop of a mid-19th-century Grahamstown jeweller is the Victorian camera obscura in the turret, which projects images of the town on to a wall.

Rhodes University

Artillery Road.
Tel *(046) 603-8111.*
multi-entry ticket.
www.ru.ac.za

This beautiful old university complex also houses the world-famous **JLB Smith Institute of Ichthyology**, where the most interesting displays are two rare embalmed coelacanth specimens. This prehistoric species of deep-water fish was presumed extinct until its "discovery" in East London in 1939. There is also a collection of other marine and freshwater fish. Visitors interested in traditional African music should visit the **International Library of African Music**, which is also on the campus.

JLB Smith Institute of Ichthyology

Rhodes University. ***Tel*** *(046) 603-8425.* *8am–1pm, 2–5pm Mon–Fri.* *Good Fri, 25 Dec.*

International Library of African Music

Rhodes University. ***Tel*** *(046) 603-8557.* *by appointment.*

For hotels and restaurants in this region see pp337–40 and pp365–7

National English Literary Museum

Beaufort St. **Tel** *(046) 622-7042.* *8:45am–4:30pm Mon–Fri.* *Good Fri, 25 Dec.* **www**.ru.ac.za/nelm

Preserved here are documents, early manuscripts and personal letters relating to South Africa's most important writers.

1820 Settlers Monument

Gunfire Hill. **Tel** *(046) 603-1100.* *8am–4:30pm Mon–Fri.*

Reminiscent of an old fort, this monument on Gunfire Hill was built in 1974 in the shape of a ship and commemorates the British families who arrived in the area in 1820. The modern Monument Theatre complex nearby is the main venue for the popular 11-day National Arts Festival *(see p41)* held here annually. Many paintings decorate the impressive foyer.

The Old Provost was once a military prison

Environs: 34 km (21 miles) north of Grahamstown lies the 445-sq-km (172-sq-mile) **Great Fish River Reserve**. After the Fifth Frontier War of 1819, the land between the Keiskamma and Great Fish rivers was declared neutral territory, and British settlers were brought in to act as a buffer against the Xhosa incursions. Today, the area is the largest wildlife reserve in the Eastern Cape province, home to kudu, eland, hartebeest, hippo, black rhino, buffalo and leopard.

Accommodation is provided in comfortable lodges. A two-day guided trail follows the river; hikers stay overnight in a tented camp.

Great Fish River Reserve

Fort Beaufort Rd. **Tel** *(040) 653-8010.*

Camera obscura in the Observatory Museum

VISITORS' CHECKLIST

Road map D5. *200,000.* *Port Elizabeth, 127 km (79 miles) to NE.* *High Street.* *Cathcart Arms Hotel, Market Square.* *63 High Street, (046) 622-3241.* *8:30am–5pm Mon–Fri, 8:30am–noon Sat.* *Good Fri, 25 Dec, pub hols.* *National Arts Festival (Jul).* **www**.grahamstown.co.za

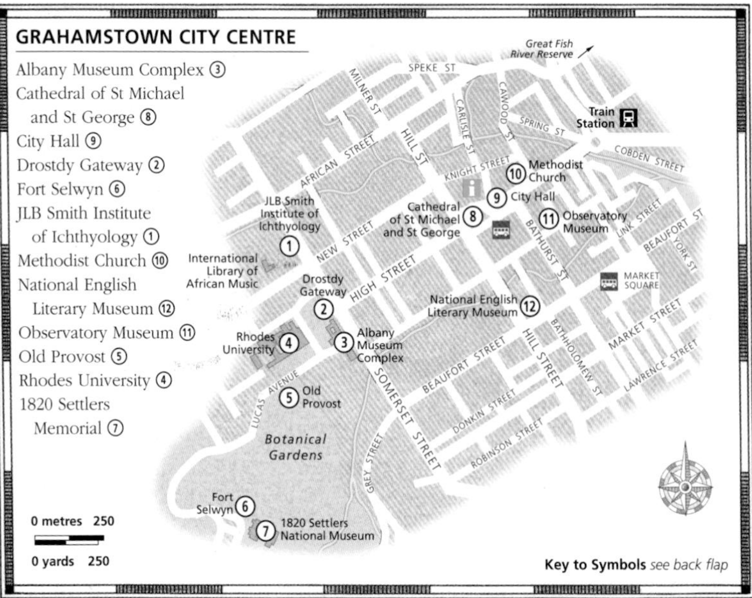

Introducing the East Coast and Interior

Crowned by Southern Africa's highest mountains, a serrated spine that runs the length of this region, the Eastern Cape, Lesotho and KwaZulu-Natal offer rugged mountain scenery, undulating hills, and superb beaches. The powerful currents of the warm Indian Ocean carve the wave-battered cliffs of the Wild Coast. Although an almost continuous chain of coastal resorts extends 160 km (100 miles) south of Durban, Africa's largest port, much of the coastline remains unspoilt and accessible only along winding dirt roads. In the far north, subtropical forests and savannah provide a haven for an abundance of big game and birds, while coastal lakes and the ocean lure fishermen and holiday-makers.

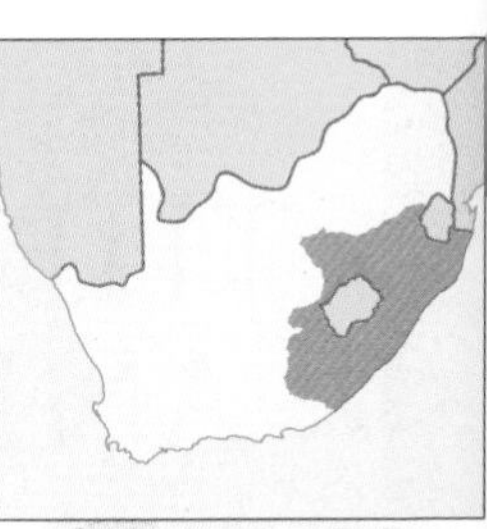

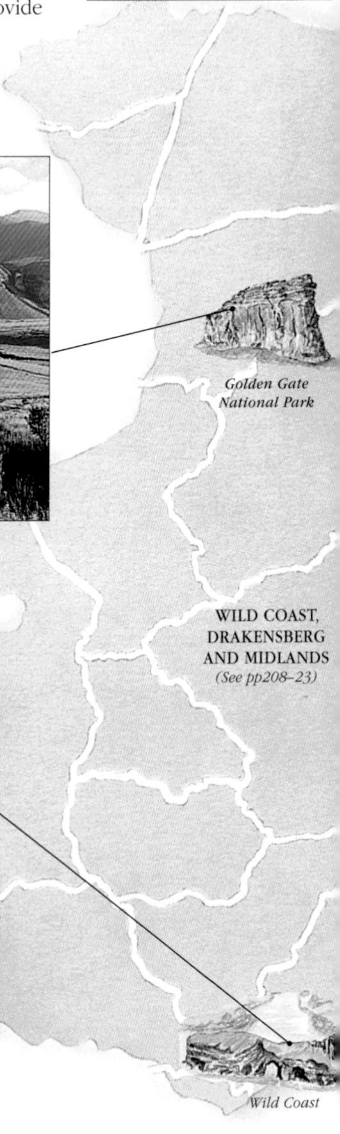

Golden Gate Highlands National Park *in the northeastern Free State lies in the foothills of the Maluti mountains. Magnificent scenery, impressive sandstone formations like Sentinel Rock, abundant wildlife and pleasant walks are the attractions in this park* (see p217).

WILD COAST, DRAKENSBERG AND MIDLANDS
(See pp208–23)

0 kilometres 100

0 miles 100

The Hole in the Wall *is situated just off the coast at the mouth of the Mpako River. It is one of the best known sites on the romantic Wild Coast* (see p213).

◁ **Loggerhead turtle hatchlings on Sodwana Bay beach, along the Maputaland Coast**

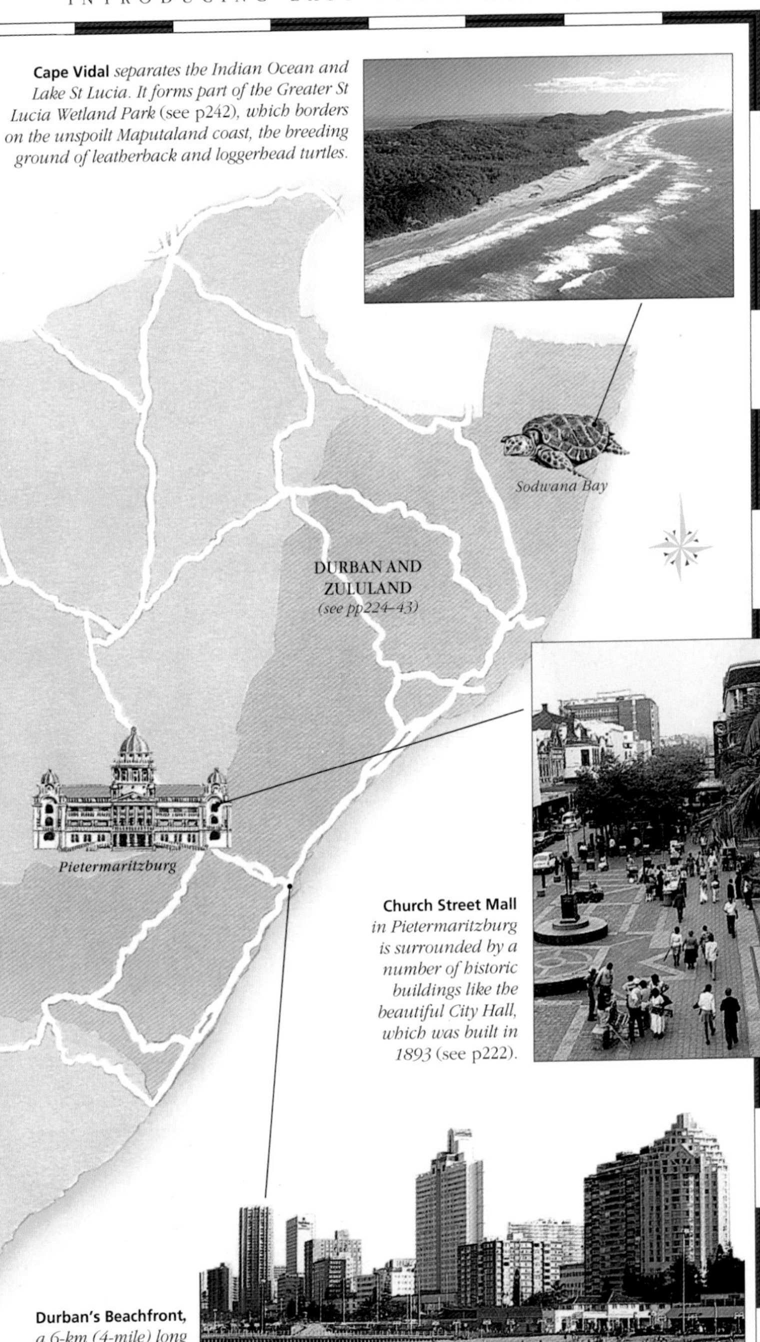

Cape Vidal *separates the Indian Ocean and Lake St Lucia. It forms part of the Greater St Lucia Wetland Park* (see p242), *which borders on the unspoilt Maputaland coast, the breeding ground of leatherback and loggerhead turtles.*

Church Street Mall *in Pietermaritzburg is surrounded by a number of historic buildings like the beautiful City Hall, which was built in 1893* (see p222).

Durban's Beachfront, *a 6-km (4-mile) long stretch of hotels, restaurants and entertainment venues along the Indian Ocean shoreline, is also known as the Golden Mile (see p228).*

Zulu Culture

Clay pot

The reputation of being a fierce warrior nation, fuelled by written accounts of the 1879 Anglo-Zulu War, has been enhanced by dramatic films like *Zulu* and, more recently, the internationally acclaimed television series *Shaka Zulu*. Many sites associated with Zulu history can be visited in the Ulundi, Eshowe and Melmoth districts of KwaZulu-Natal. It is true that the Zulu fought determinedly to defend their land, but their culture also reflects other, gentler, aspects in beadwork, pottery and basketry. In the remote Tugela River Valley and the northern parts of the province, rural people uphold many old customs and dances.

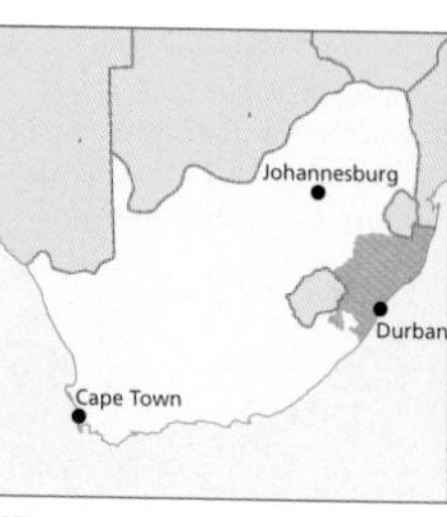

KEY

KwaZulu-Natal

Oxhide was stretched on the ground and cured to make clothing and shields.

Fence made of poles and woven reeds.

Zulu Beehive Hut
A framework of saplings is covered with plaited grass or rushes. A hide screen affords additional privacy.

Maize, the staple diet, is ground and boiled to form a stiff, lumpy porridge.

Basket weaver

ZULU CRAFTS

The Zulu people are renowned as weavers and for their colourful beadwork. Baskets and mats made from *ilala* palm fronds and *imizi* grass are very decorative and especially popular. Most baskets display the traditional triangle or diamond shape, a symbol representing the male and female elements. Shiny glass beads introduced by the early 19th-century traders created a new custom. Today, artistic beadwork forms an important part of Zulu culture. Every pattern and colour has symbolic significance, as in the *incwadi*, or love-letters, that are made by young women and presented to eligible men.

Zulu beadwork and spoon

Utshwala *(beer) is prepared by the women, using sorghum. The fermented liquid is then strained through long grass sieves to separate the husks.*

Zulu dances require stamina and agility

TRADITIONAL DANCING

In Zulu society, social gatherings almost always involve dancing. Most Zulu dances require a high level of fitness – and a lack of inhibition. While ceremonial dances can involve large crowds of gyrating, clapping and stamping performers, small groups of performers need only the encouragement of an accompanying drum and singing, whistling or ululating onlookers. Lore and clan traditions may be related through the dance; alternatively, the movements may serve as a means of social commentary.

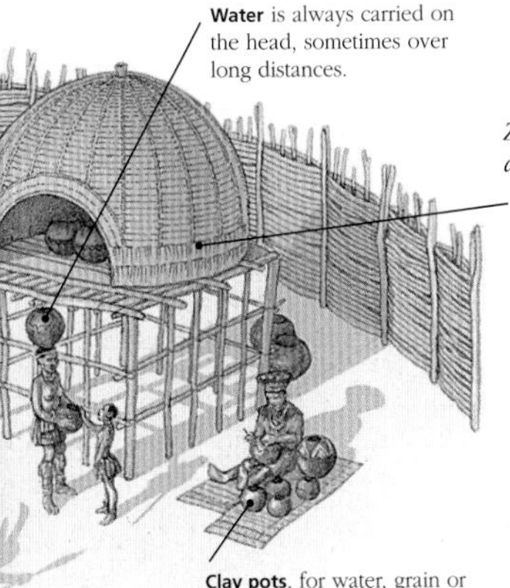

Water is always carried on the head, sometimes over long distances.

Grain Storage *To protect their grain from birds and rodents, the Zulu stored maize and sorghum in a hut on long stilts.*

Clay pots, for water, grain or sorghum beer, are smoothed and decorated before firing.

Cattle *are a symbol of wealth and play an important part in Zulu society. They are kept in a kraal (securely fenced enclosure) at night.*

THE ZULU KRAAL

Historically the *imizi* (Zulu kraal) was a circular settlement that enclosed several *uhlongwa* (beehive-shaped grass huts) grouped around an enclosure in which the cattle were corralled at night. Although the principle of the kraal continues, traditional architectural styles are seldom seen nowadays. Cement, bricks, concrete blocks and corrugated iron sheeting are the modern choices.

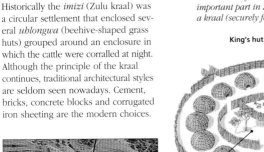

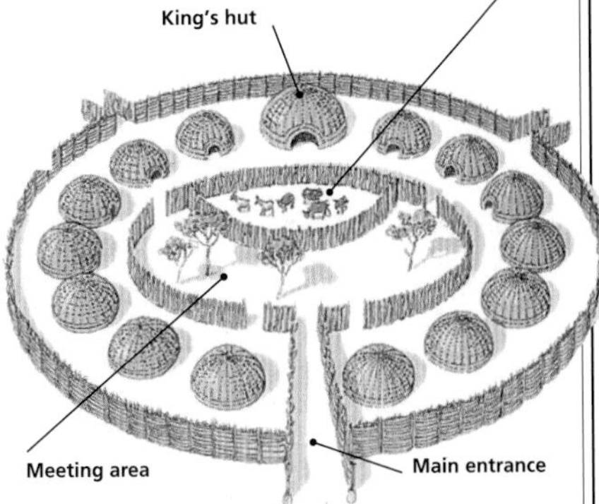

Traditional weapons *are still an integral part of Zulu culture, even today, and men often carry wooden staffs and clubs. At political meetings and rallies, tempers tend to flare, and as a result the carrying of traditional weapons has been outlawed.*

Durban's Surfing Scene

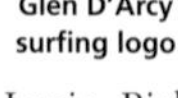
Glen D'Arcy surfing logo

In the 1960s, fibreglass surfboards replaced the canvas-covered wooden versions, causing a surge in devotees to the sport. Durban, with its warm currents, consistent waves and wide beaches, quickly became the surfing capital of the country. Some of the international greats the city has produced were Max Wetland, Shaun Thomson and Martin Potter, while current champions include David Weare, Travis Logie, Ricky Basnett and Jordy Smith. Although surfing venues can vary, favourite Durban hotspots are North Beach, New Pier, the Bay of Plenty and Snake Park. For the more experienced surfer, there is Cave Rock Bluff, south of the harbour.

Jordy Smith, *one of a new breed of young surfers to come out of Durban, was crowned champion at the ISA World Surfing Games in California in October 2006.*

"Bottom turn" *is the term used to describe the manoeuvre at the base of a wave; it is often followed by a "floater", which is when the surfer floats across the top of the wave to generate speed.*

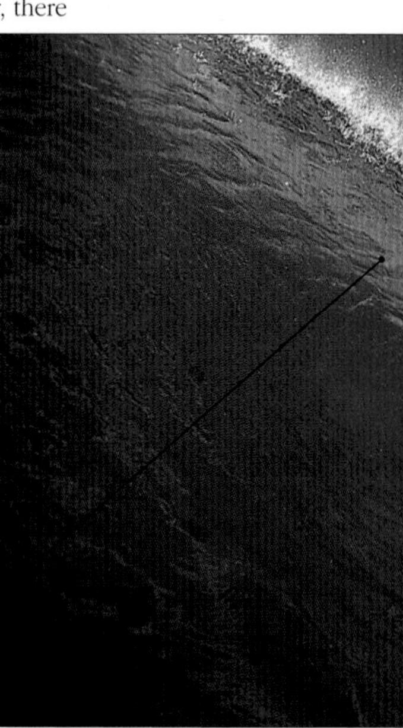
The perfect wave provides an exhilarating ride. Durban is famous for its superb waves.

CAVE ROCK

Cave Rock is Durban's premier big-wave surf spot. The presence of a deep ocean channel *(see p25)* and a reef near the shore produces powerful big waves that compare with those that made Hawai'i world-famous.

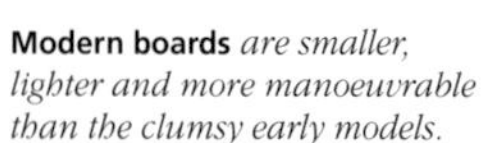
Modern boards *are smaller, lighter and more manoeuvrable than the clumsy early models.*

Competition long boards must exceed 2.8 m (9 ft) in length and weigh between 5.2–7 kg (11–15 lbs).

Short boards are lighter, more manoeuvrable, and are not allowed to exceed 3.2 kg (7 lbs) to qualify for contests.

Wax is rubbed on the top of the board to improve the surfer's grip.

Shaun Thomson *(middle) became a local hero and surfing icon when he won the World Championship title in 1977.*

SURFING CULTURE

Surfing has produced a unique life-orientation and philosophy followed by dedicated devotees around the globe. Laid-back and easy-going, it strives for simplicity and centres on the enjoyment of one of nature's most powerful forces: water. Graffiti and murals in Durban integrate the thrills and spills of surfing with the cityscape, transforming the bland walls into roaring tubes of salt and spray.

The lip forms as the base of the wave encounters the reef.

The tube of the wave curls up and around behind the surfer.

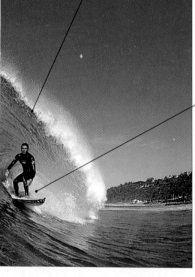

Surf-wear fashion *is a lucrative spin-off industry. Imaginative creations that reflect surfing's way of life are produced by brands such as Quiksilver and Billabong and command designer-wear prices.*

Surfing heroes, *such as Kelly Slater, attract cult status wherever they go. Each year, big surf contests draw devoted surf "groupies" and autograph hunters to Durban's beachfront.*

The Gunston 500, *South Africa's premier surfing event, takes place over six days every July. First staged in 1969 with prize money of R500 (which gave rise to the contest's name), it was the first professional surfing event to be held outside Hawai'i.*

SURFING LINGO

Tube – ride through the concave curve formed by the body of the wave.
Lip – the tip of the wave (its most powerful part).
Barrel – ride through the curve of a wave that ends in the wave breaking on the surfer.
Bomb – enormous wave.
Filthy – excellent surf.
Grommet – a beginner.
Shundies – thank you.
Tassie – a young woman.
Cactus – any person that surfers do not like.

The Wild Coast ❶

The second-largest city in the Eastern Cape and the country's only river port, East London is a good starting point for exploring the shores of the former Transkei *(see p199)*. Appropriately named "Wild Coast", this area is one of South Africa's most under-developed, where rural communities adhere to age-old traditions, and spectacular beaches front a section of the Indian Ocean that is notorious for its shipwrecks. Much of the land here is communally owned by the Xhosa-speaking inhabitants.

East London's Orient Beach is popular with bathers and surfers

Exploring the Wild Coast

The Wild Coast is an outdoor paradise with rugged cliffs, an unspoilt coastline, sheltered bays, pounding breakers and dense coastal forests. Most resorts, reserves and villages are accessible from the N2, but many roads are untarred and in poor condition. There is no public transport to speak of, the best option is the Baz Bus, which covers the N2.

East London

Road map E5. 808,000. *R72, 12 km (7 miles) W of East London. Station Rd. Oxford St. Shop 1 & 2, King's Tourism Centre Esplanade (043) 722-6015.*

East London is a pleasant seaside town on the Buffalo River. Several good swimming beaches are washed by the warm waters of the Indian Ocean.

Among several interesting sites is the statue in front of the City Hall of Black Consciousness leader, Steve Biko. Born in the Eastern Cape, he died under dubious circumstances while in police custody.

Latimer's Landing, the city's waterfront, offers good river and harbour views.

Rock angling is a popular sport

COELACANTH

In 1938 a boat fishing off the Chalumna River mouth near East London netted an unusual fish. The captain sent it to the East London Museum, whose curator, Marjorie Courtenay-Latimer, contacted Professor JLB Smith, ichthyologist at Rhodes University. The fish belonged to a species believed to have become extinct with the dinosaurs. The reward offered for another *Latimeria chalumnae* was claimed only in 1952, when one was netted off the Comoros Islands. The coelacanth is steel-blue and covered in heavy scales; it is distinguished by its six primitive, limb-like fins.

The coelacanth

East London Museum

319 Oxford St. ***Tel*** *(043) 743-0686* *9am–4pm Mon–Fri, 10am–1pm Sat, 10am–3pm Sun.* *Good Fri, 25 Dec.*

Kwelera

Road map E4. 26 km (17 miles) E of East London. *Yellow Sands Resort, (043) 734-3043.*

Kwelera is one of the most attractive estuaries in the region. There is a resort on the north bank and canoeists can paddle upriver, past hills dotted with huts and cycads, and which echo with the cries of fish eagles. An extensive coastal forest reserve, south of the river mouth, is an ideal habitat for bushbuck.

Morgan's Bay and Kei Mouth

Road map E4. Off the N2, 85 km (53 miles) E of East London. *Morgan's Bay Hotel, (043) 841-1062.*

These coastal villages lie on a stretch of coast renowned for its scenery. At Kei Mouth, a pont transports vehicles across the Great Kei River to the former Xhosa "homeland" known as Transkei. The Morgan's Bay Hotel adjoins the beach, and the Ntshala Lagoon offers safe swimming. Walks along the cliffs afford superb views of the sea.

Further south, at Double Mouth, a spur overlooking the ocean and estuary provides one of the finest views in the whole country.

Kei Mouth to Mbashe River

Road map E4. 95 km (59 miles) E of East London. (043) 841-1004.

The Kei River marks the start of the Wild Coast. Twenty rivers enter this 80-km (50-mile) long stretch, along which is strung a succession of old-fashioned family hotels. Kei Mouth is only an hour's drive from East London, making it a popular weekend destination.

Further north, Dwesa Nature Reserve extends along the coast from the Nqabara River. The reserve is home to rare tree dassies and samango monkeys. The grassland,

Traditional Xhosa huts dot the hillsides of the former Transkei

coastline and forest are all pristine. The Haven is on the banks of the Mbashe River within the Cwebe Nature Reserve. Adjoining reserves conserve 60 sq km (23 sq miles) of dense forest, home to bushbuck and blue duiker, as well as coastal grasslands inhabited by eland, hartebeest, wildebeest and zebra. A hiking trail follows the entire Wild Coast, but the section from Mbashe to Coffee Bay is the most spectacular.

Coffee Bay

Road map E4. Off the N2. *Ocean View Hotel, (047) 575-2005/6.*

Allegedly named after a ship carrying coffee which was wrecked at the site in 1863, Coffee Bay is popular for fishing, swimming and beach walks. There are a number of superbly sited hotels set above the sandy beaches. A prominent detached cliff, separated from the mainland by erosion, has been named Hole in the Wall; it is a conspicuous landmark located 6 km (4 miles) south along the coast. Many centuries of swirling wave action have carved an arch through the centre of the cliff.

Umngazi Mouth

Road map E4. 25 km (16 miles) S of Port St Johns. *Umngazi River Bungalows, (047) 564-1115/6/8/9.*

An idyllic estuary framed by forested hills, the Umngazi offers superb snorkelling, canoeing and board-sailing. Umngazi River Bungalows *(see p342)*, on the northern bank, and renowned for its food and service, is one of the leading resorts on the Wild Coast. There is a lovely, sandy beach and the rugged coastline extends south to the cliffs that are known in Xhosa as *Ndluzulu*, after the crashing sound of the surf.

Mkambati Nature Reserve

Road map E4. Off R61 N of Port St Johns. *Eastern Cape Tourism Board, (043) 742-4450.*

Wedged between the Mzikaba and Mtentu rivers, Mkambati is the Wild Coast's largest nature reserve. Apart from conserving a 13-km (8-mile) long strip of grassland and unspoilt, rocky coastline, the reserve is known for its endemic plants such as the Mkambati palm, which is found only on the north banks of the rivers. Cape vultures breed in the Mzikaba Gorge. The Mkambati River flows through the reserve in a series of waterfalls of which Horseshoe Falls, near the sea, is the most striking.

Accommodation ranges from a stone lodge to cottages. Outdoor activities include swimming, fishing and horse riding. Animals include eland, springbok, blesbok, impala, blue wildebeest and zebra. An added attraction is that the reserve is near the Wild Coast Sun Hotel and Casino *(see p234)*.

The Xhosa word for Hole in the Wall, *esiKhaleni*, means "the place of sound"

Lesotho ❷

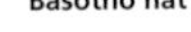
Basotho hat

Surrounded by South Africa, this mountain kingdom, or "Kingdom in the Sky" as it is sometimes referred to, achieved independence from Britain on 4 October 1966. The rugged highlands of Lesotho, which encompass the Drakensberg, Maluti and Thaba-Putsoa mountains, are a popular destination for visitors who enjoy camping, hiking and climbing. Lesotho also boasts fertile river valleys, a rich variety of flora and fauna, and a strong cultural heritage that is very much kept alive by the Basotho people.

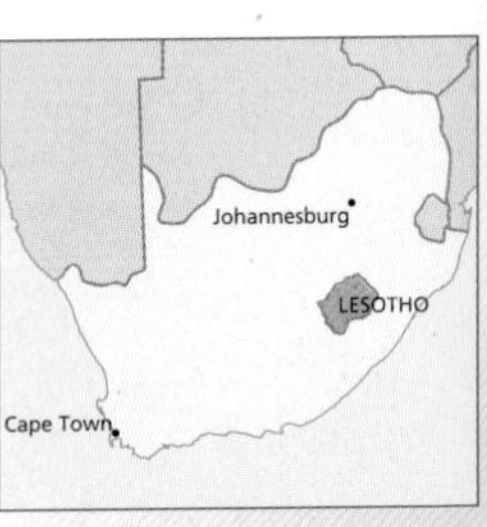

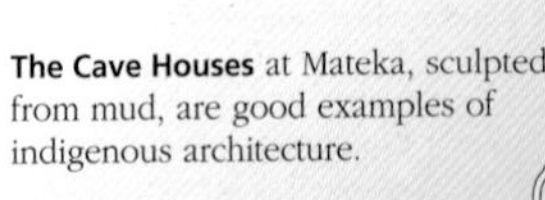

The Cave Houses at Mateka, sculpted from mud, are good examples of indigenous architecture.

★ Teyateyaneng
This town, easily accessible from Maseru, is the "craft capital" of Lesotho. The colourful woven jerseys, carpets and wall-hangings are a local speciality.

Maseru
Founded by the British in 1869, Maseru lies on the Caledon River. Buildings and roads destroyed in political turmoil toward the end of 1998 are being restored and rebuilt.

Ficksburg · Peka · Moletsa · Cave · Mateka · Ladybrand · N8 · Teyateyaneng · A1 · Sefikeng · MASERU · Thaba Bosiu · Mazenod · Roma · Likalaneng · Makhaleng · Caledon · Kolo · Morija · Ramabanta · A2 · A20 · Mafeteng · Rock Paintings · Semonkong · Bird Park · Thabana Morena · Dinosaur Tracks · Cannibal Caves · Mohale's Hoek · Mount Moorosi · Telle-Bridge · A4 · Dinosaur Tracks · Moyeni (Quthing)

STAR FEATURES

★ Teyateyaneng

★ Katse Dam

★ Sani Pass

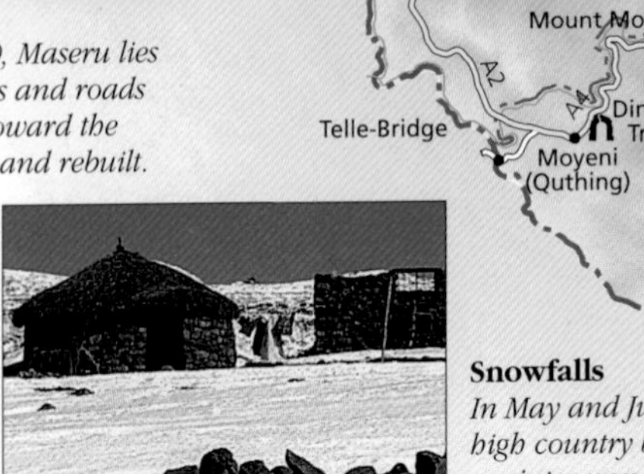

Snowfalls
In May and June the high country becomes a winter wonderland, but no commercial skiing ventures exist.

For hotels and restaurants in this region see pp340–42 and pp367–8

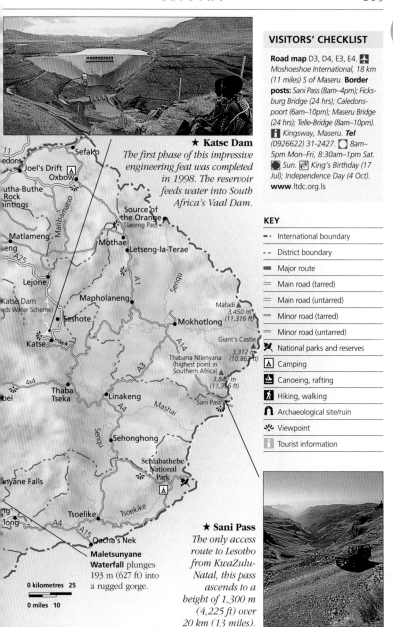

★ Katse Dam
The first phase of this impressive engineering feat was completed in 1998. The reservoir feeds water into South Africa's Vaal Dam.

VISITORS' CHECKLIST

Road map D3, D4, E3, E4. *Moshoeshoe International, 18 km (11 miles) S of Maseru.* **Border posts:** *Sani Pass (8am–4pm); Ficksburg Bridge (24 hrs); Caledonspoort (6am–10pm); Maseru Bridge (24 hrs); Telle-Bridge (8am–10pm).* *Kingsway, Maseru.* **Tel** *(0926622) 31-2427.* *8am–5pm Mon–Fri, 8:30am–1pm Sat.* *Sun.* *King's Birthday (17 Jul); Independence Day (4 Oct).* **www**.ltdc.org.ls

KEY

- International boundary
- District boundary
- Major route
- Main road (tarred)
- Main road (untarred)
- Minor road (tarred)
- Minor road (untarred)
- National parks and reserves
- Camping
- Canoeing, rafting
- Hiking, walking
- Archaeological site/ruin
- Viewpoint
- Tourist information

Maletsunyane Waterfall plunges 193 m (627 ft) into a rugged gorge.

0 kilometres 25

0 miles 10

★ Sani Pass
The only access route to Lesotho from KwaZulu-Natal, this pass ascends to a height of 1,300 m (4,225 ft) over 20 km (13 miles).

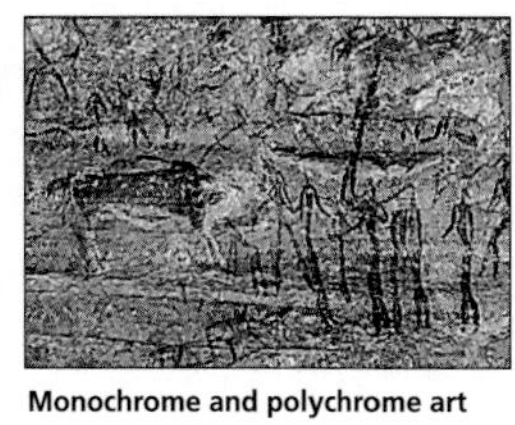
Monochrome and polychrome art

ROCK PAINTINGS AND DINOSAUR TRACKS

Due to its remoteness, Lesotho has remained relatively uncommercialized. The high mountains, where stout Basotho ponies are often the only form of transport, contain some of the finest examples of rock art in Southern Africa. Thaba Bosiu near Maseru and the Sekubu Caves at Butha-Buthe in the north are just two of the more than 400 worthwhile sites. Fossilized dinosaur tracks are found at places like Moyeni (Quthing), and the Tsikoane Mission at Hlotse.

Kamberg ❸

Road map E3. Estcourt. *KwaZulu-Natal Nature Conservation, (033) 845-1000.* *8am–6pm Mon–Thu, 8am–4:30pm Fri, 8am–noon Sat & Sun.*

Situated in the Mooi River valley, Kamberg is known for its trout fishing locations. There are several small dams near the trout hatchery, which is open to the public and offers guided tours. Walking trails explore the valley or meander along the river.

Shelter Cave has superb San Bushman rock paintings and can be visited with a guide; the return walk takes about four hours. A small chalet camp overlooks the valley.

Kamberg offers good trout fishing in a beautiful setting

Giant's Castle ❹

Road map E3. Estcourt. *KwaZulu-Natal Nature Conservation, (033) 845-1000.* *as Kamberg.*

In 1903 a sanctuary was established in this area to protect some of the last surviving

The high-lying Giant's Castle is covered with snow in winter

eland in South Africa. They now number around 1,500 – one of the largest populations in the country.

A camouflaged hide allows visitors to view endangered bearded vultures (lammergeier), an estimated 200 pairs of which are found here.

Accommodation is in comfortable bungalows and small cottages. The main camp overlooks the Bushman's River, with Giant's Castle (3,314 m; 10,770 ft) dominating the skyline. A number of trails leads off from the camp and a short walk brings visitors to a cave where 500 San Bushman rock paintings, some of which are 800 years old, can be seen.

Champagne Castle ❺

Road map E3. Winterton.

Champagne Castle, at 3,377 m (10,975 ft), is the second-highest peak in South Africa. It juts out from the surrounding escarpment and dominates the horizon in a delightful valley. A 31-km (19-mile) connecting road from the N3 provides convenient access to a cluster of luxury hotels and timeshare resorts, such as the The Nest and the luxurious Drakensberg Sun. Famous institutions like the internationally acclaimed Drakensberg Boys' Choir School, as well as the Dragon Peaks and Monk's Cowl caravan parks are found in this region.

Natal Drakensberg Park ❻

Road map E3. Winterton. *KwaZulu-Natal Nature Conservation, (033) 845-1000.* *as Kamberg.*

The Drakensberg's dramatic and rugged escarpment provides an awesome backdrop to much of the pastoral KwaZulu-Natal Midlands.

The Natal Drakensberg Park covers an area of 2,350 sq km (907 sq miles) and preserves some of South Africa's finest wilderness and conservation area, as well as its highest mountain peaks. Secluded valleys and mist-shrouded,

THE DRAKENSBERG RANGE

The Drakensberg, "dragon mountains", is South Africa's greatest mountain wilderness. It follows the border of Lesotho for 250 km (155 miles) – an escarpment that separates the high, interior plateau from the subtropical coast of KwaZulu-Natal. The Drakensberg is divided into the rocky High Berg and the pastoral Little Berg. Both are superb hiking venues.

For hotels and restaurants in this region see pp340–42 and pp367–8

dense forests are home to an abundance of wildlife, while many rock overhangs shelter some of the finest remaining examples of San Bushman rock art in South Africa today. Since these ancient paintings and etches represent a priceless cultural heritage they must never be touched, or, even worse, be splashed with water to enhance their colours.

KwaZulu-Natal Nature Conservation has established five rest camps within the park which can accommodate 370 visitors, and there are many pleasant campsites, mountain huts and caves that cater for hikers and mountaineers. On the boundaries of the park, particularly in the Cathkin Peak valley, many hotels and resorts offer comfortable accommodation and outdoor sports.

Cathedral Peak ❼

Road map E3. Winterton.

Some of the Drakensberg's finest scenery is found in this region, and the area around Cathedral Peak offers some of the best hiking in the entire range.

The road from Winterton winds for 42 km (26 miles) through Zulu villages that are scattered across the gentle folds of the Mlambonja Valley. The Drakensberg's towering peaks form a dramatic backdrop. From the conservation office near the Cathedral Peak hotel, Mike's Pass gains 500 m (1,625 ft) in 5 km (3 miles). Ndedema Gorge, where many San Bushman paintings adorn rocky overhangs, protects the largest forest in the range.

Royal Natal National Park ❽

Road map E3. Winterton. *Tendele camp, (036) 438-6411.* ***Tel*** *National Parks Board Reservations: (012) 428-9111, (031) 304-4934, or (0338) 45-1000.* *daily.* **www**.saparks.co.za

The Royal Natal National Park has some of Africa's most spectacular scenery. The awe-inspiring Amphitheatre, a crescent-shaped basalt wall 6 km (4 miles) wide, soars to a height of 1,500 m (4,875 ft). Here, the Tugela River plunges 948 m (3,080 ft) into the valley below, making it the second highest waterfall in the world.

Tendele rest camp, above the Tugela River, provides unrivalled views of the countryside below.

In the valleys, the Royal Natal Hotel and Mahai campsite provide easy access to an extensive network of trails that explore the 88-sq-km (34-sq-mile) reserve.

Bearded vulture

Golden Gate Highlands National Park ❾

Road map E3. Clarens. ***Tel*** *National Parks Board Reservations: (012) 428-9111, (058) 255-0012.* *daily.* **www**.saparks.co.za

Situated in the foothills of the Maloti Mountains in the eastern Free State, Golden Gate Highlands National Park encompasses 48 sq km (18 sq miles) of grassland and spectacular sandstone formations.

The park was proclaimed in 1963 to protect the sandstone cliffs above the Little Caledon valley.

Black wildebeest, grey rhebok, oribi, blesbok and mountain reedbuck can be seen, as well as the endangered bearded vulture (lammergeier), black eagle and steppe buzzard.

Accommodation in Glen Reenen Camp consists of chalets and a caravan park, while Brandwag Lodge offers more sophisticated cottages.

The Royal Natal National Park, an unspoilt wilderness

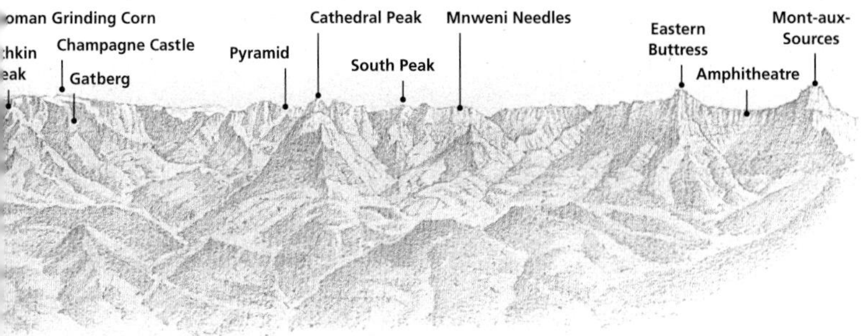

Cattle grazing at the foot of the mighty Drakensberg Mountains ▷

Battlefields Tour ⑩

The peaceful, rolling grasslands and treed hills of northwestern KwaZulu-Natal retain few reminders of the bloody battles that were waged in this corner of South Africa during the 19th century. In the 1820s, Zulu king Shaka's campaign to seize control over the scattered tribes plunged the entire region into turmoil. Over the following 80 years many wars were fought, pitting Zulu against Ndwandwe, Afrikaner against Zulu and English against Afrikaner and Zulu. A detailed guide to the battlefields lists over 50 sites of interest and is available from the local publicity associations and the Talana Museum, where expert guides can be hired as well.

Monument at Rorke's Drift

Elandslaagte ②
The Boer and British forces clashed here on 22 October 1899, during a severe storm. The British were forced to retreat to nearby Ladysmith.

Talana Museum ③
This museum commemorates the first battle of the South African War (20 October 1899) when 4,500 British soldiers arrived in Dundee to defend the town and its coal mines.

Ladysmith ①
On 2 November 1899, Boer general Piet Joubert laid siege to Ladysmith and its 12,000 British troops for 118 days.

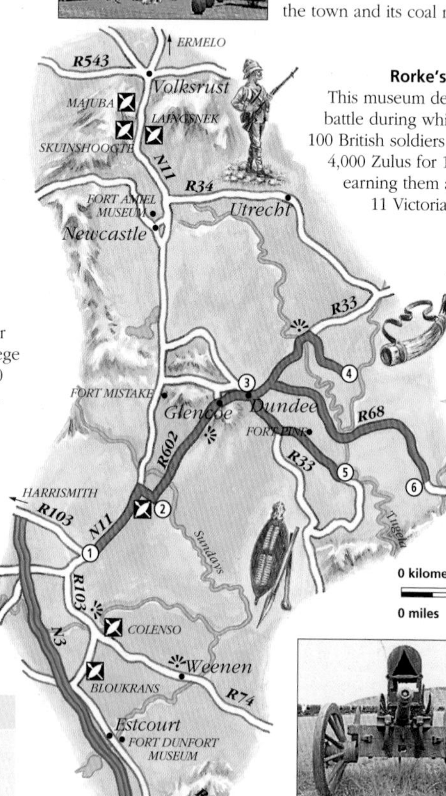

Rorke's Drift ⑤
This museum depicts the battle during which some 100 British soldiers repelled 4,000 Zulus for 12 hours, earning them a total of 11 Victoria crosses.

KEY

- Motorway
- Tour route
- Other roads
- Viewpoint
- Battle site

TIPS FOR DRIVERS

Length: 380 km (236 miles).
Stopping-off points: The towns of Ladysmith and Dundee have restaurants and accommodation. Audio tapes can be bought from the Talana Museum in Dundee and at Fugitives Drift, which also offers guided tours and accommodation.

Isandlhwana ⑥
Zulu *impis*, angered by an invasion of their territory, attacked a British force on 22 January 1879.

Blood River ④
For years seen as a symbol of the Afrikaners' victory over the Zulus, this battle gave rise to a public holiday – 16 December, now called Day of Reconciliation.

Midmar Dam is surrounded by a tranquil nature reserve

Spioenkop Nature Reserve ⓫

Road map E3. 35 km (22 miles) SW of Ladysmith on Winterton Rd. ***Tel*** *(036) 488-1578.* *6am–6pm daily.*

The picturesque dam nestles at the foot of the 1,466-m high (4,764 ft) Spioenkop which was scene of a decisive battle between British and Boer forces in 1891 during the South African War *(see p55)*. Countless graves and memorials are scattered across the mountain's summit as a grim reminder.

Today, Spioenkop is very popular with outdoor enthusiasts. The dam offers fishing and boating, while eland, hartebeest, zebra, giraffe, kudu, buffalo and white rhino can be seen in the surrounding nature reserve. Here, there is also a pleasant campsite, as well as a swimming pool, battlefields museum, tennis courts, children's playground and a slipway on the southern shore. Picnic sites are situated along the southern shoreline, and two short trails encourage visitors to view game on foot.

Two bush camps offer luxury accommodation. Ntenjwa overlooks the peaceful upper reaches of the large dam and is only accessible by private boat or the ferry service provided by Nature Conservation.

Iphika, at the foot of Spioenkop on the northern shore, is a secluded tented safari camp, reached by a private track. As other vehicles are not permitted in this sector, visitors are offered a unique wilderness experience.

The monument to the Battle of Spioenkop overlooks the dam

Midlands Meander ⓬

Road map E3 Mooi River *(033330) 8195.*

The undulating hills of the Natal Midlands, with their green patches of forest and their dairy farms, have long been a retreat favoured by artists and craftspeople. In 1985 six studios established an arts and crafts route: the Midlands Meander. The route quickly gained popularity and now consists of around 140 participating members and studios.

Tapestry detail, Rorke's Drift

There are four routes that meander between the small towns of Hilton, Nottingham Road and Mooi River. Goods on offer include herbs, cheese, wine, pottery, woven cloth, leather itms, furniture, stained glass and antiques.

Of interest is a monument on the R103, just past Midmar Dam, that marks the spot where Nelson Mandela *(see p59)* was arrested by security police on 5 August 1962.

Accommodation along the way ranges from idyllic country hotels, tranquil guest farms and picturesque lodges to comfortable bed and breakfast establishments. There is also a well-known health spa and many quaint country pubs and eateries.

Street-by-Street: Pietermaritzburg ⓭

From its humble beginnings as an irrigation settlement established by Afrikaner farmers in 1836, Pietermaritzburg has developed into the commercial, industrial and administrative centre of the KwaZulu-Natal Midlands. An intriguing blend of Victorian, Indian, African and modern architecture and culture combine to produce a distinctly South African city. Many historic buildings and monuments, as well as galleries and museums, are located around the city centre and in the western suburbs, which nestle at the foot of a range of densely wooded hills. Visitors can ramble through the surrounding forests and botanic gardens, and visit several nature reserves and recreation resorts located within the city or a few minutes' drive away.

Gandhi Statue
In Pietermaritzburg, in 1893, Gandhi had to leave a first-class train, because he wasn't white.

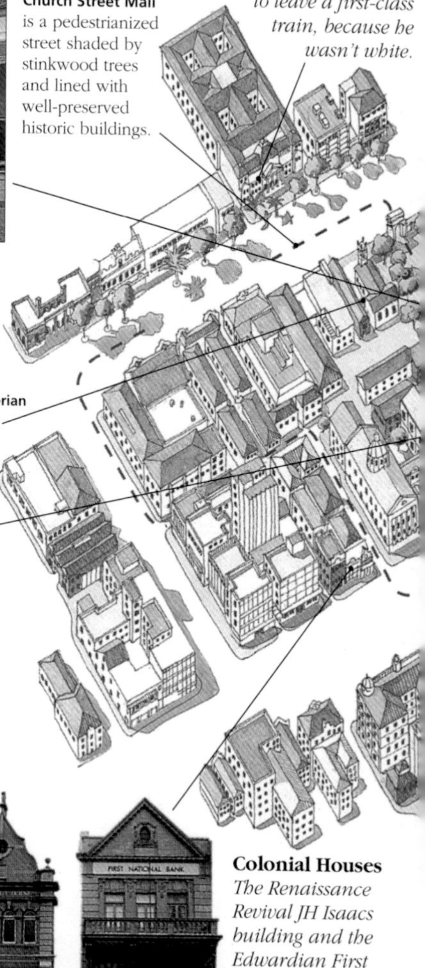

Church Street Mall is a pedestrianized street shaded by stinkwood trees and lined with well-preserved historic buildings.

★ Tatham Art Gallery
Housed in the old Supreme Court, displays at this gallery include works by South African artists, as well as European masters like Edgar Degas, Henri Matisse and Pablo Picasso.

Presbyterian Church

Parliament Building
The seat of the colonial government prior to 1910, it now houses KwaZulu-Natal's provincial legislature.

KEY

 Suggested route

Colonial Houses
The Renaissance Revival JH Isaacs building and the Edwardian First National Bank are two examples of colonial architecture in Longmarket Street.

STAR SIGHTS

★ Tatham Art Gallery

★ City Hall

★ Natal Museum

For hotels and restaurants in this region see pp340–42 and pp367–8

VISITORS' CHECKLIST

Road map E3. 928,000. Durban, 80 km (49 miles) SE Msunduzi Airport, S of the city Top of Church Street. Publicity House, Cnr Langalibalele and Chief Albert Luthuli streets. Publicity House (033) 345-1348. 8am–5pm Mon–Fri, 8am–1pm Sat & public hols. Royal Agricultural Show (May). **www**.pmbtourism.co.za

★ City Hall

This handsome red-brick building was completed in 1893. The clock tower, a later addition commissioned in 1900, rises 47 m (153 ft) above the street.

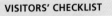

Voortrekker Museum

The Church of the Vow, built by the Voortrekkers after the Battle of Blood River (see p53), *is the focus of the Voortrekker Museum on the corner of Longmarket and Boshoff streets.*

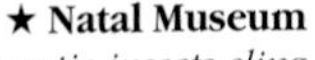

★ Natal Museum

Gigantic insects cling to the outside walls of this museum, whose superb displays include African mammals, birds and dinosaurs.

Exploring Pietermaritzburg

The town is a treasure trove of architecture and lends itself well to walking excursions. One of the oldest quarters, the Lanes – a labyrinth of narrow alleys between Church and Longmarket streets – gives an idea of what Pietermaritzburg was like in days gone by.

Environs: Midmar Dam, a weekend and holiday venue for watersports enthusiasts and fishermen, lies 27 km (17 miles) north of Pietermaritzburg in the **Midmar Dam Resort**. A small wildlife reserve on the southern shore is home to several antelope species, among them black wildebeest, eland, hartebeest, springbok, blesbok and zebra.

The origins of Howick, some 18 km (11 miles) north of Pietermaritzburg, date back to 1850. In the town, a viewing platform and restaurant overlook the beautiful Howick Falls, equal in height to the Victoria Falls in Zimbabwe.

On the Karkloof Road, just outside Howick, the **Umgeni Valley Nature Reserve** offers hiking trails through the steep-sided, boulder-strewn valley carved by the Umgeni River. The track leading from the entrance gate provides scenic views of the gorge.

Midmar Dam Resort
Howick. ***Tel*** *(033) 330-2067.*
24 hours daily.

Umgeni Valley Nature Reserve
Howick. ***Tel*** *(033) 330-3931.*
8am–4:30pm daily.
25 Dec.

The Howick Falls

Durban ❶

Life ring

Vasco Da Gama's Port Natal was renamed Durban in honour of Cape Governor Benjamin D'Urban after Zulu chief Shaka gave the land to the British in 1824. Today the former trading post is the holiday capital of KwaZulu-Natal. Sunny days and the warm Indian Ocean draw visitors to a beachfront flanked by high-rise hotels and holiday apartments. Attractions such as Water World and the Umgeni River Bird Park lie north of South Africa's principal harbour.

An aerial view of the Paddling Pools on Durban's Golden Mile

Exploring Durban

Most of the city's attractions are located along the beachfront, close together and within walking distance from the hotels. But Durban is not only about seaside fun; the city centre has many historic buildings, as well as museums, theatres and exciting markets. For safety reasons, visitors are advised not to explore the city on their own but to join one of the many organized tours.

The Golden Mile

Marine Parade.

The land side of this 6-km (4-mile) long holiday precinct is lined with a continuous row of hotels, while the seaward edge consists of amusement parks, an aerial cableway, craft sellers, pubs, restaurants, ice-cream parlours, piers, sandy beaches and a promenade.

Along the Golden Mile is where visitors will find many brightly decorated rickshaws. Their colourful drivers, festooned in beads and tall, elaborate headdresses, are a curious amalgamation of traditional African practices and Indian influences.

uShaka Marine World offers an excellent aquarium and dolphinarium. The aquarium's main tank is home to many species of tropical fish, turtles and sting rays. Scuba divers enter the tank twice a day to feed the fish. Shows at the dolphinarium feature dolphins, seals and penguins. The **FitzSimons Snake Park** exhibits indigenous snakes, as well as crocodiles, lizards and tortoises. It also plays the vital role of being South Africa's major producer of snake-bite serum.

uShaka Marine World
1 Bell St, Point Road. ***Tel*** *(031) 328-8000.* *9am–5pm daily.*
www.ushakamarineworld.co.za

FitzSimons Snake Park
248 Lower Marine Parade, Golden Mile. ***Tel*** *(073) 156-9606.* *9am–4:30pm Sun–Fri (to 5pm Sun).*

Durban Waterfront

Victoria Embankment.

The bright murals and pink staircase that lead to the **BAT Centre** (Bartel Arts Trust) are an appropriate introduction to Durban's innovative dock-side art-and-music scene.

The centre has a 300-seat theatre and music venue, a dance studio, art galleries and shops. Next door, are a pub and a fine restaurant, both of which overlook the harbour.

Photographs and memorabilia of Durban's seafaring past are displayed in the **Natal Maritime Museum**. The tugboats *Ulundi* and *JR More* and the minesweeper SAS *Durban* form part of the exhibits.

BAT Centre
Victoria Embankment. ***Tel*** *(031) 332-0451.* *8:30am–4:30pm Mon–Fri, 10am–2:30pm Sat.* *public hols.*

Natal Maritime Museum
Victoria Embankment. ***Tel*** *(031) 311-2230.* *8:30am–4pm Mon–Sat, 11am–3:30pm Sun.*

The Wheel

55 Gillespie St. *(031) 332-4324.* *9am–5pm daily.* *1 Jan.*

The top floor of this shopping centre, which comprises 140 shops and restaurants and 12 cinemas, is modelled after a Moroccan village, but the main focus is a gigantic ferris wheel.

Modern art exhibit at the BAT Centre

The mock-Tudor façade of The Playhouse

VISITORS' CHECKLIST

Road map F3. KwaZulu-Natal Province. *3,200,000. 14 km (9 miles) SW of city centre. New Durban Station, Umgeni Rd. New Durban Station. Old Station Bldg, 160 Pine Street. (031) 304-4934. Comrades Marathon (Jun); Rothmans July Handicap (Jul); Gunston 500 (Jul).* **www**.durban.kzn.org.za

Central Durban
Beautifully restored buildings and interesting museums can be found in the city centre. All are situated within walking distance of one another. The cafés and restaurants that line the streets offer respite from the heat and humidity.

Completed in 1910, Durban's **City Hall** was modelled after that of Belfast, in Northern Ireland. The central dome is 48 m (156 ft) high while statues symbolizing art, literature, music and commerce flank the four smaller domes.

The **Natural Science Museum** is situated on the ground floor of the City Hall. Exhibits vary from a display of South African wildlife to a geological collection, a bird hall, a dinosaur exhibit and an Egyptian mummy. Fascinating, if disturbing, are the oversized insects featured in the *Kwa-Nunu* section of the museum.

Upstairs, the **Durban Art Gallery** began collecting black South African art in the 1970s, the first in the country to do so.

What was once Durban's Court now houses the **Local History Museum**. It contains relics of early colonial life in what was then Natal.

The Playhouse, opposite City Hall, offers top-class entertainment, ranging from opera to experimental theatre.

Natural Science Museum
City Hall, Smith St. ***Tel** (031) 311-2256. 8:30am–5pm daily (from 11am Sun). Good Fri, 25 Dec.*

Durban Art Gallery
City Hall, Smith St. ***Tel** (031) 311-2264. 8:30am–4pm daily (from 11am Sun). Good Fri, 25 Dec.*

Local History Museum
Cnr Smith & Aliwal sts. ***Tel** (031) 311-2225. 8:30am–4pm daily (from 11am Sun). Good Fri, 25 Dec.*

The Playhouse
231 Smith St. ***Tel** (031) 369-9555.*

In the Natural Science Museum

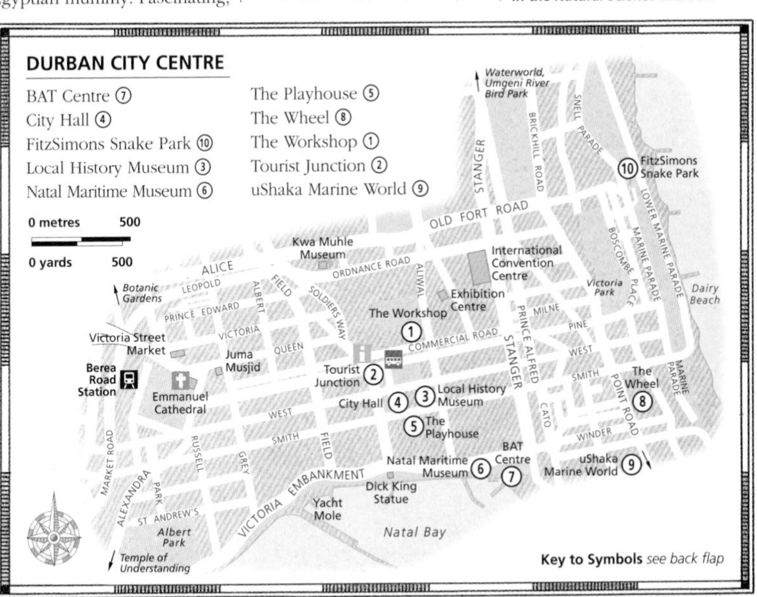

Exploring Durban

Away from the city centre, beautiful mosques, richly decorated temples and vibrant street markets await the visitor. Nature reserves and sanctuaries are situated on the outskirts of Durban, among them the Umgeni River Bird Park, north of the city, which houses exotic birds in walk-through aviaries. Water World is a perfect destination on a hot day, while the Hindu Temple of Understanding, in the suburb of Chatsworth, never fails to impress with its grandiose opulence. Tour operators offer tailor-made coach trips to all of these sights.

Tourist Junction

Station Building, 160 Pine St. ***Tel** (031) 304-4934.* *8am–5pm Mon–Fri, 9am–2pm Sat & Sun.*

Tucked between Commercial and Pine streets stands the former railway station. The four-storey, red-brick building was completed in 1894 and now houses the tourist centre. In the entrance of the building stands a statue in memory of Mahatma Gandhi, who bought a train ticket to Johannesburg here in June 1893.

The building's most curious feature is the roof, designed to carry the weight of 5 m (16 ft) of snow. The London firm of architects accidentally switched plans – and the roof of Toronto station caved in during the first heavy snowfalls.

The Tourist Junction has a comprehensive range of maps and brochures, and the staff can advise on several walking tours of the city centre. There is also a useful booking office for accommodation at the national parks (the only other offices are in Cape Town and Pretoria) and a booking office for long-distance bus tours.

The Workshop

99 Aliwal St. ***Tel** (031) 304-9894.* *8:30am–5pm Mon–Fri, 10am–4pm Sat & Sun.*

Durban's premier shopping experience, The Workshop is housed in a vast, steel-girded Victorian building that was once the railway workshop.

Extensive renovations have transformed it into a postmodern complex, with "old-world" touches like fanlights, brass- and wrought-iron trimmings.

The Workshop houses over 120 shops, boutiques, jewellers, a supermarket and several cinemas, as well as a large fast food and restaurant area.

Opposite The Workshop, on the opposite side of Aliwal Street, in the direction of the beach, are the big grounds of the Durban Exhibition Centre. A bustling outdoor market is held here on every Sunday morning. It is very popular and draws many shoppers to its craft, fruit and vegetable stalls and the colourful curio displays.

Bananas

Exotic curry and masala spice

Victoria Street Market

Cnr Queen & Victoria sts. ***Tel** (031) 306-4021.* *6am–6pm Mon–Fri, 6am–2pm Sat, 10am–2pm Sun.*

At the end of the N3 flyover, where the highway meets the streets of central Durban, is the Victoria Street Market. The building is a striking city feature – each one of its 11 domes was modelled on a notable building in India.

In this crowded and noisy bazaar, visitors can sample the tastes and aromas of the Orient as they browse through 116 stalls offering spices and incense. Upstairs, 56 shops sell silk, linen and other fabrics, as well as brassware, leather goods and ceramics.

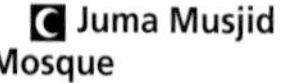

Juma Musjid Mosque

Cnr Queen & Grey sts. ***Tel** (031) 306-0026.* *10am–noon, 2–3pm Mon–Sat.* *book in advance.*

The impressive Juma Musjid Mosque, also known as Grey Street Mosque, lies across the road from the Victorian Street Market. Completed in 1927, it is the largest mosque on the African continent.

Visitors are allowed inside at certain times. A strict dress code is enforced, and shoes must be removed before entering the building.

Durban Botanic Gardens

Sydenham Rd. ***Tel** (031) 201-1303.* *7:30am–5:15pm Apr–Sep; 7:30am–5:45pm Sep–Apr.*

Heading north on Grey Street, the Durban Botanic Gardens is located near the Greyville

The Workshop houses a wide variety of shops

racecourse. It was established in 1849 as an experimental station for tropical crops.

The Ernest Thorp Orchid House, named after an early curator, gained renown as the first naturalistic botanical display in South Africa.

The spectacular cycad and palm collection on the 15-ha (38-acre) property is one of the largest of its kind in the world. It includes several rare species, like a male *Encephalartos woodii* from the Ngoye forest, which was successfully transplanted in 1916.

Among the garden's 480 tree species are the oldest jacarandas in South Africa, originally imported from Argentina.

Other attractions include a Braille trail, a sunken garden, a herbarium, an ornamental lake and a tea garden.

Durban's Botanic Gardens is the perfect setting for a picnic

The Temple of Understanding in Chatsworth

Waterworld

Battery Beach Rd. ***Tel*** *(031) 903-3034.* *9am–5pm Mon–Fri, 8am–5pm Sat & Sun.*

This theme park is based on having fun in the water and is easily accessible from the northern beaches which are situated along the Golden Mile.

Given Durban's hot, at times even sultry, climate throughout most of the year, Water World is an extremely popular destination. It offers thrilling water slides, cool wave pools and water chutes in a tropical setting framed by palm trees.

Umgeni River Bird Park

490 Riverside Rd, Northway. ***Tel*** *(031) 579-4600.* *9am–4pm daily.* *25 Dec.*

Bordered on three sides by steep cliffs, and overlooking the north bank of the Umgeni River, 1.5 km (1 mile) from its mouth, the Umgeni River Bird Park enjoys a superb location. Four waterfalls cascade down the cliffs into ponds fringed by palms and lush vegetation. The four large walk-through aviaries allow visitors a face-to-face encounter with some of the 3,000 birds. Among the 400 resident species are rare exotic parrots, toucans, cranes macaws, and hornbills.

Entertaining bird shows are held daily at 11am and 2pm, except Mondays.

Temple of Understanding

Chatsworth. ***Tel*** *(031) 403-3328.* *4:30am–8pm daily.*

This large, ornate temple of the International Society for Krishna Consciousness was designed by the Austrian architect, Hannes Raudner. It is encircled by a moat and a beautiful garden laid out in the shape of a lotus flower.

The daily guided tours take in the awe-inspiring marble temple room and the inner sanctuary, as well as an interesting audio-visual show.

THE HINDU POPULATION OF DURBAN

When the first sugar was produced from sugar cane in 1851, the Natal Colony experienced a major economic boom. Cheap labour was required to work in the plantations, and the colony entered into negotiations with the colonial government in India. Between 1860 and 1911, a total of 152,000 indentured labourers was shipped to Durban from Madras and Calcutta. Tamil and Hindi were the main languages spoken. At the end of their five-year contracts, the workers were offered a free passage back to India. Over half of them opted to remain in South Africa, and became active as retailers and vegetable farmers; in later years many entered commerce, industry and politics. Of the current population of over one million (the largest Indian community outside of Asia), an estimated 68 per cent are Hindu. Deepavali is their most important festival, and begins with the lighting of a lamp for the Goddess of Light, symbolizing the conquest of good over evil.

Statue of Bhaktivedanta Swami, a respected religious teacher

The South Coast ❷

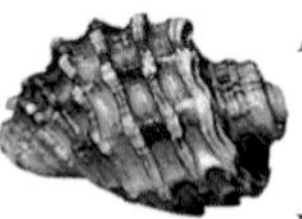
Furry-ridged triton

A year-round combination of sunshine, sand, sea and surf has created an irresistible drawcard for visitors coming from the cooler inland climates or the Northern Hemisphere. Some 30 inviting resort towns form a coastal playground that stretches for 162 km (100 miles) from the Eastern Cape border to Durban. The attractions entail much more than the obvious seaside fun. From nature reserves and bird sanctuaries to glittering casinos – this coast has it all.

Port Edward

Road map E4. N2, 20 km (12 miles) S of Margate. ✈ 🚌 *Margate.* ℹ *Panorama Parade, Margate, (039) 312-2322.*

The village of Port Edward on the Umtamvuna River is the southernmost beachside resort in KwaZulu-Natal. Port Edward is popular for swimming, fishing and boating, and the estuary is navigable far upstream, making it ideal for ski-boats.

The lush Caribbean Estates on the north bank is rated as one of the country's top timeshare resorts.

Between 1976 and 1994 the land south of the Umtamvuna River bridge fell within the homeland known as Transkei. At that time, gambling was illegal under South African law and a casino resort, the Wild Coast Sun, was built here to lure visitors from Durban and the South Coast. Today, it overlooks an unspoilt coastline covered in dense forest and grassland. A challenging 18-hole golf course stretches from the banks of the river to the shores of the lagoon.

The Mzamba Village Market opposite the resort's main entrance offers a range of locally crafted curios, such as woven grass baskets, stone and wood carvings and beadwork. The **Umtamvuna Nature Reserve**, some 8 km (5 miles) north of Port Edward protects a 30-km (19-mile) section of the Umtamvuna River gorge. The trails that explore the dense, subtropical forest are excellent for bird-watching.

Umtamvuna Nature Reserve
Port Edward. Road to Izingolweni. ***Tel*** *(039) 311-2383.* ℹ *Ezemwelo Kzn Wildlife Service, (033) 845-1000.* 🕐 *daily.*

The swimming pool of the Wild Coast Sun

Margate

Road map E4. N2. 👥 *45,000.* ✈ *4 km (2.5 miles) inland.* 🚌 *Beachfront.* ℹ *Panorama Parade, (039) 312-2322.* **www**.sunnymargate.com

Margate is the tourist capital of the South Coast. Daily flights from Johannesburg land at the town's small airport.

Margate's focal point is a broad expanse of golden sand lined by the tall, white towers of dozens of hotels and apartments. Marine Drive, which runs parallel to the coast one block inland, is the town's main business centre, and banks, restaurants, pubs, fast-food outlets, shops, estate agencies and cinemas all compete for the available street frontage.

The approach to the sandy beach leads across well-tended palm-shaded lawns that attract many sunbathers. Along the main beachfront a variety of attractions compete for the holiday-maker's attention. Among these are the paddling pools, a fresh-water swimming pool, water slides, a mini-golf (putt-putt) course, paddle boats and many ice-cream parlours.

Margate's fishing area is one of the drawcards of the town

Uvongo

Road map E4. N2, 12 km (7 miles) N of Margate. 👥 *11,000.* ℹ *Panorama Parade, Margate, (039) 312-2322.*

Just before it empties into the sea, the Vungu River plunges down a 23-m (75-ft) waterfall into a lagoon. High cliffs, overgrown with wild bananas, protect the sheltered lagoon. With its spit of sandy beach separating the river from the ocean, Uvongo is one of the most attractive features along the South Coast.

Boating is popular in the lagoon and the beach, a safe playground for children, is also the site of a daily craft, fruit and basketry market. A restaurant, timeshare resort, tidal pool and paddling pool are a short walk inland.

On the main road, less than 2 km (1.2 miles) south of the beach, the small Uvongo Bird Park is home to many species of exotic birds.

For hotels and restaurants in this region see pp342–4 and pp368–70

THE HIBISCUS COAST

Lying approximately 120 km (74.5 miles) south of Durban, the Hibiscus Coast extends from Hibberdene in the north to Port Edward in the south. As well as beaches and golf courses, this stretch of coastline is home to the famous "Sardine Run". Every June or July, millions of the tiny silver fish head north from their spawning grounds off the Eastern Cape to reach the waters of Port Edward. They are followed by predators such as dolphins, sharks and seals, while numerous sea birds rain down from above to take their fill. The Sardine Run lasts for several weeks, then lessens as the shoal continues its northbound migration.

Birds diving into a shoal of fish during the Sardine Run

Oribi Gorge Nature Reserve

Road map E4. 21 km (13 miles) inland of Port Shepstone. ***Tel*** *(033) 845-1000.* *daily.*

In a region where population densities are high and where sugar cane plantations and coastal resort developments have replaced most of the natural vegetation, the ravine carved by the Umzimkulwana River is a delight for nature lovers. The impressive gorge is 24 km (15 miles) long, up to 5 km (3 miles) wide and 300 m (975 ft) deep.

The reserve has a small rest camp with eight huts perched on the southern rim of the chasm. There is a scenic circular drive, three walking trails and many beautiful picnic spots along the river.

Small, forest-dwelling animals like bushbuck, duiker, samango monkey and leopard occur in the dense forest, which comprises some 500 different tree species.

Oribi Gorge was formed by the Umzimkulwana River

Scottburgh's beaches and lawns are popular with sunbathers

Scottburgh

Road map E4. N2, roughly 30 km (19 miles) S of Amanzimtoti. *9,000.* *Scott St, (039) 976-1364.*

An almost continuous carpet of sugar cane plantations lines this stretch of South Coast, and the town of Scottburgh was once used as a harbour for exporting the crop. Today, the neat and compact little town has a distinct holiday atmosphere, and is a popular beach resort. It occupies the prominent headland overlooking the mouth of the Mpambanyoni River, and most of the hotels and holiday apartments offer superb sea views.

In the previous century, a spring used to cascade from the bank above the river, but today a large water slide occupies the site. A restaurant, small shops, a miniature railway and tidal pool are added attractions. Further south, a caravan park adjoins the beach and the town's popular golf course has a prime site overlooking the Indian Ocean surf.

Amanzimtoti

Road map F4. N2, 27 km (17 miles) S of Durban. *16,300.* *Durban.* *95 Beach Rd, (031) 903-7498.*

It is claimed that Amanzimtoti derives its name from a remark made by Shaka Zulu *(see p51)*. In the 1820s, returning home from a campaign further down the South Coast, Shaka drank from a refreshing stream and is said to have exclaimed, "*amanzi umtoti*" (the water is sweet). Today, Amanzimtoti is a lively coastal resort. Its beaches are lined with hotels, holiday apartments, take-away outlets, restaurants and beachwear shops.

Frangipani

The most popular beach extends for 3 km (2 miles) north of the Manzimtoti River and offers safe bathing, picnic sites and a fine salt-water pool.

The N2 passes within 400 m (1,300 ft) of the coast, providing easy access to the town's attractions, such as the small bird sanctuary, a nature reserve and two fine golf courses in the vicinity of the beach.

North Coast ❸

This subtropical region is renowned for its attractive towns, sheltered bays and estuaries, uncrowded beaches and forested dunes that give way to a green carpet of sugar cane and timber plantations. Northern KwaZulu-Natal has escaped the rampant development that characterizes the South Coast and offers unspoilt nature at its best.

One of the guest rooms at the cross-cultural bush lodge of Simunye

Umhlanga Rocks

Road map F3. 20 km (12 miles) NE of Durban. *22,000.* *Umhlanga Express.* *Chartwell Drive, (031) 561-4257.*

The premier holiday resort on the North Coast, Umhlanga Rocks has excellent beaches, timeshare resorts, hotels and restaurants. This is a fast-growing, upper-income town, but the stylish outdoor cafés and bistros, make it seem more like a peaceful coastal centre than a fast-paced resort. The promenade, which extends along the coastline for 3 km (2 miles), provides stunning views of the golden sands that have made Umhlanga famous.

Further north, at the mouth of the Ohlanga River, forested dunes fringing the beach form part of a nature reserve. Here a boardwalk crosses the river and the forest teems with blue duiker, birds, monkeys.

Hibiscus flower

Ballito

Road map F3. N2, 30 km (19 miles) N of Umhlanga Rocks. *14,000.* *Baz Bus.* *Dolphin Coast Publicity, Cnr Ballito Dr/Link Rd, (032) 946-1997.*

Ballito and the neighbouring Salt Rock, extend for 6 km (4 miles) along a coast known for its beaches, rocky headlands and sheltered tidal pools alive with a menagerie of sea creatures. Lining the main coastal road are many good restaurants. Accommodation ranges from luxury holiday apartments and timeshare resorts to family hotels and attractive caravan parks.

Mtunzini

Road map F3. N2, 29 km (19 miles) SW of Richards Bay. *Baz Bus.* *Hely-Hutchinson St, (035) 340-1421.*

The pretty village, whose name means "in the shade", is set on a hillside overlooking the sea. Its streets are lined with coral trees and in winter their red flowers add splashes of colour to the townscape. A golf course adjoins the main shopping street, and near the railway station there is a grove of raffia palms. The nearest known group of these plants is on the Mozambique border, 260 km (163 miles) north. The rare palm-nut vulture is a fruit-eating raptor that may be spotted here, and the swamp forest and raffia palms can be seen from a raised boardwalk.

Mtunzini lies in a belt of unspoiled coastal forest that falls within the Umlalazi Nature Reserve. Comfortable log cabins, tucked into the forest, border a broad marsh, and along the banks of the Mlazi River there is a circular walk through a mangrove swamp that is alive with crabs and mud-skimmers.

From the picnic site on the bank of the Mlazi River, a boat trip to the river mouth will reveal glimpses of fish eagles and kingfishers, and walking trails lead through the forest to a wide, sandy beach. Along the many trails, shy forest animals such as vervet monkey, red duiker and bushbuck are often seen.

Holiday apartments and hotels line the beach at Ballito

Simunye Lodge ❹

Road map F3. Melmoth. D256. ***Tel*** *(035) 450-3111.* *7am–5pm daily.* **www**.proteahotels.com

A unique lodge tucked into the Mfule Valley 6 km (4 miles) from Melmoth allows visitors to experience both traditional and contemporary Zulu culture. The creation of linguist Barry Leitch, Simunye overlooks the Mfule River in a

◁ **Shaka's Rock, near Ballito, is a subtropical holiday resort, typical of the North Coast**

typical Zululand scenery of thorn trees and grassy hills. To reach the lodge, visitors have to ride on horseback for 6 km (4 miles), then continue by ox- or donkey-cart.

Overnight guests have the option of staying in a stone lodge or traditional Zulu *kraal* *(see pp204–5)*. Guides tell the fascinating history of the Zulu nation, and there are demonstrations of traditional dances, sparring and spear-throwing. Guests also visit working Zulu homesteads for a first-hand experience of rural Zulu life.

The entrance to the cultural village of Shakaland

Shakaland ❺

Road map F3. Eshowe. R68, Norman Hurst Farm, Nkwalini.
Tel *(035) 460-0912.* *6am–9pm daily.* *11am, 2pm daily.*
www.shakaland.com

For the production of the TV series *Shaka Zulu*, several authentic 19th-century Zulu *kraals* were constructed in 1984. The series was sold to many overseas networks and principal actor, Henry Cele, became a star. For the series' grand finale, the villages were set alight; only that of Shaka's father was spared and opened to the public as Shakaland.

The unique Zulu village is open for day visits, while those wishing to stay overnight are accommodated in one of the Protea Hotel chain's most unusual destinations. A video explaining the origin of the Zulu people is shown, and guests sleep in beehive huts and enjoy traditional Zulu fare, followed by a dancing display.

On a tour of the 40-hut village, visitors are introduced to a variety of traditional skills such as hut building, spear-making, beer brewing, artistic beadwork and pottery.

Zulu "love-letter" pouch, Shakaland

Framed by thorn trees and aloes, Goedertrou Dam in the valley below is an attractive body of water. The sunset river boat cruises are an added attraction.

In the hills east of Shakaland, and commanding a superb view over the wide Mhlatuze Valley, is the site of Shaka's famed military stronghold, KwaBulawayo. Construction of this historic facility began in 1823, but today, almost nothing remains of the citadel that once held so much of Southern Africa in its grasp.

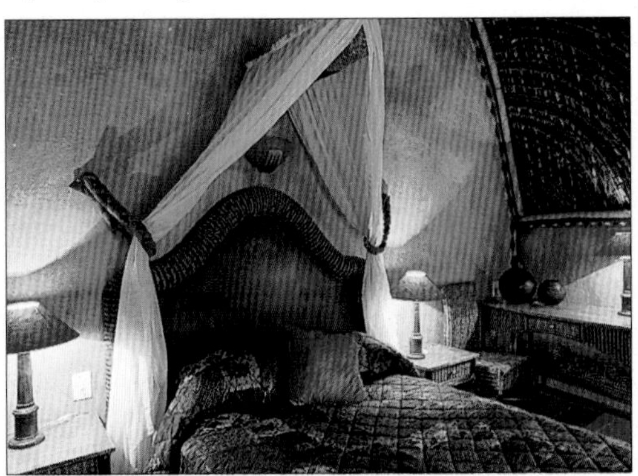
Shakaland offers unusual hotel accommodation

TRADITIONAL HEALING

In traditional Zulu society, the *inyanga* (herbalist) was male and concentrated on medicinal cures, while the *isangoma* (diviner) was a woman who possessed psychic powers and the ability to communicate with the ancestral spirits. Today, this strict division is no longer accurate. *Muthi* is an assortment of medicine and remedies made from indigenous bulbs, shrubs, leaves, tree bark and roots. Animal products like fat, claws, teeth and skin are also often used. Despite the advances of Western culture, the faith in traditional healing methods is still wide-spread in rural and urban settlements. In order to meet the demand for the plants and to ensure a regular supply, special "*muthi* gardens" have been established in a number of nature reserves.

Zulu *inyanga* (herbalist)

Hluhluwe-Umfolozi Park ❻

Road map F3. *30 km (18 miles) W of Ulundi, or from N2.* (035) 562-0255 or (033) 845-1000. *Apr–Sep: 6am–6pm daily; Nov–Feb: 5am–7pm; Oct & Mar: 8am–7pm.* **www**.kznparks.co.za

An unspoilt wilderness of rolling hills, subtropical forest, acacia woodland and palm-fringed rivers, the 964-sq-km (372-sq-miles) park is world-renowned for its rhino conservation programme.

In 1895 two wildlife reserves, Hluhluwe and Umfolozi, were established to protect the last rhinos in South Africa. In the early 1950s a corridor of land between the two was added. The park was consolidated in 1989, and is now the fourth largest in the country. One of Africa's leading wildlife sanctuaries, it is home to an astonishing diversity of wildlife. The varied vegetation supports large herds of nyala, impala, wildebeest, kudu, zebra and buffalo, as well as elephant, rhino, giraffe, lion, leopard, hyena and cheetah.

Over the years, animals that had become extinct in this region were re-introduced.

In 1958 a single male lion suddenly appeared – possibly from the Kruger National Park some 350 km (220 miles) to the north. Two lionesses were relocated from the Kruger park some time later, and their offspring have re-established prides throughout the park.

Southern bald ibis roosting site in the Hluhluwe-Umfolozi Park

Elephants, first transported from Kruger in 1981, have adapted extremely well to their new environment and now number around 200.

Nyalazi Gate, the park's main entrance, is reached from the N2 at Mtubatuba. It is a perfect starting point for exploring the park's 220-km (138-mile) road network. Heading south, the route traverses open woodland before fording the Black Umfolozi River. Then it ascends to Mpila Camp, which has magnificent views over the reserve.

A trio of exclusive reed-and-thatch rest camps on the banks of the Black Umfolozi, Sontuli, Gqoyeni and Nselweni rivers allow visitors to savour the most secluded corners of this wilderness. Game rangers conduct game-viewing walks.

From Nyalazi Gate north, the route follows a tarred road that curves across rolling hills teeming with wildlife. The journey to Hluhluwe climbs a range of hills, 400 m (1,300 ft) above the Hluhluwe River.

These hills trap moisture-laden clouds resulting in an average rainfall of 985 mm (38 inches) per year. In the dense woodland and forests live red duiker, bushbuck, nyala and samango monkey. Buffalo, zebra, white rhino and elephant can be seen roaming the northeastern grasslands near Memorial Gate.

Hilltop Camp, at an altitude of 450 m (1,460 ft), offers panoramic views over the surrounding countryside and can accommodate up to 210 guests in its chalets. Facilities at the central complex include a restaurant, bar, shop, petrol station and swimming pool.

A short trail through the adjoining forest is excellent for bird-watching.

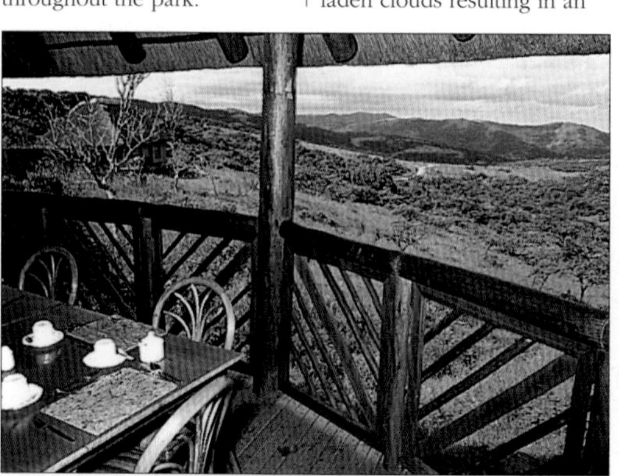

Hilltop Camp at Hluhluwe-Umfolozi Park

A female waterbuck at Hluhluwe-Umfolozi Park

Itala Game Reserve ❼

Road map F3. Vryheid. R69 via Louwsburg, 50 km (31miles) NE of Vryheid. ***Tel*** *(033) 845-1000.* *Nov–Feb: 5am–7pm daily; Mar–Oct: 6am–6pm daily.* **www**.kznparks.co.za

From the unhurried village of Louwsburg on the R69, a tarred road descends a steep escarpment to the wilderness of Itala, a 296-sq-km (114-sq-mile) tract of grassland with dramatic mountain scenery and densely wooded valleys.

The reserve was established in 1972, and over the years 13 farms have become one of South Africa's top sanctuaries. The Phongolo River flows along the northern boundary

For hotels and restaurants in this region see pp342–4 and pp368–70

Mhlangeni Bush Camp, Itala Game Reserve

for some 37 km (23 miles). Seven tributaries have carved the deep valleys that dissect this park and enhance its scenic splendour. The Ngoje escarpment rises dramatically to 1,446 m (4,700 ft), providing a striking backdrop to Itala's game-viewing roads.

A 7-km (4-mile) tarred road leads from the entrance to the prestigious Ntshondwe Camp, which nestles at the foot of an imposing escarpment. Its 40 self-catering chalets have been carefully tucked away between boulders and wild fig trees. The central complex contains a reception area, restaurant, store and coffee shop, and offers panoramic views over the entire reserve. In front of the building, an extensive wooden platform overlooks a reed-fringed water hole and is perfect for bird-watching. As no fences surround the camp, animals such as warthog often wander between the chalets. A path leads to a swimming pool tucked into a clearing at the base of the mountain.

An additional three exclusive bush camps offer guided walks led by resident rangers. Ntshondwe Lodge is a lavish, three-bedroomed cabin perched on a hill top. The far-reaching vista from its wooden deck and sunken swimming pool is arguably Itala's finest.

Game-viewing at Itala is excellent. Visitors will see white rhino, giraffe, hartebeest, kudu, eland, impala, wildebeest, warthog and zebra, as well as the only population in KwaZulu-Natal of the rare tsessebe antelope. Elephant, buffalo, leopard and black rhino are also present, but are generally more difficult to locate.

Ngubhu Loop, a 31-km (19-mile) circuit, which crosses a broad basin backed by the escarpment and then hugs the cliff face on the return journey, is the best drive in the park. Another route winds down the thickly wooded Dakaneni Valley to the Phongolo River. Although game is not as plentiful here as on the higher grasslands, the scenery is spectacular.

Game-viewing in the Itala Game Reserve

A white (square-lipped) rhino

THE WHITE AND THE BLACK RHINO

At first glance, it may seem impossible to classify the grey hulks, yet there are a number of clear distinguishing factors between the white *(Ceratotherium simum)* and black *(Diceros bicornis)* rhino. The term "white" does not describe colour, but is a bastardization of the Dutch *wijd* (wide), referring to the lips of the animal. The white rhino is a grazer that carries its large, heavy head close to the ground as it rips off grass with its wide, square lips. The black rhino, on the other hand, is a browser and holds its small head up to feed off leaves with its elongated, prehensile upper lip. Black rhinos are smaller and occur singly or in very small groups, while white rhinos may weigh up to 2,300 kg (5,000 lb) and gather in larger social groups. Today the Hluhluwe-Umfolozi Park protects a total of 1,200 white and 400 black rhino.

African fish eagle

Greater St Lucia Wetland Park ❽

Road map F3. St Lucia. Approx. 53 km (33 miles) NE of Empangeni. *(035) 550-4059.* *daily, some areas are restricted.* www.stlucia.org.za

Lake St Lucia, 368 sq km (142 sq miles) in size, is the focal point of the third largest wildlife sanctuary in South Africa. Stretching from the game-filled Mkuzi plains in the north to the St Lucia Estuary in the south, the 1,700-sq-km (656-sq-mile) Greater St Lucia Wetland Park encompasses a diversity of habitats: mountain, bushveld, palm groves, sand forest, grassland, wetland, coastal forest, coral reef and ocean.

The coastal village of St Lucia is a popular holiday destination, with a range of facilities and accommodation. Regular cruises offer close-up views of hippos, crocodiles, pelicans, fish eagles and rare waterbirds. The Crocodile Centre, north of the village, is the finest in the country.

Cape Vidal, 32 km (20 miles) north of St Lucia Estuary, boasts a reef-shielded beach, tropical waters, deep-sea fishing and a freshwater lake.

The coastline from Cape Vidal to Ponta Do Ouro is a protected marine reserve; the sandy beaches provide vital nesting sites for loggerhead and leatherback turtles. Fishing is allowed in certain areas.

Located 65 km (41 miles) north of St Lucia Estuary, along an unspoilt and uninhabited coastline, **Sodwana Bay** is a popular destination for deep-sea fishing and scuba diving expeditions.

The road from Sodwana to the N2 passes the southern boundary of the **Mkuzi Game Reserve**; its four game-viewing hides are renowned for their close-ups. **KwaJobe Cultural Village** near Mantuma camp gives visitors an insight into traditional Zulu culture.

GREATER ST LUCIA WETLAND PARK

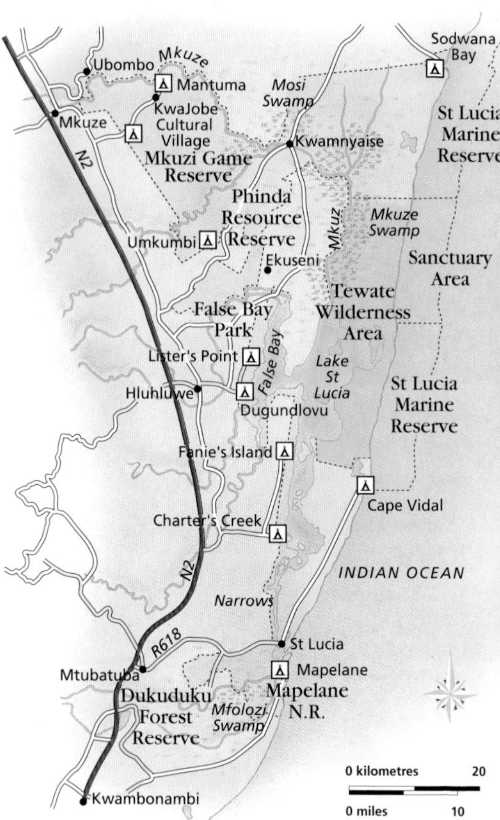

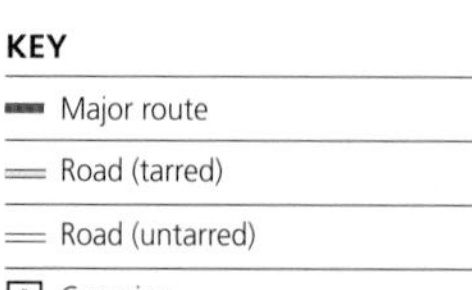

St Lucia Estuary offers excellent shore-based fishing

For hotels and restaurants in this region see pp342–4 and pp368–70

One of the beaches at Kosi Bay, the northernmost part of KwaZulu-Natal

Sodwana Bay
Tel (035) 571-0051.

Mkuzi Game Reserve
Tel (035) 562-0255.

KwaJobe Cultural Village
Tel 035) 573-9004.

Phinda Resource Reserve 9

Road map F3. 80 km (50 miles) NE of Empangeni. ***Tel** (011) 809-4300.* *restricted access.* **www**.ccafrica.com

Extending over 170 sq km (65 sq miles) of bushveld, wetland, savannah and sand forest, luxurious privately-owned Phinda adjoins the Greater St Lucia Wetland Park. Activities on offer include sunset cruises on the beautiful Mzinene River, outdoor meals under a spreading acacia tree, game-viewing drives led by experienced rangers as well as bush walks and fishing or diving expeditions to the nearby coast. Wildlife is abundant and includes nyala, kudu, wildebeest, giraffe, zebra, elephant, white rhino, lion and cheetah. Visitors can stay in Nyala Lodge, which offers panoramic views over the surrounding bushveld, or in the exclusive, glass-walled Forest Lodge, which is so much a part of the sand forest that its rooms are framed by trees and enclosed by dense foliage. The reserve has its own air strip and arranges regular air transfers from Johannesburg, or road transfers from Richards Bay.

Kosi Bay 10

Road map F2. Approx. 155 km (96 miles) NE of Mkuze. ***Tel** (033) 845-1000.* *restricted access.*

Kosi Bay Nature Reserve is an 80-sq-km (31-sq-mile) aquatic system that incorporates an estuary, mangrove swamps and four interconnecting lakes. It can be reached from Mkuze, just south of Pongolapoort Dam. The system hosts many fresh- and salt-water fish species, and angling and boating are popular. Tonga fish traps (fences built from sticks and reeds) have been a feature of the Kosi system for over 500 years. There is a campsite and a few thatched chalets, and guided walks and boat trips can be arranged. A 4-day circular trail allows hikers to explore the lakes on foot.

Environs: About 50 km (31 miles) west of Kosi Bay is the **Ndumo Game Reserve**, renowned for the richness of its riverine life, particularly its water-related birds – an amazing 420 species have been recorded. Hides on the Nyamithi and Banzi pans afford excellent views. The pans also sustain large hippo and crocodile populations, and animals such as nyala, red duiker, and white and black rhino can be seen. To appreciate the beauty of the pans, book one of the guided Land Rover tours. A small rest camp and a tented safari camp overlook Banzi Pan.

Ndumo Game Reserve
***Tel** (033) 845-1000.* *daily.*

Tembe Elephant Park 11

Road map F3. Approx. 110 km (68 miles) N of Mkuze. ***Tel** (031) 202-9090.* *restricted access.* **www**.tembe.co.za

This 290-sq-km (112-sq-mile) wilderness reserve bordering South Africa and Mozambique protects the flood plain of the Phongolo River along the northern boundary of KwaZulu-Natal. The park was established in 1983 to protect the KwaZulu-Natal elephants. Access is limited to 4WD vehicles, and only ten visitors are allowed in per day. There is a small, tented camp near the entrance, and two hides overlook areas where elephants come to drink. The park has South Africa's largest population of suni antelope and 430 species of birds.

Loggerhead turtles lay their eggs on sandy beaches

Introducing Gauteng and Mpumalanga

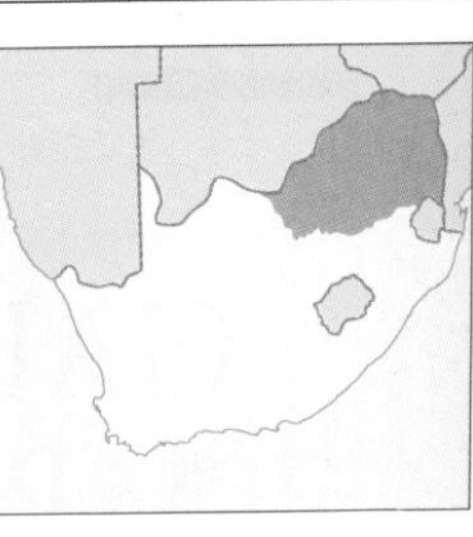

From natural wonders and wildlife to the "City of Gold", this region offers something for everyone. Johannesburg is the throbbing life of the streets and the sophistication of exclusive suburbs, while Soweto, Johannesburg's "other half", provides an insight into the daily lives of the country's urban black people. To the east, the land drops over 1,000 m (3,281 ft) to the hot Lowveld plains and the Kruger National Park. West lies the arid heartland of the subcontinent, and beyond, the Magaliesberg range seems to rise from the waters of the Hartbeespoort Dam. The most fascinating destination of all, perhaps, is glittering Sun City and the near-mythical grandeur of the Lost City.

The Palace of the Lost City, *a part of the opulent Sun City resort and casino complex, is a spectacular architectural indulgence of age-stressed concrete, beautifully crafted pillars and ornate domes set in a man-made tropical garden and surrounded by a variety of water features such as Roaring Lagoon.*

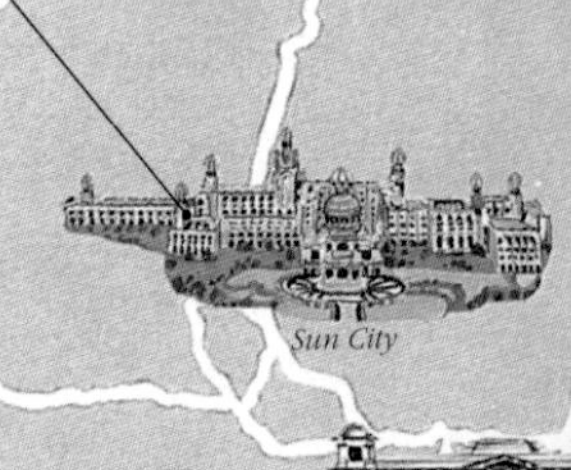

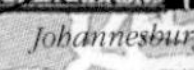

GAUTENG AND SUN CITY
(See pp252–71)

Johannesburg *is the largest city in South Africa and the one in which extremes are most evident. Poverty and wealth, historic buildings and modern office blocks, create stark contrasts.*

◁ **The lion is one of the "Big Five" African animals, seen here in the Kruger National Park**

Lions *(Panthera leo) can live in almost any habitat except desert and thick forest. They are both nocturnal and diurnal and occur in prides of 3 to 40 individuals (although 6 to 12 is more usual). In the Kruger, which is accessible through several gates, they are often seen resting in the shade of a tree.*

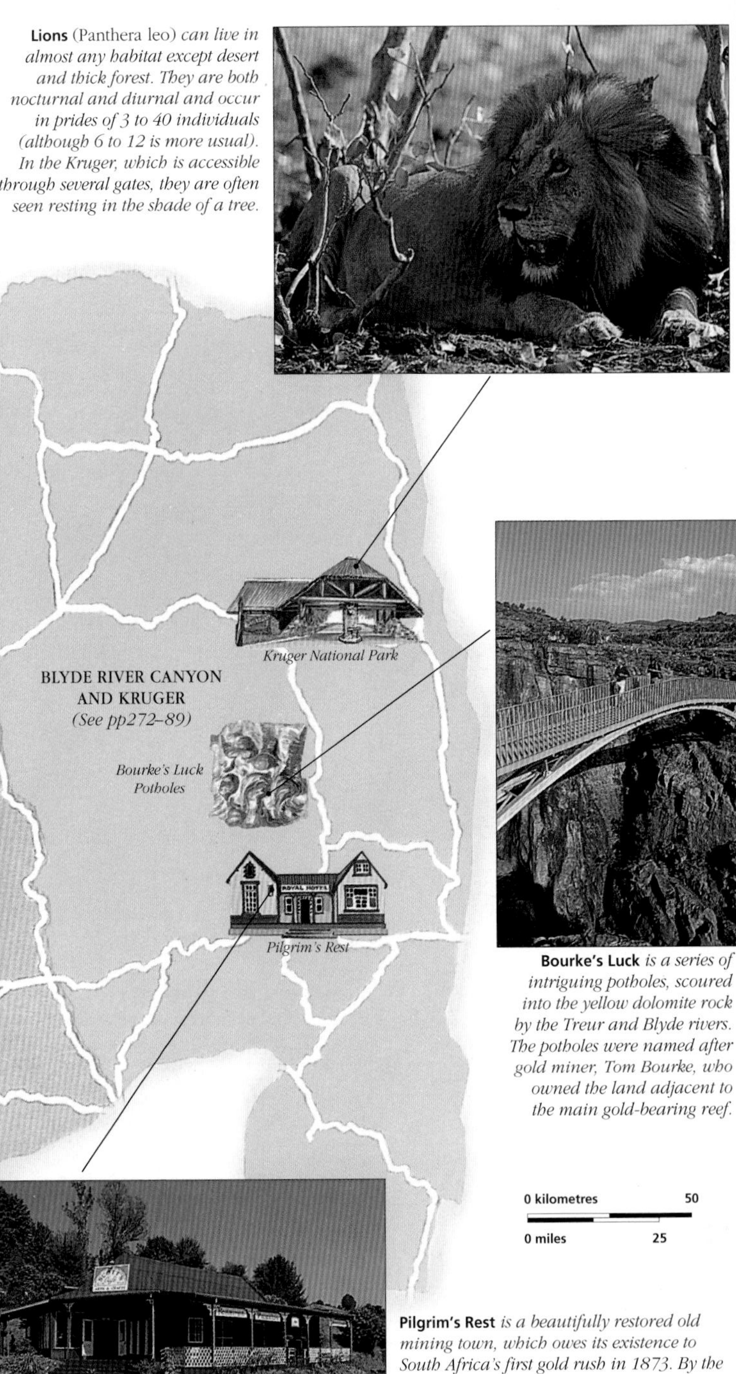

Bourke's Luck *is a series of intriguing potholes, scoured into the yellow dolomite rock by the Treur and Blyde rivers. The potholes were named after gold miner, Tom Bourke, who owned the land adjacent to the main gold-bearing reef.*

Pilgrim's Rest *is a beautifully restored old mining town, which owes its existence to South Africa's first gold rush in 1873. By the end of that year, more than 1,500 diggers had converged on the area and Pilgrim's Rest had grown into a large mining camp.*

National Parks Board logo

Conservation in the Kruger National Park

The Kruger National Park stretches for 352 km (220 miles) along South Africa's northeastern border. The 19,633-sq-km (7,580-sq-mile) conservation area supports an astounding array of fauna and flora. Although the park sustains the animals in their natural habitat, a fence along much of its boundary does restrict their free movement. Wildlife is concentrated in the lusher southern parts, which calls for careful management. Periodically, rangers have to limit the numbers this contained ecosystem can safely support by translocating young and healthy animals to other reserves.

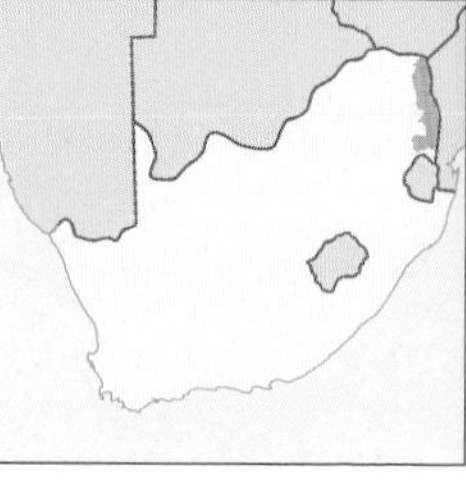
EXTENT OF THE KRUGER NATIONAL PARK

Park boundaries

Dry hills provide a habitat for kudu and eland, animals that do not need to drink water regularly.

Zebra flourish when artificial water points are provided. Large zebra herds have a negative impact on animals who require tall grass, like roan, sable and reedbuck.

The Olifants River *is the largest of the park's seven major watercourses. Since water is scarce, artificial water points have allowed elephants to move into areas that were previously only accessible in wet summer months.*

Tall trees along the riverbed shelter animals such as baboon, grey duiker, bushbuck and giraffe.

MANAGING FOR DIVERSITY

Scientists are only now beginning to understand the complicated African savannah. In an effort to manage the ecosystem in a way that maintains its diversity, artificial water points, which caused habitat-modifiers like elephant to flourish (to the detriment of other species), are now being closed.

Giraffe *are the tallest of the browsers and favour areas where acacias are abundant.*

Kudu *are large antelope that do not need to drink frequently and occur in dense woodland.*

Sable *antelope require tall grass of a high quality that grows on well-drained soils.*

Radio tracking *enables scientists to monitor the endangered predators. Only 180 cheetah and 400 wild dog inhabit the park's vast expanse. Research has shown that competition from the more aggressive lion is a major limiting factor.*

DROUGHT STATISTICS

Although park managers endeavour to limit the impact of drought, animal populations in the park are never static. Some species like wildebeest and giraffe are hardly affected, while buffalo, sable and roan antelope exhibit sharp declines.

SPECIES	1992	1995	2005
Elephant	7,600	8,371	11,672
White rhino	1,803	2,800	4,509
Wildebeest	13,960	12,723	9,612
Giraffe	4,600	4,902	5,114
Impala	101,416	97,297	85,869
Buffalo	21,900	19,477	27,000
Sable	1,232	880	550
Roan	60	44	70

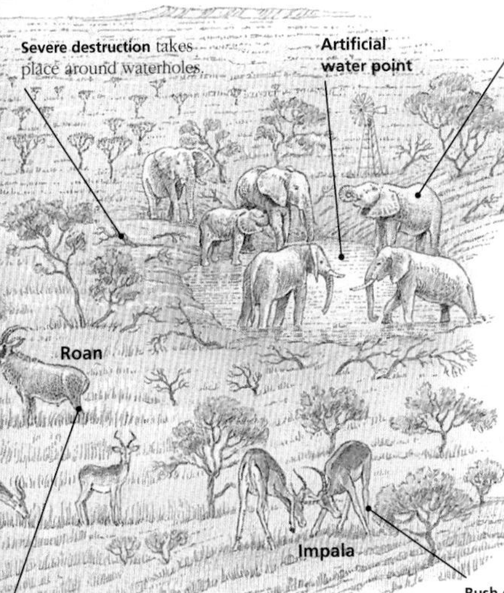

Elephant are termed habitat-modifiers, because they destroy trees, which brings about significant changes in vegetation.

Destructive feeders, *elephants strip bark off umbrella thorn acacias and fever trees. Kruger's 8,700 elephant each consume up to 250 kg (550 lb) of vegetation daily and comprise one-quarter of the park's total biomass.*

Endangered roan antelope require open woodland, with tall grass to hide their young, and are unable to adapt to the short-grass conditions caused by an increase in zebra herds around artificial water points.

Bush encroachment, resulting from elephants damaging tall trees and from concentrations of grazing animals near water, benefits browsers like impala, kudu and giraffe.

TOURIST GUIDELINES

To ensure the safety of visitors and maintain the park's essential attributes, a few regulations are necessary. It is important to observe speed limits, as the animals, too, use the roads as thoroughfares. Since camp closing times are strictly enforced, a good rule of thumb is to calculate an average travelling speed, including stops, at 20 kph (12 mph). Visitors are not permitted to leave their cars except at the 22 designated picnic sites and facilities at 13 of the larger camps – all of the animals are wild and unpredictable, and the predators are superbly camouflaged. Although baboons and vervet monkeys may beg for food, particularly on the road between Skukuza and Lower Sabie, feeding is a punishable offence. It disrupts natural behaviour, and often produces aggression, particularly in male baboons.

Feeding is illegal

Visitors blatantly ignoring the rules

Gold Mining

Kruger rands

Vast natural resources make South Africa one of the richest countries on earth. Ancient sediments in this geological treasure chest yield silver, platinum, chromite, uranium, diamonds – and gold. Over the years, small-scale miners have left behind evidence of their labour all around the country. The most poignant of these historic sites is Pilgrim's Rest *(see p278)*, a well-preserved mining town in Mpumalanga. Today, controlled by giant corporations, South Africa produces about one-quarter of the world's gold.

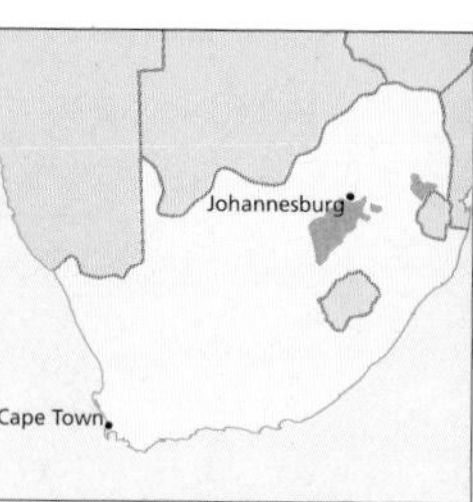

EXTENT OF GOLD FIELDS

Main mining operations

Johannesburg in 1889 *was a sprawling tent settlement. Three years earlier, a prospector named George Harrison had discovered the greatest gold reef in history on a farm named Langlaagte, just west of today's Johannesburg.*

The processing plant produces gold bars of 90 per cent purity, ready for transport to the refinery.

Office blocks house the administration and human resources staff, as well as engineers, geologists, surveyors, mechanics and planners.

SHAFT 9 – VAAL REEFS

This vast gold mine near Klerksdorp straddles the North West and Free State provinces. It is the world's largest gold-mining complex, and is now in the process of selling some of its 11 shafts to black empowerment groups such as Rainbow Mining.

The main shaft, *sunk to a depth of 60 m (197 ft), is encased in a concrete "collar" to support the headgear. South African gold-mine shafts are the deepest in the world, because the reefs are located several miles underground.*

Miners *work underground on eight-hour shifts. Rock temperatures in the confined working place (stope) may reach up to 55°C (131°F).*

Canteen staff *have to cater for the different traditional diets of miners, as well as their exceptionally high calorie intake.*

The ore *is crushed and pumped into a leach tank where cyanide is added to dissolve it. The product is then heated to remove impurities and smelted into gold bars of about 90 per cent purity. A yield of one troy ounce (31.1 grams) of gold from a ton of ore is considered very rich indeed.*

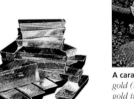

e headgear, set up after the initial aft has been sunk, carries the ropes, heels and other mining equipment.

Mine dumps, *yellow heaps on the outskirts of Johannesburg, contain the waste solids of the extraction process. 'Greening' the dumps has seen the return of smaller animals and birds.*

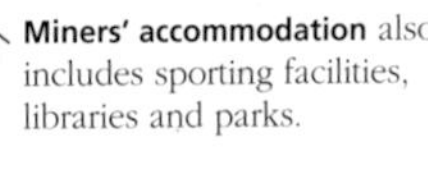

Miners' accommodation also includes sporting facilities, libraries and parks.

The gold price *is determined twice daily (except on weekends and British bank holidays) by a group of London bullion dealers. It is quoted in US dollars per troy ounce.*

A carat *denotes the purity of gold (measured per part of gold in 24 parts other metal).*

THE KRUGER MILLIONS

Legend has it that when Paul Kruger, last president of the Zuid-Afrikaansche Republiek (1883–1900), left to go into exile in Europe in 1900, all the gold in the State Mint at Pretoria travelled with him to keep it out of the hands of the advancing British army. At the town of Nelspruit (Mpumalanga), the presidential train was delayed while mysterious wooden crates were unloaded and carried away into the bush. Kruger had little money (or any assets at all) in Europe, and it is surmised that the missing gold – in Kruger pounds, coin blanks and bars – still awaits discovery somewhere between Nelspruit and Barberton. The search continues to this day.

President Paul Kruger

Exploring Gauteng and Sun City

The rocky Witwatersrand – ridge of white waters – lies about 1,600 m (5,250 ft) above sea level and stretches for 80 km (50 miles) from west to east. Johannesburg and its satellites have grown, literally, on gold. Here live almost half of South Africa's urban people. Although hot and lush in summer, languid afternoons are frequently torn apart by short, violent thunderstorms. The Highveld grasslands do experience frost and occasional snow in winter. To the northwest, Sun City and The Palace of the Lost City are part of a glittering complex offering superb accommodation, casinos and fast-paced entertainment.

History comes alive in Gold Reef City

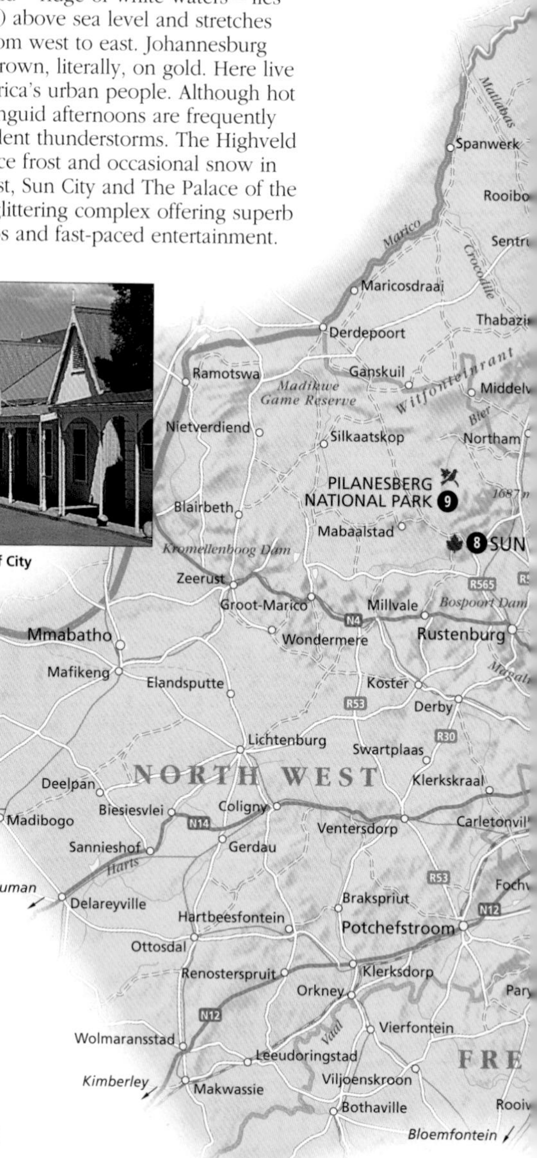

SIGHTS AT A GLANCE

Gold Reef City pp260–61 ❷
Hartbeespoort Dam ❻
Johannesburg ❶
Pilanesberg National Park ❾
Pretoria/Tshwane ❼
Sandton and Randburg ❹
Soweto ❸
Sun City ❽
Palace of the Lost City pp270–71

Tour

Touring Gauteng pp264–5 ❺

KEY

- Motorway
- Main road
- Minor road
- Untarred road
- Scenic route
- Main railway
- Minor railway
- International border
- Provincial border
- Summit

For additional map symbols *see back flap*

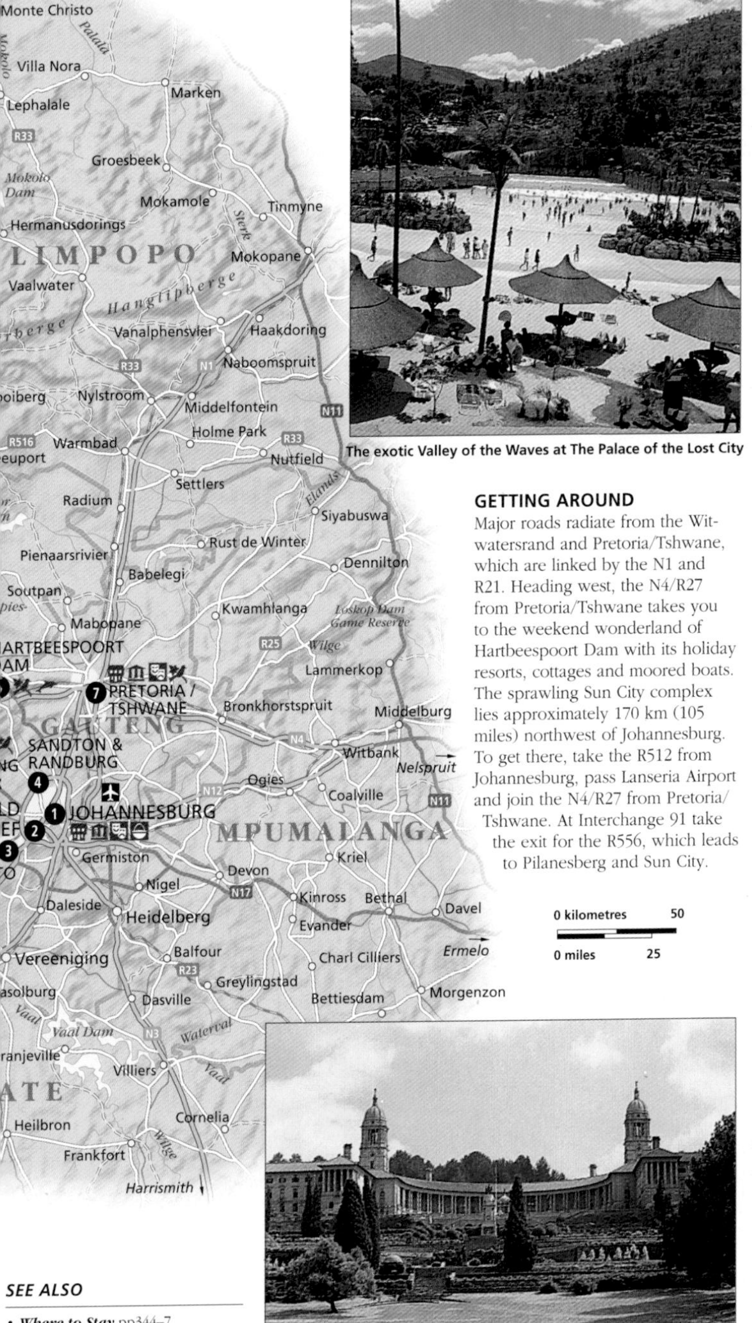

The exotic Valley of the Waves at The Palace of the Lost City

GETTING AROUND

Major roads radiate from the Witwatersrand and Pretoria/Tshwane, which are linked by the N1 and R21. Heading west, the N4/R27 from Pretoria/Tshwane takes you to the weekend wonderland of Hartbeespoort Dam with its holiday resorts, cottages and moored boats. The sprawling Sun City complex lies approximately 170 km (105 miles) northwest of Johannesburg. To get there, take the R512 from Johannesburg, pass Lanseria Airport and join the N4/R27 from Pretoria/Tshwane. At Interchange 91 take the exit for the R556, which leads to Pilanesberg and Sun City.

The Union Buildings, the seat of parliament in Pretoria/Tshwane

SEE ALSO

• ***Where to Stay*** pp344–7

• ***Where to Eat*** pp370–72

Johannesburg ❶

A taste of Africa

The densely populated city of Johannesburg is the country's financial and commercial heartland. The city has many names, and most of them, like Egoli and Gauteng, mean "place of gold". Indeed, gold and, of course, glamour are close companions in this place, which has grown from primitive mine camp to metropolis in little over a century. The city pulsates with entrepreneurial energy while, at the same time, it retains the spirit of a frontier town. It lies at an altitude of 1,763 m (5,784 ft) above sea level but at the Western Deep gold mine, the shafts reach an astonishing 3,777 m (12,388 ft) below ground.

Traditional arts and crafts are sold at many markets

Exploring Johannesburg

Johannesburg is undergoing considerable change, with the once quiet neighbourhoods of Sandton and Randburg, north of the city, fast becoming fashionable places to live. The city centre, however, has a host of interesting sights.

Johannesburg is not a safe city to explore on foot and with a poor public transport system, visitors are advised to embark on an organized tour.

City Centre

University of the Witwatersrand

Cnr Jorissen & Bertha sts. ***Tel*** *(011) 717-1000.* *8:30am–4:30pm Mon– Fri, Sat (bookings only).* *public hols.*

Splendid African carvings and ceremonial and ritual objects can be seen at the Gertrude Posel Gallery on the campus.

The James Kitching Gallery of the Bernard Price Institute has the largest collection of prehistoric fossils in the country.

Market Theatre Complex

Bree Street. ***Tel*** *(011) 832-1641.* *9am–5pm daily.*

The Market Theatre Complex is the centre of the Newtown Cultural Precinct that includes the SAB World of Beer, the Workers' Museum and Library, and MuseuMAfricA. A great effort has been made to make Newtown a safe place to visit.

Originally an Indian fruit market, it now houses three theatres, two art galleries, restaurants, cafes and shops. Each Saturday morning, flea-market traders gather on the square outside to sell all kinds of curios.

Opposite the Market Theatre, but part of the complex, the Africana Museum (1935) was relaunched in 1994 as **MuseuMAfricA**. The theme is Johannesburg and its people at various stages of socio-political transformation.

Situated west of the Market Theatre and along Jeppe Street, the **Oriental Plaza** bazaar is permeated by the exotic aroma of Eastern spices. Here, some 300 shops and stalls sell everything from carpets to clothing. Many of the traders here are the descendants of Indians who came to the Witwatersrand in the 19th century after their contracts on the sugar plantations had expired.

MuseuMAfricA

Newtown. ***Tel*** *(011) 833-5624.* *9am–5pm Tue–Sun.*

Oriental Plaza

Main & Bree Sts. ***Tel*** *(011) 838-6752.* *8:30am–5pm Mon–Fri, (8:30–2pm Sat).* *public hols.*

Johannesburg Stock Exchange Building

Diagonal St. ***Tel*** *(011) 298-2800.* *to the public.*

This rather impressive glass-walled building is set somewhat incongruously in a downtown area that is busy with street vendors and tiny shops selling everything from plastic buckets to blankets and traditional herbal medicines. The building once housed the Johannesburg

MuseuMAfrica, part of the Market Theatre Complex in Newtown

For hotels and restaurants in this region see pp344–7 and pp370–72

Stock Exchange (JSE) on one of its floors, but the exchange has now moved to new premises in Sandton.

SAB World of Beer, a museum tour with refreshments

SAB World of Beer

15 President St. (entrance in Gerard Sekoto St.), Newton Cultural Precinct. ***Tel*** *(011) 836 4900*
10am–6pm daily.

South African Breweries (SAB), which was established in 1895, is the largest brewer by volume in the world, boasting 150 brands and a production of 120 million barrels annually. In this modern museum there is an entertaining display of the company's long history. Other exhibits focus on the development of brewing in ancient Mesopotamia and illustrate how beer-brewing came to Africa and Europe, with excellent reconstructions of a "gold rush" pub, a traditional Soweto *shabeen*, and a full-scale brewhouse where you can see how the brewing process works.

At the end of the tour, adult visitors will be pleased to know that they are rewarded with two ice-cold "frosties". Those under 18 are given a choice of several non-alcoholic cocktails.

KwaZulu Muti

14 Diagonal St. ***Tel*** *(011) 836-4470.*
8am–5pm Mon–Fri, 8am–1pm Sat. *Sun, public hols.*

This working herbalist shop represents a traditional side of Africa that is very much a part of daily life for many South Africans. It offers a variety of herbs and plants, both dried and fresh, for sale. Not all the remedies, potions and medicines are herbal, however. Its fascinating stock includes animal skins, bones, horns and claws, as well as dried bats, frogs and insects.

VISITORS' CHECKLIST

Road map E2. Gauteng Province. *712,500.* *20 km (12 miles) E of the city.* *Rotunda terminal, cnr Rissik and Wolmarans sts, Braamfontein.* *Rotunda terminal.* *Sandton Mall, Level 4, Entrance 6, Sandton, (011) 784–9596/7/8* *daily.* *FNB Vita Dance Umbrella (Feb–Mar); Windybrow Festival (Mar); Arts Alive (Sep); Johannesburg Biennale (Oct, only in odd-numbered years).* **www**.gauteng.net

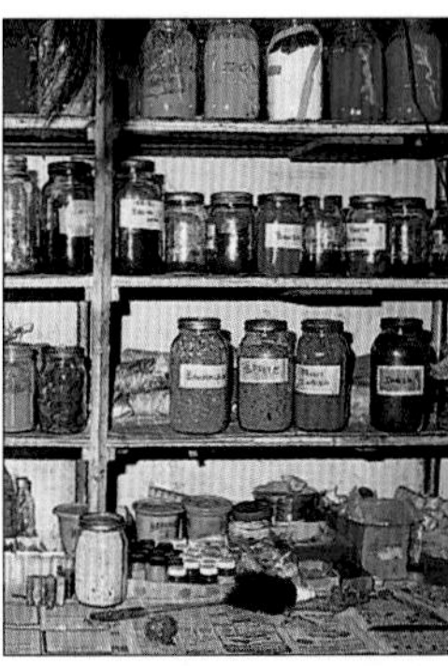

Traditional African herbal remedies

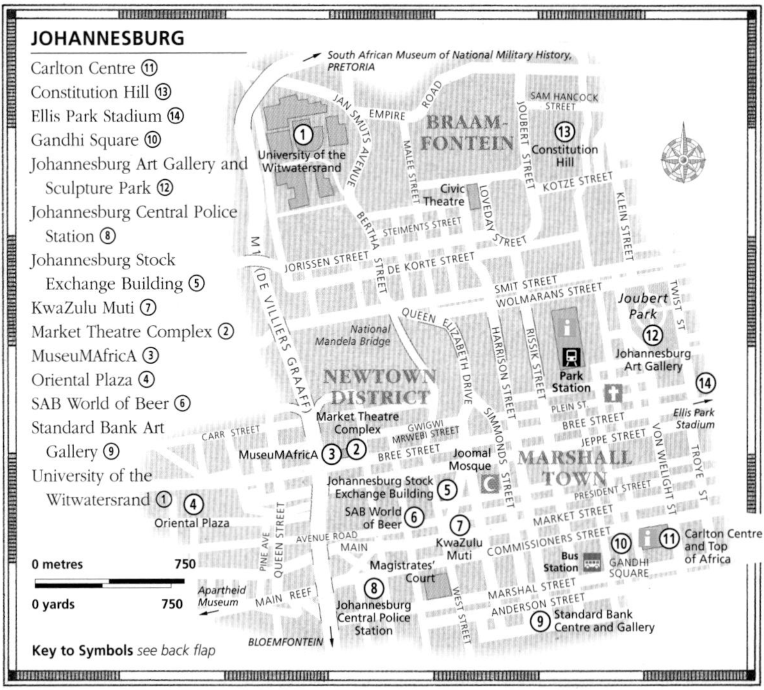

JOHANNESBURG

- Carlton Centre ⑪
- Constitution Hill ⑬
- Ellis Park Stadium ⑭
- Gandhi Square ⑩
- Johannesburg Art Gallery and Sculpture Park ⑫
- Johannesburg Central Police Station ⑧
- Johannesburg Stock Exchange Building ⑤
- KwaZulu Muti ⑦
- Market Theatre Complex ②
- MuseuMAfricA ③
- Oriental Plaza ④
- SAB World of Beer ⑥
- Standard Bank Art Gallery ⑨
- University of the Witwatersrand ①

0 metres 750
0 yards 750

Key to Symbols *see back flap*

The impressive Carlton Centre, a landmark on the downtown Johannesburg skyline

Johannesburg Central Police Station

Commissioner St. ***Tel*** *(011) 375-5911.* *to the public.*

Formerly known as the infamous John Vorster Square, this was the nerve centre of apartheid repression, a place that in its own way was as sinister as the KGB or the Gestapo headquarters. The nondescript blue and white building, was the home of the dreaded Security Branch, where many were held, tortured and died while in custody. Renamed, it still functions as a police station.

Standard Bank Art Gallery

Cnr Simmonds and Fredericks Sts. ***Tel*** *(011) 631-1889.* *8am–4:30pm Mon–Fri, 9am–1pm Sat.* *public hols.*

The unusual setting of a working bank conceals a sophisticated gallery that provides a remarkable showcase for talented local and international artists. As well as changing exhibitions, the display features part of the Standard Bank's own extensive collection. This started as an informal project and was augmented by approved art purchases of each successive chairman of the bank. The gallery has easy-to-follow explanations of both the collection and the African fine art form. The building also hosts recitals and concerts.

Across the road in the Standard Bank's headquarters is Ferreira's Stope – an interesting old mine shaft with a small museum attached.

Gandhi Square

Built in 1893 as Government Square, this central business district plaza has undergone many transformations. In 1949, it was remodelled and renamed Van der Byl Square after a prominent local politician. The area then became a bustling and anarchic bus station before being thoroughly refurbished in 2002, as part of a wider redevelopment of the surrounding district. The Square was also given a new name, after the prominent Indian politician Mahatma Gandhi, who came to Johannesburg in 1903 and worked as a lawyer and civil rights activist. Gandhi's profession often brought him to the Transvaal Law Courts (now demolished), which were located in the square.

In 2003, a life-size statue of Gandhi, by sculptor Trinka Christopher, was unveiled here. Although buses still pass through the area, albeit in a more orderly fashion, there is also a row of trendy shops, restaurants and cafés lining the southern side of the square. A pleasant arcade was added in 2005 to provide a link with Marshall Street, and the retail space created was sold out in days.

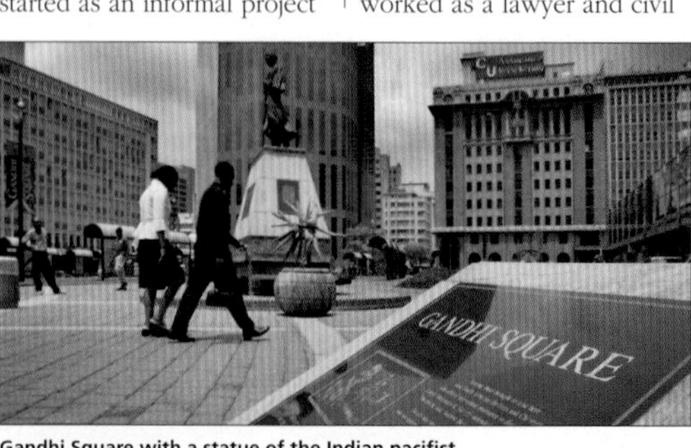

Gandhi Square with a statue of the Indian pacifist

Carlton Centre

150 Commissioner Street. ***Tel*** *(011) 368-1331.* *9am–7pm daily.*

A key downtown landmark, the Carlton Centre is 50 storeys or 223 m (730 ft) tall, making it the African continent's highest building. For a small fee visitors can take the lift up to the Top of Africa observation deck on the 50th floor where amazing panoramic views of the city can be seen. The building was completed in 1973 as part of a five-star hotel complex, and sold in 1999 to Transnet, the South African Transport Organisation.

The Carlton Centre is linked to the Carlton Hotel by an underground shopping mall, in which there are more than 180 shops, several restaurants and an ice-skating rink. At ground level a useful information office for visitors, a popular plaza and the country's largest car parking arcade can be found.

Johannesburg Art Gallery and Sculpture Park

Klein St, Joubert Park. ***Tel*** *(011) 725-3130.* *10am–5pm Tue–Sun.* *Good Fri & 25 Dec.*

This gallery in Joubert Park has displays of traditional, historical and modern South African art, as well as works from European schools. There are also collections of ceramics, sculpture, furniture and textiles on view.

Unfortunately, the small park here has now become a haven for hustlers, so visitors must be on their guard.

Constitution Hill

San Hancock St. ***Tel*** *(011) 274-5300.* *9am–5pm daily.* *Good Fri, 25 Dec.* *except Tue.*

This remarkable development is a living museum documenting South Africa's turbulent past and its transition to democracy. The site incorporates the Old Fort Prison Complex, a notorious jail for over a century where many, including Nelson Mandela, were imprisoned. South Africa's Constitutional Court, established in 1994 after the country's first democratic elections, now occupies the eastern side of the complex.

Hillbrow

One of Johannesburg's oldest suburbs, Hillbrow is densely populated. Active and lively, it offers many restaurants and entertainment venues. Due to the high crime rate, visitors should join an organized tour.

A Blackburn Buccaneer on display in the Museum of Military History

Ellis Park Sports Stadium

Cnr Cerrey and Staib sts. ***Tel*** *(011) 402-8644.* *fm Rotunda terminal.* *Ellis Park station.*

Home ground of the Gauteng Lions rugby team, this 60,000-seat stadium was built in 1982. It hosts regular matches and fixtures, and also features an Olympic-sized swimming pool.

Environs

South of the city, **Santarama Miniland** houses landmark buildings, accurately reconstructed on a miniature scale.

Santarama Miniland

Rosettenville Rd, Wemmerpan. ***Tel*** *(011) 435-0543.* *9am–5pm daily.*

South African National Museum of Military History

Saxonwold 2132. ***Tel*** *(011) 646 5513* *9am-4:30pm daily.* *Good Friday & 25 Dec*

Initially opened by then prime minister Field Marshall Jan Smuts in 1947 to commemorate South Africa's role in the two world wars, this outstanding museum also covers the Anglo-Zulu War, the Anglo-Boer War and the South African resistance movements. It displays more than 44,000 items, divided into 37 separate categories, including the nation's official war art and war photography collections. It also has a vast library of books, journals and archive material, along with some of the world's rarest military aircraft, including the only extant night fighter version of the feared German Me 262 pioneer aircraft.

Apartheid Museum

Northern Parkway and Gold Reef Road, Ormonde. ***Tel*** *(011) 309 4700* *10am–6pm Tue–Sun*

The darkest days of South Africa's turbulent past are chillingly evoked at this fascinating museum. To set the mood there are separate entrances for whites and non-whites. Documenting the triumph of the human spirit over adversity, the displays recall the National Party's apartheid policy after their election to power in 1948, which turned 20 million non-whites into legally defined second-class citizens. Particularly powerful exhibits include a room with 131 nooses representing the number of political prisoners hanged during apartheid, BBC footage taken in 1961 of Nelson Mandela when he was in hiding from the authorities and a series of evocative photographs taken by Ernest Cole before he was sent into exile during the late 1960s.

The entry to the Apartheid Museum with its separate doorways

Gold Reef City ❷

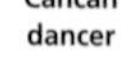

This lively and imaginative reconstruction of Johannesburg of the 1890s is situated some 8 km (5 miles) south of the city. It was built around Shaft 14, a gold mine that was in use from 1887–1971. The Gold Reef City theme and fun park aims to recapture that transient time during which Johannesburg slipped, quite unobtrusively, from mining camp to city. There are interesting museums to visit and an informative underground tour of the now disused mine. Daily displays of tribal, gumboot and cancan dancing complement the festive atmosphere.

Cancan dancer

Golden Loop
The daring loop is one of 26 rides that can be enjoyed free of charge.

Main Gate
People short enough to pass under the miner's hands without touching (1.2 m; 4 ft) enter free of charge.

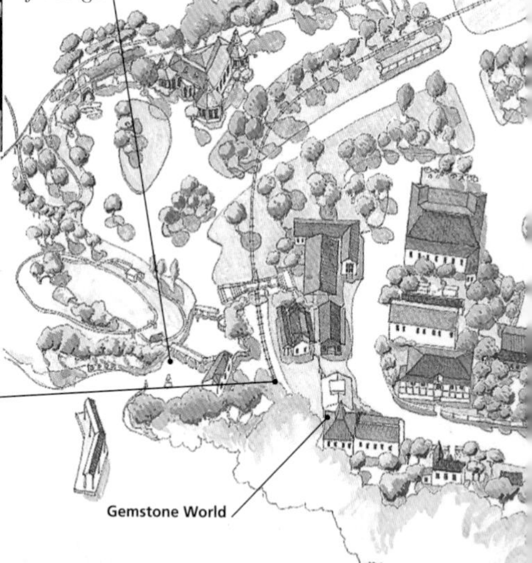

Gemstone World

Gold Reef City Train
For visitors wishing to gain an overview of the theme park, the Gold Reef City Train offers a leisurely mode of transport and stops at three different stations.

★ Gumboot Dancing
The gumboot dance is said to be based on an Austrian folk dance that was taught by missionaries who were scandalized by "pagan" African dances. The deliberately heavy-footed response is a gentle rebuke to those who saw merit only in their own customs.

STAR FEATURES

★ Gumboot Dancing

★ Main Street

★ Gold Pouring

For hotels and restaurants in this region see pp344–7 and pp370–72

★ Main Street
Restaurants, pubs, shops, banking facilities, and the Gold Reef City Hotel line this wide street, which also acts as a stage for impromptu dance displays.

VISITORS' CHECKLIST

Road map E2. Shaft 14, Northern Parkway, Ormonde, Johannesburg. ***Tel*** *(011) 248-6800.* *55 from city centre; major hotels offer shuttle buses.* *9:30am–5pm Tue–Sun.* *25 Dec.* *incl. all rides & shows.* *multilingual.* **www**.goldreefcity.co.za

The Digger Joe's Prospector Camp
Here visitors can experience the thrill of panning for gold in a swift-running stream. An experienced gold digger is on hand to explain the process and give expert advice.

Victorian merry-go-round

Town square

Scale model of the gold mine

Vintage car display

0 metres 50

0 yards 50

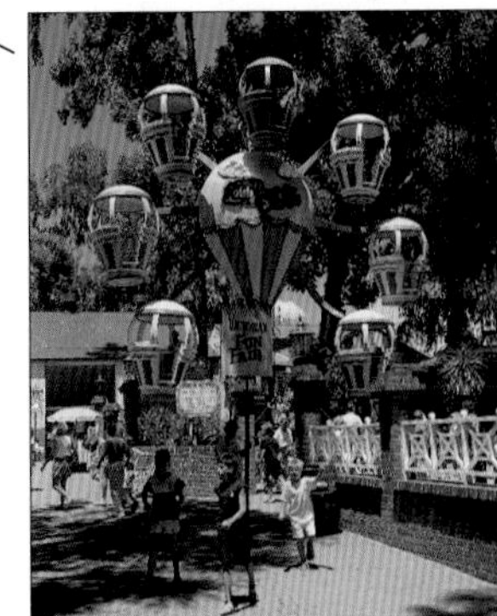

Victorian Funfair
This fair is suitable for visitors of all ages and available to use at no additional cost. The fair affords a unique opportunity to experience authentic, Victorian-era rides.

★ Gold Pouring
Gold Reef City is the only venue in the entire country where the public can attend a gold pouring demonstration.

The Spirit of Sophiatown

Sophiatown – 10 km (6 miles) from Johannesburg's city centre in the 1950s – was a rather seedy shanty town, yet it was also the cradle of a developing urban black culture, and became part of South Africa's mythology. Much of the creative black African talent of Johannesburg lived in this overcrowded slum. Artists and journalists from *Drum* (the first "black" magazine in the country), stylish dressers and musicians would meet in the vibrant dance halls and debate politics in the shebeens (illegal bars). But the magic ended abruptly in the 1950s when the government ordered the forcible removal of the community to Meadowlands, a characterless settlement on the far edge of the city – and the white suburb of Triomf replaced Sophiatown.

Township shuffle

Sophiatown Gangs
Gangsters looked to the USA for role models. The most admired gang in Sophiatown was a snappily dressed, limousine-driving group known as "The Americans".

Shebeens
The Casbah Gang Den was the most notorious shebeen. At these illegal drinking spots, workers and teachers, both white and black, would meet.

Tap water was unavailable in most homes.

Skokiaan was a potent, back-yard-brewed cocktail.

Building materials were bits of wood, cardboard boxes, tin and old sacks.

ESSENCE OF SOPHIATOWN

Despite the poverty, squalor, petty crime and violence, Sophiatown's stimulating vibe differed from that of other townships in the country. People of all races could (and did) buy and own properties here.

The Sounds of Music
The sounds of the penny whistle, saxophone, harmonica, piano, trumpet and clarinet filled the streets and halls.

Leaving Sophiatown
It took four years to remove all of the inhabitants to Meadowlands (now Soweto). By 1959 Sophiatown had been demolished.

Graffiti on a wall in Soweto

Soweto ❸

Road map E2. *5.5 million.*
118469 Senokonyana St, Orlando West, (011) 982-1050.
8:30am–5pm Mon–Fri.

Few white South Africans have visited Soweto or any of the other townships built beyond the limits of the once "whites-only" suburbs. Soweto has few parks or reserves, museums or malls, but it is home to at least five or six million people.

It was in Soweto, in 1976, that the final phase of resistance to apartheid began. The anniversary of this uprising, 16 June, is commemorated as Youth Day. There is a modest monument in the suburb.

Numerous reliable tour companies *(see p381)* organize day trips to Soweto, usually including a visit to a traditional shebeen, as well as a backyard, or spaza, shop. It is not advisable for visitors to enter Soweto alone.

Sandton and Randburg ❹

Road map E2. *600,000.*
Johannesburg International.
Magic Bus, (011) 394-6902.
Village Walk, cnr Rivonia Rd & Maud St, (011) 783-4620. 9am–4:30pm Mon–Sat, 9am–1pm Sun.

North of Johannesburg, the metropolitan sprawl blends into expensively laid-out residential areas with high walls, spacious gardens, swimming pools and tennis courts.

Affluent Sandton is a fashionable shoppers' paradise, with Sandton City reputedly the most sophisticated retail centre in the Southern Hemisphere. It is especially noted for its speciality shops, trendy boutiques, jewellers and dealers in African art, curios and leatherwork. The centre also has 16 cinemas and 20 superb restaurants and bistros. A number of five-star graded hotels adjoin the Sandton City complex and Sandton Square, where an Italianate fountain is the focal point in a little piazza that is lined with coffee shops and restaurants. The Village Walk, close to Sandton City, has restaurants, cinemas and up-market boutiques selling clothing and accessories that have been imported from fashion centres in Europe.

Situated about 10 km (6 miles) northwest of Sandton City is another of Johannesburg's more vibrant suburbs – Randburg – which is a sought-after residential area.

Sandton's Village Walk mall

Randburg's pedestrian mall was among the first in the country. The Randburg Waterfront is a lakeside centre with a variety of shops, pubs, restaurants, craft markets, cinemas, live musical shows, an entertainment area for children and a floodlit musical fountain in the evenings.

On the Witkoppen Road, north of Randburg and Sandton, the Klein Jukskei Vintage Car Museum features a collection of early vehicles.

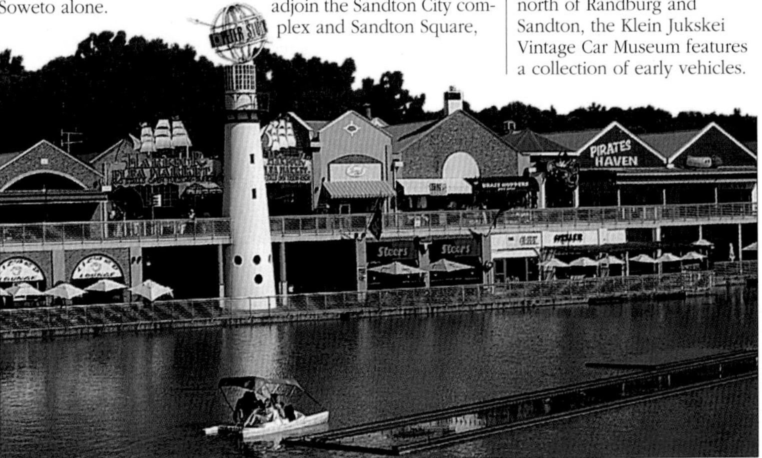

The Randburg Waterfront is a popular entertainment venue in Johannesburg's northern suburbs

Touring Gauteng ❺

Although much of Gauteng consists of the industrial areas that have helped to shape the national wealth, the vibrant metropolitan centres of Johannesburg and Pretoria/Tshwane are surrounded by a green belt that offers various facilities for outdoor recreation. Popular destinations like the De Wildt cheetah station, Hartbeespoort Dam and the hiking trails of the Magaliesberg mountain range are accessible via an excellent network of highways.

Mask, Heia Safari Ranch

De Wildt Wildlife Reserve ⑦
This sanctuary near Brits initiated a breeding programme for captive king cheetahs in 1971. The project is a great success. Booking is essential.

The Magaliesberg Range ⑥
This chain of low hills between Pretoria/Tshwane and Rustenburg is popular with hikers. The area has many hotels, guest farms, caravan parks and camp sites.

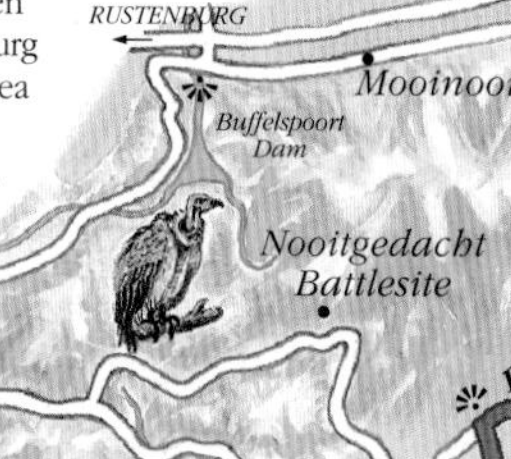

KEY

- Motorway
- Tour route
- Other roads
- Viewpoint

Roodepoort Museum ⑤
A series of displays on local history, including the discovery of gold and development of Roodepoort from mining camp to city.

Sterkfontein Caves and Robert Broom Museum ④
This extensive cavern network – a World Heritage site – is one of the world's most important archeological locations. Guided tours leave every 30 minutes.

Aloe Ridge Game Reserve ②
At this reserve near Muldersdrift, visitors can see white rhino, buffalo, hippo and many antelope and bird species. There is also a Zulu craft centre.

TIPS FOR DRIVERS

Length: *200 km (124 miles) Hartbeespoort Dam is an hour's drive from Pretoria/Tshwane and Johannesburg.*
Stopping-off points: *There are good restaurants at Heia Safari, the Aloe Ridge Game Reserve and around the Hartbeespoort Dam area.*

Hartbeesport Dam ⑧
A 17-sq-km (6.6-sq-mile) water surface makes this a prime weekend destination for Johannesburg and Pretoria/Tshwane citizens.

Crocodile River Arts and Crafts Ramble ⑨
Visitors driving along this route can stop off at a variety of workshops to watch the craftspeople in action and buy fine art, furniture and metalware.

Lion Safari Park ⑩
A one-way road passes through a 200-ha (493-acre) lion enclosure and a separate park stocked with blesbok, black *wildebeest* (gnu), impala, gemsbok and zebra, to reach a picnic site.

Witwatersrand National Botanical Gardens ①
The Witpoortje Falls form the focus of the gardens, where indigenous highveld flora like aloes and proteas attract many bird species.

Heia Safari Ranch ③
Impala, blesbok and zebra wander freely through the grounds, which also incorporate a conference centre, restaurant, and bungalows on the banks of the Crocodile River.

Power-boating is popular on Hartbeespoort Dam

Hartbeespoort Dam ❻

Road map E2. On R514 take cableway turnoff. ℹ *(012) 251-0992.*

This dam forms part of the **Hartbeespoort Nature Reserve**. Boating is permitted and the dam is popular with waterskiers, boardsailors and yachtsmen, while anglers cast for *kurper* (a species of bream), carp and yellowfish.

The circular drive includes a short tunnel leading to the dam wall, on which you experience wide views over the captive waters of the Crocodile and Magalies rivers.

Other attractions include what is said to be the largest freshwater aquarium in Africa. It houses most species of South African freshwater fish, crocodiles, penguins and seals.

The **Gauteng Elephant Sanctuary** (www.elephantsanctuary.co.za) is also nearby. Visitors can feed, ride and walk hand-in-trunk with the pachiderms, or observe them from a tree-house deck.

Environs: In the Ysterhout Kloof is the **Magaliesberg Canopy Tour**. Enjoy the magnificent greenery of the ancient Magaliesberg range from 11 platforms connected by cables. Tours start from the Sparkling Waters Hotel & Spa.

Magaliesberg Canopy Tour
Ysterhout Kloof. ***Tel*** *(014) 535-0000.* *Summer: 7am–4:30pm daily; winter: 8am–3:30pm daily.*

The Cascades Hotel at Sun City

Sun City ❽

Road map D2. Rustenburg. N4, take R565 turnoff. *6 km (4 miles) from Sun City.* *Johannesburg (011) 780-7800.* ***Tel*** *(014) 557-1000.* *daily.*

Set in a fairly bleak part of Southern Africa, two hours by road from the metropolitan centres of the Witwatersrand, "the city that never sleeps" is a glittering pleasure resort. Sun International *(see p325)* and Computicket *(see p377)* offer regular coach tours from Gauteng and there are daily flights from Johannesburg International Airport.

Sun City is the inspiration of self-made multimillionaire hotelier Sol Kerzner. In the 1970s, when the complex was built, the land formed part of the quasi-independent "republic", Bophuthatswana, where gambling, officially banned in South Africa at the time, was legal. The casino was a key element in the resort's initial success, which then included only one luxury hotel, a man-made lake and a challenging 18-hole golf course designed by the former South African golfing champion, Gary Player.

Within a few years, it became apparent that the complex could not cope with the influx of visitors, and a further two hotels were added in 1980 and 1984 respectively, the Cabanas and the attractive Cascades. Accommodation at the 284-room Cabanas Hotel caters mainly for families and day visitors with outdoor interests, and costs slightly less than elsewhere in the resort.

Although recent changes in gambling legislation mean that casinos have sprung up around the country and punters no longer have to drive to Sun City, the resort continues to attract visitors due to its many other features, particularly the entertainment centre, still one of the principal attractions. Not only does it offer a chance of winning a fortune at the spin of a wheel, there are also elaborate stage shows featuring lines of sequinned dancers, music concerts, beauty pageants and a variety of sports events. The complex also houses a vast array of restaurants, curio shops, boutiques and coffee shops. **The Palace of the Lost City** *(see pp270–71)* is the latest addition to the complex.

Casino entrance

In the vicinity of Sun City are several worthwhile natural attractions that should n ot be missed. Located at the entrance to the resort is the fascinating

Sun City is a spectacular man-made oasis in the North West Province

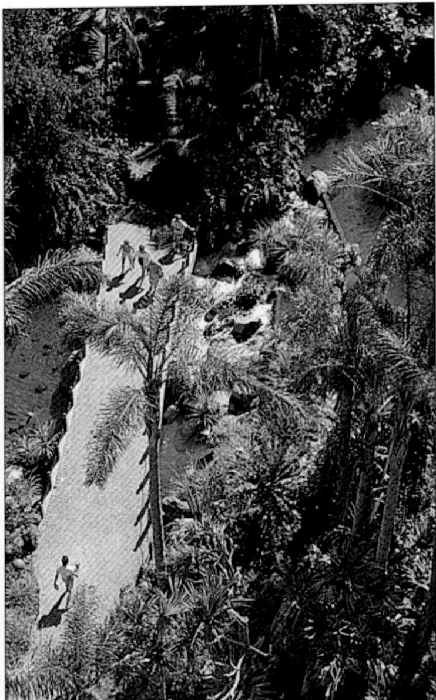
Paths and bridges wind through the jungle gardens

Kwena Gardens, where Nile crocodiles can be viewed in their natural habitat, with special walkways leading to observation areas.

Kwena Gardens
Sun City. ***Tel*** *(014) 552-1262.*
10am–6pm daily. Feeding: 4:30pm daily.

Pilanesberg National Park ❾

Road map D2. Take Mogwase turnoff from R510. ***Tel*** *(014) 555-5351/52.*
6am–6pm daily (times may vary).

The circular layout of the park can be traced to prehistoric times, when this area was the fiery crater of a volcano. Around the central Mankwe Dam lie three rings of little hills – mounds of cooled lava – and the whole area is raised above the plain.

The decision to establish a reserve here was economic: to benefit the local people, and to complement the nearby resort of Sun City.

Re-stocking the overgrazed farmland turned into one of the most ambitious game relocation ventures ever attempted in South Africa. Appropriately called Operation Genesis, it involved the release of 6,000 mammals of 19 species into the new reserve. To ensure the success of the ambitious venture, alien plants were removed and replaced with indigenous ones, telephone lines were diverted, farming structures demolished and the ravages of erosion repaired.

Elephant, black rhino and leopard head an impressive list of wildlife that can be seen at Pilanesberg today. Qualified rangers take guests on safaris in open vehicles. For visitors staying overnight, there is the excitement of night drives.

The Pilanesberg is also home to a number of birds, notably a variety of raptors. Cape vultures nest on the steep cliffs of the Magaliesberg mountains and a number of feeding stations have been established to encourage the survival of this endangered bird.

Pilanesberg National Park offers a choice of accommodation, from the luxurious Kwa Maritane Lodge, Tshukudu Bush Camp and Bakubung Lodge, which overlooks a hippo pool, to tented camps and thatched huts. In the vicinity is a private camp with bungalows and a pleasant caravan park.

HOT-AIR BALLOONING IN THE PILANESBERG

Hot-air balloon trips over the Pilanesberg National Park and Sun City complex are a popular safari option. Suspended in total silence, tourists drift over the herds of wildlife that peacefully graze within the rim of the extinct volcano, experiencing the wonderful calm high above the pyramids and domes of the Sun City leisure resort – except when a brief blast from the burners redresses a loss of height. Since the wind determines the flight direction, balloon ascents are only undertaken on calm days.

A hot-air balloon glides over the bushveld

Young elephants in the Pilanesberg National Park

The Palace of the Lost City

In an ancient volcanic crater, some 180 km (112 miles) northwest of Johannesburg, lies the mythical "lost city" of a vanished people, where time seems to have stood still. Here, innovative design and fanciful architecture in a lush, man-made jungle have created a complex that promises an unforgettable holiday experience: luxurious hotels, world-class golf courses, the glamorous Superbowl entertainment centre, glittering casinos, hanging bridges and blue waves lapping white, palm-fringed beaches.

Palace light

The King's Suite
Maple panelling, a private library, bar and panoramic views make this the hotel's most opulent suite.

King Tower

Buffalo Wing

Lost City Golf Course
This 18-hole championship course offers a choice of tees. A crocodile pool at the 13th hole is a unique water hazard.

Cheetah Fountain
This superb bronze sculpture shows impala, frozen in flight from the feared predator.

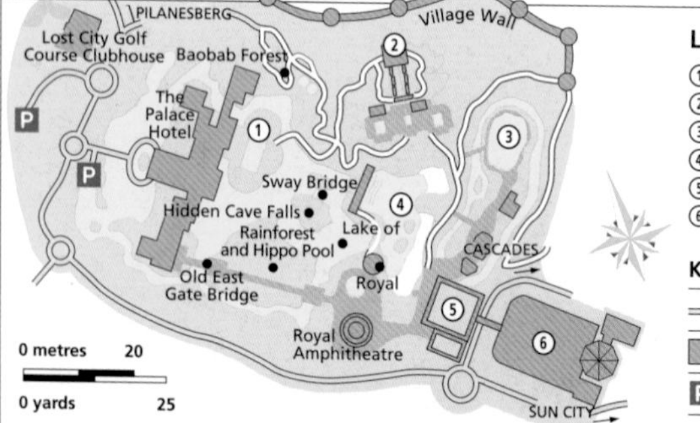

LOST CITY COMPLEX

① Grand Pool
② Temple of Courage
③ Adventure Mountain
④ Roaring Lagoon
⑤ Bridge of Time
⑥ Superbowl

KEY

Road (tarred)
Building
P Parking

For hotels and restaurants in this region see pp344–7 and pp370–72

★ Elephant Atrium and Shawu Statue
This sculpture honours an elephant bull that roamed the Kruger National Park, until his death in 1986, aged 80. It graces a large chamber at the end of the vaulted Elephant Atrium.

VISITORS' CHECKLIST

Road map D2. N4 from Rustenburg, then R565; or R556, 70 km (43 miles) past Brits. North West Province. *Sun City: Airlink (011) 978-1111.* *from Johannesburg (014) 557-1684.* *Sun International Central Reservations (011) 780-7800.* ***Tel*** *The Palace of the Lost City (014) 557-1000.* *daily.* **www**.suninternational.co.za

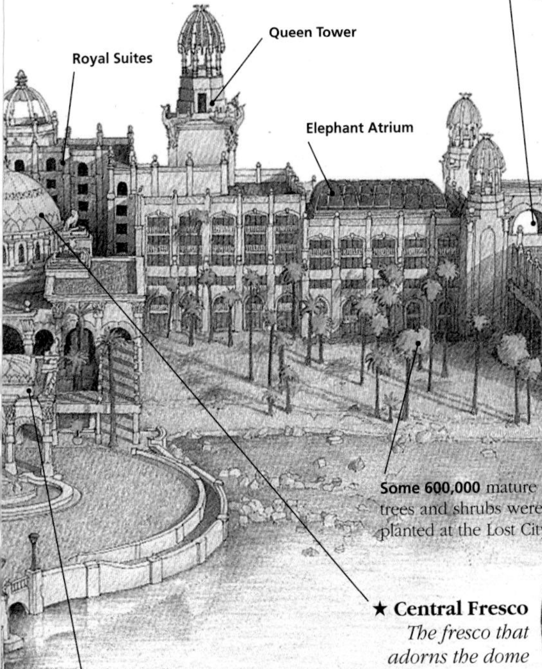

Queen Tower

Royal Suites

Elephant Atrium

Some 600,000 mature trees and shrubs were planted at the Lost City.

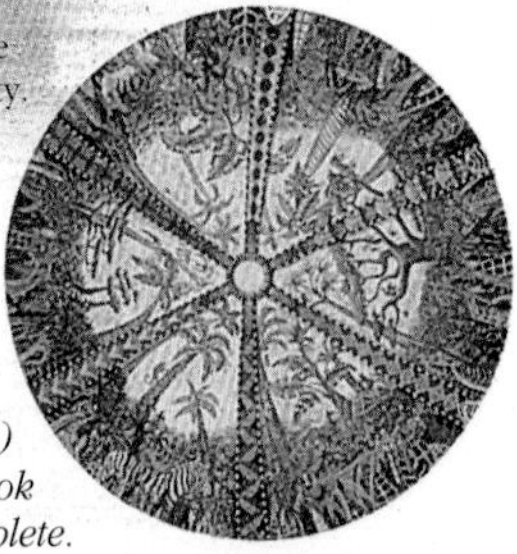

★ Central Fresco
The fresco that adorns the dome of the reception area measures 16 m (52 ft) in diameter and took 5,000 hours to complete.

The porte-cochère leads to the domed lobby.

Roaring Lagoon
Every 90 seconds a 2-m (6.56 ft) wave rolls onto the white sand beach.

STAR FEATURES

- ★ Elephant Atrium and Shawu Statue
- ★ Central Fresco

Exploring the Blyde River Canyon and Kruger

Early prospectors flocked to the eastern part of the country in search of gold, and found it in the rivers and streams. Today, visitors are attracted by the natural beauty and the superb nature reserves. Here, the Blyde River has cut a mighty canyon, and close by, the edge of the Drakensberg range rises from the grassy plains a kilometre below. This is wildlife conservation country, home of the renowned Kruger National Park and a cluster of exclusive private reserves. There are airstrips and excellent accommodation – just a few hours' drive away from the Witwatersrand.

SIGHTS AT A GLANCE

Tour

SEE ALSO

• ***Where to Stay*** pp348–50
• ***Where to Eat*** pp372–3

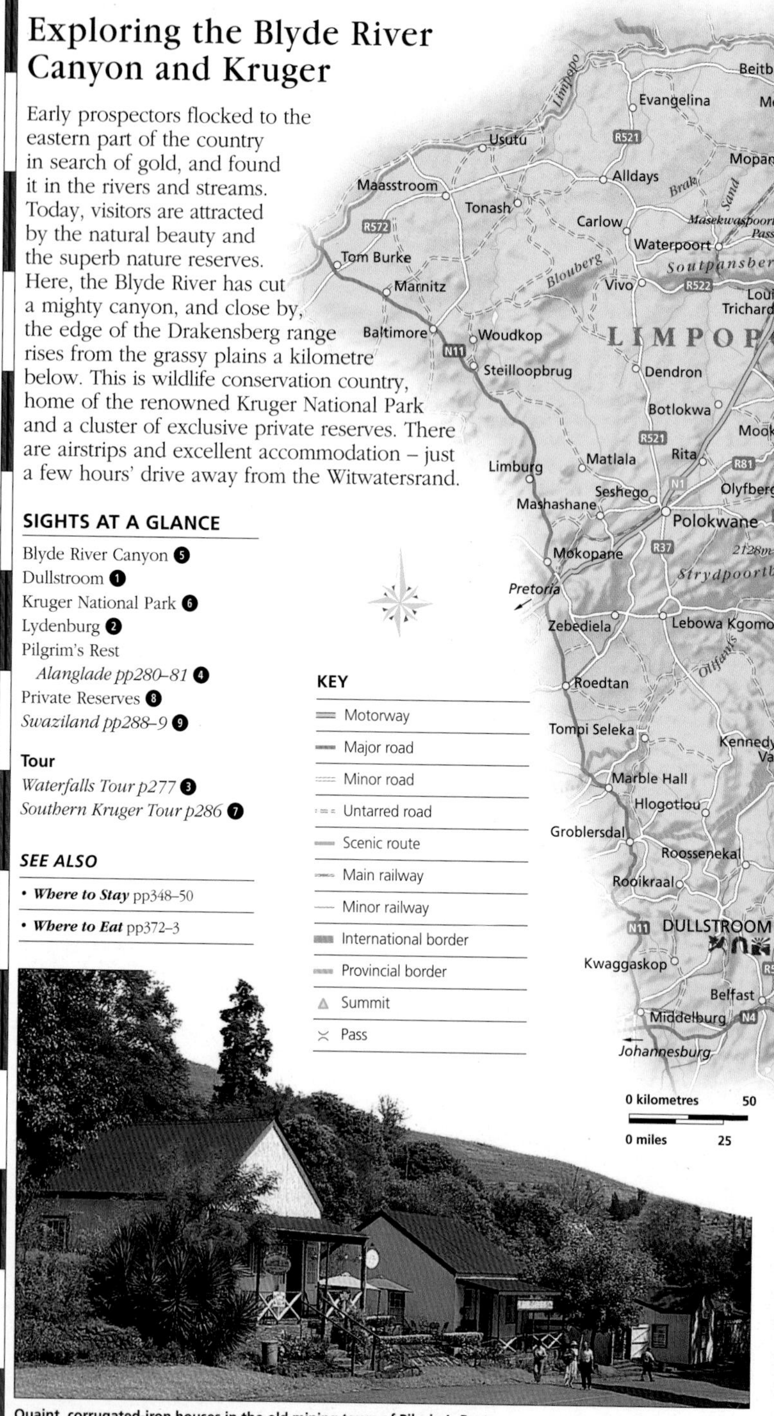

Quaint, corrugated-iron houses in the old mining town of Pilgrim's Rest

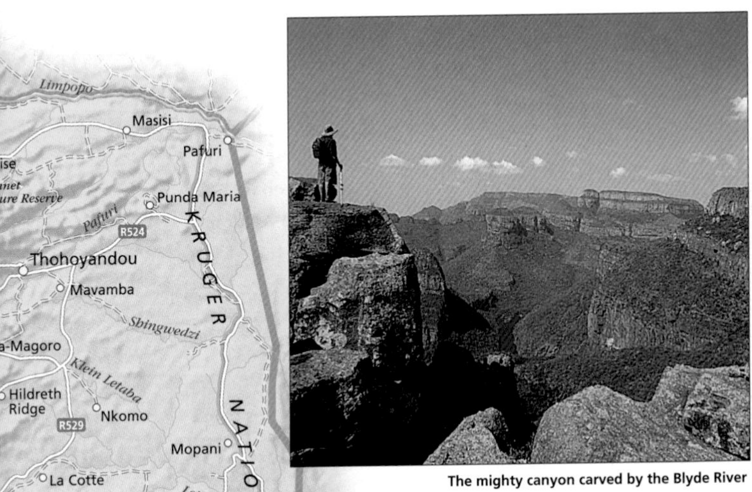

The mighty canyon carved by the Blyde River

GETTING AROUND

The N4 national road, running east from Pretoria/ Tshwane, is the smoothest and most direct route to the border of Mozambique. Leave Johannesburg on the N12, which joins the N4 near Witbank. For destinations in the Kruger Park or at Blyde River, turn north onto other good, tarred roads – a few of the escarpment passes may seem narrow and steep. The Panorama Route, one of the highest and most scenic roads in South Africa, includes the picturesque old mining village of Pilgrim's Rest *(see pp278–9)*. Slow down and use the car's headlamps and fog lights in misty conditions (usually during late winter and early summer).

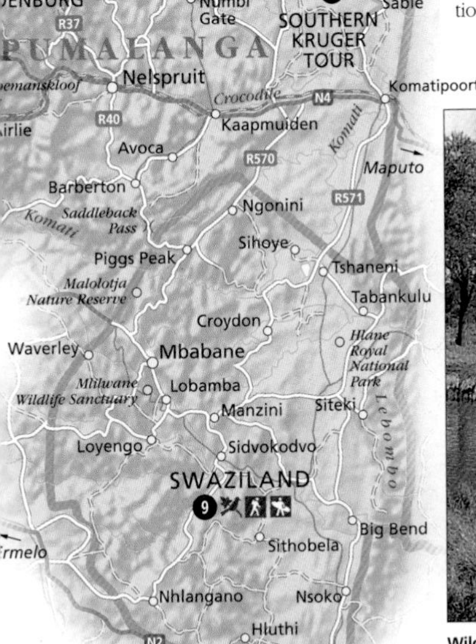

Wildlife gathers at a waterhole in the Kruger National Park

The serpentine curves of Long Tom Pass near Lydenburg

Dullstroom ❶

Road map E2. Middelburg. *500.*
Huguenote St, (013) 254-0254.
www.dullstroom.biz

Named in 1893 after a Dutch official called "Dull" and the *stroom* (stream) of the Crocodile River, Dullstroom is South Africa's fly-fishing centre. It has the highest railway station in South Africa, at 2,076 m (6,811 ft) above sea level. In winter, temperatures can drop to -13°C (9°F).

Environs: The **Dullstroom Dam Nature Reserve**, on the eastern outskirts of the town, is an area of attractive wooded gorges surrounding a tranquil dam known for its trout fishing. Sheltered camping and caravan sites lie close to the shores amid the unusual and luxuriant sub-alpine vegetation. Bird life is rich, and the countryside is traversed by scenic hiking trails like Misty Valley, Ratelspruit and Salpeterkrans.

Verloren Vlei Nature Reserve lies 14 km (9 miles) by road north of Dullstroom, at the heart of a wetlands conservation area boasting a wealth of floral species. The endangered wattled crane is the subject of a conservation project, which aims to release the bird back into the wild.

Along the road to Nelspruit, the **Sudwala Caves** are filled with bizarre dripstone formations. There are regular guided tours. The network of caverns, is named after a Swazi leader who took refuge here during the mid-1800s.

A short walk from the caves is an interesting timeline of the developement of man, as well as a park with life-sized models that portrays prehistoric wildlife in a convincing setting of palms, shrubs and cycads.

Dullstroom Dam Nature Reserve
Tel *(013) 254-0151. daily.*

Verloren Vlei Nature Reserve
Tel *(013) 254-0799.*
by appointment.

Sudwala Caves
Tel *(013) 733-4152. daily.*

Lydenburg ❷

Road map F2. 58 km (36 miles) N of Dullstroom. *6,000.*

Lydenburg means "town of suffering" and refers to the failed attempt to establish a town in the malaria-infested area to the north. Survivors headed south in 1850 to found a new settlement. Interesting historic buildings from that early period are the old church and the Voortrekker school.

The most interesting exhibits in the **Lydenburg Museum** are replicas of the Lydenburg Heads *(see p47)*, seven large, unique terracotta masks dating back to about AD 500 and believed to have been used in ceremonial rituals.

Lydenburg Museum
Long Tom Pass Rd. ***Tel*** *(013) 235-2213. 8am–1pm, 2–4:30pm Mon–Fri, 8am–5pm Sat–Sun. 25 Dec.*

Environs: Sabie, some 53 km (33 miles) east of Lydenburg, is surrounded by vast forestry plantations and is reached via the scenic **Long Tom Pass**, originally part of a wagon road. In places the rocks still bear the marks of metal-rimmed wheel ruts. In the 19th century exotic, fast-growing trees were planted around Sabie to provide timber for use in the many local gold mines. Timber is still the area's mainstay. The **Safcol Forestry Industry Museum** is dedicated to wood and its many uses.

Safcol Forestry Museum
10th Ave, Sabie ***Tel*** *(013) 764-1058. 8:30am–4pm Mon–Fri, 10am–3pm Sat & Sun.*

TROUT FISHING IN DULLSTROOM

In 1890, brown trout were successfully introduced to the inland waters of KwaZulu-Natal for the first time and were later distributed in cold streams throughout the country. The rainbow trout with its sparkling reddish-mauve side stripe was introduced in 1897. The trout-rich waters around Dullstroom allow for dam and river angling, mostly from private ground. Temporary membership of the Dullstroom Fly-Fishers' Club allows temporary access to sites, as well as sound advice from experienced local anglers. Details may be obtained on admission to Dullstroom Dam, or from the Town Clerk. Accommodation in the district ranges from wooden cabins to luxurious guesthouses.

Tranquil dam near Dullstroom

The Waterfalls Tour ❸

High-lying ground, generous rainfall and heavy run-off have created spectacular waterfalls in this old gold-mining area along the Drakensberg escarpment. There are, in fact, more waterfalls here than anywhere else in Southern Africa. Several of them can be seen on an easy round trip of under 100 km (60 miles) between the towns of Sabie and Graskop. Most are well signposted and easy to reach by car. Enchanting as they are, waterfalls can be slippery and dangerous and visitors are urged to heed the warning notices.

Lisbon Falls ⑥
The Lisbon Falls crash 90 m (295 ft) down a rocky cliff. The old miners named many local places after towns in their home countries.

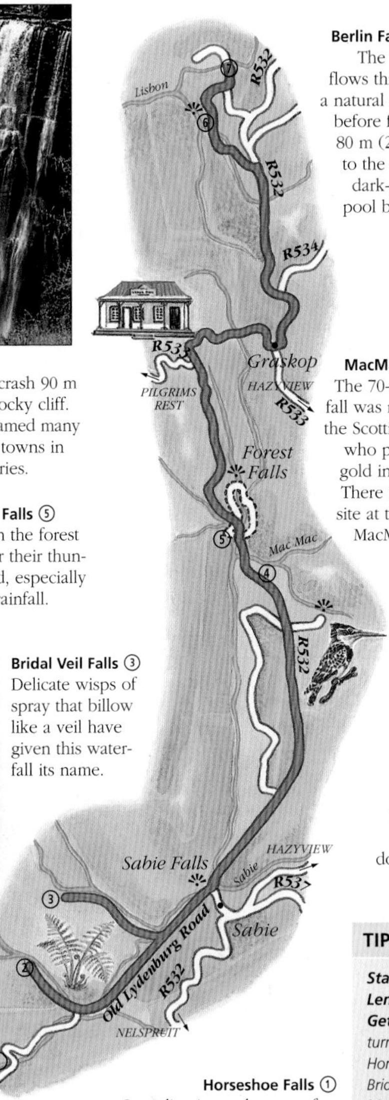

Berlin Falls ⑦
The water flows through a natural sluice before falling 80 m (263 ft) to the deep, dark-green pool below.

MacMac Falls ④
The 70-m (230-ft) fall was named for the Scottish miners who panned for gold in this area. There is a picnic site at the nearby MacMac pools.

Maria Shires Falls ⑤
These falls in the forest are noted for their thundering sound, especially after heavy rainfall.

Bridal Veil Falls ③
Delicate wisps of spray that billow like a veil have given this waterfall its name.

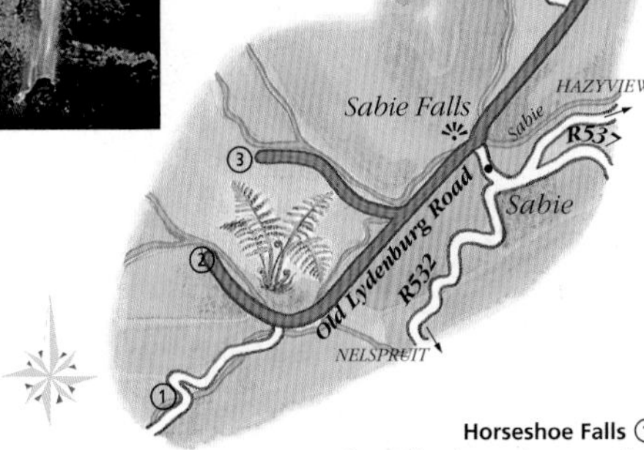

KEY

- Tour route
- Other roads
- Trail
- Viewpoint

Lone Creek Falls ②
From almost 70 m (230 ft), the spray of the falls drifts down onto dense pockets of fern and mountain forest.

Horseshoe Falls ①
Cascading in an almost perfect horseshoe, these falls are on private land and reached after a short walk through a campsite.

TIPS FOR DRIVERS

Starting point: *Sabie.*
Length: *100 km (60 miles).*
Getting there: *From Sabie, turn left on to the R532 for the Horseshoe, Lone Creek and Bridal Veil falls. For the MacMac, Maria Shires, Lisbon, Berlin and Forest falls, take the R532 from Sabie towards Graskop.*

Pilgrim's Rest ❹

Gravestone

Prospectors struck it rich in 1874, ending their search for gold in a picturesque Lowveld valley. Their original village, today restored to its modest glory, is unique: the diggers built in "tin and timber" thinking that, once the gold was exhausted, they would move on. But the gold lasted almost 100 years, and Pilgrim's Rest, 15 km (10 miles) west of the Drakensberg escarpment, is a living part of history.

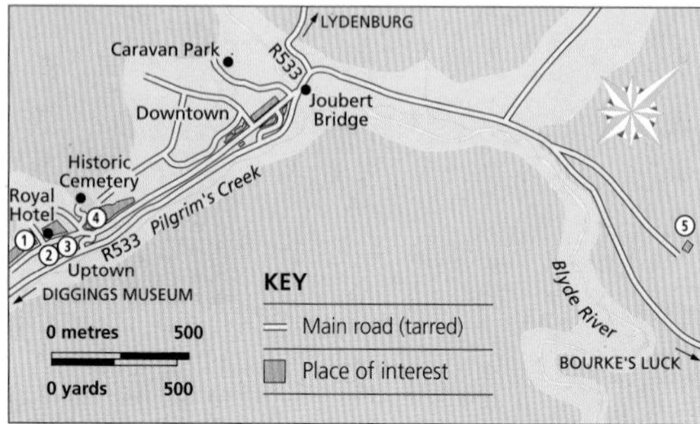

KEY TO TOWN PLAN

The Old Print House ①
Information Centre ②
The Miner's House ③
Dredzen & Company ④
Alanglade ⑤

Exploring Pilgrim's Rest

The entire village, situated 35 km (21 miles) north of Sabie, is a national monument. A single ticket, available from the Information Centre, affords access to the buildings.

A leisurely downhill stroll from St Mary's Church to the Post Office passes the old "uptown area", where one can visit the cemetery. Most interesting of all the tombstones is the enigmatic Robber's Grave.

At the Diggings Site, on the bank of Pilgrim's Creek, visitors may try their luck at panning for alluvial gold.

The Old Print House is typical of local buildings: corrugated iron sheets on a timber frame. Newspapers were the only news medium in days gone by, and printers were among the town's early residents.

The Miner's House puts the life of prospectors into perspective: they may have been surrounded by gold, but their way of life was simple.

Dredzen & Company, the general dealer, displays essential household requisites of a century ago.

Stately Alanglade, the mine manager's residence, was situated in a wooded glen, well away from the dust and noise of the village *(see pp280–81)*.

The bar of the Royal Hotel was once a chapel

VISITORS' CHECKLIST

Road map F2. *(013) 768-1060.* *9am–4pm daily.* *multi-entry.* *(013) 768-1367.* **www**.pilgrims-rest.co.za

Dredzen's store with its colourful bargains from a bygone era

Environs: Timber and tourism are the mainstays of this area on the dramatic escarpment of the Drakensberg mountains.

From the village, the tarred R533 winds across Bonnet Pass to Graskop, a convenient centre for exploring both the escarpment and the Kruger National Park, whose main camp, Skukuza, is just 70 km (44 miles) away.

View from God's Window

The R534, also known as the Panorama Route, starts 3 km (2 miles) north of Graskop and passes cliff-top sites and lovely waterfalls *(see p277)*. The escarpment drops almost 1,000 m (3,281 ft) to the Lowveld plains below. In places, the view extends 100 km (60 miles) towards Mozambique. The scenery in this area has been called the most beautiful in South Africa, and the vistas are spectacular.

The Three Rondavels in the Blyde River Canyon

Blyde River Canyon ❺

Road map F2. On R534.
Tel *(013) 761-6019.* 7am–5pm daily.

The fast-flowing Blyde River has, over the centuries, carved its way through 700 m (2,300 ft) of shale and quartzite to create a scenic jumble of cliffs, islands, plateaus and bush-covered slopes that form a 20-km (12-mile) canyon. At the heart of this canyon lies the Blydepoort Dam.

The forested slopes of the ravine are home to several large antelope species, as well as smaller mammals, birds, hippo and crocodile. Only in the Blyde River Canyon are all the Southern African primates found: chacma baboon, vervet and samango monkeys, and both species of bushbaby. The abundant flora ranges from lichens and mosses to montane forest, orchids and other flowering plants.

Exploring the Blyde River Canyon Nature Reserve

A 300-km (186-mile) circular drive from Graskop via Bosbokrand, Klaserie, Swadini and Bourke's Luck affords panoramic vistas of the escarpment rising above the plains, the Blydepoort Dam and the breathtaking view deep into the canyon itself. There are several overnight trails and short walks, and accommodation is available at the resorts of Swadini and Blydepoort.

Kowyn's Pass

The tarred R533 between Graskop and the Lowveld provides views of the escarpment and its soaring cliffs. It also passes the scenic Panorama Gorge with its feathery waterfall.

Aventura Swadini

Tel *(015) 795-5141.* *daily.*
www.aventura.co.za

This resort, set deep in the canyon on the shores of Blydepoort, offers accommodation, a restaurant and a base for boating trips on the dam. The visitors centre and low-level view site have information on the dam and the Kadishi Falls, the world's largest active tufa (calcium carbonate) formation.

Three Rondavels

Resembling the traditional cylindrical huts of the Xhosa or Zulu, these three hills were shaped by the erosion of soft rock beneath a harder rock "cap" that eroded more slowly. The capping of Black Reef quartzite supports a growth of evergreen bush. The Three Rondavels is one of three sites that can be viewed from the road which overlooks the canyon – the other two are World's End and Lowveld View.

Bourke'sLuck potholes

Bourke's Luck

Tel *(013) 761-6019.*
7am–5pm daily.

Grit and stones carried by the swirling waters at the confluence of the Blyde ("joyful") and Treur ("sad") rivers have carved potholes, from which early prospectors extracted large quantities of gold. Off the R532, Bourke's Luck is the reserve's headquarters, with an information centre.

The Pinnacle, Panorama Route

Panorama Route

The 18-km (11-mile) stretch of the R534 that loops along the top of the cliff, right at the very edge of the escarpment, is a scenic marvel. Wonderview and God's Window may sound like purely fanciful names until one explores the sites and stands in silent awe at the breathtaking scenery.

The Pinnacle

This impressive column of rock, also on the Panorama Route, appears to rise sheer from a base of evergreen foliage. Optical illusions seem to place it almost within reach. Exposed layers of sandstone show the rock's sedimentary origins. It becomes clear that, even at this lofty height above present sea level, the top of the escarpment was once covered by a primordial sea.

Pilgrim's Rest: Alanglade

Palatial by Pilgrim's Rest standards, Alanglade was occupied by a succession of Transvaal Gold Mining Estate managers. It is, however, most strongly associated with its first occupants. Alan and Gladys Barry moved into the newly built house with their young family in 1916. Today, the mansion is a period museum furnished in the Edwardian style, and seems to await the return of its first owners.

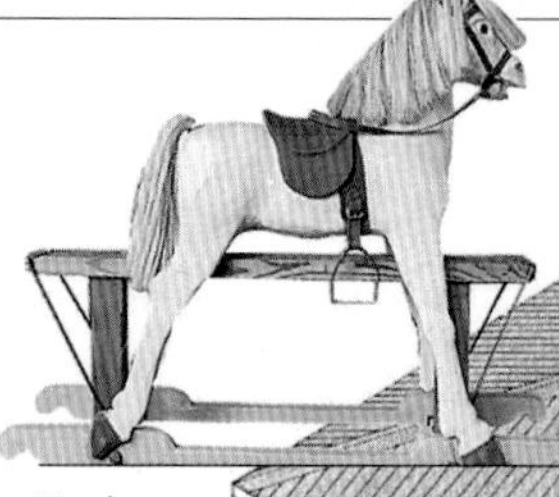

Wooden rocking horse

★ The Kitchen
The kitchen staff had to cook for many people, so the kitchen includes two pantries, a larder, scullery and milk room.

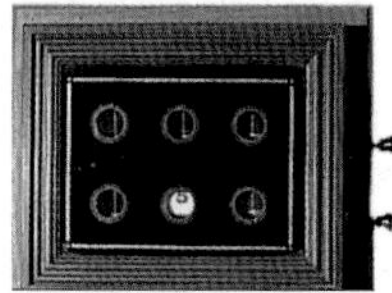

Electric Bell
An ingenious bell system connected to a numbered, glazed box informed the staff in which room service was required.

Blocks of local stone line the base of the house.

Glazed double doors separate the rooms and let in light.

Arched windows offset the entrances from the rest of the house.

Enclosed Verandahs
Airy verandahs doubled as sleeping space for the Barry household, which included seven children and many servants.

STAR FEATURES

★ The Kitchen

★ Erica's Bedroom

VISITORS' CHECKLIST

Pilgrim's Rest. 3 km (2 miles) NE at R533 fork. *(013) 768-1060.* *11am, 2pm daily. Book ahead.* **www**.pilgrims-rest.co.za

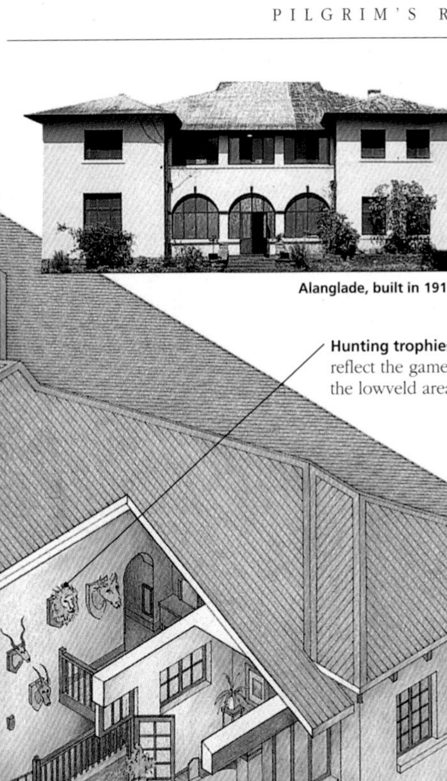

Alanglade, built in 1915

Hunting trophies reflect the game of the lowveld area.

★ Erica's Bedroom
The eldest daughter, Erica, was the only child to have her own bedroom, even though she only visited during school holidays.

Antique Furniture
Museum Services furnished Alanglade with a number of exquisite antiques, such as this rosewood armoire.

Day nursery

Floor coverings consist of woven mats made of coir, grass or sisal fibre.

The Rose Garden
Only the small rose garden still displays the strict, original period layout of bold lines, geometric patterns and herbaceous borders.

ALAN BARRY'S LEGACY

On 15 August 1930, Richard Alan Barry, the General Manager of Transvaal Gold Mining Estates Ltd, wrote this diary entry: "Leave Pilgrim's Rest. A very sad parting from work and friends and associates." This, the third Alanglade (the other two were in Johannesburg), had been the family's home for 14 years and had seen a new generation of Barrys grow up. So strong was the association with these first owners that the house is called Alanglade to this day.

Three of the Barry children

The Kruger National Park 6

Kruger is South Africa's largest national park, and unquestionably one of the best wildlife sanctuaries in the world. From the Limpopo River in the north to the Crocodile in the south, the park extends for 352 km (220 miles), and averages 60 km (38 miles) from east to west. This vast wilderness covers an area of 19,633 sq km (7,580 sq miles), equivalent in size to Israel. The park has 16 distinct sections, based on the type of vegetation found there.

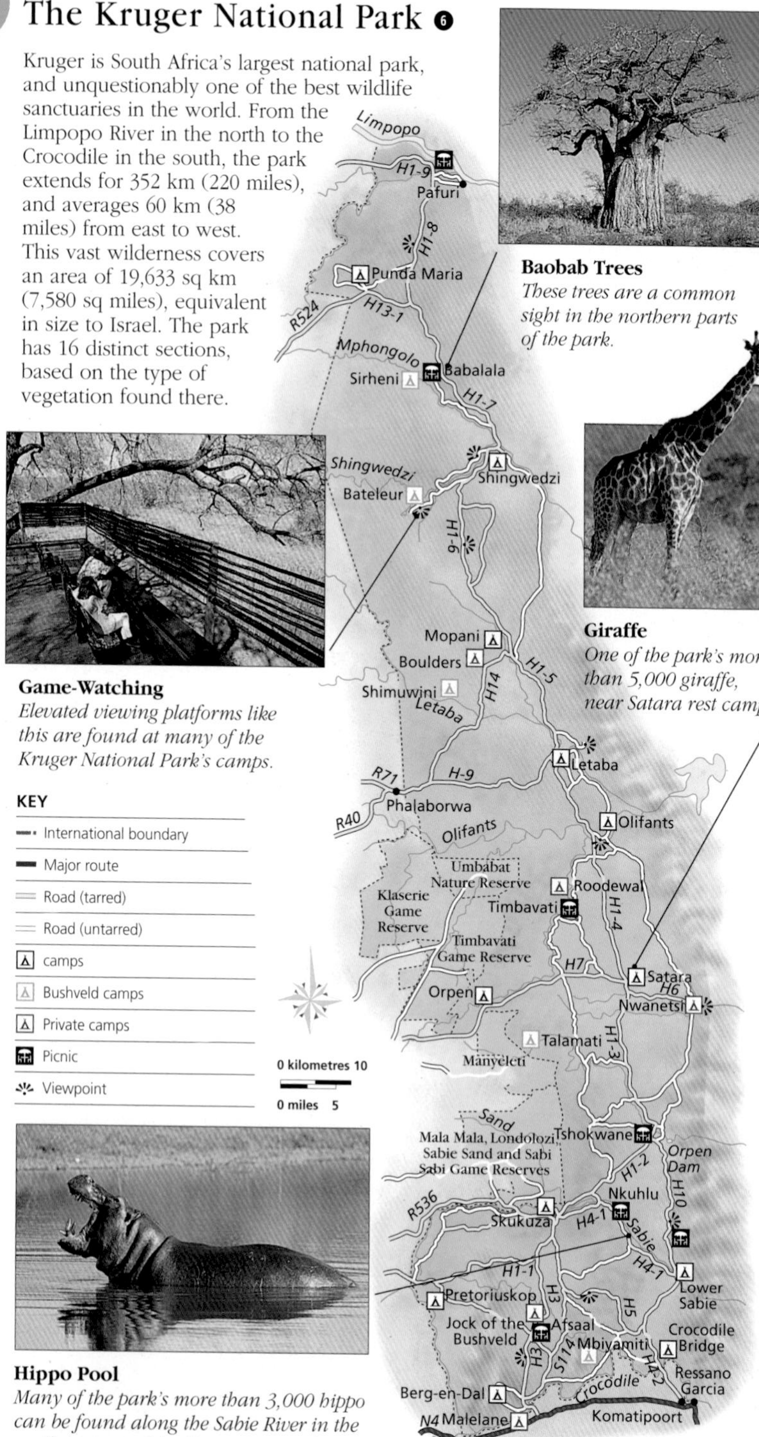

Baobab Trees
These trees are a common sight in the northern parts of the park.

Giraffe
One of the park's more than 5,000 giraffe, near Satara rest camp.

Game-Watching
Elevated viewing platforms like this are found at many of the Kruger National Park's camps.

KEY

- International boundary
- Major route
- Road (tarred)
- Road (untarred)
- camps
- Bushveld camps
- Private camps
- Picnic
- Viewpoint

Hippo Pool
Many of the park's more than 3,000 hippo can be found along the Sabie River in the southern part of the Kruger National Park.

◁ **Zebra and impala share a drink at one of the Kruger National Park's many waterholes**

Mopane trees and red sand near Punda Maria in northern Kruger

VISITORS' CHECKLIST

Road map F1–2. *Skukuza, Phalaborwa, Nelspruit.*
***Tel* Central bookings:** *National Parks Board. (012) 428-9111 or (021) 975-4472. 5:30am–6:30pm Sep–Mar, 6am–6pm Apr–Aug. Malaria precautions are necessary.*
www.saparks.co.za

NORTHERN KRUGER

Kruger's semi-arid northern region is an immense, arid wilderness of mopane trees. Several rivers, often little more than sandy courses, sustain some of the park's most intriguing habitats. Apart from providing sanctuary for large herds of elephant and buffalo, the north also hosts antelope species such as sable, roan, eland, Lichtenstein's hartebeest, tsessebe and grysbok.

Punda Maria

The remote northernmost corner of Kruger will appeal to visitors seeking solitude. Punda Maria's huts date back to 1933. The Pafuri picnic spot, at the northern extremity of the park, attracts bird-watchers in pursuit of the exquisite crimson-and-green Narina trogon. Longtailed starlings, crested guinea fowl and white-fronted bee-eaters are also found in this tranquil haven within the park. Wild fig, fever, mahogany, ebony and baobab trees border the Luvuvhu River, where nyala feed quietly in the shade.

Shingwedzi and Mopani

Shingwedzi, 47 km (29 miles) south, occupies a hill summit overlooking the Pioneer Dam. In this hot, dry region, the camp's swimming pool offers year-round relief. Mopani, 63 km (39 miles) further, is an ideal base from which to explore the area. A network of roads follows both banks of the beautiful Shingwedzi River, which sustains elephant, buffalo, nyala, waterbuck, lion and leopard.

Letaba

Enjoying a commanding position on the south bank of the Letaba River is one of Kruger's finest camps. Chalets are arranged in semi-circles overlooking the river. In the Elephant Hall is a display of tusks from the "Magnificent Seven", believed to be the largest tusks ever found in Southern Africa.

CENTRAL KRUGER

Although no major rivers flow across the flat plains of Kruger's central region, the open grassland supports large herds of antelope and other game. As prey animals are plentiful, half of the park's lions inhabit this region and are regularly sighted. During winter, large herds of impala, zebra, wildebeest, buffalo and giraffe gather to drink at the artificial waterholes and dams that have been constructed across sandy riverbeds.

There are some superb vantage points on the road north from Lower Sabie that overlook the Kruger's dams. Mlondozi Dam has good picnic facilities and a shady terrace overlooking the valley. The very popular Nkumbe lookout point offers unparalleled views over the plains below. The water of Orpen Dam, at the foot of the N'wamuriwa hills, attracts kudu, elephant and giraffe.

Crested guinea fowl

Olifants

This attractive camp overlooks the broad flood-plain of the Olifants River. This area supports large herds of elephant. Lion, antelope and buffalo can often be found along the roads that follow the river.

Satara and Orpen

Satara, the second largest camp, is located in an area where lion are common. Gravel roads along the Sweni, Nuanetsi and Timbavati rivers offer superb game-viewing. To the west of Satara, Orpen camp is close to the private Timbavati Game Reserve.

Near Satara, zebra and giraffe enjoy fresh grazing after the summer rains

For hotels and restaurants in this region see pp348–50 and pp372–3

Southern Kruger Tour ❼

Although the Southern region covers only about one-fifth of the Kruger National Park's total area, it attracts the most visitors, as it is easily accessible from Gauteng. Three of the five largest camps are found here, and the traffic volume can be high, but it is considered to be the best game-viewing area. It is also a very scenic region, where granite *koppies* (outcrops) punctuate the woodland, and the Sabie River carves a verdant corridor across the plains.

Skukuza ①
The largest camp, able to accommodate around 1,000 visitors, is at the centre of the Kruger's best wildlife-viewing area. Camp facilities include an airport, car-hire service, bank, post office, museum, library, restaurant, shop and bakery.

Tshokwane Picnic Site ②
A pleasant place for breakfast, lunch or a cup of tea, refreshments can be bought from the kiosk. Tshokwane is located on the old transport wagon trail, cut through the bush in the 1880s.

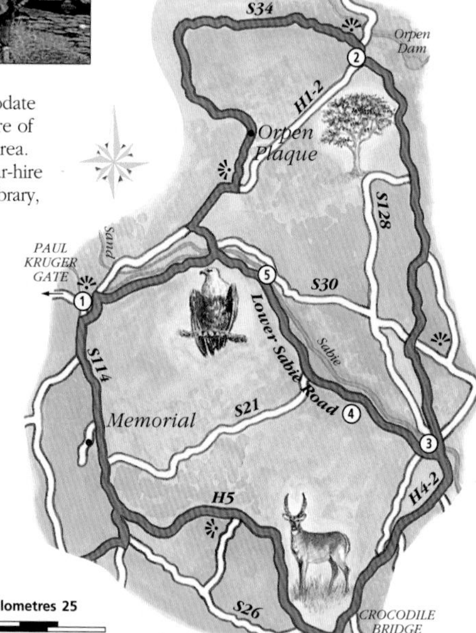

Nkuhlu Picnic Site ⑤
On the shady banks of the Sabie River, the picnic spot is often visited by monkeys who descend from the trees to snatch food off plates. Fish eagles may be seen, and crocodiles float in the river.

Lower Sabie Road (H4-1) ④
Connecting Skukuza to Lower Sabie, the road closely follows the Sabie River for 43 km (27 miles). It is the most popular road in the park, as there is much wildlife in the area.

KEY

- Tour route
- Other roads
- Viewpoint

Lower Sabie ③
At the modest-sized Lower Sabie camp, many of the chalets survey an expanse of the Sabie River where elephant, buffalo, hippo, ducks and herons are often seen.

TIPS FOR DRIVERS

Starting point: *From Paul Kruger Gate to Skukuza, Tshokwane and Lower Sabie, and onto the H4-1.*
Length: *100 km (62 miles).*
Getting there: *Take the N4 from Nelspruit, the R538 to Hazyview and R536 to Paul Kruger Gate.*

Private Reserves ❽

Along the western boundary of the national park, and bordered by the Sabie and Olifants rivers, a mosaic of private reserves provides a vital buffer between the densely populated areas of Lebowa and Gazankulu, and the Kruger. A fence, erected along the park's boundary in the 1960s to prevent the spread of diseased animals, also blocked migration routes. An agreement between all parties made possible its removal, and by 1994 herds were free once again to trek along their ancient paths.

Hippo in the natural pool at Sabi Sabi Game Reserve

Exploring the Private Reserves

Luxury lodges, often recipients of international awards for service excellence, offer exclusive "bush experiences" to small groups of visitors. Emphasis is placed on personal attention, and experienced rangers guide visitors on night drives and interesting bush walks.

Sabie Sand Complex

Mpumalanga. ***Tel*** *bookings: Selati and Bushlodge (011) 483-3939; Mala Mala and Londolozi (011) 809-4300.* *restricted access.* *fully incl.* **www**.ccafrica.com

This famous complex includes the Mala Mala, Londolozi and Bushlodge reserves and shares a 33 km (21 mile) boundary with Kruger. Sightings of the Big Five are virtually guaranteed, and hyena, cheetah and wild dog may also be seen.

The choice of accommodation alternatives ranges from exclusive bush camps to luxury lodges. Popular camps like Selati, Sabie River, the Bushlodge, Mala Mala and Londolozi offer access to the southern Sabi-Sabi region with its abundant wildlife.

Manyeleti Reserve

Mpumalanga. ***Tel*** *(013) 692-8780.* *restricted access.* *fully incl.* **www**. safarilodges.co.za

This reserve adjoins the Orpen area of the Kruger National Park, known for its varied wildlife. Visitors can stay either in the comfortable tented Honeyguide Camp, or at the luxurious Khoka Moya chalets.

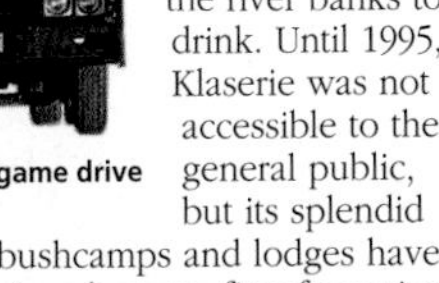

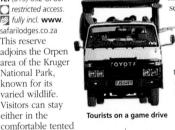

Tourists on a game drive

A luxurious lounge at Mala Mala Private Reserve

Timbavati Game Reserve

Mpumalanga. ***Tel*** *bookings for the different lodges: (021) 424-1037.* *restricted access.* *fully incl.*

The 550-sq-km (210-sq-mile) Timbavati reserve, adjoining Kruger's central region, has some of the best game-viewing in South Africa. Five lodges each with access to a different part of the reserve offer drives and guided walks.

M'bali, a tented camp, and Umlani Bush Camp are situated in the north, while the luxurious Kambaku, Ngala and Tanda Tula lodges lie in the central region.

Klaserie

Mpumalanga. ***Tel*** *bookings: Thornybush (011) 883-7918; King's Camp (015) 793-1123; Umhlali (012) 346-4028; Motswari (011) 463-1990.* *restricted access.* *fully incl.* **www**.thornybush.co.za

Klaserie is an area that encompasses many private reserves, making it the second largest private sanctuary in the country. It extends over 620 sq km (235 sq miles) and borders on the Kruger National Park, as well as on the Olifants River. The Klaserie River meanders across the semi-arid bushveld and is the reserve's central focus as countless birds and animals gather on the river banks to drink. Until 1995, Klaserie was not accessible to the general public, but its splendid bushcamps and lodges have since become firm favourites.

Swaziland ❾

Traditional Swazi hut at Mlilwane

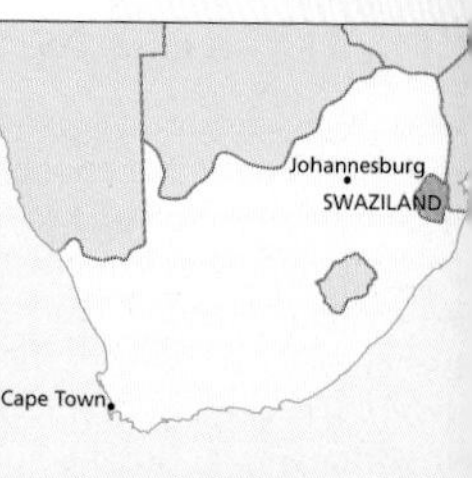

The kingdom of Swaziland achieved its independence from Britain on 6 September 1968. King Mswati III has ruled the almost one million Swazis since 1986. In the west of the country, the highlands offer many opportunities for hikers. The middleveld has the perfect growing conditions for tropical fruit and is known for its arts and crafts. In the east, lush sugar cane plantations contrast with the dense brown bushveld of game reserves and ranches.

★ Mbabane

Swaziland's capital city developed around the site where Michael Wells opened a pub and trading post at a river crossing in 1888. Today, trade is brisk at the Swazi Market.

★ Mlilwane Wildlife Sanctuary

Mlilwane, which supports white rhino, giraffe, zebra and antelope, covers 45 sq km (17 sq miles). The rest camp's Hippo Haunt restaurant overlooks a hippo pool.

STAR SIGHTS

- ★ Mlilwane Wildlife Sanctuary
- ★ Mbabane
- ★ Peak Craft Center, Piggs Peak
- ★ Hlane Royal National Park

Manzini

Swaziland's biggest town is situated close to the airport. An industrial centre, it also has colourful markets that sell fresh produce, crafts and fabric.

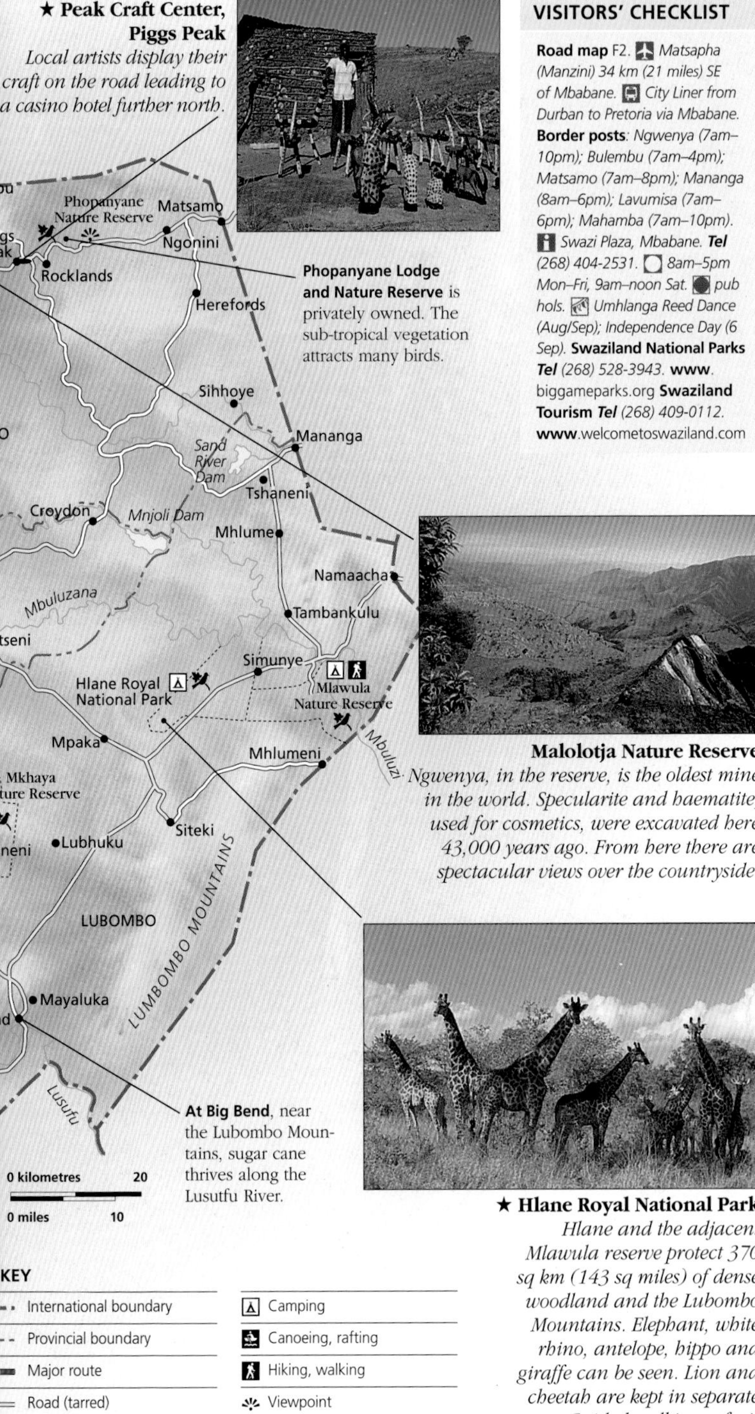

★ Peak Craft Center, Piggs Peak
Local artists display their craft on the road leading to a casino hotel further north.

Phopanyane Lodge and Nature Reserve is privately owned. The sub-tropical vegetation attracts many birds.

At Big Bend, near the Lubombo Mountains, sugar cane thrives along the Lusutfu River.

Malolotja Nature Reserve
Ngwenya, in the reserve, is the oldest mine in the world. Specularite and haematite, used for cosmetics, were excavated here 43,000 years ago. From here there are spectacular views over the countryside.

★ Hlane Royal National Park
Hlane and the adjacent Mlawula reserve protect 370 sq km (143 sq miles) of dense woodland and the Lubombo Mountains. Elephant, white rhino, antelope, hippo and giraffe can be seen. Lion and cheetah are kept in separate camps. Guided walking safaris can be arranged on request.

VISITORS' CHECKLIST

Road map F2. *Matsapha (Manzini) 34 km (21 miles) SE of Mbabane.* *City Liner from Durban to Pretoria via Mbabane.* **Border posts***: Ngwenya (7am–10pm); Bulembu (7am–4pm); Matsamo (7am–8pm); Mananga (8am–6pm); Lavumisa (7am–6pm); Mahamba (7am–10pm).* *Swazi Plaza, Mbabane.* ***Tel*** *(268) 404-2531.* *8am–5pm Mon–Fri, 9am–noon Sat.* *pub hols.* *Umhlanga Reed Dance (Aug/Sep); Independence Day (6 Sep).* **Swaziland National Parks** ***Tel*** *(268) 528-3943.* **www.**biggameparks.org **Swaziland Tourism** ***Tel*** *(268) 409-0112.* **www.**welcometoswaziland.com

KEY

- International boundary
- Provincial boundary
- Major route
- Road (tarred)
- Road (untarred)
- Camping
- Canoeing, rafting
- Hiking, walking
- Viewpoint
- Tourist information

Introducing the Arid Interior

The semi-arid, sparsely populated Karoo extends across the Northern Cape and parts of the Free State, Eastern and Western Cape provinces. Sleepy country towns and villages, often treasure chests of Cape Dutch and Victorian architecture, serve as supply centres for surrounding farms. North of the Orange River lie the red dunes of the Kalahari desert, one of South Africa's finest wilderness areas. A rich assortment of wildlife inhabits this remote territory. In the Northern Cape, the most famous diamond mines in the world extract shining riches from the earth.

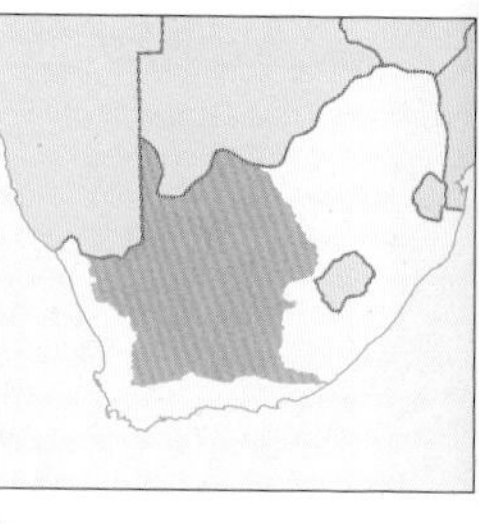

The Richtersveld *is a bleak moonscape with curious flora such as the* kokerboom *(quiver tree), from which Khoina hunters made arrows.*

The Camel Rider Statue *in Upington honours the memory of the policemen and their tireless mounts who patrolled the Kalahari in the early 20th century.*

◁ A ***kokerboom*** **(quiver tree) in the barren semi-desert of the Augrabies Falls National Park**

Kimberley's diamond mines, *once owned by De Beers Mining Company, are nowadays controlled by the Anglo-American Corporation. Impressive headgear dominates the skyline on the outskirts, while in the town itself lie many beautiful historic buildings, like the City Hall.*

Bloemfontein's Civic Centre, *a tall modern structure of glass and concrete, represents a bold departure from the traditional, stately sandstone buildings in the town.*

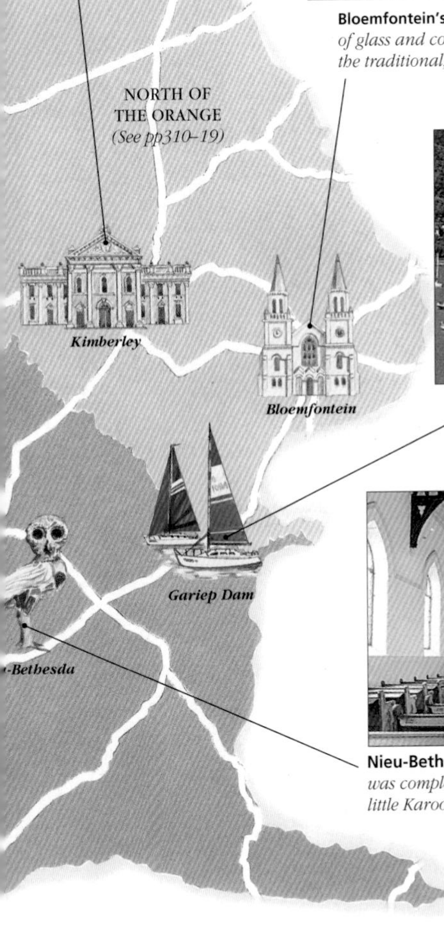

NORTH OF THE ORANGE
(See pp310–19)

The Gariep Dam *is the largest water project on the Orange River and has become a popular weekend resort.*

-Bethesda

Nieu-Bethesda's *quaint Dutch Reformed Church was completed in 1905. The main drawcard of this little Karoo town, however, is the bizarre Owl House.*

0 kilometres 100

0 miles 50

Life in the Desert

Velvet mite

The Kalahari Desert forms part of a vast inland steppe that stretches from the Orange River to the equator. It extends across portions of the Northern Cape and Namibia, and also covers much of Botswana. Rainfall in this region varies from 150–400 mm (6–16 in) per year and is soon soaked up or simply evaporates. There is little surface water and the flora consists mainly of grass, shrubs and the hardy camelthorn acacias that line the dry beds of ancient rivers. Although the landscape may appear to be lifeless, it supports an astonishing variety of wildlife that is superbly adapted to survive in this harsh environment.

Seasonal river beds, *such as that of the Auob, carry water only every few years usually after exceptionally heavy downpours.*

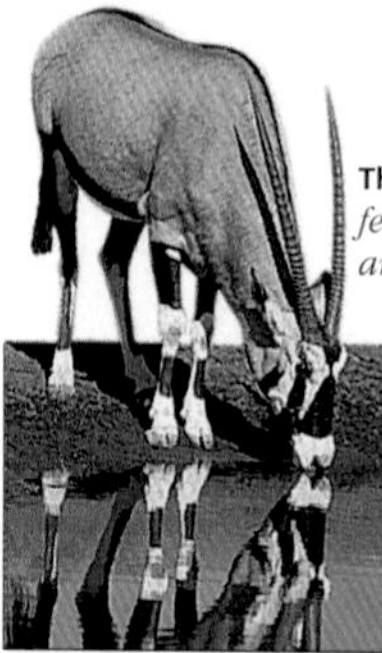
The *Gemsbok* (oryx) *feeds on grass, leaves and roots, and can do without water. The animal's temperature fluctuates in response to climatic changes: during the day it may soar to above 45°C (113°F).*

The quiver contains arrows poisoned with the juice of beetle larvae.

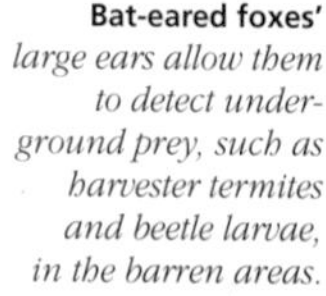
Kalahari lions *are unique to the Kgalagadi Transfrontier Park, and have learned to depend on smaller prey, taking porcupines and bat-eared foxes when antelope migrate.*

Bat-eared foxes' *large ears allow them to detect underground prey, such as harvester termites and beetle larvae, in the barren areas.*

The brown hyena *is primarily a scavenger, but also eats wild fruit, beetles, termites, birds' eggs and small animals. Restricted to the drier desert regions of Southern Africa, it can survive without fresh water for extended periods of time.*

The *Tsama* melon's *bitter-tasting flesh is eaten by Bushmen and animals, as it is a vital source of vitamin C and moisture.*

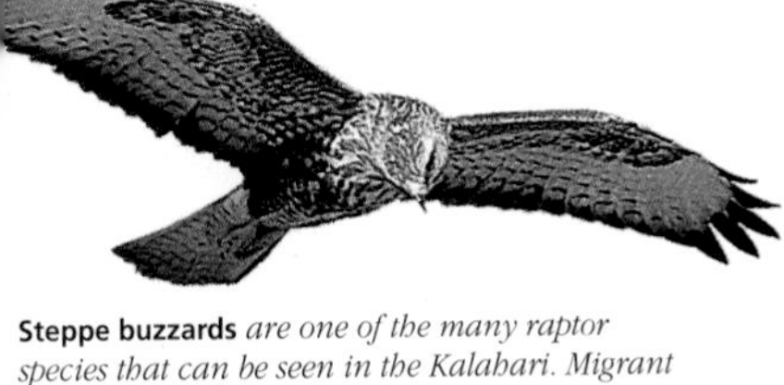

Steppe buzzards *are one of the many raptor species that can be seen in the Kalahari. Migrant visitors, they arrive in Southern Africa during October and depart in March.*

Namaqua sandgrouse *males fly distances of up to 60 km (37 miles) every three to five days to drink and to soak their specially adapted chest feathers. The water retained in these feathers sustains the chicks.*

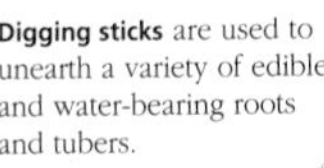

Digging sticks are used to unearth a variety of edible and water-bearing roots and tubers.

Ostrich eggs are a source of moisture and protein.

The puff adder *is highly poisonous and bites readily when threatened. The snake propels itself forward leaving deep, straight tracks which can sometimes be seen on the Kalahari sand dunes.*

THE BUSHMEN

These nomads have all but vanished from the subcontinent. A small band lives on land south of the Kgalagadi Transfrontier Park allocated to them in 1997. The modern age has severely affected their culture. Even in the remote reaches of Botswana, clans now live in settlements around waterholes – the nomadic lifestyle replaced by a sedentary existence. Before these camps were established, water and food were obtained from the bush: the Bushmen knew of 20 edible insects and 180 plants, roots and tubers.

Barking geckos *herald sunset in the desert by emitting a series of sharp clicking sounds. When threatened they tend to freeze, camouflaged against the red sand.*

The *Sparrmannia flava* *scarab has a furry coat which enables it to remain active at night when temperatures can drop drastically.*

Wind mills *pump precious water from below the surface into metal reservoirs. Agricultural activities in the Kalahari region include Karakul sheep, goat and wildlife farming, while hardy Afrikander cattle only survive where a water supply is assured.*

The Orange River

South Africa is predominantly a dry country, with precipitation decreasing from east to west and only 8 per cent of rainfall reaching the few major rivers. The mighty Orange and its tributaries drain 47 per cent of the country. For much of the 2,450-km (1,530-mile) long journey from its source in northeast Lesotho to the Atlantic Ocean, the Orange meanders across the arid plains of the Northern Cape. Here, wooden wheels draw the precious water from canals to sustain a narrow, fertile corridor of vineyards, date palms, lucerne and cotton fields, tightly wedged between the river and the unrelenting desert.

Quiver tree

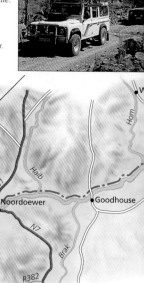

Alexander Bay *is the site of large-scale diamond dredging operations. The nearby Orange River estuary is a wetland renowned for its splendid birdlife.*

Richtersveld National Park *is located in a jagged, mountainous landscape crisscrossed by 4WD trails. UNESCO is currently evaluating the area as a possible World Heritage site.*

The Fish River Canyon lies across the Namibian border.

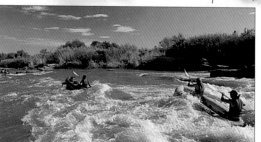

Orange River canoe trips (see p380) *have become increasingly popular since the 1990s. Several Cape Town-based adventure companies offer exciting canoeing and rafting tours that include camping along the river banks.*

Augrabies Falls, *christened* Aukoerebis *("place of great noise") by the early Khoina inhabitants of this region, is where the Orange River plunges 56 m (182 ft) into a constricted granite gorge. The falls and surrounding area were declared a national park in 1966.*

Onseepkans, a small settlement and border post, serves as a departure point for canoe trips down the Orange River.

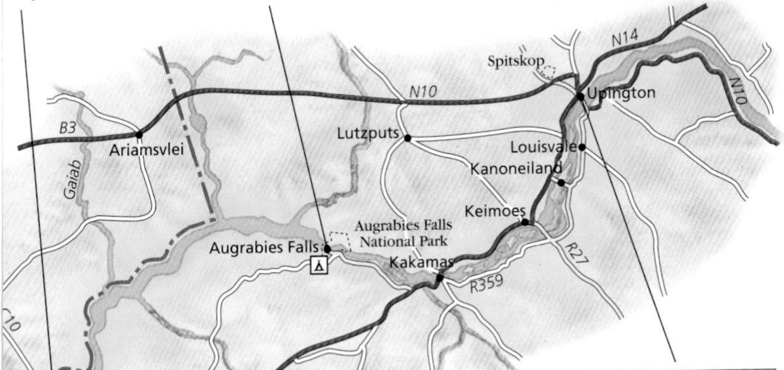

N14
Spitskop
Upington
N10
N10
B3
Lutzputs
Ariamsvlei
Louisvale
Gaiab
Kanoneiland
Keimoes
Augrabies Falls National Park
Augrabies Falls
R27
Kakamas
R359
C10
pkans
R358
N14
Pella
Pofadder

Upington, *on the north bank of the Orange River, is the largest town along its course. An important centre for the dried fruit industry, a common sight along the road are sultanas drying in the sun. The municipal resort, on an island in the river, is a popular stop-over.*

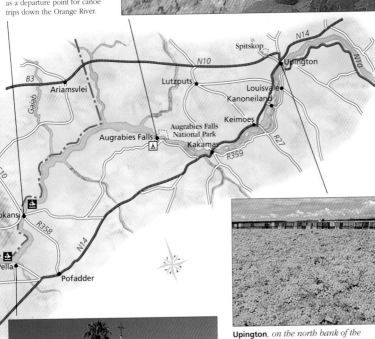

Pella Mission, *with its rows of date palms and the tall spire of its Catholic church, exudes a distinctly Mexican ambience. The church was built by two missionaries whose only building manual was an encyclopaedia.*

KEY

- International boundary
- Major route
- Road (tarred)
- Road (untarred)
- Camping
- Canoeing / rafting

Exploring South of the Orange

The Karoo is a region of endless vistas and clear blue skies, where the road runs straight as an arrow to the distant horizon. Large sheep farms produce much of South Africa's mutton and wool. Steel windmills, standing in the blazing sun, supply the area's life-blood: water. Only 70 small towns and villages, of which Beaufort West is the largest, cling tenaciously to the drought-prone land. Many of them, for example Graaff-Reinet, are architectural treasure chests. At Beaufort West, Graaff-Reinet and Cradock, nature parks conserve the characteristic landscape, fauna and flora of the region.

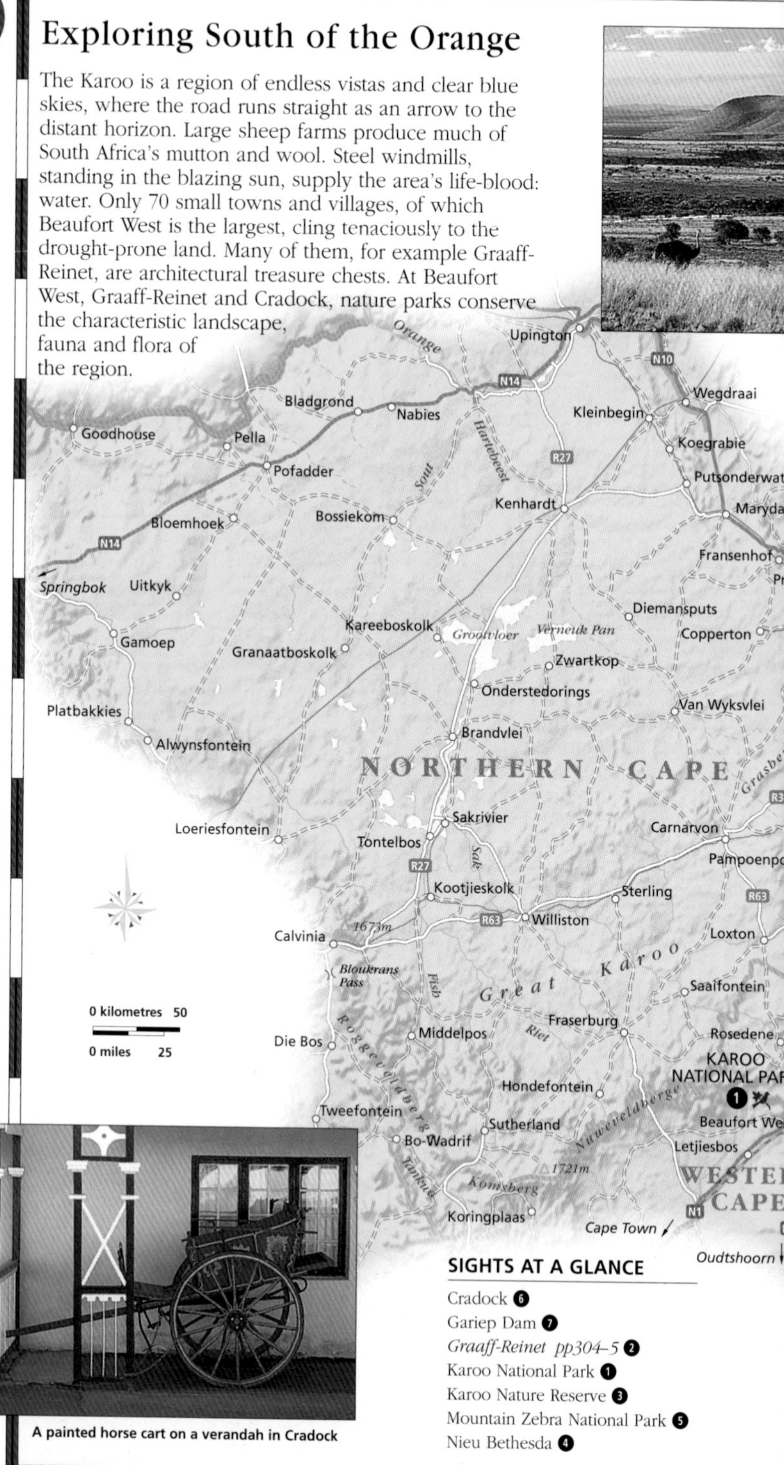

A painted horse cart on a verandah in Cradock

SIGHTS AT A GLANCE

Cradock 6
Gariep Dam 7
Graaff-Reinet pp304–5 2
Karoo National Park 1
Karoo Nature Reserve 3
Mountain Zebra National Park 5
Nieu Bethesda 4

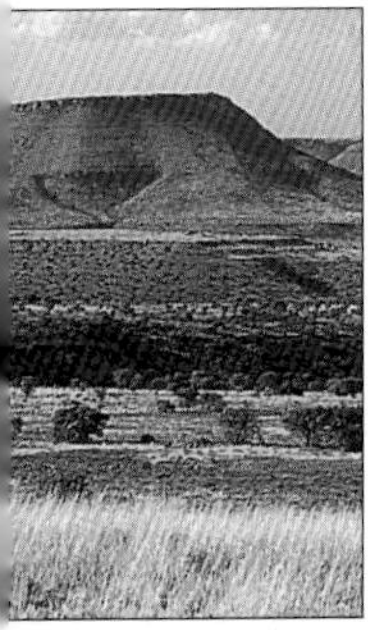

Ostrich in the Mountain Zebra National Park

GETTING AROUND

The N1 national route that links Cape Town and Johannesburg passes right through Beaufort West. The N9, which connects Graaff-Reinet to the Southern Cape coast, branches off the N1 at Colesberg. Cradock and the nearby Mountain Zebra National Park to the west of the town are located on the N10. Tarred provincial roads connect most of the smaller villages, allowing visitors to explore the more remote parts of the region. Although distances are great, traffic volumes are moderate and many of the Karoo towns have comfortable bed-and-breakfast establishments and restaurants. The long-distance bus companies stop in Beaufort West, Graaff-Reinet and Cradock.

The Drostdy in Graaff-Reinet, a typical example of a Cape Dutch-style magistrate's office

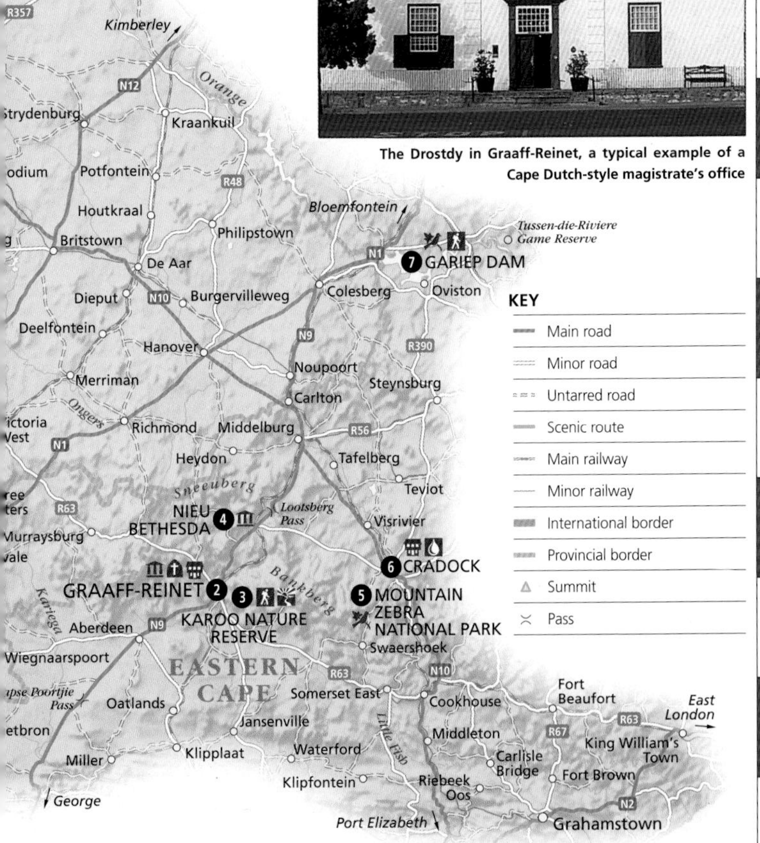

Kimberley
Strydenburg
Kraankuil
Orange
Potfontein
Houtkraal
Britstown
De Aar
Philipstown
Bloemfontein
Tussen-die-Riviere Game Reserve
7 GARIEP DAM
Colesberg
Oviston
Dieput
Burgervilleweg
Deelfontein
Hanover
Noupoort
Merriman
Steynsburg
Carlton
Richmond
Middelburg
Heydon
Tafelberg
Teviot
Sneeuberg
4 NIEU BETHESDA
Lootsberg Pass
Visrivier
Murraysburg
6 CRADOCK
2 GRAAFF-REINET
3 KAROO NATURE RESERVE
5 MOUNTAIN ZEBRA NATIONAL PARK
Aberdeen
Swaershoek
Wiegnaarspoort
EASTERN CAPE
Somerset East
Cookhouse
Fort Beaufort
East London
Oatlands
Jansenville
Middleton
King William's Town
Miller
Klipplaat
Waterford
Carlisle Bridge
Fort Brown
Klipfontein
Riebeek Oos
George
Port Elizabeth
Grahamstown

KEY

- Main road
- Minor road
- Untarred road
- Scenic route
- Main railway
- Minor railway
- International border
- Provincial border
- Summit
- Pass

SEE ALSO

- *Where to Stay* pp350–51
- *Where to Eat* p373

Karoo National Park ❶

Road map C4. N1, 2 km (1 mile) S of Beaufort West. *(023) 415-2828.* ***Tel*** *booking: (086) 111-4845.* *5am–10pm daily.* **www**.saparks.co.za

The Karoo National Park was established on the outskirts of Beaufort West in 1979, to conserve a representative sample of the region's unique heritage. It has been enlarged over the years and now encompasses vast, flat plains as well as the rugged Nuweveld Mountains. Animals such as mountain reedbuck, grey rhebok, kudu, steenbok, jackal and aardwolf occur naturally, while reintroduced species include springbuck, hartebeest, gemsbok (oryx), black wildebeest (gnu), Cape mountain zebra and the endangered black rhino and riverine rabbit. Some 196 bird species have been recorded, and the park also sustains more than 20 black eagle pairs.

A comfortable rest camp is set at the base of the Nuweveld Mountains. Its spacious Cape Dutch chalets provide a convenient overnight stop that is easily accessible from the N1. The camp has a shop, swimming pool, restaurant and caravan park. Nearby, the historic Ou Skuur Farmhouse contains the park's information centre. A 4WD trail has been laid out in the rugged western region of the park, and night drives provide the very best chances of seeing many of the region's shy nocturnal animals, such as the aardwolf.

Springbok once roamed the Karoo plains in their thousands

The short Fossil and Bossie trails are accessible from the rest camp and allow visitors to learn about the Karoo's fascinating 250-million-year-old geological history and its unique vegetation. The Fossil Trail accommodates wheelchairs and incorporates braille boards. An easy circular day hike of 11 km (7 miles) is also accessible from the rest camp.

Graaff-Reinet ❷

See pp304–5.

Karoo Nature Reserve ❸

Road map C4. Graaff-Reinet. *(04989) 2-3453.* *6am–6pm Apr–Sep; 6am–7pm Oct–Mar.* **www**.graaffreinet.co.za

In a bid to conserve typical Karoo landforms and wildlife, an area of 145 sq km (56 sq miles) around Graaff-Reinet *(see pp304–5)* was set aside. West of the town is the Valley of Desolation, a popular landmark in the reserve. Here, spectacular columns of weathered dolerite tower 120 m (390 ft) over the valley floor.

A 14-km (9-mile) road leads to a view site and a short walk, while the circular day hike is reached from the Berg-en-dal gate on the western edge of town. A two- to three-day hike explores the scenic mountainous terrain in the southeast.

The eastern region of the nature reserve includes the Driekoppe peaks, which rise 600 m (1,950 ft) above the plains. This section sustains more than 220 species of bird. The population of Cape mountain zebra, buffalo, hartebeest, springbok, kudu and blesbok is expanding, and many of them may be seen.

There are game-viewing roads and picnic sites around the Van Ryneveld's Pass Dam in the centre of the reserve, and both boating and fishing are permitted.

The Valley of Desolation in the Karoo Nature Reserve

The back yard of the Owl House is populated with many strange figures

Nieu Bethesda 4

Road map C4. 50km (31 miles) N of Graaff-Reinet. 950. *Church St, (049) 892-4248.*

The turn-off to this village lies on the N9, 27 km (17 miles) north of Graaff-Reinet. From there, a good dirt road traverses the Voor Sneeuberg ("in front of snow mountain") and leads to Nieu-Bethesda.

The Kompasberg (Compass Peak), at 2,502 m (8,131 ft), is the highest point in the Sneeuberg range. It received its name in 1778 when Cape Governor Baron van Plettenberg, accompanied by Colonel Jacob Gordon, visited the mountain while on a tour of the interior and noted that the surrounding countryside could be surveyed from its summit.

Nieu-Bethesda was founded by Reverend Charles Murray, minister of the Dutch Reformed Church in Graaff-Reinet. The fertile valley in the arid terrain reminded him of the Pool of Bethesda *(John 5:2)*, and so he named the town after it.

In 1875 he acquired a farm in the valley and by 1905 the church (now in Parsonage Street) was completed. It cost £5,600 to build, but at the time of its consecration two-thirds of the amount was still outstanding. To raise funds, arable church land was divided into plots and sold at a public auction. The debt was finally settled in 1929.

Owl statue

Today, Martin Street, the quaint main road, is lined with pear trees, and many of the bordering properties are framed by quince hedges. Irrigated fields and golden poplar trees complement and soften the rugged Karoo mountains, which create a bold contrast.

Pienaar Street crosses over the Gat River to its western bank, and passes an old water mill that was built in 1860 by the owner of the original farm, Uitkyk. The first water wheel was made of wood, but was later replaced with the existing steel wheel.

In recent years, the peaceful village has attracted much artistic talent, including one of South Africa's leading playwrights, Athol Fugard, who achieved world acclaim for his thought-provoking plays such as *Master Harold and the Boys* *(see p194)*.

The Owl House

River St. *8am–6pm daily.*
***Tel** (049) 841-1603.*

The Owl House is considered one of South Africa's top 50 heritage sites. Its garden is cluttered with an intriguing assembly of concrete statues: owls, sheep, camels, people, sphinxes and religious symbols, created over more than 30 years by Helen Martins and her assistant, Koos Malgas. The walls, doors and ceilings of the house are decorated with finely ground coloured glass. Mirrors reflect the light from candles and lamps. Her work, unusual in its quantity and range of subject, has been classified as "Outsider Art" (art that falls outside the artistic mainstream as a result of isolation or insanity) and "Naive" (an expression of innocence and fantasy).

HELEN MARTINS (1897–1976)

Born in Nieu-Bethesda on 23 December 1897, Helen left home to study at a teachers' training college in Graaff-Reinet, and later married a young diplomat. The relationship did not last. Neither did a second marriage, and Helen returned home to nurse her irascible, elderly father. After his death, the naturally retiring woman retreated increasingly into her own fantasy world, and began to populate her garden with bizarre figures, an expression of her personal, mythical universe. In later years her eyesight began to fail due to having worked with ground glass over a long period of time. In August 1976, aged 78, she committed suicide by drinking a lethal dose of caustic soda. As an artist she remains an enigma.

The bedroom with its "wallpaper" of ground glass

Street-by-Street: Graaff-Reinet ❷

Display in Urquhart House

In 1786 a *landdrost* (magistrate) was appointed by the Dutch East India Company to enforce Dutch law and administration along the remote eastern Karoo frontier. The settlement that grew up around the magistrate's court was named after Governor Cornelis Jacob van de Graaff and his wife, Hester Cornelia Reinet. Nine years later, the citizens of Graaff-Reinet expelled the *landdrost* and declared the first Boer Republic in South Africa. Within a matter of a few months, however, colonial control was re-established.

The War Memorial
The memorial honours the fallen of both World Wars.

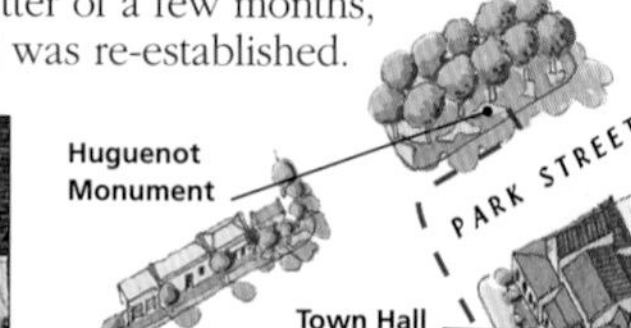

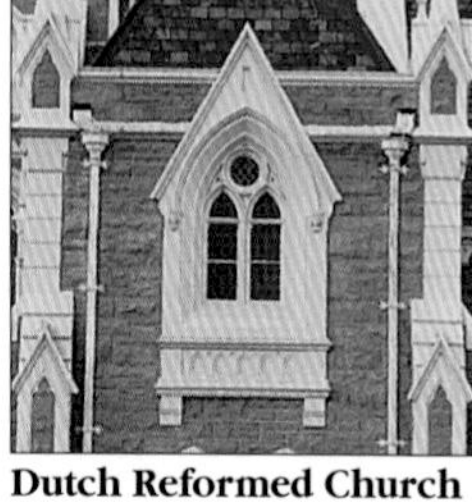

Dutch Reformed Church
The beautiful Groot Kerk *(great church), completed in 1887, was constructed using two different types of local stone.*

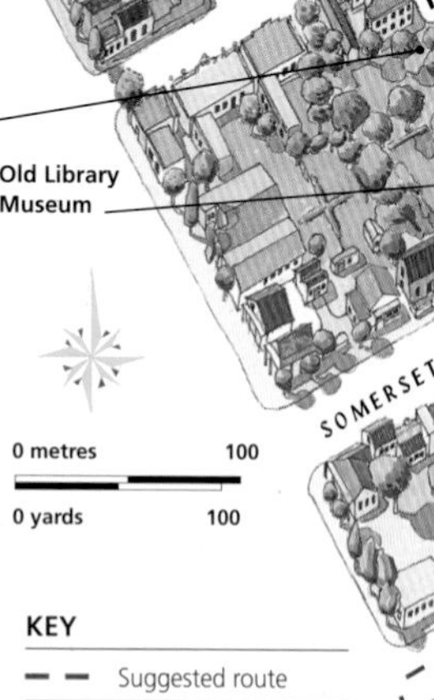

The South African War Memorial
This monument, unveiled in 1908, commemorates the efforts of Boer soldiers against the British troops.

KEY

– – Suggested route

★ Stretch's Court
These cottages were built in the 1850s to house labourers and freed slaves.

STAR SIGHTS

★ Stretch's Court

★ Reinet House

★ The Old Residency

Spandau Kop looms over the town

VISITORS' CHECKLIST

Road map C4. 60,000. *Port Elizabeth, 236 km (147 miles) SE.* *Kudu Motors, Church St.* *Publicity Association (049) 892-4248.* *8am–5pm Mon–Fri, 9am–noon Sat, Sun.* **Reinet House** ***Tel*** *(049) 892-3801.* *8am–12:30pm, 2–5pm Mon–Fri, 9am–3pm Sat, 9am–noon, 2–5pm Sun.* **www**.graffreinet.co.za

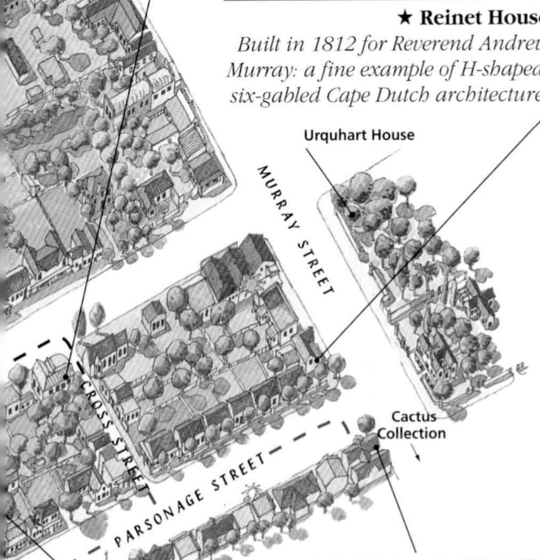

St James' Church

★ Reinet House

Built in 1812 for Reverend Andrew Murray: a fine example of H-shaped, six-gabled Cape Dutch architecture.

Urquhart House

MURRAY STREET

CROSS STREET

PARSONAGE STREET

Cactus Collection

Hester Rupert Art Gallery

The Drostdy

Heraldic detail on a plaque at the Drostdy (magistrate's court), a building designed by French architect Louis Michel Thibault in 1804.

★ The Old Residency

This imposing, gabled Cape Dutch manor was completed in the 1820s, and the original fanlight can still be seen above the front door. Today the manor is an annex of Reinet House.

Exploring Graaff-Reinet

Graaff-Reinet lies in a valley eroded by the Sundays River. The gardens and tree-lined avenues form a striking contrast to the bleak expanse of the surrounding Karoo. Many of the town's historic buildings have been painstakingly restored, and over 200 houses have been declared national monuments. The main architectural attractions lie between Bourke and Murray streets.

Dutch Reformed Church

This beautiful church is considered to be the finest example of Gothic architecture in the country. Completed in 1886, it was modelled on Salisbury Cathedral.

Stretch's Court

In 1855 Captain Charles Stretch bought land near the Drostdy for his labourers. Restored in 1977, the cottages are now an annex of the Drostdy Hotel.

Old Library Museum

Church St. ***Tel*** *(049) 892-3801.* *9am–12:30pm, 2–5pm Mon–Fri.* Completed in 1847, this building displays Karoo fossils, historic photographs and reproductions of rock art.

Hester Rupert Gallery

Church St. ***Tel*** *(049) 892-2121.* *10am–noon, 3pm–5pm Mon–Fri, 10am–noon Sat, Sun.* On display in this former Dutch Reformed Mission Church are works by contemporary South African artists, among them the well known Cecil Skotnes *(see p318)* and Irma Stern.

The Dutch Reformed Church

A Cape mountain zebra in the Mountain Zebra National Park

Mountain Zebra National Park ❺

Road map D4. 26 km (16 miles) W of Cradock. ***Tel*** *(048) 881-2427.* *7am–6pm May–Sep; 7am–7pm Oct–Apr.* **www**.parks-sa.co.za

While the national park west of Cradock is the second smallest in the country, its modest acreage in no way detracts from the visitor's enjoyment. It was originally conceived as a sanctuary that was intendend to rescue the Cape mountain zebra from imminent extinction. When the park was proclaimed in 1937, there were six zebra; by 1949 only two remained. Conservation efforts were successful, however, and the park now protects about 270 zebra. Several breeding herds have been relocated to other parks, but the Cape mountain zebra still remains rare. Also to be seen are springbok, hartebeest, eland, mountain reedbuck and black wildebeest. When additional land is acquired, cheetah and black rhino will be reintroduced.

The rest camp, which overlooks a valley, consists of chalets, a caravan park, a restaurant, shop and information centre. A short walk leads past the chalets to the swimming pool set at the base of a granite ridge.

For convenience, the park can be divided into two sections. From the camp, a circular drive of 28 km (18 miles) explores the wooded Wilgeboom Valley, noted for its rugged granite land forms. The road passes the Doornhoek Cottage where *The Story of an African Farm* was filmed, and leads to a shady picnic site at the base of the mountains.

The northern loop, which starts just before Wilgeboom, climbs steeply to the Rooiplaat Plateau, which offers splendid views across the vast Karoo and where most of the park's wildlife congregates. The early mornings and late afternoons are the best times to visit the area. Alternatively, a three-day circular hike, which begins at the camp, explores the southern part of the park, where the granite Bankberg mountains are at their most spectacular.

Cradock ❻

Road map D4. *20,000.* *Church St.* *Struwig Motors, Voortrekker St.* *Stockenstroom St, (048) 881-2383.*

In 1812, towards the end of the Fourth Frontier War, Sir John Cradock established two military outposts to secure the eastern border. One was at Grahamstown, the other at Cradock. Merino sheep flourished in this region, and Cradock soon developed into a sheep-farming centre.

The Dutch Reformed Church in Cradock

The Dutch Reformed Church was inspired by London's St Martin's-in-the-Fields. Completed in 1867, it dominates the town's central square. The **Great Fish River Museum** behind the town hall preserves the history of the early pioneers.

In Market Street, **Die Tuishuise** *(see p351)* is the result of an innovative project to restore a series of 14 mid-19th-century houses and create comfortable bed-and-breakfast establishments. Each portrays the architectural style of a particular era.

About 5 km (3 miles) north of town, the **Cradock Spa** is renowned for its indoor and outdoor swimming pools that are fed by hot sulphur springs.

The Great Fish River Museum

87 High St. ***Tel*** *(048) 881-5251.* *8am–1pm, 2–4pm Tue–Fri; 9am–noon Sat.* *Mon, Sun.*

OLIVE EMILIE SCHREINER (1855–1920)

The Story of an African Farm is widely regarded as the first South African novel of note. Olive Schreiner began writing while she worked as a governess on farms in the Cradock district. The manuscript was released in 1883 under the male pseudonym Ralph Iron, and was an immediate success. Schreiner, an active campaigner for women's equality and a supporter of "Native" rights, wrote extensively on politics. She died in Wynberg (Cape Town) in 1920. Her husband, Samuel Cronwright-Schreiner, buried her on Buffelskop, 24 km (15 miles) south of Cradock, beside their daughter who had died 25 years earlier just 18 hours after her birth, and Olive's dog.

Olive Schreiner

Cottages with striped awnings and painted stoeps verandahs) line the streets of Cradock

Cradock Spa
Marlow Rd. ***Tel*** *(048) 881-2709.*
7am–6pm daily.

Gariep Dam 7

Road map D4. NE of Colesberg on R701. ***Tel*** *(051) 754-0060 (Gariep Hotel).*

The Orange River is South Africa's largest and longest river. Together with its tributaries (excluding the Vaal River) it drains a total of one-third of the country.

In 1779, when Colonel Robert Gordon reached the banks of a watercourse that was known to the Khoina as *Gariep,* he renamed it the Orange River, in honour of the Dutch Prince of Orange. Little did he know that a dam would be constructed at this point nearly 200 years later.

In 1928 Dr AD Lewis advanced the idea of building a tunnel linking the Orange River to the Eastern Cape. Although a report was presented to the government in 1948, it was only in 1962 that then prime minister Hendrik Verwoerd gave the ambitious project the go-ahead. Work began in 1966 and in September 1970 the last gap in the wall was closed. The Gariep is South Africa's largest body of water. The dam wall rises 90 m (297 ft) above its foundations and has a crest length of 948 m (3,110 ft). At full supply level it covers an area of 374 sq km (144 sq miles).

At Oviston, midway along the shoreline, the Orange-Fish Tunnel diverts water along a stretch of 83 km (52 miles) to the headwaters of the Great Fish River near Steynsburg. This tunnel, completed in 1975, is the second longest water conduit in the world. With a diameter of 5 m (17 ft) it can divert one-quarter of the Orange River's water flow.

A corridor of bushveld surrounds the Gariep Dam, and the land that lies between the Caledon and the Orange rivers has been developed into three beautiful nature reserves with a combined area of 452 sq km (174 sq miles). Springbok, blesbok and the rare Cape mountain zebra and black wildebeest have been successfully re-introduced here.

The **Aventura Midwaters** resort, at the dam wall, offers comfortable chalets, a campsite and a range of outdoor activities including boating, fishing, golf, tennis, horse riding and swimming.

At the headwaters of the dam, an aptly-named game reserve, **Tussen-die-Riviere** ("between the rivers"), supports herds of springbok, black wildebeest, hartebeest, eland, gemsbok, zebra and white rhino. Chalets overlook the confluence of the rivers, and hiking trails explore the eastern half of the reserve.

Aventura Midwaters
Gariep Dam. ***Tel*** *(051) 754-0045.*
daily.

Tussen-die-Riviere Game Reserve
Gariep Dam. ***Tel*** *(051) 754-0060.*
daily.

Chalets built on the water's edge at the Gariep Dam

Ancient mountains provide a dramatic backdrop to the guest cottages in the Karoo National Park ▷

NORTH OF THE ORANGE

The red dunes of the Kalahari Desert stretch north of the Orange River like the waves of an inland sea. Three mountain ranges break the monotony until the dunes give way, at last, to the grasslands of the Highveld plateau. In this remote wilderness, oasis-like towns such as Upington welcome the traveller, and in a narrow band along the river, vineyards produce sultana grapes and fine wines.

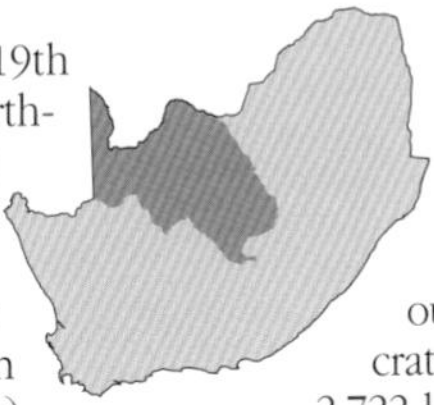

At the beginning of the 19th century, the uncharted Northern Cape was home to the last nomadic hunter-gatherers, the San Bushmen. In 1820, Robert and Mary Moffat built a mission and school in Kuruman, 263 km (163 miles) northeast of Upington, and devoted 50 years to translating and printing the Bible in the Setswana language. The journeys of exploration undertaken by their son-in-law, David Livingstone, focused European attention on Africa.

In the Cape Colony Afrikaner farmers became increasingly discontented with the British administration and many trekked north in search of new land. In 1836, a group of Voortrekkers *(see pp52–3)* crossed the Orange River and settled near Thaba Nchu, east of the present-day Bloemfontein, where they established an independent republic, the Orange Free State, in 1854.

The discovery of diamonds in 1866 transformed South Africa's economy. At the town of Kimberley, countless fortune-seekers carved out the Big Hole, an enormous crater that had yielded a total of 2,722 kg (5,988 lb) of diamonds by the time work stopped in 1914.

Further west along the Orange River, a local Griqua leader invited early missionary, Reverend Christiaan Schröder, to establish a mission station on the banks of the river, and the town of Upington was founded. Irrigation canals soon transformed the desert into a fertile crescent of vineyards, orchards, wheat and lucerne fields.

Although mining is still the main contributor to the region's economy, today visitors are enticed by the area's history, desert scenery and diverse wildlife, such as various raptor species and the unique Kalahari lion.

Suricates, or slender-tailed meerkat, live in closely knit family groups

◁ **A *halfmens*, or half-human, *(Pachypodium namaquanum)* stands out over misty Richtersveld plains**

Exploring North of the Orange

Upington is the perfect base for exploring South Africa's last frontier: the red-dune wilderness bordering the Kalahari Desert. Although no permanent rivers have flowed across this ancient landscape for thousands of years and grass-covered dunes seem to stretch to infinity, wildlife is abundant. Kimberley was once the scene of the world's greatest diamond rush and retains many reminders of its frenetic heyday. Driving eastward, annual rainfall increases. The grasslands of the Free State support cattle and sheep, as well as fields of sunflowers and maize. Historic Bloemfontein, once the capital of a Boer republic named Orange Free State, has many superb old buildings.

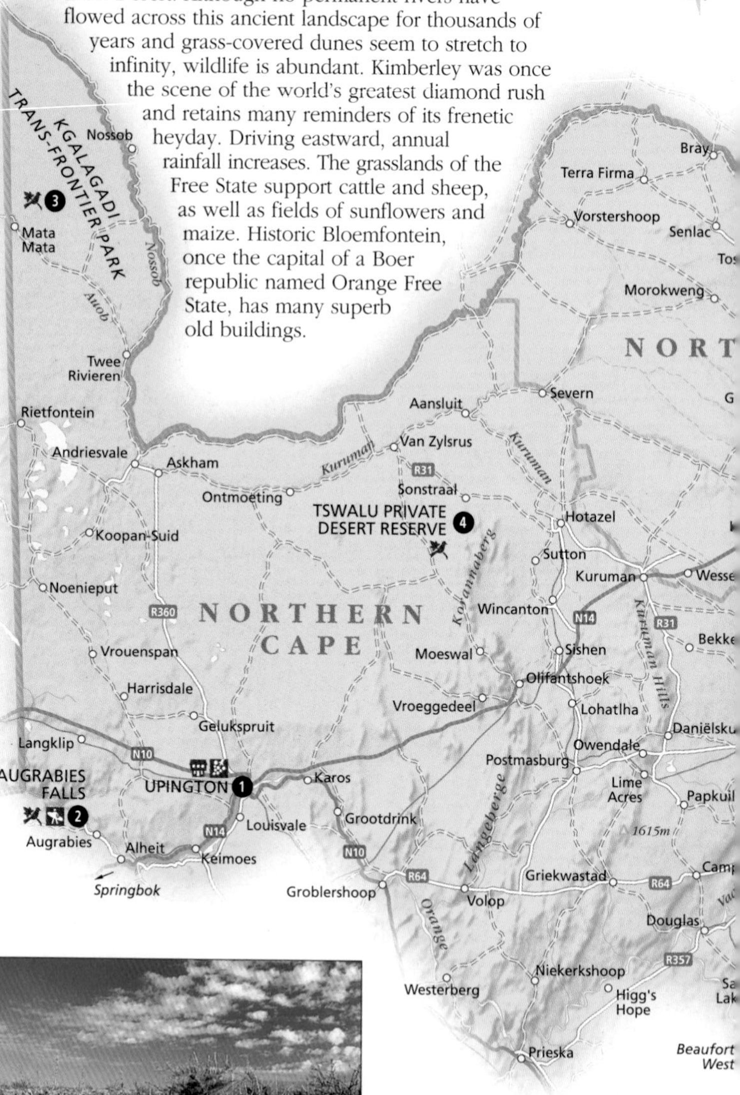

Devil's claw plant, Kgalagadi Transfrontier Park

SIGHTS AT A GLANCE

Augrabies Falls National Park 2
Bloemfontein 6
Kgalagadi Transfrontier Park 3
Kimberley 5
Tswalu Private Desert Reserve 4
Upington 1

For additional map symbols *see back flap*

KEY

- Major road
- Minor road
- Untarred road
- Scenic route
- Main railway
- Minor railway
- International border
- Provincial border
- Summit

0 kilometres 50

0 miles 25

The Big Hole in Kimberley, begun in the 1870s

GETTING AROUND

Most of the towns north of the Orange River lie more than 200 km (125 miles) apart, and there are few petrol stations or refreshment stops along the way. But as traffic volumes are low and all the main roads are tarred, travel in this region need not be arduous. The R360 runs north from Upington to the Kgalagadi Transfrontier Park. Although the roads in the park are sandy, 4WD vehicles are not required. National roads link the major regional centres to Johannesburg and to the Western and Eastern Cape. The east–west R64 connects Upington, Kimberley and Bloemfontein. There are regional airports in all three centres, and long-distance coaches provide links to other towns.

SEE ALSO

- ***Where to Stay*** pp351
- ***Where to Eat*** p373

Sunflowers constitute one of the Free State's major crops

The Reverend Christiaan Schröder's cottage in Upington

Upington ❶

Road map B3. 76,000.
Schröder St, (054) 332-6064.
7 km (4 miles) NE of town.
Upington station.

Upington lies in a vast plain dotted with low shrubs. Only where the road reaches the Orange River does the landscape change abruptly, as the river paints a green stripe across the barren territory.

The Northern Cape's second largest town after Kimberley, Upington serves a district of lucerne, cotton, fruit and wine farms lining a fertile corridor on the river.

In the late 19th century the Northern Cape was a wild frontier. The nomadic bands of Khoina hunter-gatherers resented the intrusion of the white settlers into this region and frequently stole livestock from them. In 1871, however, at the request of Korana chief Klaas Lukas, the Reverend Christiaan Schröder established a mission station in the wilderness and the first irrigation canals were dug. His original church is part of the **Kalahari-Oranje Museum** in Schröder Street. Here too, is the statue of a camel and rider, which honours the policemen and their tireless mounts who once patrolled this desert region.

Occupying an island in the Orange River, just outside town, Die Eiland is one of the finest municipal resorts in South Africa. Sunset cruises down the river depart from here.

The five wine cellars in this arid region all belong to the **OranjeRivier Wine Cellars**, which offers tours and tastings. On the southern bank of the river, the South African Dried Fruit Co-op on Louisvale Road is capable of processing up to 250 tonnes of dried fruit daily.

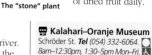

The "stone" plant

Kalahari–Oranje Museum
Schröder St. ***Tel*** *(054) 332-6064.* *8am–12:30pm, 1:30–5pm Mon–Fri.*

OranjeRivier Wine Cellars
Tel *(054) 337-8800.* *8am–5pm Mon–Fri, 9am–noon Sat.* *public hols.*

Augrabies Falls National Park ❷

Road map B3. 100 km (62 miles) W of Upington. ***Tel*** *(054) 452-9200.* *daily.* ***Tel*** *bookings: (012) 343-1991.*
www.parks-sa.co.za

The Augrabies Falls National Park was established in 1966 to protect the Augrabies Fall, which rushes through the largest granite gorge in the world. During periods of normal flow, the main waterfall plunges 56 m (182 ft) into the gorge. The lesser Bridal Veil Waterfall, located along the northern wall of the gorge, cascades 75 m (244 ft) into the river below.

At the main complex near the entrance to the park is a shop, restaurant and bar. Paths lead from here down to the falls. Despite safety fences to prevent visitors from falling into the chasm, you should take care near the waterfall, as the rocks are very slippery.

Apart from the waterfall itself and the attractive rest camp which consists of 59 chalets, three swimming pools and an extensive campsite, Augrabies has much to offer. The 39-km (24-mile) long Klipspringer Trail explores the southern section of the park and affords superb views of the gorge and surrounding desert. The Black Rhino Adventure Company offers trips downriver in a rubber dinghy, as well as tours of the park's northern section where black rhino may be seen.

The Augrabies Falls in the national park of the same name

For hotels and restaurants in this region see p351 and p373

Kgalagadi Transfrontier Park ❸

Road map B2. 280 km (174 miles) N of Upington. *(054) 561-2000.* **Tel** *bookings: (012) 991-0758.* *daily.*
www.saparks.co.za

An immense wilderness of grass-covered dunes traversed by two dry, ancient riverbeds, this national park (formerly the Kalahari Gemsbok National Park) is Africa's largest and extends over 34,390 sq km (13,278 sq miles) across territory almost twice the size of the Kruger National Park. Jointly managed by South Africa and Botswana, the border within the park is unfenced and the wildlife is free to migrate.

From Upington the new R360 cuts a course across a landscape that seems devoid of human habitation. The tar roads ends near Andriesvale and a sandy track hugs the border fence for 58 km (36 miles) before reaching the southern entrance. A dusty campsite is situated near the gate, while the nearby camp of Twee Rivieren offers chalets, a restaurant and a swimming pool. From Twee Rivieren, two roads follow the dry courses of the Auob and Nossob rivers on their way to the camps of Mata Mata and Nossob. There are four lovely picnic spots along the Nossob.

Although Twee Rivieren is situated in the most arid region of the park, wildlife is surprisingly plentiful. The Kgalagadi does not support the diversity of antelope found in savannah parks, but an astonishing 19 species of carnivore are present, including the black-maned Kalahari lion, cheetah, brown hyena, wild cat and honey badger. Raptors such as martial, tawny and bateleur eagles as well as the pale chanting goshawk are commonly sighted.

A total of 40 windmills have been erected in the riverbeds, providing water for wildlife.

Springbok *(Antidorcas marsupialis)*, Kgalagadi Transfrontier Park

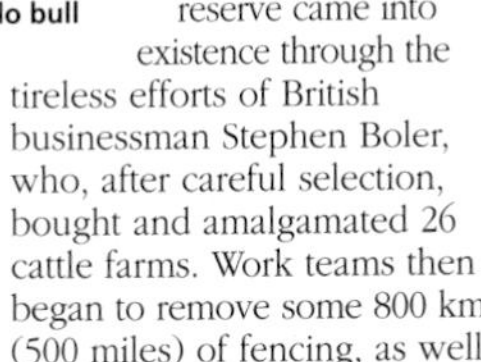

Buffalo bull

Tswalu Private Desert Reserve ❹

Road map C2. 115 km (71 miles) NW of Kuruman. *information and bookings: (053) 781-9211.*
www.tswalu.com

An ambitious project without equal, Tswalu is South Africa's largest private reserve. It protects 750 sq km (285 sq miles) of red Kalahari dunes and the picturesque Korannaberg mountains. The reserve came into existence through the tireless efforts of British businessman Stephen Boler, who, after careful selection, bought and amalgamated 26 cattle farms. Work teams then began to remove some 800 km (500 miles) of fencing, as well as 2,300 km (1,440 miles) of electric lines, 38 concrete dams and the farmsteads. Approximately 7,000 cattle were sold off and the reserve was fenced.

Boler has invested over R54 million to develop the reserve. A total of 4,700 animals, representing 22 species, have been reintroduced, including lion, leopard, cheetah, white rhino, buffalo, zebra, giraffe, sable, tsessebe, eland and gemsbok. But the jewels in Tswalu's crown are, without doubt, the eight black desert rhinos (subspecies *Diceros bicornis bicornis*) relocated with the permission of the Namibian government. The rhinos were later followed by seven desert elephants.

Tswalu's very expensive luxury lodge has its own tarred airstrip and is managed by the Conservation Corporation. Guests are accommodated in nine thatched units and there is an attractive swimming pool.

SIR LAURENS VAN DER POST (1906–96)

Soldier, writer, philosopher, dreamer and explorer, Laurens van der Post was the son of an Afrikaner mother and a Dutch father. During World War II he obtained the rank of colonel and was a prisoner of the Japanese in Java until 1945. Upon his return to South Africa, he began his journeys into the wilderness. A fascinating account of his expedition in search of the San Bushmen of the Kalahari was published in 1958. *The Lost World of the Kalahari* was one of the first books to detail this intriguing and highly spiritual culture. A personal friend of the British Royal Family, the late Van der Post is remembered for his insightful, philosophical writings, most of which deal with the moral and social issues of his time.

Sir Laurens van der Post

Kimberley ❺

The first Diamond Rush in the Kimberley district took place in 1869 when diamonds were found in the walls of a house on the farm Bultfontein. In July 1871 prospectors camped at the base of a small hill, 4.5 km (3 miles) to the northwest. The party's cook was sent to the summit as punishment for a minor offence and returned with a diamond. Within two years, New Rush tent town, renamed Kimberley in 1873, had become home to 50,000 miners. By the time Cecil John Rhodes *(see p54)* arrived, 3,600 claims were being worked.

A re-created street scene at the Kimberley Mine Big Hole

Exploring Kimberley

The angular street pattern of Kimberley is in contrast to the neat, parallel, grid pattern characteristic of other South African cities, a legacy from its formative, tent-town years. Although reminders of the past are not always apparent, Kimberley has several interesting historic landmarks that are well worth visiting.

Kimberley Mine Big Hole

West Circular Rd. ***Tel*** *(053) 833-1557.*

The quaint museum village, laid out around the rim of the Big Hole, consists of cobbled streets lined with diverse historic buildings. A small church, the pharmacy, an assortment of shops and an old bar are all decorated with authentic fittings.

Kimberley Club

70–72 Du Toitspan Rd. ***Tel*** *(053) 832-4224.* *daily.*

Completed in 1896, this luxurious club was the meeting place of the mining magnates and saw much wheeling and dealing. In keeping with tradition, women are not permitted in the main bar.

Oppenheimer Memorial Gardens

Jan Smuts Blvd.

In the gardens, five bronze miners surround the Digger's Fountain. A marble colonnade contains a bust of Sir Ernest Oppenheimer, the German-born diamond buyer who in 1917 founded the giant Anglo American Corporation.

VISITORS' CHECKLIST

Road map D3. *1 million.* *7 km (4 miles) S of town.* *Old de Beers Rd.* Shell Ultra City. *121 Bultfontein Rd, (053) 832-7298.*

William Humphreys Art Gallery

Cullinan Crescent. ***Tel*** *(053) 831-1724.* *10am–4:30pm Mon–Sat, 2–5pm Sun.* *free on Wed and first weekend of month.*

Across the road from the Memorial Gardens, the gallery houses a superb collection of paintings by European masters and South African artists.

McGregor Museum

Egerton Rd. ***Tel*** *(053) 839-2700.* *8am–5pm Mon–Sat, 2–5pm Sun.*

Cecil John Rhodes stayed in this building, completed in 1897, during the South African War. It now houses a museum of natural and cultural history and has important ethnological and archeological displays, as well as rock paintings.

Duggan-Cronin Gallery

Egerton Rd. ***Tel*** *(053) 839-2700.* *9am–5pm Mon–Sat, 2–5pm Sun.*

The gallery contains 8,000 photographs of anthropological interest taken over a 20-year period by Alfred Duggan-Cronin, who, having arrived in Kimberley in 1897, became deeply interested in the indigenous people of the Northern Cape.

Honoured Dead Memorial

Dalham & Oliver rds.

The memorial, designed by Sir Herbert Baker, honours the memory of the British soldiers who died during the siege of Kimberley in 1899. It is flanked by Long Cecil, a cannon built in the De Beers workshops.

The McGregor Museum, Kimberley

For hotels and restaurants in this region see p351 and p373

The Kimberley Diamond Rush

Kimberley Mine, or the Big Hole, as it is known, is the only one of four diamond mines in the Kimberley area that is still open. Within two years of the discovery of diamond-bearing kimberlite pipes in 1871, the claims were being worked by up to 30,000 miners at a time. Early photographs reveal a spider's web of cables radiating upward from the edge of the excavation. With little more than picks and shovels to aid them, the miners dug deep into the earth, and by 1889 the hole had reached an astounding depth of 150 m (488 ft). The deeper the miners delved, the more difficult it became to extract the diamond-bearing soil, and the chaotic arrangement of cables, precipitous paths and claims lying at varying heights encouraged the diggers to form syndicates. These groupings were absorbed into various companies that were later acquired by Cecil John Rhodes.

Barney Barnato

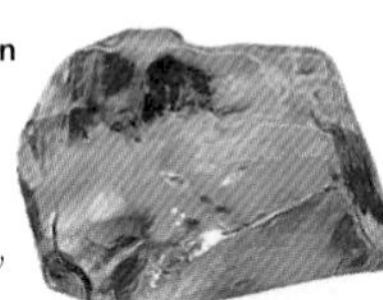

The Cullinan Diamond *is the largest diamond ever found. A replica is displayed at the Kimberley Mine Museum.*

Cecil John Rhodes, *depicted as victorious empire builder in this 19th-century* Punch *cartoon, was one of the most influential people in Kimberley.*

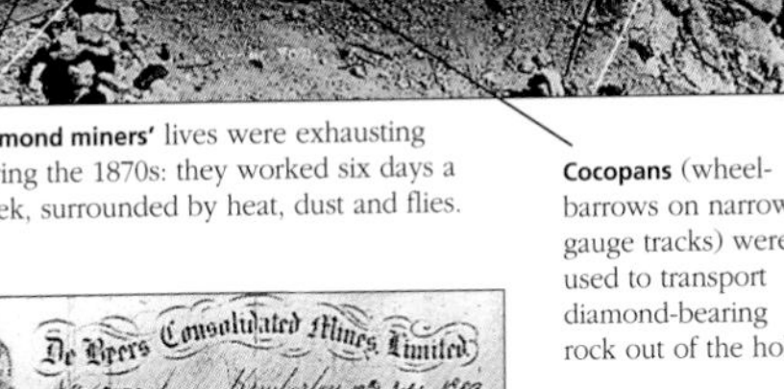

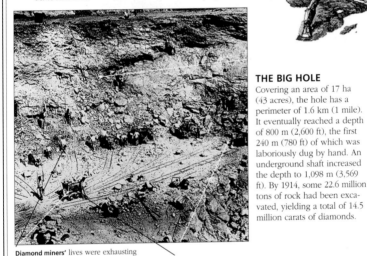

THE BIG HOLE

Covering an area of 17 ha (43 acres), the hole has a perimeter of 1.6 km (1 mile). It eventually reached a depth of 800 m (2,600 ft), the first 240 m (780 ft) of which was laboriously dug by hand. An underground shaft increased the depth to 1,098 m (3,569 ft). By 1914, some 22.6 million tons of rock had been excavated, yielding a total of 14.5 million carats of diamonds.

Diamond miners' lives were exhausting during the 1870s: they worked six days a week, surrounded by heat, dust and flies.

Cocopans (wheelbarrows on narrow-gauge tracks) were used to transport diamond-bearing rock out of the hole.

De Beers Consolidated Mines Limited
No 5050 Kimberley 18th July 1889
The Cape of Good Hope Bank Limited
Kimberley Branch
Pay ... or Order
£5,338,650

De Beers Consolidated Mines, *owned by Cecil John Rhodes, bought Barney Barnato's diamond mines for the sum of £5,338,650 in 1889.*

The Big Hole *was closed as a working mine in 1914. It is the largest man-made hole in the world, and the central focus of the Kimberley Open-Air Mine Museum.*

Bloemfontein ❻

Situated in the heartland of South Africa, Bloemfontein, capital of the Free State and seat of the province's parliament, is also the judicial capital of South Africa. It lies at the hub of six major routes that traverse the country. An altitude of 1,400 m (4,550 ft) means that summers are moderate and winters mild to cool. The city was named after a fountain, west of the present business district, where early travellers stopped on their treks through the interior. The city's history, and many of its stately old sandstone buildings, are firmly connected with the Afrikaners' struggle for independence. In 1854, when Major Henry Warden, the region's official British representative, was recalled to the Cape, the Afrikaners established a republic with Bloemfontein as their capital.

The Appeal Court building, Bloemfontein

Exploring Bloemfontein
Although Major Warden's fort has long disappeared, a portion of Queen's Fort, dating back to 1848, can still be seen south of the city centre.

President Brand Street is lined with many fine old sandstone buildings, such as the **Appeal Court**, built in 1929, opposite the **Fourth Raadsaal**, which now houses the Free State's provincial legislature. This brick-and-sandstone building was constructed around 1893, during the presidency of Frederick Reitz.

Detail of the Women's Memorial

The National Museum
36 Aliwal St. ***Tel*** *(051) 447-9609.* *8am–5pm Mon–Fri, 10am–5pm Sat, noon–5:30pm Sun & pub hols.*
www.nasmus.co.za
This museum contains a good collection of dinosaur fossils, and a reconstruction of a typical 19th-century Bloemfontein street, complete with a cluttered general dealer's store.

National Museum for Afrikaans Literature
Cnr President Brand & Maitland sts. ***Tel*** *(051) 405-4711.* *8am–5pm Mon–Fri, 9am–noon Sat.*
Near the Appeal Court, this museum is devoted to leading Afrikaans writers, even those who, like André Brink *(see p31)*, opposed apartheid.

Old Presidency
President Brand St.
Tel *(051) 448-0949.*
10am–4pm Mon–Fri.
Three blocks south from the Literature Museum lies the Old Presidency, completed in 1861. The attractive building stands on the site once occupied by the homestead of Major Warden's farm.

First Raadsaal
St George's St. ***Tel*** *(051) 447-9610.*
10am–1pm Mon–Fri.
This, the oldest building in the city, is a white, unpretentious structure near the National Museum. Built by Warden in 1849, it was used as a school. After Warden had been withdrawn in 1854, it became the meeting place of the republic's *Volksraad* (people's council).

Tweetoringkerk
Charles St. ***Tel*** *(051) 430-4274.*
Dedicated in 1881, the Dutch Reformed Tweetoringkerk (twin-spired church) is unique in the country. It was inspired by Europe's Gothic cathedrals and designed by Richard Wocke. The interior, too, is Gothic. Especially noteworthy is the woodwork around the pulpit and organ.

King's Park and Zoo
King's Way. ***Tel*** *(051) 405-8483.*
On the western edge of the city, this park will appeal to lovers of the outdoors. Shade trees, flower beds and rolling lawns surround a lake, Loch Logan, and a small zoo.

National Women's Memorial and War Museum
Monument Rd. ***Tel*** *(051) 447-3447.*
8am–4:30pm Mon–Fri, 10am–4:30pm Sat, 2–4:30pm Sun.
South of the city, this site commemorates the countless Boer and Black African women and children who died in British concentration camps during the South African War.

Emily Hobhouse, a British woman who campaigned for better treatment of the prisoners, is buried at the foot of the monument.

Environs: North of the city centre, the **Franklin Nature Reserve** occupies Naval Hill. The name originated during the South African War when a cannon was mounted here by the British Naval Brigade.

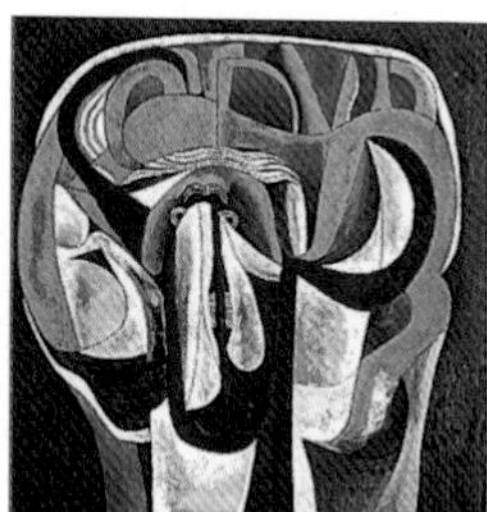

Abstract painting by Cecil Skotnes, Oliewenhuis Art Gallery

Exterior of the Oliewenhuis Art Gallery, Bloemfontein

In 1928, the University of Michigan (USA) built an observatory on the summit. Over 7,000 star systems were discovered before it closed in 1972. It now houses a theatre.

Further north of the city, on Harry Smith Street, the **Oliewenhuis Art Gallery** is set in a spacious garden. This gallery is renowned for its superb collection of South African art.

Several excellent wildlife reserves can be found north of Bloemfontein. The **Soetdoring Nature Reserve** borders on the expansive Krugerdrif Dam whose wall, at 5 km (3 miles), is one of the longest in South Africa.

The river and shoreline of this reserve provide excellent picnic spots and attract many birds. Antelope species like black wildebeest and gemsbok roam free, while predators like lions and wild dogs are kept in a large separate camp.

The turn-off to the **Willem Pretorius Game Reserve** lies some 150 km (93 miles) north of Bloemfontein on the N1. The grassland around the Allemanskraal Dam supports large herds of gazelle. The hills on the northern shore are home to kudu, eland, buffalo, giraffe and white rhino. Birds like korhaan and double-banded courser are also commonly seen.

Franklin Nature Reserve
Union Ave, Naval Hill. *daily.*

Oliewenhuis Art Gallery
Harry Smith St. ***Tel*** *(051) 447-9609.* *8am–5pm Mon–Fri, 10am–5pm Sat, 1–5pm Sun.*

Soetdoring Nature Reserve
R64 (Kimberley Rd). ***Tel*** *(051) 433-9002.* *7am–6pm daily.*

VISITORS' CHECKLIST

Road map D3. *200,000.* *N8, 10 km (6 miles) E of the city.* *Harvey Rd.* *Tourist Centre.* *Bloemfontein Tourist Centre, 60 Park Rd. (051) 405-8489.* *8am–4:15pm Mon–Fri, 8am–noon Sat.* *Bloemfontein Show (Mar); Rose Festival (Oct).* **www**.bloemfontein.co.za

Willem Pretorius Game Reserve
N1 to Kroonstad. ***Tel*** *(057) 651-4003.* *daily.*
www.sa-venues.com/game-reserves/fs_willempretorius.htm

Giraffe, Franklin Nature Reserve on Naval Hill, Bloemfontein

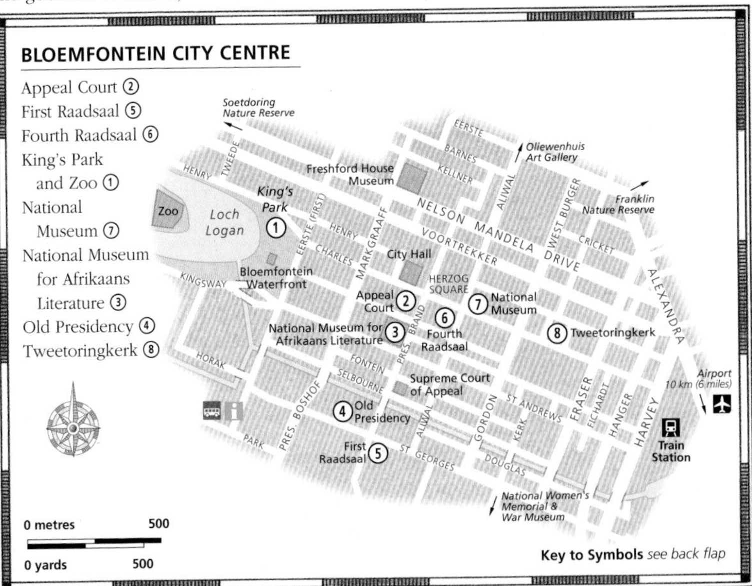

TRAVELLERS' NEEDS

WHERE TO STAY

The slow journeys of earlier centuries, when the vast distances between settlements had to be covered on horseback or by ox wagon, led to a proud local tradition. In South Africa "hospitality" is more than a catchword, and establishments, from the largest hotel chain to the smallest bed-and-breakfast, do their utmost to make the modern traveller feel welcome. The wide range of accommodation available is a reflection of the diversity of the country itself. A fantasy resort hotel like the Palace of the Lost City at Sun City *(see pp270–71)* and Cape Town's elegant colonial hotel, the Mount Nelson *(see p328)*, offer every conceivable luxury and bear comparison with the best in the world. Charming alternatives are the guest cottages found in most *dorpe* (country villages), where tranquillity and hearty, home-cooked fare is valued far more than modern convenience. Farmsteads and safari lodges provide a lavish and expensive Africa experience, while camp sites and backpacker's hostels offer basic amenities and cater for younger visitors on limited budgets.

Doorman at the Mount Nelson Hotel

WHERE TO LOOK

Visitors touring South Africa by car may be worried by the distances that separate cities and towns. Fortunately, hotels, bed and breakfasts, motels and self-catering cottages are found in even the remotest villages. Farm accommodation is also plentiful.

South Africa's cities offer a great variety of places to stay, whether you want family, luxury or business accommodation. In well-visited country and resort areas, there is also accommodation to suit every taste and pocket: many game parks, for example, offer luxurious lodges as well as basic camp sites, while most coastal resorts offer hotels, camp sites, B&Bs and guesthouses. Enquire at the local tourist information office (usually well signposted) or contact one of the many umbrella associations such as the AA Travel Information Centre, The National Accommodation Selection, Youth Hostel Association or the Guesthouse Association of Southern Africa *(see p325)*. If you are travelling through the smaller towns without having made prior arrangements, ask at the post office, one of the local stores or police stations for accommodation advice.

If you are seeking quiet surroundings, try the smaller and more simple hostelries, inland or away from obvious attractions on the coast. Most private game reserves offer superb safari lodges.

HOTEL PRICES

Prices tend to be per room rather than per person, but may be advertised as "per person sharing". Taxes (and sometimes gratuities) are usually included in the rates, but tips are appreciated.

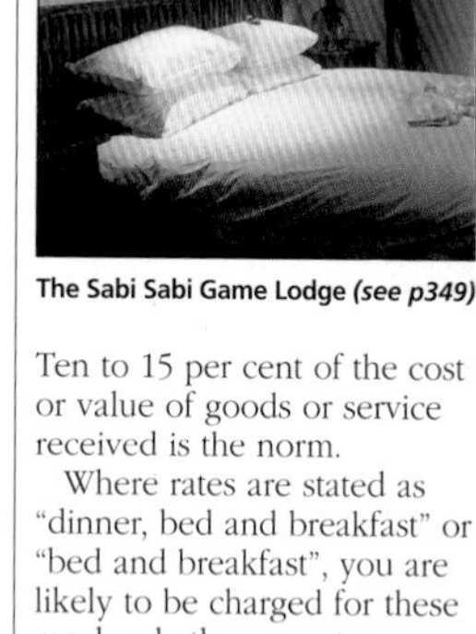

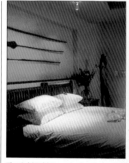

The Sabi Sabi Game Lodge *(see p349)*

Ten to 15 per cent of the cost or value of goods or service received is the norm.

Where rates are stated as "dinner, bed and breakfast" or "bed and breakfast", you are likely to be charged for these meals whether or not you take them. If you advise the host in time, it may be possible to avoid payment for advertised meals that are not taken. Also notify the hosts in advance if you are vegetarian, for example. "Special offers" are seldom further negotiable.

Rooms with a shower are usually cheaper than those with a bath, and those with views are more expensive.

Prices vary slightly, outside of high season (Nov–Feb, Easter weekend and the mid-year school holidays). But do ask your travel agent about possible special offers made by hotel groups, or contact them directly. Hotels do not close during winter (May–Aug).

Thatched rondavels at Olifants camp, Kruger National Park *(see p285)*

◁ A herd of elephant makes its way across the Addo Elephant Park near Port Elizabeth

The pool at the Singita Private Game Reserve *(see p349)*

HOTEL GRADING

South African hotels are classified by a number of organizations, such as **Satour**, the national tourism authority, and **Portfolio of Places**. Satour divides hotels into five categories, indicated by a plaque carrying from one to five stars. A typical five-star hotel is luxurious, offering suites as well as rooms and a wide range of services, such as hair dressing, dry cleaning and room service. In a country town, a one-star hotel may prove to be comfortable and entirely satisfactory, while in a city it may be little more than a liquor outlet or a noisy local rendezvous spot.

Many charming hotels have lower ratings, and some hotels with higher ratings – although they boast more than the required minimum of facilities and service – turn out to be impersonal business warrens.

Some self-catering cottages and guesthouses are also accredited by Satour.

FACILITIES

Facilities vary according to location and grading. Parking is usually available, but is not always under cover or supervised by a guard. Some hotels offer a daily car-wash, and may also have courtesy vehicles for hire, either with or without a driver.

Most hotels provide a telephone in the bedroom, but it is usually cheaper to use a public telephone. Television sets in rooms (without cable channels) are fairly common, and there is almost always a set in the guests' lounge.

Central heating in winter is not the norm, although most places of accommodation do provide portable heaters. Many self-catering cottages, particularly those on farms, have indoor fireplaces.

Some more upmarket small guesthouses and B&Bs offer an "honesty bar" with cold beers, wine, soft drinks and mineral water.

In country towns, the hotel frontage may be on the main street. If there is no bypass road, the noise level may be uncomfortable, especially at night. Before asking to be moved to a room at the back, however, check that there are no large cooling units tucked away, as those are likely to be even more disturbing.

Hotels usually have a locked and secure safe where guests can deposit valuables.

HOTEL GROUPS

Many of the better class hotels are controlled by one of the national hotel chains *(see p325)*, offering incentives or package deals that include lower family rates or out-of-season tariffs. Some, however, are graded lower than others, so have a different rates' structure.

CHILDREN

Don't presume that your venue of choice will cater for children. Many upmarket hotels, guesthouses and safari lodges do not accept children under the age of ten.

Where children are accepted, families may be able to share a room at little extra cost, as tariffs are "per room" rather than "per person".

BOOKING

If possible, confirm a telephone booking in writing, by fax or by email. It is likely that a deposit will be required, which you will forfeit if you cancel your booking at short notice.

The hotel is legally obliged to inform you if there has been a tariff increase since you made your booking.

Even if you have reserved a specific room, ask to see it before you sign the register. And if you require special arrangements, first ensure that these are satisfactory.

Unless otherwise stated, the occupation period generally extends from noon to noon.

Reception area in the Palace of the Lost City at Sun City *(see pp270–71)*

SELF-CATERING

Choice in style and price of self-catering accommodation in South Africa is vast, with cottages sometimes also referred to as chalets, bungalows or *rondavels* (if they are round and grass-thatched).

Many of the game parks have luxurious, East African-style safari tents with private outdoor kitchens, while farm-style cottages in the vast Karoo *(see pp302–3)* feature large, indoor hearths to fend off the bitter cold on winter nights. Municipal chalets in caravan parks may offer only the mere basics, while cottages on the wine estates of the Cape *(see pp136–49),* for example, may even be equipped with microwaves and satellite television.

Club Mykonos, Langebaan *(see p159)*

The larger resorts and game reserves will usually have a selection of cottages. These may be self-contained units or have shared kitchen, laundry and bathroom facilities. Self-catering cottages usually have well-equipped kitchens, are comfortably furnished and may even include towels and bedding, although it is always advisable to ask beforehand.

Upon arrival, a member of staff may check to ensure that all the items on the inventory are supplied and intact. You could also be asked to pay a small deposit (refundable at the end of your stay) to cover potential loss or breakage.

It is advisable to approach individual tourist information offices of towns or regions for the addresses and contact numbers of self-catering cottages. Agencies like **Roger & Kay's Travel Selection** may also be able to assist.

Guest cottage at the Blyde River Canyon resort *(see p279)*

COUNTRY COTTAGES

Cottages on farms and in peaceful villages are to be found in Mpumalanga (**Jacana Country Homes and Trails**), the KwaZulu-Natal Midlands (**The Underberg Hideaway**), and in the wine- and fruit-farming areas around Cape Town. A memorable aspect of a stay in the country is the hospitality and catering in true local style.

Entrance of the Table Bay Hotel, on Cape Town's V&A Waterfront *(see p331)*

BED AND BREAKFAST

Accommodation in private homes has become very popular, especially along the Garden Route and in bigger cities like Cape Town, Port Elizabeth and Johannesburg. The hosts, who concentrate on a small number of guests staying only a night or two, take pride in being able to provide personal attention.

GUEST FARMS

Relatively inexpensive outdoor family holidays are provided by guest- or holiday-farms all around the country. Visitors stay in the farmhouse or in a nearby cottage. Sometimes meals are eaten with the resident family, otherwise there are equipped kitchens. Guests can also take part in daily activities, such as collecting the eggs and milking the cows.

GAME LODGES

Game lodges in most private reserves *(see pp386–91)* cater for affluent visitors. They typically offer excellent cuisine, luxurious pseudo-rustic accommodation, highly skilled staff and game rangers who ensure that guests see as much of the African wildlife as possible. National parks are much more basic, yet very comfortable.

BUDGET ACCOMMODATION

Hosteling International provides accommodation in several hostels. The YMCA and YWCA offer similar basic facilities. No age limit is imposed on guests, although preference is usually given to the younger travellers.

Backpackers' lodges are more suited to young people, as facilities and meals are few and privacy is non-existent. Staying in a youth hostel may be fairly accurately described as "roughing it".

CARAVAN PARKS

You don't have to tow a caravan to qualify for residence, as many caravan parks have caravans to let, along with prefabricated or rustic cottages. Allocated sites are usually connected to water mains and electricity supplies.

Larger caravan parks have a shop, restaurant and swimming pool, and sometimes even tennis courts or a bowling green.

Most campers do their own cooking– the method of choice is the South African *braaivleis* or barbecue. Cooking-places or "braai sites" are provided – one per site – and good, dry firewood is usually available from the park office.

Camping in the Natal Drakensberg Park *(see p216)*

Camping sites can be noisy at night, so choose a spot well away from the entrance gate, which usually also serves as the exit point. The **AA Travel Services** will be able to supply contact details of caravan parks and camping sites.

REST CAMPS

Rest camps are the "standard" version of the luxurious game lodge and are found in national parks and provincial game reserves *(see pp386–91)*. Most of them offer a variety of facilities such as swimming pools, shops and communal dining areas, with accommodation options ranging from bungalows to bigger chalets.

UNDER CANVAS

Numerous camping grounds are situated along South Africa's major rivers or at the sea. Sites are separated from each other by calico screens or hedges. Communal ablution blocks are provided. Many of the camp sites are run as part of a local caravan park.

MINERAL SPRINGS

There are resorts at most South African hot springs, such as the one at Cradock *(see p306)*. The attraction is the water itself, in swimming pools or in the form of medicinal baths. Accommodation is in hotels or at camp sites.

DIRECTORY

HOTEL GROUPS BOOKING OFFICES

Aventura Resorts
Tel *(011) 423-5660.*

City Lodge
Tel *(011) 884-0660.*

Formule 1 Hotel
Tel *(011) 392-1453.*

Holiday Inn Garden Court
Tel *(0861) 447-744.*

Portfolio of Places
Tel *(011) 880-3414.*

Protea Hotels
Tel *(0861) 119-000.*

Southern Sun
Tel *(0861) 447-744.*

Stay
Tel *(012) 460-1050.*

Sun International
Tel *(011) 780-7800.*

COUNTRY HOMES

Jacana Country Homes and Trails
Box 95212, Waterkloof, Pretoria, 0145.
Tel *(012) 346-3550.*

The Underberg Hideaway
Box 1218, Hilton, KwaZulu-Natal, 3245.
Tel *(033) 343-1217.*

CAMPING

Aventura Resorts
Tel *(011) 423-5660.*

KZN Wildlife
Tel *(033) 845-1000.*
www.kznwildlife.com

National Parks Board Bookings
Tel *(012) 428-9111 or (011) 678-8870.*
www.saparks.co.za

GUESTHOUSES AND B&BS

Bed 'n' Breakfast Bookings
Box 91309, Auckland Park, Gauteng, 2006.
Tel *(011) 234-5045.*
www.bedandbreakfast.co.za

Guest House Association of Southern Africa
Box 18416, Wynberg, Cape Town, 7824.
Tel *(021) 762-0880.*
www.gaza.co.za

Roger & Kay's Travel Selection
Box 405, Bergvliet, Cape Town, 7864.
Tel *(021) 715-7130.*

GENERAL

AA Travel Services
Box 7118, Johannesburg, 2000.
Tel *(011) 799-1400.*
www.aatravel.co.za

Hosteling International
Tel *(021) 421-7721.*

South African Tourism
Private Bag X10012, Sandton, 2146.
Tel *(011) 895-3000.*
www.southafrica.co.za

Choosing a Hotel

The hotels in this guide have been selected from a wide price range for their good value or exceptional location, comfort and style. The chart highlights some of the factors that may influence your choice and gives a brief description of each hotel. Entries are listed by price categories within the towns.

PRICE CATEGORIES
The following price ranges are for a standard double room per night, including tax and service charges, but not including breakfast.
® Under R400
®® R400–R800
®®® R800–R1,200
®®®® R1,200–R2,000
®®®®® Over R2,000

CAPE TOWN

CITY BOWL Daddy Long Legs ®®
134 Long Street, 8000 ***Tel*** *(021) 424-1403* ***Fax*** *(021) 422-3446* ***Rooms*** *13* ***Map*** *5 2A*

Each room in this hostel has been put together by a different local artist, and the results are individual, irreverent and representative of Cape Town's lively cultural landscape. Daddy Long Legs is one of the city's most unique places to stay, located on a bustling strip that hosts much of Cape Town's thriving nightlife. **www.daddylonglegs.co.za**

CITY BOWL Formula 1 Hotel ®®
J Smuts Ave & M Hammerschlag Way, Foreshore, 8000 ***Tel*** *(021) 418-4664* ***Rooms*** *64* ***Map*** *6 1D*

A viable budget option, Formula 1 is a basic but clean hotel. The central location on the foreshore behind the Artscape Theatre is perfect for sightseeing; from here it is a mere two-minute drive to the bustling V&A Waterfront. All rooms are en-suite and accommodate up to three people each. **www.hotelformule1.co.za**

CITY BOWL Lions Kloof Lodge ®®
26 Higgo Crescent, Higgovale, 8001 ***Tel*** *(021) 426-5515* ***Fax*** *(021) 422-2047* ***Rooms*** *5* ***Map*** *4 E4*

Located between Table Mountain and Signal Hill, this hotel features expansive wooden decking jutting out over a lush, exotic garden. The ambience is relaxed, and the decor comprises simple elegant furnishings punctuated by pieces of African art. Massages and beauty treatments are available in the wellness studio. **www.lionskloof.co.za**

CITY BOWL Palm Tree Manor ®®
11 Glynville Terrace, Gardens, 8001 ***Tel*** *(021) 461-3698* ***Fax*** *(021) 462-3330* ***Rooms*** *4* ***Map*** *5 1A*

A restored and sedate Victorian terraced house just off historic Dunkley Square. The National Gallery, the Houses of Parliament and many great restaurants can be found nearby. Decor is colonial meets African. All rooms are en suite, and three of them open on to balconies. **www.africa-adventure.org/p/palmtree/index.htm**

CITY BOWL Acorn House ®®®
1 Montrose Avenue, Oranjezicht, 8001 ***Tel*** *(021) 461-1782* ***Fax*** *(021) 461-1768* ***Rooms*** *8* ***Map*** *5 A4*

Acorn House was originally built for the editor of a local newspaper and has a 1904 Herbert Baker-designed edifice. Today the house is the home of Bernd and Beate, who have made a name for this hotel in Cape Town's German quarter through their meticulous hospitality, beautiful decor and passionately compiled wine list. **www.acornhouse.co.za**

CITY BOWL Cape Town Hollow Boutique Hotel ®®®
88 Queen Victoria Street, 8001 ***Tel*** *(021) 423-1260* ***Fax*** *(021) 423-2088* ***Rooms*** *56* ***Map*** *5 B2*

Situated in Cape Town's old centre, overlooking the Dutch East India Company Gardens, this four-star boutique hotel offers tasteful modern furnishings and a relaxing wellness centre. For excellent views of Table Mountain, request a room on the fifth floor or above, facing the gardens. **www.capetownhollow.co.za**

CITY BOWL Leeuwenvoet House ®®®
93 New Church Street, Tamboerskloof, 8001 ***Tel*** *(021) 424-1133* ***Fax*** *(021) 424-0495* ***Rooms*** *12* ***Map*** *4 2F*

An excellent guesthouse in a lovingly restored Victorian building, Leeuwenvoet is situated around the corner from trendy Kloof Street, with its superb restaurants and boutiques. Start the day with a hearty breakfast and then head over Kloof Nek to the beach. Alternatively, ask your friendly hosts for daytripping tips. **www.leeuwenvoet.co.za**

CITY BOWL Table Mountain Lodge ®®®
10a Tamboerskloof Road, Tamboerskloof, 8001 ***Tel*** *(021) 423-0042* ***Fax*** *(021) 423-4983* ***Rooms*** *8* ***Map*** *4 F2*

This large, colourfully restored Cape Dutch farmhouse on the slopes of Signal Hill has received a four-star grading from the South African Tourism Council. Freshly cut flowers adorn the halls of the house, and there are eight en-suite rooms all furnished in a classically elegant style. **www.tablemountainlodge.co.za**

CITY BOWL Underberg Guesthouse ®®®
6 Tamboerskloof Road, Tamboerskloof, 8001 ***Tel*** *(021) 426-2262* ***Fax*** *(021) 424-4059* ***Rooms*** *10* ***Map*** *4 F2*

A beautifully renovated Victorian house at the bottom of Kloof Nek, with ten en-suite rooms available. Wireless Internet and a self-service honesty bar are available to guests. Your hosts are on hand to help with travel tips, airport transfers and any theatre or restaurant reservations. **www.underbergguesthouse.co.za**

Key to Symbols *see back cover flap*

CITY BOWL Villa Lutzi ®®®

6 Rosmead Avenue, Oranjezicht, 8001 **Tel** *(021) 423-4614* **Fax** *(021) 426-1472* **Rooms** *11* **Map** *4 F4*

Located on the slopes of the mountain in Oranjezicht, a ten-minute walk from the city, Villa Lutzi offers a luxurious home away from home, with an exotic garden and a large pool deck overlooking the Lions Head. Hosts Dagmar and Eric are clued up on local restaurants and nightlife and keen to point guests in the right direction. **www.villalutzi.com**

CITY BOWL Cape Heritage Hotel ®®®®

Heritage Square, Bree Street, 8001 **Tel** *(021) 424-4646* **Fax** *(021) 424-4949* **Rooms** *15* **Map** *5 1B*

Contemporary design meets colonial charm at this four-star luxury boutique hotel in a historic 18th-century building. Cape Heritage borders a shady courtyard around which five independent restaurants compete for business. All 15 rooms are individually decorated and full of Old World character. **www.capeheritage.co.za**

CITY BOWL Townhouse Hotel ®®®®

60 Corporation Street, 8001 **Tel** *(021) 465-7050* **Fax** *(021) 465-3891* **Rooms** *107* **Map** *5 B2*

Among the facilities on offer at this four-star hotel in the city centre are an indoor heated pool, a fitness room and a shuttle service to the V&A Waterfront. The Townhouse was extensively renovated in 2006, and all rooms are well appointed, with satellite television, electronic safes and high-speed Internet access. **www.townhouse.co.za**

CITY BOWL Urban Chic Boutique Hotel ®®®®

172 Long Street, 8001 **Tel** *(021) 426-6119* **Fax** *(021) 423-2086* **Rooms** *20* **Map** *5 A2*

The ultimate in cosmopolitan and contemporary boutique hotels. Sip cocktails in the cigar lounge, while you make use of the wireless Internet connection, or step outside into the throbbing heart of Cape Town's nightlife. Each room has a large corner window affording great views of Table Mountain and Signal Hill. **www.urbanchic.co.za**

CITY BOWL Arabella Sheraton Hotel ®®®®®

Convention Square, Lower Long Street, 8000 **Tel** *(021) 412-9999* **Fax** *(021) 412-9001* **Rooms** *483* **Map** *5 1B*

State-of-the-art technology and uncompromising luxury permeate the guest's experience at this architectural landmark, from the slick, contemporary furnishings and African art on the walls, to the oversized beds and e-butler facility, which passes your requests to the relevant member of staff. **www.starwoodhotels.com/sheraton**

CITY BOWL Kensington Place ®®®®®

38 Kensington Crescent, Higgovale, 8001 **Tel** *(021) 424-4744* **Fax** *(021) 424-1810* **Rooms** *8* **Map** *4 F4*

An award-winning and unique place to stay in exclusive Higgovale, on the slopes of Table Mountain. Setting a high benchmark for intimate boutique hotels, Kensington focuses on sexy contemporary stylings with unobtrusive yet attentive service. Featured on *Tatler*'s 2006 list of the 101 Best Hotels in the World. **www.kensingtonplace.co.za**

CITY BOWL Mount Nelson Hotel ®®®®®

76 Orange Street, 8001 **Tel** *(021) 483-1000* **Fax** *(021) 483-1001* **Rooms** *201* **Map** *5 A3*

A colonial masterpiece and Cape Town institution, the "Pink Lady" is located at the foot of Table Mountain. The hotel is spread over a large plot of lovely gardens, and has been voted the Best Hotel in South Africa in the *World Travel Awards* for several years running. Nelson Mandela celebrated his 79th birthday here in 1998. **www.mountnelson.co.za**

V&A WATERFRONT Breakwater Lodge ®®

Portswood Road, V&A Waterfront, 8001 **Tel** *(021) 406-1911* **Fax** *(021) 406-1070* **Rooms** *250* **Map** *1 1A*

A budget hotel built in a converted 19th-century prison, Breakwater Lodge is comfortable, inexpensive and full of character. Rooms overlook Table Bay on one side of the hotel, and Table Mountain on the other. The hotel is linked with the UCT Graduate School of Business, and its conference facilities are impressive. **www.bwl.co.za**

V&A WATERFRONT Victoria Junction ®®®®

210 Victoria Jct, Prestwich St, Green Point, 8005 **Tel** *(021) 418-1234* **Fax** *(021) 418-5678* **Rooms** *172* **Map** *2 D5*

Half in Green Point and half inside the V&A, the Victoria Junction offers the full designer hotel experience. The industrial interior is offset by chic furnishings, and the rooms have the feel of contemporary loft-style apartments. The excellent in-house restaurant is constructed around a working film set. **www.proteahotels.com**

V&A WATERFRONT Cape Grace ®®®®®

West Quay Road, V&A Waterfront, 8002 **Tel** *(021) 410-7110* **Fax** *(021) 419-7622* **Rooms** *122* **Map** *1 2B*

A member of the Leading Small Hotels of the World group, the Cape Grace is the stately jewel in the crown of the Waterfront's crop of hotels. It has scooped numerous international awards since the Brand family first opened the doors in 1996. The atmosphere is intimate, with exquisite decor and personalized service. **www.capegrace.co.za**

V&A WATERFRONT Radisson Hotel ®®®®®

Beach Road, Granger Bay, V&A Waterfront, 8002 **Tel** *(021) 441-3000* **Fax** *(021) 441-3520* **Rooms** *181* **Map** *1 3C*

The Radisson is a well-established hotel located on a Granger Bay promontory that overlooks a private marina. The plentiful modern facilities include an in-house spa and multiple restaurants. The service is always impeccable, but never intrusive. All rooms offer either mountain or sea views. **www.radissonsas.com**

V&A WATERFRONT The Table Bay Hotel ®®®®®

Quay 6, V&A Waterfront, 8002 **Tel** *(021) 406-5000* **Fax** *(021) 406-5656* **Rooms** *329* **Map** *1 1C*

Exuding the nautical charm of a cruise liner, the Table Bay Hotel has a heated salt-water pool, perhaps the only tropical sea water you'll find during your stay in the Western Cape. Other features include an in-house spa, a small gym, an elegant ballroom, an executive boardroom and dramatic sea views. **www.thetablebay.co.za**

V&A WATERFRONT Victoria & Alfred Hotel ®®®®®

Pier Head, V&A Waterfront, 8002 ***Tel*** *(021) 419-6677* ***Fax*** *(021) 419-8955* ***Rooms*** *120* ***Map*** *1 2B*

The Victoria & Alfred is the original waterfront hotel, offering spacious rooms with expansive panoramas of the mountain or the basin. Service is prompt and includes a chauffeur facility if required. For the less demanding commuter, a shuttle bus takes guests to and from the centre of town on a regular basis. **www.vahotel.co.za**

ATLANTIC SEABOARD Albatross B&B ®®

24 Queens Road, Sea Point, 8005 ***Tel*** *(021) 434-7624* ***Rooms*** *8*

This comfortable bed and breakfast in Bantry Bay offers non-smoking en-suite and triple rooms. The house itself is spacious, with two large palm trees presiding over the garden. Children over the age of nine are welcome, and Cape Town tours, airport transfers and car rental can all be arranged. **www.safarinow.com/go/albatross**

ATLANTIC SEABOARD Lions Head Lodge ®®

319 Main Road, Sea Point, 8005 ***Tel*** *(021) 434-4163* ***Fax*** *(021) 439-3813* ***Rooms*** *49*

Located in the heart of Sea Point, this great-value hotel offers both serviced rooms and self-catering flats. There is an Internet café inside the lodge, as well as a small pool and a restaurant. Be sure to ask the management how to get around Sea Point, since the main road can be dangerous after dark. **www.lions-head-lodge.co.za**

ATLANTIC SEABOARD The Hout Bay Manor Hotel ®®®

Baviaanskloof, off Main Road, Hout Bay, 7872 ***Tel*** *(021) 790-0116* ***Fax*** *(021) 790-0118* ***Rooms*** *21*

The Manor dates back to 1871 and offers the ultimate in rest and relaxation for visitors to the self-proclaimed "Republic of Hout Bay". The beach is a short walk away, and there are shops, restaurants and an excellent weekend craft market nearby. All rooms are child-friendly and furnished with sleeper couches. **www.houtbaymanor.co.za**

ATLANTIC SEABOARD Villa Rosa Guesthouse ®®®

277 High Level Road, Sea Point, 8005 ***Tel*** *(021) 434-2768* ***Fax*** *(021) 434-3526* ***Rooms*** *7*

Villa Rosa is a Victorian family home located at the foot of Lions Head, in upper Sea Point. Breakfasts are a hearty affair, with muesli, breads, eggs and home-made jam to order. This is an established and safe bet for a warm welcome and a comfortable stay. **www.villa-rosa.com**

ATLANTIC SEABOARD Villa Sunshine ®®®

1 Rochester Road, Bantry Bay, 8001 ***Tel*** *(021) 439-8224* ***Fax*** *(021) 439-8219* ***Rooms*** *7*

The four-star Villa Sunshine offers B&B accommodation in seven individually decorated en-suite rooms. All modern home comforts are provided, as well as high-speed Internet, a beautiful salt-water pool and a secluded location on spectacular Bantry Bay. **www.wheretostay.co.za/villasunshine**

ATLANTIC SEABOARD Ambassador Hotel ®®®®

34 Victoria Road, Bantry Bay, 8005 ***Tel*** *(021) 439-6170* ***Fax*** *(021) 439-6336* ***Rooms*** *97*

This large, established four-star hotel is located along Bantry Bay's jagged coastline, wedged between the main road and the surf-weathered rocks below. The building has just undergone a major refurbish, with luxury finishes added to the rooms. All rooms have dramatic views of the surrounding granite cliffs. **www.ambassador.co.za**

ATLANTIC SEABOARD Bateleurs House ®®®®

81 Theresa Avenue, Camps Bay, 8001 ***Tel*** *(021) 438-1697* ***Fax*** *(021) 438-9588* ***Rooms*** *3*

At the top of Camps Bay's network of mountainside avenues is Jasper and Zonia's five-star establishment. There are two spacious suites with king-size beds and a third, slightly smaller option with a private entrance. All rooms have lovely views across Camps Bay and the Atlantic Ocean beyond. **www.bateleurshouse.co.za**

ATLANTIC SEABOARD The Cape Cove ®®®®

11 Avenue Deauville, Fresnaye, 8005 ***Tel*** *(021) 434-7969* ***Fax*** *(021) 434-8191* ***Rooms*** *8*

This boutique hotel has made a name for itself as a luxury retreat with the emphasis on cutting-edge design. A large wooden deck with an infinity pool extends outwards over the granite face of Lions Head. Inside, immaculately selected pieces of wood and leather furniture are interspersed with contemporary and African artworks. **www.capecove.com**

ATLANTIC SEABOARD O on Kloof ®®®®

Cnr King & Kloof Roads, Bantry Bay, 8005 ***Tel*** *(021) 439-2081* ***Fax*** *(021) 439-8832* ***Rooms*** *6*

Olaf Dambrowski is no stranger to the hospitality business, and O is his most sophisticated venture yet. This impeccably decorated villa on the slopes of Lions Head is all about attention to detail. The wooden deck of the honeymoon suite on the top floor is the ideal location to enjoy panoramas of both mountains and ocean. **www.oonkloof.co.za**

ATLANTIC SEABOARD Primi Royal ®®®®

32 Camps Bay Drive, Camps Bay, 8001 ***Tel*** *(021) 438-2741* ***Fax*** *(021) 438-1718* ***Rooms*** *10*

The theme at this boutique hotel belonging to the Primi Group is the fusion of African and Asian styles. Suites afford spectacular views that take in Lions Head, Bakoven and the vast expanse of Atlantic inbetween. Popular Camps Bay Beach is just across the road, with plenty of restaurants on the main thoroughfare. **www.primi-royal.com**

ATLANTIC SEABOARD Villa Clifton ®®®®

7 Leckhampton Court, 234 Kloof Road, Clifton, 8005 ***Tel*** *(021) 919-1752* ***Fax*** *(021) 919-1758* ***Rooms*** *2*

Positioned high on Kloof Road, this self-catering house has a large deck overlooking some of the world's most beautiful beaches. The Atlantic seaboard's spectacular sunsets are best enjoyed with a well-stirred cocktail in hand and the sound of the crashing waves below. **www.villaclifton.com**

Key to Price Guide *see p326* **Key to Symbols** *see back cover flap*

ATLANTIC SEABOARD Winchester Mansions ®®®®

221 Beach Road, Sea Point, 8001 ***Tel*** *(021) 434-2351* ***Fax*** *(021) 434-0215* ***Rooms*** *53*

A renowned, privately owned four-star hotel on Sea Point's coastal boulevard. Tailor-made tours to the Winelands or to Cape Point can be arranged through consultation with the management. The hotel restaurant, Harveys, is run by an award-winning local chef. **www.winchester.co.za**

ATLANTIC SEABOARD The Bay Hotel ®®®®®

69 Victoria Road, Camps Bay, 8005 ***Tel*** *(021) 430-4444* ***Fax*** *(021) 438-4433* ***Rooms*** *78*

This large hotel has a prime position on Camps Bay's main drag. The grounds are large, with plenty of activities to keep restless guests happy. The Bay Hotel boasts four swimming pools, a tennis court and a luxury wellness centre for those in need of pampering. The city is five minutes' drive away, over Kloof Nek. **www.thebay.co.za**

ATLANTIC SEABOARD Ellerman House ®®®®®

180 Kloof Road, Bantry Bay, 8005 ***Tel*** *(021) 430-3200* ***Fax*** *(021) 430-3215* ***Rooms*** *11*

A historical landmark on the granite outcrops of Bantry Bay, this classic turn-of-the-century mansion is recognized as one of the top boutique hotels in the world. The emphasis is on immaculate service and perfection at every level. Ellerman Villa next door is available as a serviced home for a hefty nightly fee. **www.ellerman.co.za**

ATLANTIC SEABOARD The Twelve Apostles Hotel & Spa ®®®®®

Victoria Road, Oudekraal, Camps Bay, 8005 ***Tel*** *(021) 437-9000* ***Fax*** *(021) 437-9055* ***Rooms*** *70*

Sandwiched between the mountains and the Atlantic Ocean, this secluded five-star retreat has uninterrupted views of the pristine coastline. Rooms are beautifully appointed, though guests may wish to trade their king-size four-poster bed for a little extra elbow room in one of the smaller standard suites. **www.12apostleshotel.com**

GREEN POINT AND MOUILLE POINT Brenwin ®®

1 Thornhill Road, Green Point, 8001 ***Tel*** *(021) 434-0220* ***Fax*** *(021) 439-3465* ***Rooms*** *16* ***Map*** *1 4C*

Built in 1830 to accommodate Cape Town's port captain, Brenwin can be found in cosmopolitan Green Point, just off High Level Road, overlooking the Waterfront. Rooms range from spacious doubles with extra sleeper couch to self-contained apartments that can be booked as either B&B or self-catering. **www.brenwin.co.za**

GREEN POINT AND MOUILLE POINT La Splendida Luxury Suites ®®

121 Beach Road, Mouille Point, 8001 ***Tel*** *(021) 439-5119* ***Fax*** *(021) 439-5112* ***Rooms*** *22* ***Map*** *1 3B*

Situated on Mouille Point's coastal boulevard, La Splendida offers clean, modern accommodation at a good price, although it should be noted that the emphasis here is not on round-the-clock or overly attentive service. A two-storey penthouse is also available. The V&A Waterfront is a ten-minute walk away. **www.lasplendida.co.za**

GREEN POINT AND MOUILLE POINT 18 on Crox ®®®

18 Croxteth Road, Green Point, 8005 ***Tel*** *(021) 439-3871* ***Fax*** *(021) 433-2318* ***Rooms*** *3* ***Map*** *1 4C*

Formerly one of Cape Town's best-kept secrets, in the past few years this classy, small guesthouse has grown enormously in renown. The furnishings and lighting are immaculate, with gowns and slippers provided along with the down duvets. Due to the increased popularity in this hotel it is best to book well in advance. **www.18oncrox.com**

GREEN POINT AND MOUILLE POINT Jambo Guest House ®®®

1 Grove Road, Green Point, 8005 ***Tel*** *(021) 439-4219* ***Fax*** *(021) 434-0672* ***Rooms*** *5* ***Map*** *1 4B*

Relax in a hot Jacuzzi surrounded by tropical foliage at this B&B. Hosts Barry and Mina Thomas are on hand to advice on local places of interest. Decor varies in theme from African animal skins to the ornately colonial. Jambo has won several AA Accommodation Awards in recent years and offers good value for money. **www.jambo.co.za**

GREEN POINT AND MOUILLE POINT Romney Park Luxury Suites ®®®®

Cnr Hill & Romney Roads, Green Point, 8005 ***Tel*** *(021) 439-4555* ***Fax*** *(021) 439-4747* ***Rooms*** *18* ***Map*** *1 B4*

Afro-colonial decor has been carefully selected for the well-appointed, spacious suites at Romney Park. Facilities are extensive, with a lap pool outside and a wellness spa offering all kinds of invigorating treatments. Rooms have creamy carpets and are painted in neutral tones, which offsets the mahogany furniture. **www.romneypark.co.za**

KHAYELITSHA Majoro's ®

69 Helena Crescent, Graceland, 7784 ***Tel*** *(021) 361-3412* ***Fax*** *(021) 361-3412* ***Rooms*** *2*

Maria Maile offers visitors a warm welcome at her B&B. If you want to find out how the vast majority of South Africans live, staying at Majoro's is the way to do it. A traditional African meal is served at dinner time, and guests are also invited to visit the local shebeen to share in the latest township gossip. **sonke@telkomsa.net**

KHAYELITSHA Vicky's B&B ®

C685a Kiyane Street, Site C, Khayelitsha, 7784 ***Tel*** *(0)82 225-2986* ***Fax*** *(021) 364-9660* ***Rooms*** *2*

Vicky's B&B is constructed in the typical cut-and-paste style of most township dwellings, forged from a collage of corrugated iron, tree trunks and hardboard. Inside, however, guests want for nothing, particularly warmth and hospitality. The house is directly opposite the "original" V&A waterfront shebeen. **vickysbandb@yahoo.com**

LANGA Ma Neo's ®

30 Zone 7, Langa, 7455 ***Tel*** *(021) 694-2504* ***Fax*** *(021) 695-0661* ***Rooms*** *3*

Ma Neo's is a warm, friendly family home where visitors are invited to share in the host's vast knowledge and recollections of local history and culture. This is the ideal place to learn about the seismic changes South Africa has undergone through the apartheid years to the present. **maneo@absamail.co.za**

SOUTH PENINSULA Afton Grove Country Guesthouse ®®

Main Road, Noordhoek, 7979 ***Tel*** *(021) 785-2992* ***Fax*** *(021) 785-3456* ***Rooms*** *13*

Located in rural Noordhoek, at the southern end of breathtaking Chapmans Peak Drive, Afton Grove is a classy four-star guesthouse offering B&B or self-catering cottages. All mod cons are available, as well as poolside dinners and picnic baskets on request. Nearby activities include horse riding and surfing. **www.aftongrove.co.za**

SOUTH PENINSULA Lord Nelson Inn ®®

58 St George's Street, Simon's Town, 7975 ***Tel*** *(021) 786-1386* ***Fax*** *(021) 786-1009* ***Rooms*** *10*

A traditional inn in this well-preserved former Royal Navy town, the Lord Nelson is located close to Cape Point Nature Reserve and Boulders Beach, with its renowned jackass penguin colony. Also nearby are tennis courts and a golf course. Rated three stars by the South African Tourism Grading Council. **www.lordnelsoninn.co.za**

SOUTH PENINSULA Toad Hall ®®

9 AB Bull Road, Froggy Farm, Simon's Town, 7975 ***Tel*** *(021) 786-3878* ***Fax*** *(021) 786-3878* ***Rooms*** *2*

Toad Hall is a B&B in a quiet cul-de-sac on the outskirts of Simon's Town. Watch the sun come up over False Bay, and expect to see whales between late August and early November. Your hosts can arrange a boat trip for you to get a closer look. Explore nearby Cape Point, or visit Kalk Bay and its fantastic restaurants. **www.toad-hall.co.za**

SOUTH PENINSULA Boulders Beach Guest House ®®®

Boulders Place, off Bellvue Road, Simon's Town ***Tel*** *(021) 786-1758* ***Fax*** *(021) 786-1825* ***Rooms*** *14*

Only a few short strides from Boulders Beach and its penguins, this hidden gem offers an east-facing location for spectacular sunrises, great food and no TV to distract you from the glorious environs. Double or twin rooms are available in the lodge, while self-catering units sleep a maximum of six. **www.boulderbeach.co.za**

SOUTH PENINSULA Villa St James ®®®

36 Main Road, St James, 7945 ***Tel*** *(0)82 784-8000* ***Rooms*** *8*

A landmark building on the False Bay coast, with 360-degree views of the ocean and the mountains. The villa has a fascinating history, and over the years it has played host to many VIPs, including Greek royalty and South African premier Jan Smuts. Down the road is Kalk Bay, with its quirky shops and cafés. **www.villastjames.co.za**

SOUTH PENINSULA Glenview Cottage ®®®®

56 Camilla St, Glencairn Heights, Simon's Town, 7975 ***Tel*** *(021) 782-1324* ***Fax*** *(021) 782-9406* ***Rooms*** *2*

A finalist in the 2006 AA Accommodation Awards, Glenview has a wonderful location high above Glencairn Beach. The house looks down on the valley and Simon's Town beyond. Expect tranquillity, excellent hospitality and a tasty breakfast on the patio, while False Bay's tides wash over the beach below. **www.glenviewcottage-sa.com**

SOUTH PENINSULA Whale View Manor ®®®®

402 Main Road, Murdoch Valley, Simon's Town, 7995 ***Tel*** *(021) 786-3291* ***Fax*** *(021) 786-5453* ***Rooms*** *8*

This stately manor house is perched upon a strip of lawn that runs down to Fisherman's Beach. The interior is impressively furnished, with high ceilings that convey an airy colonial ambience. The penguin colony at Boulders Beach is a short walk along the coast. A four-star haven in this secluded corner of the deep south. **www.whaleviewmanor.co.za**

SOUTH PENINSULA The Long Beach ®®®®®

1 Kirsten Avenue, Kommetjie, 7976 ***Tel*** *(021) 794-6561* ***Fax*** *(021) 794-2069* ***Rooms*** *6*

In the fishing village and popular surfing spot of Kommetjie is The Long Beach, the least metropolitan of Cape Town's boutique hotels, and one of The Last Word Group's trio of luxury small hotels. Each room faces the sea, and the tranquil ambience fills this undiscovered corner of the Cape Peninsula. **www.thelongbeach.com**

SOUTHERN SUBURBS Allandale Holiday Cottages ®®

72 Swaanswyk Road, Tokai, 7945 ***Tel*** *(021) 715-3320* ***Fax*** *(021) 712-9744* ***Rooms*** *17*

Allandale is located at the end of a cul-de-sac on the slopes of Constantiaberg, adjacent to the Tokai Forest Reserve. Cottages are self-catering, with metered telephones. Towels and bedding are also provided. A pool and all-weather tennis court are available and mountain-bike hire is arranged on request. **www.safarinow.com/go/allandaleholidaycottages**

SOUTHERN SUBURBS Dongola House ®®

30 Airlie Place, Constantia, 7806 ***Tel*** *(021) 794-8283* ***Fax*** *(021) 794-9024* ***Rooms*** *7*

Wake up to the sound of the guinea fowl's call in this B&B. The interior is chic-contemporary-meets-traditional-African. The Constantia Wine Route starts nearby, and the beaches and restaurants of the Southern Peninsula are a short drive away. Host Peter Eckstein is on hand to provide travel tips and advice. **www.dongolahouse.co.za**

SOUTHERN SUBURBS Hampshire House ®®

10 Willow Road, Constantia, 7806 ***Tel*** *(021) 794-6288* ***Fax*** *(021) 794-2934* ***Rooms*** *3*

The English and continental breakfast buffet is renowned at this sedate Constantia home with a large secluded garden. Ricky and Carole Chapman are charming and obliging hosts with a wicked sense of humour. Four-star graded and winner of the AA's Guest House of the Year for three years running. **www.hampshirehouse.co.za**

SOUTHERN SUBURBS Welgelee Guesthouse ®®

Dressage Close, off Spaanschemat Road, Constantia, 7800 ***Tel*** *(021) 794-7397* ***Fax*** *(021) 794-4320* ***Rooms*** *8*

A four-star guesthouse on a former working farm, Welgelee houses six double en-suite rooms, as well as offering two private self-catering cottages with fully fitted kitchens. The ambience is relaxed, and hosts Peter and Anna Buchanan are happy to help with travel tips, transfers and car hire. **www.welgelee.co.za**

Key to Price Guide *see p326* **Key to Symbols** *see back cover flap*

SOUTHERN SUBURBS The Wild Olive Guest House ®®

4 Keurboom Road, Newlands, 7708 ***Tel*** *(021) 683-0880* ***Fax*** *(021) 671-5776* ***Rooms*** *7*

The Wild Olive is nestled amid leafy suburban Newlands, close to Newlands Cricket Ground and the shopping mecca of Cavendish Square. The property has spacious grounds that feature a pool, a gym and a sauna. The atmosphere is serene and welcoming, with rooms that offer luxurious decor in warm earthy tones. **www.wildolive.co.za**

SOUTHERN SUBURBS Constantia Lodge ®®®

Duntaw Close, Constantia, 7806 ***Tel*** *(021) 794-2410* ***Fax*** *(021) 794-2418* ***Rooms*** *7*

On the southern slopes of Table Mountain, in serene and densely wooded Upper Constantia, lies the Constantia Lodge. Suites are decorated with simple elegance, and they are reasonably priced for the location. There are wonderful views across False Bay from the front garden and pool area. **www.constantialodge.com**

SOUTHERN SUBURBS Houtkapperspoort ®®®

Constantia Nek Estate, Hout Bay Main Rd, 7806 ***Tel*** *(021) 794-5216* ***Fax*** *(021) 794-2907* ***Rooms*** *24*

Houtkapperspoort is spread out across an ample piece of Constantia Nek, the pass that takes you to Hout Bay on the other side of the mountain. Despite four- and five-star gradings for the cottages, prices are remarkably affordable. Tennis, a heated pool and high-speed Internet access are all available. **www.houtkapperspoort.co.za**

SOUTHERN SUBURBS Alphen Hotel ®®®®

Alphen Drive, Constantia, 7806 ***Tel*** *(021) 794-5011* ***Fax*** *(021) 794-5710* ***Rooms*** *21*

This converted manor house and national monument dates back to 1753. Situated in Cape Town's most exclusive and leafy suburb, at the heart of a now-defunct wine estate, the Alphen includes a hair studio and a health and beauty salon. Personalized tours and transfers to the airport are available on request. **www.alphen.co.za**

SOUTHERN SUBURBS The Bishops Court ®®®®

18 Hillwood Avenue, Bishopscourt, 7708 ***Tel*** *(021) 797-6710* ***Fax*** *(021) 797-0309* ***Rooms*** *5*

This five-star boutique hotel perched at the top of elite Bishopscourt boasts discrete and attentive staff and unparalleled views. The lawn rolls downhill past the pool and the tennis court, accompanied by bursts of greenery all the way to Kirstenbosch Botanical Gardens and Table Mountain beyond. **www.thebishopscourt.com**

SOUTHERN SUBURBS Greenways Hotel ®®®®

1 Torquay Avenue, Upper Claremont, 7708 ***Tel*** *(021) 761-1792* ***Fax*** *(021) 761-0878* ***Rooms*** *15*

Commanding six acres of rolling manicured gardens, the five-star Greenways offers boutique-hotel attentiveness and individual charm in a Cape Dutch manor house built in the 1920s. There are five golf courses nearby, and the hotel is also close to Kirstenbosch Botanical Gardens and the Cavendish Square shopping mall. **www.greenwayshotel.co.za**

SOUTHERN SUBURBS Southernwood Country House ®®®®

19 Avenue Bordeaux, Constantia, 7806 ***Tel*** *(021) 794-3208* ***Fax*** *(021) 794-7551* ***Rooms*** *4*

Five minutes' drive from Kirstenbosch Botanical Gardens and close to the legendary Cellars Hohenort restaurant, Southernwood is a typical airy Constantia home in large grounds on a leafy avenue. Each of the rooms has a private entrance, and scenic mountain and forest walks start right on your doorstep. **www.southernwood.co.za**

SOUTHERN SUBURBS Andros ®®®®®

Cnr Newlands & Phyllis Rds, Claremont, 7700 ***Tel*** *(021) 797-9777* ***Fax*** *(021) 797-0300* ***Rooms*** *10*

A Herbert Baker-designed Cape Dutch homestead in the heart of leafy Claremont, Andros is a B&B-cum-boutique hotel with an in-house chef and wonderfully elegant rooms. The shopping at Cavendish Square, just around the corner, is on a par with what's on offer at the Waterfront and is an altogether less brash retail experience. **www.andros.co.za**

SOUTHERN SUBURBS Cellars Hohenort ®®®®®

93 Brommersvlei Road, Constantia, 7800 ***Tel*** *(021) 794-2137* ***Fax*** *(021) 794-2149* ***Rooms*** *55*

Home to the famous restaurant of the same name, this five-star hotel is a luxury country-living experience in close proximity to everything that Cape Town has to offer. As well as luxury doubles, standard doubles, suites and single rooms, there is a private cottage and another detached suite within the grounds. **www.collectionmcgrath.com**

SOUTHERN SUBURBS Constantia Uitsig Country Hotel ®®®®®

Spaanschemat Road, Constantia, 7800 ***Tel*** *(021) 794-6500* ***Fax*** *(021) 794-7605* ***Rooms*** *16*

A working vineyard since the 17th century, the Uitsig offers superior accommodation and unparalleled gastronomic treats as two of South Africa's top restaurants – Constantia Uitsig and La Colombe – are within the hotel grounds. Sixteen garden rooms offer stunning panoramas of the Constantia Valley. **www.constantiauitsig.co.za**

SOUTHERN SUBURBS Steenberg Hotel and Winery ®®®®®

10802 Steenberg Estate, Tokai Road, Constantia, 7945 ***Tel*** *(021) 713-2222* ***Fax*** *(021) 713-2251* ***Rooms*** *30*

Set on a working wine farm up against the Constantiaberg Mountains, Steenberg offers a supremely tranquil setting and tremendous views across the vineyards. The hotel itself is housed entirely within the original listed Cape Dutch buildings. There is a twice-daily shuttle service to the V&A Waterfront for guests. **www.steenberghotel.com**

SOUTHERN SUBURBS Vineyard Hotel ®®®®®

Colington Road, Newlands, 7700 ***Tel*** *(021) 657-4500* ***Fax*** *(021) 657-4501* ***Rooms*** *173*

A four-star hotel with three excellent restaurants on its premises. The health and fitness centre is well appointed, and there are two pools to choose from – indoors and open-air, both heated. The Cavendish Square shopping mall is nearby, and the city centre and the V&A Waterfront are only 15 minutes away by car. **www.vineyardhotel.co.za**

CAPE WINELANDS

FRANSCHHOEK Auberge Bligny ®®

28 van Wijk Street, Franschhoek, 7690 ***Tel*** *(021) 876-3767* ***Fax*** *(021) 876-3483* ***Rooms*** *8*

An 1860 homestead in the historic centre of Franschhoek, this Huguenot home is furnished with period antiques that add to the period atmopshere. Some of South Africa's greatest restaurants are within easy walking distance. In the summer months, breakfast is served on the terrace, with a view of the pool and the mountains beyond. **www.bligny.co.za**

FRANSCHHOEK Franschhoek Country House & Villas ®®

Main Road, Franschhoek, 7690 ***Tel*** *(021) 876-3386* ***Fax*** *(021) 876-2744* ***Rooms*** *26*

At this restored manor house and perfumery, the emphasis is on classic luxury, attention to detail and utter indulgence. The venue's Monneaux restaurant, headed up by chef Adrian Buchanan, has been scooping accolades since the mid-1990s. Spectacularly furnished villa suites and a wine cellar were added in 2006. **www.fch.co.za**

FRANSCHHOEK La Fontaine Guest House ®®®

21 Dirkie Uys Street, Franschhoek, 7690 ***Tel*** *(021) 876-2112* ***Fax*** *(021) 876-2112* ***Rooms*** *12*

This beautiful guest house is centrally located in the village, and it offers great value for money. Rooms in the main house afford beautiful mountain views. Among the activities on offer at La Fontaine are fly fishing, horse riding and hiking, and children of all ages are welcome. **www.lafontainefranschhoek.co.za**

FRANSCHHOEK Plumwood Inn Guest House ®®®

11 Cabriere Street, Franschhoek, 7690 ***Tel*** *(021) 876-3883* ***Fax*** *(0)86 672-6030* ***Rooms*** *7*

Seven rooms all sumptuously and uniquely decorated in a contemporary style are available here. The Plumwood experience offers unrivalled pampering, superb views and a daily soundtrack of garrulous birdlife. Franschhoek's cosmopolitan centre is a mere two minutes away on foot. **www.plumwoodinn.com**

FRANSCHHOEK Akademie Street Guesthouses ®®®®

5 Akademie Street, Franschhoek, 7690 ***Tel*** *(021) 876-3027* ***Fax*** *(021) 876-3293* ***Rooms*** *3*

Three separate guesthouses that are effectively individual cottages, each with its own private pool and garden attended by cooing doves and chirping crickets. Rooms have been nominated as the Winelands' best for honeymoons, and the Akademie was the AA's Best Small Guest House in South Africa in 2006. **www.aka.co.za**

FRANSCHHOEK Rusthof Guesthouse ®®®®

12 Huguenot Street, Franschhoek, 7690 ***Tel*** *(021) 876-3762* ***Fax*** *(021) 876-3682* ***Rooms*** *7*

This small and exclusive guesthouse hosts a maximum of 16 guests at a time. The Rusthof is on the main street of Franschhoek, within a minute's walk of the town's restaurants and delis. A wide range of activities can be arranged, including wine tours, horseback wine tastings, hot-air ballooning and scenic drives to Route 62. **www.rusthof.com**

FRANSCHHOEK Le Quartier Français ®®®®®

16 Huguenot Road, Franschhoek, 7690 ***Tel*** *(021) 876-2151* ***Fax*** *(021) 876-3105* ***Rooms*** *15*

Focusing on "ultimate luxury and romantic charm", Le Quartier Français was named Best Small Hotel in the World by *Tatler* in 2005. The innovative restaurant regularly appears on international top-50 lists. In-room beauty therapy is available, with some rooms featuring private pools and iPod docking stations. **www.lqf.co.za**

HERMON Bartholomeus Klip Farmhouse ®®®®

Hermon, 7308 ***Tel*** *(022) 448-1820* ***Fax*** *(022) 448-1829* ***Rooms*** *5*

Endless farmland vistas, herds of antelope roaming the extensive *fynbos* nature reserve, mountains turning pink as the sun dips below the horizon: the Bartholomeus Klip enjoys a magical setting. Explore the farm and nature reserve on a mountain bike, chill by the lake, or visit the quagga- and buffalo-breeding projects. **www.parksgroup.co.za**

KUILSRIVER Zevenwacht Country Inn ®®®

Langverwacht Road, Kuils River, 7579 ***Tel*** *(021) 903-5123* ***Fax*** *(021) 906-1570* ***Rooms*** *25*

All modern comforts are installed in these air-conditioned luxury suites with private terraces and views across False Bay. The Zevenwacht's working wine farm is also an integral part of the Stellenbosch Wine Route. Cellar tours, cheese and wine tastings, horse riding and quad biking are all available on the premises. **www.zevenwacht.co.za**

MONTAGU Monteco Nature Reserve ®

Gats Kraal, Montagu, 7560 ***Tel*** *(028) 572-1922* ***Fax*** *(028) 572-1290* ***Rooms*** *5*

An award-winning nature-reserve accommodation option, Monteco focuses on ecotourism and adventure trails. The cottages are self-catering, with game drives, guided walks and quad-bike excursions available to help you seek out the reserve's 40 mammal and 160 bird species. There is also a camp site for outdoorsy types. **www.monteco.co.za**

MONTAGU Mimosa Lodge ®®®

Church Street, Montagu, 6720 ***Tel*** *(023) 614-2351* ***Fax*** *(023) 614-2418* ***Rooms*** *16*

Sleek modern decor adorns the spacious rooms in this intimate Edwardian hotel renowned for its hospitality. The food is also well-regarded, presided over by owner-chef Bernard Hess. Montagu is central to Route 62 and affords easy exploration of this increasingly popular alternative to the Garden Route. **www.mimosa.co.za**

Key to Price Guide *see p326* **Key to Symbols** *see back cover flap*

MONTAGU Montagu Country Hotel ®®®

27 Bath Street, Montagu, 6720 **Tel** *(023) 614-3125* **Fax** *(023) 614-1905* **Rooms** *26*

Simple country charm and relaxation are the key themes at this airy hotel with Art Deco accents. Staff are on hand to pamper with massages, facials and all manner of organic beauty treatments. Fruit trees line the streets in this Winelands oasis and infuse the dry air with their aromas in the spring and summer. **www.montagucountryhotel.co.za**

PAARL Lemoenkloof Gastehuis ®

396a Main Street, Paarl, 7646 **Tel** *(021) 872-3782* **Fax** *(021) 872-7520* **Rooms** *20*

A 19th-century listed Victorian homestead with an indigenous manicured garden. There is a secluded pool area and a sun terrace where you can sunbathe after enjoying a generous cooked breakfast. The ambience is one of great tranquillity. Horse riding on neighbouring farms is available by arrangement. **www.lemoenkloof.co.za**l

PAARL Goedemoed Country Inn ®®

Cecilia Street, Paarl, 7646 **Tel** *(021) 863-1102* **Fax** *(021) 863-1104* **Rooms** *8*

A Cape Dutch manor house on a working wine farm, this B&B also offers dinner by prior arrangement. Surrounded by Shiraz and Chardonnay vineyards, Goedemoed is in close proximity to both the Berg River and a superb 18-hole golf course. Eight double rooms are available, all with free high-speed wireless Internet. **www.goedemoed.com**

PAARL Pontac Manor Hotel and Restaurant ®®®®

16 Zion Street, Paarl, 7646 **Tel** *(021) 872-0445* **Fax** *(021) 872-0460* **Rooms** *22*

An historic piece of 18th-century architecture tucked below Paarl Rock, the Pontac Manor is surrounded by stately oak trees and imbued with the generous spirit and hospitality of the Boland region. An award-winning and gastronomically accomplished restaurant is installed in a restored barn on the estate. **www.pontac.com**

PAARL Roggeland Country House ®®®®

Dal Josaphat Valley, Northern Paarl, Paarl, 7623 **Tel** *(021) 868-2501* **Fax** *(021) 868-2113* **Rooms** *11*

Run by the Minkley family, this exclusive hotel in a Cape Dutch national monument houses only 21 guests when it is at full capacity. The rooms are spacious, with large en-suite bathrooms. The menu and wine-list change on a daily basis. Children are welcomed subject to prior arrangement with the management. **www.roggeland.co.za**

PAARL Grande Roche Hotel ®®®®®

Plantasie Street, Paarl, 7646 **Tel** *(021) 863-5100* **Fax** *(021) 863-2220* **Rooms** *34*

Another historic Paarl manor house, this 18th-century building was recently restored to add a sophisticated contemporary flavour to the decor. The hotel facilities include floodlit tennis courts, two swimming pools, an award-winning restaurant, gym, massage parlour, hair salon, sauna and steam bath. **www.granderoche.co.za**

ROBERTSON Rosendal Winery and Wellness Retreat ®®®

Klaas Voogds West, Robertson, 6705 **Tel** *(023) 626-1570* **Fax** *(023) 626-1571* **Rooms** *8*

Breathtaking Breede River Valley views, game drives embarking from the doorstep, an intimate wine cellar, one of the area's most accomplished restaurants and, of course, the beautifully appointed wellness centre combine to create an outstanding hotel. A stay at Rosendal is always a special experience. **www.rosendalwinery.co.za**

SOMERSET WEST Helderberg Cottages ®®

48 Almond Drive, Somerset West, 7130 **Tel** *(021) 855-0100* **Fax** *(021) 855-0932* **Rooms** *5*

Heldeberg's self-catering cottages are located on the fringe of the Winelands and within half an hour of Cape Town. The one- or two-bedroom lodgings offer great value for money, and they come with fully equipped kitchens and an outdoor barbecue (*braai*) area. Bedding, linen and towels are also provided. **www.hbcc.co.za**

SOMERSET WEST Ivory Heights Boutique Hotel ®®®®

17 L Botha Ave, Monte Sereno, Somerset West, 7130 **Tel** *(021) 852-8333* **Fax** *(021) 852-8886* **Rooms** *10*

An award-winning boutique hotel offering splendid views of False Bay from the infinity pool, as well as free wireless Internet, pool, satellite TV, gym, tennis and squash courts. Contemporary architecture and sleek decor set the mood in this airy and elegant five-star establishment. **www.ivoryheights.co.za**

SOMERSET WEST Straightway Head Country Hotel ®®®®

175 Parel Valley Road, Somerset West, 7129 **Tel** *(021) 851-7088* **Fax** *(021) 851-7091* **Rooms** *19*

A luxury country hotel close to Cape Town, the Straightway Head offers four-star accommodation in 19 cottages. There's a large swimming pool to relax in and around, with the Helderberg Mountains in the background. Golf is five minutes away at Erinvale, or you can head for Gordons Bay and relax on the beach. **www.straightwayhead.com**

STELLENBOSCH Knorhoek Guest House ®®

Off R44, off N1 between Stellenbosch and Klapmuts, 7600 **Tel** *(021) 865-2114* **Fax** *(021) 865-2627* **Rooms** *7*

The wine farm here dates back to 1710. Enjoy a traditional Cape breakfast as the farmyard hubbub fizzes around you. During harvest time, you will be invited to sample the first fermentations of the year and enjoy the award-winning wines on offer. In addition to the seven en-suite rooms, there is also one self-catering suite. **www.knorhoek.co.za**

STELLENBOSCH Dorpshuis Boutique Hotel ®®®

22 Dorp Street, Stellenbosch, 7600 **Tel** *(021) 883-9881* **Fax** *(021) 883-9884* **Rooms** *22*

Elegant country-style accommodation close to the University of Stellenbosch is on offer at the Dorpshuis. The hotel houses seven luxury suites and 15 standard rooms with all modern conveniences. Light meals are available throughout the day, and the bar service runs around the clock. **www.dorpshuis.co.za**

STELLENBOSCH Eendracht Boutique Hotel ®®®

161 Dorp Street, Stellenbosch, 7600 ***Tel*** *(021) 883-8843* ***Fax*** *(021) 883-8842* ***Rooms*** *12*

Ideally located in the heart of old Stellenbosch, Eendracht was highly commended by the AA in 2005. The emphasis here is firmly placed on luxury and traditional Afrikaans hospitality. Next door to the hotel is the fascinating village-museum complex, which consists of the four oldest houses in town. **www.eendracht-hotel.com**

STELLENBOSCH Ryneveld Country Lodge ®®®

67 Ryneveld Street, Stellenbosch, 7600 ***Tel*** *(021) 887-4469* ***Fax*** *(021) 883-9549* ***Rooms*** *10*

Luxurious antiques adorn the halls of this national monument. Self-catering cottages, as well as individually furnished en-suite rooms, are available. Children are welcome, and golf and wine tours can be arranged on request. The management have been collecting accolades and awards since 1999. **www.ryneveldlodge.co.za**

STELLENBOSCH Batavia House Boutique Hotel ®®®®

12 Louw Street, Stellenbosch, 7600 ***Tel*** *(021) 887-2914* ***Fax*** *(021) 887-2915* ***Rooms*** *5*

Winner of the AA's Best Boutique Hotel Award in both 2005 and 2006, Batavia House offers something exclusive and unique in the heart of Stellenbosch. Renovated from a derelict house in 2003 by the inspired hand of Matilda de Bod, the hotel stands just off Dorp Street, in the historic heart of Stellenbosch. **www.bataviahouse.co.za**

STELLENBOSCH D'Ouwe Werf Country Inn ®®®®

30 Church Street, Stellenbosch, 7600 ***Tel*** *(021) 887-4608* ***Fax*** *(021) 887-4626* ***Rooms*** *32*

In business since 1802, this four-star inn lends new meaning to the word "established". It offers a heated outdoor pool, free valet parking and 32 individually decorated en-suite rooms. The staff pride themselves on their attentive service. D'Ouwe Werf is also renowned as a fine dining destination. **www.ouwewerf.com**

STELLENBOSCH Summerwood Guest House ®®®®

28 Jonkershoek Road, Mostertsdrift, Stellenbosch, 7600 ***Tel*** *(021) 887-4112* ***Fax*** *(021) 887-4239* ***Rooms*** *9*

This turn-of-the-century mansion has been lovingly restored by an Italian architect so as to appeal to contemporary tastes. The grounds are extensive and there are only nine rooms, so guests never feel overcrowded. Staff are always on standby to help with tips on Stellenbosch, guided wine tours or golfing outings. **www.summerwood.co.za**

STELLENBOSCH The Village at Spier ®®®®

R310 Lynedoch Road, Lynedoch, Stellenbosch, 7600 ***Tel*** *(021) 809-1100* ***Fax*** *(021) 881-3141* ***Rooms*** *155*

At this luxury wine-estate village, the grounds are immense and dotted with pretty self-contained cottages. The estate dates back to 1692 and is now a throbbing cultural hub in the area. The complex also plays host to four excellent restaurants, including the unique Moyo, as well as art collections and the Camelot Spa. **www.spier.co.za**

STELLENBOSCH Lanzerac Manor and Winery ®®®®®

Lanzerac Road, Stellenbosch, 7599 ***Tel*** *(021) 887-1132* ***Fax*** *(021) 887-2310* ***Rooms*** *48*

The Lanzerac is one of South Africa's finest examples of Cape Dutch architecture. It is located amid landscaped gardens and surrounded by ancient oak trees that add to the historic atmosphere. The rooms include Presidential and Royal Pool suites, the latter with its own private pool, as the name would suggest. **www.lanzerac.co.za**

STELLENBOSCH Sante Hotel and Wellness Centre ®®®®®

Simonsvlei Road, Paarl-Franschhoek Valley, 7625 ***Tel*** *(021) 875-8100* ***Fax*** *(021) 875-8111* ***Rooms*** *90*

Focusing entirely on health and lifestyle, Sante is the only African spa to feature in Taschen's eponymous art book on the subject. *Condé Nast Traveller* has also heaped praise on the establishment. The wellness centre's signature "vinotherapy", or grape cure, is said to relax, rejuvenate and de-stress. **www.santewellness.co.za**

TULBAGH De Oude Herberg ®®

6 Church Street, Tulbagh, 6820 ***Tel*** *(023) 230-0260* ***Fax*** *(023) 230-0260* ***Rooms*** *4*

Originally established in 1885, this guesthouse has been a national monument since it was rebuilt after the town's devastating 1969 earthquake. Occupying a prime position near the centre of the village, it has four double en-suite rooms decorated in a simple contemporary and elegant style. **www.deoudeherberg.co.za**

TULBAGH Rijk's Country Hotel ®®®

Middelpos Road, Tulbagh, 6820 ***Tel*** *(023) 230-1006* ***Fax*** *(023) 230-1125* ***Rooms*** *15*

On the outskirts of town and part of a new wine estate, the Rijk's offers secluded and luxurious tranquillity. Each room has its own patio overlooking the lake and pool. Three self-catering cottages are also available. Despite being a new farm, awards have already begun to come in for the wines, which are available for tasting. **www.rijks.co.za**

WELLINGTON Diemersfontein Wine and Country Estate ®®

Jan van Riebeck Drive, (R301), 7654 ***Tel*** *(021) 873-2671* ***Fax*** *(021) 864-2095* ***Rooms*** *14*

Diemersfontein has been turning heads in the wine trade since its first selection of reds in 2001. Its heavenly pinotage is now very hard to find. There is no better way to pick up a case than to go to the source. Rooms are furnished in a comfortable country style, and activities include mountain biking and horse riding. **www.diemersfontein.co.za**

WORCESTER Church Street Lodge ®®

36 Church Street, Worcester, 6850 ***Tel*** *(023) 342-5194* ***Fax*** *(023) 342-8859* ***Rooms*** *18*

Situated in the historical and most attractive part of town, Church Street Lodge offers a Roman-themed swimming pool, fountains and a serene leafy garden in which to relax. All rooms are air-conditioned, with fridges and TVs with M-Net (subscription channels). Self-catering units are also available. **www.churchst.co.za**

Key to Price Guide *see p326* **Key to Symbols** *see back cover flap*

WESTERN COASTAL TERRACE

CEDERBERG Mount Ceder ®

Grootrivier Farm, Cederberg **Tel** *(023) 317-0113* **Fax** *(023) 317-0543* **Rooms** *21*

A river etches a path through rugged mountain scenery at this Cederberg retreat. There are nine self-catering cottages available, and a small country shop is nearby, allowing guests to stock up on essentials without having to travel too far. Hiking, canoeing, bird-watching, swimming and walks are all on offer. **www.mountceder.co.za**

CITRUSDAL Treetops ®

Take Citrusdal turnoff off N7, Citrusdal, 7340 **Tel** *(022) 921-3626***Fax** *(022) 921-3626* **Rooms** *4*

Experience tranquil treetop living in these riverside cabins on stilts, connected by elevated boardwalks. One of them features a barbecue area on the verandah overlooking the Olifants River. Canoes are available for paddling down the river, and a hot spring with swimming pools is a short drive away. **www.citrusdal.info/kardouw**

CLANWILLIAM Saint du Barry's Country Lodge ®®

13 Augsberg Road, Clanwilliam, 8135 **Tel** *(027) 482-1537* **Fax** *(027) 482-2824* **Rooms** *6*

Hosts Wally and Joan foster an atmosphere of light-hearted generosity in this luxurious home away from home. Bedrooms are all en suite, with high ceilings and wooden rafters. The Saint du Barry's is highly commended by the AA, and the enchanting hospitality here leaves guests longing to return. **www.saintdubarrys.com**

CLANWILLIAM Bushmanskloof Wilderness Reserve ®®®®

Over Pakhuis Pass, towards Wuppertal, 8135 **Tel** *(021) 685-2598* **Fax** *(021) 685-5210* **Rooms** *20*

The Bushmanskloof features one of the densest concentrations of rock art in South Africa: paintings date back 10,000 years and are found on 130 separate sites. In spring, the landscape bursts with colour as wild flowers carpet the ground. Guided walks and botanical tours allow you to explore the local eco-system. **www.bushmanskloof.co.za**

LANGEBAAN The Farmhouse Hotel ®®

5 Egret Street, Langebaan, 7357 **Tel** *(022) 772-2062* **Fax** *(022) 772-1980* **Rooms** *18*

Built on the hill above the lagoon in 1860, this dignified Cape Dutch building exudes a stately charm with its reed ceilings, oversized fireplaces and majestic vistas. Stretch your legs on a hike in the adjacent nature reserve, or head out to Langebaan's bars and restaurants to experience the local culture. **www.thefarmhouselangebaan.co.za**

MOOREESBURG Sewefontein ®

Follow Palaisheuwel Road, in Piekenierskloof Pass, off N7 **Tel** *(022) 921-3301* **Fax** *(022) 921-2502* **Rooms** *2*

A working farm at the top of majestic Piekenierskloof with two self-catering houses available for hire. A great option for independent travellers on a budget, Sewefontein is also a good base from which to explore the surrounding areas of Clanwilliam and Lamberts Bay, or the Cederberg and Kouebokkeveld. **www.citrusdal.info/sewefontein/**

PIKETBERG Dunn's Castle Guesthouse ®®

R399 Veldrif Road, Piketberg, 7320 **Tel** *(022) 913-2470* **Fax** *(022) 913-3065* **Rooms** *24*

A Herbert Baker-designed home in the heart of the Swartland, the Dunns Castle has cosy rooms with a Victorian feel, each with its own fireplace. Nineteen self-catering cottages were recently added to the accommodation options. The hosts are renowned for their caring and helpful hospitality. **www.dunnscastle.8k.com**

RIEBEEK KASTEEL The Royal Hotel ®®®®

33 Main Street, Riebeeck Kasteel, 7307 **Tel** *(022) 448-1378* **Fax** *(022) 448-1073* **Rooms** *10*

Refurbished in 2005, the Royal now boasts four stars, a state-of-the-art kitchen and an outdoor amphitheatre. The fittings are of excellent quality: contemporary, but full of character. The porch has been described as "the most convivial stoep south of the Limpopo", so expect a lively atmosphere with plenty of locals. **www.royalinriebeek.com**

RIEBEEK WEST Riebeek Valley Hotel ®®

4 Dennehof Street, Riebeek West, 7306 **Tel** *(022) 461-2672* **Fax** *(022) 461-2692* **Rooms** *16*

A well-appointed country house that exudes tranquillity, the Riebeek Valley Hotel overlooks a picture-postcard valley of vineyards, with the Cederberg beyond. The en-suite bedrooms and suites are mostly spacious and adorned in a romantic fashion. High-quality fusion cuisine is served at Bishops restaurant. **www.riebeekvalleyhotel.co.za**

ST HELENA BAY The Oystercatcher Lodge ®®®

1st Avenue, Shelley Point, St Helena Bay, 7382 **Tel** *(022) 742-1202* **Fax** *(022) 742-1201* **Rooms** *6*

The Oystercatcher is quietly positioned at the water's edge and presents spellbinding views across the dunes from the private verandahs. In the spring you can watch the whales from your room, or take a stroll down to the nine-hole golf course. The decor has a Mediterranean beach house feel to it. **www.oystercatcherlodge.co.za**

VELDRIF Doornfontein Bird and Game Lodge ®

R399, Veldrif, 7368 **Tel** *(022) 783-0853* **Fax** *(022) 783-0853* **Rooms** *9*

The Doornfontein is a working farm, and hosts Nick and Petra go all out to ensure a genuine West Coast experience for their guests. A riverboat is available for bird-watching and sundowner cruises through the wetlands. Choose from rooms in the restored farmstead or the cottage adjacent to the indoor heated pool. **www.doornfonteinfarm.co.za**

VELDRIF Kersefontein Farm ®®

Between Hopefield & Velddrif, 7355 **Tel** *(022) 783-0850* **Fax** *(022) 783-0850* **Rooms** *6*

This family-run farm dates back to 1770, when it was established by settler Martin Melck. Today Julian Melck's large en-suite bedrooms are lovingly furnished with period antiques salvaged from the farm's attics. The *Architectural Digest* described the farm as "...appearing to exist in a glorious and romantic time warp". **www.kersefontein.co.za**

YZERFONTEIN Emmaus on Sea ®®

30 Versveld Street, Yzerfontein, 7351 **Tel** *(022) 451-2650* **Fax** *(022) 451-2650* **Rooms** *6*

This well-appointed retreat is only one hour's drive from Cape Town and 19 km (12 miles) from the West Coast Nature Reserve. Enjoy picturesque views over the quaint fishing harbour, long walks on unspoilt beaches, and opportunities for whale- and bird-watching. **www.emmaus.co.za**

SOUTHERN CAPE

BETTY'S BAY Buçaco Sud Guesthouse ®®

2609 Clarence Drive, Betty's Bay, 7141 **Tel** *(028) 272-9750* **Fax** *(028) 272-9750* **Rooms** *6*

Individually decorated rooms with a Provençal feel are found at this beautiful Betty's Bay guesthouse. The Kogelberg Mountains behind are South Africa's first UNESCO Biosphere Nature Reserve, while the bay in front is a popular destination for whale-watchers. One of the country's most romantic hideaways. **www.bucacosud.co.za**

BREEDE RIVER Breede River Lodge ®®

Malgas, Breede River, 6858 **Tel** *(028) 537-1631* **Fax** *(028) 537-1650* **Rooms** *23*

Located at the mouth of the Breede River, this lodge organizes a wide range of activities for its guests, from deep-sea fishing charters to skippered boat hire, spearfishing, horse riding, kayaking and quad biking. The hotel has been graded as three-star accommodation; the self-catering option has four stars. **www.breederiverlodge.co.za**

GANSBAAI Crayfish Lodge Sea and Country Guest House ®®®®

2–4 Killarney Street, De Kelders, 7220 **Tel** *(028) 384-1898* **Fax** *(028) 384-1898* **Rooms** *5*

Great sea and *fynbos* views can be enjoyed from this fine contemporary building. There is a large heated swimming pool and a sandy beach just a short stroll down the hill. The Crayfish Lodge boasts its own wellness clinic. Two luxury suites and three superior garden rooms are available, each with its own private patio. **www.crayfishlodge.co.za**

GREYTON The Greyton Lodge ®®

52 Main Road, Greyton, 7233 **Tel** *(028) 254-9800* **Fax** *(028) 254-9672* **Rooms** *15*

A former police station renovated as a series of cottages, this hotel is evocative of the unique, elegant Greyton character. The GL restaurant offers award-winning cuisine and a superb selection of local and international wines, while the adjacent gallery hosts regular exhibitions by local artists. **www.greytonlodge.com**

HERMANUS Harbour Vue ®®®

84 Westcliff Road, Hermanus, 7200 **Tel** *(028) 312-4860* **Fax** *(028) 312-4860* **Rooms** *4*

Tastefully decorated en-suite rooms with high-quality finishes in this four-star luxury B&B. Watch the whales from your bedroom, or stroll down to the cliff paths and breathe in the heady *fynbos* aromas. The dining room also features large glass panels that can be opened to enjoy the sounds of the waves crashing below. **www.harbourvue.co.za**

HERMANUS Whale Rock Lodge ®®®

26 Springfield Avenue, Westcliff, Hermanus, 7200 **Tel** *(028) 313-0014* **Fax** *(028) 313-2932* **Rooms** *11*

One of the most pristine and lovingly maintained old buildings in Hermanus, Whale Rock Lodge is covered in heavy thatch, which hints at the cosy ambience inside. Breakfast is served in the sun room, with a view over the koi pond and pool below. Water sports such as kayaking, scuba diving and fishing can be arranged. **www.whalerock.co.za**

HERMANUS The Marine ®®®®

Marine Drive, Walker Bay, Hermanus, 7200 **Tel** *(028) 313-1000* **Fax** *(028) 313-0160* **Rooms** *43*

Individually decorated bedrooms and suites, each with its own facilities, can be found here. The Marine boasts a spa and heated salt-water swimming pool in the large central courtyard. A dip in the tidal pool in front of the hotel gives the impression of swimming with the whales, which can often be seen off shore. **www.marine-hermanus.com**

MCGREGOR The Old Mill Lodge ®®

McGregor, 6708 **Tel** *(023) 625-1841* **Fax** *(023) 625-1941* **Rooms** *4*

Consisting of four cottages, each with two separate en-suite bedrooms, the Old Mill has been lovingly restored and provides a perfectly secluded spot along the world's longest wine route. A delightfully cosy bar and lounge overlooks the vineyards and the majestic Langeberg Mountains. **www.oldmilllodge.co.za**

OUDTSHOORN De Oude Meul Country Lodge ®®

Near Cango Caves, 6620 **Tel** *(044) 272-7190* **Fax** *(0)82 272-7190* **Rooms** *30*

Halfway between the Cango Caves and Oudtshoorn, in the beautiful Schoemanspoort Valley and surrounded by mountains, is the four-star De Oude Meul. Owners Boy and Marianne assure their guests of a supremely comfortable stay and a delicious ostrich steak at dinner time. **www.deoudemeul.co.za**

OUDTSHOORN Feather Nest Guest House ®®

12 Tiran Street, West Bank, Oudtshoorn, 6620 ***Tel*** *(044) 272-3782* ***Fax*** *(0)86 617-7793* ***Rooms*** *2*

Roger and Cynthia Longworth's home is comfortable, relaxed and affordable. Recline beside the pool and listen to the sound of hundreds of birds chattering in the lush foliage above, or take in the spectacular Karoo sunset with a cocktail in hand on the spacious balcony. **www.feathernest.co.za**

OUDTSHOORN La Plume Guest House ®®

Volmoed, Route R62, 6620 ***Tel*** *(044) 272-7516* ***Fax*** *(044) 272-7516* ***Rooms*** *9*

La Plume is a working ostrich and alfalfa farm with wonderful views over the Olifants River all the way to the Swartberg Mountains. Hosts Bartel and Karin offer extraordinarily warm hospitality, great service and high levels of personal attention. Winner of an AA award in 2002. **www.laplume.co.za**

OUDTSHOORN Queens Hotel ®®®

Baron van Reede Street, Oudtshoorn, 6625 ***Tel*** *(044) 272-2101* ***Fax*** *(044) 272-2104* ***Rooms*** *40*

Children are welcome at this popular Oudsthoorn hotel, the third-oldest in South Africa, having been built in colonial style in 1880. Last renovated in 2006, the Queens hotel is close to shops and restaurants in the centre of town. All 40 rooms have their own bath and shower. **www.queenshotel.co.za**

OUDTSHOORN Rosenhof Country Lodge ®®®®®

264 Baron van Reede Street, Oudtshoorn, 6625 ***Tel*** *(044) 272-2232* ***Fax*** *(044) 272-3021* ***Rooms*** *14*

A collection of antiques offsets the original exposed yellow-wood beams and ceilings. The two executive suites are separated from the main house for extra privacy, and they have their own swimming pools, too. There are excellent wellness and fitness facilities available to work off the restaurant's cordon bleu meals. **www.rosenhof.co.za**

STANFORD Mosaic Farm ®®

Hermanus Lagoon, Provincial Road, 7210 ***Tel*** *(028) 313-2814* ***Fax*** *(028) 313-2811* ***Rooms*** *9*

Mosaic Farm wraps around the edge of Stanford's Kleinrivier Lagoon. Spacious en-suite rooms under thatch and canvas are seamlessly integrated with the surroundings, which feature magnificent *fynbos*, ancient milkwood thickets and the craggy Overberg Mountains. There are many nature-related activities on offer. **www.mosaicfarm.net**

SWELLENDAM Aan de Oever Guest House ®®

21 Faure Street, Swellendam, 6740 ***Tel*** *(028) 514-1066* ***Fax*** *(028) 514-1086* ***Rooms*** *7*

Run by the friendly van de Venter family, the Aan de Oever offers spacious, open-plan rooms with simple but elegant furnishings. Casual luxury abounds in this serene location. Relax by the salt-water pool, play a round of golf on the nine-hole course or watch the birdlife through the telescope in the garden. **www.aandeoever.com**

SWELLENDAM Adin and Sharon's Hideaway ®®®

10 Hermanus Steyn Street, Swellendam, 6740 ***Tel*** *(028) 514-3316* ***Fax*** *(028) 514-3316* ***Rooms*** *3*

Adin and Sharon have been inducted into the AA Hall of Fame for their peerless hospitality and elegant cottage. Adin handmakes his own furniture and is also renowned for his delicious breakfasts. The Hideaway is often listed as one of South Africa's best guesthouses. **www.adinbb.co.za**

SWELLENDAM De Kloof Luxury Estate ®®®

8 Weltevrede Street, Swellendam, 6740 ***Tel*** *(028) 514-1303* ***Fax*** *(028) 514-1304* ***Rooms*** *6*

De Kloof offers guests daily complimentary wine tastings, as well as a cigar lounge, a pool and a fully equipped gym. Extra-long beds and oversized duvets add to the ambience of sheer indulgence in the deluxe and honeymoon suites. Chartered flights can be arranged on request for some aerial whale-watching along the coast. **www.dekloof.co.za**

SWELLENDAM Klippe Rivier ®®®®

Klippe Rivier Homestead, 6740 ***Tel*** *(028) 514-3341* ***Fax*** *(028) 514-3337* ***Rooms*** *13*

Klippe Rivier's Cape Dutch manor house lies at the end of a winding road lined with peach orchards and vineyards. The main complex is furnished with Victorian and Dutch antiques. The upstairs rooms are located under the sweet-smelling thatch, and they come with private balconies and air-conditioning as standard. **www.klipperivier.com**

GARDEN ROUTE TO GRAHAMSTOWN

ADDO Cosmos Cuisine Guesthouse ®®®

Sunland, Addo, Sundays River Valley ***Tel*** *(042) 234-0323* ***Fax*** *(042) 234-0796* ***Rooms*** *13*

Ten minutes from Addo Elephant Park, Cosmos draws visitors in with traditional country hospitality in the heart of the Sundays River Valley. The restaurant has been voted one of the best in South Africa, and its sumptuous five-course gastronomical extravaganzas are a welcome respite after a long day's game driving. **www.cosmoscuisine.co.za**

THE CRAGS Hog Hollow Country Lodge ®®®®®

Askop Road, The Crags, Plettenberg Bay, 6600 ***Tel*** *(044) 534-8879* ***Fax*** *(044) 534-8879* ***Rooms*** *15*

A unique eco-venture and a labour of love set on the edge of an indigenous forest and private nature reserve, the Hog Hollow is a little slice of paradise on the Garden Route. Beautifully decorated log cabins offer sweeping vistas of the surrounding woodlands. The superb team of friendly staff comes from the local community. **www.hog-hollow.com**

GEORGE Protea Hotel King George ®®®

King George Drive, King George Park, George, 6529 ***Tel*** *(044) 874-7659* ***Fax*** *(044) 874-7664* ***Rooms*** *64*

Close to the George Golf Course, this hotel offers attentive service and a wide range of amenities, including two swimming pools, a tennis court and a children's playground. A bowling green, squash courts and hiking trails are all nearby. There's also a terrace overlooking the majestic Outeniqua Mountain Range. **www.proteahotels.com**

GEORGE Hilltop Country Lodge ®®®®

Victoria Bay, George, 6529 ***Tel*** *(044) 889-0142* ***Fax*** *(044) 889-0199* ***Rooms*** *8*

A country guesthouse in a private reserve overlooking the Indian Ocean. The lodge layout takes full advantage of the incredible panoramas, with big windows and glass doors opening on to lawns that roll down to lush forests and the sea. Hosts Magda and Hennie will provide advice for your daytrips and meals. **www.hilltopcountrylodge.co.za**

GEORGE Fancourt Hotel and Country Club ®®®®®

Montague Street, Blanco, George, 6529 ***Tel*** *(044) 804-0000* ***Fax*** *(044) 804-0700* ***Rooms*** *146*

Cape colonial decor has been tastefully applied at the Fancourt, and a variety of restaurants offer gourmet treats for weary fairway trudgers. Facilities include two Gary Player-designed golf courses and a golf school, four tennis courts, a squash court, lawn bowls and outdoor swimming pools. **www.fancourt.co.za**

GRAHAMSTOWN The Cock House Guest House ®®

10 Market Street, Grahamstown, 6139 ***Tel*** *(046) 636-1287* ***Fax*** *(046) 636-1287* ***Rooms*** *9*

The Cock House is a G-Town landmark and former winner of the heritage category in the AA Travel Awards. The interior is adorned with yellow-wood floors, sublime fabrics and attractive antiques. The library played host to novelist André Brink, of *A Dry, White Season* fame, who wrote four of his novels here. **www.cockhouse.co.za**

GRAHAMSTOWN 7 Worcester Street ®®®®

7 Worcester Street, Grahamstown, 6139 ***Tel*** *(046) 622-2843* ***Fax*** *(046) 622-2846* ***Rooms*** *10*

This restored Victorian residence is close to the town centre, where you can enjoy many shopping opportunities, as well as numerous cultural events. Expect boutique hotel-style luxury, a warm welcome from the attentive staff and an eclectic art collection ranging from the Ming dynasty to contemporary African pieces. **www.worcesterstreet.co.za**

JEFFREY'S BAY Stratos Guest House ®®®

11 Uys Street, Jeffrey's Bay, 6330 ***Tel*** *(042) 293-1116* ***Fax*** *(042) 293-3972* ***Rooms*** *7*

On the beach at Jeffrey's Bay, renowned for its surfing waves, is this four-star guesthouse, located in a modern two-storey building. The swimming pool is heated, and the balconies afford spectacular sunrise views, as well as the chance for dolphin, whale and penguin watching. Stratos is also close to game reserves. **www.stratos-za.com**

KNYSNA Point Lodge Luxury Guest House ®®

The Point, Knysna, 6570 ***Tel*** *(044) 382-1696* ***Fax*** *(044) 382-1652* ***Rooms*** *9*

Ryk and Amanda Cloete's guesthouse offers panoramic views across the lagoon to the Knysna Heads. Point Lodge is a good base from which to explore Knysna; bicycle and canoe hire are both available. The ambience is quiet and peaceful, with a wide variety of birds to be found in the garden. **www.waterfront-lodge.co.za**

KNYSNA The Lofts ®®®

Long Street, Thesen Island, Knysna, 6570 ***Tel*** *(044) 302-5710* ***Fax*** *(044) 302-5711* ***Rooms*** *12*

This small boutique hotel is tucked away in a boatshed on Thesen Island. Amenities include a heated pool and a lounge bar. The rooms have balconies with lagoon views, and the harbour and a plethora of fine restaurants and interesting shops are a mere seven-minute walk away. **www.thelofts.co.za**

KNYSNA Belvidere Manor ®®®®

Belvidere Estate, Duthie Drive, Knysna, 6570 ***Tel*** *(044) 387-1055* ***Fax*** *(044) 387-1059* ***Rooms*** *34*

Belvidere Manor is a historic estate dating from 1834. Guests stay in free-standing serviced cottages – each with its own verandah, fireplace and overhead fan. There are extensive, rambling gardens with sweeping views of the Knysna lagoon, and the town centre is a five minute drive away. **www.belvidere.co.za**

KNYSNA St James of Knysna ®®®®

The Point, Knysna, 6570 ***Tel*** *(044) 382-6750* ***Fax*** *(044) 382-6756* ***Rooms*** *15*

A five-star country hotel on the shores of the lagoon, the St James is owner-managed and offers an exclusive retreat on the outskirts of Knysna. The emphasis here is firmly on privacy and high standards of service. Guests are afforded lots of individual attention in this hotel, which is set on a beautifully landscaped estate. **www.stjames.co.za**

MATJIESFONTEIN The Lord Milner Hotel ®®

Matjiesfontein, off the N1 Karoo, 6901 ***Tel*** *(023) 561-3011* ***Fax*** *(023) 561-3020* ***Rooms*** *58*

The Lord Milner is a well-preserved colonial vestige of what was once a glamorous Victorian spa town. In the early 1900s, this building was used as a military hospital during the Anglo-Boer War. The colonial atmosphere extends to the daily raising of the Union Jack on the turret of the hotel. **www.matjiesfontein.com**

MOSSEL BAY Linkside 2 Guesthouse ®®®

72 21st Avenue, Mossel Bay, 6506 ***Tel*** *(044) 690-4364* ***Fax*** *(086) 5599* ***Rooms*** *2*

Enjoy your stay in this beautiful guesthouse, with its breathtaking views across Mossel Bay. Breakfast is enjoyed on the patio while watching whales play in the waters below. The Mossel Bay Golf Course is situated just 800 m (half a mile) from your doorstep. **www.bellasombra.co.za**

Key to Price Guide *see p326* **Key to Symbols** *see back cover flap*

MOSSEL BAY Cheetah House ®®®

Take R328 Hartenbos/Oudtshoorn, Brandwag ***Tel*** *(044) 694-0029* ***Fax*** *(044) 694-0029* ***Rooms*** *5*

African decor, an outdoor *braaivleis* area and a heated pool are some of the attractions at Cheetah House. A variety of birdlife and buck can be spotted within the grounds. The management will be pleased to arrange activities such as game drives, deep-sea fishing, quad-bike rides and bird-watching. **www.cheetahlodge.com**

MOSSEL BAY Eight Bells Mountain Inn ®®®

Robinson Pass, R328, between Mossel Bay & Oudtshoorn ***Tel*** *(044) 631-0000* ***Fax*** *(044) 631-0004* ***Rooms*** *25*

Great bed-and-breakfast hospitality is on offer from the Brown family, who have run Eight Bells for more than 30 years. Accommodation options range from thatched rondavels, to log cabins and rooms in the main house. Horse riding and tennis courts are available on the premises. **www.eightbells.co.za**

MOSSEL BAY The Point Hotel ®®®

Point Road, The Point, Mossel Bay, 6506 ***Tel*** *(044) 691-3512* ***Fax*** *(044) 691-3513* ***Rooms*** *50*

A four-star hotel built upon the rocks below the lighthouse, The Point is a three-minute drive from Mossel Bay town and offers spectacular views of the breakers crashing on to the jagged shoreline. Whales swim by regularly in the spring. The St Blaise hiking trail that hugs the coastline starts nearby. **www.pointhotel.co.za**

PLETTENBERG BAY Anlin Place ®®

33 Roche Bonne Avenue, Plettenberg Bay, 6600 ***Tel*** *(044) 533-3694* ***Fax*** *(044) 533-3394* ***Rooms*** *6*

The Indian Ocean and white sands of Robberg Beach are only a short walk away from this guesthouse, also known as Anlin Beach House. The two apartments are fully equipped with all mod cons for self-catering. Suites are serviced daily and offer satellite TV and wireless Internet connections. Decor is contemporary African. **www.anlinplace.co.za**

PLETTENBERG BAY Crescent Budget Hotel ®®

Piesang Valley Road, Plettenberg Bay, 6600 ***Tel*** *(044) 533-3033* ***Fax*** *(044) 533-2016* ***Rooms*** *39*

Budget accommodation in Plettenberg Bay is increasingly rare, however, this established and clean hotel offers great-value B&B lodgings within walking distance of Robberg Beach. There are good recreational facilities including canoeing, pony rides, tennis and volleyball. **www.crescenthotels.com**

PLETTENBERG BAY Mallard River Lodge ®®®®

End of Rietvlei Rd, off N2, after Plettenberg Bay, 6600 ***Tel*** *(044) 533-2982* ***Fax*** *(044) 533-0687* ***Rooms*** *5*

All lodges at the Mallard River are individually and stylishly furnished and accommodate one couple each, apart from the family lodge, which sleeps four. All feature wooden decks overlooking the sprawling wildlife-rich Bitou River wetlands. Bathrooms include under-floor heating and open-air showers. **www.mallardlodge.com**

PLETTENBERG BAY Tsala Treetops Lodge ®®®®®

From Plettenberg Bay, take N2 west for 10 km, 6600 ***Tel*** *(044) 532-7818* ***Fax*** *(044) 532-7878* ***Rooms*** *10*

Tsala is a unique and luxurious forest-canopy living experience: glass-and-wood huts are perched high on stilts and connected by wooden boardwalks above the Tsitsikamma forest floor. Each treetop dwelling has its own plunge pool, fireplace and sunken bathtub. **www.hunterhotels.com**

PORT ALFRED Fort d'Acre Reserve ®®®

Box 394, Port Alfred, 6170 ***Tel*** *(082) 559-8944* ***Fax*** *(046) 675-1095* ***Rooms*** *4*

Enjoy sweeping views of both the ocean and the grassland bushveld at this exclusive private game park situated at the mouth of the Great Fish River. The thatched safari lodge is decorated with African art and artifacts. Game drives and horse trails with a qualified ranger can be organized by the management. **www.fortdacre.com**

PORT ALFRED The Halyards ®®®

Albany Road, Port Alfred, 6170 ***Tel*** *(046) 604-3300* ***Fax*** *(046) 624-2466* ***Rooms*** *36*

All guests at this New England-style landmark hotel have complimentary access to the hotel's lodge and spa on the east bank of the river, which also has an indoor heated pool. A range of activities is available, including deep-sea fishing and game drives at the Halyards-owned Mansfield Private Reserve. **www.halyardshotel.com**

PORT ELIZABETH Brighton Lodge ®®

21 Brighton Drive, Summerstrand, Port Elizabeth, 6001 ***Tel*** *(041) 583-4576* ***Fax*** *(041) 583-4104* ***Rooms*** *11*

A boutique hotel-styled establishment close to the airport and central shopping areas of the city, Brighton Lodge is positioned to cater for both leisure and business travellers. As well as Internet and fax facilities, a swimming pool and airport shuttle service are available on request. **www.brightonlodge.co.za**

PORT ELIZABETH Villa Hestia ®®

14 Tenth Avenue, Summerstrand, Port Elizabeth, 6001 ***Tel*** *(041) 583-3927* ***Fax*** *(041) 503-8513* ***Rooms*** *7*

A theme of Greek mythology runs through this guesthouse named after the goddess of the hearth and home. On the activities front, a sportfisher boat named *Chico* is on hand for guests keen to try a bit of deep-sea fishing. Other facilities include an honesty bar, a swimming pool and several built-in *braais*. **www.villahestia.co.za**

PORT ELIZABETH Beach Hotel ®®®

Marine Drive, Port Elizabeth, 6001 ***Tel*** *(041) 583-2161* ***Fax*** *(041) 583-6220* ***Rooms*** *58*

A standard hotel on Port Elizabeth's beachfront, close to shopping centres and the dolphinarium. Nearby are the famous Hobie Beach, Addo Elephant National Park and a variety of watersports and recreational activities. Non-smoking rooms, Jacuzzis and separate showers are available on request. **www.beach-hotel.co.za**

PORT ELIZABETH Hacklewood Hill Country House ®®®®

152 Prospect Road, Walmer, Port Elizabeth, 6070 **Tel** *(041) 581-1300* **Fax** *(041) 581-4155* **Rooms** *8*

A luxurious, serene and private country house full of Victorian character. All rooms have a large bathroom and several also have a balcony; the grounds include a crystal-clear pool and a tennis court. The decor is made up of rich and sumptuous colours, exquisite fabrics and a considerable antiques collection. **www.hacklewood.co.za**

PORT ELIZABETH Shamwari Game Reserve ®®®®®

R342 to Paterson, off N2, Grahamstown, 6139 **Tel** *(042) 203-1111* **Fax** *(042) 235-1224* **Rooms** *52*

The Wildlife Department at Shamwari, South Africa's leading malaria-free game reserve, has received the Global Nature Fund Award for Best Conservation Practice. The reserve and its ecosystem are meticulously maintained by a dedicated team of experts. After a long day game driving, relax at the luxury spa. **www.shamwari.com**

SEDGEFIELD Lakeside Lodge ®®

Wilderness National Park, Wilderness, 6560 **Tel** *(044) 343-1844* **Fax** *(044) 343-1844* **Rooms** *7*

An eco-tourism retreat on the banks of the Swartvlei Lake inside the Wilderness National Park. There are either lake-facing self-catering rooms or B&B accommodation. The limited number of rooms at Lakeside Lodge – and the fact that it is closed to non-residents – guarantees a private and exclusive stay. **www.lakesidelodge.co.za**

TSITSIKAMMA Tsitsikamma Lodge ®®

Storms River, Tsitsikamma, 6308 **Tel** *(042) 280-3802* **Fax** *(042) 280-3702* **Rooms** *32*

Winner of the AA Award for Best Leisure Hotel in South Africa, Tsitsikamma Lodge is comprised of a series of en-suite log cabins with access to all amenities and the resort's own spa bath. Several spectacular trails are nearby, including the famous Striptease River Trail and Indigenous Forest Trail. **www.tsitsikamma.com**

WILDERNESS Ballots Bay Coastal Lodges ®®

Victoria Bay turnoff, George Industria, 6536 **Tel** *(044) 880-1153* **Fax** *(044) 880-1153* **Rooms** *8*

Ballots Bay is a rocky cove that nestles between the steeply falling cliffs of a rugged coastline. Beautiful rustic timber homes are available for hire in this dramatic private nature reserve, the ideal retreat for nature lovers who appreciate hiking, fishing, and bird- and game-watching. There are magnificent views over the *fynbos*-covered hills.

WILDERNESS Bay Tree House ®®®

898 Eighth Avenue, Wilderness, 6560 **Tel** *(044) 877-0488* **Fax** *(044) 877-0441* **Rooms** *3*

A roomy and well-appointed five-star guesthouse set in spectacular Wilderness, the secluded heart and soul of the Garden Route. Local activities include canoeing, surf fishing, swimming, paragliding and golfing at Fancourt. The house includes under-floor heating, goose-down duvets, a spa pool and an honesty bar. **www.baytreehouse.co.za**

WILD COAST, DRAKENSBERG & MIDLANDS

BALGOWAN Granny Mouse Country House ®®®

Box 22, Balgowan, KwaZulu-Natal, 3275 **Tel** *(033) 234-4071* **Fax** *(033) 234-4429* **Rooms** *20*

The deluxe thatched cottages of Granny Mouse are found at the foot of the Drakensberg Mountains, in the heart of the Natal Midlands. Located among golf courses and battlefields, the four-star hotel has an award-winning restaurant and spa. Canopy tours, quad biking and hot-air ballooning can all be arranged. **www.grannymouse.co.za**

BARKLY EAST Reedsdell Guest Farm ®®

Box 39, Barkly East, Eastern Cape, 9786 **Tel** *(045) 974-9900* **Fax** *(045) 974-9900* **Rooms** *7*

This working holistic farm is located in mountain country, close to the highest passes of the Southern Drakensberg. The scenic surroundings, which include waterfalls, sheer cliffs, pristine grasslands and rock art, are perfect for hikers to explore. The farm organizes arts and crafts courses, as well as skiing tuition in the winter. **www.snowvalley.co.za**

BERGVILLE Mont aux Sources Hotel ®

Mont aux Sources, Bergville, 3350 **Tel** *(036) 438-6243* **Fax** *(036) 438-6566* **Rooms** *107*

The Mont aux Sources Hotel lies in the spectacular setting of the Amphitheatre area of the Drakensberg, where the Tugela River creates the second-highest waterfall in the world, plunging more than 950 m (3,000 ft). Outdoor activities include giant chess, a playground, ball games, hiking and climbing. **www.places.co.za**

BUTHA BUTHE, LESOTHO Afri-Ski Leisure Kingdom ®®

Mahlasela Pass, Lesotho **Tel** *(011) 888-8881* **Fax** *(011) 888-1263* **Rooms** *40*

The ideal destination for active holiday-makers: as well as a ski slope and lift, there is an Austrian-operated ski school, an après-ski restaurant and several bars. In the summer, facilities include the highest Gary Player golf course on earth, fishing, mountain and quad biking, rock climbing, rafting and trekking. **www.afriski.co.za**

BUTHA BUTHE, LESOTHO New Oxbow Lodge ®®

Box 60, Ficksburg, Free State, 9730 **Tel** *(051) 933-2247* **Rooms** *35*

This lodge is made up of thatched and tin-roofed rondavels on the banks of the Malibamatsoe River, in the Lesotho Maluti Mountains. This is strictly 4x4 territory, and a haven for bird-watching, hiking and climbing. There is a ski slope with equipment for hire at Mahlasela Hill, 11 km (7 miles) away. Children under 12 stay free. **www.oxbow.co.za**

Key to Price Guide *see p326* **Key to Symbols** *see back cover flap*

CHAMPAGNE VALLEY Inkosana Lodge ®

Box 60, Winterton, 3340 **Tel** *(036) 468-1202* **Fax** *(036) 468-1202* **Rooms** *15*

Surrounded by luxuriant indigenous gardens, Inkosana offers a variety of accommodation options, including dorms. Good climbing opportunities await nearby, and the lodge offers advice and guidance for climbers, as well as white-water rafting. Dinner is often a barbecue. Winner of the AA Overnight Backpackers Award. **www.inkosana.co.za**

DUNDEE Royal Country Inn ®

61 Victoria Street, Dundee, 3000 **Tel** *(034) 212-2147* **Fax** *(034) 218-2146* **Rooms** *26*

The Royal Country Inn, located on the Battlefields Route, offers a mix of well-appointed bedrooms and economical backpackers' lodgings. Hiking, bird-watching, mountain biking, abseiling and white-water rafting are all available. There are several nature reserves nearby, as well as the Zulu Cultural Experience. **www.royalcountryinn.com**

EAST LONDON Bunkers Inn ®®

23 The Drive, Bunkers Hill, East London, 5241 **Tel** *(043) 735-4642/(0)82 659-8404* **Fax** *(043) 735-1227* **Rooms** *10*

Located on a golf course in a quiet suburb, the Art Deco-style Bunkers Inn attracts visitors thanks to its proximity to game reserves and museums. A snake park, an aquarium and the beach are also nearby. There is an Internet connection in every room, and picnics can be arranged by the management. **www.portfoliocollection.com**

EAST LONDON Kennaway Hotel ®®®

Esplanade Street, Beach Front, East London, 6280 **Tel** *(043) 722-5531* **Fax** *(043) 722-5531* **Rooms** *83*

This three-star, seven-storey balconied block on the Esplanade offers a vast array of lodgings, including spacious rooms, suites, family rooms and honeymoon suites. Nearby, visitors will find a spa and an aquarium, as well as whale-watching opportunities. Township tours can also be arranged. **www.katleisure.co.za**

GONUBIE The White House ®®

10 Witthaus Street, Gonubie, Eastern Cape, 5120 **Tel** *(072) 140-0344* **Fax** *(072) 140-4898* **Rooms** *11*

Fifteen minutes from East London, on a Blue Flag beach and the Gonubie River, is this attractive accommodation four-star accommodation, which also offers self-catering rooms. Surfing, sailing, waterskiing and boating are all available. A casino and a game park are nearby. **www.wheretostay.co.za/thewhitehouse**

HOWICK Mulberry Hill Guest House ®®

Curry's Post Road, Howick, 3290 **Tel** *(033) 330-5921/(0)82 465-9978* **Fax** *(033) 330-4424* **Rooms** *6*

Located on an estate near the Howick Falls, the four-star Mulberry Hill Guest House is on the Midlands Meander Art & Craft Route. There are two trout dams for fishing enthusiasts, as well as glorious mountain views and forest walks. Riding, bird-watching, croquet, polo and golf are all available nearby. **www.mulberryhill.co.za**

LIDGETTON Pleasant Places ®®

Lidgetton Valley, KwaZulu-Natal, 3270 **Tel** *(033) 234-4396/(0)82 456-2717* **Fax** *(033) 234-4396* **Rooms** *6*

Lying in the green Natal Midlands, this thatched country house is surrounded by forests and farming country. Guests can either relax in the rambling garden or opt for more energetic pursuits in the nearby river and rapids. Nature lovers should also keep an eye out for the otters and birds that frequent this area. . **www.pleasantplaces.co.za**

MAZEPPA BAY Mazeppa Bay Hotel ®®®

Mazeppa Bay, Eastern Cape **Tel** *(047) 498-0033* **Fax** *(047) 498-0034* **Rooms** *49*

On its own island, reached by a suspension bridge, the Mazeppa Bay Hotel was completely renovated a few years ago. Thatched single-storey rooms and rondavels cluster around a central building. Among the activities available are fishing, hiking, volleyball, tennis, sandboarding and mountain biking. **www.mazeppabay.co.za**

MOOI RIVER Sycamore Avenue Treehouse ®®®

PO Box 882, Mooi River, 3310 **Tel** *(033) 263-2875* **Fax** *(033) 263-2134* **Rooms** *6*

Located in the Giants Castle area of the Drakensberg, one of the most scenic parts of KwaZulu-Natal, Sycamore Avenue offers beautifully appointed wooden pavilions up in the trees. All rooms come with with balconies and Jacuzzis. Children under 12 stay at half price; those under the age of two for free. **www.sycamore-ave.com**

MOOI RIVER Hartford House ®®®®

Giants Castle Road, Mooi River, 3300 **Tel** *(033) 263-2713* **Fax** *(033) 263-2818* **Rooms** *16*

The former home of Natal's prime minister, Hartford House is now a luxurious boutique hotel. It is surrounded by beautiful gardens and boasts a wellness centre and a helipad. The management offers guided tours of nature reserves, as well as drives and picnics to Bushman painting sites and battlefields. **www.hartford.co.za**

NEWCASTLE Newcastle Inn ®®

Cnr Hunter & Victoria Roads, Newcastle, 2940 **Tel** *(034) 312-8151* **Fax** *(034) 312-4142* **Rooms** *167*

Situated in the economic heart of KwaZulu-Natal, with views of both downtown Newcastle and luxuriant gardens, the Newcastle Inn is conveniently located for the Zululand Battlefield tour. Bird-watching, fishing and hiking are all on offer, and there is a casino nearby, as well as a golf course. **www.africanskyhotels.com**

NOTTINGHAM ROAD Rawdon's Hotel ®®

Box 7, Nottingham Road, Midlands, KwaZulu-Natal, 3280 **Tel** *(033) 266-6044* **Fax** *(033) 266-6044* **Rooms** *28*

Officially described as a "hotel and fly-fishing estate", Rawdon's Hotel provides warm, friendly hospitality in a building with a thatched roof, dormer windows and log fires. Restaurants, a coffee shop and a brewery offer welcome refreshment after activities such as tennis, bowls and volleyball. **www.rawdons.co.za**

NOTTINGHAM ROAD Fordoun Spa ®®®®

Notthingham Road, Midlands, KwaZulu-Natal, 3280 **Tel** *(033) 266-6217* **Fax** *(033) 266-6630* **Rooms** *17*

Built in the 1880s, this dairy farm amid scenic rolling grasslands was turned into a boutique hotel and restaurant. Relax in the steam room or the hydrotherapy bath. Alternatively, go fishing with the local guru, or try horse riding, hot-air ballooning or mountain biking. There is also a golf course nearby. **www.fordounspa.co.za**

PIETERMARITZBURG Hilton Hotel ®®®

Box 35, Hilton, 3245 **Tel** *(033) 343-3311* **Fax** *(033) 343-3722* **Rooms** *38*

The privately owned Hilton Hotel has been welcoming guests since 1936. Housed in a Tudor building located amid rolling green grounds, the terrace has a swimming pool, a tennis court and several *braais*, on which the hotel's speciality, sheep-on-a-spit are cooked. A good base for the Midlands Meander Art & Craft Route. **www.hiltonhotel.co.za**

PORT ST JOHNS Khululeka Retreat ®

Box 128, Port St Johns, 5120 **Tel** *(039) 253-7636* **Fax** *(086) 672-4096* **Rooms** *10*

Off the beaten track, the Khululeka Retreat offers catered or self-catering cottages in indigenous forest on a hill with views of the sea and the estuary of the Ntafufu River. Meet the local tribal people, visit the Magwa tea plantation or the Isinuka sulphur springs. Fishing, whale-watching, hiking and biking are all available. **www.khululekaretreat.co.za**

PORT ST JOHNS Umzimvubu Retreat ®®

380 Golf Course Drive, First Beach, Port St Johns, 5120 **Tel** *(047) 564-1741* **Fax** *(047) 564-1310* **Rooms** *11*

This recently restored guesthouse is within walking distance of the town centre. Overlooking the mouth of the Great Unzimvubu River and the Indian Ocean, the three-star Umzimvubu is ideally located for exploring the Wild Coast. Enjoy local crafts, angling, canoeing, biking and forest trails. **www.geocities.com/umzimvuburetreat**

PORT ST JOHNS Umngazi River Bungalows ®®®

Box 75, Port St Johns, Wild Coast, 5120 **Tel** *(047) 564-1115/19* **Fax** *(031) 701-7006* **Rooms** *64*

Spacious thatched bungalows, a spa and fresh local food are just some of the reasons for staying here. Add pristine beaches, breathtaking views, indigenous forests and mangrove swamps, and the Umngazi River Bungalows becomes a very appealing proposition. Activities include fishing, tennis, snooker and table tennis. **www.umngazi.co.za**

QOLORA MOUTH Trennery's ®®®

Southern Wild Coast, Eastern Cape, 4960 **Tel** *(047) 498-0004/(0)82 908-3134* **Fax** *(047) 498-0011* **Rooms** *37*

Thatched rondavels and bungalows provide the accommodation in lush, tropical gardens close to the lagoon and the river. Among the activities on offer are tennis, bowls, golf, sailing, fishing, 4x4 adventures and sea cruises. Saturday nights see Trennery's famous Seafood Extravaganza. A good place for children. **www.trennerys.co.za**

RORKE'S DRIFT Fugitives' Drift Lodge ®®®®®

PO Rorke's Drift, KwaZulu-Natal, 3016 **Tel** *(034) 271-8051/(034) 642-1843* **Fax** *(034) 271-8053* **Rooms** *17*

David and Nick Rattray are pioneers of historical tourism, and their stylish guesthouse plays host to an impressive collection of Zulu and Anglo-Boer war-related memorabilia. The lodge is located in a vast malaria-free nature reserve with abundant wildlife, including zebras, giraffes and over 250 species of bird. **www.fugitives-drift-lodge.com**

WINTERTON Dragon Peaks Mountain Resort ®®

PO Winterton, 3340 **Tel** *(036) 468-1031* **Fax** *(036) 468-1104* **Rooms** *30*

Choose between B&B and self-catering accommodation at this family- and pet-friendly resort. Cottages, chalets and campsites are located in the shadow of Champagne Castle, the second-highest peak in South Africa, and the Cathkin Mountains in the Ukhahlamba World Heritage Site. A game reserve is nearby. **www.dragonpeaks.com**

WINTERTON Cathedral Peak Hotel ®®®®®

Winterton, Drakensberg, KwaZulu-Natal, 3340 **Tel** *(036) 488-1888* **Fax** *(036) 488-1889* **Rooms** *94*

A collection of thatched buildings on a hillside in the Drakensberg, this three-star hotel was started in 1939 and renovated in 2001. Located in a dramatic setting, it has a wedding chapel among its facilities, along with a helicopter pad, children's programmes, biking, fishing, riding and hiking trails. **www.cathedralpeak.co.za**

DURBAN AND ZULULAND

BALLITO Dolphin Holiday Resort ®®

Compensation Road, Dophin Crescent, Ballito, 4420 **Tel** *(032) 946-2187* **Fax** *(032) 946-3490* **Rooms** *16*

This informal resort with cottages, caravan stands and campsites is situated in a peaceful forest north of Durban. Shopping facilities, beaches, golf and restaurants are all available nearby. Outdoor chess, volleyball, trampolines and a playground make it a great destination for families with young children. **www.dolphinholidayresort.co.za**

BALLITO Izulu Hotel ®®®®®

Rey's Place, Ballito, 4420 **Tel** *(032) 946-3444* **Fax** *(032) 946-3494* **Rooms** *18*

The five-star Izulu Hotel is a mere five-minute walk from the sea and offers splendid views of subtropical dunes. Relax in the luxuriously appointed beauty spa, or take part in more active pursuits such as visits to the nearby crocodile farm, animal reserve, and historic and cultural sites, including battlefields. **www.hotelizulu.com**

Key to Price Guide *see p326* **Key to Symbols** *see back cover flap*

DOLPHIN COAST The Lodge at Prince's Grant ®®®®

Prince's Grant, Dolphin Coast, 4404 **Tel** *(032) 482-0005* **Fax** *(032) 482-0040* **Rooms** *15*

The four-star Lodge at Prince's Grant is situated on the KwaZulu-Natal golf estate, in the vicinity of other golf courses. As well as a private lagoon, guests can enjoy the beautiful unspoilt coastline near Rorke's Drift, not to mention the stunning views of the Indian Ocean. **www.princesgrantlodge.co.za**

DURBAN Garden Court South Beach ®

73 Marine Parade, Durban, 4001 **Tel** *(031) 337-2231* **Fax** *(031) 337-4640* **Rooms** *414*

A modern Art Deco building on the beach, close to the city centre and several attractions, including the Umaa Masjid Mosque (the largest in the southern hemisphere), the Indian market, the Botanical Gardens and the BAT Arts Centre. The rooms are standard but well turned out, with coffee- and tea-making facilities. **www.southernsun.com**

DURBAN 164 Guest House ®®

164 St Thomas Road, Musgrave, Berea, Durban, 4001 **Tel** *(031) 201-4493* **Fax** *(031) 201-4496* **Rooms** *7*

In the heart of trendy Musgrave, the 164 benefits from its proximity to boutiques, cafés, shops and bars. Built in 1928 in luxurious colonial style, this five-star guesthouse also offers self-catering cottages. A wealth of activities, such as riding, cycling, fishing, golf, bird-watching and paragliding, is available nearby. **www.164.co.za**

DURBAN Protea Hotel Edward ®®

149 Marine Parade, Durban, 4001 **Tel** *(031) 337-3681* **Fax** *(031) 332-1692* **Rooms** *101*

This elegant four-star hotel on the Golden Mile is located within walking distance from Durban's central business district, the convention centre, the casino and the shops. Built in 1911, the Edward has been constantly updated. It features an internationally recognized restaurant. Children under 12 stay free. **www.proteahotels.com**

DURBAN Riviera Hotel ®®

127 Victoria Embankment, Durban, 4001 **Tel** *(031) 301-3681* **Fax** *(031) 301-3681* **Rooms** *66*

A modern low-budget option on the edge of the central business district, the Riviera is located opposite the yacht harbour, near the BAT Arts Centre, and five minutes' drive from the convention centre, the Marine World and the casino. Rooms are simple but clean and comfortable, and many have sea views. **www.sa-venues.com/kzn/riviera**

DURBAN Elangeni Hotel ®®®

63 Snell Parade, Durban, 4001 **Tel** *(031) 362-1300* **Fax** *(031) 332-5527* **Rooms** *447*

Part of the Southern Sun group, the fashionable Elangeni is situated on the beach, within walking distance from shops and restaurants, and close to attractions such as Durban's Snake Park, Seaworld and a flea market. Tennis, bowling, squash, fishing and windsurfing can be arranged by the management. **www.southernsun.com**

DURBAN North Beach Hotel ®®®

83 Snell Parade, Durban, 4001 **Tel** *(031) 332-7361* **Fax** *(031) 337-4058* **Rooms** *295*

North Beach is a world-famous surfers' paradise, but within walking distance of this three-star establishment you will also find museums and art galleries. The hotel is close to the convention centre, Durban's Snake Park and Mini Town. A pool on the 32nd floor offers amazing views of the Indian Ocean. **www.southernsun.com**

DURBAN Audacia Manor ®®®®

11 Sir Arthur Road, Morningside, 4001 **Tel** *(031) 303-9520* **Fax** *(031) 303-2763* **Rooms** *101*

Built in 1928, this restored family home in a secluded cul-de-sac is a grand dame of the Durban hotel scene, exuding a genteel charm. Sit in the drawing room or on the Arts and Crafts-style verandah, cooled by the breezes of the Berea. Among the services on offer are a beautician, chauffeur service and croquet on the lawn. **www.audaciamanor.com**

DURBAN City Lodge ®®®®

Old Fort/Brickhill Roads, Durban, 4001 **Tel** *(031) 332-1447* **Fax** *(031) 332-1483* **Rooms** *160*

This reliable chain hotel strikes the right balance between corporate and leisure hospitality. City Lodge is centrally located and is only a couple of minutes from relaxing beaches and the convention and exhibition centres. Although the rooms are basic luscious gardens and a swimming pool add to the appeal. **www.citylodge.co.za**

DURBAN Quarters Hotel ®®®®

101 Florida Road, Morningside, 4001 **Tel** *(031) 303-5246* **Fax** *(031) 303-5269* **Rooms** *24*

Four gracious Victorian houses provide a successful combination of Old World charm and modern sophistication. The rooms are exquisitely appointed, with balconies, air-conditioning and double-glazed windows, and the Brasserie Restaurant offers a wide-ranging menu. Minutes from the sea and the city's dining district. **www.quarters.co.za**

DURBAN Royal Hotel ®®®®

267 Smith Street, Durban, 4001 **Tel** *(031) 333-6000* **Fax** *(031) 333-6002* **Rooms** *213*

This 150-year-old grand hotel in Durban's city centre is decorated with warm indigenous yellow wood and blue tones. The butler service adds a touch of luxurious sophistication, and there is a women-only floor, massage and sauna facilities. Six restaurants, three bars and a yacht harbour all contribute to the appeal. **www.theroyal.co.za**

ESHOWE Shakaland ®®®®

Normanhurst Farm, Nkwalini, Eshowe, 3816 **Tel** *(035) 460-0912* **Fax** *(035) 460-0824* **Rooms** *48*

Experience the disappearing Zulu culture at this resort overlooking Umhlatuze Lake. Shakaland is an authentic re-creation of a historic Zulu village, Shaka's Great Kraal. Guests stay in traditional beehive huts and enjoy Zulu activities such as tribal dancing, spear-making, beadwork and a beer-drinking ceremony. **www.shakaland.com**

HLUHLUWE Zululand Tree Lodge ®®®®®

PO Box 116, Hluhluwe, 3960 **Tel** *(035) 562-1020/(0)82 902-5972* **Fax** *(035) 562-1032* **Rooms** *48*

Enjoy an unusual accommodation experience in these thatched houses on stilts in a fever-tree forest, part of the Ubizane Game Reserve. Each tree lodge includes a luxury bedroom, en-suite bathroom and private balcony. Guided bush walks and drives, boat cruises, bird-watching and cheetah projects can all be arranged. **www.threecities.co.za**

KOSI BAY Rocktail Bay Lodge ®®®®®

Manguzi, Kosi Bay, KwaZulu-Natal, 3886 **Tel** *(021) 424-1037* **Fax** *(021) 424-1036* **Rooms** *11*

Located in the Greater St Lucia Wetland Park, Rocktail Bay Lodge has easy access to 29 km (18 miles) of ocean coast. The Maputaland Marine Reserve lies just offshore, providing unique diving and snorkelling opportunities. Accommodation is in thatched tree-house chalets with balcony and en-suite bathrooms. **www.wilderness-safaris.com**

LINKHILLS Zimbali Lodge & Country Club ®®®®®

PO Box 943, Linkhills, 3652 **Tel** *(031) 765-4446* **Fax** *(031) 765-4446* **Rooms** *76*

A five-star boutique hotel overlooking the Indian Ocean and set within a conservation area rich in local flora and fauna. The luxurious rooms are located in lodges with viewing decks and furnished with wooden furniture. Bird- and butterfly-watching, golf, horse riding and swimming are just some of the activities on offer. **www.zimbali.org**

NORTH KWAZULU White Elephant Safari Lodge & Bush Camp ®®®®®

Pongola Game Reserve, North KwaZulu **Tel** *(034) 413-2489/(0)82 945-7173* **Fax** *(034) 413-2499* **Rooms** *8*

Surrounded by the majestic Lebombo Mountains and Lake Jozini are these eight luxury safari tents, all featuring private verandahs, bathrooms with views and outdoor showers. The Kors family are conservation pioneers and organize elephant-viewing programmes, game drives and bush walks. **www.whiteelephant.co.za**

SAN LAMEER Mondazur Resort Estate Hotel ®®®®

Old Main Road, San Lameer, 4277 **Tel** *(011) 679-2994* **Fax** *(086) 511-6122* **Rooms** *40*

The beneficiary of a recent multimillion-rand renovation, this resort hotel is located on a lagoon on the Indian Ocean. Mondazur is a great option for a beach holiday, but it also has plenty to keep more active guests happy: abundant wildlife, boat rides, tennis courts, a golf course, volleyball and squash. **www.kwazuluhotelguide.co.za**

SOUTH COAST Rock Inn Backpackers ®

835 Tegwan Road, Ramsgate, 4285 **Tel** *(039) 314-4837* **Fax** *(039) 314-4393* **Rooms** *8*

The young and active are the target audience of this century-old stone lodge located on a scenic stretch of the coastline. Nearby areas to explore include beaches, the Ramsgate lagoon, a river and the tropical nature reserve in a malaria-free area. Sea kayaking, horse riding and PADI dive courses are available to guests. **www.sa-venues.com**

UMHLANGA ROCKS The Oyster Box ®®®®

2 Lighthouse Road, Umhlanga Rocks, 4319 **Tel** *(031) 561-2233* **Fax** *(031) 561-4072* **Rooms** *72*

This Art Deco building from the 1930s has been renovated and extended, but it maintains its original atmosphere of old-fashioned elegance. Right on the beach, and featuring its own lighthouse, The Oyster Box is also close to the city centre and its amenities. The hotel is famous for high tea and oysters served in many ways. **www.oysterbox.co.za**

UMHLANGA ROCKS Beverly Hills Hotel ®®®®®

Lighthouse Road, Umhlanga Rocks, 4320 **Tel** *(031) 561-2211* **Fax** *(031) 561-3711* **Rooms** *88*

A favourite luxurious modern hotel on the seafront, with superb views of the Indian Ocean and miles of unspoilt beaches within easy access. The recently refurbished rooms are decorated in brown and cream tones; the suites have rich suede and leather furnishings and plasma TV screens. Close to amenities and shops. **www.southernsun.com**

GAUTENG AND SUN CITY

DUNKELD Backpackers Ritz ®

1a North Road, Dunkeld, 2196 **Tel** *(011) 325-7125* **Fax** *(011) 325-2521* **Rooms** *15*

Basic accommodation, friendly service and tourist tips are available at the Backpackers Ritz, the longest-established hostel in Johannesburg. Located in a beautiful mansion on a large property, part of which was a fort during the Anglo-Boer War, it boasts a swimming pool, a bar and pretty views. Ample parking. **www.backpackingafrica.com**

DUNKELD Ten Bompas ®®®®®

10 Bompas Rd, Dunkeld, 2196 **Tel** *(011) 325-2442* **Fax** *(011) 341-0281* **Rooms** *10*

Ten suites, each individually decorated by a different interior designer with their own interpretation of "Home from Home in Africa". Neutral colours and cherrywood furniture are used throughout. The restaurant serves classic dishes and old home favourites. A magnificent wine cellar overlooks the swimming pool. **www.tenbompas.com**

EASTERN SUBURBS Brown Sugar Backpackers ®

75 Observatory Avenue, 2198 **Tel** *(011) 648-7397* **Fax** *(011) 648-7138* **Rooms** *10*

This "castle-like" mansion was built by a Mozambiquan mafioso in the 1970s. Rooms are clean and comfortable, and many offer great views of Johannesburg. In-house entertainment includes a bar, a pool table and a swimming pool; the Bruma flea market and Johannesburg International Airport are nearby. **www.brownsugar.web.za**

Key to Price Guide *see p326* **Key to Symbols** *see back cover flap*

FOURWAYS Inchanga Ranch Resort ®

Inchanga Road, 2021 ***Tel*** *(011) 708-1304* ***Fax*** *(011) 798-1310* ***Rooms*** *12*

Located in the Northern Suburbs, Johannesburg's only resort hotel is a charming horse ranch with a swimming pool, Jacuzzi and tennis courts. Choose to stay in luxury chalets, en-suite log cabins or the 100-year-old ranch house. Hear lions from the nearby Lion Park roar, and bird-watch by the picturesque river. **www.inchangaresort.co.za**

FOURWAYS Palazzo Intercontinental Montecasino ®®®®®

Montecasino Blvd, 2021 ***Tel*** *(011) 510-3000* ***Fax*** *(011) 510-4001* ***Rooms*** *246*

This Tuscan-style villa built in 2000 in the upmarket suburb of Fourways, close to the major highways, houses a massive gaming, leisure, entertainment and retail complex. Landscaped gardens and water features help conjure a feeling of peace and tranquillity. The acclaimed restaurant serves international dishes. **www.interconti.com**

HARTEBEESPOORT Leopard Lodge ®®®

Box 400, Broederstroom, 0240 ***Tel*** *(012) 207-1130* ***Fax*** *(012) 207-1158* ***Rooms*** *14*

Leopard Lodge offers visitors the full bush experience, including game drives, bush walks and a bush *boma*. Two swimming pools are available, as well as a bird-watching deck and an African-style pub. The restaurant overlooks the Hartebeespoort Dam, where you can enjoy a wide range of watersports. **www.leopardlodge.co.za**

JOHANNESBURG The Westcliff ®®®®®

67 Jan Smuts Avenue, 2193 ***Tel*** *(011) 481-6000* ***Fax*** *(011) 481-6010* ***Rooms*** *117*

Created in the image of a Mediterranean village, with cobbled pathways, fountains and lush greenery cascading down the hillside, The Westcliff offers high luxury and impeccable service, as well as sweeping views of Johannesburg. A club-car service is available to transport guests around the property. **www.westcliff.co.za**

KEMPTON PARK InterContinental Airport Sun ®®®®®

Johannesburg International Airport, 1620 ***Tel*** *(011) 961-5400* ***Fax*** *(011) 961-5401* ***Rooms*** *138*

Conveniently situated within walking distance from the terminals of Or Thambo International Airport outside of Johannesburg. Special features for travellers include in-room flight information, a health spa to ease the stress of travel and an indoor heated swimming pool with a panoramic view over Johannesburg. **www.southernsun.com**

MAGALIESBERG Lesedi African Lodge ®

Box 699, Lanseria, 1748 ***Tel*** *(012) 205-1394* ***Fax*** *(012) 205-1433* ***Rooms*** *30*

A unique and powerful experience, Lesedi African lodge consists of five villages, each with a different cultural theme (Zulu, Sotho, Xhosa, Pedi, Ndebele) and decorated accordingly. In the evenings, guests can witness or take part in singing, dancing and storytelling. Don't miss out on the Ndebele craft market and shop. **www.lesedi.com**

MAGALIESBERG Hunters Rest ®®®®

Box 775, Rustenburg, 0300 ***Tel*** *(014) 537-2140* ***Fax*** *(014) 537-2661* ***Rooms*** *91*

An extensive resort with excellent recreational facilities, including golf, tennis, game drives, quad bikes, hiking, dancing, heated pools and games room. Little ones can be kept entertained at the children's barnyard, and there is even a crèche on site. Weekend highlights include a Saturday lunch *braai* at the pool. **www.huntersrest.co.za**

MAGALIESBERG Mount Grace Country House & Spa ®®®®®

Old Rustenberg Road, R24, 2805 ***Tel*** *(014) 577-1350* ***Fax*** *(014) 577-1202* ***Rooms*** *81*

Elegant yet unpretentious country retreat located in 4 hectares (10 acres) of gardens. English country-style decor dominates in the stone-and-thatch bedrooms with private patios. Enjoy swimming, fishing, bird-watching, croquet and walking. A good spa, delightful cuisine and an excellent wine list add to the experience. **www.grace.co.za**

MELROSE Premiere Classe Furnished Apartments ®®

62 Corlett Drive, Melrose, 2196 ***Tel*** *(011) 788-1967* ***Fax*** *(011) 788-1971* ***Rooms*** *30*

Centrally located, this affordable, self-catering apartment hotel is suitable for both short- and long-term stays. Serviced daily, the lodgings consist of fully equipped kitchen, lounge and dining area. Telephone and subscription TV are also available, and you can arrange for breakfast to be served in the apartment. **www.premiereclasse.co.za**

MELROSE Protea Wanderers Hotel ®®®®

Cnr Corlett Drive & Rudd Road, Melrose, 2196 ***Tel*** *(011) 770-5500* ***Fax*** *(011) 770-5555* ***Rooms*** *229*

Part of the Protea Hotels group, the Wanderers Hotel offers comfortable rooms within close proximity to all business and entertainment centres. Just around the corner is the hi-tech Planet Fitness Gym, open 24 hours. Little homely touches include a fresh apple placed in each guest room every day. **www.proteahotels.com**

MELROSE Melrose Arch Hotel ®®®®®

1 Melrose Square, Melrose Arch, 2196 ***Tel*** *(011) 214-6666* ***Fax*** *(011) 214-6600* ***Rooms*** *118*

Situated in the secure urban Melrose Arch lifestyle development, this hip five-star hotel offers designer decor with warm, natural tones and mood-enhancing lighting. The stylish restaurant provides a fusion of tastes from around the world. Sink into one of the inviting leather couches at the library bar. **www.africanpridehotels.com**

MELVILLE Pension Idube ®

11 Walton Avenue, Melville, 2092 ***Tel*** *(011) 482-4055* ***Rooms*** *7*

An ideal option for budget travellers to Johannesburg. Accommodation at the Idube has personal touches by the owner, who lives on site. Facilities include a sparkling pool and patio area, fully equipped kitchen for self-catering guests, laundry service and TV lounge. Game drives can be organized on request. **www.pensionidube.co.za**

MELVILLE Die Agterplaas B&B ®®

66 Sixth Avenue, 2092 ***Tel*** *(011) 726-8452* ***Fax*** *(0)86 616-8456* ***Rooms*** *10*

Homely accommodation at the foot of the historical Melville Koppies, a short walk from the eclectic restaurants and shops of Melville. In addition to the en-suite rooms, a spacious cottage is available for longer stays. Badia's coffee shop offers delicious *bobotie* and *biryani*. **www.agterplaas.co.za**

MIDRAND The Manor Inn Country House ®®®

5 Begonia Rd, Kylami, 1684 ***Tel*** *(011) 702-1187* ***Fax*** *(011) 702-1183* ***Rooms*** *16*

This Tudor-style home provides charming accommodation. Its spacious surroundings and the presence of several dogs and cats contribute to the relaxed atmosphere. The cosy dining room offers home-cooked meals, but only takes bookings. The hotel is two minutes from the Kylami Race Track. **www.themanorinn.co.za**

MULDERSDRIFT Misty Hills Country Hotel, Conference Centre & Spa ®®®

69 Drift Boulevard Road, 1747 ***Tel*** *(011) 950-6000* ***Fax*** *(011) 957-3212* ***Rooms*** *151*

Located between Johannesburg and Pretoria/Tshwane, Misty Hills offers accommodation in stone-built thatched rooms. The restaurant is well known for its charcoal-grilled game and other traditional local meats, skewered on swords and cooked over an open fire. **www.rali.co.za**

MULDERSDRIFT Avianto ®®®®

Driefontein Road, 1747 ***Tel*** *(011) 668-3000* ***Fax*** *(011) 668-3060* ***Rooms*** *34*

Nestled along the Crocodile River is this stylish yet unpretentious hotel with a distinctive Tuscan character. Romantic touches include a calming sprig of fresh lavender on your pillow at turndown. Golf fans may want to try Qolf, a fun, challenging lawn game that combines golf and croquet. **www.avianto.co.za**

NORWOOD Garden Place ®®

53 Garden Road, Orchards, 2192 ***Tel*** *(011) 485-3800* ***Fax*** *(011) 485-3802* ***Rooms*** *25*

Garden Place provides comfortable self-catering accommodation with fully equipped kitchens. There is a communal breakfast room for those who prefer to mingle. Located near the trendy suburb of Norwood, it is a great place to relax, with a pretty tree-filled garden. A free shuttle service to surrounding areas is available. **www.gardenplace.co.za**

ORMONDE Protea Hotel Gold Reef City ®®®

Shaft 14, Northern Parkway, 2159 ***Tel*** *(011) 248-5700* ***Fax*** *(011) 248-5791* ***Rooms*** *74*

Set in a mining theme park, this Victorian-style hotel offers an experience reminiscent of a bygone era with all modern amenities. Each of the en-suite rooms is uniquely decorated and themed. Gold Reef City will keep children happily entertained with rides, clowns and other entertaining diversions. **www.proteahotels.com/goldreefcity**

PILANESBERG Bakubung Game Lodge ®®®®®

Box 294, Sun City, 0136 ***Tel*** *(014) 552-6000* ***Fax*** *(014) 552-6080* ***Rooms*** *76*

En-suite chalets on the edge of the malaria-free Pilanesberg National Park, which is situated in an ancient volcanic crater. View lions, leopards, cheetahs and a variety of antelope during game drives. There is also a regular shuttle bus to Sun City, where you can visit a crocodile farm, a casino and several theatres and cinemas. **www.legacyhotels.co.za**

PILANESBERG Kwa Maritane Bush Lodge ®®®®®

Pilanesberg National Park, Sun City, 0316 ***Tel*** *(014) 552-5100* ***Fax*** *(014) 552-5333* ***Rooms*** *143*

Luxury suites and self-catering chalets and cabanas on the doorstep of Pilanesberg National Park. Kwa Maritane is a particularly child-friendly resort, with a playground, trampoline, floodlit bush putt, outdoor chess board and water slide. Grown-ups will enjoy activities such as volleyball, tennis and swimming. **www.legacyhotels.co.za**

PILANESBERG Tshukudu Bush Lodge ®®®®®

Box 6805, Rustenburg, 0300 ***Tel*** *(014) 552-6255* ***Fax*** *(014) 552-6266* ***Rooms*** *13*

Built high on a hilltop, the six private luxury cottages offer a view of Pilanesberg National Park's bush and a waterhole where wild animals gather to drink. Cool off in the rock plunge pool in the daytime, and gather by the fire for dinner. The hotel offers twice-daily game drives and morning game walks. **www.legacyhotels.co.za**

PRETORIA/TSHWANE La Maison Guesthouse ®®

235 Hilda Street, Hatfield, 0083 ***Tel*** *(012) 430-4341* ***Fax*** *(012) 342-1531* ***Rooms*** *6*

Located close to the Hatfield Shopping Centre, this inviting guesthouse boasts a long tradition of excellence. Enjoy the views from the rooftop patio or sip a cocktail by the pool. Gustav Klimt fans will enjoy the ambience in one of the dining rooms, which features a mural depicting the Austrian artist's famous *Kiss*. **www.lamaison.co.za**

PRETORIA/TSHWANE Oxnead Guesthouse ®®

Marnewick Street, Moreleta Park, 0044 ***Tel*** *(012) 993-4515* ***Fax*** *(012) 998-9168* ***Rooms*** *9*

One of the first guesthouses established in Pretoria/Tshwane, this Cape Georgian-style manor is located in a quiet and safe suburb of the city. Most of the tastefully decorated rooms have kitchen facilities and private entrances. There is easy access to a driving range for golfing enthusiasts. **www.oxnead.co.za**

PRETORIA/TSHWANE Kievits Kroon Country Estate ®®®

Plot 41, Reier Road, Kameeldrift East, 0035 ***Tel*** *(012) 808-0150* ***Fax*** *(012) 808-0148* ***Rooms*** *99*

This Cape Dutch-inspired estate, situated in the beautiful Kameeldrift Valley, is an ideal romantic getaway. The Kievits Kroon prides itself on its catering options, which range from fine dining at the elegant restaurant to picnic baskets by the poolside. Also on offer is a state-of-the-art spa. **www.kievitskroon.co.za**

Key to Price Guide *see p326* **Key to Symbols** *see back cover flap*

PRETORIA/TSHWANE Illyria House ®®®®®

37 Bourke Street, Muckleneuk, 0002 **Tel** *(012) 344-5193* **Fax** *(012) 344-3978* **Rooms** *6*

A magnificent colonial manor boasting fine antiques, 17th-century tapestries and exquisite cuisine. Guests will enjoy the enchanting colonial lifestyle with white-gloved butlers and classical music playing in the background. Take advantage of the pampering beauty treatments in one of the wooden treatment rooms in the garden. **www.illyria.co.za**

ROSEBANK Grace in Rosebank ®®®®®

54 Bath Avenue, Rosebank, 2196 **Tel** *(011) 280-7300* **Fax** *(011) 280-7333* **Rooms** *73*

This independent five-star hotel is set in a vibrant, cosmopolitan area, with a covered, elevated walkway linking the hotel to The Mall of Rosebank, with its many shopping options. The dining room's unpretentious yet creative menu, the tranquil roof garden and outdoor heated pool make this elegant hotel a favourite. **www.thegrace.co.za**

SANDTON City Lodge Morningside ®®

Cnr Rivonia & Hill Roads, Sandton, 2146 **Tel** *(011) 884-9500* **Fax** *(011) 884-9440* **Rooms** *160*

Affordable quality accommodation is on offer at this elegant outpost of the City Lodge family. The hotel is situated in the heart of one of Johannesburg's most fashionable suburbs, close to major highways, exclusive shops and restaurants. Children sharing a room with their parents stay free. **www.citylodge.co.za**

SANDTON Melleney's Exclusive Guest House ®®

149 12th Avenue, Rivonia, 2128 **Tel** *(011) 803-1099* **Fax** *(011) 803-1190* **Rooms** *8*

An exclusive guesthouse close to the shops and restaurants in Rivonia. One of the highlights at Melleney's is the salt-water pool, which enables guests to experience a rare taste of the ocean inland. The recently renovated pub offers a friendly, relaxed atmosphere. **www.melleneys.co.za**

SANDTON Zulu Nyala Country Manor ®®®

70e Third Road, Chartwell, 2146 **Tel** *(011) 708-1969* **Fax** *(011) 708-2220* **Rooms** *30*

This thatched country manor in beautifully landscaped gardens is a mere ten-minute drive from Johannesburg and offers comfortable, spacious rooms and warm hospitality. The popular Lion Park is so close that, according to the hotel's website, you will probably hear the lions roar at night. **www.zulunyala.com**

SANDTON Protea Hotel Balalaika ®®®®

20 Maude Street, Sandton, 2196 **Tel** *(011) 322-5000* **Fax** *(011) 322-5022* **Rooms** *330*

A tranquil hotel in the heart of Sandton, the Balalaika features two private gardens and two swimming pools. The recently refurbished hotel is located at the heart of a vibrant shopping hub that includes the Sandton shopping complexes, the mall at the waterfront and the Oriental Plaza. **www.proteahotels.com/balalaika**

SANDTON Fairlawns Boutique Hotel & Spa ®®®®®

Alma Road, off Bowling Avenue, Sandton, 2191 **Tel** *(011) 804-2540* **Fax** *(011) 802-7261* **Rooms** *19*

This elegant boutique hotel was built on one of the original homesteads of the area and is inspired by the romantic architecture of 18th-century Europe. Fairlawns' cellar is renowned for the rare and vintage wines on offer, and the hotel's list appears regularly at the Diners Club's Wine List of the Year Award. **www.fairlawns.co.za**

SANDTON Michelangelo ®®®®®

135 West Street, Sandton, 2128 **Tel** *(011) 282-7000* **Fax** *(011) 282-7172* **Rooms** *242*

A member of The Leading Hotels of the World, this prestigious five-star Renaissance-style hotel is set in a piazza surrounded by many upmarket shops and restaurants. Expect discreet service and the sort of attention to detail typical of such a top-class hotel. Gourmet African cuisine is on offer in the restaurant. **www.michelangelo.co.za**

SANDTON Saxon Hotel & Spa ®®®®®

36 Saxon Road, Sandton, 2132 **Tel** *(011) 292-6000* **Fax** *(011) 292-6001* **Rooms** *24*

Set in tranquil, tree-lined Sandhurst, a five-minute drive from Sandton City, this lush boutique hotel and spa sits on 2 hectares (6 acres) of landscaped gardens and epitomizes tasteful African elegance. For total relaxation, try the signature sound therapy at the world-class spa. **www.thesaxon.com**

SUN CITY Cascades, Sun City Hotel and Cabanas ®®®®

Box 2, Sun City, 0316 **Tel** *(011) 780-7800* **Fax** *(011) 780-7443* **Rooms** *962*

Accommodation is split between three different venues at this massive five-star complex close to Sun City's casino and entertainment centre. The luxury rooms are decorated in ochre and yellow tones and feature dark-stained furniture, while the cabanas are particularly suitable for families with children. **www.suninternational.com**

SUN CITY The Palace of the Lost City ®®®®®

Box 308, Sun City, 0316 **Tel** *(014) 557-1000* **Fax** *(014) 557-3111* **Rooms** *338*

Masterminded by entrepreneur Sol Kerzner, this hotel recreates an ancient African fantasy temple rising out of a subtropical jungle. The grand architecture is complemented by animal statuary and exotic works of art. The water park, The Valley of the Waves, is a fun treat for children. **www.suninternational.com**

VEREENIGING Riviera on Vaal ®®®®

Mario Milani Drive, Vereeniging, 1930 **Tel** *(016) 420-1300* **Fax** *(016) 420-1301* **Rooms** *89*

This well-appointed boutique hotel is situated on the banks of the Vaal River, in close proximity to Johannesburg, and it caters to both corporate and leisure travellers. Each of the rooms boasts expansive panoramic river views. The hotel's well-known floating restaurant offers guests a unique dining experience. **www.rivieraonvaal.co.za**

BLYDE RIVER CANYON AND KRUGER

DULLSTROOM Walkersons ®®®

Walkersons Private Estate, Dullstroom, 1110 ***Tel*** *(013) 253-7000* ***Fax*** *(013) 253-7230* ***Rooms*** *24*

A luxurious stone-and-thatch lodge set in a vast estate in the heart of fly-fishing country. Bedrooms have lake views, private patios and fireplaces. Indulge in country cuisine and choose your wine from the award-winning cellar. Fish for rainbow trout on private rivers and lakes – all the necessary equipment is provided. **www.walkersons.co.za**

DULLSTROOM Peebles Country Retreat ®®®®

Cnr Lyon Cachet & Bosman Streets, Dullstroom, 1110 ***Tel*** *(013) 254-8000* ***Fax*** *(013) 254-8014* ***Rooms*** *10*

At this gracious family-owned country house set in the trout-fishing village of Dullstroom you can choose from a variety of activities: trout fishing, bird-watching, horse riding, clay-pigeon shooting, archery and mountain biking. Peebles offers personal service and well-appointed accommodation with attention to detail. **www.peebles.co.za**

GRASKOP Mac Mac Forest Retreat ®

Box 907, Sabie, 1260 ***Tel*** *(013) 764-2376* ***Fax*** *(013) 764-3124* ***Rooms*** *4*

Close to the thunderous Mac Mac and Forest Falls, this relaxed resort offers activities such as 4x4 trails, archery, canoeing, paintball, gold-panning and mountain biking. Accommodation is provided in renovated forestry houses, which are self-catering, with all appliances, cutlery, crockery and bedding included. **www.macmac.co.za**

GRASKOP The Graskop Hotel ®®

3 Main Street, Graskop, 1270 ***Tel*** *(013) 767-1244* ***Fax*** *(013) 767-1244* ***Rooms*** *34*

Located in malaria-free Graskop, within easy reach of Kruger National Park. The superb sights of the area include God's Window, Pilgrim's Rest and Bourke's Luck Potholes. The rooms are artistically decorated, and the food is prepared with home-grown produce and herbs. There is a crafts studio and gallery on site. **www.graskophotel.co.za**

HAZYVIEW Sabi River Sun ®®

Main Road, Perry's Farm, Hazyview, 1242 ***Tel*** *(013) 737-7311* ***Fax*** *(013) 737-7314* ***Rooms*** *60*

This resort hotel offers comfortable accommodation and unrivalled sporting activities, including an 18-hole golf course, five swimming pools, three floodlit tennis courts, a bowling green, squash court, volleyball and jogging trail. Sabi River Sun caters particularly well for children, with a daily activity programme. **www.southernsun.com**

HAZYVIEW The Windmill Wine & Cottages ®®

R536 Box 204, Hazyview, 1242 ***Tel*** *(013) 737-8175* ***Fax*** *(013) 737-8966* ***Rooms*** *7*

The Windmill is located on 22 hectares (54 acres) of malaria-free indigenous bush populated by small game, including vervet monkeys, caracal and bushbuck. The cottages are well spaced to give guests privacy. Enjoy bird-watching from your own private deck or join the wine, beer and cheese tastings at the Wine Shop. **www.thewindmill.co.za**

HAZYVIEW Rissington Inn ®®®

R40 Box 650, Hazyview, 1242 ***Tel*** *(013) 737-7700* ***Fax*** *(013) 737-7112* ***Rooms*** *14*

This affordable lodge, just ten minutes from Kruger National Park, offers stylish but relaxed accommodation. Each of the warm rooms has its own entrance and verandah, so you can enjoy the breathtaking views down the valley in privacy and comfort. Golf, riding and a host of other activities are available nearby. **www.rissington.co.za**

HAZYVIEW Thulamela Guest Cottages ®®®

R40, White River Road, Hazyview, 1242 ***Tel*** *(013) 737-7171* ***Fax*** *(086) 676-6047* ***Rooms*** *5*

This is a lovely honeymoon destination, as children under the age of 16 are not allowed. Each charming timber cabin at Thulamela has been built and decorated to ensure total privacy for its occupants: they are set in indigenous bush and feature a spa bath on the patio. Guests can expect generous breakfasts. **www.thulamela.co.za**

HAZYVIEW Blue Mountain Lodge ®®®®®

R514, Kiepersol, 1241 ***Tel*** *(013) 737-8446* ***Fax*** *(013) 737-6917* ***Rooms*** *17*

Those looking for seclusion will enjoy this hotel set in a vast expanse of indigenous forest. Each luxurious suite offers a different style, from Victorian elegance to Provençal rustic. Hot-air balloon flights, helicopter excursions, rafting adventures and bush walks can be arranged, as can beauty treatments. **www.bluemountainlodge.co.za**

HAZYVIEW Highgrove House ®®®®®

R40 Box 46, Kiepersol, 1241 ***Tel*** *(013) 764-1844* ***Fax*** *(013) 764-1855* ***Rooms*** *8*

A colonial-style, award-winning lodge with a pastoral setting. The rooms have open fireplaces, overhead fans and secluded verandahs opening on to spectacular views. Expect gourmet dishes, fine wines and personal service at the candlelit restaurant. Easy access to the area's panoramic drives and wildlife reserves. **www.highgrove.co.za**

HENDRIKSDAL Artist's Café and Guesthouse ®®

Hendriksdal Siding, Sabie, 1260 ***Tel*** *(013) 764-2309* ***Fax*** *(013) 764-2309* ***Rooms*** *4*

Accommodation quarters and a restaurant can be found in this former station, built in 1920 and surrounded by lush green forests. A changing selection of artworks creates a unique atmosphere, while the restaurant serves Tuscan fare, using fresh herbs and vegetables grown in the garden. **www.wheretostay.co.za/artistscafe**

Key to Price Guide *see p326* **Key to Symbols** *see back cover flap*

KRUGER NATIONAL PARK Satellite Camps ®

Box 787, Pretoria/Tshwane, 0001 **Tel** *(012) 428-9111* **Fax** *(012) 343-0905* **Rooms** *135*

The ideal camp for people who want to embrace nature and don't mind roughing it. Staying at Maroela, Tamboti, Tsendze, Balule, Malelane, Boulders and Roodewal camps requires booking in at the main camp. It is important to note there are no staff on site overnight. **www.sanparks.org**

KRUGER NATIONAL PARK Bushveld Camps ®®®

Box 787, Pretoria/Tshwane, 0001 **Tel** *(012) 428-9111* **Fax** *(012) 343-0905* **Rooms** *67 units*

This accommodation is great for families who are looking for a real bush experience. Bateleur, Mbyamiti, Sirheni, Shimuwini and Talamati camps offer several self-catering cottages. There is no mobile-phone signal, so you are guaranteed a quiet, uninterrupted stay. **www.sanparks.org**

KRUGER NATIONAL PARK Main Camps ®®®

Box 787, Pretoria/Tshwane, 0001 **Tel** *(012) 428-9111* **Fax** *(012) 343-0905* **Rooms** *1,636 units*

The wide variety of lodgings are perfect for first time safari visitors. Camps offer restaurants, shops and other amenities. They all have swimming pools, apart from Olifants. Berg-en-Dal, Skukuzu, Satara and Letaba camps offer children's programmes over the holidays. Skukuza is the only camp with an ATM and a post office. **www.sanparks.org**

LYDENBURG De Ark Guesthouse ®

37 Kantoor Street, Lydenburg, 1120 **Tel** *(013) 235-1125* **Fax** *(013) 235-1125* **Rooms** *9*

Dating back to 1857, this delightful guesthouse is one of the oldest remaining buildings in Lydenburg. Located at the foothills of Long Tom Pass, De Ark has been lovingly restored and decorated with eclectic period furniture. Owners François and Francis Le Roux are always pleased to advise their guests on itineraries. **www.dearkguesthouse.co.za**

MALELANE Malelane Sun ®®®®

Riverside Farm, Box 392, Malelane, 1320 **Tel** *(013) 790-3304* **Fax** *(013) 790-3303* **Rooms** *102*

These luxury thatched chalets, only a few minutes' drive from Kruger National Park, provide an ideal resort-type alternative for visitors unable to obtain a place within the park itself. A viewing deck on the river offers memorable sunrises and sunsets, while crocodiles glide by. **www.southernsun.com**

PILGRIM'S REST Crystal Springs Mountain Lodge ®®®

Robber's Pass, Pilgrim's Rest, 1290 **Tel** *(013) 768-5000* **Fax** *(013) 768-5024* **Rooms** *192*

Individual self-catering cottages situated within a game reserve high above Pilgrim's Rest. Tennis and squash courts, mini-golf and a gym surround an indoor heated pool and Jacuzzi area. You can relax in the pub, by the fireplace in your room, or on the open wooden deck of your cottage, which includes a braai. **www.crystalsprings.co.za**

ROOSSENEKAL Old Joe's Kaia Country Lodge ®®®

Schoemanskloof Valley, Roossenekal, 1207 **Tel** *(013) 733-3045* **Fax** *(013) 733-3777* **Rooms** *14*

Old Joe's is a friendly country home decorated with vibrant colours in authentic African colonial style. Choose from log cabins, rondavels or "Kaia" rooms. Meals are prepared using garden-fresh produce and can be eaten in the dining room, garden or by the river. Don't miss out on the home-baked bread. **www.oldjoes.co.za**

SABIE Hillwatering Country House ®®

50 Marula Street, Sabie, 1260 **Tel** *(013) 764-1421* **Fax** *(013) 764-1550* **Rooms** *5*

In a quiet residential area, a few minutes from the centre of Sabie, is this welcoming country home. Four of the rooms have French doors leading on to a private porch where guests can enjoy the view of the Drakensberg Mountains. Owners Hazel and Richard are happy to book day trips and other activities. **www.hillwatering.co.za**

SABIE Bohm's Zeederberg Country House ®®®

Box 94, Sabie, 1260 **Tel** *(013) 737-8101* **Fax** *(013) 737-8193* **Rooms** *10*

This farm, with its majestic views, borders the pine and eucalyptus forests of Sabie on one side and the agricultural heartland of subtropical fruit on the other. The garden has a swimming pool, sauna and Jacuzzi, as well as a variety of indigenous trees, all labelled for easy identification. **www.bohms.co.za**

SABIE Lone Creek River Lodge ®®®

Old Lydenburg Road, Sabie, 1260 **Tel** *(013) 764-2611* **Fax** *(013) 764-2233* **Rooms** *21*

Accessible from all major routes, this five-star boutique hotel offers elegant accommodation in a variety of lodgings, from self-catering timber cottages to luxury river suites located on the banks of the Sabie. Children are welcome in the timber lodges, and those under seven are accommodated at half price. **www.lonecreek.co.za**

SABIE SAND RESERVE Sabi Sabi Game Lodge ®®®®®

Box 52665, Saxonwold, 2132 **Tel** *(011) 483-3939* **Fax** *(011) 483-3799* **Rooms** *25*

This multi-award-winning establishment includes four unique rest camps – Bush, Little Bush, Selati and Earth – each of which offers the ultimate luxury safari experience. Experienced guides accompany visitors on day and night game-viewing drives on open vehicles. Fully inclusive. **www.sabisabi.com**

SABIE SAND RESERVE Singita Private Game Reserve ®®®®®

Box 23367, Claremont, 7735 **Tel** *(021) 683-3424* **Fax** *(021) 683-3502* **Rooms** *30*

Singita was voted Best Hotel in the World by *Condé Nast Traveller* in 2004, and indeed its five lodges offer exceptional standards of luxury. Gourmet cuisine, an extensive wine cellar, day and night game drives and walking safaris are all included. Suites in the Boulders Lodge feature stunning stone bathrooms and bedrooms. **www.singita.com**

SWAZILAND Mlilwane Lodge ®

Mlilwane Wildlife Sanctuary, lobamba **Tel** *(09268) 528-3963* **Fax** *(09268) 528-3924* **Rooms** *8*

At Mlilwane Lodge, you can choose between various accommodation options situated right in the sanctuary, from twin huts in the rest camp, to family huts or cottages, from traditional beehive huts to rondavels and camping sites. There is also an inexpensive youth hostel. **www.biggame.co.sz**

SWAZILAND Malolotja Lodge ®®

Malolotja Nature Reserve, Nkhaba **Tel** *(09268) 416-1151* **Fax** *(09268) 416-1480* **Rooms** *20*

Rustic log cabins and campsites are dotted throughout this scenic nature reserve catering for self-sufficient hikers. At the front of each cabin is a *braai* for evening barbecues. The reserve has many interesting walking trails, and the shop at the main gate sells basic provisions. **www.welcometoswaziland.com**

SWAZILAND Royal Swazi Spa Hotel ®®®®®

Main Road, Mbabane – Manzini **Tel** *(09268) 416-5000* **Fax** *(09268) 416-1859* **Rooms** *149*

One of a trio of hotels under the Royal Swazi Sun Valley umbrella, the Royal Swazi Spa is nestled in the scenic Ezulwini Valley. It is renowned for its superb golf course, casino and high-quality cuisine. Other facilities include tennis, squash, a games room, Camp Kwena for children, horse riding and a spa. **www.suninternational.com**

TIMBAVATI PRIVATE GAME RESERVE Tanda Tula Safari Camp ®®®®®

Box 32, Constantia, 7848 **Tel** *(021) 794-6500* **Fax** *(021) 794-7605* **Rooms** *10*

Luxury tented camp in an exclusive reserve near Kruger Park. The thatched East Africa-style tents are fitted with roll-top baths, outdoor showers and spacious wooden decks overlooking the dry river bed. All meals and drinks are included, and they can be taken on your private verandah or convivially around the *boma*. **www.tandatula.co.za**

TZANEEN Coach House ®®®®

Box 544, Tzaneen, 850 **Tel** *(015) 306-8000* **Fax** *(015) 306-8008* **Rooms** *39*

Built in 1892 to cater to travellers in the days of the Gold Rush, the Coach House is set on a high plateau. Individual chalets are set in beautiful gardens; each features a private verandah with views of the Drakenberg Mountains. The 8,000-bottle wine cellar and the renowned Coach House nougat are big attractions. **www.coachhouse.co.za**

WHITE RIVER Kirby Country Lodge ®®

Jatinga Road, White River, 1240 **Tel** *(013) 751-2645* **Fax** *(013) 750-1836* **Rooms** *11*

Only 25 minutes by car from Kruger National Park, this tranquil thatched lodge set in woodland gardens is owned by a hospitable Swiss family. They are on hand to help their guests book all sorts of activities, from game drives to gold-panning or hot-air ballooning. Families with children are welcome. **www.kirbycountrylodge.co.za**

WHITE RIVER Jatinga Country Lodge ®®®®

Jatinga Road, White River, 1240 **Tel** *(013) 751-5059* **Fax** *(013) 751-5119* **Rooms** *26*

Once a hunting lodge, this luxurious homestead dates back to the 1920s. The African colonial style and ambience have been retained even with renovations in 2001. The hammocks in the garden are a great way to wind down. The restaurant caters well for diabetics and vegetarians. **www.jatinga.co.za**

WHITE RIVER Cybele Forest Lodge ®®®®®

R40 Box 346, White River, 1240 **Tel** *(013) 764-1823* **Fax** *(013) 764-9510* **Rooms** *12*

Tucked away in forest country is this exquisite old farmhouse. The gardens are filled with the varied vivid colours of indigenous trees, and the rooms are lavish, with log fireplaces and private gardens – some with heated pools. Spa and beauty treatments, bird-watching and horse riding are some of the activities on offer. **www.cybele.co.za**

SOUTH OF THE ORANGE

BEAUFORT WEST Lemoenfontein ®®

Off Jagers Pass, Beaufort West, 6970 **Tel** *(023) 415-2847/(0)82 495-3124* **Fax** *(023) 415-1044* **Rooms** *12*

Built in 1850 as a hunting lodge, Lemoenfontein is an oasis in the heart of the arid Great Karoo, under the Nieweveld Mountains. The extensive game reserve surrounding it teems with buck, giraffes and bird life. Enjoy the views from the wide verandahs, and tuck into the hearty breakfasts and traditional Karoo dinners. **www.lemoenfontein.co.za**

BEAUFORT WEST Treetop Guest House ®®

17 Bird Street, Beaufort West, 6970 **Tel** *(023) 414-3744/(0)83-366 9784* **Fax** *(023) 415-1329* **Rooms** *7*

A pleasant residential building surrounded by a garden in a small town full of history. The Treetop offers a great home-away-from-home vibe, with a pool and *braai* facilities for the guests. Start the day with a full English breakfast, and enjoy a traditional Karoo dinner by candlelight in the evening. **www.treetopguesthouse.co.za**

COLESBERG Kuilfontein Stable Cottages ®®

Box 17, Colesberg, 9795 **Tel** *(051) 753-1364/(0)82 522-2488* **Fax** *(051) 753-0200* **Rooms** *8*

A farm that produces Karoo lamb, Kuilfontein has been in the same family for more than a century. The rooms are located in former racing stables, and activities include bird-watching and game viewing. Nearby are historical and Stone Age sites, water sports at Gariep Dam and a local museum for Karoo fossils. **www.kuilfontein.co.za**

Key to Price Guide *see p326* **Key to Symbols** *see back cover flap*

CRADOCK Die Tuishuise ®®

36 Market Street, Cradock, 5880 **Tel** *(048) 811-322* **Fax** *(048) 881-5388* **Rooms** *27*

These traditional iron-roofed Karoo cottages were restored and beautifully renovated into tourist accommodation. Each cottage is furnished with antiques and four-poster beds, reflecting the style of English and Dutch settlers in the mid-1800s. Activities include game drives, township tours and rock art. **www.tuishuise.co.za**

GRAAFF REINET Caledonia ®®

61 Somerset Street, Graaff Reinet, 6280 **Tel** *(049) 892-3156* **Fax** *(049) 892-3156* **Rooms** *6*

In the historic quarter of this interesting town – the fourth-oldest in South Africa – is this 150-year-old colonial-style stone house. Shops, banks and museums are all within walking distance, as is the Valley of Desolation, where you can see zebras, wildebeest and springbok. The restaurant serves delicious Karoo-style dishes. **www.caledonia.co.za**

KING WILLIAM'S TOWN Dreamers ®

29 Gordon Street, Hospital Hill, 5601 **Tel** *(043) 642-3012/(0)82 923-3870* **Fax** *(086) 677-6016* **Rooms** *11*

This guesthouse in historic King William's Town is a good stopover on the way to the Drakensberg Mountains. Meals are served on request, and owners Marieta and André take pride in the challenge of special-request cuisine. Given a little notice, they will also arrange a visit to a Xhosa kraal to observe local culture. **www.dreamersguesthouse.com**

LADY GREY Comfrey Cottage ®®

51–59 Stephenson Street, Lady Grey, 9755 **Tel** *(051) 603-0407* **Fax** *(051) 603-0407* **Rooms** *8*

One of four family-run cottages in a garden in a tranquil village below the Witteberg Mountains, the four-star Comfrey Cottage provides great comfort and good food. It is an ideal base from which to enjoy local attractions such as hiking, biking, fly-fishing, bird-watching and flower tours. Fully licensed. **www.comfreycottage.co.za**

NORTH OF THE ORANGE

BLOEMFONTEIN Dias Guest House ®

14 Dias Crescent, Dan Pienaar, 9301 **Tel** *(051) 436-6225/(0)83 265-0265* **Fax** *(051) 436-7733* **Rooms** *8*

Rhyno and Mariette's award-winning, gay-friendly guesthouse is located near several museums and historic monuments, including the Women's War Memorial, the War Museum and the Rugby Museum. Each room features an Internet connection, fridge and microwave. **www.diasgfi.co.za**

BLOEMFONTEIN Florentia ®®

2c Louis Botha Street, Waverley, 9301 **Tel** *(051) 436-7847/(0)82 853-7472* **Fax** *(051) 436-7847* **Rooms** *8*

On a tree-lined street at the foot of Naval Hill, this four-star guesthouse is renowned for owner Jolena van Rooyen's collection of quilts, which can be admired on the beds as well as hanging on the walls. A game reserve, orchid house and theatre are all located nearby. **www.florentia.co.za**

BLOEMFONTEIN Halevy Heritage Hotel ®®®

Markgraaff & Charles Streets, 9301 **Tel** *(051) 403-0600/(0)82 559-9443* **Fax** *(051) 403-0699* **Rooms** *21*

Originally built as accommodation for theatre-goers at the end of the 19th century, the Halevy Heritage was renovated and reopened in 2004. It has maintained its Edwardian appeal and features spacious rooms, high ceilings, dark furniture and attractive Tiffany bedside lamps. **www.halevyheritagehotel.co.za**

KIMBERLEY Protea Hotel Diamond Lodge ®®

124 Du Toits Pan Road, Kimberley, 8301 **Tel** *(053) 831-1281* **Fax** *(053) 831-1284* **Rooms** *34*

This small, comfortable, friendly hotel is conveniently located near Kimberley's central business district. The three-star Diamond Lodge is also within easy walking distance to historical and recreational facilities, including the Mine Museum. Most rooms have two double beds. **www.proteahotels.com**

KIMBERLEY Garden Court ®®®

120 Du Toits Pan Road, Kimberley, 8301 **Tel** *(053) 833-1751* **Fax** *(053) 832-1814* **Rooms** *135*

A standard city hotel that caters to both business and leisure travellers, the Garden Court is close to the main tourist attractions and to a tram stop that takes you to the Big Hole, the world's largest man-made excavation. Tours to local places of interest, including the Ghost Trail and the battlefields, can also be arranged. **www.southernsun.com**

KIMBERLEY Kimberley Club ®®®

35 Currey Street, Kimberley, 8301 **Tel** *(053) 832-4224* **Fax** *(053) 832-4226* **Rooms** *17*

Founded by a cluster of diamond magnates who missed their London clubs, the Kimberley Club has had a recent facelift and an upgrade to four-star boutique hotel in colonial style. Formal but comfortable, it is close to excellent museums, mining buildings, the Big Hole, the Magersfontein battlefield and a casino. **www.kimberleyclub.co.za**

UPINGTON Le Must Manor ®®

11 Schroeder Street, Upington, 8800 **Tel** *(054) 332-3971* **Fax** *(054) 332-7830* **Rooms** *7*

This beautiful Georgian-style guesthouse is surrounded by a splendid manicured garden on the banks of the Orange River, in the central business district of Upington. The Kalahari, the Augrabies Falls, the Kgalagadi Transfrontier Park and the Tswalu Reserve are all within a short driving distance. **www.lemustupington.com**

WHERE TO EAT

South Africa has a wide variety of restaurants and eateries, from franchise steakhouses and sizzling street-corner *boerewors* stands to elegant business venues and seafood, Oriental, French and Mediterranean-style restaurants. Whenever the weather is fine, eating is done outside, and coffee shops do a roaring trade. African eateries for the Western palate are found in the cities, while some township tours *(see p382)* include traditional meals. South Africa's multi-cultural heritage is also evident in the proliferation of Indian restaurants and stalls serving spicy eastern and KwaZulu-Natal-style curries. In the Western Cape, fragrant, sweet Malay curries are popular quick lunches and in the winelands, more formal fare.

Home delivery service

Village Walk in Sandton, Gauteng

SOUTH AFRICAN EATING PATTERNS

Restaurants are most likely to be open for lunch from Mondays to Fridays and for dinner from Tuesdays to Sundays. It is common to find restaurants closed on Mondays (Italian restaurants often close on Tuesdays). Coffee shops are open during the day, usually from 9am to 5pm, and serve breakfasts, light lunches and teas. For breakfasts, try the traditional cooked dish of eggs, bacon and sausages. Healthy muffins (also available at supermarkets, delis and even petrol-station stores) such as bran, banana and date are popular, too. Salads, open sandwiches and quiches are good choices for lunch, while cakes (carrot, chocolate and cheese) are usual afternoon-tea fare. Dinner is the main meal of the day, served from 6:30pm to 10pm. In the urban areas, bars, popular restaurants and fast-food outlets stay open until midnight or even later.

PLACES TO EAT

You can always eat well in South African cities and in the well-visited outlying and country areas and smaller towns.

The annual guide *Eat Out* magazine, available at newsagents, recommends restaurants nationwide, as do websites such as www.dining-out.co.za.

BOOKING AHEAD

It is best to phone ahead and reserve a table in order to avoid disappointment.

Established or fashionable venues may be booked up for weeks in advance. If you cannot keep a reservation, call the restaurant and cancel.

PRICES AND TIPPING

Eating out in South Africa is usually inexpensive. The average price of a three-course meal for one (excluding wine and a tip) at a good restaurant is about R140–160. But certain items, such as seafood, can increase the total substantially. A freshly-made deli sandwich with delicious fillings will seldom cost more than R30, while a large, hearty breakfast costs around R50.

Tipping should always be based on service. If simply average, leave 10 per cent; if excellent, 15 per cent. Tips are sometimes placed in a communal jar near the cashier.

Seafood *braai* at a *skerm* (sheltered barbecue area) on the West Coast

WHAT TO EAT

Try to visit one of the African, Indian (in KwaZulu-Natal) or Malay (in Cape Town) restaurants in the cities. If you're at the coast, don't miss the delicious seafood – calamari, mussels, tuna, crayfish, yellowtail and *kabeljou* (cob). On the West Coast there are scenic open-air seafood *braais* (barbecues). The cities and larger towns offer excellent international cuisine: Portuguese, Thai, Indonesian, Italian, Greek, French and Chinese. There are also typical South African restaurants, where traditional fare and drinks like *witblits*, strong spirit distilled from peaches, are served.

South Africa is a meat-loving nation; beef steaks are good, and franchise steakhouses offer great value for money; the selection of substantial salads and vegetable dishes will satisfy vegetarians, too. *Boerewors* (spicy-sausage) on a bread-roll can be bought from informal street vendors. At someone's home, you might sample a South African meat *braai* *(see p21)*, or barbecue. Pizza chains are very popular and offer good value.

Witblits
(peach brandy)

WINE CHOICES

South African wines offer something for everybody, and most restaurants stock a mainstream selection of local labels – usually with a significant price mark-up. Many serve a great variety: from easy-drinking wines to vintage bottlings. Some venues offer a choice of bottled wines by the glass, although house wines are, more usually, from an inexpensive 5-litre box. Fine-dining venues provide an international winelist, and the better Italian eateries, for example, offer Italian wines. Corkage (from R25) is charged if you bring your own bottle.

DELIVERY SERVICES

In the cities and larger towns, food-delivery services are popular. The company known as "Mr Delivery" is contracted to a variety of eateries and restaurants (not only fast-food outlets) and will deliver hot food, for a reasonable fee, during lunch times and from early to late evening. The local telephone directory will provide details.

SMOKING

Strict anti-tobacco laws are enforced in South Africa. Smoking in the main dining area of restaurants is not allowed. At present, most restaurants have a smoking section, and patrons should specify their requirements when booking.

CHILDREN

Restaurants and eateries are not always child-friendly in South Africa, especially at dinner times when, for many patrons, dining out is the entertainment for the evening and children are left at home.

Outdoor, informal and daytime venues (and their menus) are more likely to suit little people. High chairs and mini menus are not common; expect to pay three-quarters of the price for a half-size meal.

Franchises like the Spur Steakhouses are a very good bet: they all have an appetizing children's menu; crayons, colouring-in competitions, balloons and resident clowns.

The Spur Steakhouse franchise also caters for younger patrons

DRESS CODE

Many upmarket restaurants do require patrons to wear smart, but not formal attire. While you will not be able to wear jeans, shorts and sports shoes at such venues, you may comfortably do so just about anywhere else.

WHEELCHAIR ACCESS

A growing awareness for the special needs of the physically disabled visitor has led to the construction of ramps and wider toilet doors at some, mostly upmarket, venues. Many restaurants, however, still cannot accommodate visitors in wheelchairs, and it is advisable to check in advance.

Eating alfresco, on the patio of a South African restaurant

The Flavours of South Africa

In 1652, the Dutch East India Company established a refreshment station in the Cape to provide their ships with fresh supplies. These early settlers learned much from the hunter-gatherer skills of the local people and a multi-ethnic cuisine began to emerge. The spice traders brought exotic flavours to the country, and the diversity of ingredients increased with the arrival of British, Indian and German settlers. Finally the French Huguenots contributed culinary finesse. This rainbow of influences is evident today in both traditional and modern dishes.

Rooibos tea

South Africans preparing for a family *braai*

CAPE MALAY COOKING

Malay slaves were brought from Java to the Cape Colony in the late 1600s, bringing with them an intimate knowledge of spices that had a profound influence on Cape cooking. Authentic specialities can still be found in Cape Town's historic Bo-Kaap district. Although spiced with traditional curry ingredients such as turmeric, ginger, cinnamon, cardamom, cloves and chilies, Cape Malay cuisine is never fiery. Meat is often cooked with fruit, marrying sweet and savoury flavours, while fish, especially snoek and seafood, is also important. Malay cooks were much sought after by the settlers and soon learned how to prepare traditional Dutch fare such as *melktart* (custard tart), adding cinnamon and grated nutmeg to suit their own tastes. Other baked puddings and tarts show a strong Dutch influence, while the delicious fruit preserves are mainly French Huguenot in origin.

KWAZULU NATAL CUISINE

In the mid-1800s, indentured labour was brought from India to work in Natal's

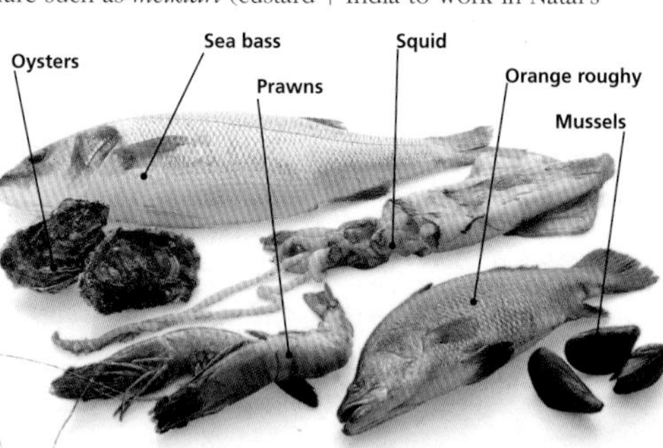

Selection of fresh South African seafood

SOUTH AFRICAN DISHES AND SPECIALITIES

Biltong

From the Malay kitchen comes *bobotie*, served with *geelrys* (rice with raisins and spices) and *blatjang* (spicy fruit chutney). Durban's most popular dish is *bunny chow* (food of the Indians), a hollowed-out loaf filled with curry and garnished with pickles. The dish dates from apartheid when black South Africans were not allowed in restaurants, so were served this portable meal through the back door. Larded saddle of venison is the signature dish of the Karoo, and venison is also dried, salted and spiced to create a type of jerky called *biltong*. The Cederberg region has its own speciality, Rooibos tea, which has a light and fruity taste. The warm Benguella and cold Atlantic currents ensure a plentiful supply of fresh fish, and snoek is a traditional favourite.

Smoorsnoek *mixes flaked snoek (a barracuda-like fish) with potato slices and tomato in a tasty braise.*

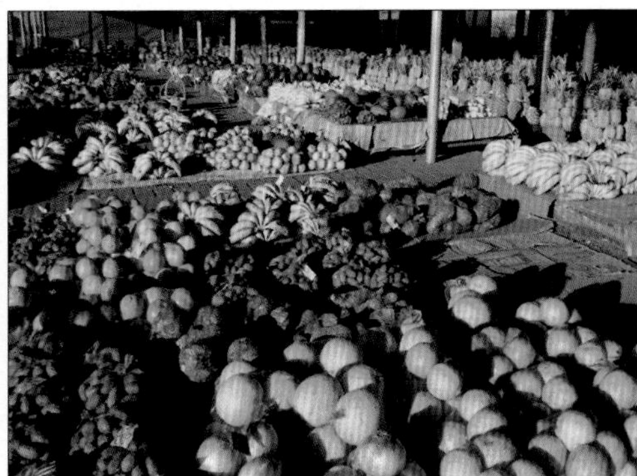
Vast array of South African fruit laid out at a Cape Town market

sugar cane fields. Many workers stayed on after their contracts expired and Gujarati traders soon began supplying traditional spices to the growing community, who blended them with local foodstuffs to create distinctly South African flavours. Today, spice stores specialize in all manner of blends, some unique to South Africa, which create delicious dishes. The early Indian settlers later gained a strong foothold in the regional fruit and vegetable trade, introducing tropical Asian fruit to KwaZulu Natal. Mangoes, lychees, banana, *paw paw* (papaya) and watermelon are enjoyed fresh, or as ingredients and accompaniments to curries.

Fresh fish is also very popular in this region and the annual sardine runs on the Natal coast are awaited with great anticipation. As soon as the fish are spotted, locals rush to the sea collecting them by the dozen. The sardines are immediately sprinkled with salt, dipped into a South African Red Spice mixture and fried.

South African bream caught by a local Natal fisherman

BRAAIVLEIS

The South African *braai* (barbecue) is much more than a meal cooked over an open fire. It is a social tradition cherished throughout the land. Lamb chops, steak, chicken, *sosaties* (kebabs) and *boerewors* (farmer's sausage) are the most common items. The Western Cape is famous for grilling whole snoek, basted with a mixture of apricot jam, white wine and fruit chutney. Grilled crayfish is another favourite *braai* dish.

ON THE MENU

Erwtensoep Dutch pea soup, slow cooked then liberally laced with diced, salted pork.

Groenmielies Corn on the cob, grilled over an open fire and thoroughly basted with butter. A favourite for a summer *braai*.

Koeksisters "Cake sisters" is a sweet Malay snack, best described as a doughnut infused with sugary syrup.

Perlemoen Tenderized and soaked in milk, abalone is lightly pan fried, which brings out the fresh sea taste.

Sosaties Skewers of meat, onions and dried fruit are marinated in a curry sauce and then grilled over an open fire.

Waterblommetjiebredie A Cape stew made of lamb and *waterblommetjies*, a water plant which resembles an artichoke.

Bobotie *is minced beef, spiced with bay and turmeric, topped with an egg custard and baked.*

Roast springbuck *or venison remains succulent when basted continously with a sour cream marinade.*

Melktert *dates back to early Cape Malay-Dutch cooking. This sweet custard tart is sprinkled with cinnamon.*

What to Drink in South Africa

South African wine may be classified as "New World", but the country actually has a long history in wine-making. The first vines were planted in the Cape of Good Hope by Commander Jan van Riebeck in 1655. The most important figure in the industry, however, was Simon van der Stel, who founded both the Stellenbosch and Constantia vineyards, the latter's dessert wine gaining an international reputation by the end of the 17th century. In 1885, the vineyards were devastated by an infestation of the phylloxera insect. The subsequent recovery led to over-production and this, along with the establishment of trade sanctions as a result of apartheid, led to a decline in quality. Recent years have seen major changes in the industry, with a move towards smaller, independent vineyards producing some world-class wines. South Africa is now the world's eighth largest producer.

Grape picker, in the scenic Dieu Donné vineyard

WHITE WINE

With its Mediterranean-style climate, the country's southwestern tip is the best area for wine production. The growing conditions are perfect for the once-ubiquitous Chenin Blanc grape used in high-volume, low-cost wines and for brandy-making. Since the quota system ended in 1992, a greater variety of grapes have been planted. Sauvignon Blanc, Chardonnay and even some German, Spanish and Portuguese vines are now well established, and have taken on their own distinctive style. Stellenbosch, Constantia and the cool-climate Walker Bay all produce some of the finest white wines.

Meerlust Estate wine

Cellars of Avondale, on Klein Drakenstein slopes, near Paarl

Morgenhof Estate bottled red, near Stellenbosch

RED WINE

The dominant red grape variety is Merlot but it now has strong competition from the homegrown Pinotage cultivar *(see pp128–29)*. South Africa still produces plenty of basic red drinking wine but producers such as Hamilton Russell with his Pinot Noir, and Neil Ellis with his Cabernet Sauvignon have dramatically expanded the country's portfolio of excellent reds.

SPARKLING AND OTHER WINES

Méthode Cap Classique is the nomenclature devised for the Champagne-style sparkling wines produced in all of the country's major wine districts *(see p134)*. The delightfully honeyed Constantina dessert wine was first produced over 350 years ago, but the wine industry has not stood still and a wide range of increasingly popular rosé wines are being produced from grapes such as Gamay and Shiraz. Additionally, South Africa offers a number of port-style fortified wines, with Calitzdorp, in the Klein Karoo region the main area of production, although Paarl and Stellenbosch also offer some good examples. Axe Hill, J P Bredell and De Krans are among the best on offer.

Graham Beck brut non-vintage

BEER

Incorporated in London in 1895, South African Breweries (SAB) has been swallowing up rival breweries and beer brands across the globe for the past two decades and is now second in size only to Belgium's InBev group. Castle is the company's ubiquitous home-brand label – it even has inspired the popular Beef & Castle pie recipe. The company operates the SAB World of Beer Museum in Johannesburg *(see p256)*, the guided tour, which illustrates the brewing process has guaranteed refreshment at the end in the form of a couple of cool "frosties".

Black label **Castle** **Hansa**

BRANDY

A KWV 10-year-old **Boplaas Potstill Brandy**

Set up in Stellenbosch in 1984, the South African Brandy Foundation represents virtually all of the country's 50 brandy trademarks. In 1997, on the 325th anniversary of South African brandy distilling, the foundation launched the world's first Brandy Route. The trail stretches from Stellenbosch through Paarl and Franschoek to the Breede River Valley town of Worcester. Attractions include the Van Ryn Brandy Cellar *(see p139)*, 8 km (5 miles) outside Stellenbosch where visitors can learn about brandy production methods; the Oude Molen Brandy Museum in Stellenbosch itself, and the tasting rooms at the Backberg Distillery near Paarl.

VARIETY	REGIONS	PRODUCERS
WHITE		
Chenin Blanc	Breede River Valley, Stellenbosch, Cederberg, Swartland	De Trafford, Kleine Zalze, Nederburg, Beaumont Hope
Sauvignon Blanc	Darling District, Elim Ward Overberg, Cape Point, Stellenbosch	Groote Post, Paul Cluver, Steenberg Vineyards, Hamilton Russell
Chardonnay	Breede River Valley, Overburg, Paarl, Swartland, Cederberg	Springfield Estate, Neil Ellis, Glen Carlou, Jordan Wines
RED		
Cabernet Sauvignon	Cederberg, Paarl Stellenbosch, Swartland, Tygerberg	Thelema Mountain Cedarberg Cellars, Neil Ellis, Rupert & Rothschild
Shiraz	Franshhoek, Paarl, Stellenbosch	Fairview, Neil Ellis, Boekehnhoutskloof
Pinotage	Overberg, Tulbagh, Breede River Valley, Stellenbosch	Rijk's Private Cellar, Fairview Primo, Graham Beck
Merlot	Constantia, Tygerberg, Paarl	Le Riche, Veenwouden, Glen Carlou
Pinot Noir	Overberg, Elgin, Constantina, Walker Bay, Darling District	Newton Johnson, Bouchard Finlayson, Paul Kluver, Groote Post
SPARKLING		
Cape Classic	Cape Peninsula	JC Le Roux, Villiera Wines, Graham Beck Wines
FORTIFIED		
(Port style)	Kleine Karoo	Axe Hill, De Krans, JP Bredell

Spectacular vineyard setting in the Franschhoek Mountains

READING THE LABEL

South Africa operates strict wine labelling laws as a guarantee of quality. According to the WO (Wine of Origin) system, information provided on the grape variety and the vintage must apply to at least 85 per cent of what's gone into the bottle. However, 100 per cent of the grapes must have come from the stated place of origin. This can be the region (for example, Olifants River, Breede Valley River or Cape Point), the precise district therein (such as Paarl, Stellenbosch and Swartland) or, narrowing it down even more, the ward (Elgin, Waterberg, Cedarberg). Top-end wines can be labelled as estate wines provided that the product is grown, vinified and bottled on one parcel of land that is farmed as a single unit and registered as such.

CITY BOWL Haiku ®®®®®

33 Church Street, 8001 ***Tel*** *(021) 424-7000* ***Map*** *5 1B*

This über-trendy offshoot of Bukhara (just around the corner) was voted Best New Restaurant in South Africa at the 2005 *Eat Out* Awards. Loud lounge music permeates the venue, but otherwise the ambience is very Zen, with soft overhead lights and black granite walls. Brighter lighting shines on the open-plan kitchen.

V&A WATERFRONT Paulaner Brauhaus and Restaurant ®®

Shop 18–19, Clock Tower Square, 8001 ***Tel*** *(021) 418-9999* ***Map*** *1 1B*

German fare dominates at this extremely popular independent brewery-cum-restaurant. A vast and varied selection of foreign beers is available, along with traditional hearty German dishes like *Schweinshaxe mit Knoedel und Krautsalat* (pigs' trotters with dumplings and sauerkraut).

V&A WATERFRONT Cape Town Fish Market ®®®

Shop 159, Kings Warehouse, Victoria Wharf, 8001 ***Tel*** *(021) 418-5977* ***Map*** *1 1B*

Part of a small chain, this busy Waterfront seafood eatery provides freshness, quality and value for money. There's a good kiddies' menu, excellent sushi and enormous portions that make eating three courses an almost-insurmountable task. Fresh seafood is also on sale for home preparation at the restaurant's fishmonger.

V&A WATERFRONT Manenberg Jazz Café ®®®

Shop 102, Clock Tower Centre, 8001 ***Tel*** *(021) 421-5639* ***Map*** *1 2B*

The live African jazz is what brings in the crowds here, with a cosmopolitan audience turning up to watch local and international acts kicking out the jams on the stage. An unpretentious menu offers a spread of seafood, chicken and steak dishes. The karoo lamb chops in sweet basting sauce is a favourite with the regulars.

V&A WATERFRONT Belthazar Restaurant and Wine Bar ®®®®

Shop 153, Victoria Wharf, 8001 ***Tel*** *(021) 421-3753* ***Map*** *1 1C*

The winner of the Fine Dining part of the Waterfront Best Restaurant Competition, as well as Best Steakhouse in SA 2005. Food is prepared to perfection, with an immensely varied and impeccable wine list to match. Having the world's largest selection of wine by the glass is an aspiration the management is striving to achieve. Book ahead.

V&A WATERFRONT Den Anker Restaurant and Bar ®®®®

Pierhead, 8001 ***Tel*** *(021) 419-0249* ***Map*** *1 2B*

The focus at Den Anker is on keeping it Belgian. The building is a glass wrap-around affair presenting views of the marina, City Bowl and the mountain beyond. Mussels with fries and mayo is a signature starter, or try the châteaubriand of springbok for a combination of European preparation and local ingredients.

V&A WATERFRONT The Green Dolphin ®®®®

Shop 2a, Alfred Mall, Pierhead, 8001 ***Tel*** *(021) 421-7471* ***Map*** *1 2B*

The Green Dolphin is a more refined option compared to the more rough-and-ready Manenberg Café. The service is friendly and highly professional, and the meals are named after local and international musicians; choose from Oscar's ostrich entrecôte, Sunny's seafood spectacular or Tiffin's trio of sorbet.

ATLANTIC SEABOARD La Cuccina ®®

Victoria Mall, Victoria Road, Hout Bay, 7872 ***Tel*** *(021) 790-8008*

A spacious deli and restaurant offering freshly baked cakes and buffet lunches. Despite being a little off the beaten path, La Cuccina is well known to most Hout Bay residents. The breakfast menu is also excellent, and the restaurant stays busy throughout the day. Plates are charged by weight at the buffet.

ATLANTIC SEABOARD Café Caprice ®®®

37 Victoria Road, Camps Bay, 8001 ***Tel*** *(021) 438-8315*

A popular haunt with models and fashionable twentysomethings, Café Caprice is always busy, particularly in the summer months. The breakfast menu is popular too, and the eggs Benedict are particularly good. In the evening a resident DJ plays in the bar, and on Sundays it becomes the place to party.

ATLANTIC SEABOARD Codfather ®®®

37 The Drive, Camps Bay, 8001 ***Tel*** *(021) 438-0782*

One of Cape Town's first dedicated sushi restaurants (although they serve other seafood as well), Codfather opened its doors to the public in 2001. The restaurant has no menu, instead waiting staff must consult with guests and help them put together tailor-made dishes. Chose a table with a panoramic view of the ocean.

ATLANTIC SEABOARD La Perla ®®®®

Beach Road, Sea Point, 8000 ***Tel*** *(021) 439-9538*

Attentive waiters deliver delicious fresh fish and shellfish at this grand old dame of seafood restaurants. For each fish on the menu, three dishes are created using different sauces and preparation. The ambience is classically elegant, but not stuffy, and children are welcome. In good weather you can sit outside and watch the breakers.

ATLANTIC SEABOARD Blues ®®®®®

The Promenade, Victoria Road, Camps Bay, 8001 ***Tel*** *(021) 438-2040*

Blues is a product of Cape Town's 80s yuppie restaurant boom. It has performed solidly over the years and was recently refurbished to include a wine cellar complete with a 12-seater table to accommodate tastings and intimate private dinners. Food is contemporary Mediterranean, with lots of seafood and dashes of global influences.

Key to Price Guide *see p358* **Key to Symbols** *see back cover flap*

GREENPOINT AND MOUILLE POINT Andiamo ®®®

Cape Quarter, 72 Waterkant Street, Green Point, 8001 ***Tel*** *(021) 421-3687* ***Map*** *2 D5*

A bustling Italian venue full of *joie de vivre* in the fashionable Cape Quarter section of Green Point. The food is blissfully unpretentious, focusing on straightforward recipes done properly. Among the signature dishes are lamb chops and fish, which is baked in the pizza oven. In the deli is a promotions table featuring tastings seven days a week.

GREENPOINT AND MOUILLE POINT Bravo ®®®

121 Beach Drive, Mouille Point, 8005 ***Tel*** *(021) 439-5260* ***Map*** *1 B3*

A family affair on Mouille Point's sea-facing boulevard, Bravo is a reliable choice for delicious alfresco pizzas or various pasta dishes. There is a children's playground nearby with a miniature train to keep the little ones occupied while you wait for your main course to arrive.

GREENPOINT AND MOUILLE POINT Anatoli ®®®®

24 Napier Street, Green Point, 8005 ***Tel*** *(021) 419-2501* ***Map*** *2 D5*

Serving up Cape Town's best Turkish cuisine since 1984, Anatoli is located in a 100-year-old warehouse. The vibrancy of Turkish culture is reflected in the decor and the cuisine, with an ever-changing list of specials. On arrival, hot flat breads and meze are carried to your table on oversized trays for immediate consumption.

GREENPOINT AND MOUILLE POINT Tank Restaurant and Sushi Bar ®®®®

Cape Quarter, 72 Waterkant Street, Green Point, 8001 ***Tel*** *(021) 419-0007* ***Map*** *2 D5*

Located in the chic Cape Quarter, Tank offers the latest in California-style sushi and Pacific Rim cuisine. The interior is dominated by crisp white walls and elegantly minimalist furnishings. Chef Frederic Faucheux's breast of duck and Norwegian salmon are both highly recommended.

GREENPOINT AND MOUILLE POINT Wakame ®®®®

Cnr Beach Drive & Surrey Road, Mouille Point, 8005 ***Tel*** *(021) 433-2377* ***Map*** *1 B3*

The dramatic interior will no doubt impress as you enter this first-floor sushi bar on Mouille Point's main street. The restaurant's mascot is a long fish skeleton that hangs above the sushi bar. Take a seat inside or choose a table in the balcony area. You may see whales in the bay during the spring and early summer months.

GREENPOINT AND MOUILLE POINT Beluga ®®®®®

The Foundry, Prestwich Street, Greenpoint, 8001 ***Tel*** *(021) 418-2948* ***Map*** *2 D5*

Another Green Point restaurant taking advantage of an industrial space, Beluga has made its home inside a century-old metalworks. Serving up a contemporary mix of seafood and grilled meats, the restaurant includes a sushi bar where you can watch Asian chefs at work slicing up the catch of the day.

GREENPOINT AND MOUILLE POINT Pigalle ®®®®®

57 Somerset Road, Greenpoint, 8001 ***Tel*** *(021) 421-4848* ***Map*** *2 5D*

Occupying a converted ice rink, no expense was spared in fitting out this upmarket eatery. Pigalle is somewhat of an anomaly in Cape Town's fickle restaurant scene, most similar ventures have lasted only a few months, but this restaurant has gone from strength to strength. Expect a smattering of celebrities enjoying a classy night out.

NORTHERN SUBURBS De Tijgerkombuis ®®

12 Old Oak Road, Bellville, 7530 ***Tel*** *(021) 914-0186*

An old-fashioned Dutch pub and restaurant serving Cape Provençal-style meals, this establishment is extremely popular with the locals. A good selection of traditional South African dishes is on offer, along with meatier favourites such as oxtail, *bobotie* and top-notch tripe.

NORTHERN SUBURBS La Masseria ®®®

Cnr Bluegum & Huguenot Streets, Durbanville, 7550 ***Tel*** *(021) 976-0036*

The emphasis is on hearty, home-made dishes at this family-run establishment. The menu is dictated by what produce is in season, and nothing is rushed to ensure that the tradition of attention to detail is maintained. Owner Lorenzo Ciman now has a deli alongside the restaurant where he does a roaring trade in cured meats and Italian cheeses.

SOUTH PENINSULA Kalky's ®

Kalk Bay Harbour, Kalk Bay, 7945 ***Tel*** *(021) 556-5555*

This is Cape Town's best fish-and-chip shop, so don't be put off by the slightly seedy harbour surrounds. Kalky's offers excellent value for money and the freshest possible ingredients. The best option is the "family meal", which will buy you enough fish, chips, calamari and bread rolls to feed a small army.

SOUTH PENINSULA The Meeting Place ®

98 St Georges Street, Simon's Town, 7975 ***Tel*** *(021) 786-1986*

A deli and coffee shop opposite Simon's Town's yacht basin and Jubilee Square, The Meeting Place has a lovely colonial-style balcony overlooking the old main road and plenty of couches to sink into on the inside. Choose from a selection of freshly baked cakes and muffins, toasted sandwiches and other light meals.

SOUTH PENINSULA The Brass Bell ®®

Kalk Bay Station, Main Road, Kalk Bay, 7975 ***Tel*** *(021) 788-5455*

Before tourism came to the area, this established live-music and drinking venue was reliant on a regular stream of patrons from the neighbouring town of Fish Hoek, which had an alcohol ban. These days it is a much smarter restaurant with good pizzas from the wood-fired oven.

SOUTH PENINSULA Cape to Cuba ®®

Main Road, Kalk Bay, 7975 ***Tel*** *(021) 788-1566*

Essentially a series of adjacent corrugated-iron shacks beside the railway line, Cape to Cuba is a marvel of South Africa's enterprising spirit. Every last piece of Latin American and African decor masking the rudimentary nature of the restaurant structure is for sale, usually with a significant price tag. Best enjoyed for cocktails and light snacks.

SOUTH PENINSULA Carla's ®®®

9 York Road, Muizenberg, 7945 ***Tel*** *(021) 788-6860*

Named after Carla, a Mozambiquan expat now happily installed in bohemian Muizenberg, the signature dish "LM prawns" is a firm local favourite, served with rice or chips and a home-made peri-peri sauce. The restaurant itself is small and cosy and presided over by Carla herself on a nightly basis. Booking is always a good idea.

SOUTH PENINSULA Il Postino ®®®

153 Main Road, Muizenberg, 7945 ***Tel*** *(021) 788-6776*

Owned and run by Daniel Evans, Il Postino is housed in the old Muizenberg post office and also hosts the odd show in the Post Box Theatre next door. The venue relies solely on a set menu, with various options chalked up on a board. Whether you go to the theatre or not, the restaurant is definitely worth visiting.

SOUTH PENINSULA Octopus' Garden ®®®

The Old Post Office Building, Main Road, St James, 7945 ***Tel*** *(021) 788-5646*

An idiosyncratic venue in St James and a delicious lemon meringue pie, which is claimed to bestow amorous skills upon the dinner, are only two of the attractions at this delightful restaurant. Children and dogs are welcome here, and the ambience is laid-back and friendly. The restaurant's hammock is the perfect place to relax after a meal.

SOUTH PENINSULA Olympia Café & Deli ®®®

134 Main Road, Kalk Bay, 7975 ***Tel*** *(021) 788-6396*

An irreverent ambience and strong culinary skills have won this café the Award for Everyday Eating. This accolade has been hung in one of the bathrooms for patrons to appreciate. The breakfasts are justifiably legendary, as is the seared tuna and other regularly rotated specials.

SOUTH PENINSULA Polana ®®®

Kalk Bay Harbour, Kalk Bay, 7945 ***Tel*** *(021) 788 4133*

Polana is a little slice of Café del Mar on the Southern Peninsula. Have a cocktail in the bar before heading for your table in the restaurant. In summer the large glass frontage is open, and the sea spray is almost tangible as you recline on the generous couches waiting for the next course to be served.

SOUTH PENINSULA The Black Marlin ®®®®

Main Road, Millers Point, Simon's Town, 7995 ***Tel*** *(021) 786-1621*

To get to Cape Town's oldest seafood restaurant at Millers Point, you have to drive through Simon's Town and past Boulders' penguin colony until the coastline is more or less deserted. The long drive is worth it for the incredible views alone. During whale season you can enjoy freshly caught crayfish while watching the giant mammals swim past..

SOUTH PENINSULA Harbour House ®®®®

Kalk Bay Harbour, Kalk Bay, 7945 ***Tel*** *(021) 788-4133*

Perhaps the most upmarket restaurant in this popular fishing village, Harbour House is located within the harbour and above two other restaurants. The interior is airy, with the bar area almost as big as the restaurant itself. Sipping a cocktail on the deck while watching the seals glide through the water below will make you feel like a millionaire.

SOUTHERN SUBURBS Peddlars on the Bend ®®

Spaanschemat River Road, Constantia, 7800 ***Tel*** *(021) 794-7747*

A local institution, Peddlars serves up consistent pub fare to a steady stream of loyal patrons. On a fine day, the garden area is full to capacity and alive with the hubbub of local gossip. Try the *ferrari prego* for the Peddlars twist on the classic steak roll, or the kingklip calabrese, with anchovies. Veggies will enjoy the spinach and lentil bake.

SOUTHERN SUBURBS Rhodes Memorial Restaurant ®®

Rhodes Memorial, Groote Schuur Estate, Rondebosch, 7740 ***Tel*** *(021) 689-9151*

Famous for its home-made desserts, this restaurant behind the granite Rhodes Memorial offers unbeatable views across the City Bowl and Cape Flats. It is also an ideal breakfast venue. Take an early morning hike along the mountain's contour path and end it here with a fry-up and some freshly squeezed orange juice – or even a beer.

SOUTHERN SUBURBS Constantia Uitsig ®®®®®

Constantia Uitsig Farm, Spaanschemat River Road, Constantia, 7800 ***Tel*** *(021) 794-4480*

A much-lauded establishment that gets it right on all levels: from the service to the food, down to the wine list. Installed in the original manor house of the Constantia Uitsig wine estate, the restaurant is hugely popular and presided over by the generous hospitality of host Frank Swainston, who opened it 13 years ago.

SOUTHERN SUBURBS La Colombe ®®®®®

Constantia Uitsig, Constantia, 7800 ***Tel*** *(021) 794-2390*

Located on the Uitsig working wine farm, La Colombe was voted 28th-best restaurant in the world by the UK's *Restaurant* magazine in 2006. The flavours are of French origin, but with a distinctive Cape accent. Ideal for special occasions that require simple elegance, the emphasis is on well-crafted meals rather than overblown service.

Key to Price Guide *see p358* **Key to Symbols** *see back cover flap*

CAPE WINELANDS

FRANSCHHOEK Bouillabaisse Champagne and Oyster Bar ®®®®

38 Huguenot Street, Franschhoek, 7690 ***Tel*** *(021) 876-4430*

Chef Camil has created a decadent restaurant serving an exotic array of tapas-sized dishes. The tasting menu is split into tantalising, delightful, sensational, marvellous and prestige sections – ask for help to create your own perfect menu. Make sure you leave room for the delicious oysters and champagne that gave the restaurant its name.

FRANSCHHOEK Haute Cabrière ®®®®

Cabriere Estate, Pass Road, Franschhoek, 7690 ***Tel*** *(021) 876-3688*

A supremely elegant cellar restaurant high up on the Franschhoek Pass. A great many of the dishes on the menu use ingredients found in the valley below, including fresh salmon and trout bred and caught in the cold-water stream that flows off the mountain. Haute Cabrière routinely features in most South African top ten restaurant lists.

FRANSCHHOEK La Petite Ferme ®®®®

Franschhoek Pass Road, Franschhoek, 7690 ***Tel*** *(021) 876-3016*

Wine magazine placed La Petite Ferme in its 2004 Top Ten Restaurants list. The cellar is impressive to say the least, and the winery has produced several award-winning vintages over the years. Head chef Olivia Mitchell and sous chef Carina Bouwer are a *tour de force* in the kitchen, crafting contemporary African and Malay masterpieces.

FRANSCHHOEK Le Quartier Français ®®®®®

16 Huguenot Road, Franschhoek, 7690 ***Tel*** *(021) 876-2151*

Voted Best Small Hotel in the World by *Tatler* magazine in 2005, Le Quartier also regularly features in *Restaurant* magazine's top 50. Chef Margot Janse is the star of the show and offers guests a choice of four-, six- or eight-course dining experiences from a menu that uses only seasonal local ingredients.

FRANSCHHOEK Reubens Restaurant & Bar ®®®®®

Oude Stallen Centre, 19 Huguenot Road, Franschhoek, 7690 ***Tel*** *(021) 876-3772*

This stylish modern café was set up by check Reuben Riffel in 2003, who has worked hard to live up to the hype that surrounding the establishment when it first opening. The relaxed ambience, great service, and particularly good seafood all make for a memorable dining experience.

PAARL Kikka ®

217 Main Street, Paarl, 7646 ***Tel*** *(021) 872-0685*

Situated just off the village main road, Kikka unusually houses both a florist and a coffee shop. Don't let the interesting trinkets that fill the shop distract you from the excellent buffet or light meals served in a comfortable and casual environment. The restaurant next door, Noop, offers more substantial dishes..

PAARL Restaurant 101 ®®

Simonsvlei Winery, Old Paarl Road (101), Paarl, 7646 ***Tel*** *(021) 863-2486*

Child-friendly, with extensive indoor and outdoor seating, 101 provides all-round value for money and is an antidote to the more gastronomic options that are found all over the Winelands. Large parties are catered for, and buffet or picnic lunches are served around the water feature in the summer months.

PAARL 42 on Main ®®®

42 Main Street, Paarl, 7646 ***Tel*** *(021) 863-0142*

A unique traditional Afrikaans establishment, 42 exudes a relaxed farmhouse ambience with the house divided into four separate dining rooms, the most popular being the *braaikamer*, or barbecue room. The menu consists of South African favourites, as well as recipes from various other cultures, including a popular Punjabi lamb dish.

PAARL Gabbemas ®®®

De Oude Paarl Hotel, 132 Main Street, Paarl, 7646 ***Tel*** *(021) 872-1002*

A gourmet restaurant in the Oude Paarl Hotel, Gabbemas has a vast selection of wines to choose from and some quite avant-garde main courses. Adventurous gastronomes might like to try the honey, *rooibos* tea and vanilla-marinated chicken *peccata* topped with a *paw paw* and chilli jam salsa and a gooseberry coulis.

PAARL Bosmans ®®®®®

The Grande Roche Hotel, Plantasie, 7646 ***Tel*** *(021) 863-2727*

Named South Africa's Top Deluxe Restaurant by *Style* magazine for two years running, Bosmans has an international team of chefs who maintain its position as one of the world's great eateries. The food is said to "reflect a sophisticated awareness of what is happening in the international culinary world". A classic fine-dining experience.

SOMERSET WEST The Avontuur Estate Restaurant ®®®

R44, Somerset West, 7130 ***Tel*** *(021) 855-4296*

Located on a wine farm between the tasting area and the cellar, Avontuur offers unhurried meals made up of fresh country ingredients with a Mediterranean flavour. In fine weather, outdoor seating is available in the patio garden, with sweeping views across the vineyards all the way to Table Mountain.

SOMERSET WEST Steffanie's Place ®®®

113 Irene Avenue, Somerset West, 7130 **Tel** *(021) 852-7584*

This ever-popular family-run business only gets better. The location is perhaps its biggest coup, as Steffanie's Place is perched right at the crest of Irene Avenue overlooking the mountains and sea beyond. Conan Garrett is a talented head chef, and dishes like grilled kingklip with Parmesan and chive sauce keep the punters coming back.

SOMERSET WEST Wine Women & Sushi ®®®

Urtell Crescent, The Triangle, Somerset Mall, 7130 **Tel** *(021) 851-0271*

Sushi is pretty much all Wine Women and Sushi does, and it does it properly, which is why this is one of the best Japanese restaurants in the Cape Winelands. The menu offers several vegetarian options as well as a takeaway service. In summer there are outdoor tables for *alfresco* dinning.

SOMERSET WEST 96 Winery Road ®®®®

Zandberg Farm, Winery Road, Somerset West, 7130 **Tel** *(021) 842-2020*

Fresh, organic local ingredients are used to great effect at this well-run Helderberg countryside restaurant. The steaks are aged for 18 days in the restaurant's purpose-built cold room, and they are particularly good. 96 Winery Road received an Award of Excellence for its wine list at the Diners Club Wine List of the Year Awards.

SOMERSET WEST Die Ou Pastorie ®®®®

41 Lourens Street, Somerset West, 7130 **Tel** *(021) 850-1660*

A country house and restaurant that has scooped a number of industry accolades. Main courses draw upon locally reared meats: the braised springbok shank and pan-seared ostrich fillet are both delicious. Vegetarians can content themselves with the butternut ravioli served with spinach *voluté*.

STELLENBOSCH Moyo at Spier ®®®®®

Spier Estate, Lynedoch Road (R310), 7603 **Tel** *(021) 809-1131*

Moyo is about much more than a meal: it's a Cape African culture experience. Food is served as a delicious buffet, while indigenous dancers and musicians entertain with traditional drumming and African storytelling. The garden is filled with bedouin tents and tree houses with water features. A great option for children.

STELLENBOSCH Terroir ®®®®®

Kleine Zalze, Techno Park turnoff, Strand Road (R44), 7600 **Tel** *(021) 880-8167*

A Provençal-inspired restaurant with award-winning wines from the host estate of Kleine Zalze. Terroir overlooks a lake, and there is additional seating outside, under the majestic oak trees. Chefs Michael and Nic have described their dishes as "deceptively simple" and are directed by the seasonality of the excellent local ingredients.

WESTERN COASTAL TERRACE

BLOUBERG The Blue Peter ®®

Blue Peter Hotel, 7 Popham Road, Bloubergstrand, 7441 **Tel** *(021) 554-1956*

Three restaurants rolled into one, including fine dining in the Upper Deck. The two informal eateries in the Lower Deck are firm child-friendly favourites with the locals, and the pizzas are highly recommended. The famous view across the bay to Table Mountain and the friendly atmosphere are the main draws here.

BLOUBERG On the Rocks ®®®

45 Stadler Road, Bloubergstrand, 7441 **Tel** *(021) 554-1988*

On the Rocks is literally that: enjoy views of the ocean and watch dolphins play in the waves as the sun dips below the Table Mountain skyline. An upmarket choice, this restaurant focuses on seafood but also has plenty to satisfy carnivores and vegetarians. Try the catch of the day, or the medallion of kingklip stuffed with basil and ham.

CLANWILLIAM Khoisan Kitchen ®®®®

Traveller's Rest, R364, Clanwilliam, 8135 **Tel** *(027) 482-1824*

Haffie Strauss serves up hearty traditional Afrikaans and Malay fare on the banks of the Brandewyn River. Mutton stew, *waterblommetjie* stew and *roosterkoek* are long-standing favourites. The Sevilla Rock Art Trail follows the river for four kilometres (2.5 miles), visiting nine sites of rock paintings left behind by the former Khoi Khoi inhabitants.

DARLING Evita se Perron ®®®

Darling Railway Station, Darling, 7345 **Tel** *(022) 492-2831*

The food is pretty good here, but this is more about the show than anything. Evita Bezuidenhout is a national treasure, the alter ego of comedian and international AIDS activist Pieter Dirk Uys. Expect a hilarious and irreverent stand-up routine that ruthlessly satirizes the Rainbow Nation and all of its chequered history.

LAMBERT'S BAY Muisbosskerm Open-Air Restaurant ®®®

Elands Bay Road, Lambert's Bay, 8130 **Tel** *(027) 432-1017*

The original West Coast seafood *skerm*, Muisbos started as a hobby to entertain family and friends, and grew into something of a phenomenon. The meal is an endless open-air buffet of seafood indulgence. As well as baked, smoked and grilled fish and crayfish, there is also a variety of *potjiekos* on offer.

LANGEBAAN Die Strandloper ®®®

On the beach, Langebaan, 7357 **Tel** *(022) 772-2490*

A visit to Die Strandloper necessitates a lengthy and indulgent meal spread out over several hours. Course after course of freshly caught and expertly prepared seafood is the speciality here. The charge is per head, with children under 12 paying according to their height, and those under five eating for free.

YZERFONTEIN Strandkombuis ®®®

16 Mile Beach, Dolphin Way, Yzerfontein, 7351 **Tel** *(022) 451-2206*

Located on the immaculate 16 Mile Beach at Yzerfontein, this is an outdoor seafood extravaganza that suits large and informal gatherings. Strandkombuis is great for family occasions: children are welcome, and there is no corkage fee. All food is prepared in a network of braai pits and stone ovens, including the freshly baked bread.

SOUTHERN CAPE

GREYTON The Jam Tin ®

Boschmanskloof, Aster Laan, Greyton, 7233 **Tel** *(028) 254-9075*

Traditional cuisine in an authentic Cape home setting is on offer at the quaint Jam Tin. If you call ahead to make a reservation, you might well be asked what your favourite dish is, and they will make it specially for you. Cape Dutch and Malay-style meals are expertly prepared. Open daily for dinner and lunch by arrangement.

HERMANUS Momo ®®

165 Main Road, Hermanus, 7200 **Tel** *(028) 313-2851*

Momo offers a reasonably priced Thai alternative to Hermanus's more traditional restaurants. The chefs only use ingredients of the highest quality to produce meals that are healthy, delicious and fresh. The restaurant is a great choice for vegetarians with a wide range of options to suit all tastes.

OUDTSHOORN The Godfather ®®®

61 Voortrekker Road, Oudtshoorn, 6620 **Tel** *(044) 272-5404*

This Italian restaurant has a reputation as the Southern Cape's own Little Italy. Ordinary and unassuming from the exterior, The Godfather is famed for the atmosphere within. Colourful murals with caricatures of celebrity visitors adorn the walls, while the menu reveals a hearty collection of grills, game and pasta dishes.

OUDTSHOORN Jemima's ®®®®

94 Baron van Rheede Street, Oudtshoorn, 6620 **Tel** *(044) 272-0808*

A gourmet food-and-wine feast is assured at Jemima's, voted as one of South Africa's ten best restaurants on several occasions. The greagarious Malherbe family love to share their culinary talents with their guests. They're also keen to recommend just the right bottle of wine to accompany the house speciality: leg of Karoo lamb.

STANFORD Marianas Home Deli & Bistro ®®®

12 Du Toit Street, Stanford, 7210 **Tel** *(028) 341-0272*

Open only for breakfast and lunch on Friday, Saturday and Sundays, Marianas is the winner of *Eat Out*'s 2005 award for South Africa's Top Farm Kitchen. Vegetables are grown organically in the field outside, and dishes such as the lamb shanks are heavenly. Booking is advisable at this superb, friendly and unpretentious foodie mecca.

SWELLENDAM Herberg Roosje van de Kaap ®®®

5 Drostdy Street, Swellendam, 6740 **Tel** *(028) 514-3001*

Part of the Roosje van de Kaap hotel, this eatery is regularly rated as a top ten Southern Cape restaurant by *Eat Out*. The menu ranges from Cape Malay to classical French dishes and gourmet pizzas. An Old World ambience is enhanced by traditional decor and soft lighting. Leave room for the wonderful desserts.

SWELLENDAM Zanddrift Restaurant ®®®

Stormsvlei on the N2, from Swellendam to Riviersonderend, 7150 **Tel** *(028) 261-1167*

Chef Edwina Kohler's country kitchen occupies the old Stormsvlei Hotel. Her preparation policy is wonderfully ad hoc, eschewing the need for a menu. She asks people what they like to eat and prepares the meal accordingly. Country stew, entrecôte with crêpes, cream and brandy, as well as ox tongue with mustard sauce, are all past triumphs.

GARDEN ROUTE TO GRAHAMSTOWN

GRAHAMSTOWN The Cock House ®®®

10 Market Street, Grahamstown, 6139 **Tel** *(046) 636-1287*

This established guesthouse and restaurant in a listed building offers home-baked breads, freshly cut herbs from the garden, an innovative menu and a lovingly compiled wine list. Former guests include Nelson Mandela. The restaurant features in Lannice Snyman's book *Reflections of the South African Table*.

KNYSNA Ile de Pain ®®

Thesen's Island Harbour Town, The Boatshed, Knysna, 6571 ***Tel*** *(044) 302-5707*

Knysna's equivalent of Kalk Bay's Olympia Café *(see p361)*, Ile de Pain has also scooped an *Eat Out* Everyday Eating Award. The bread is legendary, and all the ingredients are free range and sourced locally. For light meals, you can't go wrong here. The toasted baguette with figs, gorgonzola, rocket and balsamic vinegar is highly recommended.

KNYSNA The Knysna Oyster Company ®®

Thesen's Island, Knysna, 6570 ***Tel*** *(044) 382-6941*

This restaurant has been farming its own oysters since 1949. Enjoy the magnificent waterfront views while sipping a glass of champagne, and you're ready for the ultimate Knysna experience. Wild oysters are also available, as well as alternatives such as *zwembezi* – deep fried oysters served on a bed of spinach and *mielie pap* (polenta).

KNYSNA Persellos ®®

41 Main Road, Town Central, Knysna, 6570 ***Tel*** *(044) 382-2665*

Italian and family-run, this pizzeria is known by the locals simply as "Mamma's". If you are looking for a reasonably priced option away from the tourist hubbub of Thesen's Island, then this is the place to go. Pasta is prepared freshly on the premises, and this really can be tasted in the finished product.

KNYSNA 34 Degrees South ®®®

Quay 19, Knysna Quays, Waterfront Drive, Knysna, 6571 ***Tel*** *(044) 382-7331*

Named after Knysna's longitudinal position on the globe, 34 Degrees South is a fantastic combination of a deli and a seafood emporium. The focus is definitely on the fruits of the ocean: the hake is freshly caught as opposed to trawled, and there is fresh line fish daily. The ubiquitous Knysna oyster is also available.

KNYSNA Paquitas ®®®

The Heads, George Rex Drive, Knysna, 6570 ***Tel*** *(044) 384-0408*

Named after a three-mast German barque that ran aground and sank off the Southern coast in 1903, Paquitas is situated on the rocks at the famous Knysna Heads. This family-run restaurant serves hearty, uncomplicated fare: grills, pizzas and pasta dishes. These are best enjoyed with a bottle of wine while soaking up the spectacular setting.

KNYSNA Drydock Food Co ®®®®

Knysna Quays, off Waterfront Drive, Knysna, 6571 ***Tel*** *(044) 382-7310*

Erected on the site of Knysna's first dry dock, this reasonably priced establishment offers a wide-range of ocean-fresh seafood, decadent salads and fusion cuisine. Try the signature kingklip espatada, or the catch of the day. The bar is well stocked with local and imported beers and spirits. The cellar has a decent variety of wine too.

KNYSNA Pembreys ®®®®

Brenton Road, Belvidere, Knysna, 6571 ***Tel*** *(044) 386-0005*

Home-made pastas and local dishes infused with Mediterranean flavours rule in Peter and Viv Vadas's kitchen. The simple country setting belies the accomplished menu. Sole is a signature dish, and the desserts, including a mouth-watering *crème brûlée*, are excellent. The couple travel to Europe annually for culinary sabbaticals.

PLETTENBERG BAY Blue Bay Café ®®®

Lookout Centre, Main Street, Plettenberg Bay, 6600 ***Tel*** *(044) 533-1390*

The Blue Bay Café offers fine dining in a traditionally elegant ambience. Try specialities such as wood-smoked springbok served with rocket, crème fraîche and roasted tomato salsa, or go for the seared tuna encrusted with sesame seeds, served with soy sauce, wasabi and pickled ginger.

PLETTENBERG BAY Cornuti al Mare ®®®

Perestrella Street, Plettenberg Bay, 6600 ***Tel*** *(044) 533-1277*

Cornuti al Mare (literally, "cuckolds at the seaside") is the coastal counterpart of Piero Carrara's Johannesburg venture. Extremely popular with local patrons, it is best to book a table. The perfect crisp-based pizzas are a good option, although the coastal location also allows for the addition of seafood meze to the menu.

PLETTENBERG BAY The Lookout Deck ®®®

Lookout Beach, Plettenberg Bay, 6600 ***Tel*** *(044) 533-1379*

Lookout Beach is one of only two Blue Flag beaches in South Africa – an accolade bestowed because of its pristine condition. This restaurant is firmly established as one Plettenberg Bay's best, and it sports an unashamedly seafood-biased menu. Views of the whales, dolphins and sunsets are a wonderful distraction from the cuisine.

PORT ELIZABETH Gondwana Café ®®

Shop 2, Dolphin's Leap, Beach Road, Humewood, 6001 ***Tel*** *(041) 585-0990*

Gondwana Café in Humewood is a popular and chic lounge-cum-restaurant venue with a surprisingly eclectic menu. This "corner café" boasts floor-to-ceiling windows, so you can sip one of their excellent cocktails as you enjoy splendid views over the bay. Resident DJs spin deep-house and lounge music on the weekends.

PORT ELIZABETH Royal Delhi ®®

10 Burgess Street, Central, Port Elizabeth, 6001 ***Tel*** *(041) 373-8216*

Opened ten years ago, the family-run Royal Delhi offers the best curries in the area. The restaurant is located in a rather bland suburban building but features a light, richly decorated interior. On the menu is a wide range of curries, plus seafood, vegetarian dishes and grilled meats. There are some interesting wines on the list.

Key to Price Guide *see p358* **Key to Symbols** *see back cover flap*

PORT ELIZABETH De Kelder ®®®®

Marine Protea Hotel, Marine Drive, Summerstrand, 6001 ***Tel*** *(041) 583-2750*

Expect lots of red-meat and venison platters at this large, well-established and sophisticated Port Elizabeth restaurant. Staff are friendly and attentive, and the food is presented with loving panache. There are also popular seafood specialities on offer and excellent flambés for dessert.

WILD COAST, DRAKENSBERG & MIDLANDS

BERGVILLE Bingelela Restaurant ®®®

Needwood Farm, Box 5, Bergville, 3350 ***Tel*** *(036) 448-1336*

Nestled at the foot of the Drakensberg Mountains is this old farmhouse offering food as well as friendly B&B accommodation. Light lunches and dinners are served by owners Paula and Joss in the 68-seat restaurant or around the boma in summer. A non-smoking area is available.

BERGVILLE Caterpillar & Catfish Cookhouse ®®®®

Windmill Farm, Oliviershoek Pass, Bergville, 3350 ***Tel*** *(036) 438-6130*

Located on the crest of the Oliviershoek Pass, this B&B-cum-restaurant claims to serve trout in 30 different ways. You might want to take them up on that, or opt for turf instead, with a tasty steak followed by caramel pudding. Sit around the log fire in winter, or stay in the rooms and chalets if you indulge in too many of the wines on the list.

COFFEE BAY Lily Lodge Seafood Restaurant ®®

Box 7, Second Beach, Port St Johns, 5120 ***Tel*** *(047) 564-1171*

In the dune forests at Second Beach, overlooking the Indian Ocean and its dolphins, Lily Lodge serves a wide-ranging menu of fruits of the sea: crayfish, oysters, prawns, mussels, rock cod and cob are all complemented by a small but perfectly formed selection of Cape wines. A family-run venture staffed by local Pondoland people.

EAST LONDON Ocean Basket ®®

Vincent Park Centre, Vincent, East London, 5214 ***Tel*** *(043) 726-8809*

Owned by the largest fish retailer in South Africa and part of a popular national chain, Ocean Basket is a bright, cheerful restaurant offering reasonably priced fare, ranging from seafood to Mediterranean dishes, from Creole and Cajun food to sushi. You can bring your own wine, which will be subject to a corkage fee of R15.

EAST LONDON Michaela's at Cintsa ®®®

Steenbras Drive, Cintsa East, Eastern Cape, 5275 ***Tel*** *(043) 738-5139*

This two-storey restaurant boasts a spectacular location on top of the dunes, with views that stretch as far as the eye can see. The art and craftwork decorating the venue are all for sale. The menu is contemporary, with the accent on local seafood, but also including curries, seafood pasta and grilled meats. Good local wines are well priced.

HIMEVILLE Moorcroft Manor ®®®

Sani Road, Himeville, 3256 ***Tel*** *(033) 702-1967*

The restaurant at this award-winning five-star guesthouse in the Drakensberg Mountains offers a selection of light lunches (including a delicious ploughman's platter) and à la carte dinners. In the evening, the stylish menu features the best of local meat, trout, salads, mushrooms and cheeses. There is also an impressive wine list.

HOWICK Corner Post ®®

124 Main Street, Howick, 4200 ***Tel*** *(033) 330-7636*

This charming pub-cum-restaurant offers a country/fusion menu, which translates on the plate as old favourites with an oriental twist. Try the duck with soya, orange and sherry, and be sure to leave room for the fabulous desserts, such as home-made ice creams or *crème brûlée*. Art exhibitions are regularly held at the establishment.

HOWICK Yellowood Café ®®®

1 Shafton Road, Howick, 4200 ***Tel*** *(033) 330-2461*

In the heart of the Natal Midlands, overlooking the Howick Falls, is this country restaurant offering superb views from the verandah tables. The cuisine, based around fresh seasonal delights, matches the vistas. Select your meal from either the à la carte or pub menu, and match it with a suitable wine from the good selection.

LESOTHO Rendez-Vous Restaurant ®®®

Kingsway Street, Maseru ***Tel*** *00266 2231 2114*

Also known as the Lancer's Inn, Rendez-Vous is one of Lesotho King Letsie III's favourite restaurants. You too can eat like royalty here: the dishes available on the à la carte menu are nothing short of excellent. However, be prepared for the service to be on the slow side.

MONT-AUX-SOURCES Tower of Pizza ®®

Mont-aux-Sources, Northern Drakensberg, 3354 ***Tel*** *(036) 438-6480*

The tower is really a silo on a working farm, but it also indicates this homely Italian eatery. Wood-burning oven pizzas, pasta dishes, *tramezzini*, salads and seasonal specialities all find their way on to the menu here. The desserts are also worth trying. Local art and curios decorate the dining room of this child-friendly, informal eatery.

MOOI RIVER Hartford House
®®®®®

Hlatikulu Road, Mooi River, 3300 **Tel** *(033) 263-7713*

Fine dining is on offer at this international stud farm, which was the former home of the last prime minister of Natal. Young master chef Jacqueline Cameron has devised a sumptuous menu that has earned the restaurant many accolades, such as inclusion in the American Express Fine Dining programme. There is an extensive wine list.

PIETERMARITZBURG Turtle Bay
®®

Cascades Centre, McCarthy Drive, Pietermaritzburg, 3201 **Tel** *(033) 347-1555*

Cosmopolitan fine dining is found in this relaxed eatery in a shopping centre. Enjoy a light lunch or an afternoon tea on the terrace by the stream. Among chef Garth Bayley's best dishes are pocket of pork with prune and apricot, Moroccan fillet with dates and coriander, and vegetable strudel with sun-dried tomato pesto. Well-balanced wine list.

PIETERMARITZBURG Els Amics
®®®®

380 Longmarket Street, Pietermaritzburg, 3201 **Tel** *(033) 345-6524*

Opened in 1976 in a Victorian house, Els Amics provides an à la carte menu with a Spanish flavour. Order garlic soup, gazpacho and succulent cuts of meat with lots of fresh vegetables. There are also some great choices on the wine list. Given sufficient notice (at least six hours), owner and chef Roy Tabernor will also prepare a genuine *paella valenciana*.

TWEEDIE Snooty Fox
®®

Fernhill Hotel, Tweedie, 3255 **Tel** *(033) 330-5071*

Hearty breakfasts, filling lunches and romantic, candlelit dinners are all available at the restaurant of this five-star country hotel built in Tudor style. The food is reasonably priced, especially the renowned carvery menu, and you can enjoy it by the fireplace, your dining experience accompanied by the sound of the crackling logs. Excellent service.

UNDERBERG Pile Inn Tea Garden
®

27 Old Main Road, Underberg, 3257 **Tel** *(033) 701-2496 or (0)82 487-4998*

Popular tea garden serving good milk shakes and the best fish 'n' chips and burgers in the area. Located at the foot of Hlogoma Mountain, the Pile Inn is a good stop on the way to or from the Sani Pass. There is a cosy fireplace with logs burning if it's snowing, and a shady patio for alfresco dining in the summer.

DURBAN AND ZULULAND

BALLITO Al Pescatore
®®

14 Edward Place, Ballito, 4420 **Tel** *(032) 946-3574*

Long established and popular with the local community, this Italian restaurant is renowned for both its great views of the Indian Ocean and its hearty dishes. Try the seafood platter, or the line fish in pesto sauce, and accompany your choice with a good wine from the varied list. Live entertainment on Wednesdays and Thursdays.

DURBAN 9th Avenue Bistro & Bar
®®

Avonmore Centre, Morningside, 4001 **Tel** *(031) 312-9134*

An upmarket café-style eatery with ochre walls. Owner-chef Carly Goncalves, who runs the place with his wife Frances, aims for interesting menus featuring classic and modern fusion interpretations of Japanese and Italian dishes. The fare changes according to the seasons. 9th Avenue made the top ten Special Occasion Restaurants in *Wine* magazine.

DURBAN Fabulous Moroccan
®®

37 St Thomas Road, Durban, 4001 **Tel** *(031) 201-7292*

Located in an elegant two-storey house next to Durban's Botanical Gardens, Fabulous Moroccan impresses with its lavish decor, tapestries and mosaics, its perfumed garden and its North African food. The choice is restricted to ten starters and ten mains, including *tajines* with saffron and couscous. Enjoy a *hookah* and belly-dancing at weekends.

DURBAN Jaipur Palace
®®

Sunset Casino Boulevard, Durban, 4001 **Tel** *(031) 332-2767*

Part of the Riverside Hotel complex, Jaipur Palace was voted one of the best 100 restaurants in South Africa. As well as splendid views of the Indian Ocean, it offers a vast menu of North and South Indian dishes, and it is especially good for vegetarians and curry and tandoor lovers. Although the kitchen is halal, there is a full bar and wine list.

DURBAN Mo' Noodles
®®

Florida Centre, 275 Florida Road, Berea, 4001 **Tel** *(031) 312-4193*

Based within a suburban shopping centre, this restaurant has a great atmosphere. The food is a fusion of Thai, Japanese and Australian styles, with the spotlight firmly on noodles. Specialities include chicken in sesame and chilli peanuts on coconut noodles. There are also healthy chicken, vegetarian and salad options.

DURBAN TransAfrica Express
®®

BAT Centre, 45 Maritime Place, Victoria Embankment, Durban, 4001 **Tel** *(031) 332-0804*

Indian-influenced pan-African food with a contemporary, innovative twist is available at TransAfrica Express. Enjoy views of the small boat harbour as you tuck into the lovely meze platters, which combine Drakensberg trout, prawn chapati, roast sweet potato and parsnip, and marinated ostrich.

Key to Price Guide *see p358* **Key to Symbols** *see back cover flap*

DURBAN Vintage India ®®

20 Windermere Road, Morningside, 4001 ***Tel*** *(031) 309-1328*

An upmarket dining area decorated with warm colours, wooden furniture and traditional Indian musical instruments on the wall. The food runs the gamut of the Indian sub-continent, from Goan specialities such as the delicately spiced prawns *xacuti* to Hyderabadi dishes. There is also a vast selection of vegetarian dishes.

DURBAN Gateway to India ®®®

Palm Boulevard, Umhlanga Ridge, New Town, 4320 ***Tel*** *(031) 566-5711*

This sumptuously decorated Indian restaurant is located in an upmarket shopping mall. Everything in it comes from India: from the artworks to the chefs. The huge North Indian menu includes tandoori dishes, curries, *roghan josh* and a great and varied vegetarian selection. There is an extensive wine list, including many options by the glass.

DURBAN Oyster Bar ®®®

Wilsons Wharf, Victoria Embankment, Durban, 4001 ***Tel*** *(031) 307-7863*

One of a group of trendy restaurants right on the water. Locally fished (or cultivated) oysters are served with lemon and champagne, or you can try oysters mornay (topped with cheese), oysters wrapped in bacon, or oysters with a Thai sauce of ginger, coriander and soya, then grilled. Local and international wines appear on the list.

DURBAN Saagries House of Curries ®®®

Holiday Inn, 167 Marine Parade, Durban, 4001 ***Tel*** *(031) 332-7922*

A favourite of Zulu royalty, Saagries is a spacious, plush and elegant restaurant with good food and service. The menu offers authentic Cape Malay, South Indian and Gujarat curries. Be warned though, Durban curries tend to be very hot. End by sampling a dessert from the extensive range. The wines are expertly chosen to complement the food.

DURBAN Le Troquet ®®®®

Village Market, 123 Hofmeyr Road, Westville, 3630 ***Tel*** *(031) 266-5388*

Authentically French, this traditional bistro has been in the hands of the same family for more than 20 years. Daily specials of *cuisine regionale* include seafood or mushroom pancakes, rabbit and flamed fillet mignon. There are also some rare local wines. The interior features dark walls and furniture, rosy linen and a colonnade across the dining area.

DURBAN Roma Revolving Restaurant ®®®®

32nd Floor, John Ross House, Esplanade, Victoria Embankment, Durban, 4001 ***Tel*** *(031) 368-2275*

Situated 105 m (344 ft) above sea level, Roma gently revolves at the top of John Ross House for 360-degree views of the city. The cuisine is based on Italian and continental fare, with a good mix of seafood and game dishes. Signature dishes include crayfish Portofino, in a creamy white-wine sauce, and the fillet Old Man, flambéed in brandy.

RAMSGATE The Waffle House ®®

Marine Drive, Ramsgate, 4285 ***Tel*** *(039) 314-9424*

Attentive service, good prices and a play area for children make The Waffle House a great place to relax for families on an active holiday. Enjoy Belgian waffles on the deck overlooking the lagoon. Toppings range from hot apple and ice cream to vegetable curry or smoked salmon with avocado and cream cheese.

RAMSGATE La Petite Normandie ®®®®

73 Marine Drive, Ramsgate, 4285 ***Tel*** *(039) 317-1818*

Gallic hospitality is on offer at La Petite Normandie, where convivial owner Yvonne Cosson offers traditional French food: frogs' legs, rabbit, stuffed duck, *pâté de foie gras*, creamed asparagus, *tarte tatin* and profiteroles. Eat indoors or alfresco in the pretty garden. Winner of the Johnny Walker Top Country Kitchens award. Excellent wine list.

UMHLANGA ROCKS Razzmatazz ®®

10 Lagoon Drive, Umhlanga Rocks, 4320 ***Tel*** *(031) 561-5847*

Choose between formal dining in a terracotta-coloured room with white tablecloths, or a more casual experience alfresco, on a terrace overlooking the ocean. Signature dishes include crocodile or ostrich kebabs, and chicken in a pastry basket. Also available are seafood, game and pasta dishes. End your meal with their famous *crème brûlée*.

UMHLANGA ROCKS Tare Panda ®®

Gateway Theatre of Shopping, Umhlanga Rocks, 4320 ***Tel*** *(031) 566-3138*

Named after a cartoon character, Tare Panda has a mainly Japanese menu, although it also offers Chinese and Thai dishes. The chef uses traditional Japanese methods to prepare sushi, tepanyaki, tempura and the less familiar *shabu shabu* – rather like fondue cooking in hot soup. The bar is expertly stocked with local wine and sake.

UMHLANGA ROCKS Grill Room at the Oyster Box ®®®®

Lighthouse Road, Umhlanga Rocks, 4320 ***Tel*** *(031) 561-2233*

Located right on the beach, the Grill Room is renowned for its old-fashioned, discreet silver service. The restaurant serves oysters in a variety of ways, but the menu also includes great steaks, chops and curries. Lighter, pub-style meals are on offer on the terrace overlooking the ocean. There is a good list of South African wines.

UMHLANGA ROCKS Sugar Club ®®®®

Lighthouse Road, Umhlanga Rocks, 4320 ***Tel*** *(031) 561-2211*

The luxurious restaurant of the five-star Beverly Hills Hotel is one of the best in the country. In addition to its extensive wine list, the Sugar Club boasts an award-winning chef preparing fusion/contemporary cuisine. Signature dishes include tempura of West Coast oysters and Asian confit of duck, with truffle and stir-fried vegetables.

ROSEBANK Cranks ®®

Shop 169, Rosebank Mall, 2193 ***Tel*** *(011) 880-3442*

A lively and atmospheric restaurant, Cranks is not ideal for anyone looking for a quiet, intimate dining experience. This colourful and festive Thai/Vietnamese restaurant has been going successfully for more than 30 years. All dishes can be adapted for vegetarians. Expect live blues music on weekends.

ROSEBANK The Grillhouse ®®®®

Shop 70, The Firs Hyatt Centre, 2193 ***Tel*** *(011) 880-3945*

This New York-style grillhouse offers choice steaks – basted or pepper-coated – and in different sizes. Though it is primarily a steakhouse, the restaurant also serves seafood, line fish and poultry. The salon area, separated from the restaurant by a corridor, offers a smoking area, a bar for pre-dinner drinks and live music.

SANDTON Yo Sushi ®®

Shop 49, Village Walk Shopping Centre, 2196 ***Tel*** *(011) 783-6166*

A conveyor-belt sushi restaurant with fresh, high-quality sushi, sashimi and other Japanese staples. The plates travelling past your seat are colour-coded according to their price. Start your meal with a warm cup of sake, but switch to green tea between servings to cleanse your palate. Prices are reasonable and the vibe is relaxed.

SANDTON The Blues Room ®®®®

Village Walk Shopping Centre, 2196 ***Tel*** *(011) 784-5527*

A low-lit blues-themed restaurant that offers a varied international menu – from buffalo wings and traditional burgers to pasta dishes, via oriental stir fries and a handful of seafood options. The Blues Room features local and international blues, rock and jazz bands. It's worth leaving some room for their famously decadent desserts.

SANDTON Browns of Rivonia ®®®®

21 Wessels Road, 2128 ***Tel*** *(011) 803-7533*

Once a farmhouse, this restaurant offers a sunny garden for alfresco eating in the summer months and a fireplace in the dining room to warm up the ambience in the colder months. Their exquisite wine and cheese selection, seafood and venison options have won the restaurant several awards.

SANDTON Linger Longer ®®®®®

58 Wierda Road, 2196 ***Tel*** *(011) 884-0465*

This award-winning restaurant, one of the country's top ten, is set in a gracious colonial home with a large garden. The cuisine is a blend of eastern and western flavours, but the menu also includes classic dishes such as poached Scottish salmon or the trio of lamb, beef and venison roasts. A superb selection of wines rounds things off nicely.

SOWETO Wandies Restaurant ®®

618 Makhalemele Street, Dube, 1800 ***Tel*** *(011) 982-2796*

A warm, convivial tavern in the middle of Soweto, Wandies is extremely popular among both tour operators and locals. The buffet meals include several vegetarian dishes, including *morugu* (wild spinach cooked with herbs) and *chakalaka* (a local salad made of tomatoes, baked beans, onion and chillies).

STERKFONTEIN Greensleeves ®®®®®

Hekpoort Road, 1740 ***Tel*** *(011) 951-8900*

Take part in a unique medieval experience, indulging in a five-course feast with a goblet of mead. Try *sallamagundy* (salad with fruit, vegetables and fish bites) or pottage (soup) with home-baked bread. There is live entertainment with troubadours and minstrels, and medieval costumes are available for hire for those who want to join in the fun.

SUN CITY Crystal Court ®®®®®

Palace of the Lost City, Sun City ***Tel*** *(014) 557-4315*

Surrounded by three terraces and a picturesque lake, this 320-seat restaurant serves international cuisine in a dining room with floor-to-ceiling windows, a beautiful large chandelier and a water fountain in the middle. The high tea served in the afternoon is a delightful treat.

BLYDE RIVER CANYON AND KRUGER

GRASKOP Harries Pancakes ®®

Cnr Louis Trichard & Church Streets, Graskop, 1270 ***Tel*** *(013) 767-1273*

Famous for its traditional South African cuisine, Harries real speciality is meal-sized pancakes stuffed with a variety of sweet and savoury fillings – from traditional *bobotie* to chicken livers, and from banana with caramel to chocolate mousse. The restaurant, located next to an African arts and crafts shop, displays local art both inside and out.

HENDRIKSDAL Artists' Café ®®®

Hendriksdal Siding, 1260 ***Tel*** *(013) 764-2309*

Surrounded by lush forests, this *trattoria* in the former station master's tin-roofed house offers hearty, rural Tuscan fare. The menu changes every few months, but it always includes several home-made pasta dishes that make use of the fresh herbs and vegetables grown in the garden. The café exhibits art and tribal crafts.

Key to Price Guide *see p358* **Key to Symbols** *see back cover flap*

NELSPRUIT 10 on Russell ®®®®

10 Russell Street, Nelspruit, 1200 ***Tel*** *(013) 755-2376*

This award-winning restaurant is set in an old farmhouse with an exquisite garden, which is perfect for an alfresco meal. 10 on Russel offers a relaxed fine-dining experience, and the menu features salads, which are particularly refreshing, and excellent home-made pasta. Children's dishes can be ordered on request.

SWAZILAND Phoenix Spur ®®®

Shop 19, Mall, Mbabane, H100 ***Tel*** *(09268) 404-9103*

This relaxed family restaurant is part of a chain with a slightly overdone Native American theme. The menu consists mainly of grills and burgers, with an extensive buffet offering plenty of different salads. Phoenix Spur caters brilliantly for children, with games and a great kiddies' menu.

WHITE RIVER Oliver's Restaurant and Lodge ®®®®®

White River Country Estate, 1240 ***Tel*** *(013) 750-0479*

The first green of the White River golf course provides the perfect visual background to a leisurely lunch at Oliver's. The restaurant specializes in Mediterranean cuisine with the odd Austrian touch. Try the venison platter of kudu, eland and gemsbok, or the prawn and white-wine risotto. The menu has tasty and healthy options for kids, too.

WHITE RIVER Salt ®®®®®

Shop 7, R40, Bagdad Centre, 1240 ***Tel*** *(013) 751-1555*

A stylish restaurant renowned for its fusion menu – in particular, the duck with apricot sauce. The vibe is relaxed, with soft lighting, contemporary music playing in the background and a roaring fireplace for the winter months. Salt has an enviable cellar and serves specific wines to complement your chosen dish.

SOUTH OF THE ORANGE

GRAAFF REINET The Coldstream Restaurant ®®

3 Kerk Street, Graaff Reinet, 6280 ***Tel*** *(049) 891-1181*

Coldstream is situated in the same building as the second-oldest men's club in the country and offers a truly historic experience. Guests here can enjoy breakfast, lunch, dinner or simply a cup of tea and a slice of home-baked cake. The quality of the food on offer is consistently superlative.

GRAAFF REINET Caledonia ®®®

61 Somerset Street, Graaff Reinet, 6280 ***Tel*** *(049) 892-3156*

A Georgian building that has been an inn for more than a century. Typically Karoo breakfasts and dinners are served in a shady courtyard or the bright, airy interior. The food has been described by patrons as innovative, imaginative and truly delicious. The waiters also speak German.

NORTH OF THE ORANGE

BLOEMFONTEIN Beethoven's Café Restaurant ®®

Victoria Square, Second Avenue, Westdene, 9301 ***Tel*** *(051) 448-7223*

A delightful continental coffee shop, Beethoven's serves a variety of delicious breakfasts, coffees, teas and hot chocolates, not to mention superlative home-made cakes and pastries. Blankets are supplied for cool days for those who wish to sit at the outside tables.

BLOEMFONTEIN De Oude Kraal Country Estate ®®®®

Exit 153 on N1, south of Bloemfontein, 9301 ***Tel*** *(051) 564-0636*

Extravagant and simple, De Oude Kraal is located on a farmstead 35 km (22 miles) south of Bloemfontein. Both the dinner buffet and the six-course dinner menu are gastronomic adventures, accompanied by a wine list that has received the Diners Club Diamond Award. If dinner stretches too late for the drive back, you can stay the night.

KIMBERLEY Kimberley Club ®®®®

35 Currey Street, Kimberley, N Cape, 9320 ***Tel*** *(053) 832-4224*

Fine food is served in the elegant dining room of an updated gentleman's club with warm wooden furniture, white tablecloths and high ceilings. The adventurous chef produces traditional and modern dishes, including T-bone steaks, Karoo lamb chops and *eisbein* (pork knuckle) with apple sauce.

UPINGTON Le Must Manor ®®®®

11 Schroeder Street, Upington, 8800 ***Tel*** *(054) 332-3971*

French-influenced Kalahari cuisine made with locally sourced ingredients is available at this intimate restaurant on the river. Chef Neil Stemmet is an advocate of slow cooking and seasonal produce; try his blue-cheese *crème brûlée*, or the pork with green fig and mustard compote. A great place to stop in the middle of a sightseeing day in this area.

SHOPPING IN SOUTH AFRICA

South Africa's principal shopping attraction is, undoubtedly, its superb range of handcrafted goods, as well as jewellery made from locally mined gold, inlaid with precious or semi-precious stones. Intricate beadwork, woven rugs and carpets, decorative baskets, stone and wood carvings, wood-and-bone spoons and traditional, flowing African garments with geometric motifs are sold at curio shops and markets countrywide. Crafters from the rest of Africa, attracted by South Africa's thriving tourism industry, frequent markets in the bigger centres, selling, for example, ceremonial wooden masks and malachite bracelets. All manner of other handworks can be found in craft markets, too, from windchimes, wooden beach chairs and painted duvet covers to African chilli sauces and leather goods.

Natural cluster of amethyst crystals

Eye-catching works in malachite

SHOPPING HOURS

City shopping malls have adopted extended hours, staying open until around nine o'clock at night for the convenience of their patrons, while most small-town shops observe the nine-to-five rule. Village shops may even close at noon as siestas are still very much a part of rural South Africa.

Outdoor fleamarkets usually begin trading around 10am and end at sunset.

HOW TO PAY

Visa and MasterCard are readily accepted in malls and city shops. Similarly, Visa, American Express and Thomas Cook traveller's cheques are accepted against proof of identity. Small shops and informal traders prefer cash. In remote areas and rural villages, it is advisable to carry cash in a concealed wallet or pouch. If you need cash after hours, most banks have automatic teller machines (ATMs) that allow you to make withdrawals with your credit card or international ATM card.

BARGAINING

African traders are always prepared to bargain hard, mostly because they would rather make a sale than lose it. Indian salespeople also enjoy haggling over prices and seem to expect a little resistance from their customers.

VAT

Most goods (except basic foodstuffs) are subject to 14 per cent Value Added Tax (VAT), included in the price. Expensive antiques, art and jewellery are best bought from reputable dealers who issue foreign clients with a VAT refund document, which can be used to claim the VAT amount paid, prior to departure from the international airports.

The Workshop ***(see pp228–31)*** **in Durban during the festive season.**

Vibrant colour at a market stall

A WORD OF WARNING

Hawkers of gold jewellery and watches, theatrically concealed under a jacket or inside a folded piece of cloth, commonly hang around open-air markets and parking lots of shopping malls. Although they approach potential buyers with a very convincing act of secrecy and a lowered voice, the goods are usually cheap brass imitations. They may also be real – and perhaps stolen. In either case, decline briskly and walk away.

REFUNDS

If the merchandise you have bought is defective in any way, you are entitled to a refund. If you decide that you don't like an item, you may have to settle for a credit note or an exchange. In general, the larger the store, the more protected you are; if you are unhappy with the service, talk to the customer services department or the manager.

WHERE TO SHOP

Many interesting stores have moved away from the malls and main centres. Specialist book, design and wine stores jostle with delis and art studios in the city side streets. There are also always surprises in the small-town bric-a-brac shops. Gold and diamond jewellery, however, is best sought in the malls; the variety is more extensive.

SHIPPING PACKAGES

The post office will send parcels of up to 30 kg (66 lb) to Great Britain, Australia and New Zealand and up to 20 kg (44 lb) to the United States. They may not be larger than 2.5 sq metres (8 sq feet). A fixed handling fee is payable, with additional charges per 100 g. Insurance is an option, with an upper limit of around R2,000. Surface mail will take about 6–8 weeks; airmail one week.

Many upmarket stores will arrange all packaging and shipping. To organize your own exports, contact a shipper such as **Trans Global Cargo Pty Ltd**. They will arrange customs and packaging, and will deliver to your home or the office of their local agent. There is no maximum or minimum size or weight, and prices are competitive.

A bottle of wine to suit any taste

Swaziland is a treasure trove of woven baskets and mats

STRICTLY SOUTH AFRICAN

In Johannesburg and other large cities, you can buy almost anything. Johannesburg, in particular, attracts consumers from all over the subcontinent. It is the queen of the mall culture, and the best place to find indigenous arts and crafts. But much of the wood and stone carving is from West and Central Africa and Zimbabwe.

The crafts in Durban *(see pp228–31)* and KwaZulu-Natal *(see pp204–5)*, on the other hand, are more likely to be local. Zulu baskets are usually of outstanding quality, as are the woven beer strainers, grass brooms, pots, shields and drums. Sometimes brightly coloured baskets are made from telephone wire.

These wares, as well as many charming and often brightly painted wooden animal and bird figures, can be found on the side of the N2 highway from Durban to the game parks: Hluhluwe-Umfolozi and Mkuzi.

Gazankulu and Venda also have a reputation for crafts. Clay pots with distinctive angular designs in gleaming silver and ochre are popular, as are the woodcarvings, tapestries, fabrics and batiks.

Ndebele bead blankets, belts, aprons and dolls are also worth looking out for *(see p266)*. They can be found at Botshabelo Museum and Nature Reserve near Fort Merensky, 13 km (8 miles) north of Middelburg.

Knysna *(see pp186–7)* is yet another craftwork "capital". A major timber centre, this is the place to buy stinkwood and yellowwood chairs and tables, door knobs and other unusual decor accessories. Colourful, woven mohair blankets, shawls, cushion covers and jackets are also found in this region.

The label "Scarab Paper", represents a truly unique South African craft: handmade papers, notelets and cards in nationwide craft and curio stores – produced from (now fragrance free) elephant dung!

Swazi candles are also sold countrywide: look out for the distinctive "stained-glass" effect of these slow-burning bright candles in animal, bird and more traditional candle shapes.

Throughout the country, gift stores and jewellers offer an unusual array of necklaces, rings, earrings and bracelets using local diamonds and semi-precious stones, often combined with South African gold and platinum.

DIRECTORY

SHIPPING AGENCIES

Trans Global Cargo Pty Ltd
Tel *(021) 385-1075.*

Seaclad Maritime (shipping line)
Tel *(021) 419-1438.*

AfroMar (ship brokers)
Tel *(011) 803-0008.*

ENTERTAINMENT IN SOUTH AFRICA

Johannesburg is said to be the entertainment and nightlife hub of South Africa. In this entrepreneurial city people party as hard as they work, and there is always something happening. This does not mean, however, that other South African cities and towns are dull. Even rural places have their music, restaurant and clubbing venues. The demand for cinemas and casinos is high, and exciting new venues are opened regularly. The dramatic arts are innovative and of a very high standard, with theatre companies committed to the development of a local arts culture. The vibrant music scene spans classical, jazz and the African *genre*.

CAPAB ballet dancers

The Oude Libertas amphitheatre, Stellenbosch *(see p39)*

INFORMATION

For details of entertainment in the cities, check the local daily press and the weekly papers such as the *Mail & Guardian*, available nationwide. They review and list theatre productions, current film festivals, art exhibitions, music performances and other interesting events.

Reviews and listings also appear in a number of magazines that are sold in book stores and at newsagents. The Tonight website (www.tonight.co.za) includes restaurant reviews and details of workshops, gay and lesbian and kids' events in Cape Town, Johannesburg and Durban.

BOOKING TICKETS

Seats for most events can be reserved by calling **Computicket**, which has branches in all the major centres and larger towns countrywide.

To make telephone bookings for Ster-Kinekor cinemas, call Ticketline, or **Ticketweb**.

Most South African theatres and cinemas do not accept telephone bookings without credit card payment.

CINEMA

Mainstream Hollywood film productions and foreign-language films with subtitles are the main fare in South African cinemas, because the local film industry is still in the fledgling stage.

The cities host regular film festivals: themes range from French, Italian and Dutch to natural health, the environment and gay and lesbian.

THEATRE, OPERA AND DANCE

Comedy, satire, cabaret and musicals are particularly popular in South Africa, as are modernized and "localized" adaptations of Shakespeare.

Theatres are committed to the development of scriptwriting and directing talent, and talent-scouting festivals are becoming annual events.

Arts Alive, a Johannesburg festival held in September, is a major celebration of the performing arts. The FNB Vita Dance Umbrella, held in Johannesburg in February and March, is an important platform for new choreographers. The National Arts Festival *(see*

The South African State Theatre, Pretoria/Tshwane *(see p266)*

"Cross Roads", Rupert Museum, Stellenbosch

p61) held in Grahamstown in July is, of course, the best place to go for an overview of the innovative, exciting South African theatre, dance, artistic and musical talent.

In KwaZulu-Natal, the annual Massed Choir Festival, toward the end of the year is a celebration of African voices harmonizing oratorio, opera and traditional music. Watch the press for details.

Opera, too, is well supported. The five-month, annual Spier Festival of Music, Theatre and Opera attracts national and international artists.

Zulu dancer at Heia Safari Ranch

MUSIC

The five symphony seasons throughout the year are well supported in the cities; concerts are held in venues such as the Durban City Hall *(see p229),* Cape Town's Baxter Theatre *(see p111)* and the Johannesburg College of Music in Parktown.

Outdoor, twilight performances, for example at Durban's Botanic Gardens *(see p231)* and Kirstenbosch Gardens in Cape Town *(see p104),* are popular. Look out for the musical fireworks shows in the cities every December.

Nowadays, international bands, pop and opera singers regularly include South Africa on their world tours.

Nevertheless, local bands are far from neglected, and they offer a wide range of sounds: rock, jazz, gospel, reggae, rap and Afro-fusion. The members of the popular Soweto String Quartet charm audiences with their unique compositions and African-flavoured interpretations of classical pieces.

Local rock bands such as Springbok Nude Girls and Sons of Trout enjoy a loyal following, and appear at clubs countrywide. Check the listings guides and local radio stations for details of gigs and venues.

Music from the rest of Africa is filtering down to South Africa, and clubs are rocking to sounds from Ghana, Mali and Benin.

ART

Johannesburg, Durban, Cape Town, Port Elizabeth and Bloemfontein, as well as some of the larger towns such as Knysna, have excellent art galleries. These showcase local and international works, from the traditional to the somewhat more bizarre, from ceramics and photography to multi-media works and installations. Exhibitions change regularly, and exhibition openings are popular social events, with a high-profile speaker as well as a buffet and drinks.

Merry-go-round at the Carousel

GAMING

Investors, developers and casino operators have poured billions of rand into this industry. South Africa is said to be the one of the biggest emerging gaming markets in the world.

Spectacular gaming and entertainment centres with names like **Sun City**, **Carousel** and **Emnotweni** are now dotted all over the country. Their architectural styles are detailed and lavish, blending fun and fantasy with the latest in technology.

Limited payout machines *(see pp268–9),* one-arm bandits and slot machines are found in theme bars, while gaming tables include black-jack, roulette, poker and punto banco. Larger casinos usually have a *salon privé.*

DIRECTORY

BOOKING TICKETS

Computicket
Tel *(083) 915-8000.*
www.computicket.com

Ticketweb
Tel *(083) 915-1234.*

CINEMAS

Ster-Kinekor Ticket-Line
Tel *Cape Town, Durban, Pretoria/Tshwane and Johannesburg (0861) 300-444.*

NuMetro booking line
Tel *Cape Town, Durban, Pretoria/Tshwane and Johannesburg (0861) 100-220.*

GAMING

Tel *Carousel (012) 718-7566.*
Tel *Sun City (014) 557-1000.*
Tel *Wild Coast Sun (039) 305-9111.*
Tel *Sundome (011) 794-5800.*
Tel *Emnotweni (013) 757-0021.*

SPECIAL-INTEREST VACATIONS

South Africa, with its moderate climate, long hours of sunshine, endless coastline and varied landscape, is a country that can provide a wide range of outdoor pursuits almost all year round. South Africans, in general, enjoy the great outdoors: during summer, visitors to Cape Town may well believe that the entire city is in training for forthcoming running and cycling marathons, as locals take to the streets to get fit. Activities go beyond competitive sports, however. Whether it is canoeing on the Orange river, taking plant-hunting trips in the coastal forests of KwaZulu-Natal, mountaineering in the Drakensberg, bungee jumping along the Garden Route, board-sailing in the Western Cape or visiting historic battlefields and museums, there is something to interest everyone. Moreover, South Africa's fascinating multicultural past and present can be experienced at regional festivals *(see pp38–9)* and on special tours.

Bungee jumping

HIKING AND RAMBLING

Hiking is an extremely popular pastime. Even the smallest farms in the most remote regions have laid-out trails, with distance-marked paths and maps provided upon booking and payment. Most overnight hikes are situated on private land or state reserves, with accommodation in rustic huts, with firewood, mattresses and cold-water washing facilities usually included. Favourite trails such as the four-night Otter Trail and four-night Tsitsikamma Trail *(see pp180–81)* need to be booked more than a year in advance. Most outdoor equipment stores are able to advise on day and longer hikes, and they also sell guide books, maps and trail provisions. **Hiking South Africa** has a list of some 250 hiking clubs around the country, which can arrange weekend and day hikes for beginners and seasoned walkers. These clubs also sometimes organize longer, more challenging trails.

Hiking in KwaZulu-Natal

Kloofing, or madcap jumping into pools, a new dimension of hiking

Most private reserves and some of the provincial reserves and national parks offer guided game- and bird-watching rambles, as well as overnight bushveld and wilderness trails. The real attraction of these hikes, is the unrivalled experience of walking through the African bush, surrounded by the sounds and smells of its diverse fauna and flora.

The Kruger National Park *(see pp284–7)* offers at least seven such trails: the Bushman Trail includes finding rock paintings in the hill shelters. Due to the popularity of these walks, bookings should be made months in advance. Contact the **Wildlife Society of South Africa** for details.

KLOOFING AND ROCK CLIMBING

Kloofing is a newly popular offshoot of hiking: it involves boulder hopping and wading while following the course of a river. It requires you to have a good level of fitness and daring, with long jumps into mountain pools. The **Mountain Club of South Africa** provides information for anyone tempted to try this.

Rock climbing (whether traditional, sport or bouldering) has a large following in South Africa. Climbing equipment stores can provide enthusiasts with gear, information and route ideas. Some of the best traditional climbing is found in the KwaZulu-Natal, Drakensberg *(see pp206–7)*, while Cape Town's Table Mountain *(see pp74–5)* offers interesting challenges for experienced climbers. Coming back down from the climb can be a fast and thrilling abseil descent, or the Australian SAS created counterpart, known as a rapp jump. This is even more exciting, as it involves descending at high speed while facing forward with the rope attached to your back and your feet pounding down the rock face.

FISHING

More than a million anglers enjoy the local waters, which are subject to strict regulations – enquire at the nearest police station or through the **South African Deep Sea Angling Association**. Over 250 species of fish can be caught through fly, line, game, surf or reef fishing. The merging of the cool Atlantic and the warm Indian oceans off the Southern Cape coast creates the conditions for a high concentration of game fish, including marlin and tuna. Mpumalanga and KwaZulu-Natal offer excellent trout fishing. Kalk Bay in Cape Town has one of the few line-fishing harbours in the world, and **Grassroutes Tours** organizes day fishing trips on a tradition wooden boat.

Almost all harbours and marinas offer the opportunity to join commercial or semi-commercial boats on short trips, and many tour groups, including **Big Game Fishing Safaris** and **Lynski Deep Sea Fishing Charters,** offer fishing charters and expeditions.

Sport fishing at Cape Vidal, in the Greater St Lucia Wetlands

Hot-air ballooning, for a fabulous view of the game

AIR SPORTS

The **Aero Club of South Africa** is the controlling and co-ordinating body for all sport aviation: ballooning, hang-gliding, microlighting and parachuting. With a good head for heights, there is no finer way to see the land than from the basket of a hot-air balloon. Flights are available at many locations, but some of the most popular are the trips over the Winelands or game parks. Early morning or late evening, when the thermals guarantee plenty of lift, are the best times to book. It's important to note that flights are sometimes cancelled due to too much or too little wind. Given the relative silence of the hot-air balloon, it's a wonderful way of getting a close view of shy big game animals. Contact **Pilanesberg Safaris** for game-viewing trips *(see p269)*.

Helicopter rides are widely available and are an exciting way to take in the panorama of Cape Town *(see pp60–123)* and Table Mountain *(see pp78–79)*. It is even possible to arrange a trial lesson.

Paragliding and parachuting courses (contact the **Hang Gliding and Paragliding Association**) and tandem flights are also popular. Bridge jumping and bungee jumping are for real adrenalin junkies. Jumps must be arranged through one of the many adventure agencies, such as **Face Adrenalin** in Cape Town. Extreme jumps can be found on the Garden Route, including the spectacular 216-m (709-ft) Bloukrans Bungee Jump, which claims to be the highest commercial challenge of its kind in the world.

Mountain biking in Knysna

CYCLING

In South Africa even the cities offer spectacular cycling routes: at least 35,000 cyclists take to the streets for the annual marathon around the Cape Peninsula *(see pp64–5)*. Cycling organizations such as the **Pedal Power Association**, **South African Mountain Bike Association** and the **South African Cycling Federation** organize weekend rides, which often include off-road routes on otherwise out-of-bounds farmlands. They can also offer advice about renting bikes. Adventure holiday agencies can book a variety of cycling tours – both off-road and on smooth tar – along the Garden Route, for example, and in the Karoo. Meals, accommodation and luggage transport are provided.

A close encounter with a great white shark, while cage diving

GAME HUNTING AND CLAY TARGET SHOOTING

Game hunting is a multi-million rand industry today, and in the hunting reserves, such as in the Waterberg region of Northern Province, the area is stocked with game specifically for that purpose. However, all foreign hunters must be accompanied by a professional South African hunter by law. Contact the **Professional Hunters' Association of South Africa (PHASA)** for details of members who can organize your hunting trip and accompany you.

A more humane alternative to hunting is clay pigeon shooting. This has become a very popular sport and is easily arranged through the **Clay Target Shooting Association South Africa**.

White-water rafting on the Orange River *(see pp296–97)*

WATER SPORTS

South Africa has 2,500 km (1,553 miles) of coastline, many rivers and dams. The country has some of the world's greatest surf, and one of the best spots is Jeffrey's Bay in the Garden Route, where perfect waves abound. Windsurfing and sailing are also popular, and many resorts rent out equipment. The beaches are also ideal for sand boarding, the land-based version of surfing, which takes advantage of the country's abundance of massive sand dunes.

Scuba diving instruction is widely available (even in Johannesburg) and instructors should be accredited to the **National Association of Underwater Instructors** (NAUI) or **Professional Association of Diving Instructors** (PADI). The best diving sites are found along the St Lucia Estuary Park in KwaZulu-Natal, with coral reefs, tropical fish, turtles, sharks and game fish. In Cape Town, wreck-diving and exploring kelp forests are both popular activities.

River rafting has a growing number of fans in South Africa. **River Rafters** and **Felix Unite River Trips** are two Cape Town operators. Qualified guides can take rafters in two- or eight-person inflatable rafts on a variety of waters. From white-water running to quiet paddling, there is a trip for everyone and overnight accommodation and meals are always superb. Popular routes include the Blyde River Canyon and the Breede, Orange and Tugela rivers. One-day or overnight coastal trips from **Coastal Kayak Trails** are available too, usually around the Cape Peninsula, along the Garden Route and in KwaZulu-Natal.

For the ultimate thrill, cage diving takes participants as close to a great white shark as they would ever wish to be. A popular venue is the aptly named Shark Alley, near the fishing village of Gansbaai *(see p170)*. Several guests at a time are lowered from a catamaran in a steel cage fitted with viewing ports. **White Shark Ecoventures** offer one- to 10-day tours, which include accommodation and equipment hire.

Pony-trekking in Lesotho *(see pp214–15)*

HORSE RIDING AND PONY-TREKKING

Sport riding is controlled by the **South African National Equestrian Foundation**. Leisure riding is also very popular; sunset rides along a beach or wine-tasting trails are memorable options.

Malealea Lodge and Horse Treks in Lesotho *(see pp214–15)* offers a real African experience. Trips are organized with guides to accompany riders through unfenced landscapes to see dinosaur tracks or San Bushman rock art. Accommodation is in Basotho huts, with traditional food and dancing provided by the local people.

HIKING AND RAMBLING

Hiking South Af
358 Christoffel St,
Pretoria 0183.
Tel *(083) 535-4538.*

Wildlife and Environment Society of South Africa
Tel *(021) 701-1397.*
www.wessa.org.za

KLOOFING AND ROCK CLIMBIN

Mountain Club South Africa
97 Hatfield House,
Cape Town, 8001.
Tel *(021) 465-2412.*
www.mcsa.org.za

FISHING

Big Game Fishing Safaris
Simons Town Pier,
Cape Town 7700.
Tel *(021) 674-2203*

Grassroutes To
Waverley Business P
Mowbray.
Tel *(021) 464-4269*

Lynski Deep Se Fishing Charte
26 Manaar Rd, Uml
Rocks, Durban 432(
Tel *082 445 6600.*

South African Sea Angling Association
PO Box 4191,
Cape Town 8000.
Tel *(021) 976-445*

HUNTING

Clay Target Sh Association South Africa
PO Box 812,
Great Brak River, 6
Tel *(086) 111-458*
www.ctsasa.co.za

Professional Hunters' Association of South Africa
PO Box 10264, Ce
Pretoria 0046.
Tel *(012) 667-204*
www.phasa.co.za

Nectar-feeding Malachite sunbird, with emerald plumage

BIRD-WATCHING, FLORA AND FAUNA TRAILS

Blessed with a prodigious variety of indigenous birds, along with vast flocks of migratory birds that pass through during the colder European winters, South Africa is a bird-watchers paradise. There is also a wide range of fauna to be seen. Seal or whale watching *(see pp130–31)* are both very popular along the coast, whether you prefer to go on a boat trip or stay on dry land with binoculars. Safaris or wilderness trails both offer an amazing opportunity to view wild animals and flora in their natural habitat, and are an essential part of any trip to South Africa *(see pp386–91)*, but it is essential to book well in advance.

The **Wildlife and Environment Society of South Africa**, as well as many local birding and botanical societies (most of which belong to the **National Botanic Institute**), regularly offer courses and group outings covering topics such as medicinal plants, orchids and spiders. Contact the organizations directly.

SPECTATOR SPORTS

For those who prefer to spectate rather than participate, South Africa has much to offer. The country is known for its love of sports and world-class rugby and cricket can be enjoyed at modern stadiums, such as the Newlands grounds in Cape Town, and the Wanderers Cricket Grounds in Johannesburg. In June and July of 2010 the country is set to host a massive event – the Football World Cup. Over a million tickets will be sold to international visitors but as with all major sports events, it is best to plan ahead when booking tickets for specific matches as they may be sold out well in advance. Check the local press and **Computicket** (www.computicket.co.za) for updates of what's on locally and nationally.

Stadiums are always open-air, and while some grandstands have canopies, it is advisable to take a hat, sun protection and a good supply of water.

Beautiful view from the green of Leopard Creek golf course

GOLF

The game of golf was introduced to South Africa by British – and notably Scottish – colonialists during the early 19th century and has a long and proud tradition here. The game has produced such great golfers as Gary Player, winner of a record 163 international competitions, and more recently, Ernie Els, who upholds Springbok pride in the world's major tournaments.

Since the 1980s and the start of the global golf boom, South Africa has seen an extensive programme of course upgrades and new builds. These include Jack Nicklaus' signature course at **Paarl Valley Golf Estate and Spa** and **Fancourt Golf Club Estate**, which is picturesquely set on the Garden Route and now widely acknowledged as one of the world's best and most scenic challenges.

The most famous course of all is the **Gary Player Country Club** at Sun City, whose immaculate greens host the Million Dollar Nedbank Golf Challenge. Other top courses to have featured on the European PGA Tour, the local Sunshine Tour and the South African Open, include Durban's **Erinvale Golf and Country Club**, **Leopard Creek** and **Glendower Country Club**.

The country's terrain and balmy climate, especially in and around the Winelands *(see pp134–151)* and the Garden Route *(see pp178–187)*, are perfect for the best enjoyment of the game and the facilities are usually just as outstanding. This has led to an increase in the popularity of golf package holidays, and South Africa now claims to be the most successful golfing nation per capita in the world.

Watching cricket at Newlands grounds, with Table Mountain as a backdrop

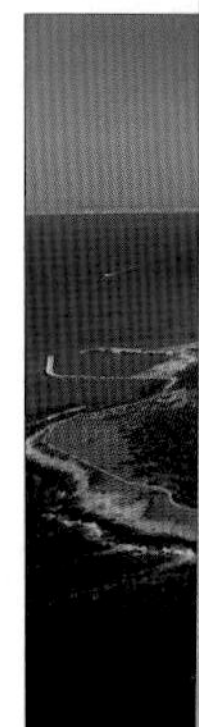

Scenic Rail Travel

An increasingly popular holiday choice is taking a land cruise, where travel between each destination is by train. Once perceived as the domain of elderly travellers, scenic train travel now attracts adults of all ages, although it is not aimed at families with young children. This is a year-round activity, but prices will be higher in the busy holiday periods. The advantages of such a tour are many: the "hotel" travels with its guests, it is possible to reach remote destinations while remaining in luxurious surroundings, and then, of course, there is the pleasure of rail travel. The lazy pace of a steam locomotive is perfect for enjoying South Africa's wonderful sights.

A Rovos Rail steam train winding through the Eastern Transvaal

CHOOSING AN ITINERARY

South Africa, with its year-long pleasant climate and beautiful scenery, is the ideal destination for luxury train travel. However, it is not a cheap holiday and it can be sensible to avoid certain times of the year. In general the cheapest fares are available in May and August, while the period from September to December can be markedly more expensive.

South Africa's land cruise itineraries are carefully chosen to reveal some truly stunning views, and reach many destinations that are difficult to access by road. It is a good idea to study the itineraries carefully. The Blue Train, for example, is best taken from south to north as this route passes through the loveliest stretches of scenery by day rather than at night. Other trips include safari expeditions and stops in neighbouring countries. Rovos Rail, in particular, offers routes to Victoria Falls in Zimbabwe and a magnificent tour to Cairo in Egypt.

CHOOSING WHICH TRAIN

There are several different companies arranging a variety of tours, from short day-trips to more lengthy affairs.

Rovos Rail, which calls itself "the most luxurious train in the world", lives up to its

The Outeniqua Choo-Tjoe steam train at Dolphin Point

reputation, with traditional furnishings and exquisite decor. Two beautifully rebuilt trains carry a maximum of 72 passengers each. All suites are of a five-star hotel standard, with air-conditioning and shower or bath facilities. The most expensive suites, occupying half-a-coach each, have a full-size Victorian roll-top bath. The trains provides 24-hour room service and there are two dining cars, which allow the entire complement of passengers to enjoy dinner at a single sitting.

In operation since 1995, the **Shongololo Express** specializes in adventure and excitement, and is therefore a big hit with the younger crowd. As a result, the style of the trains is more casual, and the cabins are fairly basic but comfortable. There are two en-suite options, but the cheaper twin or single cabins entail a walk to use shower and toilet facilities. All trains carry a fleet of air-conditioned touring cars and include a safari expedition

Crisp linens, marble-clad bathrooms, sophisticated lounges and faultless service set the tone for the magnificent **Blue Train**, one of the world's most famous scheduled services. Beautiful wood veneers and fine detail add a 1950s ambience to the train. The suites offer a choice of shower or bath and a selection of film and radio channels. The lounge cars are the perfect place to observe the panoramic views as the train winds its way through the Winelands, the Karoo desert and other impressive scenery.

ROUTES AND SIGHTS

The scheduled route for the Blue Train links Cape Town and Pretoria, and is a 2,600-km (994-mile) journey taking 27 hours through some of South Africa's most spectacular scenery. The Southern Meander tour includes two nights in a top Johannesburg hotel before transferring to the station in Pretoria. There are alternative routes from Pretoria to Durban, which include a two-night stay at the Zimbali Lodge resort with a spectacular 18-hole course. Alternatively it is possible to take the train to the Bakubung Game Lodge for a two-night stay, with optional game drives.

Rovos Rail has a variety of itineraries. Its three-day Cape Town to Pretoria route, which can be taken in either direction, includes visits to Kimberley's famous Big Hole and diamond museum, as well as the historic town of Matjiesfontein. The three-day route linking Pretoria and Durban skirts Kruger Park and instead visits Swaziland, Zululand. A game safari in Hluhluwe Game Park, home of the black and white rhino, is also included as part of the fare. Possibly the most intriguing trip is the 14-day African Adventure, which links Cape Town with Dar Es Salaam in Mozambique, passing Zimbabwe, Zambia, Victoria Falls and Selous Game Reserve – the continent's largest – on the way.

The Shongololo Express has itineraries that criss-cross South Africa dipping into neighbouring countries such as Namibia, Mozambique, Botswana, Zambia and Tanzania. There are two popular "limited edition" trips; one which focuses on wildlife and another which follows in the footsteps of Dr Livingstone.

ON-BOARD CUISINE AND SERVICE

The standard of catering and service on board will be that of a five-star hotel. These trains have a very high ratio of staff to guests, especially in the restaurant car. The Blue Train, for example, serves a menu that is of a truly gourmet standard, and in 2005 the company won platinum status in the prestigious Diner's Club International "Wine List of the Year" awards.

The Blue Train, travels past an impressive Table Mountain view

A more unusual way to travel on South Africa's luxury steam trains

WHAT TO TAKE

It pays to pack light because there are limits to the size and number of cases that can be stowed away (check with the train company). However, guests must bring formal wear for evenings as they tend to be rather grand occasions, with ladies dressing in traditional evening wear and gentlemen either in a smart lounge suit or a tuxedo. The daytime dress code is more relaxed, smart casual clothes.

WHAT IS INCLUDED

Rovos Rail include food, drink and off-train excursions by luxury coach within the fare. In addition, each suite has an inclusive mini-bar fully stocked to the passengers' choice. This is fairly typical for all the major train companies, although some may charge extra for champagne.

HEALTH AND SAFETY

All trains have a member of staff trained in first-aid and will have doctors on call along the route. It is also important to find out if the train is passing through malaria risk areas, as suitable preventative medication will need to be taken. There is little need to worry about personal security, but, as always, keep valuables locked in an on-board safe.

Dining Car 195, Shangani, a Rovos Rail train, with original teak pillars

DIRECTORY

Rovos Rail
PO Box 2837, Pretoria 0001.
Tel *(012) 315-8242*
www.rovos.co.za

Shongololo Express
PO Box 1558, Parklands, Gauteng, 2121.
Tel *(011) 781-4616*
www.shongololo.com

Blue Train
Private Bag X637, Pretoria 0001.
Tel *(012) 334-8459*
www.bluetrain.co.za

SAFARIS, NATIONAL PARKS AND WILDLIFE RESERVES

There's nothing quite as memorable as the African bush, and with the diversity of South Africa's national parks and wildlife reserves, visitors are spoiled for choice. There are backdrops of savannah, harsh semi-desert, Cape floral kingdoms, coastal parks, and grasslands.

African horn bill

The parks and wildlife reserves are world-renowned for the natural heritage they conserve, and most offer superlative game-viewing opportunities, while some concentrate on cultural or picturesque landscapes. With so many options it is helpful to plan a safari holiday in advance.

Elephants gather at a watering hole in Addo Elephant National Park

BEST TIME TO GO

The best season for game viewing is winter (July to September), when the dry weather forces animals to gather around rivers and waterholes. The disadvantages are that animals aren't in optimal condition and the winter landscape is stark.

Summer (November to January) brings high rainfall, and the landscape becomes green and lush. This is the best time of year for viewing flora, though the wildlife will be more widespread and difficult to spot. The wide availability of water also leads to a higher threat of malaria in risk areas.

While many people come for the Big Five and get a thrill in the pursuit of spotting them, it is also possible to relish the opportunity to spend quiet time in remote bush, take unbelievable hikes and view striking landscapes and lesser-known animal life. Each of the parks and reserves offers something exceptional, and the following pages will help visitors decide where they want to go.

ORGANIZED AND INDEPENDENT TOURS

Most of the safari companies operate out of Cape Town, Durban and Johannesburg, arranging accommodation and game-viewing trips as part of an organized tour. The cost of trips varies from budget excursions to more expensive holidays. Many safari companies offer package deals, which are often great value for money. It can be an easier option to let an organization take care of all the planning, but it is best to choose a company that is recognized by the **Southern African Tourism Service Association** (SATSA). Going on your own can be cheaper, and it also allows for greater flexibility to explore. Hiring a car, booking self-catering accommodation and obtaining maps and information are all easy to arrange.

PLANNING AND RESEARCH

Most of the parks fall within three groups: **South African National Parks** (SANParks), **CapeNature** and **KwaZulu Wildlife**. Contacting these organizations is a good first step, along with checking their websites and those of safari companies. Seasonal and promotional specials happen periodically and are often found in the travel sections of leading newspapers.

The Wild Card provides unrestricted access to SANParks for a year, and is a sensible investment if your itinerary includes visits to more than one reserve.

Most parks can be visited by car, since roads and gravel paths are generally well kept. However, just after the rainy season (January to April), a 4x4 vehicle is a more suitable option. It is also important to

Bontebok National Park, part of the SANParks group

A typically South African *braai* in the bush

note that petrol stations do not accept credit cards. Air-conditioning may seem a necessity when the weather is warm, however, try to keep the car windows open to experience fully the sounds and smells of the bush. The best speed for game viewing is 15 km/h (10 mph). To see which animals are in any particular area, check the sightings boards at the entrance of the camps. Wildlife identification books available in camp shops are also useful, and it may be a good investment to buy a pair of binoculars before the safari.

Essential items to pack include comfortable clothes to cover exposed areas from insects, preferably in dull colours, so as not to disturb the wildlife; a hat; sunblock; sunglasses and a camera.

ACCOMMODATION

To avoid disappointment, it is best to book as far in advance as possible, especially over school and public holidays in South Africa. Accommodation at national parks varies; there are campsites, huts, safari tents, self-contained chalets and cottages. There is generally a choice of a private or shared bathroom and kitchen. In most national parks, bedding, towels, a fridge and cooking utensils are included as part of the rate. In several of the KwaZulu-Natal parks' rest camps you are not allowed to use the kitchen; instead, the camp chef prepares and serves the meals. Once a reservation has been made, the company will send you a leaflet detailing all facilities at the camp.

The ultimate wildlife accommodation is in luxurious lodges at private game reserves, mostly around the Kruger National Park. Prices are high, but they usually include accommodation, meals, game activities and drinks. These lodges are a good option for visitors who have never experienced a safari before, since there are well-informed rangers who lead game-viewing outings, where there is a much greater chance of actually sighting some wildlife.

CHOOSING AN ITINERARY

The best times to view game are early mornings and late afternoons. Be sure to return before the camp gates shut, just before dark.

Game drives, walks and night drives can be booked at the camp offices after arrival. They usually depart at dawn, last a few hours, and are often the best way to explore the area. Wilderness trails are longer and involve staying at a remote base camp and going on walks with an armed ranger. These can be booked months in advance.

The private reserves generally plan the itinerary for their guests, although there is room for flexibility. Typical activities include drinks at dawn, followed by guided game viewing, sundowners and night drives with dinner.

SAFETY TIPS AND HEALTH ISSUES

It is recommended that you approach a sighting quietly, turn off the car engine and allow space for the vehicle in front to reverse if necessary. Never feed animals, because once they are dependant on food from humans, they become aggressive and have to be shot. Stay in your car at all times. If your car breaks down in the park, wait until a park ranger comes to help. Other visitors will be able to pass on a message to the authorities.

Water and drinks are essential to prevent dehydration. Anti-malaria prophylactics are recommended for those visiting risk areas, such as the Kruger. A doctor or travel clinic should be able to provide these. The highest-risk period is during the rainy season (December to April), when it is best to cover exposed skin with light clothing and insect repellents. A **24-hour malaria hotline** is available for further information.

Most camps in the parks provide ramped access for disabled visitors and, in many cases, accessible toilets and specially adapted accommodation.

Get a close-up view of South Africa's Big Five

CHILDREN ON SAFARI

Parks and reserves in South Africa are well equipped for families. There are excellent game reserves outside of malaria areas where you can see the Big Five, and they are the best option for families with young children. It is also essential to find out the minimum age requirement of rest camps and lodges, and whether they are fenced in. Long drives can be dull, so it's worth considering hiring a guide to keep the children interested. It is also a good idea to bring a picnic and plan stops at waterholes.

GAUTENG AND MPUMALANGA

The flagship of South Africa's game reserves and ultimate destination for the wildlife fanatic is the **Kruger National Park** with its 150 mammal and 500 bird species. There are also archaeological and historical sites of interest in the Northern areas. Trails on offer include 4x4, wilderness and mountain biking, while golfers will love the unfenced nine-hole course at Skukuza.

The **Madikwe Game Reserve** is situated in the corner of the Northwest Province that borders on Botswana. A transition zone on the edge of the Kalahari desert, where several rare species occur naturally, this is one of the few game reserves in the world that is the most sustainable land use for the area. To visit the reserve you must stay at one of the lodges.

Lying in an ancient volcano, **Pilanesberg National Park** has many attractions, including signs of early humankind in several Stone and Iron Age sites. The park is also based in the transition zone, which has a unique ecology with an enormous variety of flora and fauna. The colourful bushveld and varied topography have made this a reserve that is popular with artists and photographers.

Close to Johannesburg is the **Suikerbosrand Nature Reserve,** named after the protea (suikerbos) plant found throughout the area. The park is an excellent choice for outdoor enthusiasts as the Suikerbosrand mountain range provides excellent hiking and mountain biking opportunities. There are several day and overnight trails, plus the 700m (765yds) Toktokkie trail, which has been designed for disabled visitors with wide paved paths and several benches to stop at.

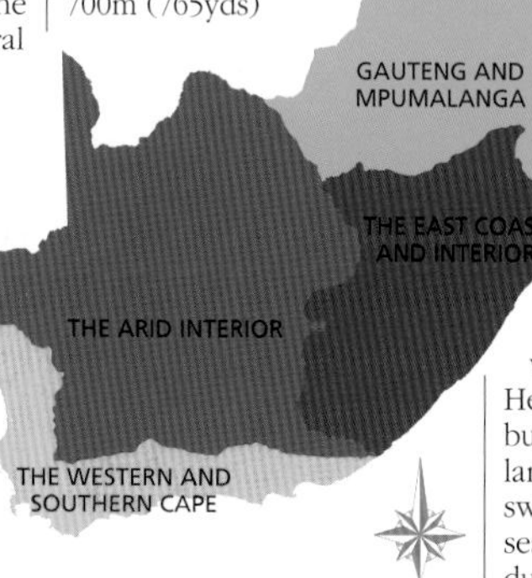

THE EAST COAST AND INTERIOR

The **Golden Gate Highlands National Park** takes its name from the beautiful sandstone rock formations that change from purple to gold at sunset. The park provides many activities including guided walks, hiking trails, abseiling, canoeing and horse riding.

Accommodation ranges from luxury log cabins in the mountains to a rest camp that is reminiscent of an eighteenth-century Basotho village. Bird-watchers should look out for the rare bearded vulture and bald ibis.

Greater St Lucia Wetland Park is South Africa's most significant wetland reserve and a World Heritage Site that incorporates bushveld, sand forest, grassland, wetland, coastal forest, swamp, beach, coral reef and sea. The best time to visit is during the turtle breeding

PLANNING YOUR TRIP

This chart is designed to help you choose your safari. The parks and reserves are listed alphabetically for each area on the map above.

	Big Five	On-Site Restaurant	Swimming Pool	On-site Fuel	Malaria Risk	Suitable for children	Suitable for disabled	Guided Game Drives	Picnic Sites	Shops	Television	Electricity	Information Centre	Internet Café	Laundry	Medical Service	Cell Phone Reception	Public Telephones	Hiking/Walking Trails	Whale-watching
GAUTENG AND MPUMALANGA																				
Kruger National Park	•	•	•	•	•	•	•	•	•	•	•	•	•	•	•	•	•	•	•	
Madikwe Game Reserve	•	•	•			•	•	•			•	•	•		•	•	•			
Pilanesberg National Park	•	•	•			•	•	•	•		•	•				•	•	•	•	
Suikerbosrand Nature Reserve						•	•		•			•					•	•	•	
THE EAST COAST AND INTERIOR																				
Golden Gate Highlands National Park		•	•	•		•	•	•	•	•	•	•			•		•	•	•	
St Lucia Estuary Park			•		•	•	•	•	•	•	•	•	•	•	•	•	•	•	•	•
Hluhluwe Umfolozi Park	•	•	•	•	•	•	•	•	•	•		•	•		•		•	•	•	
Tembe Elephant Reserve	•		•		•	•		•	•			•			•		•			
Ukhahlamba Drakensberg Park		•	•	•		•	•	•	•	•	•	•	•		•		•	•	•	
THE ARID INTERIOR																				
Ai-Ais Richtersveld Transfrontier Park				•			•		•	•		•							•	
Augrabies Falls National Park		•	•	•	•	•	•	•	•	•		•					•	•	•	
Goegap Nature Reserve						•	•		•			•	•					•	•	
Karoo National Park		•	•			•	•	•	•			•	•		•		•	•	•	
Kgalagadi Transfrontier Park		•	•	•	•	•	•	•	•	•		•	•		•		•	•	•	
Namaqua National Park						•	•		•										•	
THE WESTERN AND SOUTHERN CAPE																				
Addo Elephant National Park	•	•	•	•		•	•	•	•	•	•	•			•		•	•	•	
Bontebok National Park						•	•		•								•	•	•	
De Hoop Nature Reserve						•	•	•	•			•	•			•	•	•	•	•
Table Mountain National Park		•	•			•	•	•	•	•			•				•	•	•	•
Tsitsikamma National Park		•	•			•	•		•	•		•	•		•		•	•	•	•
Wilderness National Park			•			•	•		•	•		•	•				•	•	•	•

Thirsty big cats at a watering hole in the Kruger National Park, Gauteng and Mpumalanga area

season from October to April, or in the whale-watching season from June to December. Other animals to keep a look out for are: hippos, crocodiles, pelicans, Caspian terns and fish eagles.

Set in the heart of Zululand where tribal kings once hunted, **Hluhluwe Umfolozi Park** is renowned for rhino conservation and is home to over 1,200 white rhino and 300 black rhino. The park also has several excellent wilderness trails and guided walks. Accommodation ranges from the sumptuous Hilltop camp and lodges to more rustic bush camps.

Tembe Elephant Reserve was established in an isolated corner of KwaZulu-Natal to conserve the region's remaining elephants. Today, around 180 of the largest African elephants in the world are found here. Although the park is best known for the Big Five, it is also home to a large number of bird species. Additionally, the reserve offers a rich cultural experience with folklore stories told in song and dance around the fire in the *boma* (gathering place).

A World Heritage Site, **Ukhahlamba Drakensberg Park** encompasses the highest range south of Kilimanjaro. The park is blessed with spectacular waterfalls and streams, rocky paths and sandstone cliffs, making it a great option for hikers, rock climbers and walkers. The mountains were home to the indigenous San people for 4,000 years and the rock art is the largest and most concentrated collection in Africa. Hikers can even stay in caves that were once inhabited by the San Bushmen.

Equestrian group in the Golden Gate Highlands Park

THE ARID INTERIOR

Ai-Ais Richtersveld Transfrontier Park is truly extraordinary but it is not for visitors who want to see large game. The park is a wild landscape that seems desolate but on closer inspection reveals a treasury of the world's richest desert plants. Miniature rock gardens cling to cliff faces, and the strange stem succulents known as *half-mens* can appear almost human when viewed from a distance. The park is only accessible in 4x4 or high clearance vehicles, and other cars are not allowed to enter.

The **Karoo National Park** is the largest ecosystem in South Africa with an enormous diversity of plant and animal life. There are several species worth looking out for including the "formerly extinct" quagga, Cape mountain zebra, springbok, five species of tortoise and the rare black eagle. Activities you could try include taking a scenic drive along the Klipspringer Pass, a guided night drive, and hiking along several trails. The Karoo Fossil Trail has been specifically designed for disabled visitors.

Spectacular views of the Karoo National Park, Arid Interior region

Called the "Place of the Great Noise" by the indigenous Khoi people, **Augrabies Falls National Park** is named after the magnificent waterfall formed by the Orange River. Visitors should be aware that the approach to the falls is very slippery and people have fallen in the past. The area is known for its traditional domed huts and the excellent bird life. Sudden temperature changes are not unusual in this region, so it is worth bringing extra layers of clothing.

Colourful flowers bloom in Spring at **Goegap Nature Reserve**. The circular walks and challenging mountain bike trails attract many visitors. Accommodation includes a self-catering guesthouse, bush huts and camping sites.

Kgalagadi Transfrontier Park is a desert of glistening red sand dunes bisected by two dry rivers. It joins a vast national park in Botswana and the combined International Peace Park covers almost twice the area of the Kruger National Park *(see p388)*. Accommodation here is either in traditional rest camps or in unfenced wilderness camps, which are guarded by armed guides. These sites are always popular as guests can experience the bush at close hand during their stay. The park is also famous for its gemsbok and birds of prey.

World-renowned for its spectacular spring flower displays, where butterflies and birds can be seen among the flowers, **Namaqua National Park** is best visited from early August to September. More than 1,000 of its estimated 3,500 plant species are unique and the park is situated in the only arid biodiversity hot spot. As this is a developing park, there are no overnight accommodation facilities and the only place to stop for snacks and light refreshments is at a stall at an adjacent farm.

THE WESTERN AND SOUTHERN CAPE

Addo Elephant National Park is home to approximately 450 elephants as well as the unique flightless dung beetle. The trail has a 500-m (547-yd) boardwalk to accommodate people with mobility and sensory impairments. Overnight visitors can choose from safari tents, forest cabins, *rondavels*, and luxury guest houses, as well as caravan and camping sites.

Young baboon, De Hoop Reserve

Named after the species of antelope it was set up to conserve, **Bontebok National Park** is a World Heritage Site. The park has a wonderful view of the Langeberg mountains, and as part of the Cape Floral Kingdom it has particularly rich flora. This is an ideal spot to relax by the tranquil Breede River and take a tour of the Wine routes and surrounding areas.

Penguins at play in Table Mountain National Park, Cape Town

De Hoop Nature Reserve is a special reserve with an abundance of marine life such as dolphins, seals and whales. More than 260 species of resident and migratory birds are also found here. There are several hikes to choose from including the Whale Trail, which has five overnight stops and provides an excellent opportunity to explore the area.

Table Mountain National Park is a unique mix of natural wonders and the bustling city life of Cape Town. The park, unusually, has free access, apart from at the Cape of Good Hope, Silvermine and Boulders, which is worth visiting to see the delightful African

A floral feast for the eyes at the Namaqua National Park, the Arid Interior Region

penguins. The park is part of the Cape Floral Kingdom and has some of the best and most diverse wildlife in the world. There are plenty of activities on offer, but the scuba diving and mountain biking are most noteworthy.

Keen hikers can enjoy the illustrious Otter Trail in the **Tsitsikamma National Park**. This is a marine park where the underwater trails, scuba diving and snorkelling are also well worth experiencing. Visitors frequently catch sight of dolphins and porpoises frolicking near the shoreline and during the migration season southern right whales might be seen.

Hikers and bird-lovers alike relish the nature trails through forests and along peaceful riverbanks at the **Wilderness National Park**. Bird-watchers should keep a look-out for the Knysna lourie and the pied kingfisher here. There are plenty of other activities on offer including sports such as abseiling and paragliding.

Following the trail of otters in the Tsitsikamma National Park

DIRECTORY

PLANNING YOUR TRIP

South African Tourism Services Association (SATSA)
Tel *(086) 12 72872*
www.satsa.co.za

South African National Parks
Box 787, Pretoria, 0001.
Tel *(012) 428-9111*
www.sanparks.org

CapeNature
Belmont Park, Belmont Road, Rondebosch.
Tel (021) 426-0723
www.capenature.org.za

KwaZulu Wildlife
Box 13069, Cascades, Pietermaritzburg, 3202.
Tel *(033) 845-1000*
www.kznwildlife.com

24-Hour Malaria Hotline
(082) 234 1800

GAUTENG AND MPUMALANGA

Kruger National Park
N4, R538, R569, or R536.
Tel *(012) 428-9111*
www.sanparks.org/parks/kruger/

Madikwe Game Reserve
70km (43 miles) north of Zeerust on R49.
Tel *(018) 350-9931*
www.madikwe-game-reserve.co.za

Pilanesberg National Park
50km (31 miles) north of Zeerust on R49.
Tel *(014) 555-5354*
www.pilanesberg-game-reserve.co.za

Suikerbosrand Nature Reserve
Outside Heidelberg.
Tel *(011) 904-3930*

THE EAST COAST AND INTERIOR

Golden Gate Highlands National Park
R711 or R712.
Tel *(012) 428-9111*
www.sanparks.org/parks/golden_gate/

Greater St Lucia Wetland Park
N2 from Mtubatuba.
Tel *(035) 590-1340*
www.kznwildlife.com

Hluhluwe Umfolozi Park
N2 to signposted turn-off at Mtubatuba.
Tel *(033) 845-1000*
www.kznwildlife.com

Tembe Elephant Reserve
N2 past Mkuze, Jozini turn-off.
Tel *(031) 202-9090*
www.tembe.co.za

Ukhahlamba Drakensberg Park
N3 via Mooi River or Harrismith and Estcourt.
Tel *(033) 845-1000*
www.kznwildlife.com

THE ARID INTERIOR

Ai-Ais Richtersveld Transfrontier Park
From Springbok, N7 to Steinkopf, Port Nolloth & Alexander Bay; gravel road to Sendelingsdrift.
Tel *(012) 428-9111*
www.sanparks.org/parks/richtersveld/

Augrabies Falls National Park
N14, 120 km (74 miles) W of Upington.
Tel *(012) 428-9111*
www.sanparks.org/parks/augrabies/

Goegap Nature Reserve
E off N7; S of R14; 15 km (10 miles) SE of Springbok.
Tel *(027) 718-9906*
www.northerncape.org.za

Karoo National Park
N1 to Beaufort West.
Tel *(012) 428-9111*
www.sanparks.org/parks/karoo/

Kgalagadi Transfrontier Park
R360 from Upington.
Tel *(012) 428-9111*
www.sanparks.org/parks/kgalagadi/

Namaqua National Park
Off N7 route to Namibia.
Tel *(012) 428-9111*
www.sanparks.org/parks/namaqua/

THE WESTERN AND SOUTHERN CAPE

Addo Elephant National Park
N2 from city, then R335.
Tel *(012) 428-9111*
www.sanparks.org/parks/addo/

Bontebok National Park
Off N2.
Tel *(012) 428-9111*
www.sanparks.org/parks/bontebok/

De Hoop Nature Reserve
56 km (35 miles) E of Bredasdorp on dirt road.
Tel *(028) 425-5020*
www.capenature.co.za

Table Mountain National Park
Tel *(012) 428-9111*
www.sanparks.org/parks/table_mountain/

Tsitsikamma National Park
N2 from Plettenberg Bay.
Tel *(012) 428-9111*
www.sanparks.org/parks/tsitsikamma/

Wilderness National Park
Close to N2 highway, 15 km (10 miles) from George.
Tel *(012) 428-9111*
www.sanparks.org/parks/wilderness/

PRACTICAL INFORMATION

South Africa hosts around 4.5 million foreign visitors a year. Throughout the country, the peak seasons coincide with the South African school holidays – the busiest times are from early December to late February, especially along the south and east coasts. The Easter weekend is also busy at both inland and seaside resorts, as are the four-week winter school holidays over June and July. Although the number of tourists increases every year, the country nevertheless offers a sense of the "undiscovered". Local people still have wide, sandy beaches largely to themselves, and road travel between cities and the sea is easy. In the interior, the natural splendour of game parks and nature reserves draw crowds of visitors.

National Monument logo

WHEN TO GO

Many parts of South Africa are at their best in September and October, when the spring season's growth is fresh and the temperature comfortably warm. Game-watchers may prefer June to August, when many trees are bare and large numbers of animals converge on the diminishing number of drinking places. Winter days are usually sunny and warm, but temperatures drop as the sun sets.

Temperatures from December to February may be close to unbearable in high-lying areas such as the Northern Cape and along the East Coast, but relief is delivered through thunderstorms almost every afternoon. The moderating influence of the sea is welcome at the coast, although some people find the increased humidity difficult to deal with. The southwestern areas have winter rainfall and hot summers. Much of the southern coast receives rain throughout the year. Almost all attractions stay open all through the year.

WHAT TO TAKE

Don't underestimate South African winters, or the wind-chill factor in summer; bear in mind that central heating is the exception and pack warm clothes. Sunblock, film and specialized provisions can be bought locally, but do carry a supply of medication if you suffer from a chronic condition.

VISA AND PASSPORTS

European Union nationals need only a valid passport in order to stay in South Africa for six months. Citizens of the United States, Canada, Australia and New Zealand, who have a valid passport, can stay for three months.

Visas to enter Swaziland are issued free of charge at the border. Visa requirements for Lesotho are about to change. The South African consulate or embassy in your country will be able to advise.

All visitors must complete a temporary residence permit at the point of entry into South Africa. It shows length and purpose of the visit and a contact address. Visitors may also be asked to prove that they can support themselves financially while in the country and own a return ticket or have the means to buy one. No inoculations are necessary, however, if you arrive from a country where yellow fever is endemic you will need a vaccination certificate. Malaria is still prevalent in parts of KwaZulu-Natal and Mpumalanga, and caution is advised.

Tourist Information kiosk

TOURIST INFORMATION

Tourist offices, identified by the letter "i" on a green background, offer invaluable advice about what to see and where to go. They may also carry the name of an umbrella organisation or a local publicity association. The offices are usually sited on the main road in the smaller towns, sometimes adjoining (or inside) the offices of the local authority or forming part of the local museum or public library. You should be able to obtain advance information in your own country from **South African Tourism**.

Summer game-viewing at Addo Elephant Park, Port Elizabeth ***(see p196)***

The *John Benn* takes sightseers around the Knysna Lagoon *(see p186)*

OPENING TIMES AND ADMISSION PRICES

Most businesses (other than retail outlets), museums and galleries open from 8 or 9am until 4 or 5pm. Many, particularly in the smaller towns, close for lunch between 1 and 2pm, except during the peak summer season. Larger museums or galleries usually close for one day each week (usually on a Monday). Entry charges vary. Nature reserves, game parks and botanic gardens all charge entry fees, most of them very reasonable.

ETIQUETTE

Dress code in South African cities is casual, except for a few top restaurants and for events noted as formal. On the beach, however, it is illegal for women to either swim or sunbathe topless. The consumption of alcohol on beaches and in public places is illegal, as is smoking in buses, trains, taxis and most public buildings.

It is very important to observe religious customs when visiting mosques, temples and other places of worship.

DISABLED TRAVELLERS

Facilities for the disabled are not as sophisticated as they are in the United States and Europe, but wheelchair users, for example, will nevertheless have a satisfactory holiday. If you're renting a car, ask about a special parking disk, allowing parking concessions. Local airlines provide assistance for disabled passengers, if given prior notice. South Africa also has a growing number of hotels that cater for the disabled, and the Kruger and Karoo national parks have specially adapted huts. Contact the **Association for Persons with Physical Disabilities** *(see p397)* for further information and contact numbers.

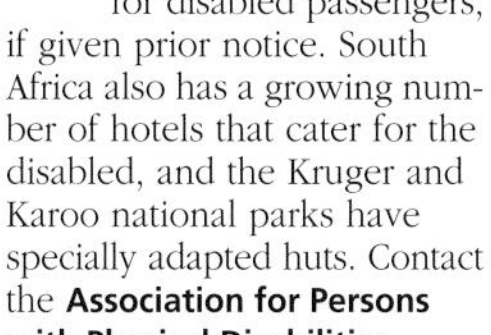

Disabled parking

VAT AND TAXES

See p374 and p405.

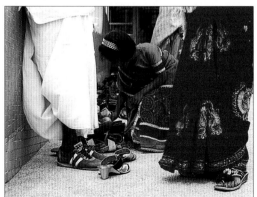

Visitors must remove their shoes before entering a Hindu temple

DIRECTORY

EMBASSIES AND CONSULATES

Australian High Commission
Pretoria/Tshwane ***Tel*** *(012) 342-3740.*
Durban ***Tel*** *(031) 208-4163.*

British High Commission
Johannesburg ***Tel*** *(011) 327-0163.*
Pretoria/Tshwane
Tel *(012) 421-7800.*
Cape Town ***Tel*** *(021) 405-2400.*

Canadian High Commission
Johannesburg ***Tel*** *(011) 442-3130.*
Pretoria/Tshwane
Tel *(012) 422-3000.*
Cape Town ***Tel*** *(021) 423-5240.*

Embassy of Ireland
Pretoria/Tshwane
Tel *(012) 342-5062.*

New Zealand High Commission
Pretoria/Tshwane
Tel *(012) 342-8656.*

US Consulate General
Johannesburg ***Tel*** *(011) 646-6900.*
Cape Town ***Tel*** *(021) 702-7300.*
Durban ***Tel*** *(031) 304-4737.*

US Embassy
Pretoria/Tshwane
Tel *(012) 421-7500.*

TOURIST OFFICES

Cape Town Tourism
Tel *(021) 405-4500.*
www.cape-town.org

Durban Publicity
Tel *(031) 426-5639.*
www.durban.co.za

Eastern Cape Tourism Board
Tel *(041) 585-7761.*

Free State Tourism
Tel *(051) 405-8111.*
www.freestate.co.za

Johannesburg Tourism
Tel *(011) 832-2780.*
www.gauteng.net

Mpumalanga Tourism
Tel *(013) 752-7001.*

Pretoria/Tshwane Tourism
Tel *(012) 358-1430.*
www.tshwane.gov.za

South African Tourism
Tel *(011) 895-3000.*

Discovery tour at Oudtshoorn's Cango Wildlife Farm *(see p176)*

TRAVELLING WITH CHILDREN

Travelling with children is fairly easy, as the sunny weather allows for a variety of outdoor entertainment. Make sure that they drink plenty of water, though, and that they wear a high-protection sun screen. Consult your doctor about travelling with children in a malaria zone.

Children can be great "ice-breakers" in getting to meet the locals, but do not let them out of your sight.

If you travel during local school holidays, you'll find that even the smaller towns offer children's activities – from aquarium and zoo tours to theatre, baking and craft workshops. The local press, libraries and the Tonight website (www.tonight.co.za) are good sources of ideas. Look out for "Touch and Feed" farms, where children can encounter farm animals.

WOMEN TRAVELLERS

South Africa has an extremely high incidence of rape *(see p398)*, although the careful tourist should be reasonably safe. There are **Rape Crisis** centres in major towns and cities. Travelling alone is not recommended. Women are potential victims of mugging, so keep to well-lit public areas during the day and night and don't exhibit any valuables. Always look as if you know where you are going and don't offer or accept a lift from anyone.

Sexual harassment is not too common, although a great many South African males do hold rather chauvinistic attitudes, so be careful not to come across as too friendly, as your interest may be perceived as sexual. The incidence of HIV/Aids is high, so don't ever have unprotected sex. Condoms are readily available at pharmacies and supermarkets.

GAY AND LESBIAN TRAVEL

Enshrined in the new constitution is a clause protecting the rights of gays and lesbians. But while Cape Town is certainly the "gay capital of Africa", the smaller towns still retain conservative attitudes.

The cities have a host of gay bars and theatre venues. The iafrica website (www.iafrica.com) has a monthly gay and lesbian event listing. **TOGS**, The Organization for Gay Sport, is among several sports organizations operating in the major cities.

The drag/theme party held in Cape Town each December by Mother City Queer Projects draws almost 10,000 party goers – at least 1,000 of them foreign visitors. In September you can join Johannesburg's annual Gay and Lesbian Pride Parade, billed as the greatest parade in Africa.

Gay and Lesbian Pride Parade

STUDENT TRAVEL

Students with a valid International Student Identity Card (ISIC) benefit from good airline travel discounts, but reduced admission to venues and events has not taken off in South Africa. The STA travel agency, which specialises in student travel, has branches world-wide, and backpacking is gaining in popularity.

Backpackers' accommodation in the centre of Cape Town

TIME

South African Standard Time (there is only one time zone) is two hours ahead of Greenwich Mean Time (GMT) all year round, seven hours ahead of the United States' Eastern Standard Winter Time and seven hours behind Australian Central Time.

PUBLIC TOILETS

There are public toilets in shopping malls and in many public buildings such as civic centres, libraries or town halls. Most large urban vehicle service stations have toilets, but these are intended for the use of clients. On major tourist routes, most garages that have refreshment centres also usually have well-kept toilets. Public toilets can be found at railway and bus stations, although these are often not very clean. Many have no soap or any means of drying your hands. An alternative is to use the toilets in a restaurant where you are a customer. Large shopping centres and tourist attractions usually have well-maintained facilities and customised toilets for wheelchair users. Baby-changing facilities are also available.

ELECTRICAL SUPPLY

Virtually all electricity (alternating current) is supplied by the state-owned utility company Eskom. Mains voltage is 220/230 volts (220V) at 50 cycles (50Hz). Most local power plugs are 5A (amperes) with twin pins, or 15A with three rounded pins, with the longest of the three carrying the earth connection (brown wire). Standard South African plugs do not contain safety fuses. An open circuit within an appliance should cause a circuit-breaker to trip at the distribution board, cutting off electricity from that board or the electricity to the section in which the fault has occurred. Seek advice about adaptors from a local electrical supplier.

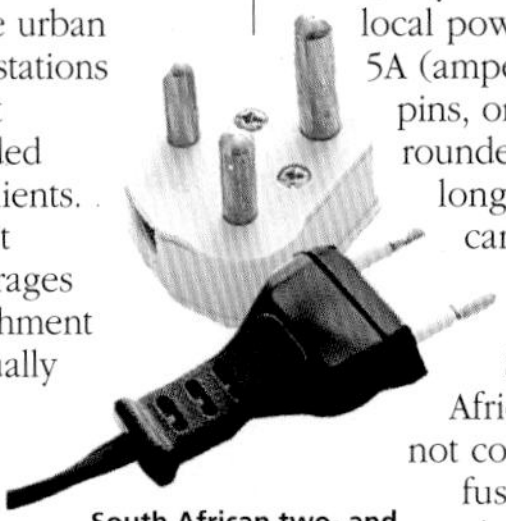

South African two- and three-prong plugs

WEIGHTS AND MEASURES

South Africa uses the metric system and SI (Système International) units. Normal body temperature of 98.4° F is equal to 37° C. If the weather chart shows 30° C, you're in for a hot day. A pressure of 30 pounds per square inch is equal to two bars.

CONVERSION CHART

Imperial to Metric
1 inch = 2.54 cm
1 foot = 30 cm
1 mile = 1.6 km
1 ounce = 28 g
1 pound = 454 g
1 pint = 0.57 litres
1 gallon = 4.6 litres

Metric to Imperial
1 mm = 0.04 inches
1 cm = 0.4 inches
1 m = 3 feet 3 inches
1 km = 0.6 miles
1 g = 0.04 ounces
1 kg = 2.2 pounds
1 litre = 1.8 pints

DIRECTORY

DISABLED TRAVELLERS

Titch Travel
26 Station Rd,
Rondebosch,
Cape Town.
Tel *(021) 686-5501.*
Tours for the physically disabled or visually impaired.
www.titchtours.co.za
@ titcheve@iafrica.com

Association for Persons with Physical Disabilities

Cape Town
Tel *(021) 555-2881.*

Durban
Tel *(031) 403-7041.*

Johannesburg
Tel *(011) 726-8040.*

Kimberley
Tel *(053) 833-3315.*

Disabled People of South Africa
Tel *(043) 743-1579.*

CHILDREN

Childline
Tel *0800-05-5555.*
National toll-free number.
www.childline.org.za

GAY AND LESBIAN

Gay and Lesbian Coalition
Cape Town
Tel *(011) 487-3810.*
www.q.co.za

Gay Travel
Cape Town.
Tel *(011) 790-0010.*
www.travel.co.za
Gay and lesbian travel.

TOGS (The Organization for Gay Sport)
Cnr Putney and Cheswick sts, Brixton, Johannesburg.
Tel *(011) 802-5589.*
www.togs.co.za

RAPE CRISIS

Cape Town
Tel *(021) 447-9762 or (083) 222-5158.*

Durban
Tel *(083) 222-5158.*

Johannesburg
Tel *(011) 642-4345 or (083) 222-5158.*

Pretoria/Tshwane
Tel *(012) 342-2222 or (086) 132-2322.*

AIDS COUNSELLING

AIDS Helpline
Tel *(08000) 12322.*

Cape Town
Tel *(021) 797-3327.*
Durban
Tel *(031) 300-3104.*

Johannesburg
Tel *(011) 725-6711.*

Pretoria/Tshwane
Tel *(012) 312-0122.*

STUDENT TRAVEL

STA Travel
Tygervalley, Cape Town.
Tel *(021) 418-6570.*

34 Mutual Gardens, Rosebank Mall, Johannesburg.
Tel *(011) 447-5414.*

Student Travel Head Office.
Tel *(086) 178-1781.*
www.statravel.co.za

Personal Security and Health

SA Police logo

South Africa is experiencing a period of profound change. For some, the rate of change is overwhelming; for others it is too slow. Democracy has at last been attained, but a great many problems – such as widespread unemployment and poverty – still need to be solved. In some areas, the incidence of serious crime is alarmingly high, but overall, South Africa is a safe place for visitors who take reasonable precautions. The wildlife should always be taken seriously and treated with respect. Bites and stings from venomous creatures are rare, but malaria and bilharzia need to be considered in certain areas.

PERSONAL SAFETY

Staying safe is a question of exercising common sense and extreme caution. While inner-city areas and townships are probably the most dangerous, villages may also have crime hot spots.

Do not go out on your own, anywhere, and don't exhibit expensive-looking accessories. Pickpockets may be a problem, and muggers may snatch at a valuable item or handbag and run away.

Police officer

Don't carry large sums of money, but do keep some change in a side pocket so that you don't have to produce your wallet whenever you need to tip.

Don't put your possessions down when you need your hands (for examining an intended purchase, perhaps). Carry with you only what you are likely to need. A money belt worn under your clothing is useful for keeping documents and banknotes.

Don't go near deserted or impoverished areas except as part of a tour group.

Avoid any place where unrestricted consumption of liquor takes place.

Leave valuables and purchases in your hotel's safe-deposit box.

Avoid any of the suburban trains at off-peak times, unless you're in a group of at least ten.

Don't go exploring without a guide. Call the **police flying squad** in an emergency, or report the incident to the nearest police station or police officer. You will need to produce identification. To make an insurance claim you will need to obtain a case reference number from the police station. A free assistance service called Eblockwatch also has a call centre which tourists can ring if they need assistance. You can register at www.eblockwatch.co.za. The centre will then send one of its members to assist you in an emergency.

Female police officer

Police officer on horseback

Tow truck

ON THE ROAD

When travelling by car, always keep the doors locked and the windows only slightly open. When you do leave the car, lock it, even if you're getting out for just a few moments *(see p408)*. Make sure that nothing of value is visible inside – leave the glove compartment open to show that there's nothing in there either. Use undercover or supervised parking wherever possible. Do not stop for hitch-hikers or to offer any help, even to an accident victim. If a hijacker or other criminal points a firearm at you, obey his or her orders.

Pharmacies offer valuable medical advice and services

MEDICAL FACILITIES

State and provincial hospitals do offer adequate facilities, but they tend to be underfunded and under-staffed. Patients who are members of medical insurance schemes are usually admitted to a private hospital, such as the **Sandton Medi-Clinic**. All visitors should take out travel insurance to cover everything, including emergencies. If you suffer from any pre-existing medical condition or are on any long-term medication, make sure those who try to help you are aware of it.

FOOD AND WATER

Tap water is safe to drink, although chlorinated. There is a wide range of bottled waters available. Be careful of river

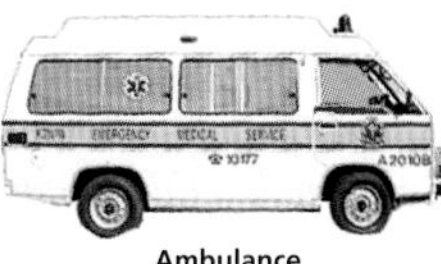
Ambulance

Police vehicle

Fire engine

or mountain water in heavily populated areas. The preparation of food in most restaurants and hotels meets international standards, but do exercise common sense. In the informal markets, avoid meat or dairy products that may have been lying in the sun, and wash all fruit and vegetables carefully.

Travellers to South Africa do not generally suffer the same stomach upsets as they may in the rest of the continent.

No fires

OUTDOOR HAZARDS

In many parts of South Africa, forest and bush fires are a major hazard, especially during the dry winter months. Don't ever discard burning matches and cigarette ends.

Always protect yourself from the harsh sun with a hat and sunblock. Before you climb or hike at high altitude, ask about the expected weather conditions. These change very quickly. If you are caught in cloud, keep warm and wait for the weather to lift. Make sure you tell a responsible person your route and the time you expect to return. Ensure that you are familiar with your route.

POISONOUS BITES AND STINGS

Few travellers are likely to find themselves in danger of being bitten or stung by any one of the venomous creatures of South Africa. People on safari or on hiking trails should nevertheless watch where they place their hands and feet.

Few snakes in South Africa are deadly, and most are not poisonous at all. They strike only when attacked or threatened. The most dangerous spider is the seldom-encountered button spider *(Latrodectus species)*. Most of the species of scorpion are only slightly venomous. In general, those with thick tails and small pincers tend to be more poisonous. Because of their lower body weight, children are more susceptible to the toxins than adults.

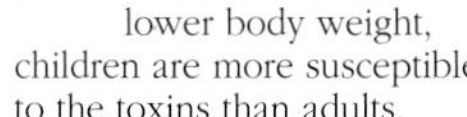

MALARIA AND BILHARZIA

Malaria is most likely to be contracted in Mpumalanga, Northern Province and northern KwaZulu-Natal. The risks of contracting malaria can be minimised by starting a course of anti-malaria tablets a week before travelling to an affected area and continuing with the treatment for a month after your return.

Bilharzia *(schistosomiasis)* results from contact (whether on the skin or by drinking) with affected water. Areas in which the disease is most likely to be contracted are Northern Province, Mpumalanga, North-West Province, KwaZulu-Natal and Eastern Cape. Suspect water should not be used for washing or bathing, and should be boiled if intended for consumption.

The charming police station in Pietermaritzburg

DIRECTORY

EMERGENCY NUMBERS

Police Flying Squad
Tel *10111 all areas.*

Ambulance
Tel *10177 all areas.*

Private Ambulance
ER24 Service
Tel *(021) 551-6823.*

Fire
Jo'burg ***Tel*** *(011) 624-2800.*
Pretoria/Tshwane ***Tel*** *10177.*
Cape Town ***Tel*** *(021) 535-1100.*
Durban ***Tel*** *(031) 361-0000.*

AA Emergency Road Service
Free call ***Tel*** *083-84322.*
24-hours, all areas.

MEDICAL FACILITIES

After-Hours Pharmacies
Jo'burg ***Tel*** *(011) 624-2800.*
Pretoria/Tshwane
Tel *(012) 460-6422.*
Cape Town ***Tel*** *(021) 797-5094.*
Durban ***Tel*** *(031) 368-3666.*

Christiaan Barnard Memorial Hospital
181 Longmarket St, Cape Town.
Tel *(021) 480-6111.*

Poison Information
Tel *0800 333-444 all areas.*

Sandton Medi-Clinic
Peter Place, Bryanston, Jo'burg.
Tel *(011) 709-2000.*

St Augustine's Hospital
107 Chelmsford Rd, Glenwood, Durban ***Tel*** *(031) 268-5000.*

Banking and Local Currency

The Standard Bank

The South African banking system is similar to that in most industrialized Western countries. There are no restrictions on the amount of foreign currency that may be brought into the country. There are, however, limits to the amount of any currency that may be taken out of South Africa. These amounts, like rates of exchange, are subject to fluctuation, so always check with your travel agent. Travellers' cheques may be exchanged at banks, bureaux de change, some hotels and some shops. Banks generally offer the best rate of exchange.

Foreign exchange bureau, V&A Waterfront, Cape Town

BANKING HOURS

In the larger towns, week day banking hours are from 9am to 3:30pm, and on Saturdays from 9am to 11am. Smaller branches and agencies may have shorter hours and be closed on Saturdays. They are all closed on public holidays. A number of sites, such as the V&A Waterfront in Cape Town and the OR Thambo airport in Johannesburg, offer a convenient, 24-hour foreign-exchange service. At all the other airports, the reception areas for international arrivals and departures have special banking facilities for international passengers.

AUTOMATIC BANKING

Automatic teller machines (ATMs) are widely distributed in the cities and towns. Cash withdrawals, up to a set limit per day per card, are made with bank-issued debit cards, but transactions may also be done with local or foreign-issued credit cards encoded with a PIN number. The cards most widely used in South Africa are Visa and MasterCard. If you find the daily limit inadequate, go to the bank and arrange to draw more. You will need your passport for any transactions at the bank counter. ATMs may run out of notes at weekends, especially if there is a public holiday on the Monday, so draw money early.

Avoid drawing money while on your own, or at deserted ATM's after-hours, and decline all unsolicited offers of "help". ATM fraud is common: a fraudster may, for example, jam the machine slot so you can't retrieve your card. While you alert the bank officials inside, the fraudster un-jams the slot and withdraws money from your account. Rather wait outside at the ATM while a companion goes for help. All ATM's display a 24-hour emergency telephone number to call in the event of any problems with your card.

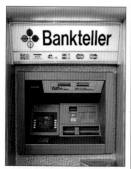

A convenient Bankteller ATM

CREDIT CARDS

Most businesses accept all major credit cards. They will be electronically validated, which usually takes no longer than a few minutes. Informal traders do not normally accept credit cards. It is not possible to purchase petrol or oil with a credit card; most banks issue a separate petrol card. Your car-rental company can help with arrangements. Find out what charges your bank will levy for use of your credit card in South Africa.

CHANGING MONEY

Among the recently introduced foreign exchange facilities are automatic teller machines in larger cities that handle only the exchange of foreign currency. While these machines are still scarce, they do offer a very convenient means of exchanging notes after hours. It is planned to install more machines.

DIRECTORY

ABSA/Maestro
National free-call, 24-hours.
Tel *0800 11 1155.*

American Express
Tel *0800 11 0929, 24-hours.*

Diners Club
Tel *(011) 358-8400.*
8am–4:45pm Mon–Fri.

First National Bank
National free-call, 24-hours.
Tel *0800 11 0132.*

MasterCard
National free-call, 24-hours.
Tel *0800 99 0418.*

Nedbank
National free-call, 24-hours.
Tel *0800 11 0929.*

Rennies Foreign Exchange Bureaux (Thomas Cook)
National free-call, 24-hours.
Tel *0800 99 8175.*

Standard Bank/ MasterCard
National free-call, 24-hours.
Tel *0800 02 0600.*

Visa International
National free-call, 24-hours.
Tel *0800 99 0475.*

TRAVELLERS' CHEQUES

These may be cashed at any bank – provided the currency of issue is acceptable. No commission is charged by a branch of the bank that issued the cheque.

CURRENCY

The South African unit of currency is the rand, indicated by the letter "R" before the amount ("rand" is short for "Witwatersrand", Gauteng's gold-bearing reef).

The rand is divided into 100 cents (c). Older issues of coins and notes are still legal tender. South African currency circulates – usually at face value – in the neighbouring Lesotho, Namibia, Swaziland and Botswana.

Bank Notes
Bank notes, on which the "Big 5" wildlife animals are represented, are issued in R10, R20, R50, R100 and R200 denominations.

R200 note

R100 note

R50 note

R20 note

R10 note

Coins (actual size)
Copper-coloured, smooth-edged coins are in denominations of 1cent, 2cents and 5cents. The 10cents, 20cents and 50cents coins are a brassy yellow and have milled edges. The R1, R2 and R5 coins are milled in a bright, silver colour.

1-cent piece

2-cent piece

5-cent piece

10-cent piece

20-cent piece

50-cent piece

R1

R2

R5

Telecommunications

Telkom logo

South African telecommunications systems are among the most advanced in the world. The national telecommunications agency is Telkom SA Limited, and a wide variety of postal options, from insured or signature-on-delivery mail to courier services, are offered by post offices countrywide. Public telephones (payphones) are found in every city and town, and include both coin- and card-operated models. Telephone cards and postage stamps may be bought at many shops and supermarkets. Some shops, especially in the rural areas, have one or more public telephone (rented from Telkom) on their premises.

TELEPHONES

Most telephone exchanges in South Africa are automatic, so it is possible to dial direct as long as the correct dialling code is used. Public telephone boxes, or payphones, are found at post offices, train stations and in shopping malls, but don't rely on finding a phone directory there. Post offices, however, usually keep a complete range of South African telephone directories. Businesses and restaurants often have a table-model payphone – aptly known as a Chatterbox. Even if you are not a patron, ask if you may use the phone. The staff are unlikely to refuse your request. Payphones accept a range of South African coins.

Telkom payphones

Telephone cards are available from most post offices, cafés and newsagents. Note that payphone models accept either coins or cards, but not both.

Reduced rates are in effect after hours, typically from 7pm until 7am on weekdays, and from 1pm Saturday to 7am Monday on weekends. Calls made from hotels may carry a substantial levy.

The AA's roadside emergency number, (011) 799 1500, is available for all members, non-members may call 10177 for the emergency services.

Stations at an Internet café

INTERNET USE

Only about ten per cent of the population of South Africa has regular access to the Internet, but there is a growing number of Internet cafés, especially in the main urban centres.

MOBILE PHONES

Mobile (or cell) phones are obtainable on contract from a private service provider. Cell-phone rental facilities can be found at the major airports. Quite often, cell phones are offered as part of a car-hire contract. Legislation forbidding the use of hand-held cell phones while driving is expected to be introduced.

Cell phone coverage is very good in most towns and cities and along the main highways.

USING A PUBLIC TELEPHONE IN SOUTH AFRICA

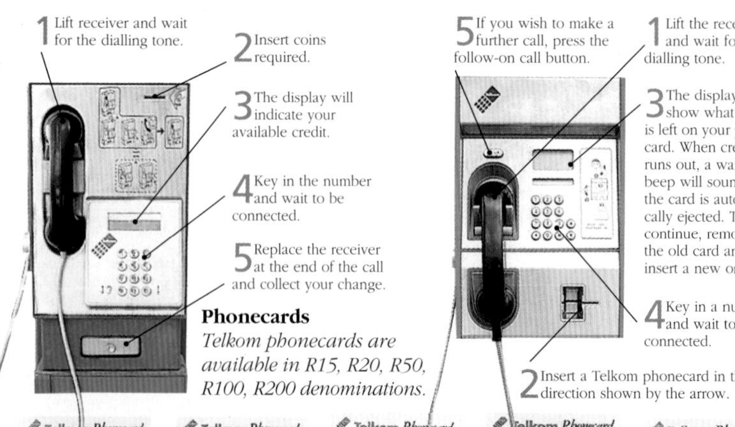

1 Lift receiver and wait for the dialling tone.
2 Insert coins required.
3 The display will indicate your available credit.
4 Key in the number and wait to be connected.
5 Replace the receiver at the end of the call and collect your change.
Phonecards
Telkom phonecards are available in R15, R20, R50, R100, R200 denominations.
5 If you wish to make a further call, press the follow-on call button.
1 Lift the receiver and wait for the dialling tone.
3 The display will show what value is left on your phonecard. When credit runs out, a warning beep will sound and the card is automatically ejected. To continue, remove the old card and insert a new one.
4 Key in a number and wait to be connected.
2 Insert a Telkom phonecard in the direction shown by the arrow.
Telkom Phonecard
R15
R20
R50
R100
R200

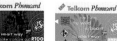

Standard South African postbox

POSTAL SERVICE

The postal service is undergoing extensive reorganization, because the delivery rate of letters and parcels is erratic. Letters or goods may be sent registered, cash-on-delivery (COD), insured, express delivery service, Fastmail and Speed Services (for guaranteed delivery within 24 hours in South Africa). Private courier services are popular. Postage stamps are sold at newsagents, grocery stores and corner cafés. Post offices are open from 8am–4:30pm on weekdays and from 8am–noon on Saturdays. Smaller centres usually close for lunch hour.

Aerograme

FACSIMILE SERVICES

Facsimile (fax), Internet and email (electronic mail) facilities are widely available. Most photocopying outlets, like **Copy Wizards** and the **Internet Café** offer international and local fax and telephone facilities, as well as email connections. You will find them in large shopping centres and business areas.

POSTE RESTANTE

If you require a "poste restante" service (there is no charge), address your request, in writing, to the postmaster of the post office in the area where you will be travelling. Supply your surname, the date on which you wish the service to begin and an address to which uncollected post should be sent. Instruct your correspondents to address all mail to the designated post office, for example, "J Jones, Poste Restante, Cape Town 8000, South Africa." Post will then safely be retained for you at that post office for a month.

NEWSPAPERS AND MAGAZINES

Daily newspapers are found in all major cities; most have both morning and afternoon papers as well as Saturday and Sunday editions. A number of national weekly or bi-weekly news tabloids are also published.

English language newspapers are widespread in the cities, but rural towns may receive fewer copies, often up to a day later. A variety of local and international magazines are widely available. Topics include travel, sport, wildlife and outdoor life. South Africa receives editions of some overseas newspapers (mainly British), as well as a number of foreign magazines. All of these are distributed through selected newsagents, such as the CNA chain, or placed in upmarket hotels.

A selection of local daily and weekly newspapers

COURIER SERVICES

Worldwide couriers like **DHL** and **Speed Services** have branches in larger South African centres. They all offer a collection service and deliver parcels, priced per kilo, country- and worldwide.

RADIO AND TELEVISION

The South African Broadcasting Corporation (SABC) is responsible for four television channels and a number of national and regional radio stations. The principal language of television is English. British and American programming dominate, but there are some good local productions. Local radio stations target specific audiences and language groups. Cable and satellite television services are provided by the private company MNet.

DIRECTORY

POSTAL SERVICES

Cape Town Post Office
Tel *(021) 464-1700.*

Johannesburg Post Office
Tel *0800 11 0226.*

Postnet
Tel *(011) 783-6810 or (021) 426-0316.*

OPERATOR ASSISTANCE

Tel *1023. (Telkom Information)*

Tel *0020. (Local long-distance)*

Tel *0900. (International call)*

Tel *1023. (Local enquiries)*

Tel *0903. (International enquiries)*

Tel *1-0118. (Telkom information service for hotels, restaurants, etc.)*

FACSIMILE SERVICES

Copy Wizards
Tel *(021) 461-9334.*

Internet Café
Tel *(021) 434-6624.*

COURIER SERVICES

DHL International
Tel *(011) 921-3600.*

Speed Services Couriers
Tel *(086) 002-3133.*

TRAVEL INFORMATION

South Africa, historically a welcome stopover for seafarers, is well served by air links with most parts of the globe and by road and rail connections to the rest of Africa. The national carrier, South African Airways (SAA), operates 45 passenger aircraft, while some 50 foreign airlines make around 180 landings in South Africa every week. There are many internal flights operated by SAA and other airlines. The rail network covers the country and extends beyond the borders to give access to Southern and Central Africa. The road system is comprehensive. Roads are generally in good condition, though the accident rate is high. Intercity bus services operate between major cities. Public transport within cities and towns is seldom satisfactory.

Tail of an SAA 747

South African Airways and Star Alliance carriers on the runway

ARRIVING BY AIR

Most visitors to the country arrive at OR Thambo International Airport, outside Johannesburg. Direct international flights also leave from and arrive in Cape Town and Durban; some flights to other African destinations are routed through Upington in the Northern Cape.

Internal destinations served by SAA, the national carrier, are Johannesburg, Durban, Cape Town, Port Elizabeth, Bloemfontein, East London, Kimberley, Ulundi, George and Upington. Smaller centres, as well as the airport at Skukuza in the Kruger National Park, are linked by regular feeder services. Air charter services are available at most of the larger airports.

Public transport to and from the major airports includes airline or privately operated shuttle buses to the city centre. Radio taxi services are also available, while most of the hotels, guesthouses and some backpackers' lodges in the larger cities, will be able to provide transport on request.

Facilities at the international airports include banking, currency exchange, car rental, post offices, information centres, duty-free shops (for outbound passengers only), restaurants and bars.

CUSTOMS

No duty is payable on any personal effects, which must be carried in unsealed or unwrapped packages.

Current customs legislation allows visitors to bring duty-free goods to the value of R3,000 into the country.

Visitors may also bring in a limited amount of perfume, 2 litres (3.5 pints) wine, 1 litre (1.75 pints) of spirits, 250 g tobacco, 200 cigarettes and 20 cigars. Further items to the value of R12,000 per person are charged at a flat rate of 20 per cent of their value. On amounts above R10,000, normal customs duties apply, plus VAT. Lesotho, Swaziland and South Africa are members

AIRPORT	INFORMATION	DISTANCE FROM CITY	TAXI FARE TO CITY	BUS TRANSFER TO CITY
Johannesburg	*Tel* (086) 727-7888	24 km (15 miles)	R230	30–35 mins
Cape Town	*Tel* (086) 727-7888	20 km (12 miles)	R200	35–50 mins
Durban	*Tel* (086) 727-7888	20 km (12 miles)	R200	20–30 mins
Port Elizabeth	*Tel* (086) 727-7888	3 km (2 miles)	R83	7–10 mins
Bloemfontein	*Tel* (086) 727-7888	15 km (9 miles)	R160	20–40 mins
East London	*Tel* (086) 727-7888	15 km (9 miles)	R160	10–15 mins
George	*Tel* (086) 727-7888	10 km (6 miles)	R130	10 mins
Skukuza *	*Tel* (013) 735-5644			

* Skukuza, the largest camp in the Kruger National Park has three flights daily arriving from Johannesburg.

Customs area

of the Southern African Common Customs Union, so there are no internal customs duties.

INTERNATIONAL FLIGHTS

Fares to South Africa are generally at their highest from September to February, but how much you pay will depend on the type of ticket you buy. Savings can also be made by booking an APEX (Advance Purchase Excursion) ticket in advance, although these are subject to minimum and maximum time limits, thus restricting the visitor's stay.

Specialist agents offer many good deals. Discount agents may also offer attractive student or youth fares.

Make sure that your booking agent is a licensed member of ABTA (the Association of British Travel Agents) or a similar authority; you will then be assured of compensation should something go wrong with your bookings.

DOMESTIC FLIGHTS

South African Airways, British Airways/Kulula.com, Itime.co.za and Nationwide offer regular inter-city services.

The current price structures are competitive, with return-fare and other attractive specials regularly on offer. In general, the earlier one books, the cheaper the fare (seven-day advance specials are common). Booking is essential.

PACKAGE HOLIDAYS

Package tours almost always offer reduced airfare and accommodation costs, making them cheaper than independent travel, unless you are travelling on a tight budget and wish to stay in backpackers' lodges, self-catering accommodation or campsites.

Popular package tours and deals include trips to Durban, Cape Town, Johannesburg, Port Elizabeth, the Garden Route, the Wild Coast, Sun City and the Palace of the Lost City, as well as the Kruger National Park.

FLY-DRIVE DEALS

Many travel agents and car-rental firms organize fly-drive packages that enable you to book a flight and have a rental car waiting for you at your destination. This is usually cheaper and involves fewer formalities than renting a car on arrival. Most major car-rental firms such as Avis, Hertz, Budget and Imperial have offices at the airports.

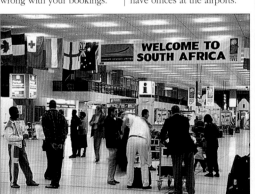

The interior of OR Thambo International Airport

AIRPORT TAX

South African Airport tax is paid upon purchase of your ticket. The tax to be paid per international departure is R116. Domestic flights are taxed at R80 per departure. The tax on flights to Botswana, Namibia, Lesotho or Swaziland is R60.

DIRECTORY

AIRPORT SHUTTLES

Cape Town Magic Bus
Domestic Arrivals Hall, Cape Town International Airport.
Tel *(021) 505-6300.*

Durban Magic Bus
Suite 7, Grenada Centre, 16 Chartwell Dr, Umhlanga Rocks.
Tel *(031) 263-2647.*

East London Shuttle
Domestic Arrivals Hall, East London National Airport.
Tel *(082) 569-3599.*

Greyhound & Mega Coach
Domestic Arrivals, Terminal 3, Johannesburg International.
Tel *(011) 249-8800.*

Pretoria/Tshwane Airport Shuttle
Cnr Prinsloo & Vermeulen sts.
Tel *(012) 991-0085.*

DOMESTIC AIRLINES

British Airways Domestic/ Kulula.com
Tel *(0861) 585-852.*
www.kulula.com

Itime.co.za
Tel *(0861) 345-345.*
www.itime.co.za

Nationwide
Tel *(0861) 737-737.*
www.flynationwide.co.za

South African Airways
Tel *(0861) 359-722.*
www.flysaa.com

CAR-RENTAL SERVICES

See p409 for information on Avis, Hertz, Imperial and Budget car-rental services.

Travelling by Train

Blue Train logo

Train travel in South Africa is quite comfortable and economical, but seldom very fast. Power is provided by electric and diesel-electric locomotives on a standard gauge of 1.65 m (3 ft 6 in). Enormously popular, particularly with foreign visitors, are the luxurious train safaris offered by the Blue Train *(see pp384-5)*. The company offers a choice of four excellent scenic routes, the unhurried journeys lasting anything from 16 hours to two days and nights. Another company, Rovos Rail, offers similar excursions to other destinations. Suburban train travel is not a very popular option among foreign tourists as routes are limited, trains run too infrequently and personal safety cannot be guaranteed.

Suburban trains are the main transport for many commuters

SUBURBAN TRAINS

Suburban services are operated by **Spoornet**, and are available in most South African cities. In Cape Town **Cape Metrorail** provides this transport service. These trains are used mainly for commuting to and from work, and they run less frequently during the off-peak times of day and at weekends. Chilren under five years of age travel for free, while children under 11 pay half the price of an adult fare.

Timetables and tickets are available at the stations. First-class tickets cost approximately twice that of those in third-class and offer better seating and security.

Tickets are clipped by train conductors, but it is essential to produce the ticket again in order to get off at the main stations (failure to do so can result in a fine). Weekly and monthly passes are available at reduced rates, but be very careful not to lose the tickets, as they have no passenger identity mark and can, therefore, be used by anyone else.

No discounts are offered for students or pensioners, however, children under seven years of age travel free, and those under 13 for half price.

It is recommended that suburban trains be used only in daylight hours, and preferably during the peak periods – early in the morning and mid- to late afternoon. It is advisable not to travel alone on suburban trains at any time.

Metrorail weekly and monthly ticket

Some suburban trains have a restaurant compartment. Try the comfortable **Biggsy's Restaurant Carriage & Wine Bar** along the False Bay coast; the trip from Cape Town to Simon's Town *(see p98)* takes about an hour.

The stately Pretoria/Tshwane Railway Station *(see p267)*

MAINLINE PASSENGER SERVICES

Mainline Passenger Services, operated by Spoornet, offers fairly comprehensive nationwide rail coverage. Daily "name" trains run between Cape Town and Johannesburg (Trans-Karoo Express), Johannesburg and Port Elizabeth (Algoa Express), Johannesburg and Durban (Trans-Natal Express) and Johannesburg and East London (Amatola Express).

It is important to remember that express trains are not particularly fast: an idea of the word "express" may be given by the Trans-Karoo, for example, which takes almost 24 hours to cover approximately 1,500 km (930 miles).

Mainline Passenger Services also provide services to two of the neighbouring states: Zimbabwe and Mozambique.

Timetables (free) and tickets are available at most central stations and Mainline offices. Third-class tickets cost about half that of first-class, and second-class tickets are somewhere in-between. First-class carriages seat four people, second-class carriages six. Seating in the third-class is open. Booking is necessary during the holiday season.

European-style discount travel passes do not apply in South Africa, although the holders of valid university student cards will receive a 40 per cent discount between February and November. Pensioners qualify for 25 per cent discount during this period. Children under five travel free all year round, children under 11 travel for half price.

A day trip by rail is a lovely way to view South Africa's landscapes

DAY TRIPS BY TRAIN

The only South African line that is routinely worked by steam train is the scenic stretch between George and Knysna on the Garden Route. The **Outeniqua Choo-Tjoe** *(see pp184–5)* offers a wonderful day's outing, taking its passengers past a landscape that includes sea, lakes, forests and mountains.

An open day at the **South African National Railway and Steam Museum** in Johannesburg is held on the first Sunday of every month. A number of steam train safaris give a taste of what train travel was about in years gone by.

From Cape Town, the **Spier Vintage Train Company** *(see p141)* runs luxury trips in gleaming vintage carriages through beautiful vineyards, directly to the estate.

Apple Express logo

Union Limited offers popular day trips through the Franschhoek Valley or across the mountains to Ceres and the six-day Golden Thread Tour travels to Oudtshoorn.

Another holiday steamer is the little **Apple Express**, which leaves from Port Elizabeth in the Eastern Cape on its 61-cm (24-inch) gauge for a trip through the countryside.

Shosholoza Meyl runs a service from Johannesburg to Port Elizabeth, Durban and Cape Town, as well as covering the route from Cape Town to Durban. Children under four travel free; those under 12 at half price.

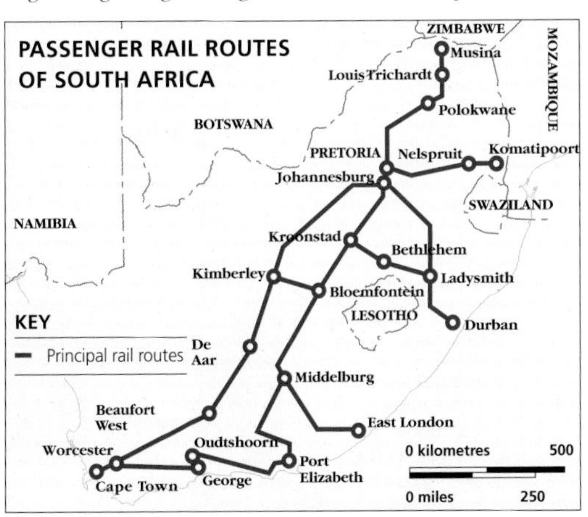

DIRECTORY

PASSENGER SERVICES

Cape Metrorail
Tel *(080) 065-6463.*
www.capemetrorail.co.za

Mainline Passenger Services
Tel *(086) 000-8888.*
www.spoornet.co.za

Spoornet
Tel *(011) 773-7743, (031) 361-3388, (041) 507-2042.*
www.spoornet.co.za

LEISURE TOURS

Apple Express
Tel *(041) 507-2333.*

Biggsy's
Tel *(021) 449-3870.*

Outeniqua Choo-tjoe
Tel *(044) 801-8288.*

SA National Railway and Steam Museum
Tel *(011) 646-5513.*

Shosholoza Meyl
Tel *(086) 000-8888.*
www.spoornet.co.za

Spier Vintage Train Company
Tel *(021) 419-5222.*

Union Limited Steam Railtours
Tel *(021) 405-4391.*

Travelling by Road

AA logo

Overall, South Africa's road network is good, although individual roads, even those that are part of the N-prefixed national road system, range from very poor to excellent. In rural areas, only main arteries may be tarred, but dirt roads are usually levelled and in good condition. Long distances and other road users, unfortunately, constitute one of the major hazards. Intercity bus services are fast, affordable and comprehensive, but own transport is necessary to visit remote areas. Most sightseeing can be done along tarred roads. Fuel is inexpensive, and busy routes have many service stations.

Service-cum-refreshment stations are welcome stop-offs on long routes

DRIVER'S LICENCE

Persons over 18, who are in possession of a locally issued driver's licence that is printed in English and includes a recent photograph of the owner, will not require an international licence to drive in South Africa. However, if you need an international licence, you must obtain one before you arrive in South Africa.

Your licence and a red warning triangle (for emergency use) must be carried in the vehicle at all times.

RULES OF THE ROAD

Traffic drives on the left side of the road. Except where granted right of way by a sign or by an official on duty, yield to traffic approaching from your right. It is common courtesy to pull over onto the hard shoulder to let faster traffic pass on the right. Seat belts are compulsory in the front and in the back. Children must be properly restrained.

Animal and rock falling warning signs

The speed limit in urban areas, whether there are regulatory signs or not, is 60 km per hour (37 mph). On freeways and roads not regulated to a lower speed, the limit is 120 km per hour (75 mph).

In the event of a vehicle breakdown, pull over onto the extreme left, activate your hazard lights and place a red warning triangle at a distance of 50 m (164 ft) behind your car. The AA provides a breakdown service for all members, call (011) 799-1500. Alternatively the emergency services can be reached on 10177.

In the event of an accident, you may move your vehicle if there are no injuries, but you have to notify the nearest police station within 24 hours. If there are any injuries, notify the police immediately and do not move the vehicles until they have arrived.

Six-lane freeway between Pretoria/ Tshwane and Johannesburg

South Africa has strict drink-driving laws. The legal blood alcohol level is 0.05 per cent maximum, which is the equivalent of one glass of beer or wine. Anyone caught driving above this limit is liable for a fine of R24,000 or up to six years' imprisonment.

SAFETY

Police advise travellers not to pick up strangers. Keep car doors locked and windows wound up. When parking, leave nothing of value in plain sight *(see p398)*. At night, park only in well-lit areas.

When passing peri-urban townships and in rural areas, be alert for pedestrians and straying livestock.

Due to the vast distances between towns, especially in the arid interior, it is advisable to refuel in good time and plan regular rest stops.

Emergency telephones are sited on some highways

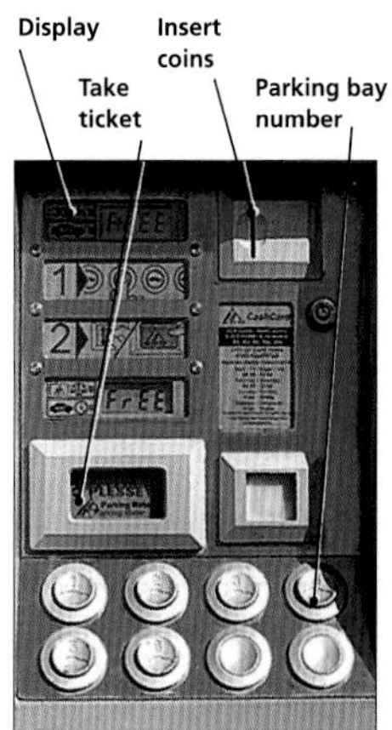

Hi-tech parking meters accept coins and low-denomination notes

PARKING

Most South African towns nowadays have parking meters, so check for numbered bays painted on the tarmac or at the kerb, and for signposts on a nearby pole. In towns and cities, unofficial "parking attendants" are a nuisance and may guide you to a no-parking zone. Many demand payment when you arrive and may also expect a tip when you leave. Some have been known to damage the cars of unobliging drivers.

Whenever you are able to do so, park in a regulated area where an official is on duty.

FUEL

Motor vehicles run on 97 Octane petrol, unleaded petrol or diesel fuel, and the unit of liquid measurement is the litre (0.22 UK gallons or 0.264 US gallons). Service station attendants see to refuelling and other checks like tyre pressure, oil, water, and cleaning the front and rear windows. A tip is always appreciated.

CAR RENTAL

Car rental is expensive in South Africa and is best arranged through fly-drive packages *(see p405)* or pre-booked with international agents at home. All the international airports have car-rental offices on site. To rent a car you must be over 23 and have held a valid driver's licence for at least five years. Check the small print for insurance cover. There are usually specials on offer.

Some of the most common and trusted car rental firms

BUS SERVICES

Greyhound, Intercape and Translux coaches travel to most towns in the country, and the journeys are safe, comfortable and fairly inexpensive – they are also faster than travelling by train. Both Greyhound and Translux coaches offer "frequent traveller" saving schemes. The City Liner hop-on/hop-off system, aimed at backpackers and budget travellers, runs along the coast between Durban and Cape Town. Trips can be booked at Computicket branches countrywide.

Conventional bus services operate along the main cross-country routes. Minibus taxis transport workers, but the service has a poor safety record and is not recommended.

There is no central system for taxis in South Africa. If you need a taxi, ask your hotel or the nearest tourism office to recommend a reliable service, or use the Yellow Pages. The AA runs a Metro Cab service in the Gauteng area.

The bus terminus in Adderley Street, Cape Town

DIRECTORY

Area codes
Johannesburg (011).
Pretoria/Tshwane (012).
Cape Town (021).
Durban (031).
Port Elizabeth (041).

CAR RENTAL

Avis
***Tel** (086) 111-3748.*
www.avis.co.za

Budget
***Tel** (086) 101-6622.*
www.budget.co.za

Hertz
***Tel** (086) 160-0136.*
www.hertz.co.za

Imperial
***Tel** (086) 113-1000.*
www.imperialcarrental.co.za

BUS SERVICES

AA Metro Cab
***Tel** (083) 692-2222.*

City Liner
***Tel** (083) 915-8000.*

Computicket
***Tel** (083) 915-8000.*
www.computicket.com

Greyhound
***Tel** (011) 249-8700.*
www.greyhound.co.za

Intercape
***Tel** (021) 380-4400.*
www.intercape.co.za

Translux
***Tel** (086) 158-9282.*
www.translux.co.za

General Index

Page numbers in **bold** type refer to main entries.

D

L

N

O

T

U

V

W

X

Y

Z

Acknowledgments

Dorling Kindersley would like to thank the following people whose contributions and assistance have made the preparation of this book possible.

Main Contributors

Michael Brett has visited many African countries, including Kenya, Malawi, Zimbabwe, Namibia and Mozambique, and has an extensive knowledge of South Africa. His first book, a detailed guide to the Pilanesberg National Park in North West Province, South Africa, was published in 1989. In 1996, he co-authored the *Touring Atlas of South Africa*. He has written *Great Game Parks of Africa: Masai Mara* and *Kenya the Beautiful*. Articles by Michael Brett have been published in several travel magazines, as well as in *Reader's Digest*.

Brian Johnson-Barker was born and educated in Cape Town, South Africa. After graduating from the University of Cape Town and running a clinical pathology laboratory for some 15 years, he turned to writing. His considerable involvement in this field has also extended to television scripts and magazine articles. Among his nearly 50 book titles are *Off the Beaten Track* (1996) and *Illustrated Guide to Game Parks and Nature Reserves of Southern Africa* (1997), both published by Reader's Digest.

Mariëlle Renssen wrote for South African general-interest magazine *Fair Lady* before spending two years in New York with *Young & Modern*, a teenage publication owned by the Bertelsmann publishing group. After returning to South Africa, several of her articles were published in magazines such as *Food and Home SA* and *Woman's Value*. Since 1995 she has been the publishing manager of Struik Publishers' International Division, during which time she also contributed to *Traveller's Guide to Tanzania*.

Additional Contributors

Duncan Cruickshank, Claudia Dos Santos, Luke Hardiman, Peter Joyce, Gail Jennings, Loren Minsky, Roger St Pierre, Anne Taylor.

Additional Photography

Charley van Dugteren, Anthony Johnson, Ian O'Leary, Jerry Young.

Additional Illustrations

Anton Krugel.

Additional Cartography

Genené Hart, Eloïse Moss.

Research Assistance

Susan Alexander, Sandy Vahl.

Additional Picture Research

Rachel Barber.

Proof Reader

Mariëlle Renssen.

Indexer

Brenda Brickman.

Revisions Editor

Anna Freiberger.

Revisions Designer

Conrad Van Dyk.

Design and Editorial Assistance

Beverley Ager, Uma Bhattacharya, Hilary Bird, Arwen Burnett, Sean Fraser, Thea Grobbelaar, Freddy Hamilton, Vinod Harish, Mohammad Hassan, Lesley Hay-Whitton, Victoria Heyworth-Dunne, Jacky Jackson, Vasneet Kaur, Vincent Kurien, Maite Lantaron, Alfred Lemaitre, Glynne Newlands, Marianne Petrou, Gerhardt van Rooyen, Sands Publishing Solutions, Mitzi Scheepers, Azeem Siddiqui.

Special Assistance

Joan Armstrong, The Howick Publicity Bureau; Coen Bessinger, Die Kaapse Tafel; Tim Bowdell, Port Elizabeth City Council; Dr Joyce Brain, Durban; Katherine Brooks, MuseuMAfrikA (Johannesburg); Michael Coke, Durban; Coleen de Villiers and Gail Linnow, South African Weather Bureau; Dr Trevor Dearlove, South African Parks Board; Louis Eksteen, Voortrekker Museum (Pietermaritzburg); Lindsay Hooper, South African Museum (Cape Town); Brian Jackson, The National Monuments Commission; Linda Labuschagne, Bartolomeu Dias Museum Complex (Mossel Bay); Darden Lotz, Cape Town; Tim Maggs, Cape Town; Hector Mbau, The Africa Café; Annette Miller, Bredasdorp Tourism; Gayla Naicker and Gerhart Richter, Perima's; Professor John Parkington, University of Cape Town; Anton Pauw, Cape Town; David Philips Publisher (Pty) Ltd, Cape Town; Bev Prinsloo, Palace of the Lost City; Professor Bruce Rubidge, University of the Witwatersrand; Jeremy Saville, ZigZag Magazine; Mark Shaw, Barrister's; Dr Dan Sleigh, Cape Town; Anthony Sterne, Simply Salmon; David Swanepoel, Voortrekker Museum; Johan Taljaard, West Coast National Park; Pietermaritzburg Publicity Association; Beyers Truter, Beyerskloof wine farm, Stellenbosch; Dr Lita Webley, Albany Museum, Grahamstown; Lloyd Wingate and Stephanie Pienaar, Kaffrarian Museum (King William's Town); and all provincial tourist authorities and national and provincial park services.

Photographic and Artwork Reference

Vida Allen and Bridget Carlstein, McGregor Museum (Kimberley); Marlain Botha, Anglo American Library; The Cape Archives; Captain Emilio de Souza; Petrus Dhlamini, Anglo American Corporation (Johannesburg); Gawie Fagan and Tertius Kruger, Revel Fox Architects (Cape Town); Jeremy Fourie, Cape Land Data; Graham Goddard, Mayibuye Centre, The University of the Western Cape; Margaret Harradene, Public Library (Port Elizabeth); Maryke Jooste, Library of Parliament (Cape Town); Llewellyn Kriel, Chamber of Mines; Professor André Meyer, Pretoria University; Julia Moore, Boschendal Manor House; Marguerite Robinson, Standard Bank National Arts Festival; Christine Roe and Judith Swanepoel, Pilgrim's Rest Museum; Dr F Thackeray, Transvaal Museum (Pretoria); Marena van Hemert, Drostdy Museum (Swellendam); Kees van Ryksdyk, South African Astronomical Observatory; Cobri Vermeulen, The Knysna Forestry Department; Nasmi Wally, The Argus (Cape Town); Pam Warner, Old Slave Lodge (Cape Town).

Photography Permissions

Dorling Kindersley would like to thank the following for their assistance and kind permission to photograph at their establishments:

African Herbalist's Shop, Johannesburg; Alanglade, Pilgrim's Rest; Albany Museum Complex, Grahamstown; Bartolomeu Dias Museum Complex, Mossel Bay; BAT (Bartel Arts Trust) Centre, Durban; Bertram House, Cape Town; BMW Pavilion, Victoria & Alfred Waterfront; Bo-Kaap Museum, Cape Town; Cango Caves, Oudsthoorn; The Castle of Good Hope; Department of Public Works, Cape Town; Drum Magazine/ Bailey's Archives; Dutch Reformed Church, Nieu Bethesda; The Edward Hotel, Port Elizabeth; Gold Reef City, Johannesburg; Groot Constantia; Heia Safari Ranch; Highgate

Ostrich Farm, Oudtshoorn; Hindu (Hare Krishna) Temple of Understanding; Huguenot Museum, Franschhoek; Johannesburg International Airport; Kimberley Open-Air Mine Museum; Kirstenbosch National Botanical Garden; Kleinplasie Open-Air Museum; Koopmans-De Wet House, Cape Town; Mal a Mala Private Reserve; MuseuMAfricA, Johannesburg; Natural Science Museum, Durban; Old Slave Lodge, Cape Town; Oliewenhuis Art Gallery, Bloemfontein; Oom Samie se Winkel, Stellenbosch; Owl House, Nieu Bethesda; Paarl Museum; Pilgrim's Rest; Rheboksklootf Wine Estate; Robben Island Museum Service; Sandton Village Walk; Shakaland; Shipwreck Museum, Bredasdorp; Simunye; South African Library; South African Museum, Cape Town; Tatham Art Gallery, Pietermaritzburg; Two Oceans Aquarium, V&A Waterfront; Victoria & Alfred Waterfront; The Village Museum Stellenbosch; Sue Williamson, Cape Town; The Workshop, Durban.

Picture Credits

t = top; tl = top left; tlc = top left centre; tc = top; tr = top right; cla = centre left above; ca = centre above; cra = centre right above; cl = centre left; c = centre; cr = centre right; clb = centre left below; cb = centre below; crb = centre right below; fcl far centre left; bl = bottom left; b = bottom; bc = bottom centre; bcl = bottom centre left; br = bottom right; d = detail.

Works of art have been reproduced with the permission of the following copyright holders: *Lead Ox*, 1995–6, © Cecil Skotnes, Incised, painted wood panel 318br; *Portrait of a Lady*, Frans Hals (1580–1666), Oil on canvas, Old Town House (Cape Town), © Michaelis Collection 70bl; *Rocco Catoggio and Rocco Cartozia de Villiers*, artist unknown, c.1842, Oil on canvas, © Huguenot Museum (Franschhoek) 145bc; Untitled work, 1998, Hannelie de Clerq, Tempera, © Stellenbosch Art Gallery 139tr.

Every effort has been made to trace the copyright holders and we apologize in advance for any unintentional omissions. We would be pleased to insert the appropriate acknowledgements in any subsequent edition of this publication.

The publisher would like to thank the following individuals, companies and picture libraries for permission to reproduce their photographs:

ACSA (Airports Company of South Africa): 404t, 405b; Shaen Adey: 1t, 28cl, 32t, 75bl, 84t, 84b, 107cr, 288tl, 288cla, 288cl, 288b, 289t, 289cr; African Pictures: Guy Stubbs 385c; Alamy Images: Bruce Coleman Inc./Michael P. Fogden 11c; Cephas Picture Library/Emma Borg 10br; Cephas Picture Library/Juan Espi 357cr; Cephas Picture Library/Alain Proust 356clb; Cephas Picture Library/Mick Rock 356cla; Dennis Cox 382br; Danita Delimont/Amos Nachoum 170tl; Danita Delimont 170tl; Reinhard Dirscherl 11br; Greatstock Photographic Library/Michael Meyersfeld 258tc; ImageState/Pictor International 13bl; Jon Arnold Images 12bl; Geof Kirby 382tl; Shaun Levick 389t; Suzanne Long 106tc, 390tr; Eric Nathan 10cl, 12tr; PCL 12c; Ben Queenborough 390c; Malcolm Schuyl 235tl; Peter Titmuss 354cla, 355c, 356tr; Travelstock 356cr; Liam West 386tc; Anita Akal: 41cl; Anglo American Corporation of South Africa Limited: 20c, 250clb, 250b, 250–251c, 251tl, 251tr, 251cr, 251r, 317t, 317bl; Apartheid Museum: 259bl; The Argus: 57bl, 58tl, 59cla; ASP Covered Images: 206tr, 207cb; AA (Automobile Association of South Africa): 408tl.

Daryl Balfour: 289b; Barnett Collection: © The Star 54cla; Barry Family Collection: 281bl; Bible Society of South Africa: 30tl, 57b; The Blue Train: 385tr; 406tl; Boomshaka/Polygram: 59tl; Boplass Family Vineyards: 357cl; Michael Brett: 31t, 248cl, 249bl, 249br, 268b, 269tl, 315c, 377b.

The Campbell Collection of The University of Natal, Durban: 56clb, 145cr; Capab (Cape Performing Arts Board): © Pat Bromilow-Downing 376t; Cango Wildlife Ranch: 176tl; Cape Archives: 4t, 30tr, 48b, 49b, 49c, 50t, 50ca, 55cr, 55br; Cape Legends: 129br; Cape Photo Library: © Alain Proust 21t; 21c, 35c, 89tl, 128cla, 128ca, 128cra, 129tr, 142cl, 143cra, 143crb; www.capespirit.com: 111tr; Cape Town City Ballet: Pat Bromilow Downing 112br; Cape Town Philharmonic Orchestra: 112tl; Cape Quarter: 106cr; Carrol Boyes Functional Art: 108bl, 108c; Zia Bird/Daniel Boshof 108bl, 108c; Corbis: Jonathan Blair 13tr; Gallo Images/Luc Hosten 172br; Gallo Images/Shaen Adey 172tl; Martin Harvey 265br; Jon Hicks 258bl, 384bc; Robert Harding World Imagery/Steve & Ann Toon 10tc; The Cory Library of Rhodes University, Grahamstown: 53cb; Ruphin Coudyzer: 30b.

De Beers: 54b; Roger de la Harpe: 5t, 34cl, 35b, 39tr, 212b, 213b, 214tl, 215t, 215cr, 216c, 218–219, 221b, 234tl, 238t, 239t, 241b, 325t, 378b, 379tr; Nigel Dennis: 24cr, 28–29c, 294tl, 295clb, 295crb, 308–309; Department of Transport: 395c; Department of Water Affairs and Forestry: 187b; Digital Perspectives: 14bl; Gerhard Dreyer: 24br, 104tl, 159cl, 162b.

The Featherbed Company: 186t; Foto Holler, © Schirmer, Hermanus: 130cl, 130–131c, 130bl.

Gallo Images: © Anthony Bannister 24cl, 25cr, 264tr, 294–295c; © David Gikey 40t; © Kevin Carter Collection 35tr; © Rod Haestier 25tr; G'echo Design: 40b; Getty Images: Gallo Images/Heinrich van den Berg 355tl; Gleanings in Africa: (1806) 131b; Benny Gool/Trace: 23c, 58–59c; Bob Gosani: 262cla; Great Stock: © Jürgen Schadeberg 262t, 262cra, 262cr, 262clb, 262b; Graham Beck Wines: Alain Proust 356br; Green Dolphin: 110b; Guardian Newspapers Limited: 57t.

Rod Haestier: 131cr, 190bl; George Hallett: 57br, 59tr; Lex Hes: 27cr, 28bc, 29bl, 29bc; Hulton Picture Company: 317cra.

i-Africa: © Nic Bothma 207t, 207cra; © Sasa Kralj 31b, 46cl; © Eric Muller 21b; International Eisteddfod: © Bachraty Ctibor 38tl; Iziko Museums, Cape Town: Cecil Kortjie 70c.

J&B Photographers: 29cra; Jacobsdal Wine Estate: 128bl.

King George VI Art Gallery, Port Elizabeth: 53crb; Klein Constantia: 101cl; Walter Knirr: 39cl, 57cr, 75cl, 75br, 220ca, 232cla, 252b, 260tr, 261br, 266b, 267t, 269tr, 269b, 279b, 352c, 374cl, 376b, 394cr, 406bl; KWV: 357fcl.

Anne Laing: 22b; Stefania Lamberti: 85cl, 233b; Grant Leversha: 381c; Levi's: 59cl; Library Of Parliament, Cape Town: © Mendelssohn Collection of watercolour paintings by Francois Vaillant 29tl; Local History Museum, Durban: 55bl; Lonely Planet Images: Craig Pershouse 171c.

Mayibuye Centre, University of the Western Cape: 56tl, 56–57c, 58clb; Meerendal Wine Estate: 128bc; Michaelis Collection (Old Town House): 70b; Military Museum, Johannesburg: 259tr; Monex Construction (Pty) Limited: 103c; Mr Delivery: 352t; Museumafrica: 9t, 46ca, 48tl, 52ca, 52cl, 53t, 61t, 125t, 201t, 245t, 291t, 321t, 393t.

Naartjie: Steve Eales 108tl; The National Archives, Pretoria: 251b; Imperial War Museum, London: 54–55; Nico Malan Theatre: 110b.

Colin Paterson-Jones: 19t, 26cra; Anton Pauw: 5c, 78b, 161tr; David Philips Publisher (Pty) Ltd: 22tl, 22tc, 31cr; Photo Access: © Getaway/C Lanz 353b; © Getaway/D Rogers 264cla; © Getaway/P Wagner 380t; © Clarke Gittens 50b; © Walter Knirr 250tl, 374b; © Photo Royal 214b; © Mark Skinner 66; © David Steele 38c, 214cla, 214clb; © Patrick Wagner 215b; © Alan Wilson 40c, 89ca; Herman Potgieter: 2–3; Photolibrary: Gerard Soury 380tl; The Port Elizabeth Apple Express:407c; Prince Albert Tourism Association: Reinwald Dedekind 173bl, 173t.

Reuters: Howard Burditt 381br; Mike Hutchings 113tl, Rheboksklloof Cellar: 135b; Robert Harding Picture Library: Yadid Levy 113br; Rovos Rail: 384cla, 385bl; Professor Bruce Rubidge: 46cb.

Sabi Sabi Private Game Reserve: 322cr; SA City Life: © Sean Laurénz 395b; SIL (© Struik Image LIBRARY): Shaen Adey 33crb, 39br, 64t, 64c, 64b, 65t, 65b, 68b, 72clb, 79bl, 79br, 88tl, 88cla, 88cl, 89cra, 89br, 97t, 100cl, 100cr, 105cra, 107tl, 128cr, 128br, 134cl, 134–135tc, 138t, 154t, 241c, 243b, 293b, 324c, 380c; Daryl Balfour 158bl; CLB (Colour Library), 25br, 26cla, 101tl, 185c, 193b, 243t, 257cr, 272, 287t, 316t; Credo Mutwa 30c; Roger de la Harpe 18, 25ca, 27crb, 34b, 85t, 92t, 107t, 200–201, 203t, 205cr, 216t, 222cl, 223cr, 226c, 239br, 240t, 240c; Nigel Dennis 19b, 26tl, 27br, 27c, 28tr, 28br, 29cr, 158cra, 158cl, 217t, 226t, 232cra, 233cra, 242tl, 244–245, 247t, 248bl, 248bc, 248br, 249t, 282–283, 284tr, 284cla, 284b, 285c, 290–291, 294tr, 294cl, 294crb, 294bl, 294br, 295tl, 295tr, 295cra, 297t, 311b, 312b; Gerhard Dreyer 26crb, 26bl, 26br, 27cla, 155t, 158crb, 162tl, 163cl, 174b, 175br, 179b, 180b, 186b, 190tl, 190tr, 190cla, 190b, 396t; Jean du Plessis 99c; Craig Fraser 39cr; Leonard Hoffman 24ca, 26tr, 27tl, 27tc, 27tr, 27cra, 27clb, 163b, 205tl, 205bl, 225b, 296tl, 375t; Anthony Johnson 71tl, 85bl; Walter Knirr 8–9, 99b, 152, 165b, 188–189, 210t, 233clb, 251cra, 255t, 268c, 276t, 313b; Mark Lewis 32bl; Jackie Murray 22b, 263t; Annelene Oberholzer 98c; Peter Pickford, 25cl, 75cra, 158tr, 158clb, 240b, 241t, 294cla, 303t; Mark Skinner 161c, 187cl; Erhardt Thiel 4b, 20t, 33tr, 37c, 38b, 65cr, 65ca, 69cra, 76cl, 77br, 80, 86–87, 93c, 98t, 100tr, 100bl, 101cr, 102t, 132b, 136tl, 162cr, 376c; David Thorpe 24t; Hein von Hörsten 44cra, 63cra, 72cla, 89crb, 95t, 104clb, 124–125, 127cl, 137bl, 139b, 163tr, 177cr, 191tl, 197t, 212t, 212c, 265tl, 265tr, 300b, 407t; Lanz von Hörsten 22c, 23t, 26clb, 41t, 73tl, 78bla, 94b, 126cla, 161tl, 161bl, 162c, 163cr, 202b, 203b, 217c, 227b, 249cr, 285t, 285b, 287b, 295b, 296cra, 298, 310, 236–237; Keith Young 60–61, 213t, 224, 228c, 235ca, 293cra, 299b, 304clb, 322b; Mark Skinner: 193c; Singita Private Game Reserve: 323tl; South African Airways: 404cla; South African Library: 48cl, 48–49c, 50cb, 51cb, 51cbr, 52b, 54tl, 54cl, 54clb, 56b, 57cl, 78tr, 88br, 315b; The South African Breweries Limited: Brett May 257tl, 357tr (all 3); South African Cultural History Museum: 48clb, 49t, 52tl, 53b; South African Museum: 47c, 47br; South African National Defence Force Archives: 56cla; The South African National Gallery: 49crb, 58clb; South African National Parks Board: 248tl' 381tl, 386br, 389br, 389c, 390b, 391tr; Addo Elephant National Park 387tl; Piet Heymans 386cla, 387cr; Geoff Spiby: 24bl, 25bl, 85br; South African Tourism: 11tl; Standard Bank 400tl; Standard Bank National Arts Festival 41b, 198tl; The Star 55t; State Archives: 29tr, 250cla, 306b, 317cl; Stellenbosch Art Gallery: 139t; Sun International: 270tr, 271crb, 324bl;.

Technically Correct: David Brooke 402tr; Telkom South Africa: 402tl, 402b; Ruvan Boshoff/ Sunday Times: 380b; Touchline: © Duif du Toit 36t; © Thomas Turck 36b; Transvaal Museum: © Dr Gerald Newlands 47ca; The Truth And Reconcilliation Committee: 59clb; Times Media; 364b; Theatre on the Bay: Bjorn De Kock 112cr; Tokara: 141tr.

University Of Pretoria: © Professor André Meyer 47t; Pieter-dirk Uys: 59cr.

Chris Van Lennep: 28cla, 206tr, 206cl, 206–207c, 207b; Chris Van Rooyen: 28cla; V&A Waterfront: 81tc, 83crb, 111bl; Hein Von Hörsten: 296cla, 297bl; André Vorster: 396c.

Wartburger Hof Country Hotel: 34cr. Ian Webb: 378cr; William Fehr Collection, Castle of Good Hope, Cape Town: 45t, 45b, 102b; W. Daniel 97b; Peter Wilson Agencies: 206br, 207cr. Keith Young: 102c.

Front Endpaper: Shaen Adey: br; SIL (© Struik Image Library): CLB (Colour Library) tr; Walter Knirr tl; Lanz von Hörsten tlc, tc; Keith Young cr; Photo Access: © Mark Skinner bl.

Jacket Front - Alamy Images: Blickwinkel c; DK Images: Roger de la Harpe clb. Back Back - Alamy Images: Peter Titmuss clb; Westend61/ Mel Stuart tl; Corbis: Lindsay Hebberd bl; DK Images: Walter Knirr cla. Spine Alamy Images: Blickwinkel t; DK Images: Shaen Adey b.

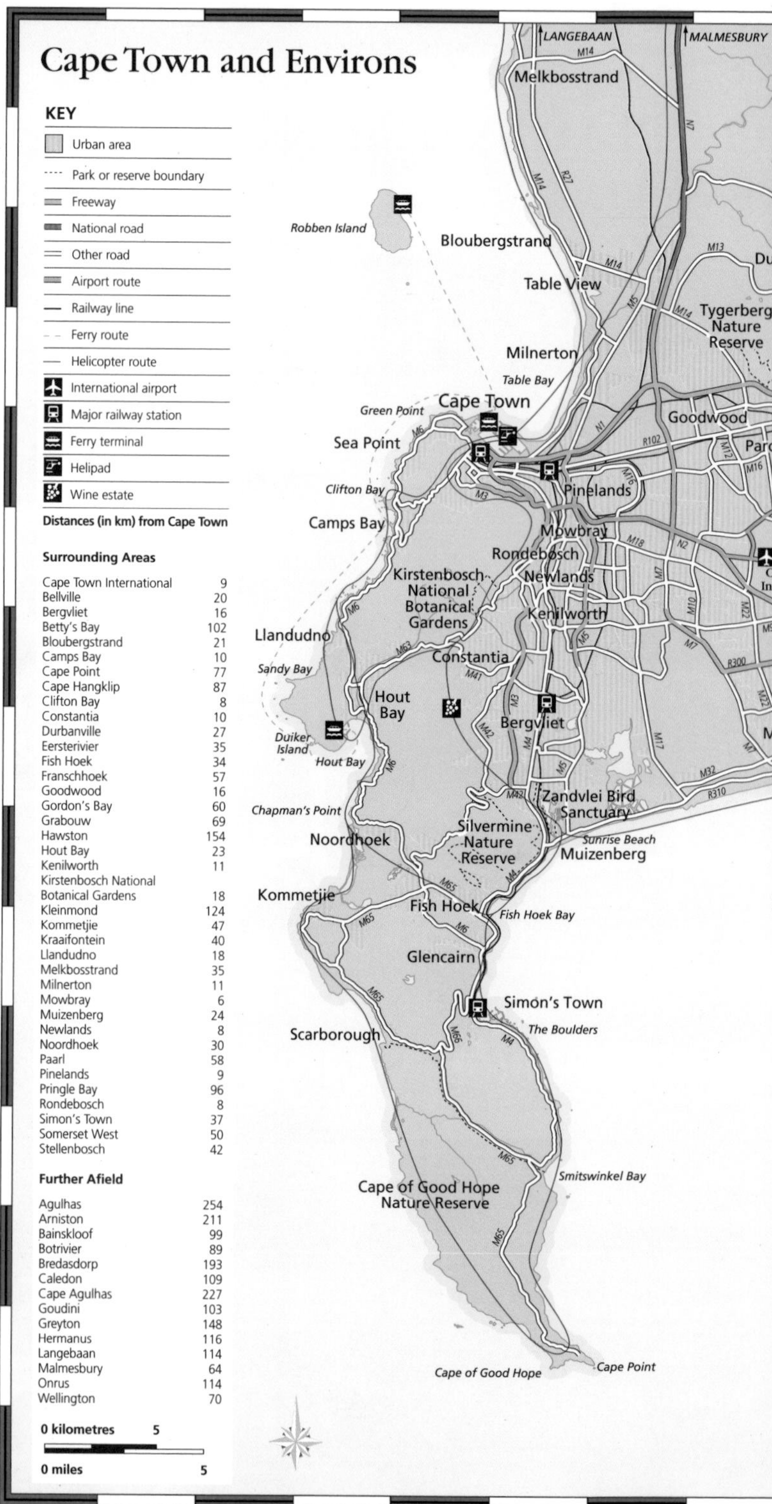
Cape Town and Environs
KEY
Urban area
Park or reserve boundary
Freeway
National road
Other road
Airport route
Railway line
Ferry route
Helicopter route
International airport
Major railway station
Ferry terminal
Helipad
Wine estate
Distances (in km) from Cape Town
Surrounding Areas
Cape Town International 9
Bellville 20
Bergvliet 16
Betty's Bay 102
Bloubergstrand 21
Camps Bay 10
Cape Point 77
Cape Hangklip 87
Clifton Bay 8
Constantia 10
Durbanville 27
Eersterivier 35
Fish Hoek 34
Franschhoek 57
Goodwood 16
Gordon's Bay 60
Grabouw 69
Hawston 154
Hout Bay 23
Kenilworth 11
Kirstenbosch National Botanical Gardens 18
Kleinmond 124
Kommetjie 47
Kraaifontein 40
Llandudno 18
Melkbosstrand 35
Milnerton 11
Mowbray 6
Muizenberg 24
Newlands 8
Noordhoek 30
Paarl 58
Pinelands 9
Pringle Bay 96
Rondebosch 8
Simon's Town 37
Somerset West 50
Stellenbosch 42
Further Afield
Agulhas 254
Arniston 211
Bainskloof 99
Botrivier 89
Bredasdorp 193
Caledon 109
Cape Agulhas 227
Goudini 103
Greyton 148
Hermanus 116
Langebaan 114
Malmesbury 64
Onrus 114
Wellington 70
0 kilometres 5
0 miles 5
LANGEBAAN
MALMESBURY
Melkbosstrand
Robben Island
Bloubergstrand
Table View
Tygerberg Nature Reserve
Milnerton
Table Bay
Cape Town
Green Point
Sea Point
Goodwood
Clifton Bay
Pinelands
Camps Bay
Mowbray
Rondebosch
Kirstenbosch National Botanical Gardens
Newlands
Kenilworth
Llandudno
Sandy Bay
Constantia
Hout Bay
Bergvliet
Duiker Island
Hout Bay
Chapman's Point
Zandvlei Bird Sanctuary
Silvermine Nature Reserve
Noordhoek
Sunrise Beach
Muizenberg
Kommetjie
Fish Hoek
Fish Hoek Bay
Glencairn
Simon's Town
The Boulders
Scarborough
Smitswinkel Bay
Cape of Good Hope Nature Reserve
Cape of Good Hope
Cape Point
M14
R27
N7
M13
M5
N1
R102
M12
M16
M6
M3
M18
N2
M7
M10
M22
M9
M63
M41
R300
M42
M4
M17
M32
R310
M65
M66